VISUAL encyclopedia

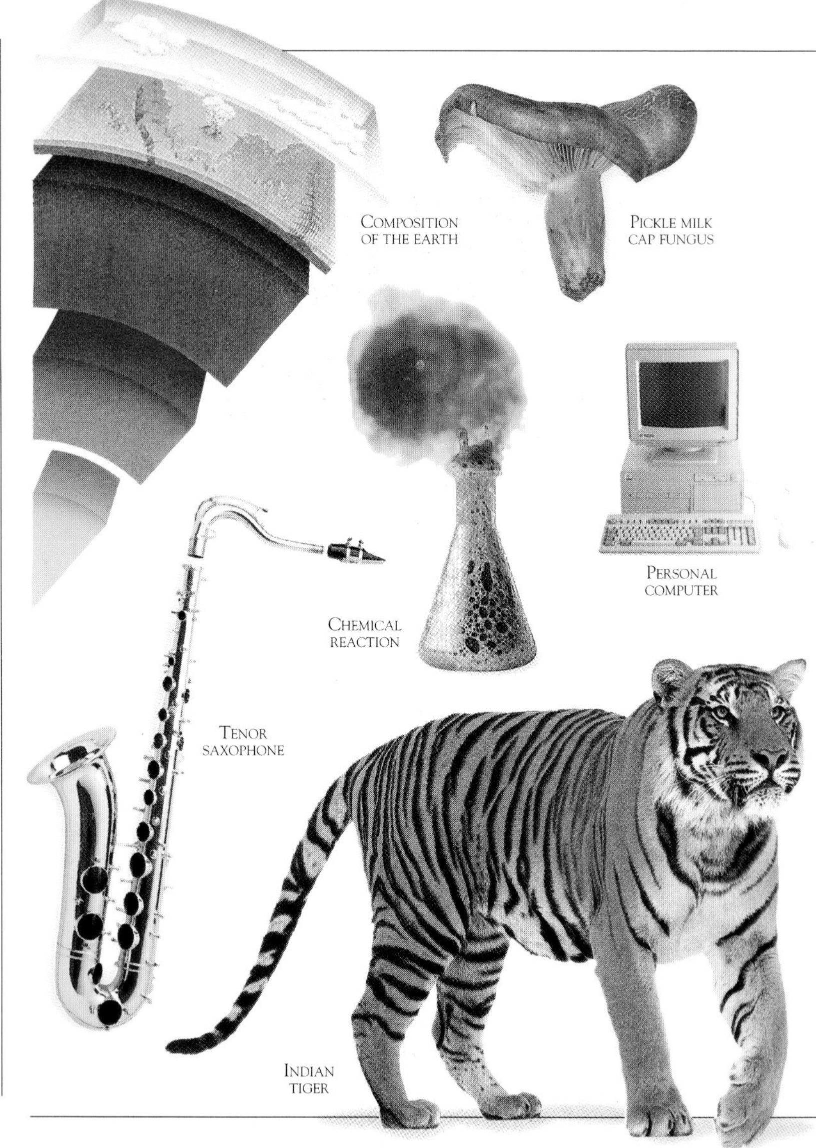
COMPOSITION OF THE EARTH
PICKLE MILK CAP FUNGUS
PERSONAL COMPUTER
CHEMICAL REACTION
TENOR SAXOPHONE
INDIAN TIGER

VISUAL encyclopedia

Written by
JOHN FARNDON

TORNADO FIGHTER PLANE

VENUS FIGURINE

OSCAR AWARD

DK

CONCISE ENCYCLOPEDIA

LONDON, NEW YORK,
MUNICH, MELBOURNE and DELHI

Produced for Dorling Kindersley by
PAGE*One*, Cairn House, Elgiva Lane, Chesham,
Buckinghamshire HP5 2JD

Project directors Bob Gordon, Helen Parker
Editor Neil Kelly
Designer Matthew Cook
DTP Designer Chris Clark

DK team Anna Kruger, Peter Bailey, Alastair Dougall, Sarah Crouch

Production Ruth Cobb
Picture research Cynthia Hole, Caroline Potts

US Editors Constance M. Robinson, Laaren Brown

Published in the United States by DK Publishing, Inc.
375 Hudson Street, New York New York 10014

Second American Edition 2003
Previously published as "Pockets Science Encyclopedia" in 1998
2 4 6 8 10 9 7 5 3

Published in Great Britain by Dorling Kindersley Limited.

A catalog for this book is available from the Library of Congress

ISBN 0-7566-0699-3

Color reproduction by Colourscan, Singapore
Printed and bound in Singapore by Star Standard

see our complete
catalog at
www.dk.com

CONTENTS

MANNED MANEUVRING UNIT

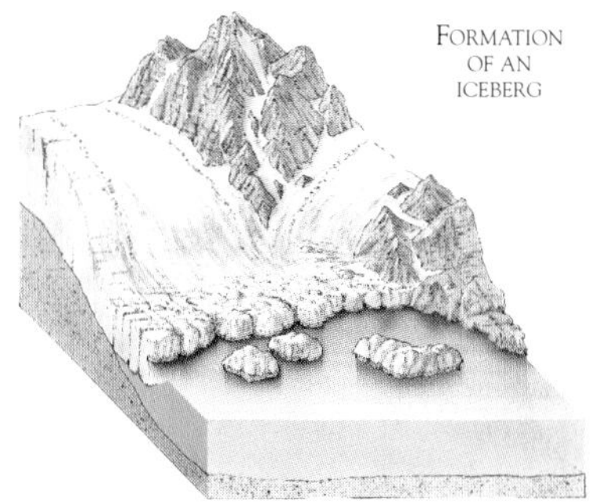
FORMATION OF AN ICEBERG

CONTENTS

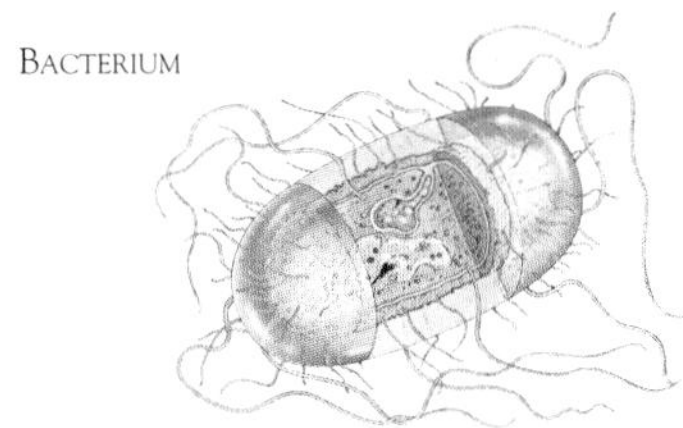
BACTERIUM

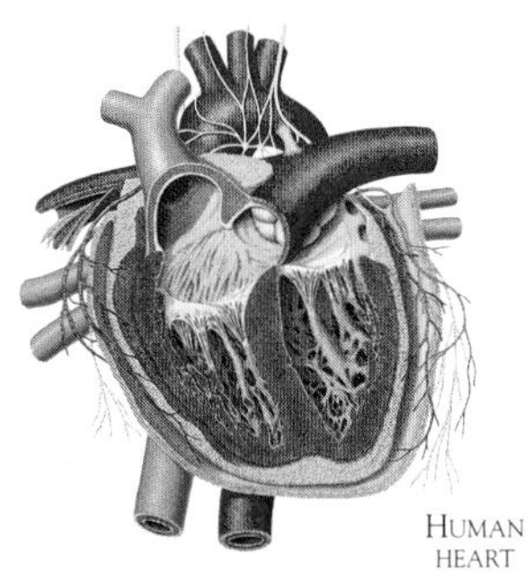
HUMAN HEART

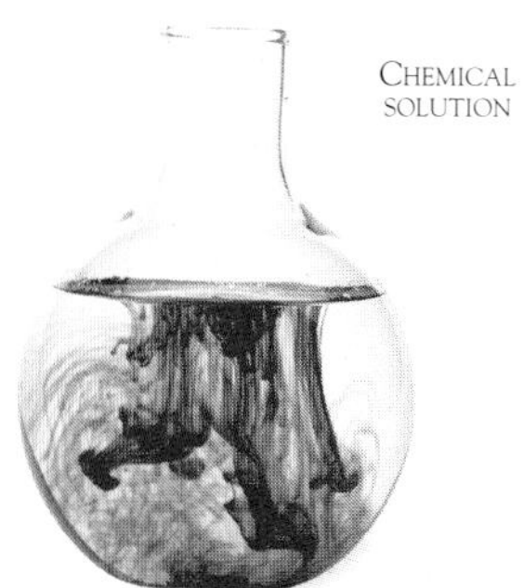
CHEMICAL SOLUTION

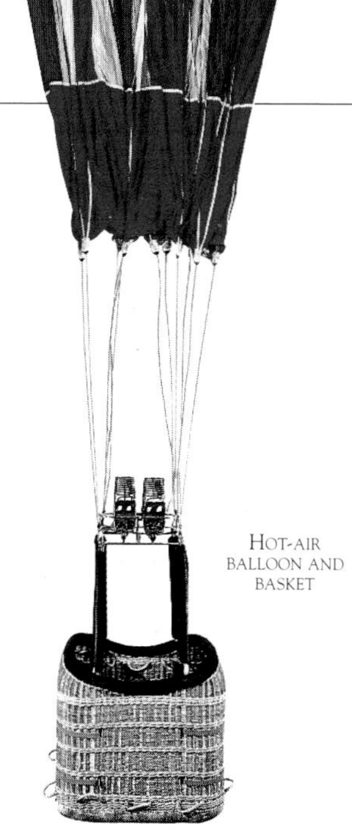
HOT-AIR BALLOON AND BASKET

CONTENTS

PATAGONIAN PUDU

ICE HOCKEY PLAYER

HOW TO USE THIS BOOK

These pages show you how to use the *DK Visual Encyclopedia*. The book is divided into nine sections of photographs, cutaway artworks, fact boxes, and illustrated timelines. At the beginning of each section there is a picture page with a list of contents.

INTRODUCTION
This provides a clear overview of the subject. After reading this, you should have an idea what the pages are about.

CORNER CODING
The corners of the pages in each section are color-coded to remind you which section you are in.

- SPACE
- PLANET EARTH
- THE LIVING WORLD
- THE HUMAN BODY
- SCIENCE AND TECHNOLOGY
- TRANSPORTATION
- THE WORLD
- PEOPLE AND SOCIETY
- HISTORY

HEADING
This describes the subject of the page. This page is about crustaceans.

LABELS
For extra clarity, some pictures have labels. They may give extra information, or identify a picture when it is not obvious from the text what it is.

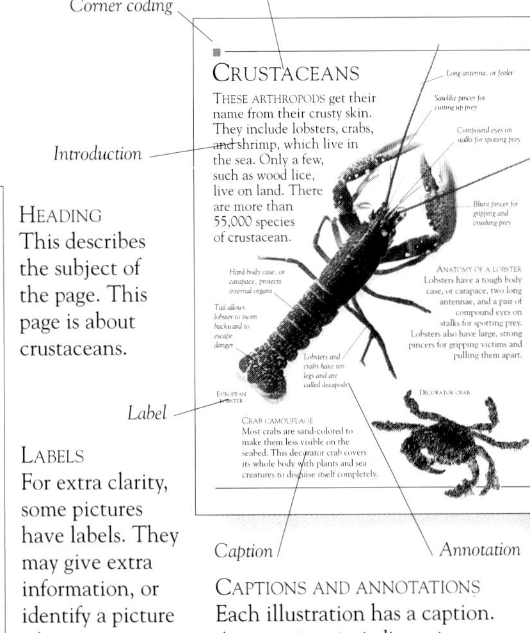
Heading
Corner coding
Introduction
Label
Caption
Annotation
CRUSTACEANS
THESE ARTHROPODS get their name from their crusty skin. They include lobsters, crabs, and shrimp, which live in the sea. Only a few, such as wood lice, live on land. There are more than 55,000 species of crustacean.
Long antenna, or feeler
Sawlike pincer for cutting up prey
Compound eyes on stalks for spotting prey
Blunt pincer for gripping and crushing prey
Hard body case, or carapace, protects internal organs
Tail allows lobster to swim backward to escape danger
Lobsters and crabs have ten legs and are called decapods
EUROPEAN LOBSTER
ANATOMY OF A LOBSTER
Lobsters have a tough body case, or carapace, two long antennae, and a pair of compound eyes on stalks for spotting prey. Lobsters also have large, strong pincers for gripping victims and pulling them apart.
DECORATOR CRAB
CRAB CAMOUFLAGE
Most crabs are sand-colored to make them less visible on the seabed. This decorator crab covers its whole body with plants and sea creatures to disguise itself completely.

CAPTIONS AND ANNOTATIONS
Each illustration has a caption. Annotations in *italics* point out features of an illustration and usually have leader lines.

RUNNING HEADS
These remind you which section you are in. The left-hand page gives the section name. The right-hand page gives the subject.

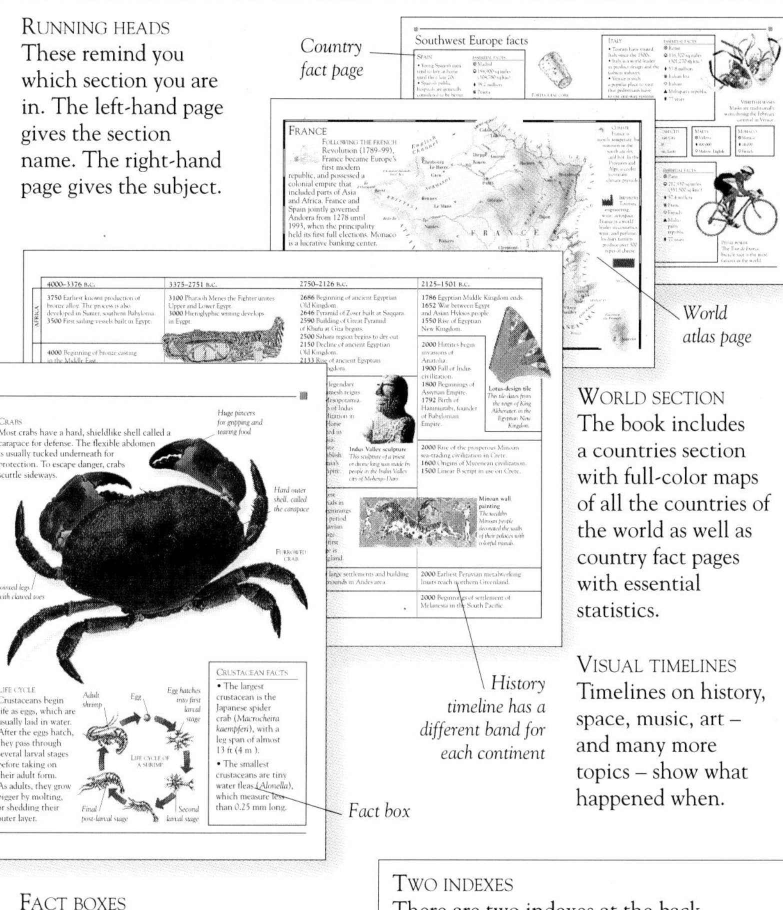

Country fact page
World atlas page
History timeline has a different band for each continent
Fact box

WORLD SECTION
The book includes a countries section with full-color maps of all the countries of the world as well as country fact pages with essential statistics.

VISUAL TIMELINES
Timelines on history, space, music, art – and many more topics – show what happened when.

FACT BOXES
Many pages have a fact box containing at-a-glance information about the subject. This fact box gives interesting information on crustaceans.

TWO INDEXES
There are two indexes at the back of the book – a gazetteer index, which lists major towns, cities, rivers, mountain ranges, and lakes that appear on the map pages, and an extensive subject index.

Space

THE UNIVERSE

FROM THE EARTH under our feet to the farthest stars, everything that exists is part of the universe. The universe is so large that it contains countless billions of stars, and it is still expanding rapidly. However, most of it consists of nothing but empty space.

LIGHT FROM A STATIONARY STAR

LIGHT FROM A MOVING STAR

LIGHT AND MOTION
If a star is moving away from Earth, its light waves are stretched out in comparison to those from other stars. The star's light becomes redder, moving towards the red end of the spectrum. This phenomenon is known as red shift.

UNIVERSE FACT

- There are an estimated 100 billion galaxies spread throughout the universe; each of these contains approximately 100 billion stars.

THE SCALE OF THE UNIVERSE
The universe is so vast that measurements such as miles and kilometers eventually become meaningless. A special unit called a light-year is used to calculate the distances between stars and galaxies. A light-year is equivalent to 5,878 billion miles (9,460 billion km), the distance that light travels in one year. The known universe spans more than 20 billion light-years.

GROUND LEVEL

FLYING AT LOW ALTITUDE 0.6 MILES (1 KM)

ORBITING AT HIGH ALTITUDE 620 MILES (1,000 KM)

EARTH FROM SPACE 62,000 MILES (100,000 KM)

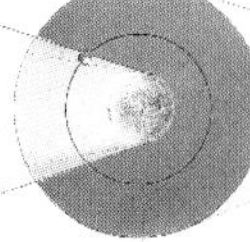

EARTH AND MOON 620,000 MILES (1 MILLION KM)

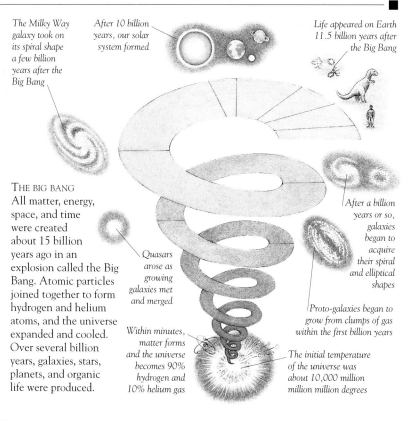

The Milky Way galaxy took on its spiral shape a few billion years after the Big Bang

After 10 billion years, our solar system formed

Life appeared on Earth 11.5 billion years after the Big Bang

THE BIG BANG
All matter, energy, space, and time were created about 15 billion years ago in an explosion called the Big Bang. Atomic particles joined together to form hydrogen and helium atoms, and the universe expanded and cooled. Over several billion years, galaxies, stars, planets, and organic life were produced.

After a billion years or so, galaxies began to acquire their spiral and elliptical shapes

Quasars arose as growing galaxies met and merged

Proto-galaxies began to grow from clumps of gas within the first billion years

Within minutes, matter forms and the universe becomes 90% hydrogen and 10% helium gas

The initial temperature of the universe was about 10,000 million million million degrees

THE SOLAR SYSTEM 6.2 BILLION MILES (10 BILLION KM)

INTERSTELLAR SPACE 620 BILLION MILES (1,000 BILLION KM)

NEAREST STARS 100 LIGHT-YEARS

MILKY WAY GALAXY 100,000 LIGHT-YEARS

LOCAL GROUP OF GALAXIES 10 MILLION LIGHT-YEARS

EXTENT OF THE KNOWN UNIVERSE 20 BILLION LIGHT-YEARS

GALAXIES

STARS ARE clustered together in enormous groups called galaxies, which were created when stars forming from spinning clouds of condensing gas were pulled toward each other by gravity. Some galaxies still rotate rapidly, maintaining a spiral shape, while others slow down and form ellipses (ovals) or less regular shapes. Large galaxies may have 1 trillion stars, but even the smallest contains a few hundred thousand.

DISTANT NEIGHBOR
The Andromeda galaxy is one of the nearest to the Milky Way, but its light still takes 2,500,000 years to reach Earth. We see the galaxy not as it is now, but as it was 2,500,000 years ago.

FOUR TYPES OF GALAXIES

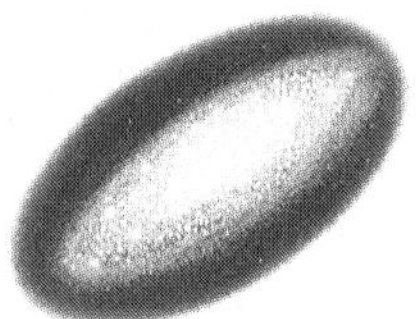

ELLIPTICAL
The most common type of galaxy, ellipticals contain mostly old stars and vary in shape from ball- to egg-like.

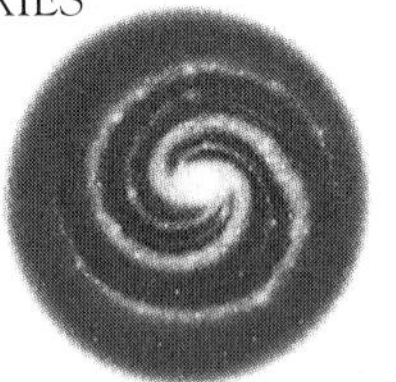

SPIRAL
These disk-shaped galaxies are flat, with a central nucleus of old stars. New stars form from clouds of gas in the spiral arms.

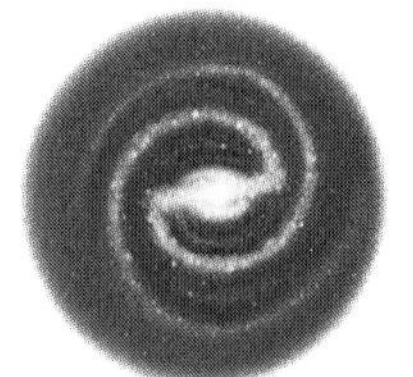

BARRED SPIRAL
One-third of spiral galaxies have a nucleus that is elongated into a bar. The vast spiral arms extend from the end of the bar.

THE MILKY WAY

The Sun is just one of 100 billion stars in our own galaxy, the Milky Way. Ours is a spiral galaxy, with a nucleus of old stars surrounded by a halo of even older stars. All the young stars are located in the spiral arms. The galaxy is called the Milky Way because it looks like a bright, creamy band of stars stretching through space when viewed from Earth.

GALAXY FACTS

- The brightest, oldest, and most distant of galaxies are "quasi-stellar objects," or quasars, some of which are 14 billion light-years away.
- There is now growing evidence that the Milky Way is a barred spiral galaxy.

MILKY WAY GALAXY: EXTERNAL SIDE VIEW

Nucleus is the brightest region of the galaxy

Galactic halo contains the oldest stars

From the side the spiral arms look like a flattened disk

MILKY WAY GALAXY: EXTERNAL OVERHEAD VIEW

Crux–Centaurus arm

Galactic nucleus

Sagittarius arm

Orion arm (Local arm)

Location of the solar system

IRREGULAR

The rarest galaxies are those that do not fit any known pattern. Some have a hint of a spiral or elliptical structure.

STARS

A STAR is an immense globe of fiery hydrogen gas powered by nuclear reactions at its core. Stars range in size from massive supergiants to small dwarf stars. The Sun is one of billions of stars scattered throughout the universe. It is a yellow star, a typical star of average size and temperature.

MAIN SEQUENCE STARS
The temperature, color, brightness, and lifespan of a star depend on its mass.

Brown dwarf 1,800°F (1,000°C)

Red dwarf 5,040°F (2,800°C)

THE SUN

Yellow star 9,900°F (5,500°C)

White star 18,000°F (10,000°C)

Blue/White star 28,800°F (16,000°C)

Blue star 43,200°F (24,000°C)

THE EVOLUTION OF A STAR

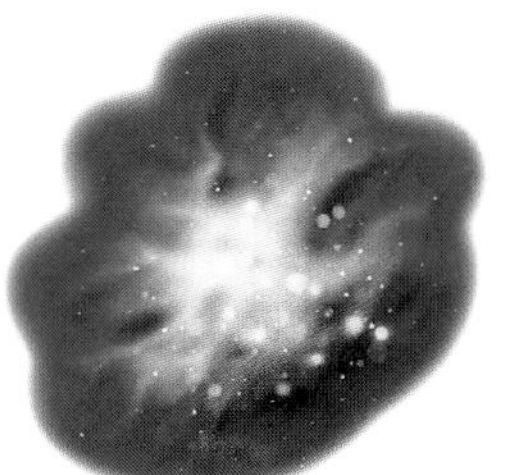

1 GAS CLOUD A star begins life as material within a nebula, an enormous cloud of gas and dust. Parts of the cloud are pulled together under their own gravity, contracting into spinning balls of gas known as protostars.

2 STARBIRTH The protostar shrinks, and its core becomes denser. Nuclear reactions begin, creating heat and light. As the star begins to shine, the leftover dust is blown away by stellar wind or forms planets around the star.

3 MAIN SEQUENCE The major period of a star's lifespan is called its main sequence. During this period, the star shines steadily, radiating energy. The bigger and brighter the star, the quicker it burns hydrogen, which reduces its lifespan.

STAR FACTS

- The biggest stars collapse to form black holes, which are so dense and have such a powerful gravitational pull that even light cannot escape.

6 SUPERNOVA
Heat from the star's core leads to a massive explosion, called a supernova. The star is as bright as a billion suns as it blows apart. The core collapses in a single second.

5 RED SUPERGIANT
Stars like the Sun fade out after the red giant stage, but more massive stars continue to swell, swallowing up any surrounding planets. The core fuses carbon atoms into iron, but lacks energy for further contraction.

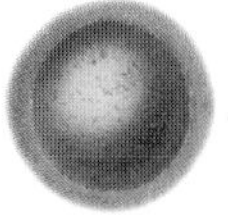

4 GROWING OLD
When its supply of hydrogen is exhausted, the star's core contracts, fusing helium atoms to make carbon. This gives out more energy, so the outer layers swell up and glow red. The star is now called a red giant.

INSIDE A STAR
A star shines because of the amount of light and heat produced by the nuclear reactions taking place within it. The fusion of hydrogen atoms, creating helium, produces so much energy that the core of a star reaches millions of degrees, making the surface glow.

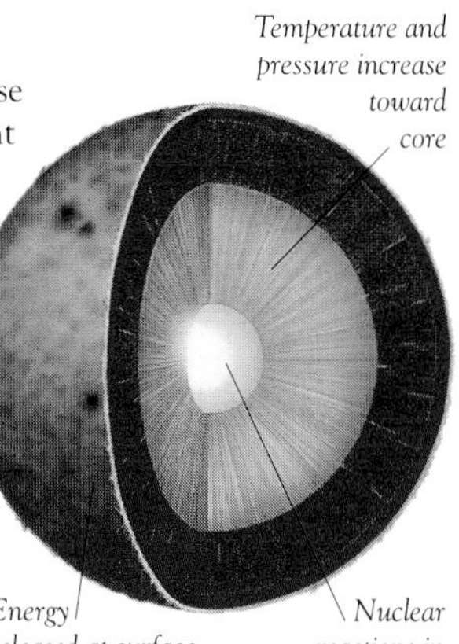
Temperature and pressure increase toward core
Energy released at surface as light and heat
Nuclear reactions in core produce energy

THE NORTHERN SKY

PEOPLE LIVING IN the Northern Hemisphere see a completely different range of stars than do people in the Southern Hemisphere. The star pattern turns steadily through the sky as Earth rotates, so the stars visible on any given night depend on the latitude, time of year, and time of night.

ORION

Arcturus

CONSTELLATIONS
Stars viewed from Earth seem to form patterns in the sky. These patterns are known as constellations. Astronomers divide the sky into 88 different constellations. Some of these, such as Orion, are supposed to represent a mythological person, creature, or object.

PROJECTED SPHERE
This sky map is a projection of the northern half of the celestial sphere onto a flat surface. Earth's North Pole is situated directly below the center of the map. The stars near the center of the sky map are called circumpolar and can be seen throughout the year. The North Star, also known as Polaris, appears to remain directly above the North Pole.

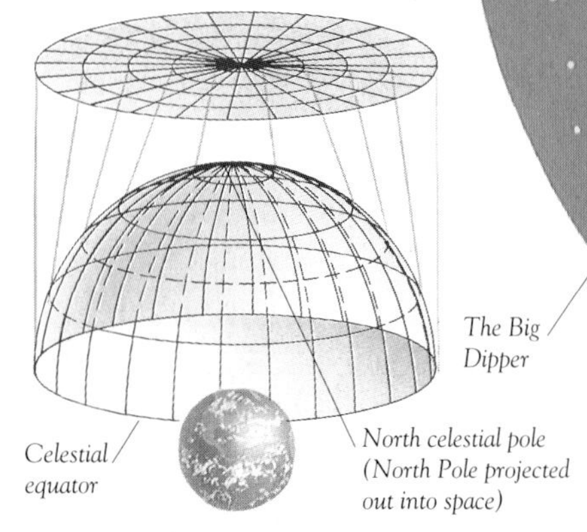
Celestial equator
North celestial pole (North Pole projected out into space)

The Big Dipper

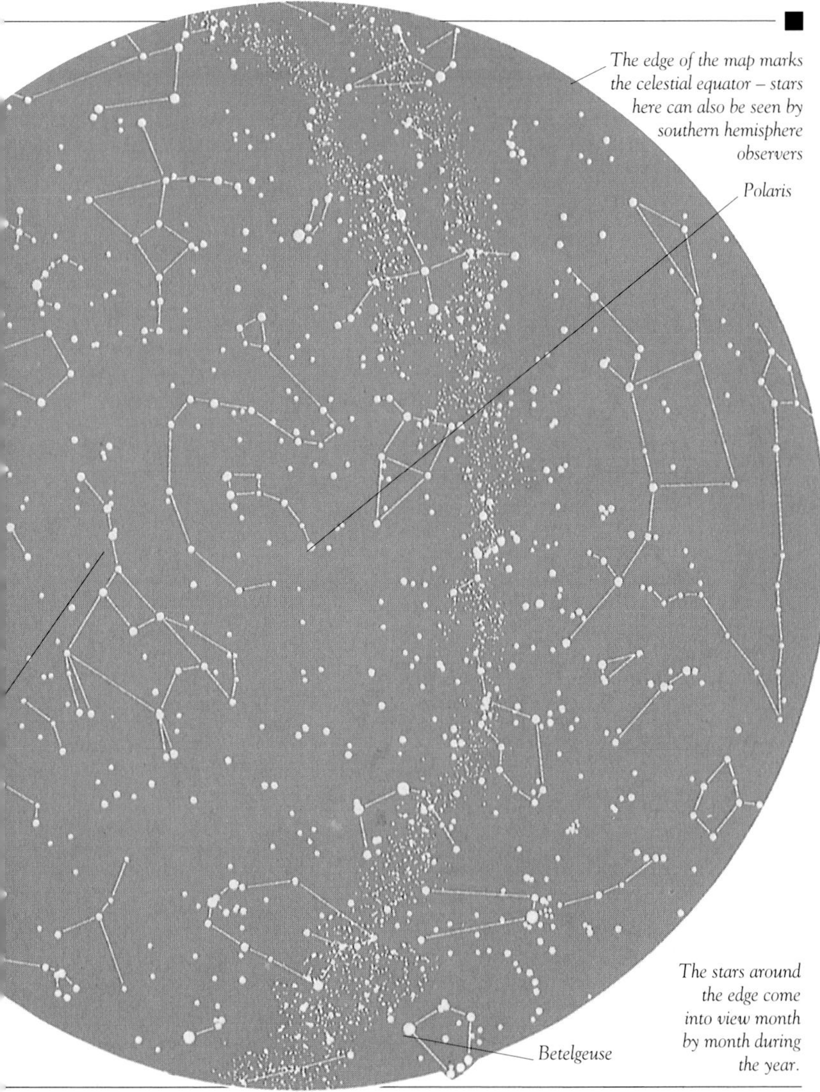
The edge of the map marks the celestial equator – stars here can also be seen by southern hemisphere observers
Polaris
Betelgeuse
The stars around the edge come into view month by month during the year.

THE SOUTHERN SKY

THE STARS VISIBLE from Earth's southern hemisphere are very different from those seen in northern skies. Which stars you can see depends on your latitude, the time of year, and the time of night. Also, you will see more stars on a clear night than on a misty or moonlit one.

THE CELESTIAL SPHERE
The stars viewed from Earth seem to be set on the inside of a giant sphere in the sky, called the celestial sphere. As Earth rotates on its axis and orbits around the Sun, different sections of the sphere are revealed. The motion of the planets can be plotted against the sphere.

Alpha Centauri

PROJECTED SPHERE
This sky map is a projection of the southern half of the celestial sphere onto a flat surface. Earth's South Pole is situated directly below the center of the map. Alpha Centauri, one of the nearest stars to the Sun, is a Southern Hemisphere star. The celestial equator is a projection of Earth's equator out into space.

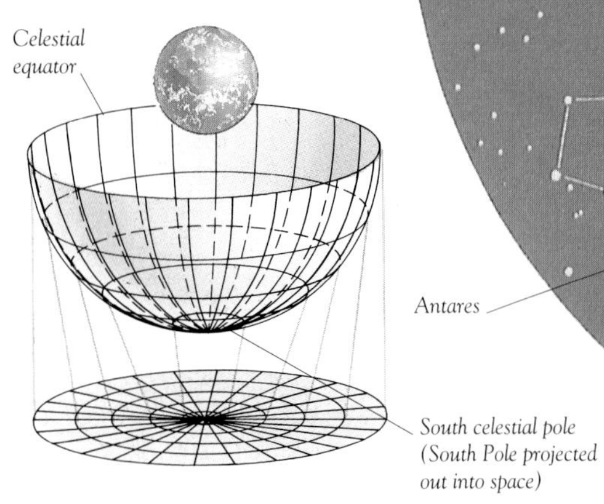
Celestial equator
Antares
South celestial pole (South Pole projected out into space)

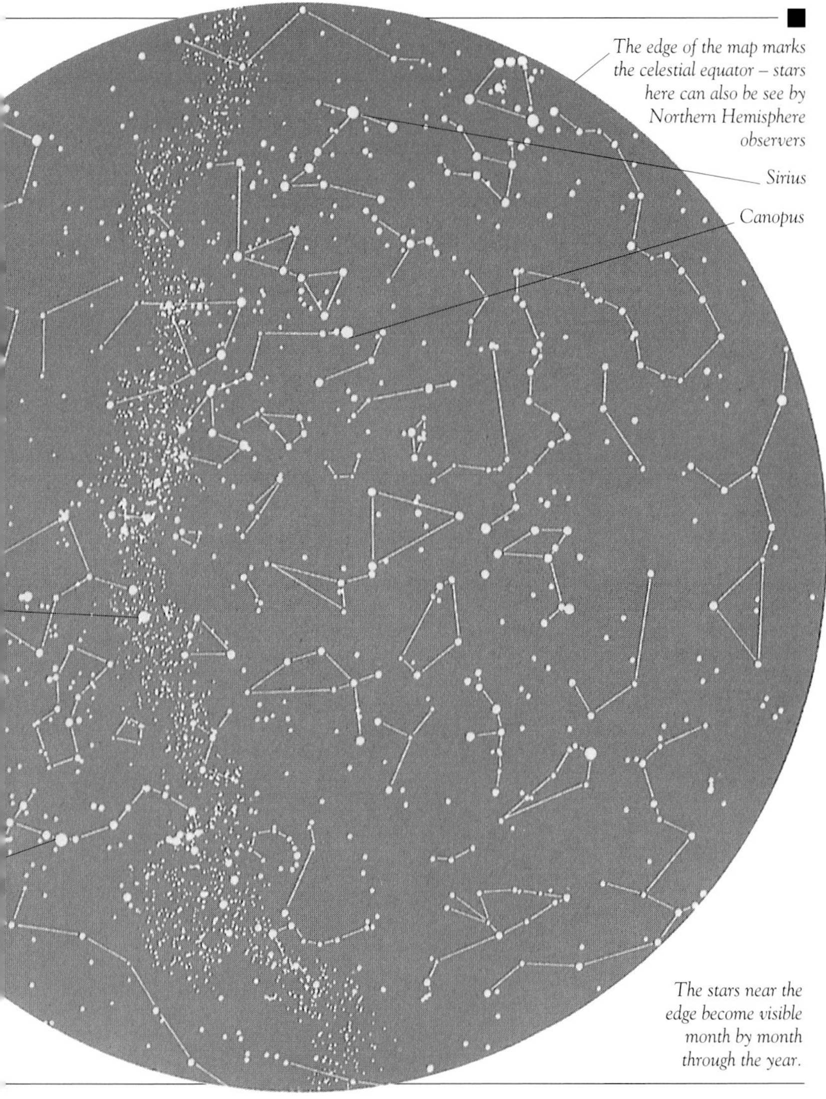
The edge of the map marks the celestial equator – stars here can also be see by Northern Hemisphere observers
Sirius
Canopus
The stars near the edge become visible month by month through the year.

THE SUN AND SOLAR SYSTEM

OUR SOLAR SYSTEM consists of the Sun and the many objects that orbit around it – nine planets, over 60 moons, and countless asteroids and comets. The system occupies a disk-shaped volume of space more than 7.45 billion miles (12 billion km) across. The Sun contains more than 99 percent of the system's mass.

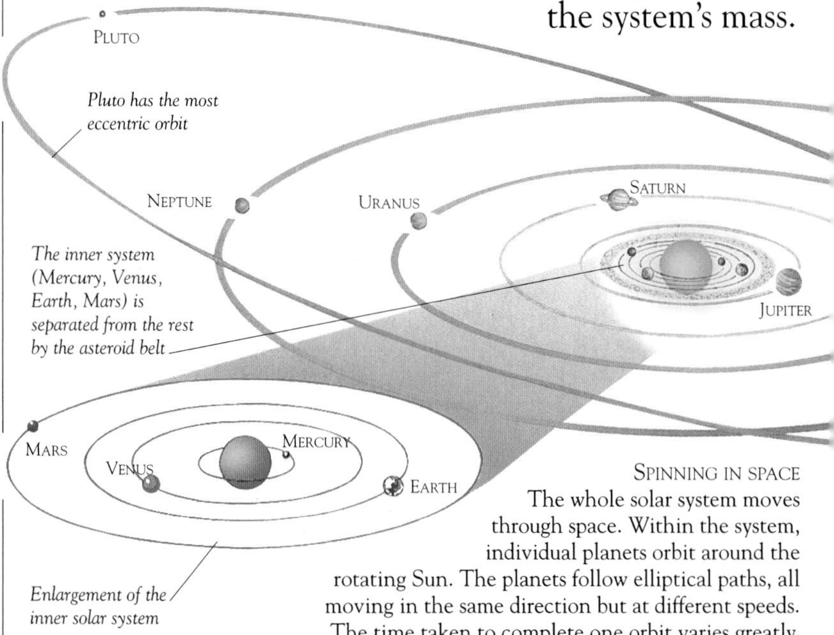

PLUTO

Pluto has the most eccentric orbit

NEPTUNE

URANUS

SATURN

JUPITER

The inner system (Mercury, Venus, Earth, Mars) is separated from the rest by the asteroid belt

MARS

VENUS

MERCURY

EARTH

Enlargement of the inner solar system

SPINNING IN SPACE

The whole solar system moves through space. Within the system, individual planets orbit around the rotating Sun. The planets follow elliptical paths, all moving in the same direction but at different speeds. The time taken to complete one orbit varies greatly, depending on the planet's distance from the Sun. In addition, each planet also spins on its axis.

STRUCTURE OF THE SUN

The Sun is a vast, fiery ball of spinning hydrogen and helium gases. Heat produced by nuclear reactions at the Sun's core erupts from its surface as millions of upsurges of gas, called granules. Sunspots are dark surface patches of cooler gas caused by disturbances in the Sun's magnetic field.

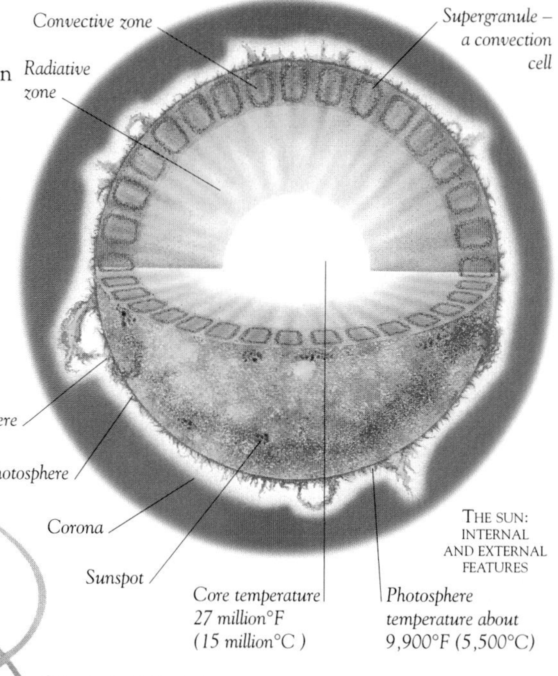
Convective zone
Supergranule – a convection cell
Radiative zone
Chromosphere
Photosphere
Corona
Sunspot
Core temperature 27 million°F (15 million°C)
Photosphere temperature about 9,900°F (5,500°C)

THE SUN: INTERNAL AND EXTERNAL FEATURES

Orbits are elliptical (oval) rather than circular

The time taken for a planet to make one orbit of the Sun is called the orbital period

SOLAR PROMINENCES

Enormous jets of hot hydrogen gas shoot out from the Sun's surface at intervals, and can stretch for many thousands of miles. The largest jets, called solar prominences, may last for several months. Some prominences are held in loops by the Sun's magnetic field.

THE INNER PLANETS

THE FOUR PLANETS closest to the Sun – Mercury, Venus, Earth, and Mars – are known as the inner planets. Each planet has a core of hot iron and a rocky crust, but surface conditions vary greatly.

MERCURY DATA

- Distance from Sun: 36 million miles (57.9 million km)
- Time taken to orbit Sun: 88 Earth days
- Diameter at equator: 3,032 miles (4,879 km)

MERCURY
A small rock world with a large, dense core, Mercury is the planet closest to the Sun. It is marked with craters, has no real atmosphere, and experiences extreme variations in surface temperature.

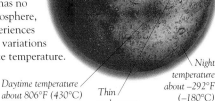

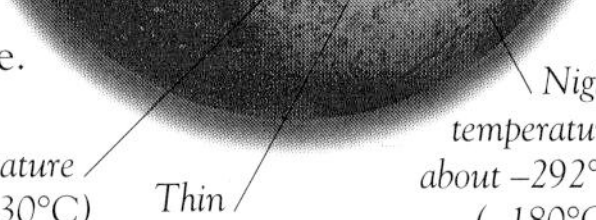
Iron core contains 80% of the planet's mass
Silicate rock mantle
NO MOONS
Night temperature about –292°F (–180°C)
Daytime temperature about 806°F (430°C)
Thin rocky crust

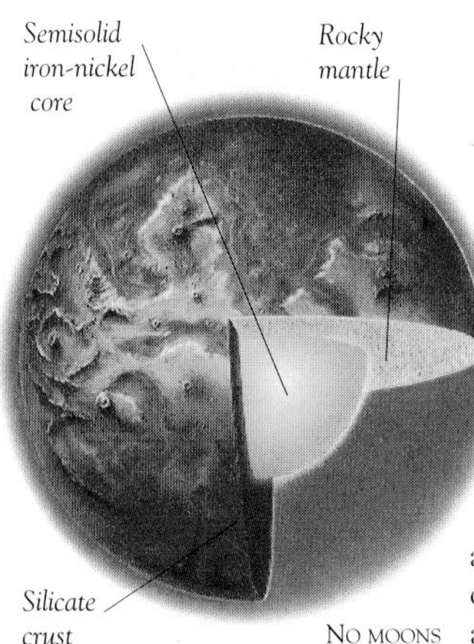
Semisolid iron-nickel core
Rocky mantle
Silicate crust
NO MOONS

VENUS
The planet Venus is about the same size as Earth. Its surface is very different, however, with intense heat, crushing pressure, and unbreathable acid air. Overhead are thick clouds of sulfuric acid droplets.

VENUS DATA

- Distance from Sun: 67.2 million miles (108.2 million km)
- Time taken to orbit Sun: 224.7 Earth days
- Diameter at equator: 7,521 miles (12,104 km)

Impact crater formation on rock planets

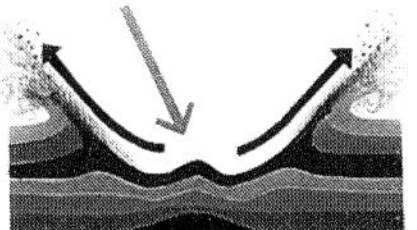

A meteorite impact blasts out a circular crater, ejecting debris.

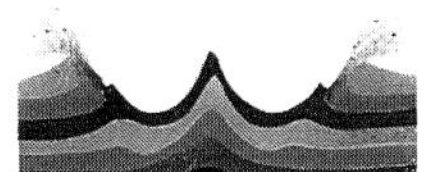

Rock compressed by the impact forms a conical central peak.

Crater gradually filled as debris slips from walls and peak.

Earth data

- Distance from Sun: 93 million miles (149.6 million km)
- Time taken to orbit Sun: 365 Earth days
- Diameter at equator: 7,926 miles (12,756 km)

Earth

The third planet from the Sun, Earth, is the only planet in the solar system with liquid water and an oxygen-rich atmosphere. These two factors make it the only known planet capable of supporting life.

1 moon

Mostly solid silicate mantle
Crust of silicate rock

2 moons

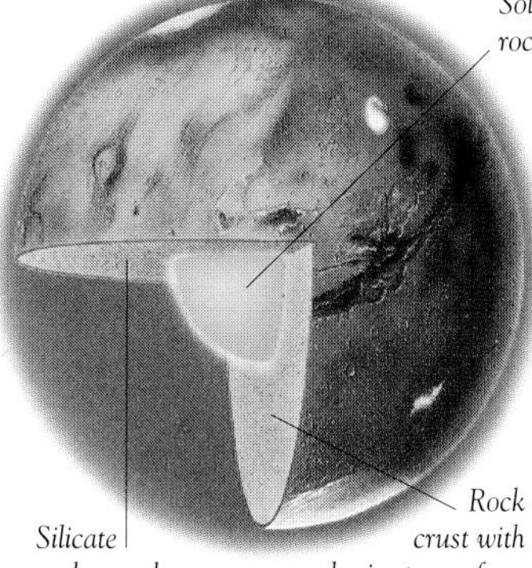
Solid rock core
Silicate rock mantle
Rock crust with under ice permafrost

Mars

A cold, barren planet with a thin atmosphere, Mars has polar ice caps, water-carved valleys, chasms, and giant volcanoes. Its red color is caused by iron oxide dust spread across its surface.

Mars data

- Distance from Sun: 141.6 million miles (227.9 million km)
- Time taken to orbit Sun: 687 Earth days
- Diameter at equator: 4,220 miles (6,792 km)

THE OUTER PLANETS

BEYOND THE ORBIT of Mars lie four giant planets formed from liquefied gas – Jupiter, Saturn, Uranus, and Neptune. Farther out still is Pluto, a small, icy rock planet.

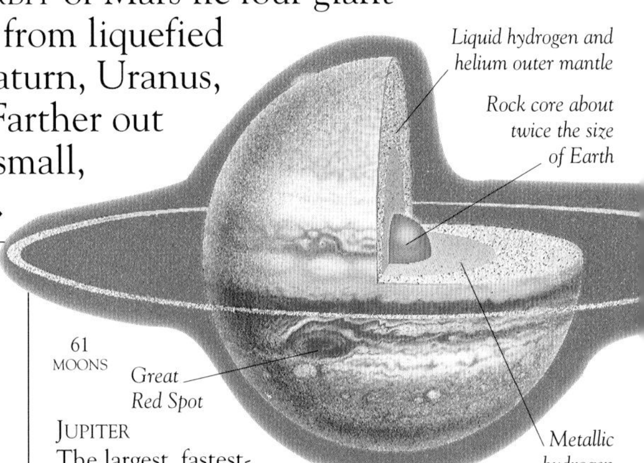

Liquid hydrogen and helium outer mantle

Rock core about twice the size of Earth

61 MOONS

Great Red Spot

Metallic hydrogen inner mantle

JUPITER DATA

- Distance from Sun: 483.7 million miles (778.4 million km)
- Time taken to orbit Sun: 12 Earth years
- Diameter at equator: 88,849 miles (142,984 km)

JUPITER

The largest, fastest-spinning planet, Jupiter could contain 1,300 Earths. Composed mainly of swirling gases, its most prominent feature is the Great Red Spot, a rotating storm bigger than the Earth.

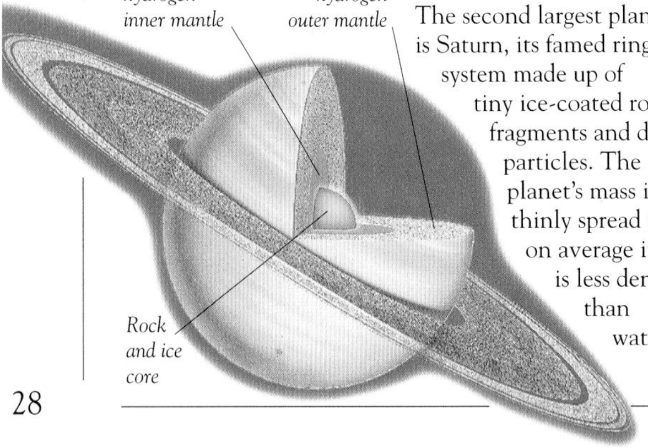

Metallic hydrogen inner mantle

31 MOONS

Liquid hydrogen outer mantle

Rock and ice core

SATURN

The second largest planet is Saturn, its famed ring system made up of tiny ice-coated rock fragments and dust particles. The planet's mass is so thinly spread that on average it is less dense than water.

SATURN DATA

- Distance from Sun: 887 million miles (1,427 million km)
- Time taken to orbit Sun: 29.5 Earth years
- Diameter at equator: 74,900 miles (120,536 km)

Rings of rock fragments about 39 in (1 m) across

27 MOONS

URANUS

The frozen methane atmosphere of Uranus gives it a blue-green appearance. The planet, and its rings and moons, are all tilted by more than 90°, traveling around the Sun on their side.

Mantle of water-ice, ammonia and methane

Solid rock core

URANUS DATA

- Distance from Sun: 1,784 million miles (2,871 million km)
- Time taken to orbit Sun: 84 Earth years
- Diameter at equator: 31,763 miles (51,118 km)

NEPTUNE DATA

- Distance from Sun: 2,795 million miles (4,498 million km)
- Time taken to orbit Sun: 165 Earth years
- Diameter at equator: 30,775 miles (49,528 km)

NEPTUNE

The outermost gas giant, Neptune's atmosphere is very similar to Uranus, but more methane in its outer layer gives it a deeper blue color. Huge, cyclonic storms form the planet's Great Dark Spot.

Silicate rock core

Methane, ammonia, and water-ice mantle

Great Dark Spot

13 MOONS

Dark, low clouds of hydrogen sulfide

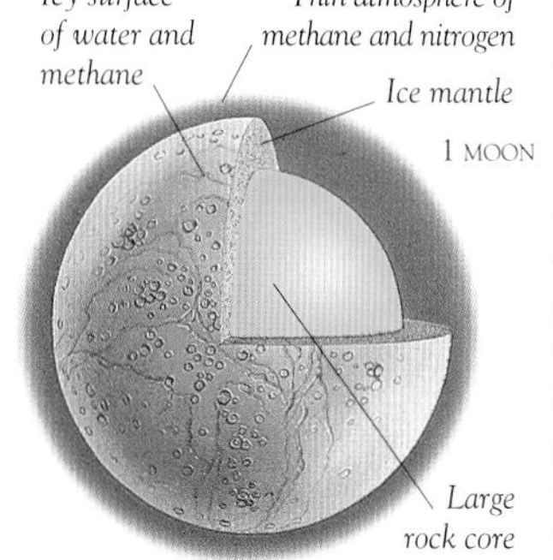
Icy surface of water and methane
Thin atmosphere of methane and nitrogen
Ice mantle
Large rock core

1 MOON

PLUTO

The smallest and most distant of all the planets, Pluto is made of ice, rock, and frozen gases. Its orbit around the Sun is uniquely tilted at 17°, and for about ten percent of its journey it is closer to the Sun than Neptune is.

PLUTO DATA

- Distance from Sun: 3,670 million miles (5,906.4 million km)
- Time taken to orbit Sun: 248 Earth years
- Diameter at equator: 1,485 miles (2,390 km)

EARTH'S MOON

THE MOON, Earth's only natural satellite, is a ball of rock held in place by our planet's gravity. A quarter of the size of Earth, the Moon is dead, waterless, and airless. As Earth orbits the Sun, the Moon in turn rotates around Earth. Each rotation, or lunar cycle, takes about a month.

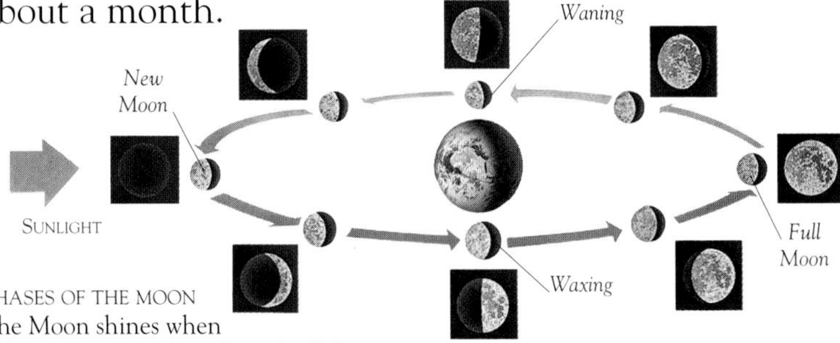
Waning
New Moon
SUNLIGHT
Full Moon
Waxing

PHASES OF THE MOON
The Moon shines when light from the Sun is reflected off the lunar surface. As it travels around Earth, the sunlit area we see changes. A monthly cycle of lunar phases is produced as it waxes (grows) from New Moon to Full Moon and wanes (shrinks) back to New Moon.

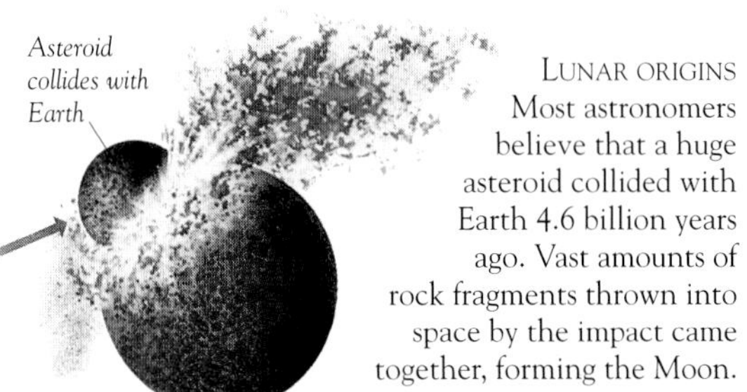
Asteroid collides with Earth

LUNAR ORIGINS
Most astronomers believe that a huge asteroid collided with Earth 4.6 billion years ago. Vast amounts of rock fragments thrown into space by the impact came together, forming the Moon.

MOON DATA

- Distance from Earth: 238,860 miles (384,400 km)
- Time to rotate on axis: 27.3 Earth days
- Diameter: 2,159 miles (3,475 km)
- Lunar temperature: –247°F to +221°F (–155°C to +105°C)

Battered surface

Meteorite impacts scar the lunar surface with craters.

3,800 million years ago
The Moon's surface receives a heavy meteorite bombardment.

The lunar seas form from volcanic lava.

2,800 million years ago
Volcanic eruptions fill the largest craters with dark lava.

Rays of rock fan out from the rim of new craters.

Today
The surface has hardly changed apart from a few recent ray craters.

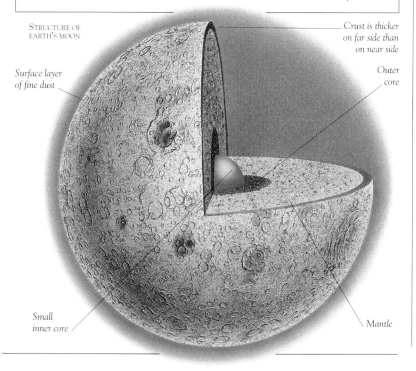

Structure of Earth's Moon

Crust is thicker on far side than on near side

Surface layer of fine dust

Outer core

Small inner core

Mantle

ASTRONOMY

VISIBLE STARLIGHT magnified by optical telescopes is only a small part of the electromagnetic spectrum, which includes all forms of radiation. Astronomers learn about the visible and invisible parts of the universe by looking at other types of radiation, such as radio waves and X-rays. Space telescopes provide the best view, collecting information from wavelengths usually absorbed by the atmosphere.

HIGH AND DRY
The Cerro Las Campanas Observatory is situated high in the mountains of Chile. A dry climate with cloud-free nights and a steady atmosphere makes this an ideal location for clear viewing through an optical telescope.

DIFFERENT IMAGES OF THE CRAB NEBULA

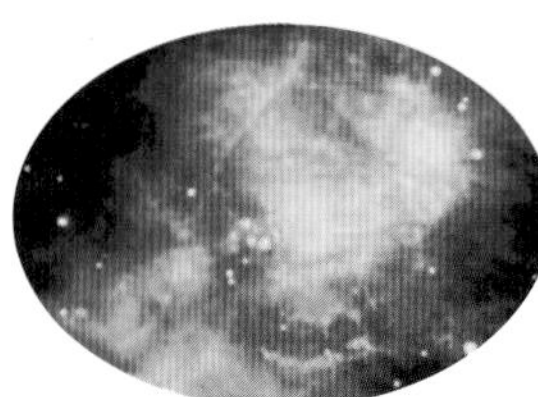

INFRARED (ABOVE)
The Crab Nebula is the remnant of a supernova explosion. When viewed in infrared light, the nebula looks like a huge cloud. The red areas represent the cooler parts of the nebula.

VISIBLE LIGHT (BELOW)
In visible light, vast filaments of hot gas can be seen. The blue glow comes from fast-moving particles accelerated by strong magnetism inside the nebula.

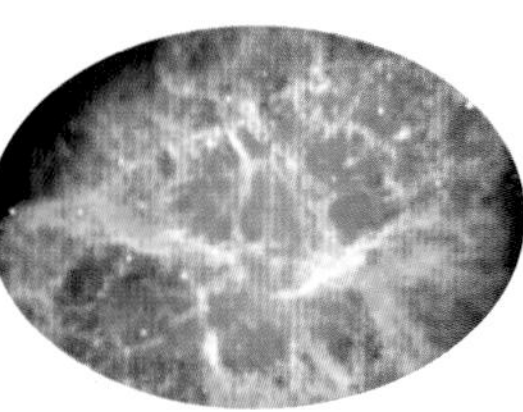

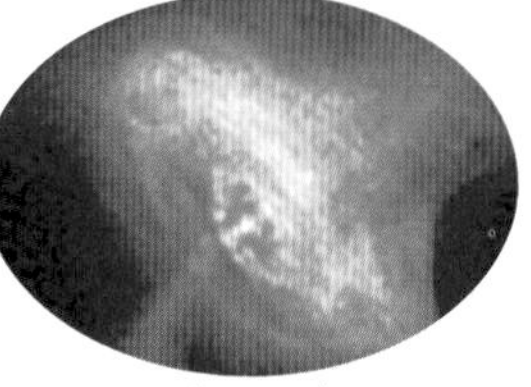

X-RAY (ABOVE)
An X-ray image reveals the magnetism's source – a rapidly spinning pulsar at the nebula's heart. The pulsar is surrounded by high-energy particles that spiral around the pulsar's magnetic field lines.

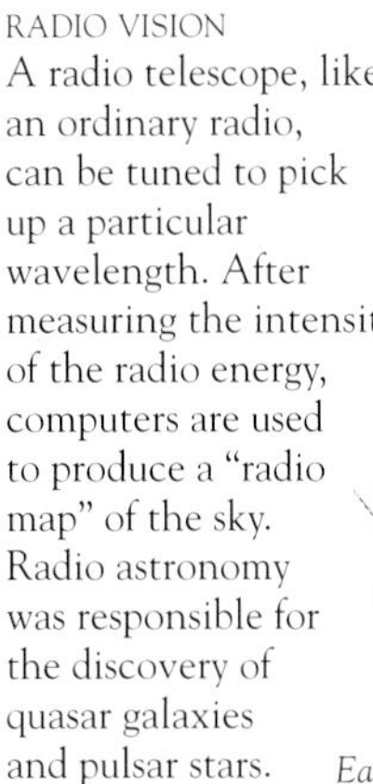

RADIO VISION

A radio telescope, like an ordinary radio, can be tuned to pick up a particular wavelength. After measuring the intensity of the radio energy, computers are used to produce a "radio map" of the sky. Radio astronomy was responsible for the discovery of quasar galaxies and pulsar stars.

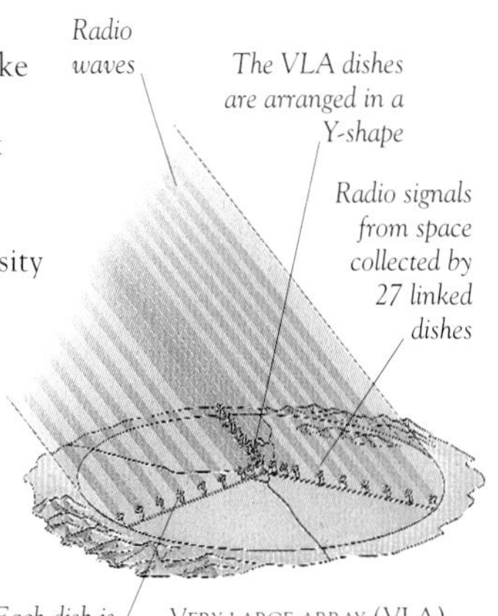
Radio waves
The VLA dishes are arranged in a Y-shape
Radio signals from space collected by 27 linked dishes
Each dish is 82 ft (25 m) across

VERY LARGE ARRAY (VLA) RADIO TELESCOPE, NEW MEXICO

ASTRONOMY FACTS

- The world's largest radio telescope is at Arecibo, Puerto Rico, with a dish 1,000 ft (305 m) across.
- The largest optical telescope is the Keck Telescope, situated at Mauna Kea, Hawaii.
- The oldest existing observatory was built in South Korea in A.D. 72.

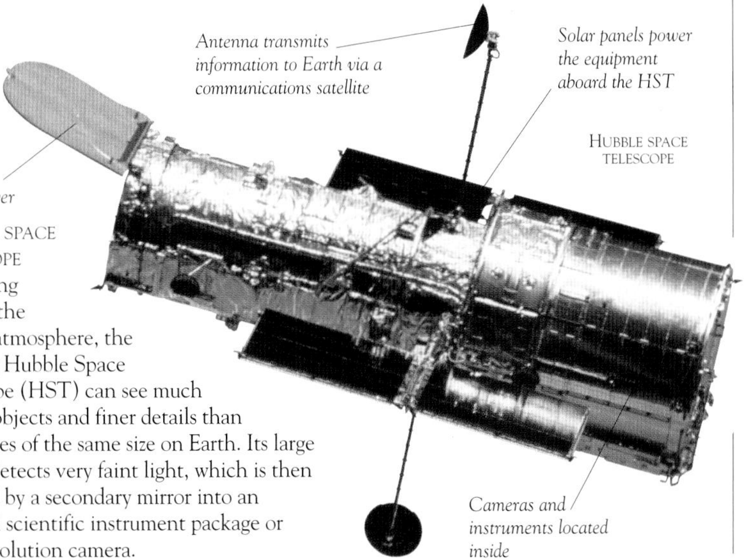

Antenna transmits information to Earth via a communications satellite

Solar panels power the equipment aboard the HST

HUBBLE SPACE TELESCOPE

Protective hinged cover

Cameras and instruments located inside

HUBBLE SPACE TELESCOPE

Operating outside the Earth's atmosphere, the orbiting Hubble Space Telescope (HST) can see much fainter objects and finer details than telescopes of the same size on Earth. Its large mirror detects very faint light, which is then directed by a secondary mirror into an onboard scientific instrument package or high-resolution camera.

ROCKETS AND SPACECRAFT

THE FIRST ARTIFICIAL satellite, Sputnik 1, was launched into space in 1957. Since then, hundreds of spacecraft have been launched, including manned missions for exploration, orbiting space laboratories, and probes to other planets. Powerful rocket engines enable spacecraft to escape the pull of Earth's gravity.

STAGE FLIGHT
Rockets are designed in separate stages, so that when all the fuel from a stage has been used up, that stage drops away and the next takes over. The giant three-stage Saturn V rocket carried astronauts to the Moon.

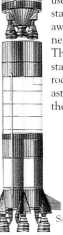

SATURN V

Solid fuel boosters jettisoned 2 mins 5 secs after liftoff, at an altitude of 28 miles (45 km). Shuttle now traveling at 4.5 times the speed of sound (Mach 4.5)

Shuttle reaches altitude of 81 miles (130 km) at Mach 15. External tank released, burning up in Earth's atmosphere

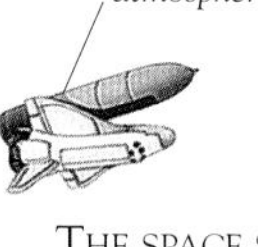

Shuttle engines put orbiter into circular orbit

Solid fuel burns for two minutes. Each solid fuel rocket produces the thrust of 11 Boeing 747 airliners at take-off

Main engines on orbiter take fuel from external tank. Two solid-fuel rocket boosters fire for liftoff

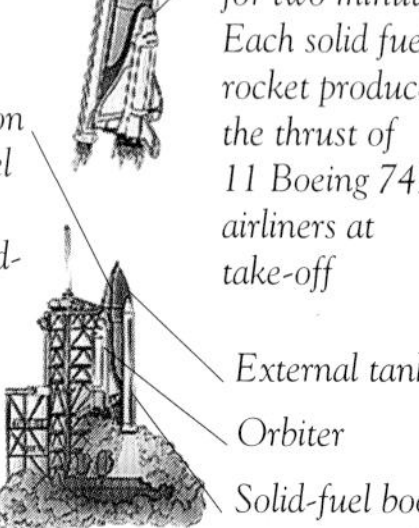

External tank

Orbiter

Solid-fuel boosters

THE SPACE SHUTTLE
The US space shuttle is the world's first reusable spacecraft. Typical shuttle missions include launching, retrieving, or repairing satellites, and carrying parts for the International Space Station. At launch, the space shuttle is propelled by reusable solid-fuel boosters, in addition to its three liquid-fueled engines.

SPACE STATION
Assembled in space by astronauts aided by tools, cranes, and a robotic arm aboard the space shuttle, the International Space Station (ISS) is a collaboration between 16 countries. Pressurized living modules for up to seven astronauts are linked to laboratories and work stations. Astronauts live and work on the ISS for up to six months at a time.

INTERNATIONAL SPACE STATION

Orbiter remains in orbit for 5–30 days to carry out mission. Cargo bay doors open, venting excess heat

Cargo bay doors close. Engines rotate orbiter into reentry position

Orbiter maneuvers into precise angle for reentry, beginning 30-minute descent into atmosphere at Mach 22.4

Parts of nose and wings reach 2,660°F (1,460°C) during reentry

Orbiter glides in to land at a speed of 214 mph (345 km/h). It is towed, or flown on the back of a Boeing 747, to the next launch site

SPACE PROBES
Computer-controlled space probes are designed to gather data about planets in the solar system. The Galileo probe, launched in 1989, was sent to collect information about Jupiter.

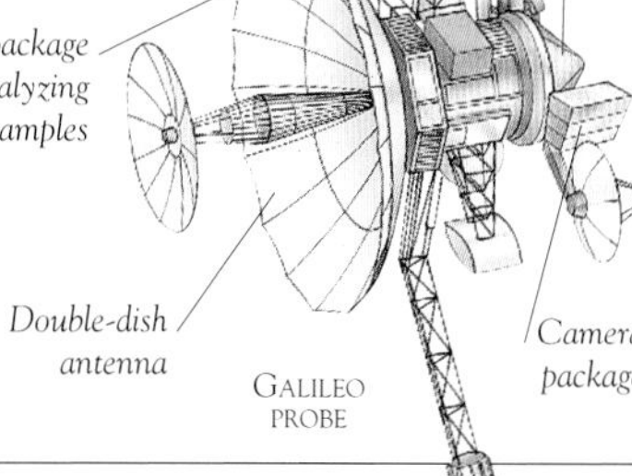
Magnetic sensors mounted on long boom to minimize interference
Atmospheric descent probe
Instrument package for analyzing atmosphere samples
Double-dish antenna
Camera package
GALILEO PROBE

1926–1968	1969–1976

1926 US engineer Robert Goddard designs and launches first liquid fuel rocket.
1942 Wernher von Braun, later to play a major role in the postwar US space program, develops Nazi Germany's rocket-powered *V2* flying bomb.
1957 Launch of USSR's *Sputnik 1*, the world's first artificial satellite.
1957 Russian dog Laika becomes first living creature in space aboard *Sputnik 2*.
1961 The first manned spacecraft, *Vostok 1*, carries Soviet cosmonaut Yuri Gagarin into Earth orbit.

Yuri Gagarin

1962 US probe *Mariner 2* flies past Venus, becoming first human-made object to "flyby" another planet.
1963 First woman in space is USSR's Valentina Tereshkova, orbiting Earth 48 times in two days in *Vostok* 6.
1965 Russian cosmonaut Alexei Leonov takes the first walk in space.
US probe *Mariner 4* finds no sign of water or life on Mars.
1966 Unmanned Soviet probe *Luna* 9 lands on Moon.
1968 US astronauts enter lunar orbit in *Apollo* 8.

1969 US astronauts Neil Armstrong and Edwin M. Aldrin are the first humans to walk on the Moon.

Edwin M. Aldrin steps onto the lunar surface

1970 USSR's *Venera 7* lands on Venus. It is the first probe to touch down on another planet.
1970 Soviet robot *Lunokhod*, the first extraterrestrial land vehicle, is driven across the Moon's surface.
1971 The first orbiting space station, the USSR's *Salyut 1*, is launched.
1972 *Apollo 17* is sixth and last US manned mission to the moon.
1973 Launch of *Skylab*, the first US space station. Close-up images of Jupiter taken by US *Pioneer 10*.
1974 US *Mariner 10* transmits first pictures of Mercury.
1975 First images of the surface of Venus sent by USSR's *Venera 9*.
1976 Surface tests carried out by US probe *Viking 1* confirm no life on planet Mars.

Martian surface

1977–1989

1977 US *Voyagers 1* and *2* start their long journey to the outer planets and beyond.
1979 US *Pioneer 11* reaches Saturn after a six-year voyage, finding a new ring and new moons. *Voyagers 1* and *2* pass Jupiter, observing active volcanoes on the moon Io.
1980 *Voyager 1* takes close-up photographs of Saturn's rings.

Saturn, photographed by Voyager 1

1981 Launch of US space shuttle *Columbia*, the first reusable spacecraft.
1986 Shuttle program halted after *Challenger* explosion kills the crew of seven. *Voyager 2* reaches Uranus and finds a ring system and 15 moons. The European probe Giotto photographs the nucleus of Halley's comet.
1987 Supernova 1987A explodes in the Large Magellanic Cloud, a neighbor of the Milky Way. It is visible to the naked eye for several months.
1988 Launch of *Discovery* resumes the US space shuttle program.
1989 *Voyager 2* reaches Neptune and discovers six new moons.

1990–2003

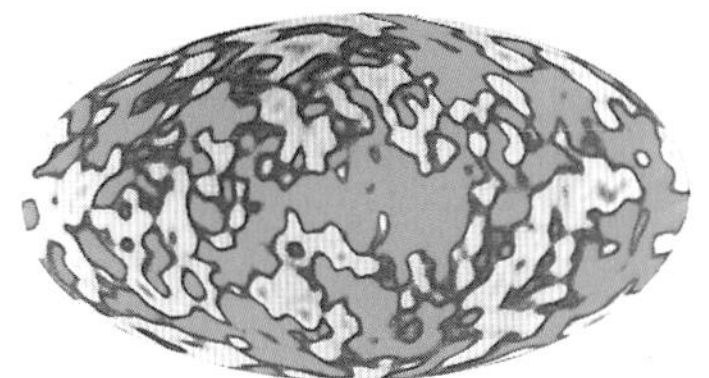

COBE image of microwave background

1990 Hubble space telescope launched (with faulty mirror).
1992 US COBE (Cosmic Background Explorer) finds hotspots in "microwave background" radio energy, providing evidence for the Big Bang theory.
1994 Fragments of Comet Shoemaker-Levy 9 hit Jupiter, producing dark marks in the planet's clouds. Hubble telescope repaired.
1995 A Jupiter-sized planet is detected around a star 50 light-years from Earth.
1996 US scientists find fossil evidence in meteorite fragments that microbes may once have existed on Mars.
1997 A small roving vehicle called *Sojourner* lands on Mars and explores the Martian surface for three months.
1998 First section of the International Space Station is launched.
2000 The NEAR-Shoemaker probe goes into orbit around the asteroid Eros. First crew begins permanent occupation of the International Space Station.
2001 Russian space station Mir burns up in the atmosphere after 15 years in orbit.
2003 Shuttle *Columbia* breaks up during reentry, with the loss of seven lives.

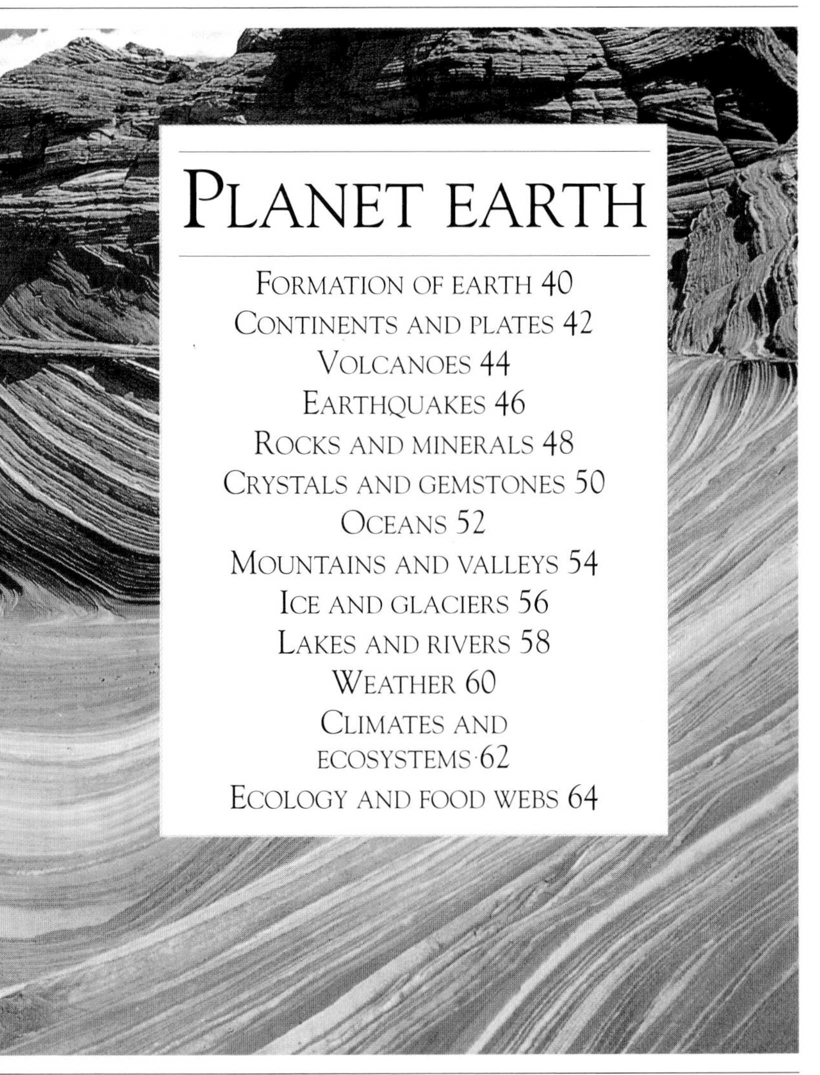

PLANET EARTH

FORMATION OF EARTH

ABOUT 4.6 BILLION years ago, the planets of the solar system were just a vast cloud of gas swirling around the newly formed Sun. Earth and the other planets formed when parts of this cloud began to cluster together.

3 EARTH'S CRUST About 4 billion years ago, Earth's crust began to form. Blocks of cooling, solid rock floated on a molten rock layer. The rock sometimes sank and remelted before rising again.

1 FORMING THE SUN A spinning cloud of dust and gas contracted to form the Sun. Cooler matter from this dust cloud combined to shape the planets.

Dense cosmic gases surrounded Earth as it formed

Sea 70.8%

Land 29.2%

PROPORTION OF LAND AND SEA

2 FORMING EARTH Radioactivity in Earth's rocks caused the planet's surface to melt. Lighter minerals floated to the surface, and heavier elements, such as iron and nickel, sank to form Earth's core.

4 MAKING THE ATMOSPHERE Over millions of years Earth's crust thickened, while gases from erupting volcanoes began to form the atmosphere. Water vapor condensed to make oceans.

EARTH DATA

- Distance from Sun: 93 million miles (150 million km)
- Time to rotate on axis: 23 hours, 56 minutes
- Time to orbit Sun: 365 days, 6 hours
- Speed of Earth's orbits of Sun: 18.5 miles/sec (29.8 km/sec)

Crust composed of rocks similar to those on surface – 4–43 miles (6–70 km) deep

Atmosphere – about 400 miles (640 km) deep

Mantle of mostly solid rock – 1,800 miles (2,900 km) deep

COMPOSITION OF EARTH

Our planet is composed of several layers of rock around a core of iron and nickel. The deeper the layer, the higher the temperature.

Outer core of liquid iron, nickel, and oxygen – 1,240 miles (2,000 km) deep

Inner core of solid iron and nickel – 1,700 miles (2,740 km) deep

5 LAND FORMS

Large landmasses, or protocontinents, began to form on the planet's crust about 3,500 million years ago. Today's continents look very different.

6 EARTH TODAY

The planet is still changing – the huge tectonic plates (see pp. 42–43) that make up Earth's crust are constantly moving, pulling some continents nearer and pushing others apart.

CONTINENTS AND PLATES

THE SEVEN HUGE landmasses that make up most of Earth's surface are called continents. They are always slowly moving, shifted around by forces deep inside Earth. This movement is known as continental drift.

The crack or boundary between two plates sliding past each other is called a transform fault

TECTONIC PLATES

Earth's crust, or lithosphere, is made up of vast pieces of rock, called tectonic plates.

Earth's tectonic plates fit together like jigsaw puzzle pieces

PLATE BOUNDARIES

Where they meet, tectonic plates may be sliding past each other, pulling apart, or colliding. These different types of motion cause earthquakes and volcanoes, create steep-sided valleys, form deep-sea trenches, and build mountains.

CONTINENTAL DRIFT

N. America
Europe
PANGAEA
Asia
India
Africa
Australia
S. America
Antarctica

1 Some 220 million years ago (mya) the continents were joined together in the giant supercontinent of Pangaea (a Greek word meaning "all lands").

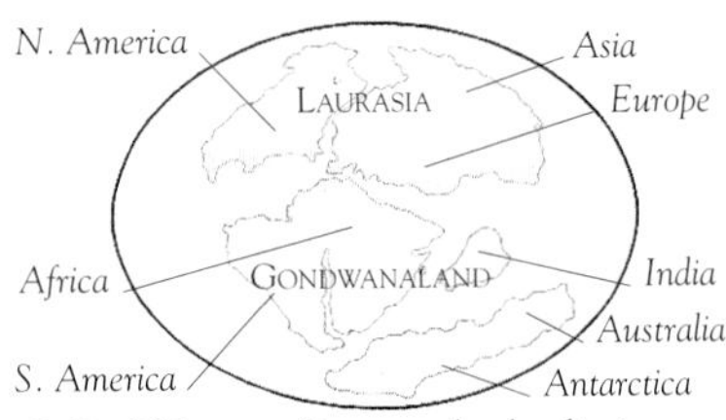
N. America
Asia
LAURASIA
Europe
Africa
GONDWANALAND
India
Australia
S. America
Antarctica

2 By 200 mya, Pangaea had split into two landmasses, Gondwanaland and Laurasia. Around 135 mya, these landmasses also began to divide.

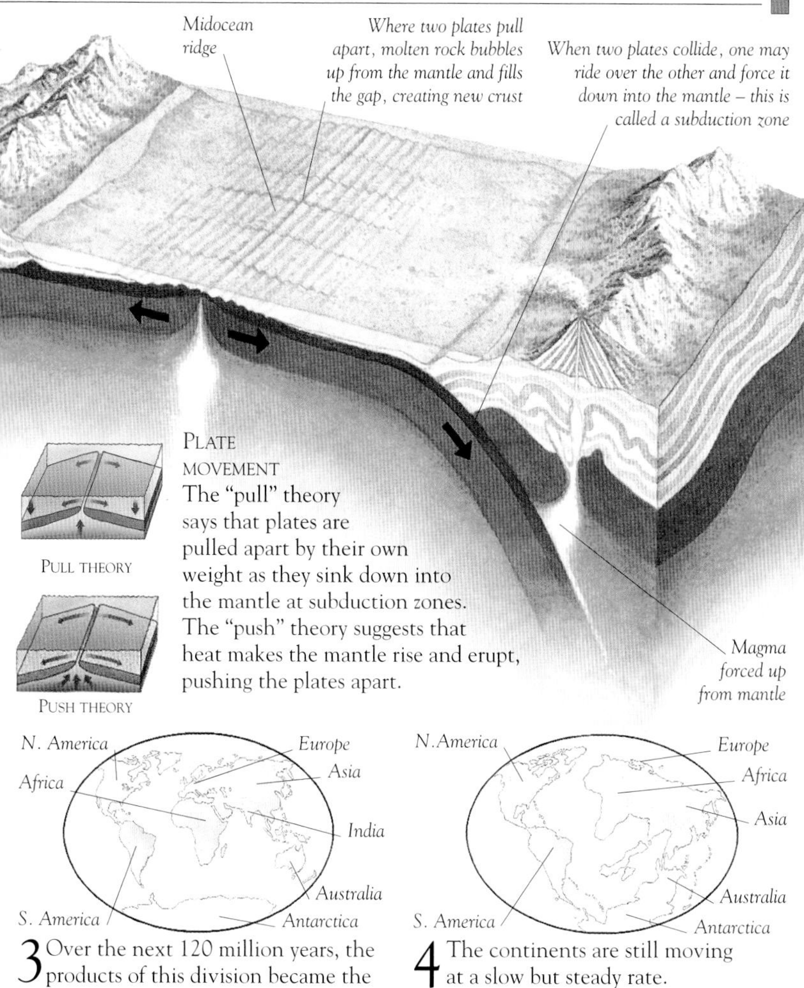
Midocean ridge
Where two plates pull apart, molten rock bubbles up from the mantle and fills the gap, creating new crust
When two plates collide, one may ride over the other and force it down into the mantle – this is called a subduction zone
Magma forced up from mantle
PULL THEORY
PUSH THEORY

PLATE MOVEMENT The "pull" theory says that plates are pulled apart by their own weight as they sink down into the mantle at subduction zones. The "push" theory suggests that heat makes the mantle rise and erupt, pushing the plates apart.

N. America
Europe
Asia
Africa
India
Australia
S. America
Antarctica

3 Over the next 120 million years, the products of this division became the continents, drifting closer or farther apart to take up their current positions.

N.America
Europe
Africa
Asia
Australia
S. America
Antarctica

4 The continents are still moving at a slow but steady rate. This is how Earth may look in 150 million years.

VOLCANOES

A VOLCANIC ERUPTION takes place when hot, molten rock called magma rises up from deep inside Earth and forces its way to the surface. The magma may erupt as a flow of red-hot lava, or explode into clouds of ash, rock, and dust.

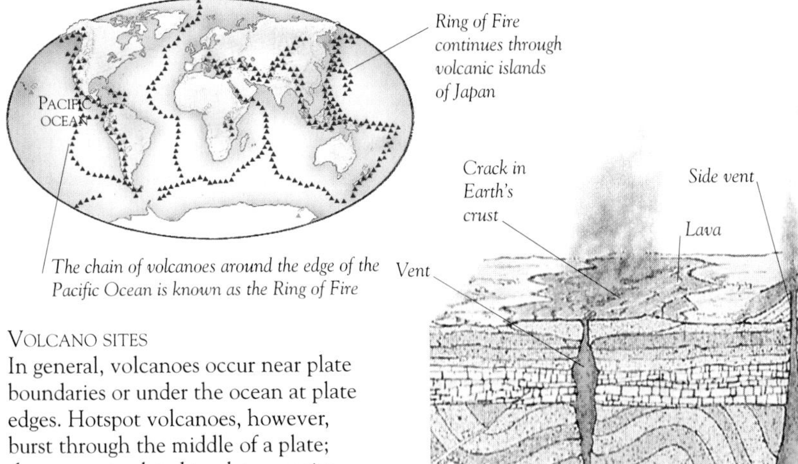
Ring of Fire continues through volcanic islands of Japan
PACIFIC OCEAN
Crack in Earth's crust
Side vent
Lava
Vent

The chain of volcanoes around the edge of the Pacific Ocean is known as the Ring of Fire

VOLCANO SITES
In general, volcanoes occur near plate boundaries or under the ocean at plate edges. Hotspot volcanoes, however, burst through the middle of a plate; they are not related to plate margins.

ERUPTION SIZES
The amount of ash thrown out during an eruption is a good indicator of the size of an eruption.

MT. ST. HELENS US 1980

MT. VESUVIUS ITALY A.D. 79

MT. KATMAI ALASKA 1912

MT. KRAKATOA INDONESIA 1883

MT. TAMBORA INDONESIA 1815

FISSURE VOLCANO
This type of volcano is a long crack in the crust. Liquid lava seeps out along its length and forms a plateau.

Volcano facts

- The worst volcanic eruption was Mount Tambora, Indonesia, which killed 92,000 people in 1815.
- Kilauea, Hawaii, is the most frequently active volcano.

Composite volcano

Cone-shaped volcanoes build up from hardening sticky lava. Inside are layers of thick lava and ash from previous eruptions. Gas builds up pressure inside the volcano until it erupts violently.

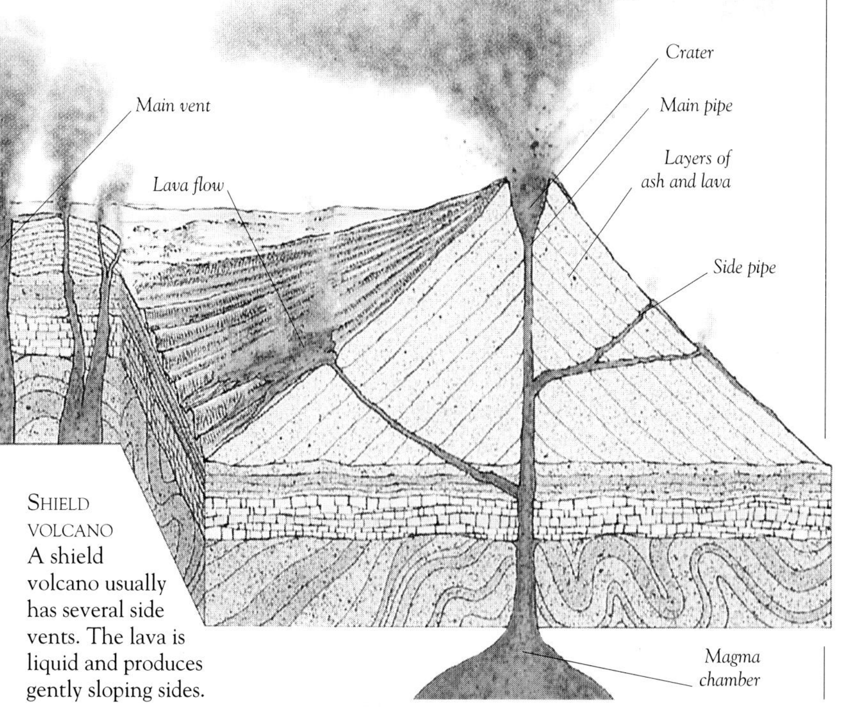
Clouds of ash, rock, and dust
Crater
Main vent
Main pipe
Lava flow
Layers of ash and lava
Side pipe
Magma chamber

Shield volcano

A shield volcano usually has several side vents. The lava is liquid and produces gently sloping sides.

EARTHQUAKES

A MAJOR EARTHQUAKE occurs when the massive tectonic plates that make up Earth's crust suddenly move. A mild earthquake can feel like a truck passing; a severe one can destroy roads and buildings and cause huge tidal waves in the ocean.

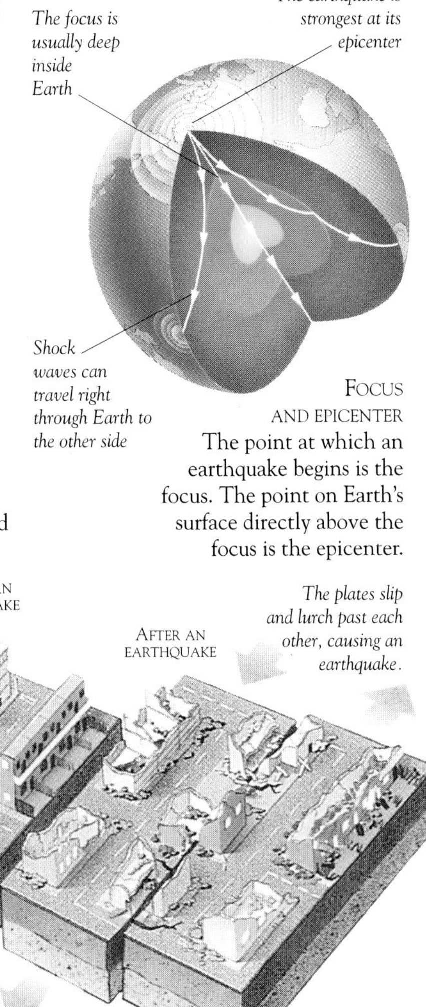
The focus is usually deep inside Earth
The earthquake is strongest at its epicenter
Shock waves can travel right through Earth to the other side
BEFORE AN EARTHQUAKE
AFTER AN EARTHQUAKE
The plates slip and lurch past each other, causing an earthquake.
This fault line marks the boundary of two plates

FOCUS AND EPICENTER

The point at which an earthquake begins is the focus. The point on Earth's surface directly above the focus is the epicenter.

CLOSE-UP OF AN EARTHQUAKE

At transform faults,where two plates are moving in opposite directions, the jagged edges of the plates may lock together. Stress builds up within the plates, until suddenly they slip, making the ground shake violently as they jolt into a new position.

Earthquake fault zones

Most earthquakes occur on or near the edges of Earth's tectonic plates (see pp. 42–43) at cracks in the crust called faults. Deep earthquakes take place where one plate is sliding under another.

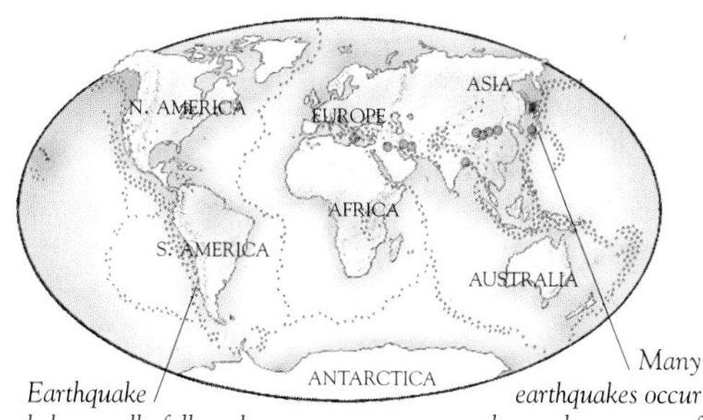
N. AMERICA
EUROPE
ASIA
AFRICA
S. AMERICA
AUSTRALIA
ANTARCTICA

Earthquake belts usually follow the edges of Earth's tectonic plates

Many earthquakes occur on the northeast coast of Asia. This is at the boundary of two of Earth's plates

Earthquake-proof buildings

In earthquake-prone areas, specially designed buildings can lessen the effects of an earthquake.

Pyramid-shaped buildings are built to withstand stress

TRANSAMERICA BUILDING, SAN FRANCISCO

The central column of the pagoda absorbs the shaking

ANCIENT BUDDHIST PAGODA, JAPAN

Earthquake facts

- The strongest known earthquake occurred in Colombia in 1906, with a magnitude of 8.9 on the Richter scale.
- The highest recorded number of deaths from an earthquake is 830,000, occurring in Shansi, China, in 1556.
- The worst earthquake damage on record took place in Kwanto, Japan, in 1923, destroying 375,000 homes and killing 144,000 people.

ROCKS AND MINERALS

THERE ARE MANY different types of rock, all of which are composed of one or more minerals. Rocks are the building blocks from which Earth's crust is formed.

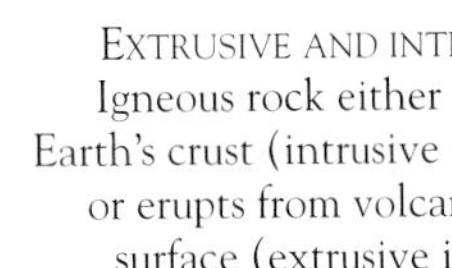
Earth's surface
Extrusive igneous rock
Intrusive igneous rock

EXTRUSIVE AND INTRUSIVE ROCKS
Igneous rock either settles within Earth's crust (intrusive igneous rock) or erupts from volcanoes onto the surface (extrusive igneous rock).

TYPES OF ROCKS

The study of rocks is called geology. All types of rocks fall into one of three categories: igneous, sedimentary, or metamorphic.

Basalt is an igneous rock.

IGNEOUS ROCK
When molten magma rising from deep within Earth begins to cool and solidify, it forms igneous rock.

METAMORPHIC ROCK
When igneous or sedimentary rock is changed by heat and/or pressure, it is called metamorphic rock.

Gneiss is a metamorphic rock.

Sandstone is a sedimentary rock.

SEDIMENTARY ROCK
Wind and rainwater deposit rock fragments as sediments in lakes, rivers, sand dunes, and on the sea floor. They are compressed over millions of years into layers of sedimentary rock.

MINERAL HARDNESS
The hardness of a mineral is graded on a scale of 1 to 10, devised by German mineralogist Friedrich Mohs (1773–1839).

MOHS' SCALE

1: TALC

2: GYPSUM

3: CALCITE

4: FLUORITE

MINERALS

A mineral is a non-living substance occurring naturally in Earth's crust. Most minerals are formed from silicates (compounds of oxygen and silicon).

Granite is composed of the minerals quartz, feldspar, and mica.

ROCK-FORMING MINERALS

Different combinations of minerals form different types of rock.

Chalcopyrite (copper ore); copper is a good conductor, widely used in the electricity industry.

ORE MINERALS

About 80 types of pure metal are extracted from ore minerals.

THE ROCK CYCLE

All rocks are constantly passing through a recycling process.

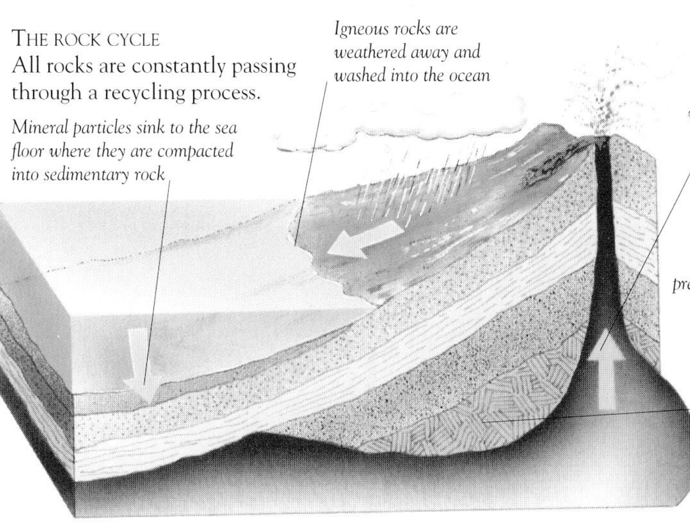
Mineral particles sink to the sea floor where they are compacted into sedimentary rock
Igneous rocks are weathered away and washed into the ocean
Rock melts and rises to the surface, where it cools to form igneous rock
Heat and pressure change sedimentary and igneous rock into metamorphic rock

5: APATITE

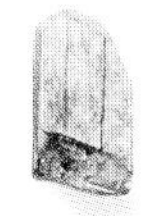

6: ORTHOCLASE

7: QUARTZ

8: TOPAZ

9: CORUNDUM

10: DIAMOND

Crystals and Gemstones

A CRYSTAL IS a solid material in which atoms are arranged in a regular pattern. Crystals form, or crystallize, either from molten minerals or from minerals that are dissolved in liquids.

Crystal habit

The characteristic general shape of a crystal is called its habit.

PRISMATIC; UNIFORM CROSS SECTION (BERYL)

DENDRITIC; TREELIKE SHAPE (COPPER)

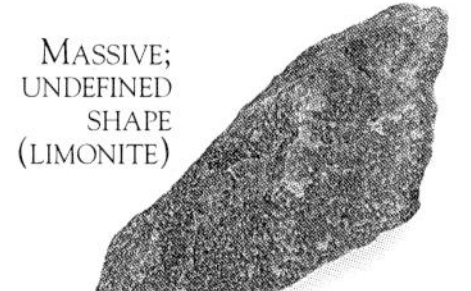

MASSIVE; UNDEFINED SHAPE (LIMONITE)

ACICULAR; NEEDLELIKE (SCOLECITE)

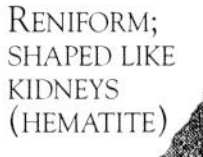

RENIFORM; SHAPED LIKE KIDNEYS (HEMATITE)

Crystal systems

The geometrical shape in which a mineral crystallizes is called its crystal system.

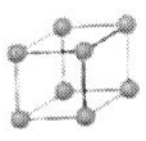

CUBIC SYSTEM
All 90° angles. All edges equal in length.

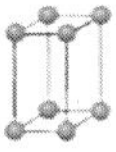

TETRAGONAL SYSTEM
All 90° angles. Two edges equal in length.

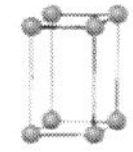

ORTHORHOMBIC SYSTEM
All 90° angles. No edges equal in length.

MONOCLINIC SYSTEM
Two edges meet at 90°. No edges equal in length.

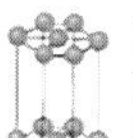

HEXAGONAL SYSTEM
Edges form angles of 90° and 120°. Two equal-length edges.

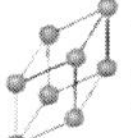

TRIGONAL SYSTEM
No angles meet at 90°. All edges of equal length.

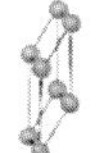

TRICLINIC SYSTEM
No edges meet at 90°. No edges equal in length.

GEMSTONES

Minerals valued for their beauty, rarity, and durability are called gemstones. There are about 100 types; the most valued include diamonds and rubies.

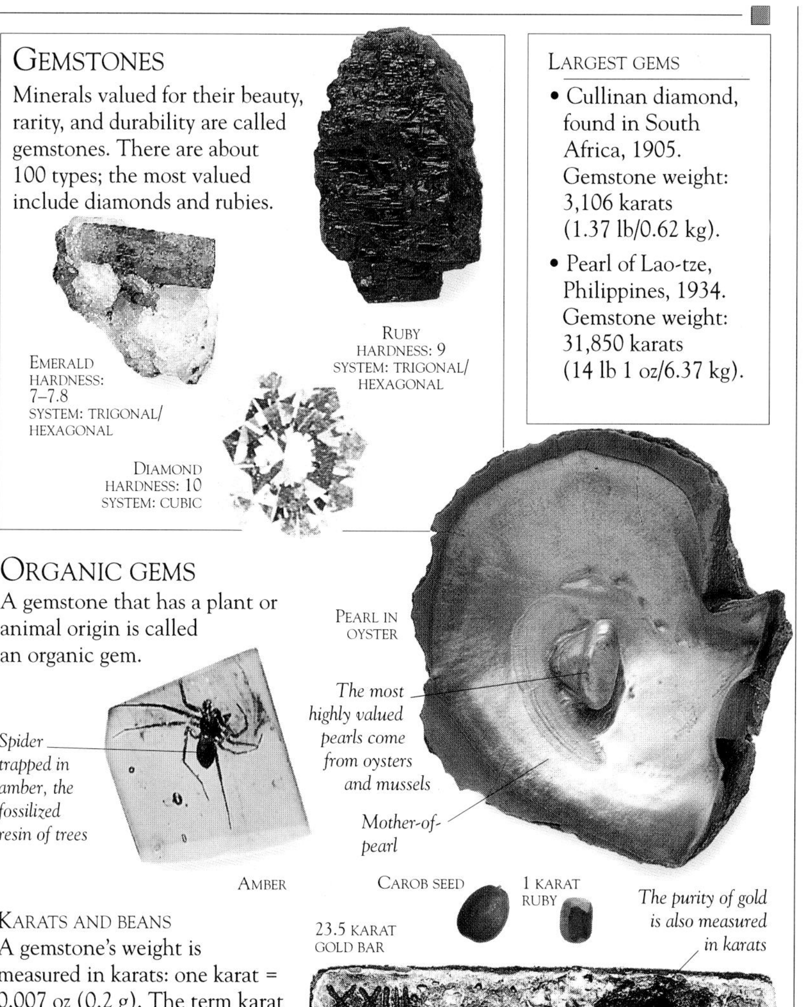
EMERALD
HARDNESS: 7–7.8
SYSTEM: TRIGONAL/ HEXAGONAL
RUBY
HARDNESS: 9
SYSTEM: TRIGONAL/ HEXAGONAL
DIAMOND
HARDNESS: 10
SYSTEM: CUBIC
PEARL IN OYSTER
The most highly valued pearls come from oysters and mussels
Mother-of-pearl
Spider trapped in amber, the fossilized resin of trees
AMBER

LARGEST GEMS

- Cullinan diamond, found in South Africa, 1905. Gemstone weight: 3,106 karats (1.37 lb/0.62 kg).
- Pearl of Lao-tze, Philippines, 1934. Gemstone weight: 31,850 karats (14 lb 1 oz/6.37 kg).

ORGANIC GEMS

A gemstone that has a plant or animal origin is called an organic gem.

KARATS AND BEANS

A gemstone's weight is measured in karats: one karat = 0.007 oz (0.2 g). The term karat is the Greek word for carob seed; these were once used as weights.

CAROB SEED
1 KARAT RUBY
23.5 KARAT GOLD BAR
The purity of gold is also measured in karats

OCEANS

MORE THAN TWO-THIRDS of Earth's surface lies under its oceans. The water in these oceans is never still; it is constant motion from currents, tides, and waves.

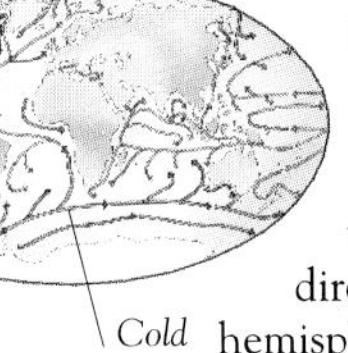
Warm current (red arrow)
Cold current (blue arrow)

OCEAN CURRENTS
Major currents circulate the oceans in a clockwise direction in the northern hemisphere and counterclockwise in the southern hemisphere. Currents may be warm or cold, flowing across the surface of the ocean or deep beneath it.

FORMATION OF AN OCEAN

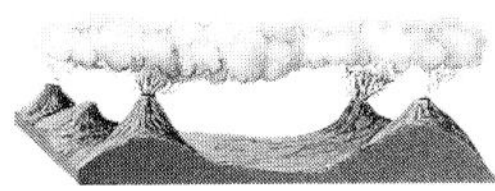

1 Volcanic gases form Earth's early atmosphere.

2 Atmospheric water vapor falls as rain and collects in vast hollows.

3 Earth cools, eruptions reduce, and sea level stabilizes.

FEATURES OF THE OCEAN FLOOR

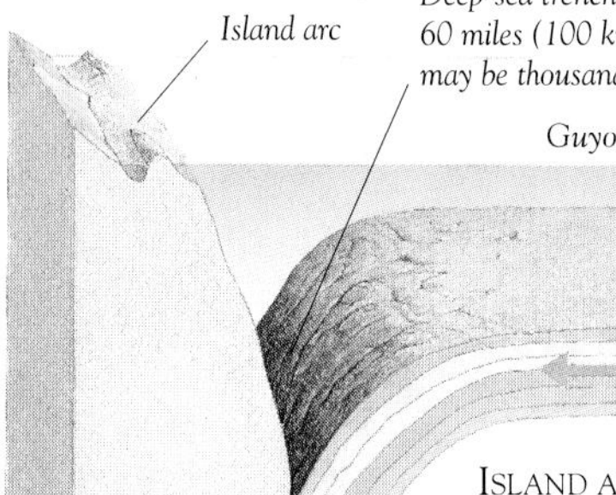
Island arc
Deep-sea trenches are about 60 miles (100 km) wide and may be thousands of miles long
Guyot (flat-topped seamount)
Escaping magma forms midocean ridge

ISLAND ARC
Molten rock from a melting, subducted oceanic plate rises through the upper plate, forming volcanic islands.

TRENCH
Where the ocean floor sinks into the mantle, long, deep trenches occur.

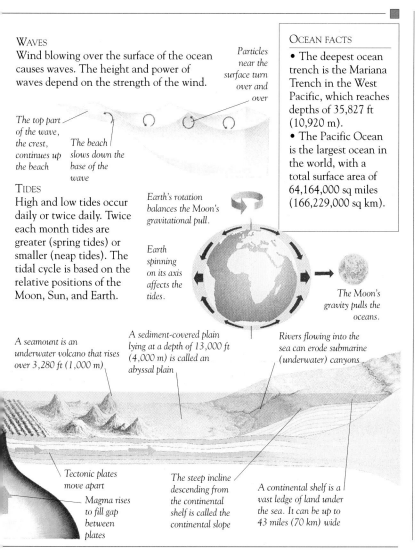

Waves

Wind blowing over the surface of the ocean causes waves. The height and power of waves depend on the strength of the wind.

Particles near the surface turn over and over

The top part of the wave, the crest, continues up the beach

The beach slows down the base of the wave

Tides

High and low tides occur daily or twice daily. Twice each month tides are greater (spring tides) or smaller (neap tides). The tidal cycle is based on the relative positions of the Moon, Sun, and Earth.

Earth's rotation balances the Moon's gravitational pull.

Earth spinning on its axis affects the tides.

The Moon's gravity pulls the oceans.

Ocean facts

- The deepest ocean trench is the Mariana Trench in the West Pacific, which reaches depths of 35,827 ft (10,920 m).
- The Pacific Ocean is the largest ocean in the world, with a total surface area of 64,164,000 sq miles (166,229,000 sq km).

A seamount is an underwater volcano that rises over 3,280 ft (1,000 m)

A sediment-covered plain lying at a depth of 13,000 ft (4,000 m) is called an abyssal plain

Rivers flowing into the sea can erode submarine (underwater) canyons

Tectonic plates move apart

Magma rises to fill gap between plates

The steep incline descending from the continental shelf is called the continental slope

A continental shelf is a vast ledge of land under the sea. It can be up to 43 miles (70 km) wide

MOUNTAINS AND VALLEYS

WHEN EARTH'S rocky tectonic plates collide, the crust may buckle and fold, forcing up lofty mountain peaks. Volcanoes also erupt at plate boundaries and sometimes build into mountains. All are slowly weathered away, as erosion wears down peaks, carves out valleys, and opens up underground caves.

LIFE OF A MOUNTAIN

1 YOUNG
High-peaked mountains that formed in the last few million years.

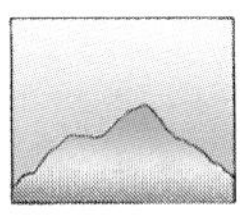

2 MATURE
Eroded mountains created several hundred million years ago.

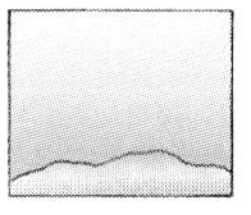

3 ANCIENT
Mountains so old and worn down that only a few hills remain.

TYPES OF MOUNTAINS

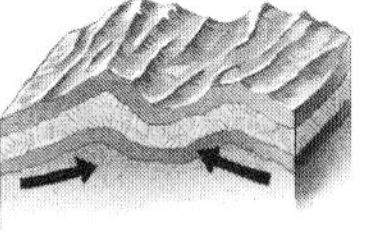

FOLD MOUNTAIN
Where two of Earth's plates collide, the rock layers buckle and bend, forcing the rocky crust up into a mountain range.

VOLCANO
Layers of volcanic lava, ash, and rock ejected from Earth's interior build up into a mountain.

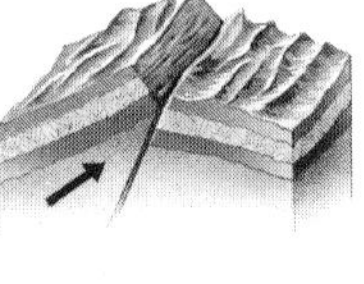

FAULT-BLOCK MOUNTAIN
When Earth's plates push together, faults or cracks appear in the crust, forcing up huge blocks of rock.

DOME MOUNTAIN
Rising magma makes the rock above bulge upward, creating a dome-shaped mountain.

MOUNTAINS AND VALLEYS

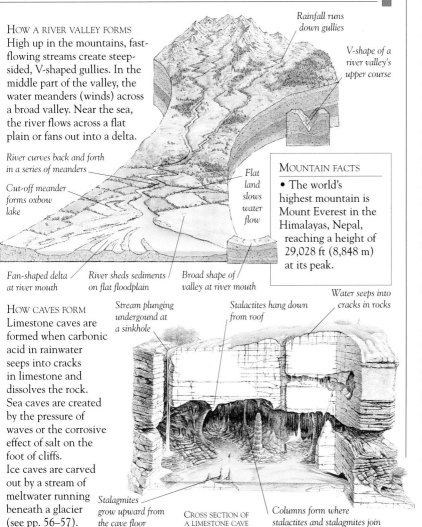

How a river valley forms

High up in the mountains, fast-flowing streams create steep-sided, V-shaped gullies. In the middle part of the valley, the water meanders (winds) across a broad valley. Near the sea, the river flows across a flat plain or fans out into a delta.

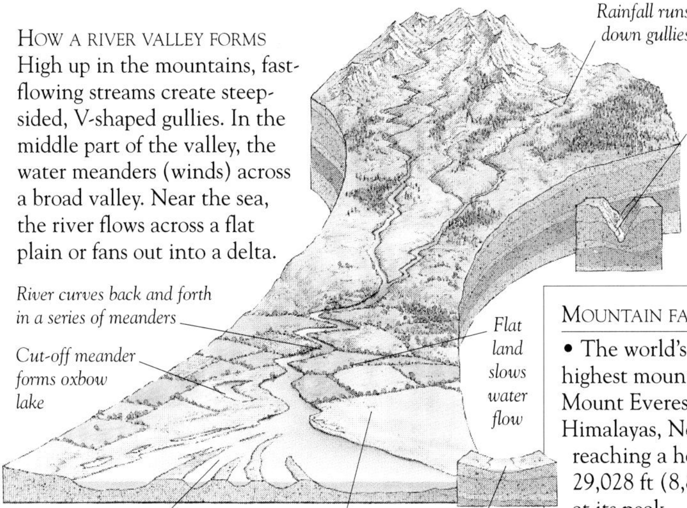

Rainfall runs down gullies

V-shape of a river valley's upper course

River curves back and forth in a series of meanders

Cut-off meander forms oxbow lake

Flat land slows water flow

Fan-shaped delta at river mouth

River sheds sediments on flat floodplain

Broad shape of valley at river mouth

Mountain facts

- The world's highest mountain is Mount Everest in the Himalayas, Nepal, reaching a height of 29,028 ft (8,848 m) at its peak.

How caves form

Limestone caves are formed when carbonic acid in rainwater seeps into cracks in limestone and dissolves the rock. Sea caves are created by the pressure of waves or the corrosive effect of salt on the foot of cliffs. Ice caves are carved out by a stream of meltwater running beneath a glacier (see pp. 56–57).

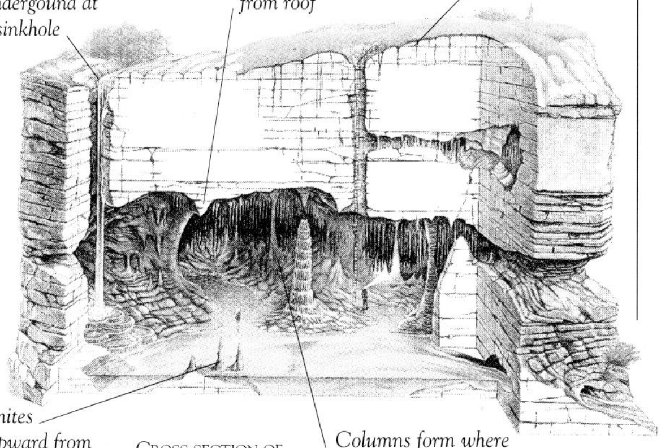

Stream plunging undergound at a sinkhole

Stalactites hang down from roof

Water seeps into cracks in rocks

Stalagmites grow upward from the cave floor

Columns form where stalactites and stalagmites join

Cross section of a limestone cave

ICE AND GLACIERS

MORE THAN ONE-TENTH of the Earth's land surface is always covered by ice. At the Poles and in high mountain regions, vast areas are covered by ice sheets and rivers of ice called glaciers.

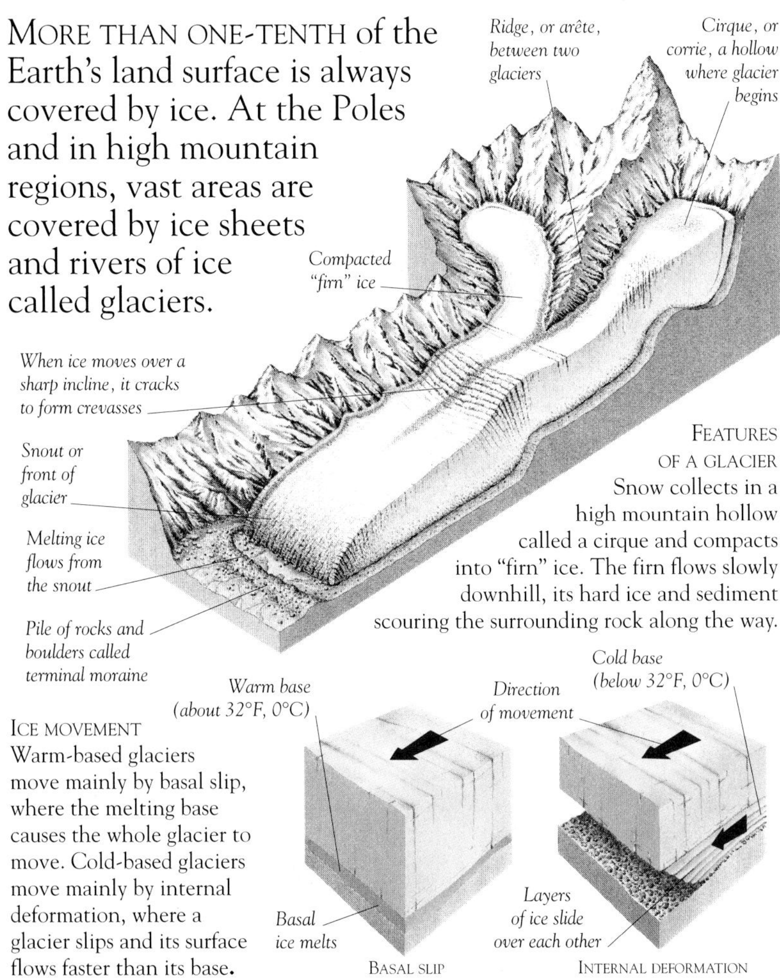
Ridge, or arête, between two glaciers
Cirque, or corrie, a hollow where glacier begins
Compacted "firn" ice
When ice moves over a sharp incline, it cracks to form crevasses
Snout or front of glacier
Melting ice flows from the snout
Pile of rocks and boulders called terminal moraine
Warm base (about 32°F, 0°C)
Direction of movement
Cold base (below 32°F, 0°C)
Basal ice melts
Layers of ice slide over each other
BASAL SLIP
INTERNAL DEFORMATION

FEATURES OF A GLACIER
Snow collects in a high mountain hollow called a cirque and compacts into "firn" ice. The firn flows slowly downhill, its hard ice and sediment scouring the surrounding rock along the way.

ICE MOVEMENT
Warm-based glaciers move mainly by basal slip, where the melting base causes the whole glacier to move. Cold-based glaciers move mainly by internal deformation, where a glacier slips and its surface flows faster than its base.

ICEBERGS

Fragments of ice that float out to sea after breaking off ice sheets, ice caps, and glaciers are called icebergs. This process is called calving. Only 12 percent of an iceberg is visible above the sea's surface.

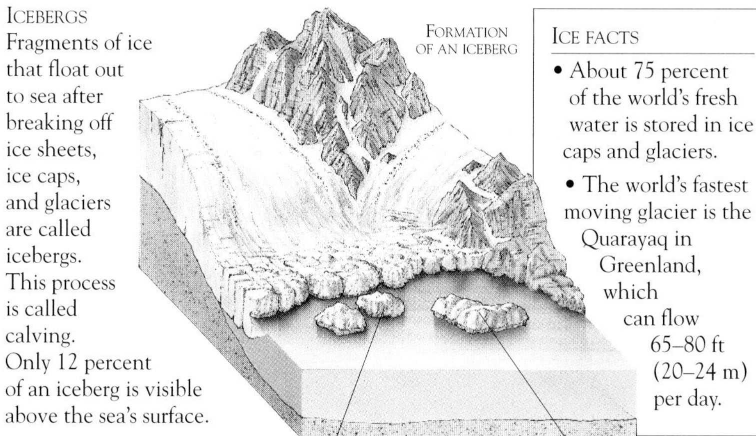
Tidal movement and buffeting by waves breaks off iceberg
An iceberg's movement is controlled by ocean currents and the wind

FORMATION OF AN ICEBERG

ICE FACTS

- About 75 percent of the world's fresh water is stored in ice caps and glaciers.
- The world's fastest moving glacier is the Quarayaq in Greenland, which can flow 65–80 ft (20–24 m) per day.

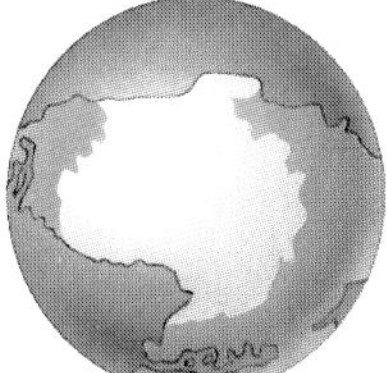

PLEISTOCENE EPOCH – THE LAST ICE AGE

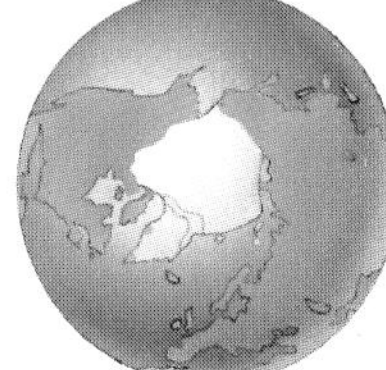

EXTENT OF ICE IN THE WORLD TODAY

ICE AGES

In Earth's history, there have been many ice ages interspersed with warmer periods called interglacials. During the most recent ice age, about 30,000 years ago, ice covered much of North America and Europe.

GLACIAL DEPOSITION

The ice in a glacier is choked with rocky debris. When the ice melts, it leaves behind piles of debris (moraine), which form small mounds or hummocks.

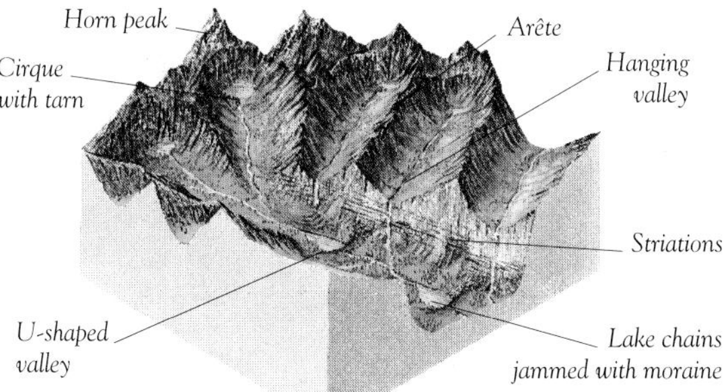
Horn peak
Arête
Cirque with tarn
Hanging valley
Striations
U-shaped valley
Lake chains jammed with moraine

LAKES AND RIVERS

WHEN RAINWATER falls on the land, it may seep into the ground, collect in lakes, or form rivers running down to the ocean. Rivers gradually mold the land, as they wear down material in some places, and re-deposit it in others.

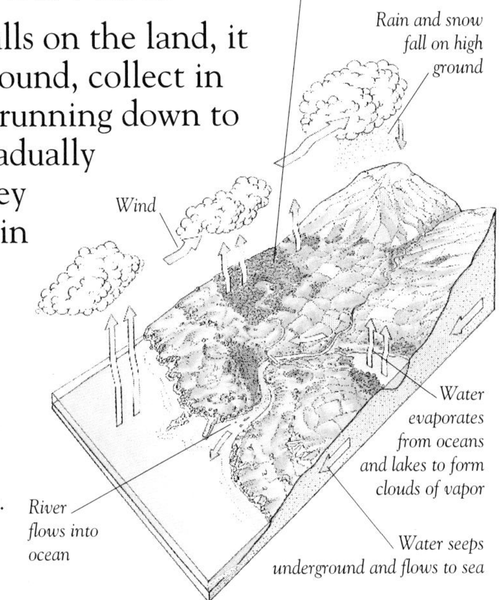
Water vapor from plants released into atmosphere
Rain and snow fall on high ground
Wind
Water evaporates from oceans and lakes to form clouds of vapor
River flows into ocean
Water seeps underground and flows to sea

THE WATER CYCLE
The Sun's heat causes water to evaporate from oceans, lakes, and rivers. As it rises into the atmosphere, the water vapor cools and condenses into clouds. Eventually the droplets fall back to Earth as rain.

TYPES OF LAKES

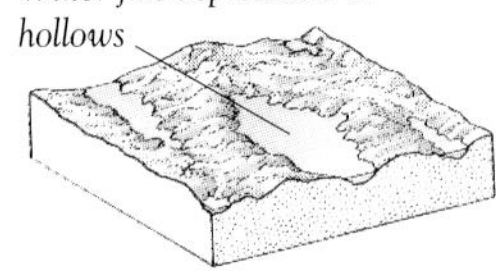
Water fills depressions or hollows

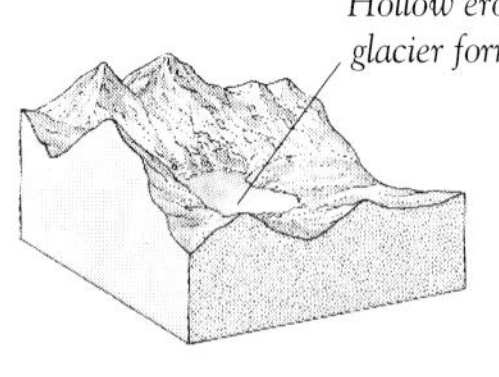
Hollow eroded by glacier forms lake

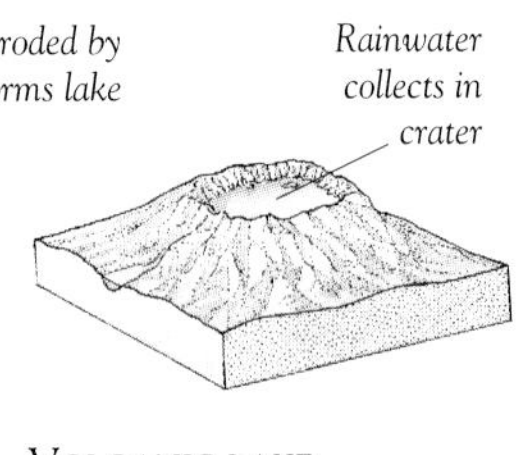
Rainwater collects in crater

KETTLE LAKE
Melting ice blocks from glaciers fill depressions in rocky glacial debris to form kettle lakes.

TARN
Circular mountain lake that forms in hollows worn by glacial erosion or blocked by ice debris.

VOLCANIC LAKE
Ancient volcanic craters fill with water, producing lakes such as Crater Lake, Oregon.

SOURCES OF RIVER WATER

All rivers receive their water, either directly or indirectly, from precipitation (rainfall).

MELTWATER

Many rivers begin as melting snow and ice from a glacier.

SPRING

Rainwater stored in the aquifer rock layer may reemerge at a spring.

OVERLAND FLOW

Rain running downhill gathers into streams.

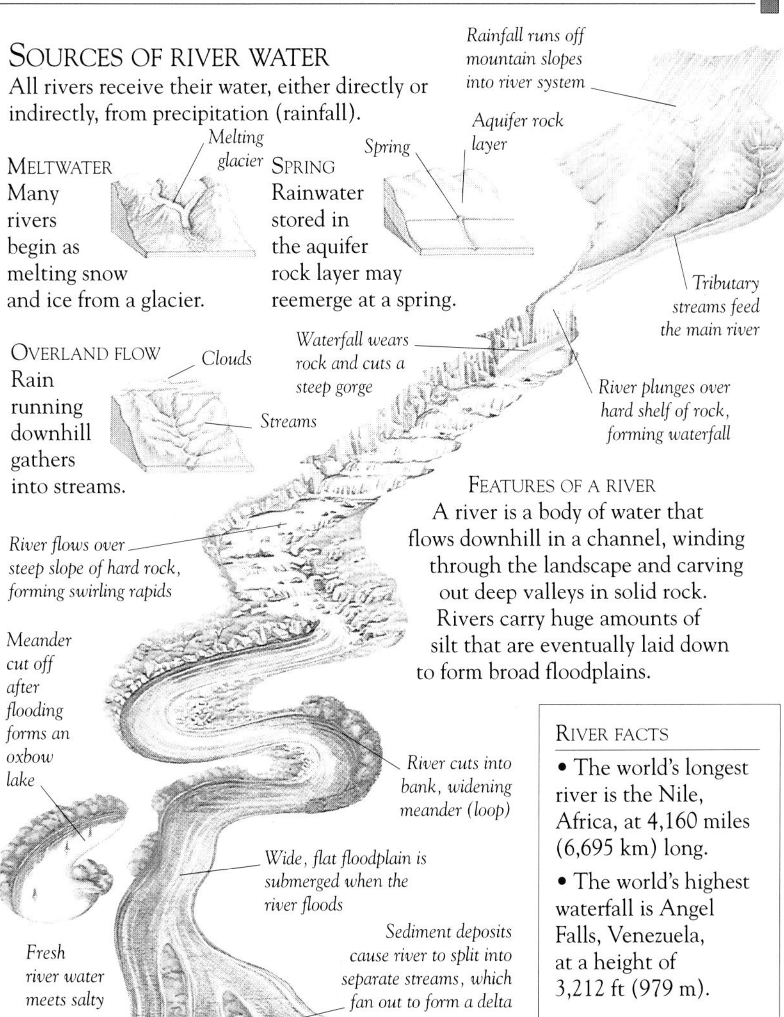
Melting glacier
Spring
Aquifer rock layer
Rainfall runs off mountain slopes into river system
Clouds
Streams
Tributary streams feed the main river
Waterfall wears rock and cuts a steep gorge
River plunges over hard shelf of rock, forming waterfall
River flows over steep slope of hard rock, forming swirling rapids
Meander cut off after flooding forms an oxbow lake
River cuts into bank, widening meander (loop)
Wide, flat floodplain is submerged when the river floods
Sediment deposits cause river to split into separate streams, which fan out to form a delta
Fresh river water meets salty seawater at estuary

FEATURES OF A RIVER

A river is a body of water that flows downhill in a channel, winding through the landscape and carving out deep valleys in solid rock. Rivers carry huge amounts of silt that are eventually laid down to form broad floodplains.

RIVER FACTS

- The world's longest river is the Nile, Africa, at 4,160 miles (6,695 km) long.
- The world's highest waterfall is Angel Falls, Venezuela, at a height of 3,212 ft (979 m).

WEATHER

THE CONSTANT motion of the lower layers of the atmosphere means that air conditions are always changing, creating weather variations such as wind and rain, snow, frost, fog, and sunshine.

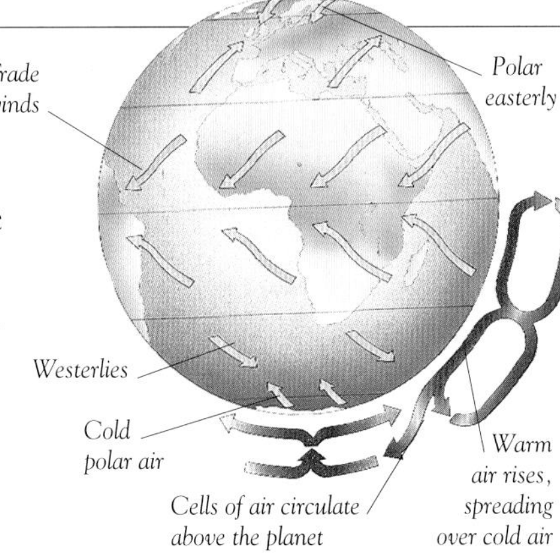
Trade winds
Polar easterly
Westerlies
Cold polar air
Warm air rises, spreading over cold air
Cells of air circulate above the planet

THE WORLD'S WINDS
Wind is simply air moving from areas of high pressure to areas of low pressure.
Three bands of prevailing (persistent) winds are found around the world – dry trade winds, warm westerlies, and cold polar easterlies.

FORMATION OF CLOUDS
Clouds form when water vapor in warm air rises, cools, and condenses.

Warm air containing water vapor rises. *Water vapor cools and condenses, forming clouds.* *Cloud continues to form as long as warm, moist air rises.*

AIR MASSES AND FRONTS
Huge bodies of air that form over continents and oceans are called air masses. They can be warm, cold, moist, or dry depending on where they form.
A front is the boundary between two air masses.

Warm air *Thick rain clouds* *The fronts are traveling from left to right* *Cold air pushes under warm air along Earth's surface*

Cold air WARM FRONT *Heavy rain* COLD FRONT

TYPES OF CLOUDS

Clouds are classified according to their shape and their height above the ground.

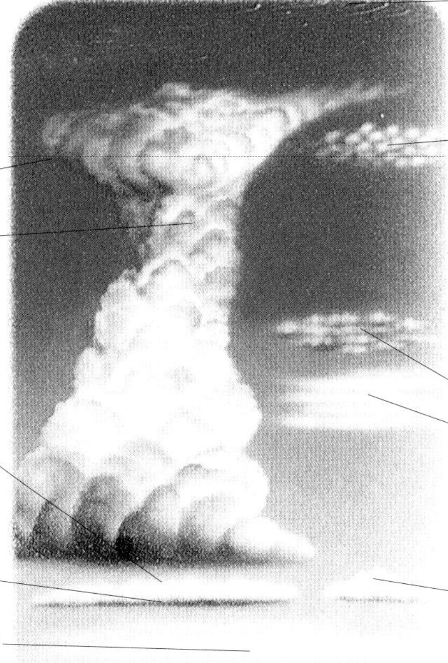
Cirrus – wisps of cloud made of ice crystals – forms at 16,000–42,000 ft (5,000–13,000 m)
Cirrocumulus – rippled ice crystal cloud like fish scales – forms at 16,000–42,000 ft (5,000–13,000 m)
Altocumulus – fluffy cloud – forms at 6,500–23,000 ft (2,000–7,000 m)
Altostratus – gray or white sheet of cloud – forms at 6,500–23,000 ft (2,000–7,000 m)
Cumulus – large, white, fluffy cloud – forms at 0–6,500 ft (0–2,000 m)
Freezing level
Cumulonimbus – giant, dark, anvil-headed thundercloud – forms at 49,000 ft (15,000 m)
Stratocumulus – white or gray lumpy cloud at top of cumulus – forms at 0–6,500 ft (0–2,000 m)
Nimbostratus – thick, gray rain cloud – forms at 0–6,500 ft (0–2,000 m)
Stratus – low-level, flat, gray sheet of misty cloud – forms at 0–6,500 ft (0–2,000 m)

TYPES OF RAIN

Most of the world's rain comes from water droplets freezing into icy particles high in a cloud. The particles grow into snowflakes, turning to raindrops as they fall. In the tropics, small raindrops join up to make bigger drops heavy enough to fall as rain.

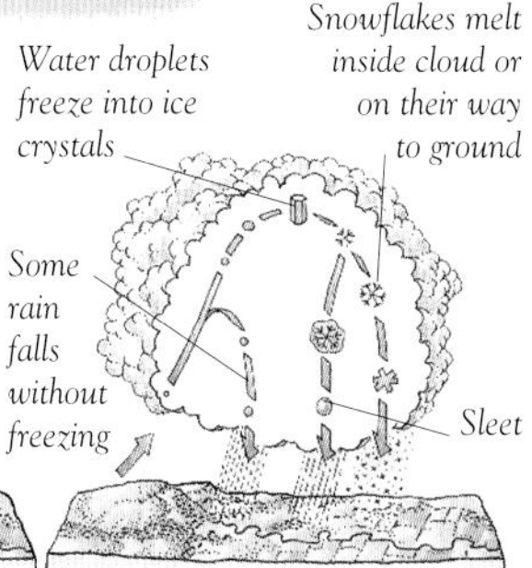
Drops smaller than 0.2 in (5 mm) fall as drizzle
Larger raindrops
Rising air
Water droplets freeze into ice crystals
Snowflakes melt inside cloud or on their way to ground
Some rain falls without freezing
Sleet

TROPICAL RAIN

MELTED SNOW

Climates and Ecosystems

THE TYPICAL LONG-TERM weather conditions of an area are referred to as its climate. A region's climate varies according to its distance from the Equator and the ocean, and its height above sea level. The interacting range of plants and animals within a climate is called an ecosystem.

MAP OF WORLD CLIMATE ZONES

TYPES OF CLIMATE
The world's climates are split into three broad zones: tropical, temperate, and polar. The farther from the Equator and above sea level a zone lies, the colder the climate. The greater distance from an ocean, the more extreme its winters and summers.

KEY TO CLIMATE ZONES
- Polar
- Taiga
- Mountain
- Temperate
- Tropical rain forest
- Hot desert

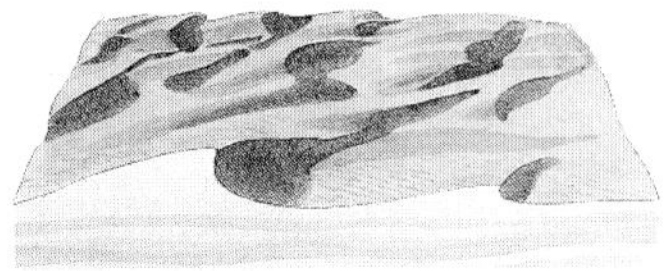

HOT DESERT
Few species can survive in desert climates. Temperatures can exceed 100°F (38°C) and it may not rain for several years.

TROPICAL RAIN FOREST
Heavy rain and high temperatures all year round make rain forests the world's richest plant and animal habitats.

POLAR AND TUNDRA

In the polar regions, temperatures rarely rise above freezing for more than a few months of the year. Fresh water is permanently frozen, and plants cannot grow. The cold, dry land bordering the ice caps is known as the tundra.

CLIMATES AND ECOSYSTEMS FACTS

- The highest recorded temperature, taken at al'Aziziyah, Libya, measured 136°F (58°C).
- The coldest inhabited place is Oymyakon, Siberia, with a temperature of –90°F (–68°C).

TAIGA (COLD TEMPERATE)

The vast coniferous forest called the Taiga stretches across Canada, Scandinavia, and the former Soviet Union. Four to six months of the year are dark, with the temperature falling well below 32°F (0°C).

TEMPERATE

Winters are cool and summers warm in temperate climates, with many plants and trees becoming dormant in winter.

MOUNTAIN REGIONS

Low temperatures prevent vegetation growing on mountain peaks; trees and plants thrive on the lower slopes.

ECOLOGY AND FOOD WEBS

THE LIVING WORLD is built on complex relationships between plants, animals, and the places they inhabit. Ecology is the study of these relationships and how communities of living things interact with their habitats.

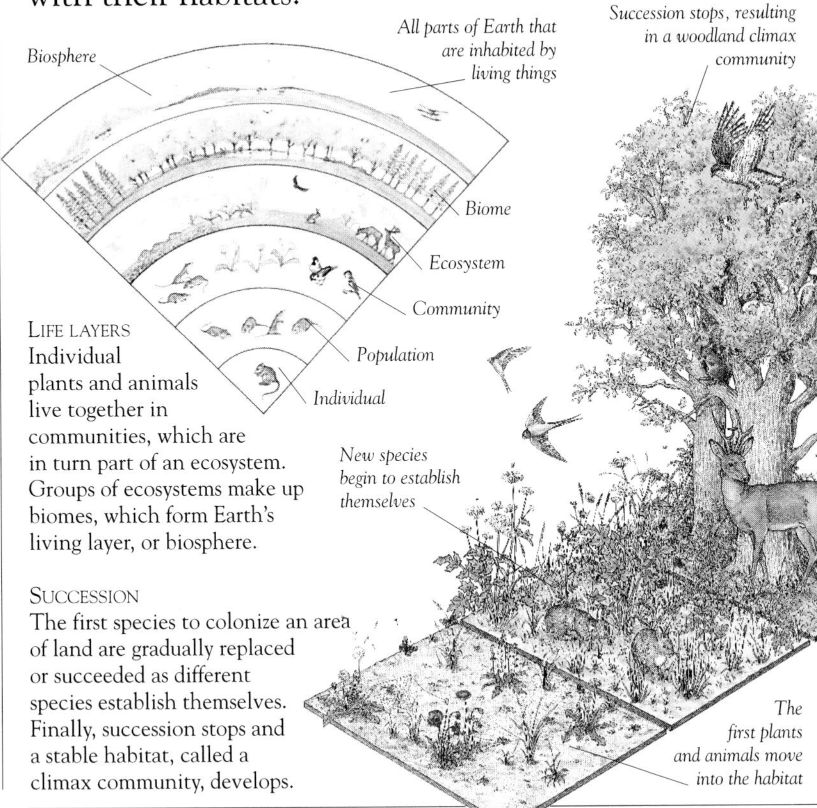

Biosphere
All parts of Earth that are inhabited by living things
Biome
Ecosystem
Community
Population
Individual
Succession stops, resulting in a woodland climax community
New species begin to establish themselves
The first plants and animals move into the habitat

LIFE LAYERS
Individual plants and animals live together in communities, which are in turn part of an ecosystem. Groups of ecosystems make up biomes, which form Earth's living layer, or biosphere.

SUCCESSION
The first species to colonize an area of land are gradually replaced or succeeded as different species establish themselves. Finally, succession stops and a stable habitat, called a climax community, develops.

FOOD WEBS

Some organisms within an ecosystem may feed off each other. In a salt marsh, for example, shrews feed on snails and marsh hawks feed on shrews. This series of feeding links is called a food chain. Each species is involved in a number of chains, and these chains link up to form interconnecting food webs.

ECOLOGY FACTS

- Earth's biosphere stretches from the ocean depths to about 9 miles (15 km) up into the atmosphere.
- The composition of nearly all plants and animals, including humans, is 75% water.

FOOD WEBS LINKING ANIMALS LIVING IN OPEN WOODLAND

Frogs link the two webs

Arrows link food source to consumer

POND FOOD WEB

MEADOW FOOD WEB

FEEDING LEVELS

In most food chains there are various stages or trophic levels.

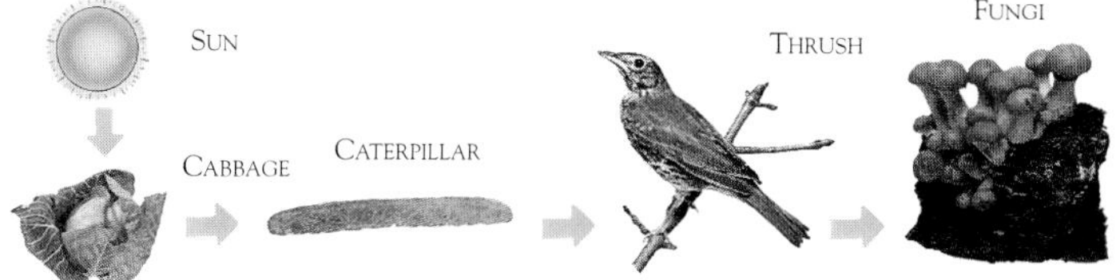
SUN
CABBAGE
CATERPILLAR
THRUSH
FUNGI

Producers
Green plants use sunlight to make their own food.

Primary consumer
Herbivores such as caterpillars eat producers.

Secondary consumer
Carnivores eat herbivores and other carnivores.

Decomposer
Fungi and bacteria decompose dead organisms.

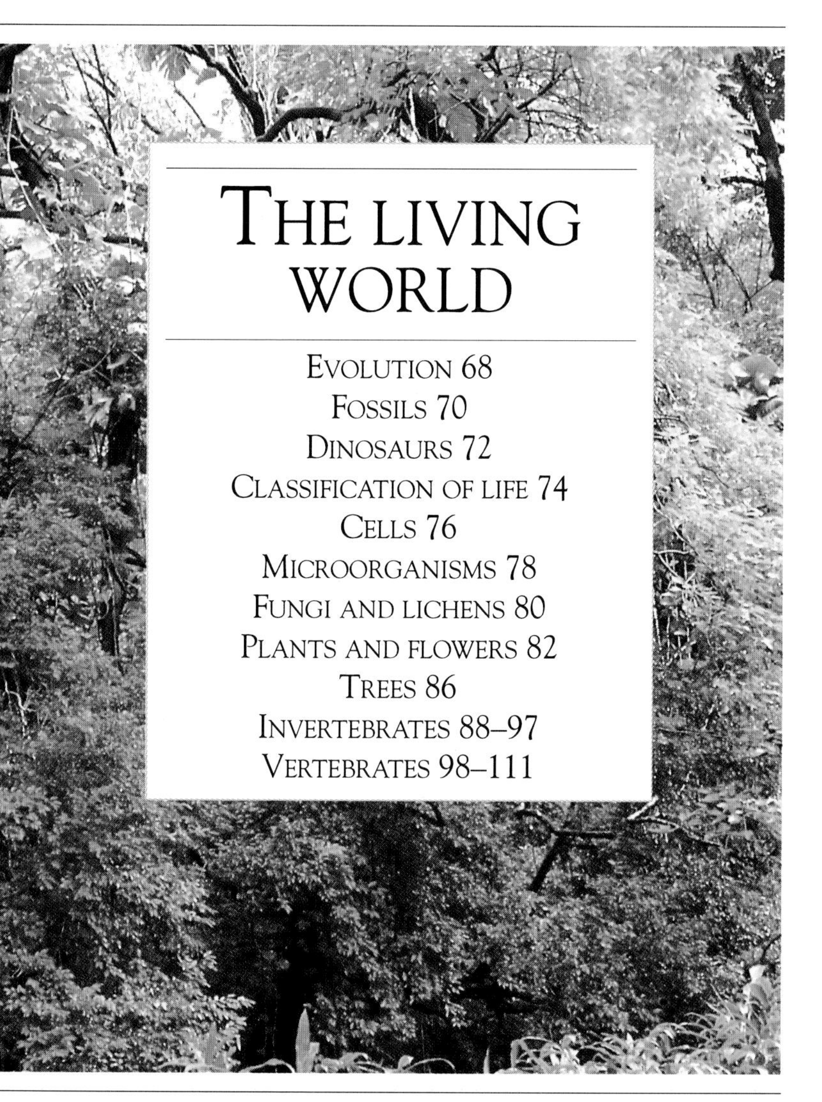

THE LIVING WORLD

EVOLUTION

SINCE LIFE appeared 3.8 billion years ago, millions of different creatures have come and gone. As habitats altered, some life forms survived by adapting to change, while others died out. This gradual change over time is known as evolution.

PORPOISE'S FRONT FLIPPER

"Finger" bones form a powerful flipper for swimming

Two sets of short "arm" bones

Two sets of long bones make up the arm

Five sets of finger bones make up the hand

HUMAN ARM

ADAPTATION

Evidence for evolution comes from the adaptation of the forearm in humans and porpoises – two related species that live in very different habitats, land and water.

LIFE FORMS THROUGH THE AGES

By working out when certain rocks formed, and then studying the fossils found in them, paleontologists – who study the life forms of the past – have built up a remarkable picture of the way species have changed since the dawn of the Cambrian period 545 million years ago. Little is known of Precambrian life forms because very few fossils remain.

PRECAMBRIAN	PALEOZOIC	
	Cambrian	Ordovician

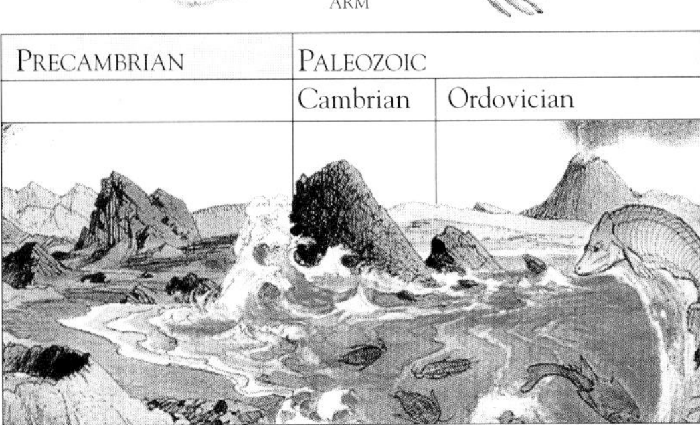

4,600–545 mya *Single-celled life forms, such as bacteria and algae, appear, then soft multi-celled life forms, such as worms and jellyfish.*	*545–495 mya* *No life on land. Invertebrates flourish in the seas. First mollusks and trilobites.*	*495–443 mya* *First crustaceans and early jawless fish appear. Coral reefs form. Sahara glaciated.*

How evolution works

According to Darwin's theory of evolution, only the best-adapted members of species survive to breed, leading to a gradual change in living organisms over millions of years. His theory challenged the accepted 19th-century view that life forms did not change after being created by a deity (god).

Charles Darwin (1809–1882)

The theory of evolution was developed by English naturalist Charles Darwin after studying animals and plants during a world voyage. He published his findings in 1859 in his book *On the Origin of Species.*

Evolution of the horse

Hyracotherium
This animal of 50 million years ago had four toes on its front feet.

Mesohippus
Mesohippus, *which lived 30 million years ago, had three toes on its front feet.*

Merychippus
One of Merychippus's *three toes formed a large hoof.* Merychippus *existed 20 million years ago.*

Equus (modern horse)
Modern horses, which have a single toe or hoof on each foot, evolved about 2 million years ago.

Silurian	Devonian	Carboniferous	Permian
443–417 *First jawed fish. Huge sea scorpions hunt in the sea. Small land plants colonize the shore.*	*417–354* *Age of sharks and fish. Insects and amphibians appear on land. Giant ferns form forests.*	*354–290 mya* *Warm swampy forests leave remains that will turn to coal. First reptiles.*	*290–248 mya* *Reptiles diversify, conifers replace tree ferns. Mass extinction as Earth turns cold.*

Fossils

THE REMAINS of living things preserved naturally, often for many millions of years, are called fossils. Most fossils are formed in rocks; however, remains can also be preserved in ice, tar, peat, and amber. Fossils tell us nearly all we know about the history of life on Earth.

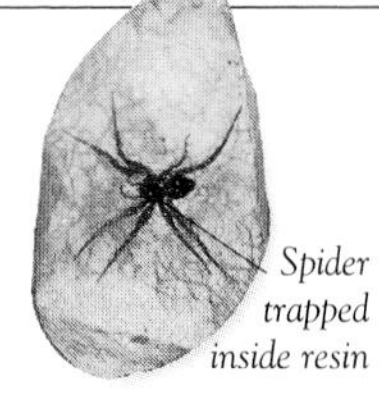
Spider trapped inside resin

SPIDER IN AMBER
Amber is fossilized tree resin that may also preserve trapped insects.

Fossilized shell

AMMONITES BECAME EXTINCT 65 MYA

KINDS OF FOSSILS
Many fossils form on the seabed, so shells and sea creatures are very common. Fossils of land animals and plants are rarer. Footprints, burrows, or droppings may also be preserved.

Mesozoic			Cenozoic	
Triassic	Jurassic	Cretaceous	Tertiary	
			Palaeocene	Eocene

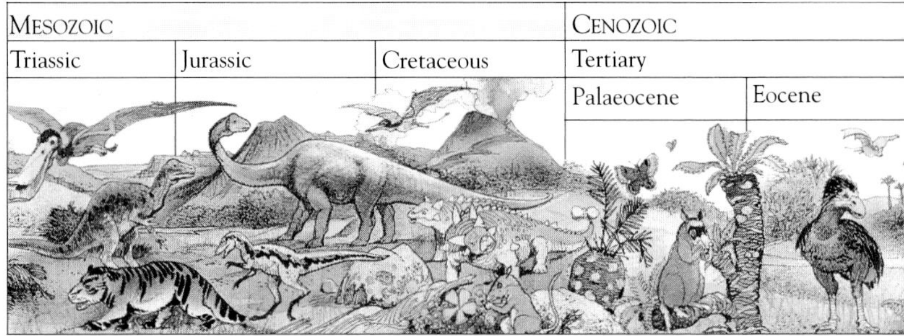

248–206 mya Mammals and dinosaurs appear. The climate warms and seed-bearing plants dominate.	*206–142 mya* The age of the dinosaurs. The first known bird, Archaeopteryx, appears.	*142–65 mya* First flowering plants. Period ends with a mass extinction that wipes out dinosaurs.	*65–55 mya* Warm, humid climate. Mammals, insects, and flowering plants flourish.	*55–34 mya* Mammals grow larger and diversify. Primates evolve.

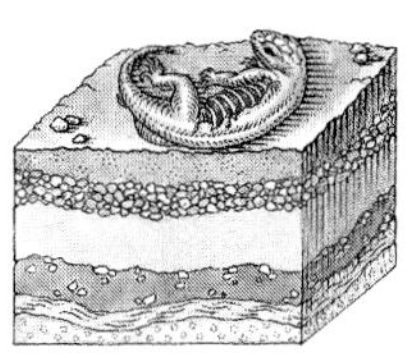

1 ANIMAL DIES The body of a dead animal lies decaying on the surface of the land.

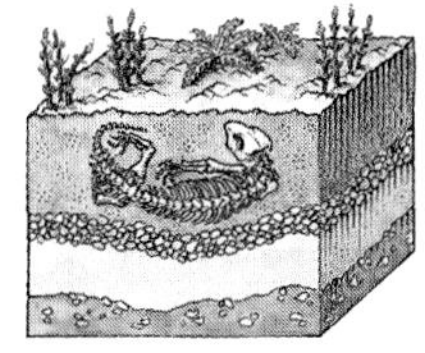

2 REMAINS SINK Gradually, the body becomes covered with sand or mud.

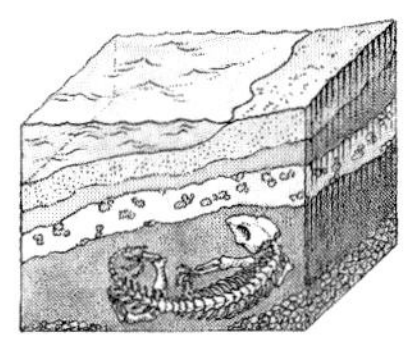

3 BONES ALTER Over time, the bones are altered, and the sand and mud turn to rock.

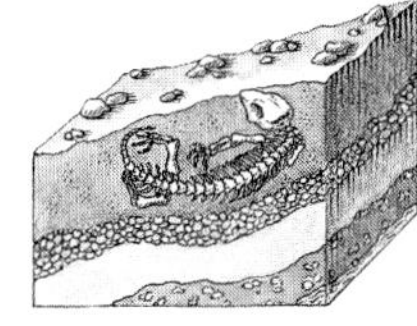

4 FOSSIL IS EXPOSED Eventually, weather and erosion expose the fossil at the surface.

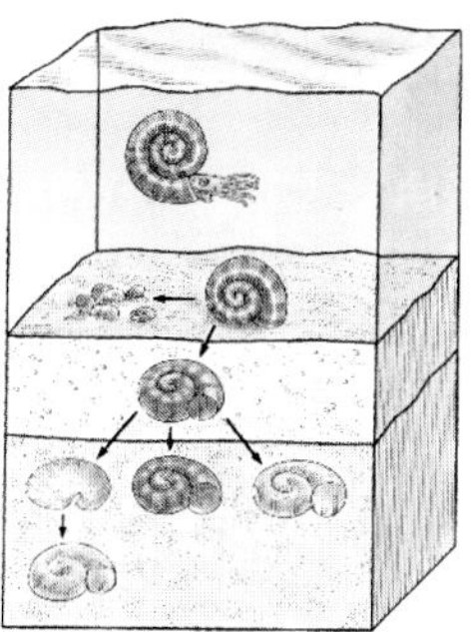

FOSSILIZATION AT SEA Dead organisms sink to the seabed and are buried. As the sediment turns to rock, their remains are either chemically altered or dissolve to leave a cavity, which may fill with minerals to form a cast.

			Quaternary	
Oligocene	Miocene	Pliocene	Pleistocene	Holocene

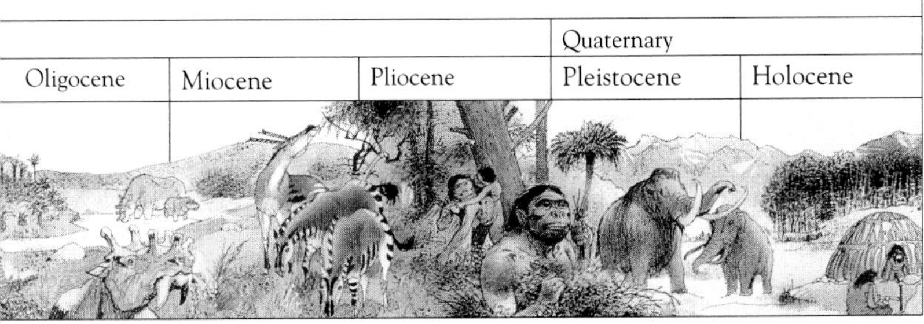

Oligocene	Miocene	Pliocene	Pleistocene	Holocene
34–24 mya *First humanlike creatures appear. Hunting birds thrive. Some mammals die out.*	*24–5 mya* *Climate cools, and forests shrink. Deerlike hoofed mammals flourish. First hominids.*	*5–2 mya* *Cold and dry. Mammals reach maximum diversity. Many modern mammals appear.*	*2 mya–10,000 ya* *Ice Ages. Homo sapiens evolves. Mammoths and saber-toothed tigers die out.*	*10,000 ya to present* *Humans develop agriculture and technology. Human activity threatens many species.*

DINOSAURS

FOR 160 MILLION YEARS, Earth was dominated by giant reptiles called dinosaurs, including *Seismosaurus*, the longest creature ever to walk on land. Then, 65 million years ago, all the dinosaurs mysteriously died out.

Light bones for flying

Wings of skin

Furry body

PTEROSAUR
While dinosaurs ruled the land, giant reptiles, like Pterosaur, flew in the air.

DINOSAUR GROUPS
Scientists divide dinosaurs into two orders according to the arrangement of their hipbones. Saurischians have lizardlike hips and include both plant and meateaters. Ornithischians have bird-like hips and are all plant eaters. The two orders are divided into five subgroups.

Muscular tail balanced the front of the body

Long neck for browsing in treetops

Ruff

Horn

SALTASAURUS

STYRACOSAURUS

Sauropods (Saurischians) *were huge, long-necked four-legged planteaters.*

Marginocephalians (Ornithiscians) *had a bony ruff and horns for self-defense.*

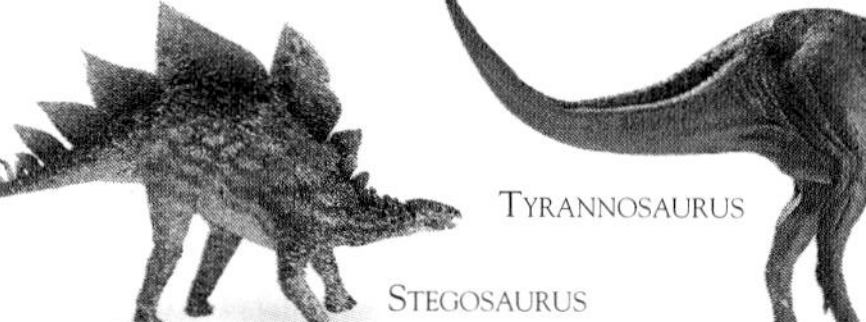
TYRANNOSAURUS
STEGOSAURUS

CORYTHOSAURUS

Thyreophorans (Ornithischians) *were spiny-backed planteaters.*

Theropods (Saurischians) *were two-legged meateaters.*

Ornithopods (Ornithischians) *had a horny beak and birdlike feet.*

One lower hip bone points forward and the other points backward
Skull
Ribs
Backbone
TYRANNOSAURUS REX (SAURISCHIAN, OR LIZARD-HIPPED)
Both lower hip bones point backwards
IGUANODON (ORNITHISCHIAN, OR BIRD-HIPPED)
Tough, waterproof skin was covered with scales
TYRANNOSAURUS REX
Strong neck muscles for holding prey
Powerful jaws for crushing bones
Serrated teeth up to 7 in (18 cm) long for slicing through flesh and bones
Clawed hands for gripping prey
Thick, heavy legs to support weight
Huge claws for holding prey on the ground

DINOSAUR SKELETONS

By studying the fossils of dinosaur bones, scientists can learn more about the lives and habits of these giant reptiles that lived millions of years ago. The way the hips are arranged helps them to group the dinosaurs.

GIANT REPTILE?

Dinosaurs may look like reptiles, but some walked with their limbs directly under their body, like birds and mammals, and may have been warm-blooded.

DINOSAUR FACTS

- Over 350 dinosaur species have so far been identified.
- Some dinosaurs may have lived 200 years.
- Dinosaur means "terrible lizard."

CLASSIFICATION OF LIFE

THE NATURAL WORLD contains millions of living things, which can be classified according to the features they have in common. The largest groups are the five kingdoms: animals, plants, fungi, protists, and monerans.

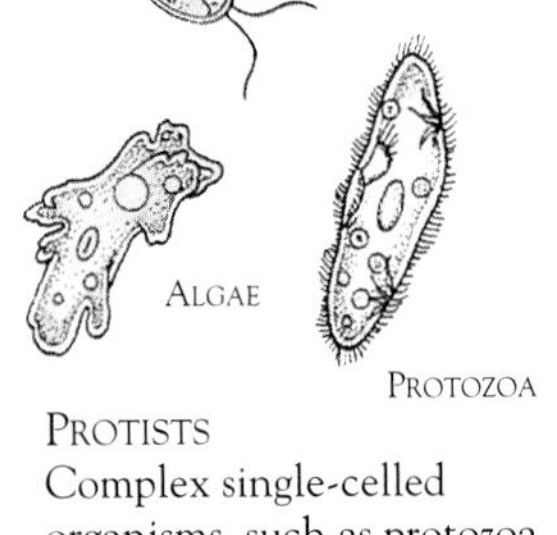
ALGAE
PROTOZOA

MONERANS
These simple single-celled organisms, such as bacteria, are visible only under a microscope. They were the first life forms and there are now more than 5,500 species.

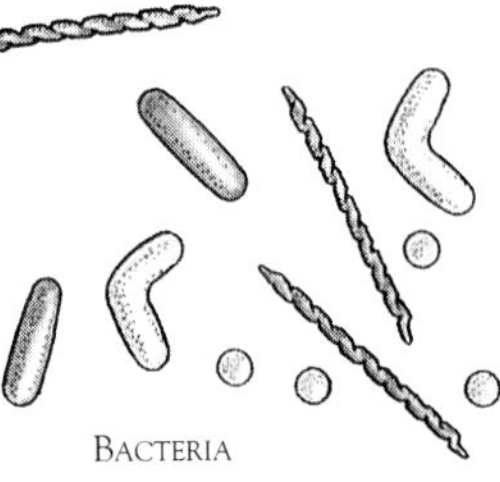

BACTERIA

PROTISTS
Complex single-celled organisms, such as protozoa and amoebas, are called protists. Protozoa are like animals. Algae are like plants. There are over 65,000 protist species.

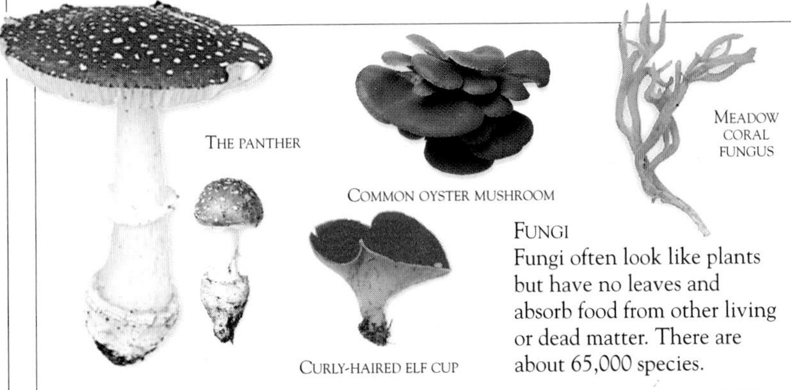
THE PANTHER
COMMON OYSTER MUSHROOM
MEADOW CORAL FUNGUS
CURLY-HAIRED ELF CUP

FUNGI
Fungi often look like plants but have no leaves and absorb food from other living or dead matter. There are about 65,000 species.

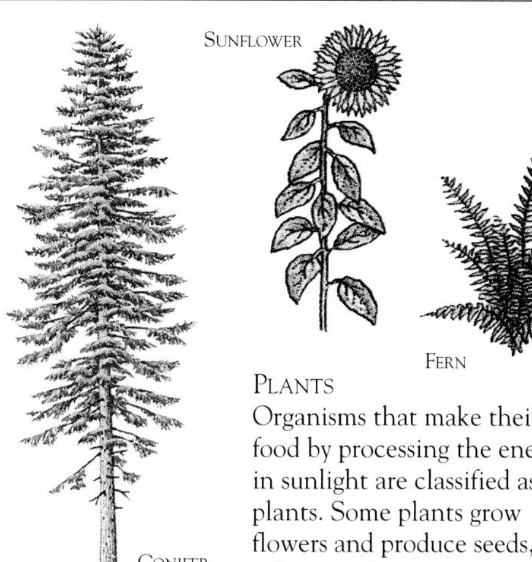
SUNFLOWER
FERN
CONIFER

PLANTS
Organisms that make their food by processing the energy in sunlight are classified as plants. Some plants grow flowers and produce seeds, other simpler species do not. There are over 250,000 species.

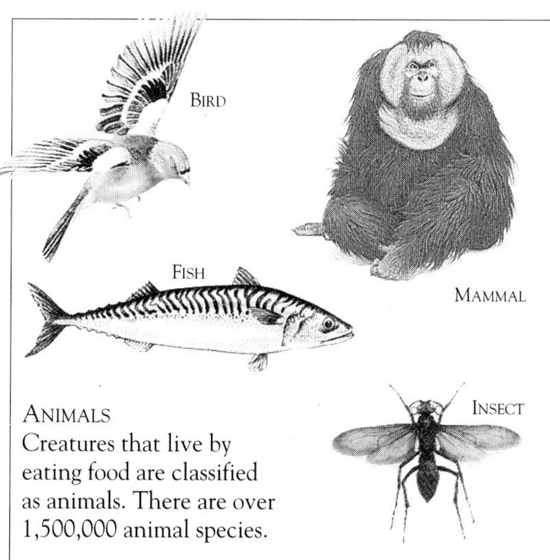
BIRD
MAMMAL
FISH
INSECT

ANIMALS
Creatures that live by eating food are classified as animals. There are over 1,500,000 animal species.

CLASSIFICATION
Each kingdom is divided into smaller and smaller groups according to its characteristics. This is how a serval (*Felis serval*) would be classified.

Kingdom
Animal (Animalia)
Many-celled, must find food

Phylum
Chordate (Chordata)
Single nerve cord during life

Class
Mammal (Mammalia)
Suckles young

Order
Carnivores (Carnivora)
Adapted to hunting

Family
Cats (Felidae)
Sharp, retractable claws

Genus
(*Felis*)
Short tail, tufted ears

Species
serval
(*Felis serval*)

FELIS SERVAL

CELLS

ALL LIVING THINGS are made up of tiny, self-contained units called cells, usually so small that they are visible only under a microscope. A cell takes in energy and uses it to grow and reproduce. Some organisms consist of just a single cell, others have trillions.

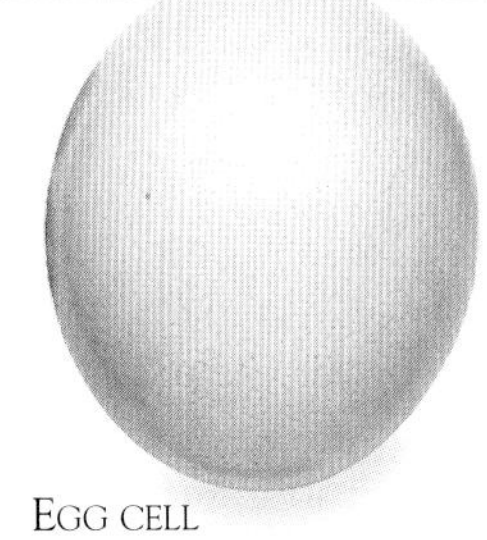

EGG CELL
Cells vary in size from minute fractions of an inch to eggs, which are the largest cells of all.

ANIMAL CELL
An animal cell is a tiny jelly-filled sac with a soft and flexible skin or membrane. Different kinds of cells, such as blood cells and skin cells, perform different tasks in the body. Inside each, there are organelles that control and run the cell.

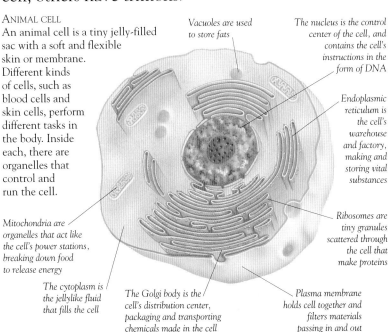

Vacuoles are used to store fats

The nucleus is the control center of the cell, and contains the cell's instructions in the form of DNA

Endoplasmic reticulum is the cell's warehouse and factory, making and storing vital substances

Ribosomes are tiny granules scattered through the cell that make proteins

Mitochondria are organelles that act like the cell's power stations, breaking down food to release energy

The cytoplasm is the jellylike fluid that fills the cell

The Golgi body is the cell's distribution center, packaging and transporting chemicals made in the cell

Plasma membrane holds cell together and filters materials passing in and out

Plant cell

The features of a plant cell are very similar to those of an animal cell, but plant cells are enclosed in a rigid shell of cellulose. They also have organelles called chloroplasts, made bright green by a pigment called chlorophyll. Chloroplasts are like solar batteries, enabling plants to trap energy from the sun in a process called photosynthesis.

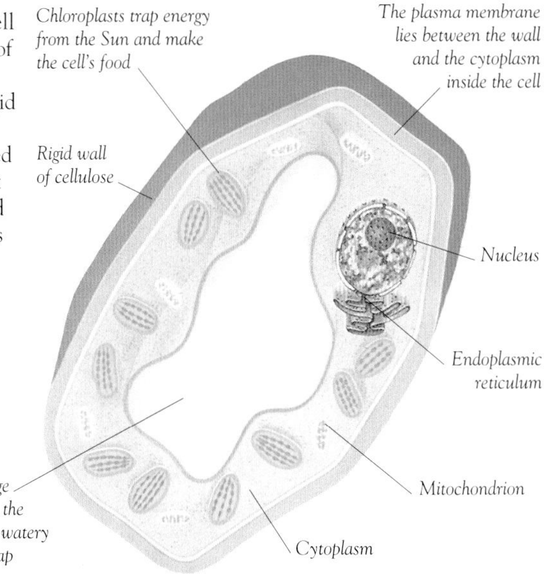
Chloroplasts trap energy from the Sun and make the cell's food
The plasma membrane lies between the wall and the cytoplasm inside the cell
Rigid wall of cellulose
Nucleus
Endoplasmic reticulum
Mitochondrion
Cytoplasm
Vacuoles are large storage spaces in the cell containing a watery fluid called cell sap

Cell division

Living cells multiply by splitting in two again and again. This is how worn-out cells are replaced and plants and animals grow. To ensure that the chromosomes (the cell's life-plan) are passed on to each new cell equally, most cells divide by a complex process called mitosis.

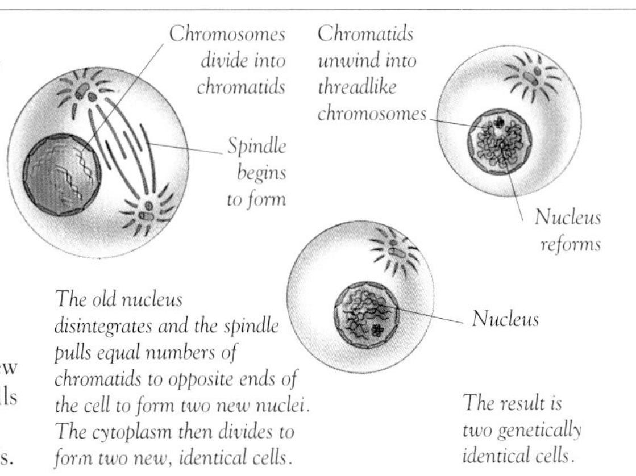
Chromosomes divide into chromatids
Spindle begins to form
Chromatids unwind into threadlike chromosomes
Nucleus reforms
Nucleus
The old nucleus disintegrates and the spindle pulls equal numbers of chromatids to opposite ends of the cell to form two new nuclei. The cytoplasm then divides to form two new, identical cells.
The result is two genetically identical cells.

MICROORGANISMS

THE MOST NUMEROUS living things in the world are usually too small to see except under a microscope. These microorganisms, including bacteria and protists, are found everywhere – there are 100,000 billion in your body alone. All are made of just a single cell.

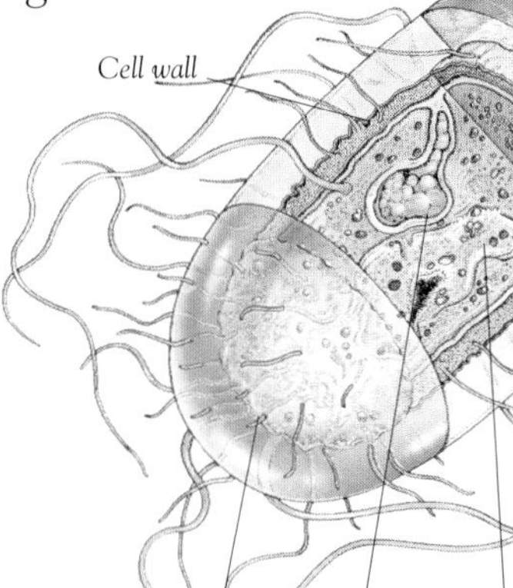

A tough, slimy capsule protects the cell wall
Long, hairlike flagella on some bacteria whip from side to side to move the cell along
Cell wall
Ribosome for making protein
Tiny hairlike pili attach the cell to food or other cells
Folded plasma membrane
A free-floating nucleoid region contains the bacteria's instructions

BACTERIA
The most abundant living things on Earth, and among the most ancient, bacteria live everywhere from the upper atmosphere to the ocean depths. Many feed on dead matter and help to recycle nutrients. Others, called germs, feed on living things and cause disease. Bacteria cells are prokaryotic, which means they have no nucleus.

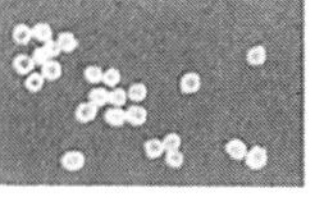
COCCUS

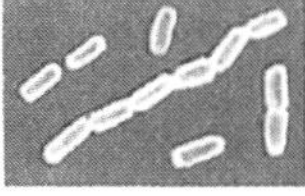
BACILLUS

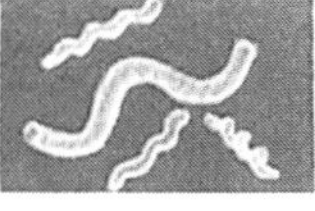
SPIRILLUM

BACTERIA SHAPES
Bacteria may be classified by shape – coccus (round), bacillus (rod-shaped), or spirillum (coiled).

Protists

Like bacteria, protists are single-celled organisms, but they have a nucleus and grow much bigger. They live in damp habitats, like soil, ponds, and oceans. Amoebae are protists with no fixed shape. They move by changing shape, and feed by engulfing food. Some live in water and soil. Others are parasites living inside plants and animals.

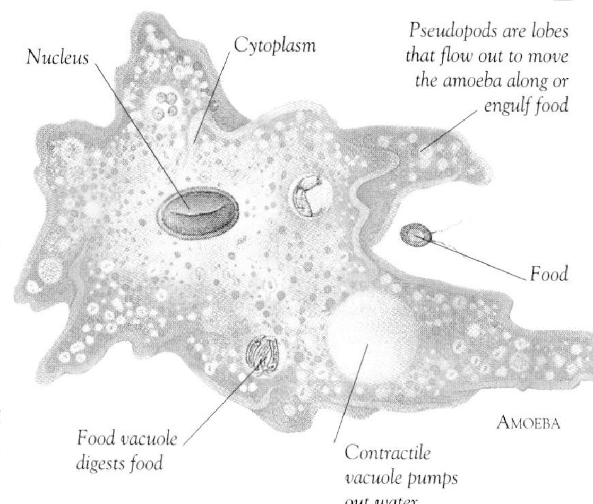
Nucleus
Cytoplasm
Pseudopods are lobes that flow out to move the amoeba along or engulf food
Food
Food vacuole digests food
Contractile vacuole pumps out water

AMOEBA

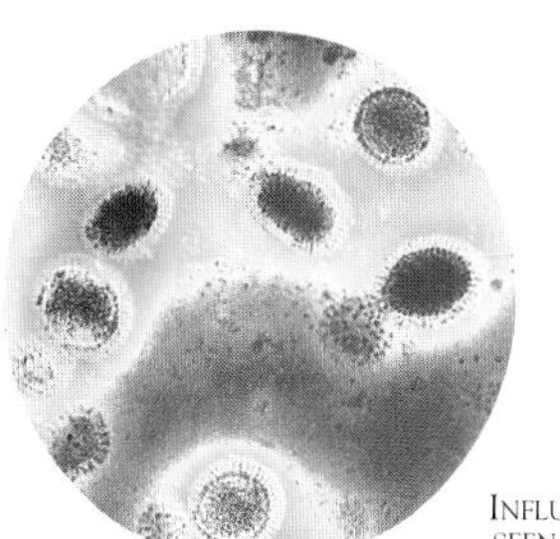

INFLUENZA VIRUSES SEEN THROUGH AN ELECTRON MICROSCOPE

Viruses

A virus is a tiny package of chemicals coated with protein. It is not a living organism – it relies on invading living hosts to reproduce itself.

Protist and bacteria facts

- A gram of soil may contain 150,000 protists.
- There may be 2,000 bacteria per square inch of human armpit.
- Extinct protists called nummulites grew to 6 in (15 cm) across!
- Viruses are visible only under an electron microscope.

Useful bacteria

Bacteria play a vital role in breaking down dead matter and recycling nutrients, helping us digest food. Bacteria are important in the production of many foods such as cheese, yogurt, vinegar, and beer.

YOGURT

CHEESE

VINEGAR

FUNGI AND LICHENS

MUSHROOMS, toadstools, mildew, and mold are all kinds of fungi. Like plants, fungi often grow in soil, but they cannot make food from sunlight. Instead they absorb chemicals from living and dead plants and animals, manure, and other organic material.

FUNGUS VARIETY
There are fungi of all shapes and sizes. Some are good to eat, but many are so poisonous they can kill.

FUNGUS STRUCTURE
The stalk and head of the toadstool are the fungi's "fruiting body," which releases tiny, seed-like spores. Wherever these spores land, they send out new hyphae (threads).

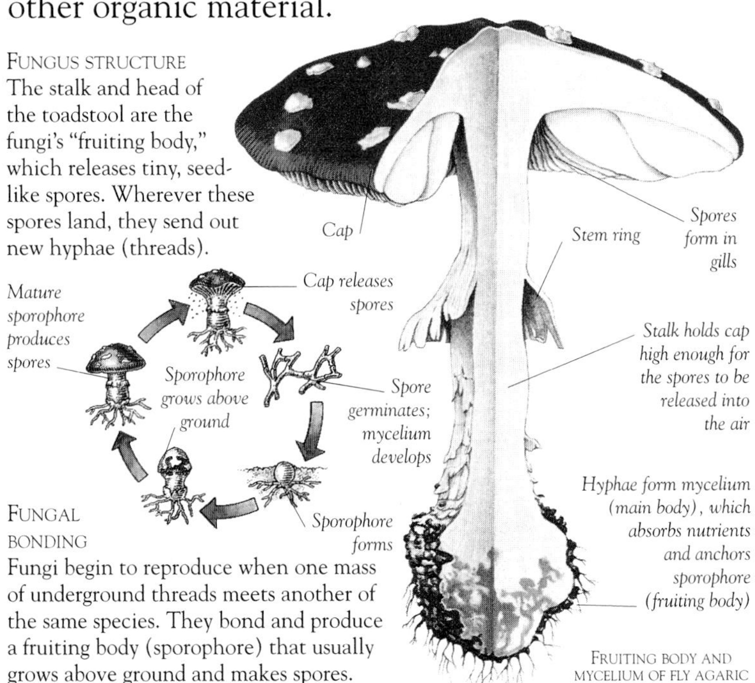
Cap
Stem ring
Spores form in gills
Stalk holds cap high enough for the spores to be released into the air
Hyphae form mycelium (main body), which absorbs nutrients and anchors sporophore (fruiting body)
Cap releases spores
Mature sporophore produces spores
Sporophore grows above ground
Spore germinates; mycelium develops
Sporophore forms

FUNGAL BONDING
Fungi begin to reproduce when one mass of underground threads meets another of the same species. They bond and produce a fruiting body (sporophore) that usually grows above ground and makes spores.

FRUITING BODY AND MYCELIUM OF FLY AGARIC

BRACKET FUNGI

Instead of growing in soil, some fungi grow in tiers on dead or dying trees and logs. Knowing which types of wood attract which types of fungus makes it easier to identify different fungus species.

Fruiting bodies grow in tiers on dead wood

LICHENS

STRUCTURE

Lichens are a partnership between fungi and algae, a little like a sandwich, with fungal bread and algal filling. The green algae trap sunlight to make food to feed the fungi, which in turn protect the algae and retain water.

Lichens attach themselves to stones or wood. They eventually break down rocks and help to form soil.

FOLIOSE (*Hypogymnia physodes*)

The many species of lichens grow in five distinct ways. Three are shown here.

FRUTICOSE (*Cladonia portentosa*)

SQUAMULOSE (*Cladonia floerkeana*)

PLANTS

PLANTS make their own food out of water, air, and sunlight. This makes them the starting point of most food chains, and most other living organisms depend on them for food. Plants have adapted to the most extreme habitats, from hot desert to icy tundra.

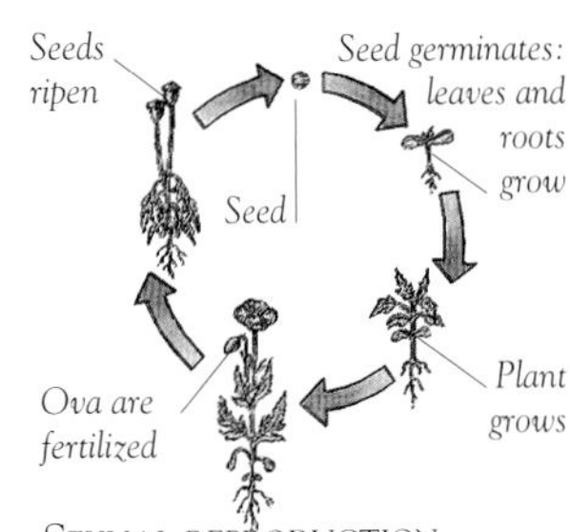
Seeds ripen
Seed germinates: leaves and roots grow
Seed
Plant grows
Ova are fertilized

SEXUAL REPRODUCTION
Many plants reproduce by ova being fertilized by pollen, whether from the same flower or plant or a different one. This is sexual reproduction.

ASEXUAL REPRODUCTION
Many plants can reproduce without pollination or fertilization taking place. This is called asexual reproduction.

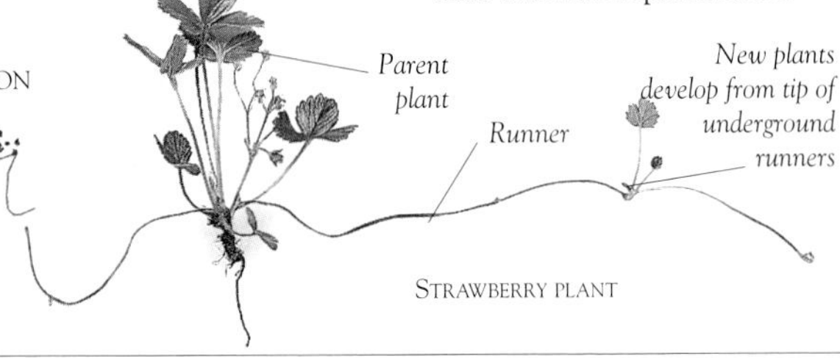
Parent plant
Runner
New plants develop from tip of underground runners

STRAWBERRY PLANT

TYPES OF PLANTS
The earliest plants on Earth did not have flowers or produce seeds. Simple plants like this still exist, but now they share Earth with their flowering relatives. Plants come in all shapes and sizes, from tiny algae to grasses and giant trees.

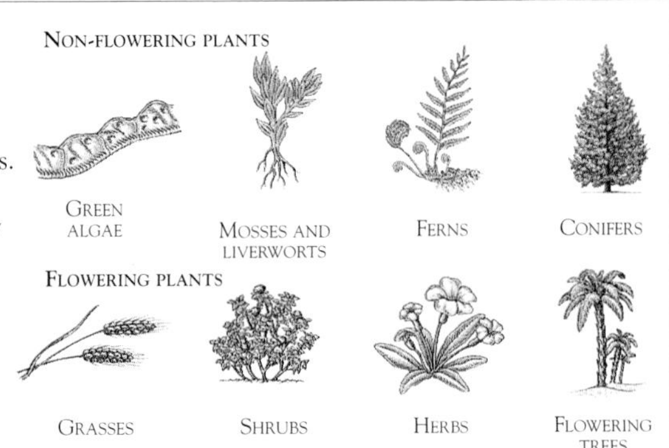
NON-FLOWERING PLANTS
GREEN ALGAE
MOSSES AND LIVERWORTS
FERNS
CONIFERS
FLOWERING PLANTS
GRASSES
SHRUBS
HERBS
FLOWERING TREES

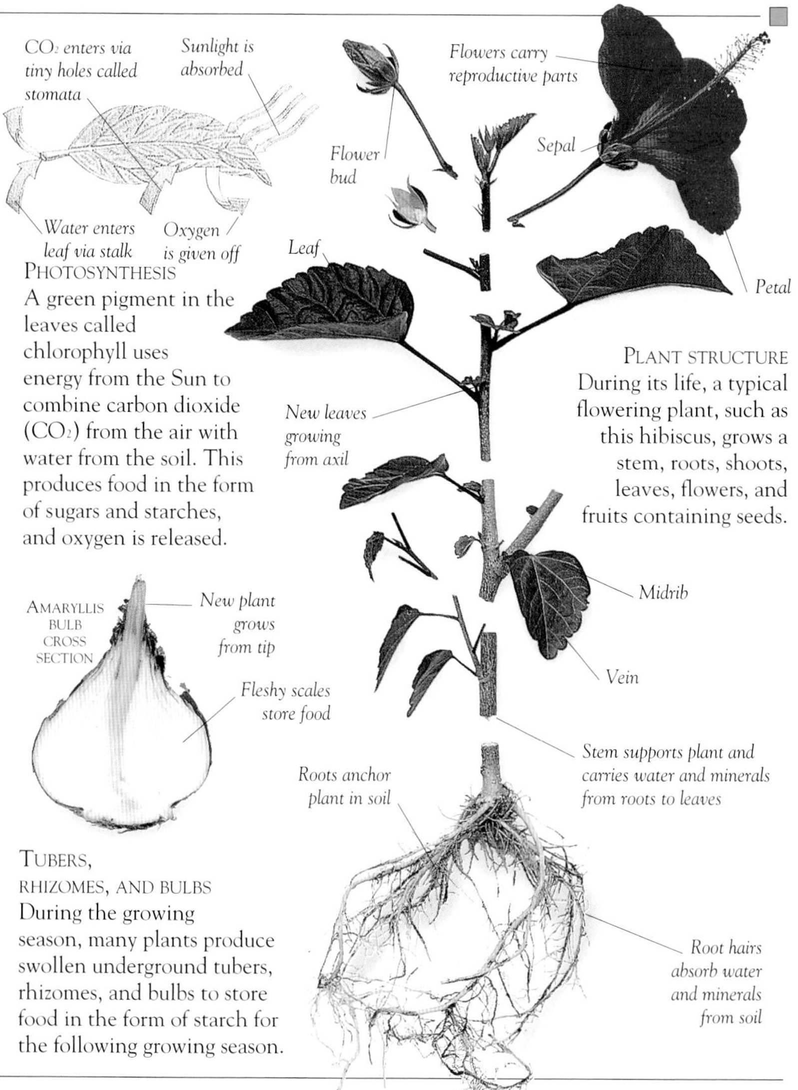
CO_2 enters via tiny holes called stomata
Sunlight is absorbed
Water enters leaf via stalk
Oxygen is given off
Flower bud
Flowers carry reproductive parts
Sepal
Leaf
Petal
New leaves growing from axil
Midrib
Vein
New plant grows from tip
Fleshy scales store food
Stem supports plant and carries water and minerals from roots to leaves
Roots anchor plant in soil
Root hairs absorb water and minerals from soil

PHOTOSYNTHESIS
A green pigment in the leaves called chlorophyll uses energy from the Sun to combine carbon dioxide (CO_2) from the air with water from the soil. This produces food in the form of sugars and starches, and oxygen is released.

PLANT STRUCTURE
During its life, a typical flowering plant, such as this hibiscus, grows a stem, roots, shoots, leaves, flowers, and fruits containing seeds.

AMARYLLIS BULB CROSS SECTION

TUBERS, RHIZOMES, AND BULBS
During the growing season, many plants produce swollen underground tubers, rhizomes, and bulbs to store food in the form of starch for the following growing season.

FLOWERS AND FRUITS

FLOWERS help ensure that a plant is pollinated so that it can produce seeds and fruit. A fruit is anything that contains a seed or seeds, from a coconut to a tomato.

Tough, bumpy surface

POLLEN GRAIN
Microscopic pollen grains, which look like orange dust, are produced by a flower's anthers. A plant is fertilized when a single grain lands on the stigma of the same type of flower.

FLOWER PARTS
The reproductive organs of a flowering plant are found in the flower. The flowerheads of some plants have a stamen (male parts) and a carpel (female), while in others they are separate.

Filament

Anther – pollen is made in pollen sacs inside anther, which split open when ripe to release the pollen

Stigma – sticky head for trapping pollen

Stamens – the male parts of the flower that consist of an anther and a filament

Style carries pollen from the stigma to the ovary

Carpel – female parts of the flower consisting of an ovary, stigma, and style

Ovary – where the ova (eggs) are made. Once the ova are fertilized, the ovary swells to become a fruit

Sepal – protects flower when it is in bud

Petal – guides insects to anthers and stigma

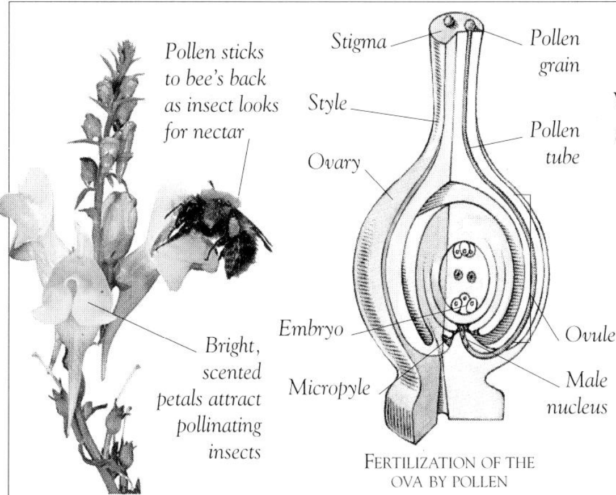
Pollen sticks to bee's back as insect looks for nectar
Bright, scented petals attract pollinating insects
Stigma
Pollen grain
Style
Pollen tube
Ovary
Embryo
Ovule
Micropyle
Male nucleus

FERTILIZATION OF THE OVA BY POLLEN

POLLINATION AND FERTILIZATION

When pollen lands on a stigma, probably carried there on the back of an insect, it grows a tube that probes into the style and penetrates the ovule (the egg container) via a hole called the micropyle. Two male sex cells from the pollen ease their way through the tube to fertilize the egg.

FRUIT

Once fertilized, the ovules form seeds, and the ovary becomes a fruit. If the seeds are spread by animals, the fruit is soft and juicy. If they are spread by the wind, it is hard and dry.

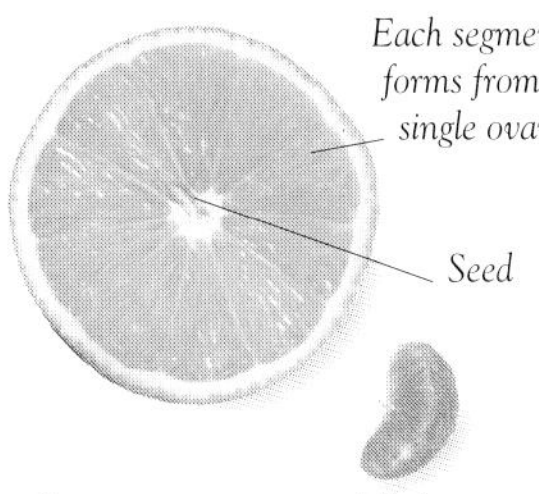
Each segment forms from a single ovary
Seed

Oranges are compound fruits – developed from several ovaries.

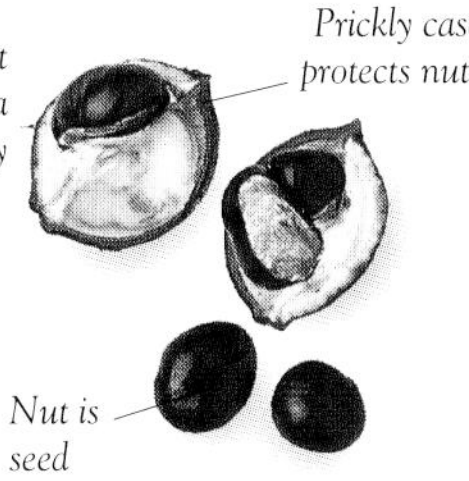
Prickly case protects nuts
Nut is seed

Horse chestnuts are nuts – single seeds in a hard, dry case.

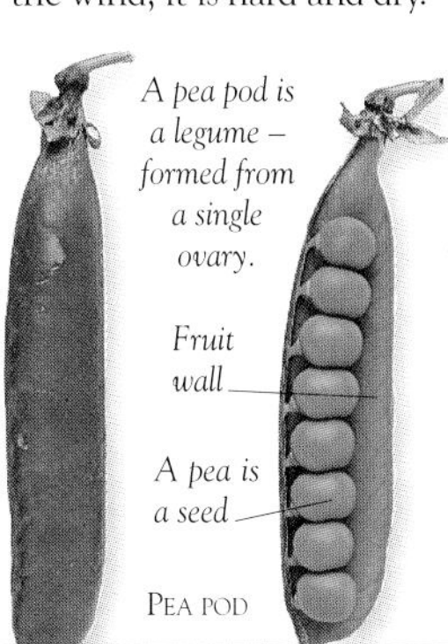
A pea pod is a legume – formed from a single ovary.
Fruit wall
A pea is a seed

PEA POD

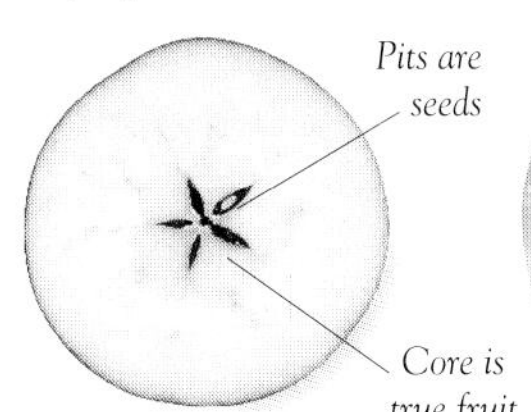
Pits are seeds
Core is true fruit

Apples are false fruits – the apple is the swollen base of the flower.

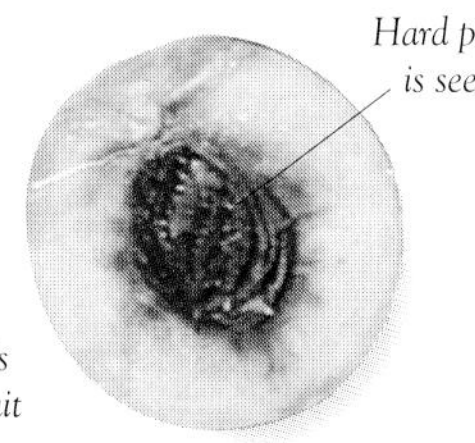
Hard pit is seed

Nectarines are drupes – fleshy fruits containing a hard seed.

TREES

TREES ARE WOODY PLANTS, which means they have hard stems and grow for years – often to immense sizes. Leaves can be broad, like oaks and beeches, or narrow, such as pine needles, or palm fronds.

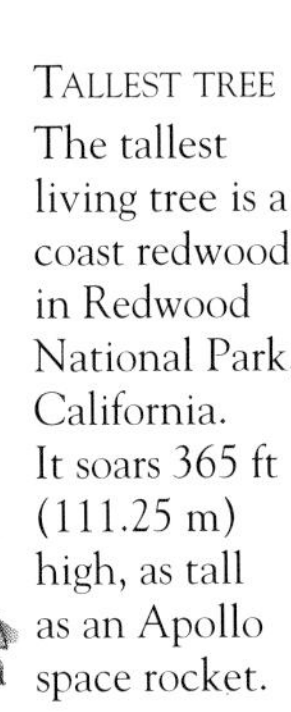

TALLEST TREE
The tallest living tree is a coast redwood in Redwood National Park, California. It soars 365 ft (111.25 m) high, as tall as an Apollo space rocket.

Leaves range from long "needles" like these to short, flat scales.

CONIFERS
Most conifers are evergreen with leaves that last three to four years and often have a dark, waxy skin to help save water.

Most conifers bear their seeds under the scales of hard cones.

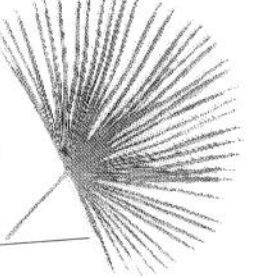

Palm trees get their name because leaves are sometimes shaped like a hand

Palm trees are flowering plants

PALM TREES
Palm trees grow mainly in the tropics. They have no branches; instead giant multiple leaves grow from a single point, called the apical bud.

BROAD-LEAVED TREES

Most broad-leaved trees are deciduous, which means they shed their leaves seasonally to save water.

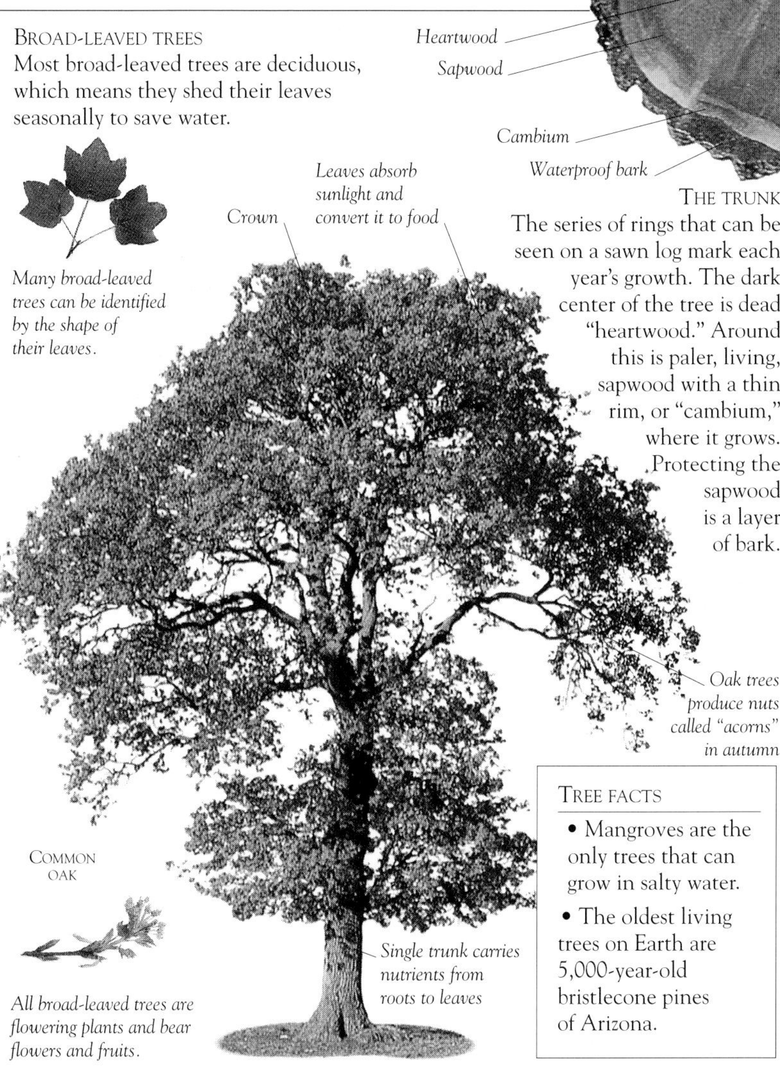

Heartwood
Sapwood
Cambium
Waterproof bark
Crown
Leaves absorb sunlight and convert it to food
Oak trees produce nuts called "acorns" in autumn
Single trunk carries nutrients from roots to leaves
COMMON OAK

Many broad-leaved trees can be identified by the shape of their leaves.

All broad-leaved trees are flowering plants and bear flowers and fruits.

THE TRUNK

The series of rings that can be seen on a sawn log mark each year's growth. The dark center of the tree is dead "heartwood." Around this is paler, living, sapwood with a thin rim, or "cambium," where it grows. Protecting the sapwood is a layer of bark.

TREE FACTS

- Mangroves are the only trees that can grow in salty water.
- The oldest living trees on Earth are 5,000-year-old bristlecone pines of Arizona.

INVERTEBRATES

NINETY-FIVE PERCENT of all animals are invertebrates, which means they have no backbone. They include jellyfish, sponges, starfish, coral, worms, crabs, spiders, and insects.

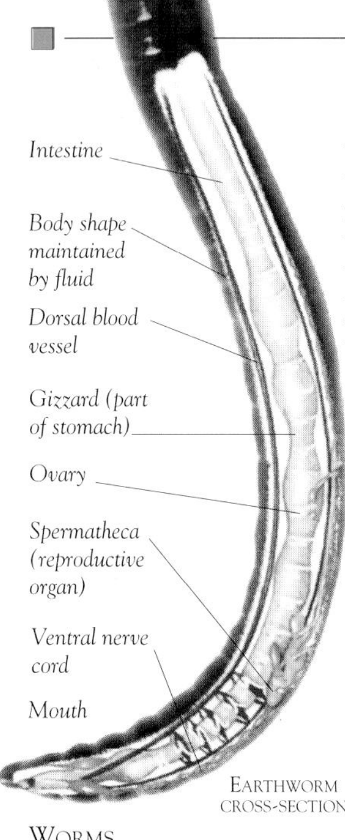
Intestine
Body shape maintained by fluid
Dorsal blood vessel
Gizzard (part of stomach)
Ovary
Spermatheca (reproductive organ)
Ventral nerve cord
Mouth

EARTHWORM CROSS-SECTION

Hard shell to protect soft body
Soft body
Eyes on stalks

MOLLUSKS
These soft-bodied invertebrates are often protected by a hard shell. Most mollusks, such as squid and octopuses, clams, mussels, and scallops, live in water, but some, like snails and slugs, live on land.

WORMS
A worm is an animal with a long soft body and no legs. There are many different kinds, including flatworms, tapeworms, earthworms, roundworms, and leeches.

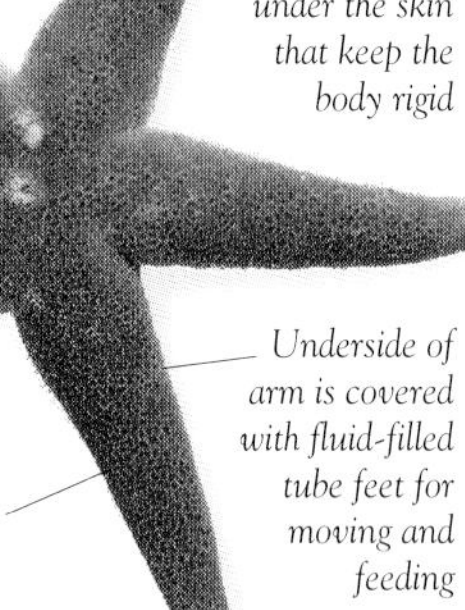
Echinoderms have a five-part body plan.
Ossicles are hard plates just under the skin that keep the body rigid
Arm
Underside of arm is covered with fluid-filled tube feet for moving and feeding
Arm

STARFISH AND URCHINS
Starfish, sea urchins, and sea cucumbers are all of echinoderms. All are predators, and most have sucker-tipped "tube feet" through which they pump water to move along and feed. The five broad arms of a starfish can wrench open a shellfish to suck out the contents.

LIFE CYCLE
Each invertebrate has its own life cycle, but most species lay eggs. Some go through several larval stages; others hatch as miniature adults.

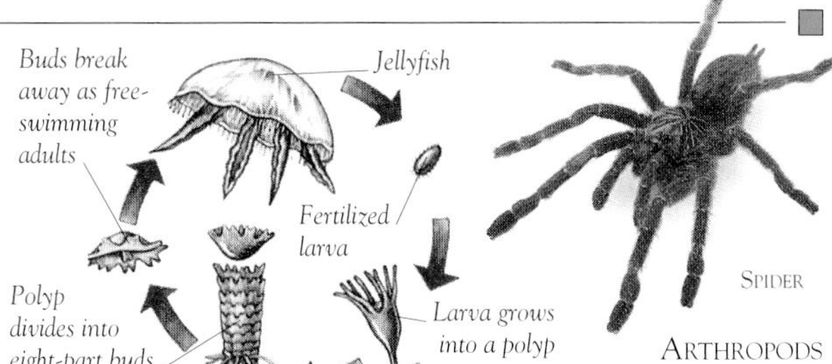

Buds break away as free-swimming adults
Jellyfish
Fertilized larva
Larva grows into a polyp
Polyp divides into eight-part buds

SPIDER

ARTHROPODS
Insects, spiders, and lobsters are all arthropods. They have jointed limbs and a tough external skeleton.

CROSS SECTION OF A JELLYFISH

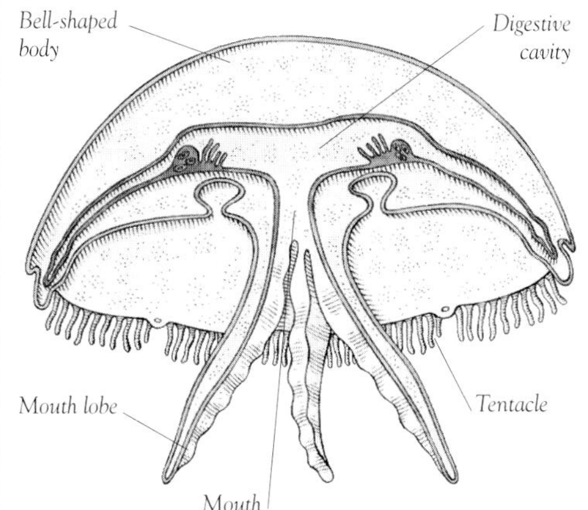

Bell-shaped body
Digestive cavity
Mouth lobe
Tentacle
Mouth

Jellyfish, anemones, and coral are all kinds of cnidarians – sea creatures with a mouth surrounded by tentacles. These tentacles usually carry a sting to stun or kill prey. Some cnidarians, called polyps, always attach to solid objects, such as a rock; others, called medusas, move by contracting their bell-shaped bodies.

SPONGES
These primitive sea creatures feed by drawing water into the holes in their soft bodies and filtering out any food.

INVERTEBRATE FACTS

- Up to 500 million hookworms may be found in a single human.
- Roundworms are probably the most numerous animals on Earth.

MOLLUSKS

AFTER ARTHROPODS, mollusks are the largest group of animals on Earth. There are over 50,000 species, ranging from tiny snails to giant squid as big as sperm whales. Most mollusks, except slugs, squid, cuttlefish, and octopuses, have soft, moist bodies protected by hard shells.

MOLLUSK SHELLS
The shells produced by mollusks are made of layers of calcium carbonate, and form in many shapes, sizes, patterns, and colors.

WHELK

COCKLE SHELLS

ROYAL CLOAK SCALLOP

PACIFIC THORNY OYSTER

TYPES OF MOLLUSK

GASTROPODS
There are 40,000 gastropod species, including snails, slugs, and whelks.

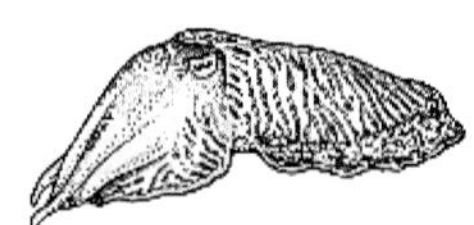

CEPHALOPODS
There are 650 species of these complex mollusks including octopus, squid, and cuttlefish.

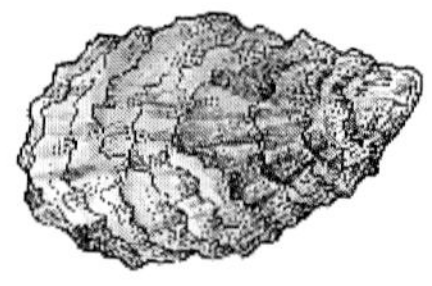

BIVALVES
There are 8,000 species of these double-shelled mollusks, such as oysters, clams, and cockles.

SNAILS AND SLUGS

Slugs and snails are gastropods. They move by a wave of contractions that runs from the rear of the foot to the front, sliding along on a trail of slime. They have soft bodies, but snails are protected by a hard, coiled shell.

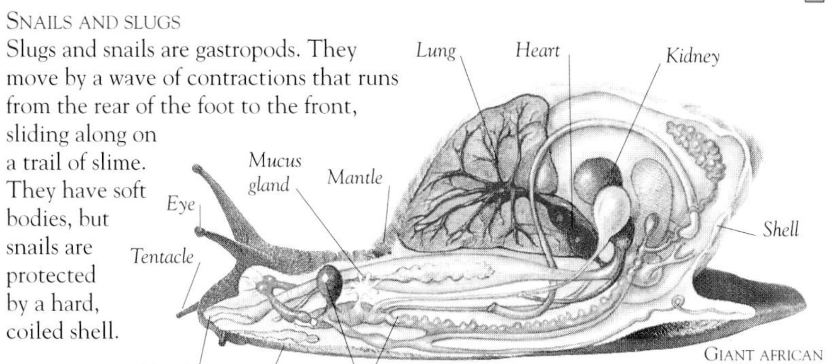

Lung
Heart
Kidney
Mucus gland
Mantle
Eye
Shell
Tentacle
Mouth
Foot
Reproductive organs

GIANT AFRICAN LAND SNAIL

LIFE CYCLE

Mollusks start life as eggs. Many marine mollusks, like this oyster, hatch first as larvae and then develop into adults. Land snails, however, hatch as miniature adults.

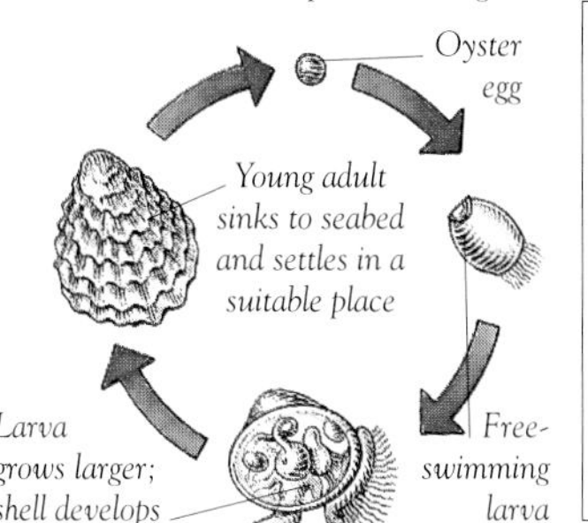

Oyster egg
Young adult sinks to seabed and settles in a suitable place
Free-swimming larva
Larva grows larger; shell develops

MOLLUSK FACTS

- Great gray slugs mate for 7–24 hours, hanging from a trail of mucus.
- Giant clams can live for over 200 years.
- Limpets' teeth are so strong that they leave scratch marks on rocks.

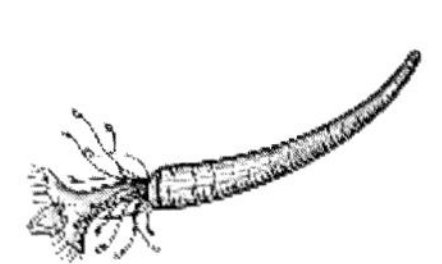

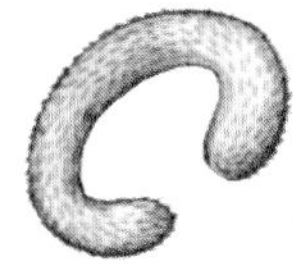

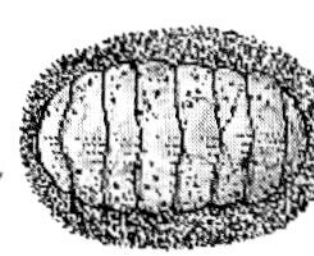

TUSK SHELLS

There are 350 species of these rare sea creatures with tusk-shaped shells.

SOLENOGASTERS

There are 250 species of these wormlike marine mollusks.

MONOPLACOPHORANS

There are only 11 species of these limpets. They live in the depths of the ocean.

CHITONS

There are 600 species of these coat-of-mail shelled creatures.

INSECTS

INSECTS MAY BE TINY, but there are more of them than all other animals put together. About one million species, from tiny flies to giant beetles, are known, and there may be over 200 million insects for every human. They have existed for over 400 million years and are found everywhere from the Arctic to the Sahara.

WASP'S HEAD

Antenna

Compound eye

COMPOUND EYES

The compound eyes of most insects have six or more facets. Dragonflies have 30,000 facets in each eye, which help to spot movement.

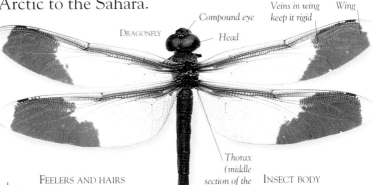

DRAGONFLY

Compound eye

Head

Veins in wing keep it rigid

Wing

Thorax (middle section of the body), which bears the legs

Abdomen (rear part of the body)

FEELERS AND HAIRS

Insects use antennae to sense the world in different ways. Most work by smell or touch. Ants, bees, and wasps use their antennae for tasting.

BEETLE ANTENNAE

Branched antennae are supersensitive

INSECT BODY

An insect's body is divided into three parts – head, thorax, and abdomen – and it has six legs. The body is encased in a tough shell, or exoskeleton, made of a substance called chitin. Some insects have two or four wings.

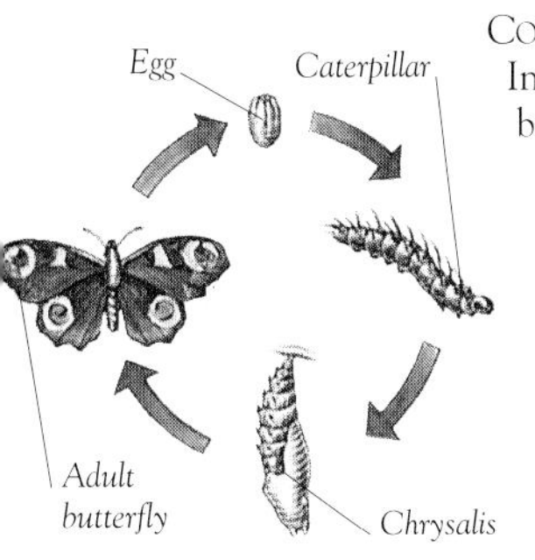
Egg
Caterpillar
Adult butterfly
Chrysalis

COMPLETE METAMORPHOSIS
Insects such as butterflies, beetles, and flies start life as larvae, which hatch from eggs. The larvae then turn into pupae, from which an adult emerges. This process is known as complete metamorphosis. The larva bears no resemblance to the adult it becomes.

Nest of chewed wood

WASPS' NEST

INSECT NESTS
Some insects, such as bees, wasps, termites, and ants, live in ordered societies and build elaborate homes.

INCOMPLETE METAMORPHOSIS
Insects such as grasshoppers or damselflies hatch into wingless "nymphs" before molting and growing into adults. This is known as incomplete metamorphosis.

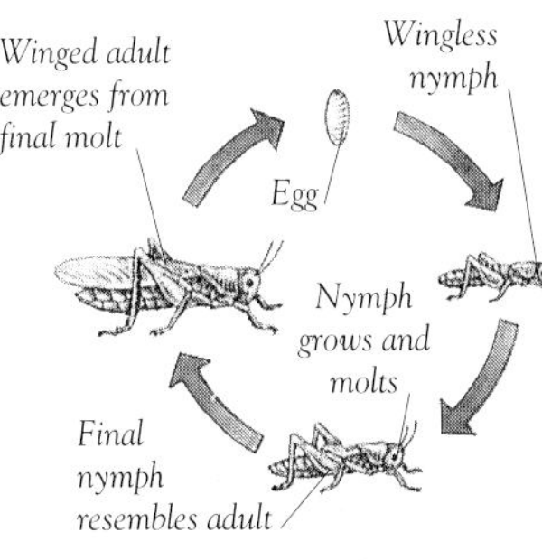
Winged adult emerges from final molt
Wingless nymph
Egg
Nymph grows and molts
Final nymph resembles adult

INSECT FACTS

- A queen termite lays 440 million eggs – one per second for 14 years.
- A bee must visit more than 4,000 flowers to make one tablespoon of honey.

MOLTING
A young insect's tough exoskeleton cannot stretch. Instead it is discarded and replaced with a new one several times. This sequence shows the final molt of a damselfly as it changes from nymph to adult.

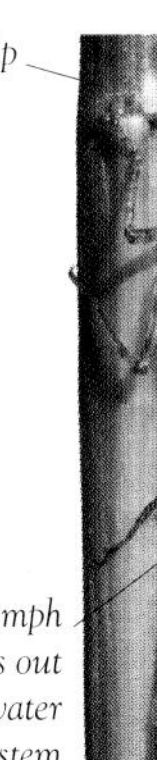
Legs grip stem
Wing buds
Nymph crawls out of water up a stem

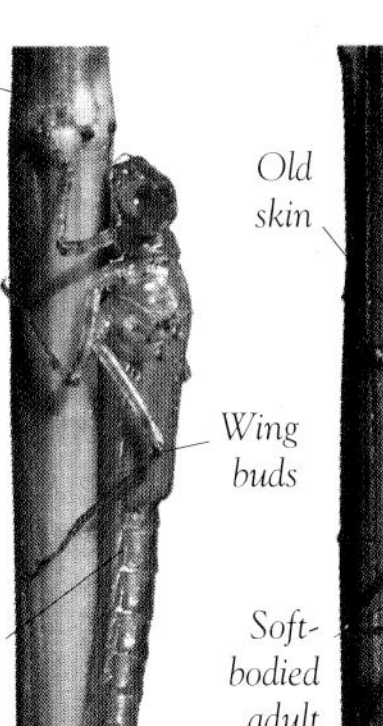
Old skin
Soft-bodied adult emerges

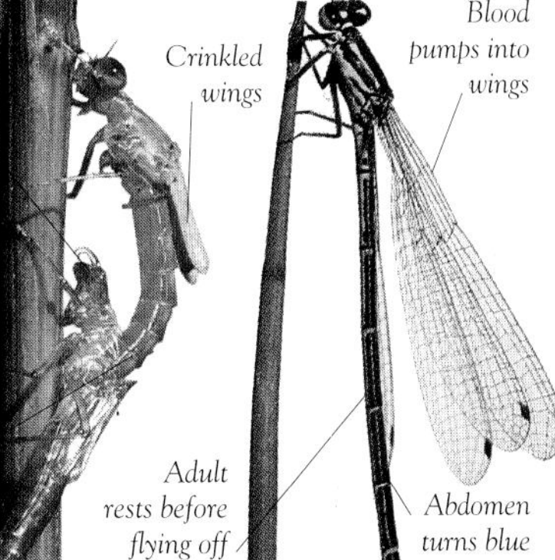
Crinkled wings
Blood pumps into wings
Adult rests before flying off
Abdomen turns blue

Types of insects

Insects range from fairyfly wasps only 0.008 in (0.2 mm) long, to giant stick insects, up to 17.7 in (45 cm) long. They are divided into 32 orders, six of which are shown here. Other insects include flies, grasshoppers, earwigs, and fleas.

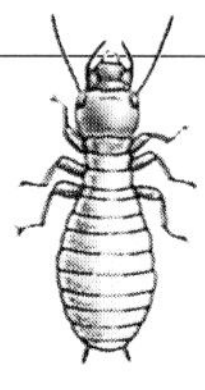

TERMITES (ISOPTERA) 2,300 SPECIES

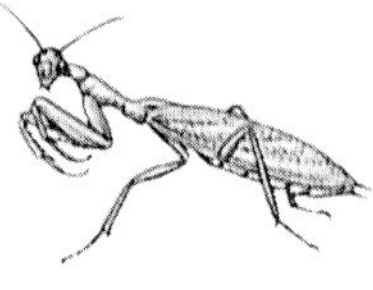

PRAYING MANTIDS (MANTODEA) 1,800 SPECIES

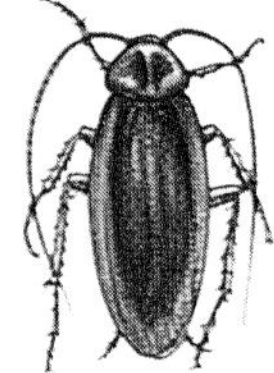

COCKROACHES (BLATTODEA) 3,700 SPECIES

ANTS, BEES, WASPS (HYMENOPTERA) 125,000 SPECIES

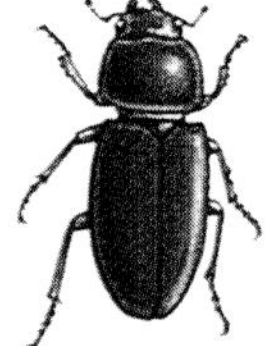

BEETLES (COLEOPTERA) 300,000 SPECIES

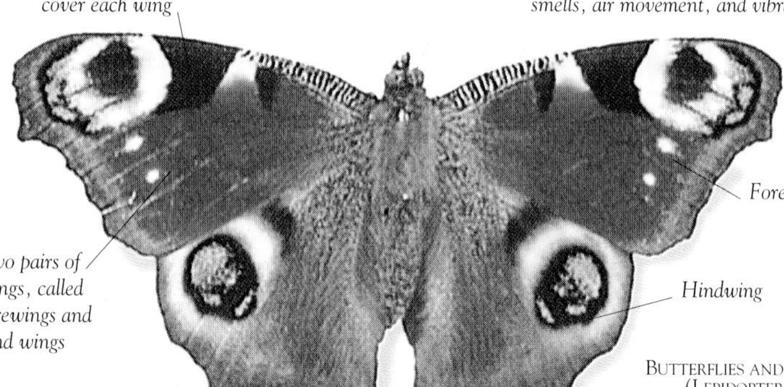

Tiny overlapping scales cover each wing
Sensitive feelers, called antennae, detect smells, air movement, and vibrations.
Forewing
Two pairs of wings, called forewings and hind wings
Hindwing

PEACOCK BUTTERFLY

BUTTERFLIES AND MOTHS (LEPIDOPTERA) 136,800 SPECIES

ARACHNIDS

SPIDERS, SCORPIONS, ticks, and mites belong to a group of arthropods called arachnids. There are more than 73,000 species, living in almost every habitat.

Eight jointed legs
Powerful jaws
CHILEAN RED-LEG SPIDER

SPIDERS
All spiders are meat-eaters. Some jump on prey; others trap prey in a web, paralyze it with venom, then eat it.

MITES AND TICKS (ACARI)
30,000 SPECIES

SPIDERS (ARANEAE)
35,000 SPECIES

ARACHNID ANATOMY
Arachnids usually have eight legs and their body is divided into the cephalothorax (front and middle) and the abdomen (rear). Scorpions have six legs and two pincer-like pedipalps for gripping prey.

Poisonous sting in the tail for paralyzing prey

Waterproof, flexible outer covering, or exoskeleton

Legs are jointed in several places for flexibility

Powerful claws, called pedipalps, hold on to prey

SCORPION

ARACHNID FACTS

- The biggest arachnid is a bird-eating spider (*Theraphosa leblondi*), with a leg span of 11 in (28 cm).
- The largest web is spun by the tropical orb spider (*Nephila*), and measures up to 10 ft (3 m) across.

CRUSTACEANS

THESE ARTHROPODS get their name from their crusty skin. They include lobsters, crabs, and shrimp, which live in the sea. Only a few, such as wood lice, live on land. There are more than 50,000 species of crustacean.

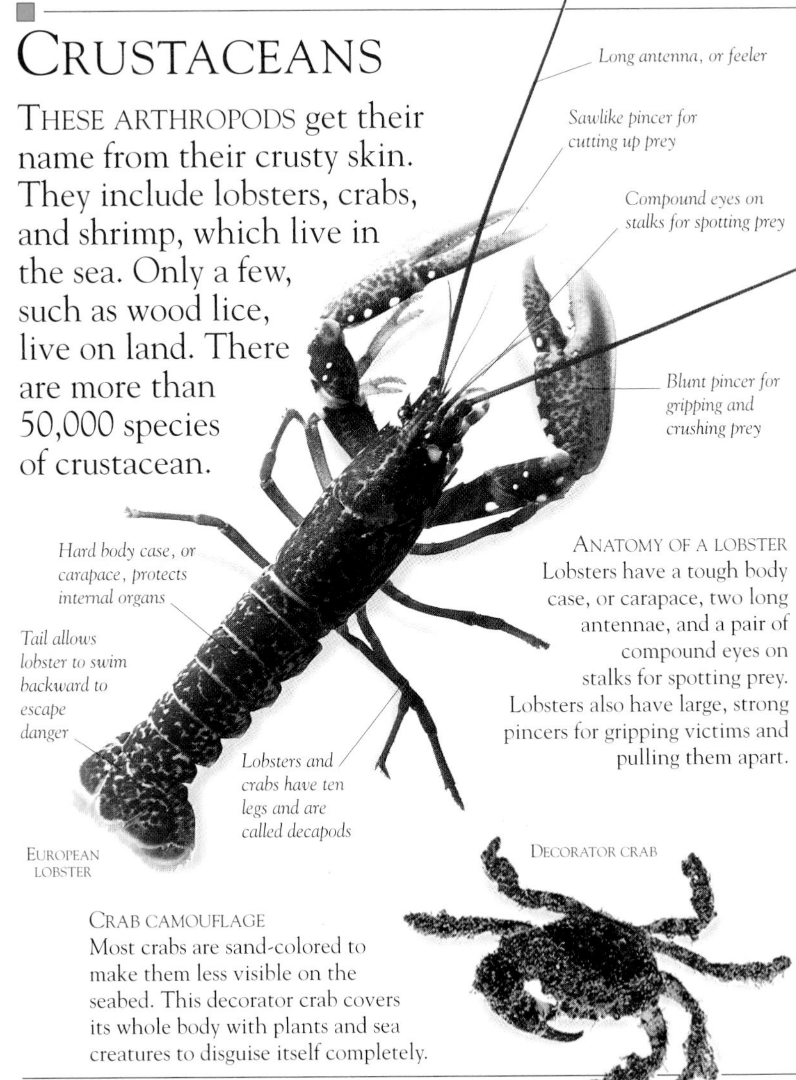
Long antenna, or feeler
Sawlike pincer for cutting up prey
Compound eyes on stalks for spotting prey
Blunt pincer for gripping and crushing prey
Hard body case, or carapace, protects internal organs
Tail allows lobster to swim backward to escape danger
Lobsters and crabs have ten legs and are called decapods
EUROPEAN LOBSTER
DECORATOR CRAB

ANATOMY OF A LOBSTER
Lobsters have a tough body case, or carapace, two long antennae, and a pair of compound eyes on stalks for spotting prey. Lobsters also have large, strong pincers for gripping victims and pulling them apart.

CRAB CAMOUFLAGE
Most crabs are sand-colored to make them less visible on the seabed. This decorator crab covers its whole body with plants and sea creatures to disguise itself completely.

Crabs

Most crabs have a hard, shieldlike shell called a carapace for defense. The flexible abdomen is usually tucked underneath for protection. Crabs move by scuttling sideways.

Huge pincers for gripping and tearing food

Hard outer shell, called the carapace

Jointed legs with clawed toes

FURROWED CRAB

Life cycle

Crustaceans begin life as eggs, which are usually laid in water. After the eggs hatch, they pass through several larval stages before taking on their adult form. As adults, they grow bigger by molting, or shedding their outer layer.

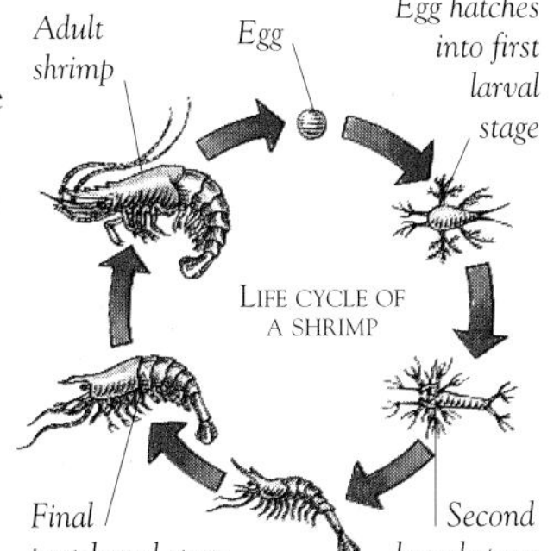
Adult shrimp
Egg
Egg hatches into first larval stage
LIFE CYCLE OF A SHRIMP
Second larval stage
Final post-larval stage

Crustacean facts

- The largest crustacean is the Japanese spider crab (*Macrocheira kaempferi*), with a leg span of almost 13 ft (4 m).
- The smallest crustaceans are tiny water fleas (*Alonella*), which measure less than 0.25 mm long.

VERTEBRATES

GORILLA SKELETON

ONLY ABOUT five percent of all animals have backbones, and these are called vertebrates. There are more than 50,000 different species of vertebrate, divided into classes of mammals, birds, fish, reptiles, and amphibians. Their sense organs and nervous systems are well developed, and they have adapted to almost every habitat.

BACKBONE
Vertebrates have a skeleton of bone, with a backbone, two pairs of limbs, and a skull that protects the brain. Inside are the heart, lungs, and other organs.

REPTILES
Lizards, snakes, crocodiles, and geckos are reptiles. They all have a tough, scaly skin. Young reptiles hatch from eggs, and look like tiny versions of their parents. This chameleon is a type of lizard.

Spines along backbone give protection from attack

Scaly skin

MADAGASCAN CHAMELEON

Prehensile tail for holding onto branches

Female frog lays eggs, called frogspawn

Male fertilizes spawn

ANIMAL REPRODUCTION
In vertebrates, offspring are created when males and females come together and the male's sperm join the female's eggs. This is called sexual reproduction, and usually involves mating. A few animals are neither male nor female, and they reproduce asexually.

SENSES

Mammals and other vertebrate animals have senses to help them find their way, locate food, and avoid enemies. For land animals, such as this caracal, sight, hearing, and smell are the most important senses. Sea creatures rely more on smell and taste to escape danger and find food.

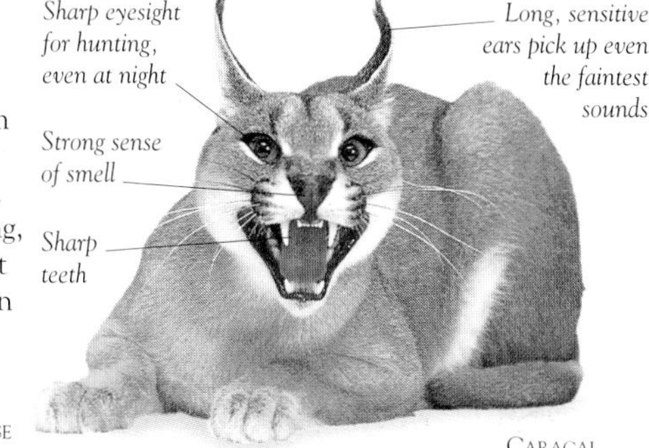
Sharp eyesight for hunting, even at night
Long, sensitive ears pick up even the faintest sounds
Strong sense of smell
Sharp teeth

CARACAL

FISH

With streamlined bodies covered in slippery scales, these vertebrates are perfectly suited to life in the water.

TWINSPOT WRASSE

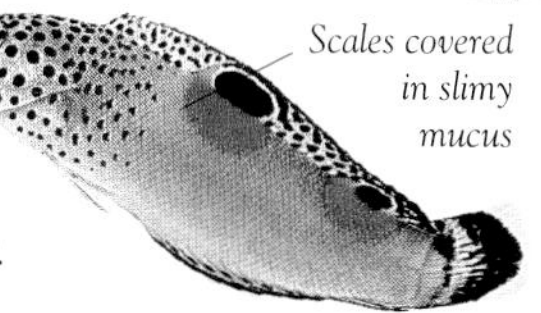
Scales covered in slimy mucus

BIRDS

The only animals that have feathers are birds, and most of them are powerful fliers. Birds have a beak, or bill, instead of teeth, and all reproduce by laying eggs.

COUNT RAGGI'S BIRD OF PARADISE

RED-EYED TREE FROG

Large eyes spot prey
Long legs for jumping

AMPHIBIANS

Frogs, toads, newts, and salamanders are amphibians. These vertebrates spend part of their lives in water and part on land. They all reproduce by laying eggs.

PORCUPINE

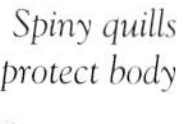
Fur helps keep body warm
Spiny quills protect body

MAMMAL

A mammal is usually covered by fur or hair. It gives birth to live young, which it feeds with milk.

AMPHIBIANS

THERE ARE more than 4,000 species of amphibian. They begin life in water as fish-like tadpoles, after hatching from clusters of eggs called spawn. Soon the tadpoles grow legs and lungs for life on land. Young amphibians breathe using gills, and the adults can breathe through their skin.

TIGER SALAMANDER

Damp skin absorbs oxygen

Bright warning spots

NEWTS AND SALAMANDERS
Salamanders have long bodies, short, thin legs, and cylindrical tails. They usually spend their adult life on land and breathe by absorbing oxygen through their damp skin. The bright color of their skin is a warning to predators.

Large, bulging eyes for spotting prey

Round external eardrum called a tympanum

Thick, bumpy skin covered with warts

Squat body

FROGS AND TOADS
Both frogs and toads have short, compact bodies, and strong back legs for jumping long distances. As they grow up from tadpole to adult, they lose their tails. There is no clear distinction between frogs and toads, but frogs tend to spend more of their life in or near water, while toads can survive in damp spots on land, returning to water to breed.

Feet are webbed for swimming

EUROPEAN COMMON TOAD

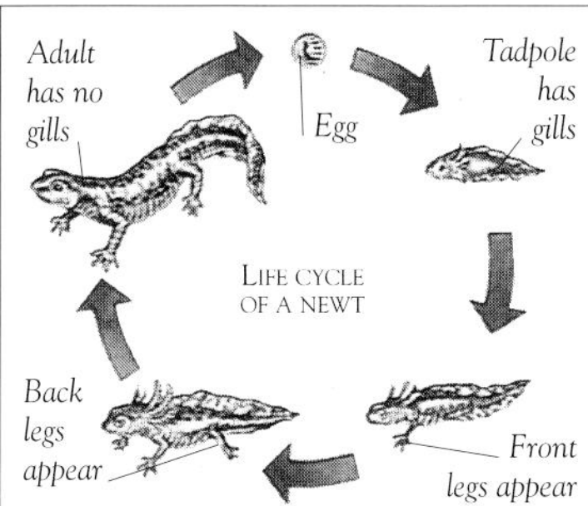
Adult has no gills
Egg
Tadpole has gills
LIFE CYCLE OF A NEWT
Back legs appear
Front legs appear

Life cycle of an amphibian

Amphibians lay their eggs in water; the eggs are not waterproof and would dry out on land. After a week or so, the eggs hatch into tadpoles, and these become strong swimmers. In newts, the front legs appear about three weeks after hatching. The back legs appear at seven to eight weeks. Finally, the gills disappear and the newt metamorphoses (changes) into an adult.

Midwife toad

The female midwife toad lays about 50 eggs. After the male has fertilized the eggs, he carries them on his back for up to one-and-a-half months until they are ready to hatch.

Male wraps eggs around back legs
MIDWIFE TOAD (MALE)

Vivid colors act as warning signal to predators
POISON-DART FROG

Deadly poisons

Some amphibians produce powerful poisons from glands in their skin. These creatures are often brightly colored to warn predators of the danger. Poison-dart frogs are the most poisonous amphibians.

Amphibian camouflage

Some amphibians manage to avoid predators by the unusual colors and patterns on their bodies. This yellow-bellied toad hardly shows up against tree bark.

Patches of green complete the toad's disguise
YELLOW-BELLIED TOAD

REPTILES

SCALY-SKINNED crocodiles, lizards, and snakes are all reptiles. There are about 6,500 species. Reptiles are found on land and in water, but they cannot live in cold places because they need the sun's warmth to give them energy.

EGGS
Most reptiles hatch from eggs with thick, leathery shells that stop them from drying out. Some reptiles are "viviparous," giving birth to live young.

IGUANA
These large American lizards often have a crest on their backs.

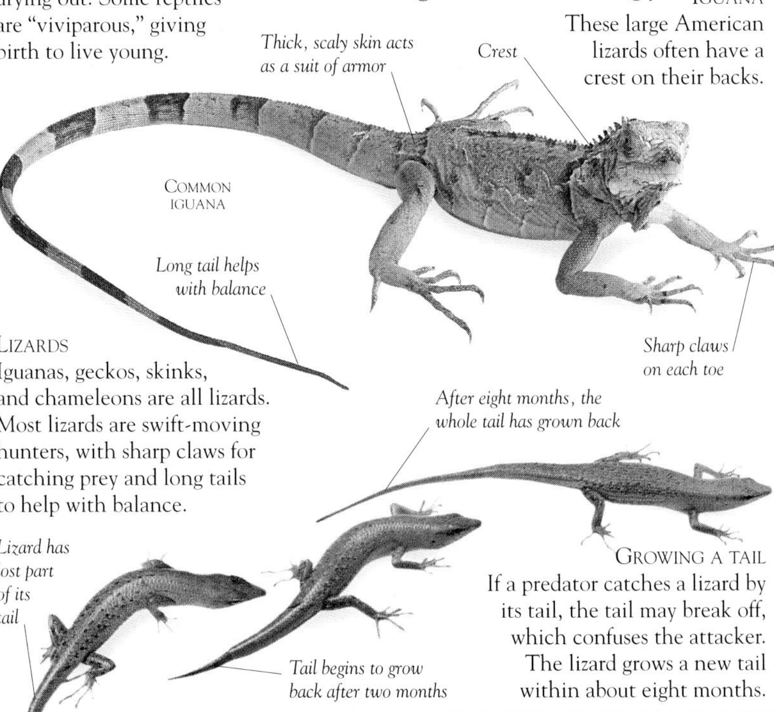
Thick, scaly skin acts as a suit of armor
Crest
COMMON IGUANA
Long tail helps with balance
Sharp claws on each toe
After eight months, the whole tail has grown back
Lizard has lost part of its tail
Tail begins to grow back after two months

LIZARDS
Iguanas, geckos, skinks, and chameleons are all lizards. Most lizards are swift-moving hunters, with sharp claws for catching prey and long tails to help with balance.

GROWING A TAIL
If a predator catches a lizard by its tail, the tail may break off, which confuses the attacker. The lizard grows a new tail within about eight months.

Turtles and tortoises

Tortoises, turtles, and terrapins are called chelonians. They have a hard shell made of bony plates. By hiding inside the shell they can escape most predators, so they do not need to move quickly. Tortoises live on land and terrapins and turtles live in water.

Shell made of horn
Starred tortoise shell
Red-eared terrapin

Cobra inflates hood to make itself appear bigger

Monocled cobra

Long, thin body

Snakes

Snakes are long, legless reptiles. They hunt prey by smelling the air with their forked tongue. Constrictors such as pythons coil around prey and suffocate them. Venomous snakes such as this cobra stun or kill their prey with poison from hollow teeth called fangs.

Reptile facts

- A giant turtle found in Mauritius in 1766 survived for another 152 years.
- The venom glands of the Australian taipan snake hold enough poison to kill 200 people.

Crocodiles and alligators

Alligators, crocodiles, caimans, and gavials are called crocodilians. These hunters with huge jaws and sharp teeth live in tropical swamps and rivers.

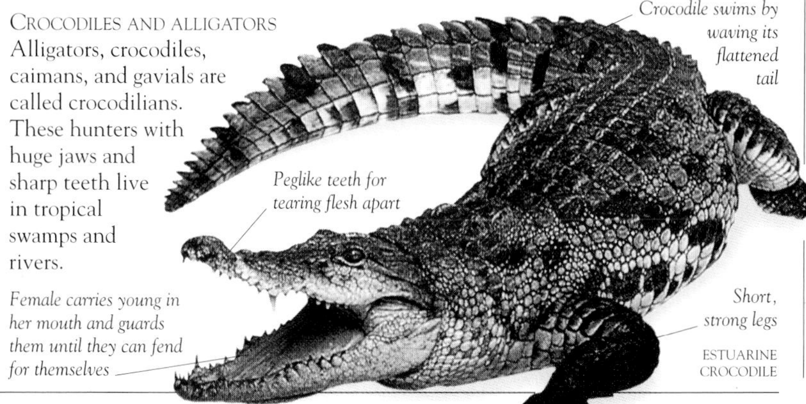
Crocodile swims by waving its flattened tail
Peglike teeth for tearing flesh apart
Female carries young in her mouth and guards them until they can fend for themselves
Short, strong legs
Estuarine crocodile

FISH

THERE ARE more than 25,000 species of fish, all of which live in water from deep oceans to ponds, rivers, and lakes. Most fish have streamlined, scaly bodies, fins for swimming, and gills for breathing. They reproduce by laying eggs.

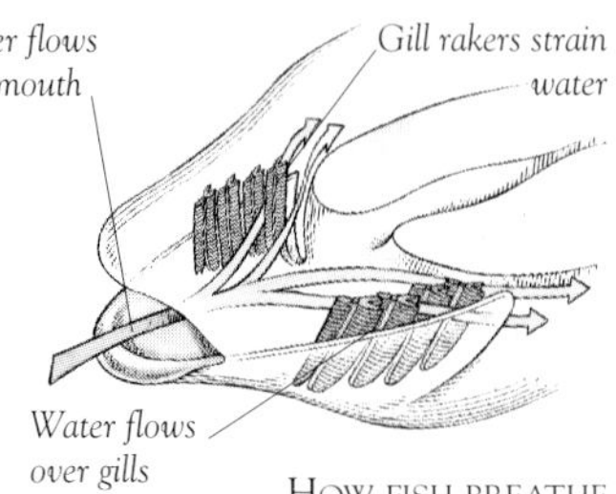
Water flows into mouth
Gill rakers strain water
Water flows over gills

HOW FISH BREATHE
Fish are able to breathe underwater using their gills. As water flows over the gills, oxygen passes into the bloodstream through special, thin skins called membranes.

BONY FISH
The largest group of fish includes carp and other bony fish. These fish have bony skeletons and an internal air bag called the swim bladder that keeps them afloat in the water.

Dorsal fin
Scales
Eye
Mouth
Caudal fin
Gill cover
Anal fin
Pelvic fin
Pectoral fin

CARP

HOW CARTILAGINOUS FISH SWIM
A cartilaginous fish, such as a dogfish, swims by swinging its tail in an "S" shape; it steers by waving its pectoral and pelvic fins. The dorsal fin helps keep the fish upright as it swims. Bony fish swim by moving their fins only.

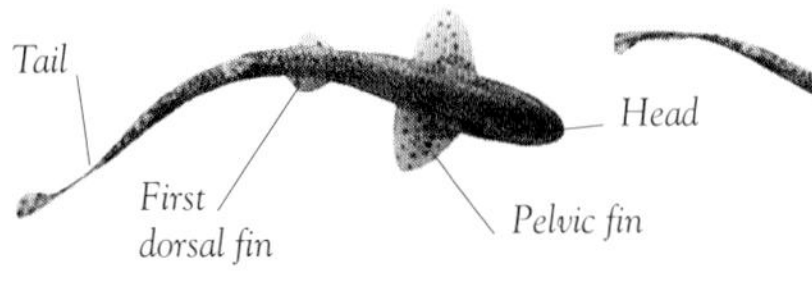
Tail
Head
First dorsal fin
Pelvic fin

The fish swings its head to the right, and an S-shaped wave begins to travel along the body.

CARTILAGINOUS FISH

Sharks, skates, and rays are cartilaginous, as their skeletons are made of rubbery cartilage instead of bone. There are about 800 species, and most of them are hunters.

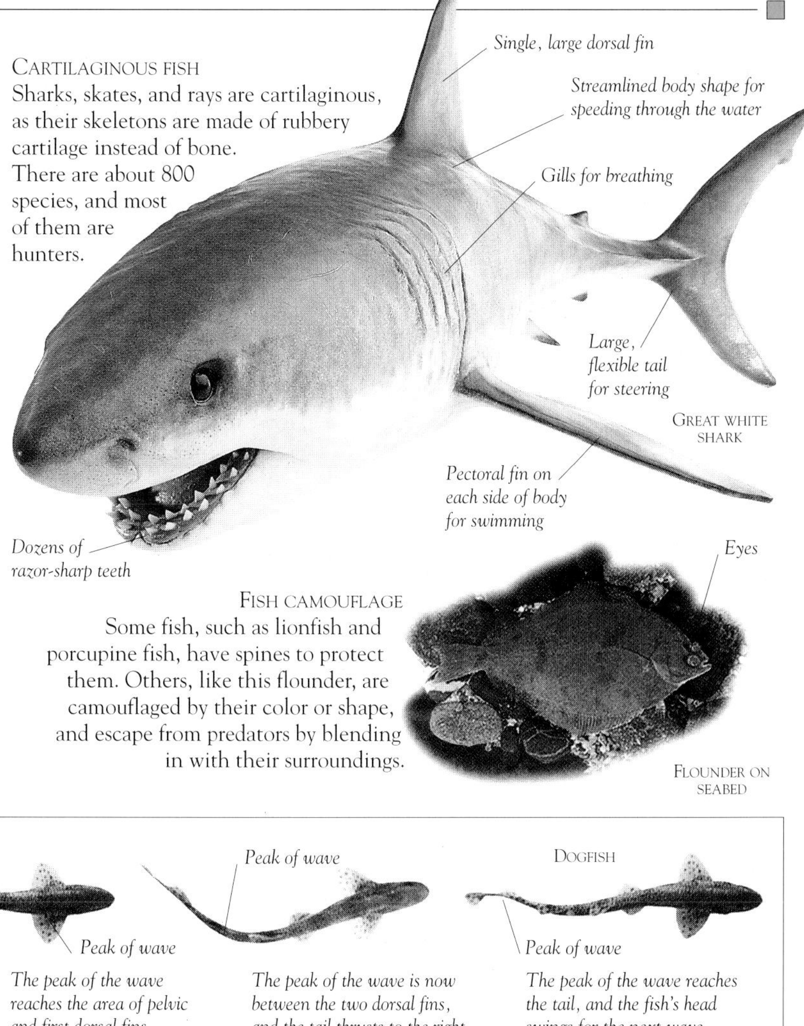
Single, large dorsal fin
Streamlined body shape for speeding through the water
Gills for breathing
Large, flexible tail for steering
Pectoral fin on each side of body for swimming
Dozens of razor-sharp teeth
Eyes

GREAT WHITE SHARK

FISH CAMOUFLAGE

Some fish, such as lionfish and porcupine fish, have spines to protect them. Others, like this flounder, are camouflaged by their color or shape, and escape from predators by blending in with their surroundings.

FLOUNDER ON SEABED

DOGFISH

Peak of wave

Peak of wave

Peak of wave

The peak of the wave reaches the area of pelvic and first dorsal fins.

The peak of the wave is now between the two dorsal fins, and the tail thrusts to the right.

The peak of the wave reaches the tail, and the fish's head swings for the next wave.

RED-TAILED MINLA

BIRDS

FROM THE TINY BEE hummingbird, which weighs only 0.056 oz (1.6 g), to the ostrich, which weighs up to 344 lb (156 kg) and grows up to 8.9 ft (2.7 m) tall, birds are the only animals with feathers. They also have wings and beaks, and most are expert fliers. Birds reproduce by laying eggs.

Wing size and shape depends on a bird's lifestyle

Wing feathers spread in flight to give lift

Beak made of bone covered by layer of horn

Scaly, clawed feet for gripping branches

Tail helps bird to balance and change direction

BIRDS IN FLIGHT
Birds fly by flapping their wings, or by gliding. Each bird has its own flight pattern. Small birds have a bouncing flight, and glide between flaps to save energy. Larger birds fly level and flap their wings all the time. Some birds take to the air for a few minutes at a time; others stay airborne for weeks or even months.

FROM EGG TO CHICK
As a chick develops inside an egg, the parent birds sit on the egg to keep it warm. This is called incubation. Small birds incubate their eggs for two weeks, eagles for seven weeks, and albatrosses for eleven weeks.

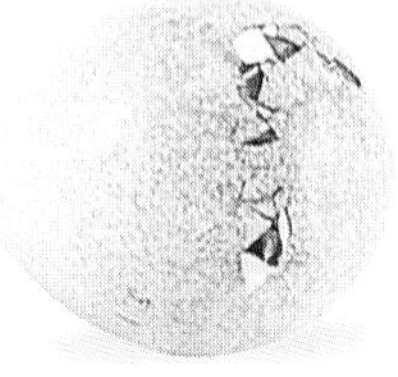
The chick hatches by pecking the shell with the "egg tooth" on its bill.

The chick pecks a circle around the top of the egg and pushes.

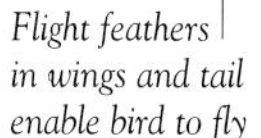

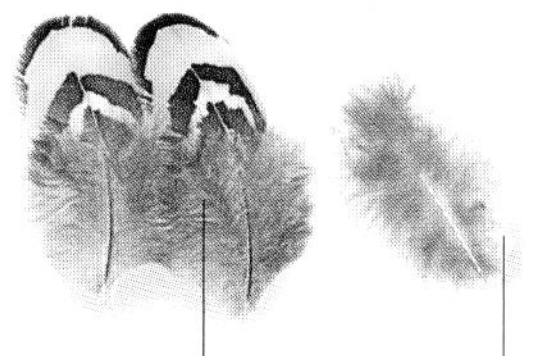

Flight feathers in wings and tail enable bird to fly

Body feathers overlap and keep bird waterproof

Down feathers trap warm air next to the skin

Tail feathers are extra long for steering, balancing, and braking

BIRD FACTS

- A wren has about 1,000 feathers; a swan has about 25,000.
- Ostrich eggs are the largest single living cells on Earth.
- A peregrine falcon (*Falco peregrinus*) can dive at 112 mph (180 km/h).

FEATHERS

A bird's feathers keep it warm and enable it to fly. Feathers are light yet strong because each strand is linked together with hooks called barbs and barbules.

NESTS AND YOUNG

Most birds build nests. A nest keeps the eggs warm and safe until they are ready to hatch, and provides a home for the newly hatched young. Each bird species has its own way of building a nest. Magpies build nests of twigs in trees; weaverbirds weave elaborate nests from grass.

NESTLINGS

CHICK EMERGING FROM EGG

The top of the shell breaks off and the chick struggles free. Its feathers are still wet.

The fluffy down soon dries out and will be replaced by feathers as the chick grows.

Types of bird

Birds have adapted to life in almost all parts of the world. Some, like birds of prey, are meat-eaters, while others eat only seeds and fruits. There are at least 9,600 species divided into 27 orders.

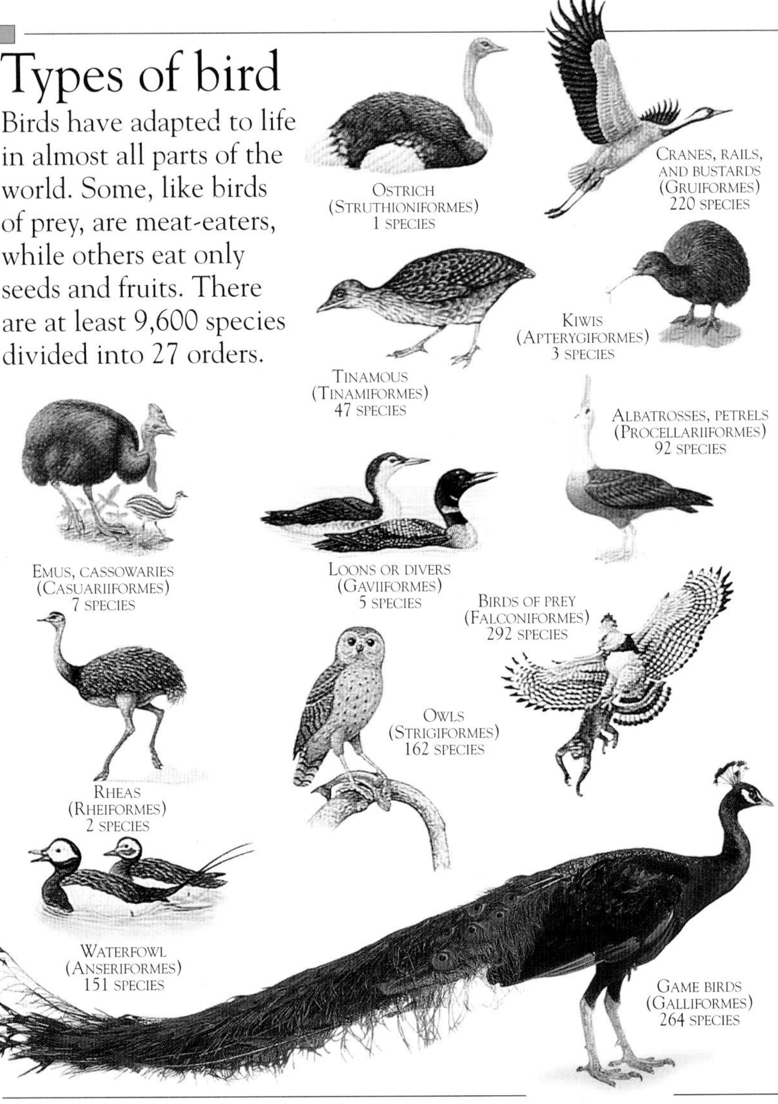
Ostrich
(Struthioniformes)
1 species
Cranes, rails, and bustards
(Gruiformes)
220 species
Tinamous
(Tinamiformes)
47 species
Kiwis
(Apterygiformes)
3 species
Albatrosses, petrels
(Procellariiformes)
92 species
Emus, cassowaries
(Casuariiformes)
7 species
Loons or divers
(Gaviiformes)
5 species
Birds of prey
(Falconiformes)
292 species
Owls
(Strigiformes)
162 species
Rheas
(Rheiformes)
2 species
Waterfowl
(Anseriformes)
151 species
Game birds
(Galliformes)
264 species

SHOREBIRDS, GULLS, TERNS, AUKS (CHARADRIIFORMES) 337 SPECIES
PARROTS, LORIES, COCKATOOS (PSITTACIFORMES) 330 SPECIES
PELICANS, GANNETS, CORMORANTS (PELECANIFORMES) 55 SPECIES
MOUSEBIRDS (COLIIFORMES) 6 SPECIES
HERONS, STORKS, IBISES (CICONIIFORMES) 110 SPECIES
NIGHTJARS, FROGMOUTHS (CAPRIMULGIFORMES) 102 SPECIES
SWIFTS, HUMMINGBIRDS (APODIFORMES) 404 SPECIES
PASSERINES (PASSERIFORMES) 5,712 SPECIES
KINGFISHERS, BEE-EATERS, HOOPOES (CORACIIFORMES) 206 SPECIES
CUCKOOS, TURACOS (CUCULIFORMES) 150 SPECIES
PIGEONS (COLUMBIFORMES) 320 SPECIES
WOODPECKERS, TOUCANS, BARBETS (PICIFORMES) 378 SPECIES
GREBES (PODICIPEDIFORMES) 19 SPECIES
PENGUINS (SPHENISCIFORMES) 17 SPECIES
TROGONS (TROGONIFORMES) 39 SPECIES

Mammals

DOLPHIN

ALL MAMMALS are warm-blooded animals, so their blood is always at the correct temperature for their body processes to work well. To keep warm, mammals usually have thick fur or a layer of fat or blubber. Mammals are found all over the world, on land, in water, and even in the air.

Carnivores

Some mammals are carnivores (meat-eaters), and most carnivores are hunters. The deadliest hunters of the mammal world are the big cats, such as lions, tigers, cheetahs, and leopards. They have strong, agile bodies for chasing prey, and sharp claws and teeth for killing it.

Sea mammals

Whales and dolphins spend their lives in the sea and come to the surface to breathe. They are called cetaceans.

Excellent hearing
Good senses of sight and smell
Striped pattern camouflages tiger in long grass
Powerful, low-slung body
Body covered in fur for warmth
Massive paws and sharp claws can strike a fatal blow

INDIAN TIGER

HERBIVORES
Mammals that eat only plants are called herbivores. Some herbivores, such as giraffes, browse on the buds of bushes and trees. Others, including zebras and cattle, graze on grass. Herbivores often have special teeth for grinding plant matter.

GUERNSEY COW

Tiny newborn kangaroo crawls into pouch

MARSUPIALS
Kangaroos, koalas, and other marsupial mammals have a pouch into which their newborn baby crawls. The young animal lives in its mother's pouch until it is fully developed and able to fend for itself.

GRAY KANGAROO

Young kangaroos are called joeys

EGG-LAYERS
Monotremes, such as this Australian duck-billed platypus, are the only mammals that lay eggs.

MOTHER'S MILK
Mammals are the only animals to feed their young on milk, produced in the mother's body. Milk is nourishing, and it contains substances that protect the young from disease.

Kittens feed on their mother's milk

MAMMAL FACTS

- Pygmy shrews lose body heat quickly because of their small size, so they must eat three times their body weight of food every day to survive.
- Elephants eat about 500 lb (228 kg) of vegetation every day.

Types of mammal

Mammals range from Kitti's long-nosed bat, which is the size of a bee, to the massive blue whale, which is the size of a jumbo jet. There are more than 4,600 species of mammal, found all over the world. Mammals are divided into 21 orders, shown here.

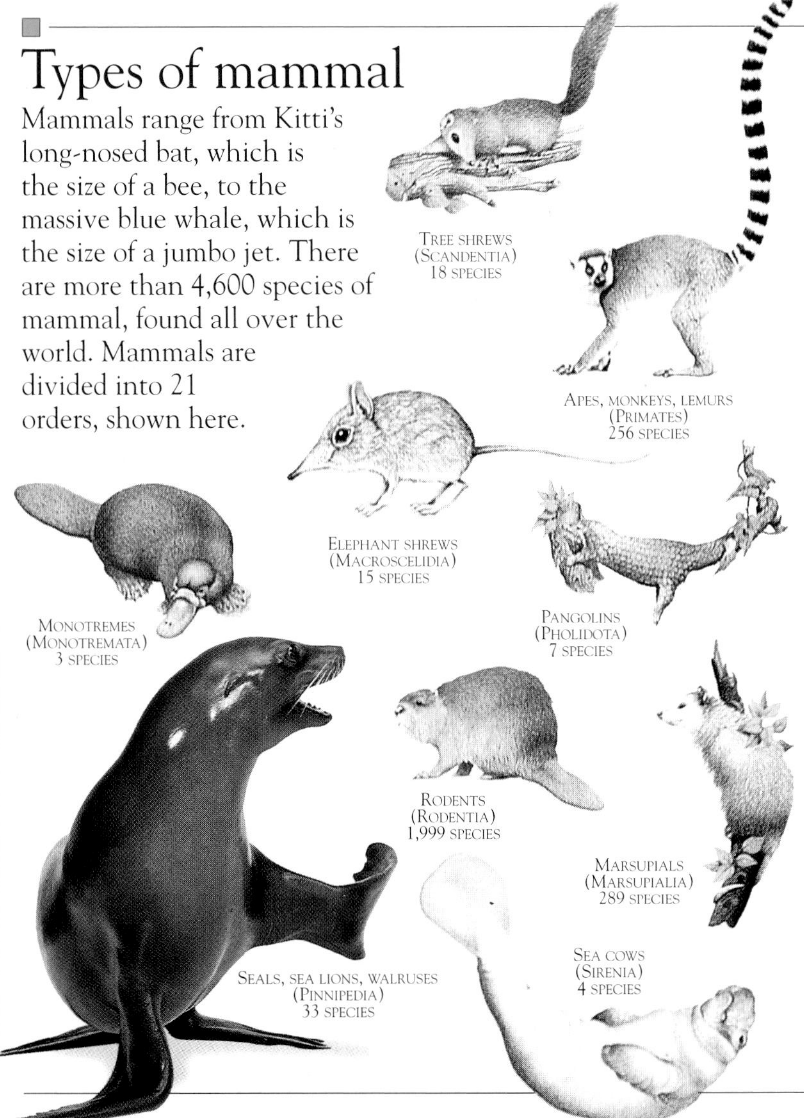

TREE SHREWS (SCANDENTIA) 18 SPECIES

APES, MONKEYS, LEMURS (PRIMATES) 256 SPECIES

ELEPHANT SHREWS (MACROSCELIDIA) 15 SPECIES

MONOTREMES (MONOTREMATA) 3 SPECIES

PANGOLINS (PHOLIDOTA) 7 SPECIES

RODENTS (RODENTIA) 1,999 SPECIES

MARSUPIALS (MARSUPIALIA) 289 SPECIES

SEA COWS (SIRENIA) 4 SPECIES

SEALS, SEA LIONS, WALRUSES (PINNIPEDIA) 33 SPECIES

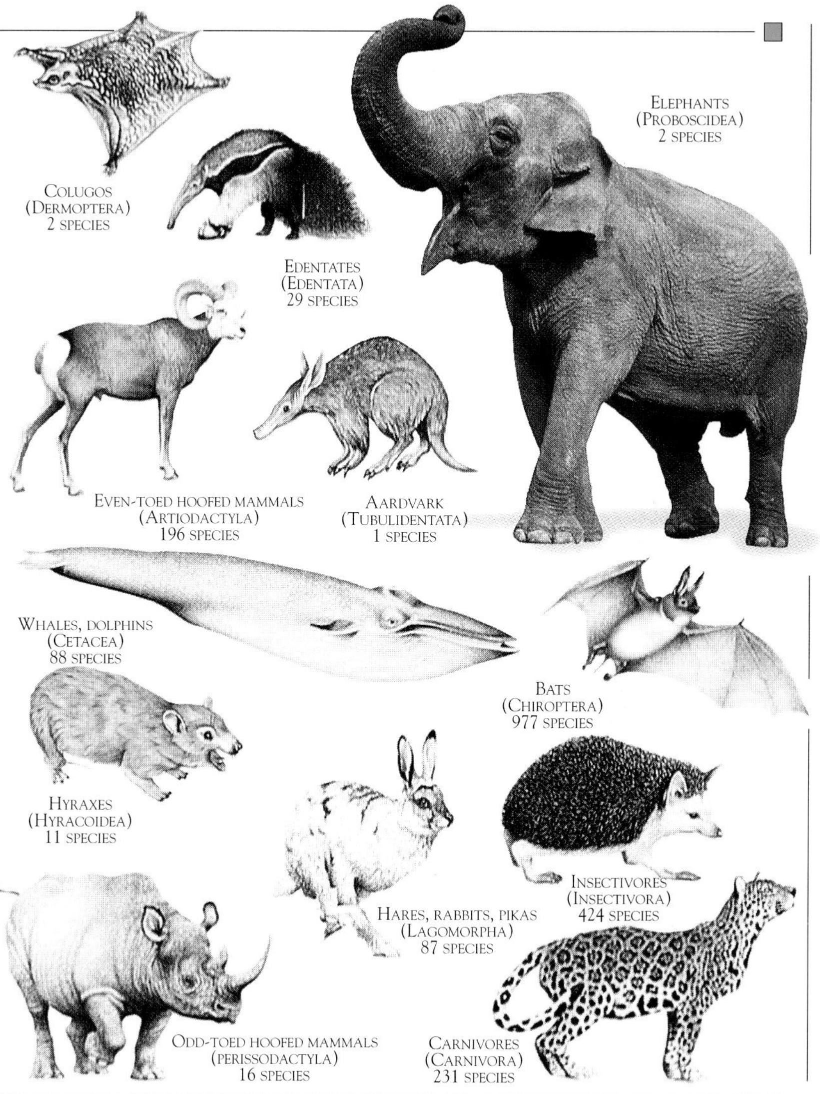
Colugos
(Dermoptera)
2 species
Edentates
(Edentata)
29 species
Elephants
(Proboscidea)
2 species
Even-toed hoofed mammals
(Artiodactyla)
196 species
Aardvark
(Tubulidentata)
1 species
Whales, dolphins
(Cetacea)
88 species
Bats
(Chiroptera)
977 species
Hyraxes
(Hyracoidea)
11 species
Insectivores
(Insectivora)
424 species
Hares, rabbits, pikas
(Lagomorpha)
87 species
Odd-toed hoofed mammals
(perissodactyla)
16 species
Carnivores
(Carnivora)
231 species

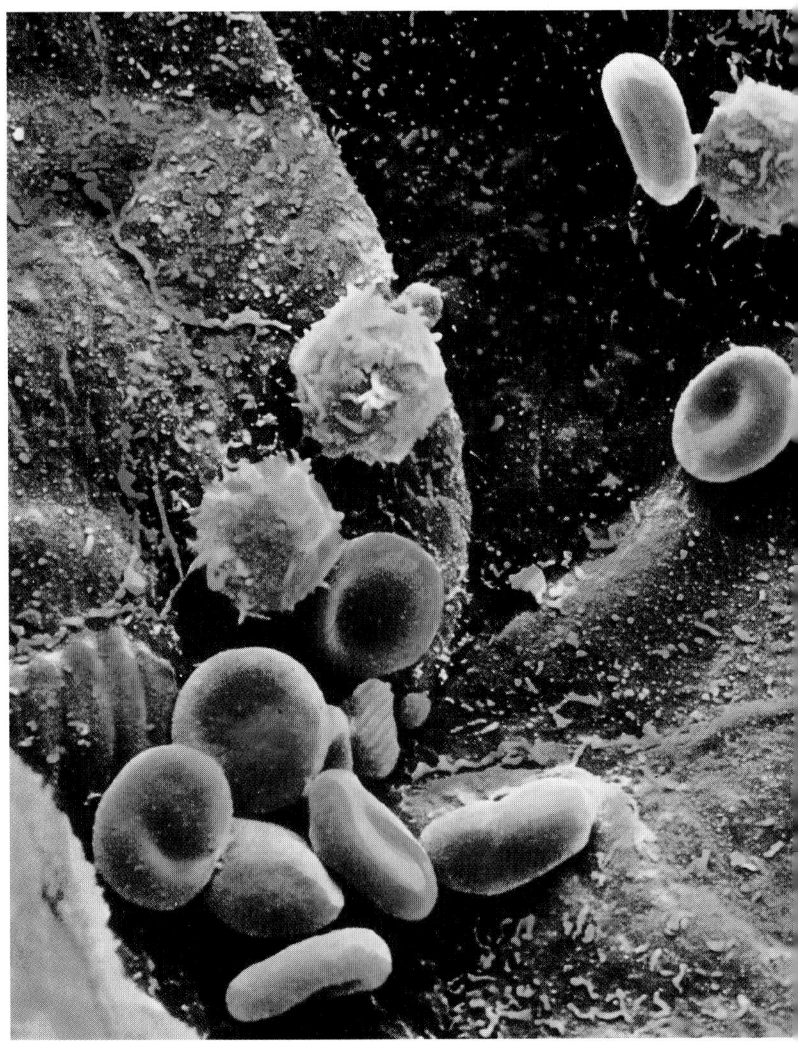

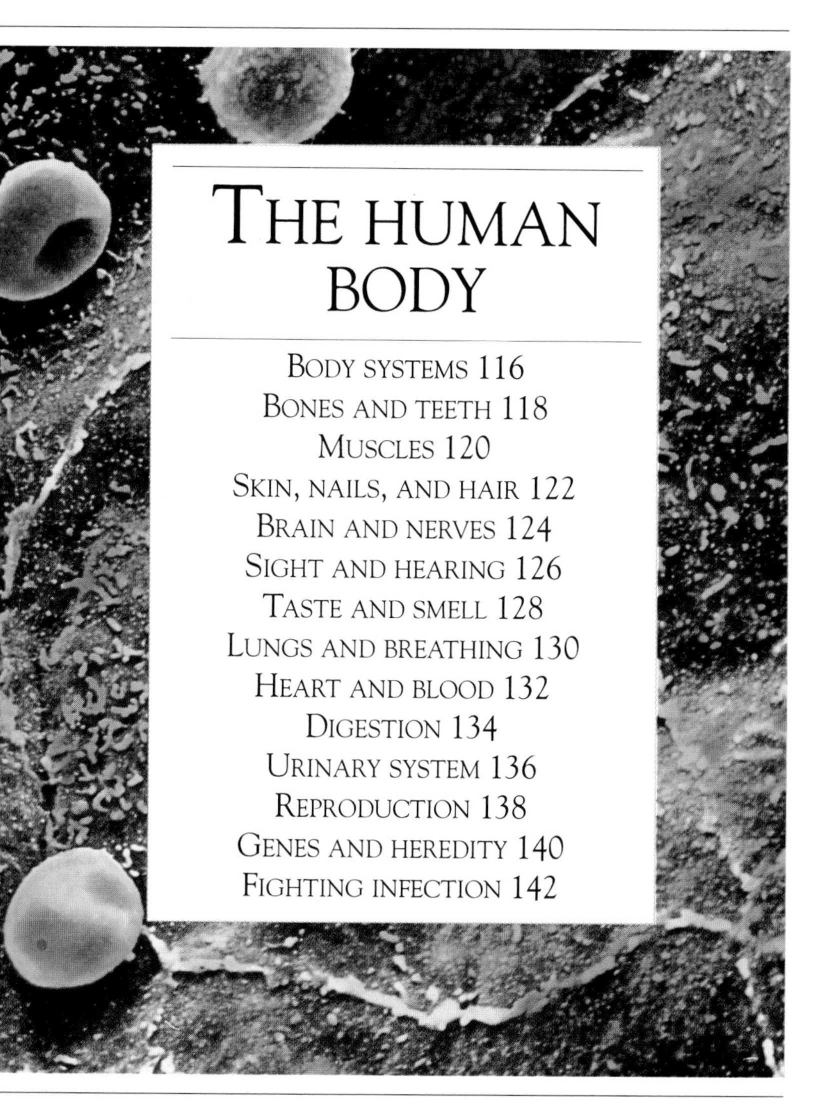

THE HUMAN BODY

BODY SYSTEMS

THE HUMAN BODY is an amazingly complex organism made up of 100 trillion microscopic cells. There are more than 200 kinds of cell, all organized into a dozen or so body systems, each with its own function. Here are the major systems that are common to all humans.

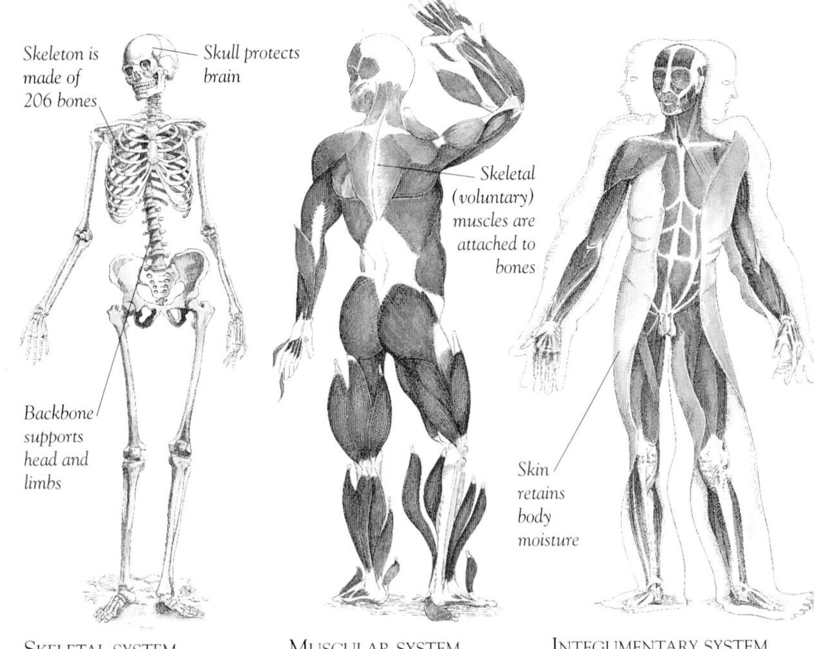
Skeleton is made of 206 bones
Skull protects brain
Backbone supports head and limbs
Skeletal (voluntary) muscles are attached to bones
Skin retains body moisture

SKELETAL SYSTEM
The skeleton is the rigid framework of bone that supports the body and protects its internal organs.

MUSCULAR SYSTEM
Every movement of the body (both involuntary and voluntary) is caused by muscles contracting.

INTEGUMENTARY SYSTEM
This system consists of the skin, hair, and nails. Skin and hair cover the body, and help to protect it.

RESPIRATORY SYSTEM
This takes oxygenated air into the lungs and pushes out waste gases.

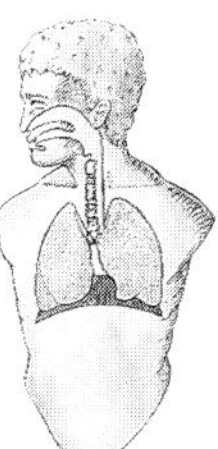

DIGESTIVE SYSTEM
The digestive tract breaks down and absorbs food, and gets rid of solid waste.

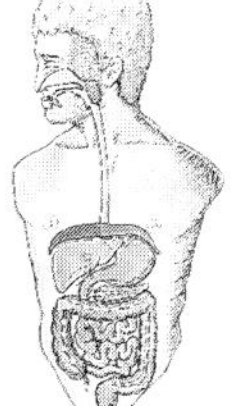

URINARY SYSTEM
This filters soluble wastes from the blood for disposal as urine.

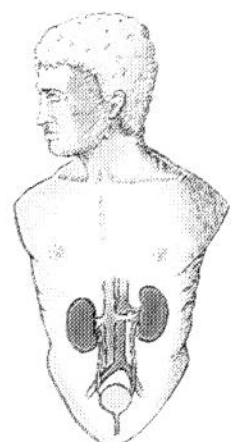

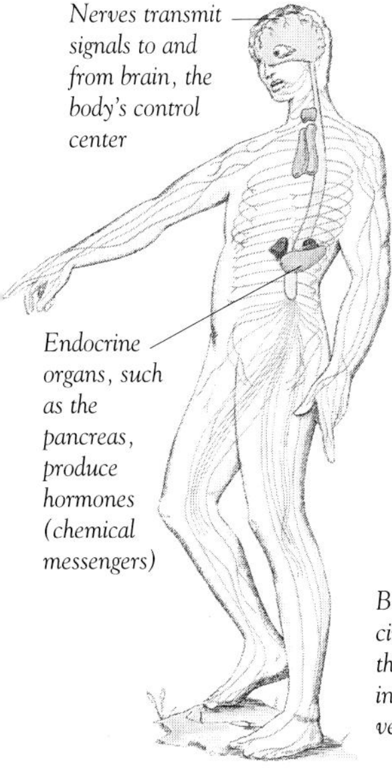

Nerves transmit signals to and from brain, the body's control center

Endocrine organs, such as the pancreas, produce hormones (chemical messengers)

Heart constantly pumps blood around body

Blood circulates through body in blood vessels

Lymph nodes filter lymph and cleanse it of infection

NERVES AND HORMONES
The nervous system and hormones coordinate all the body systems and direct our actions.

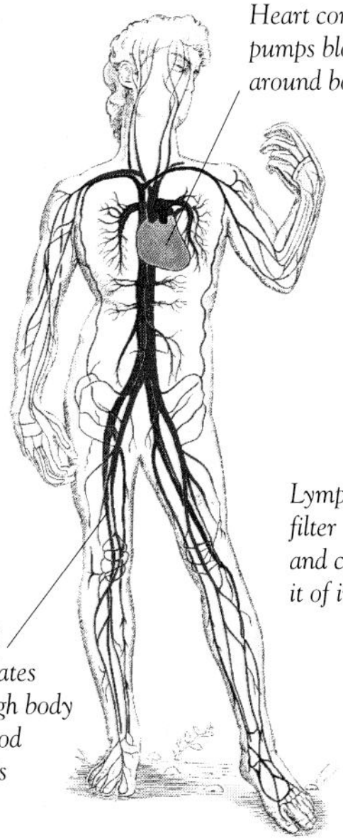

CARDIOVASCULAR SYSTEM
Blood pumped around the body by the heart supplies tissues with oxygen and removes waste products.

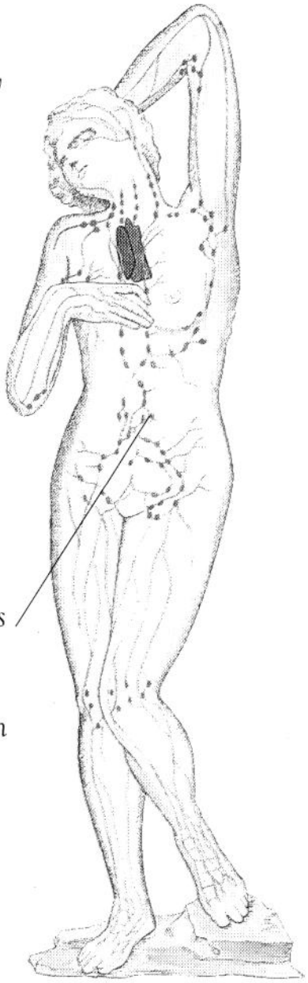

LYMPHATIC SYSTEM
Lymph, containing immune cells, is collected by a network of lymph vessels.

BONES AND TEETH

THE INNER FRAMEWORK of the human body consists of interconnecting bones that form the skeleton. Without a skeleton we could not stand or move.

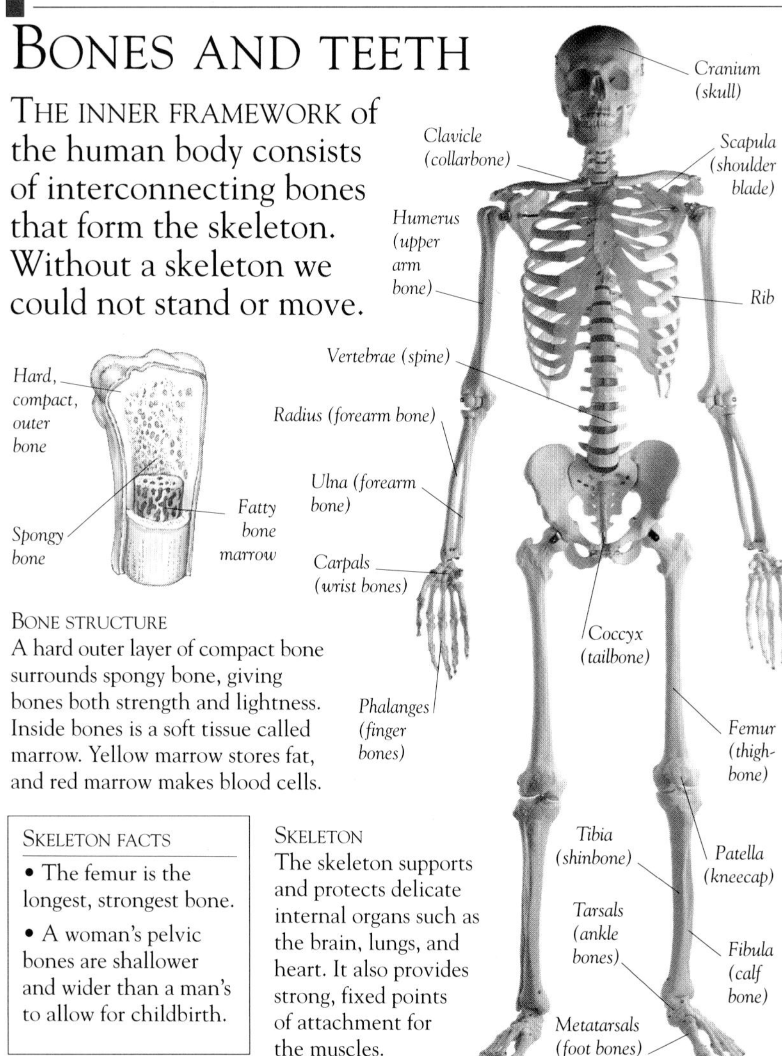
Hard, compact, outer bone
Spongy bone
Fatty bone marrow
Cranium (skull)
Clavicle (collarbone)
Scapula (shoulder blade)
Humerus (upper arm bone)
Rib
Vertebrae (spine)
Radius (forearm bone)
Ulna (forearm bone)
Carpals (wrist bones)
Coccyx (tailbone)
Phalanges (finger bones)
Femur (thigh-bone)
Tibia (shinbone)
Patella (kneecap)
Tarsals (ankle bones)
Fibula (calf bone)
Metatarsals (foot bones)

BONE STRUCTURE
A hard outer layer of compact bone surrounds spongy bone, giving bones both strength and lightness. Inside bones is a soft tissue called marrow. Yellow marrow stores fat, and red marrow makes blood cells.

SKELETON FACTS

- The femur is the longest, strongest bone.
- A woman's pelvic bones are shallower and wider than a man's to allow for childbirth.

SKELETON
The skeleton supports and protects delicate internal organs such as the brain, lungs, and heart. It also provides strong, fixed points of attachment for the muscles.

JOINTS

Where bones meet, a joint forms. In a mobile joint, the bone surface is coated with slippery cartilage and is lubricated with synovial fluid. Most joints are held together by cords called ligaments.

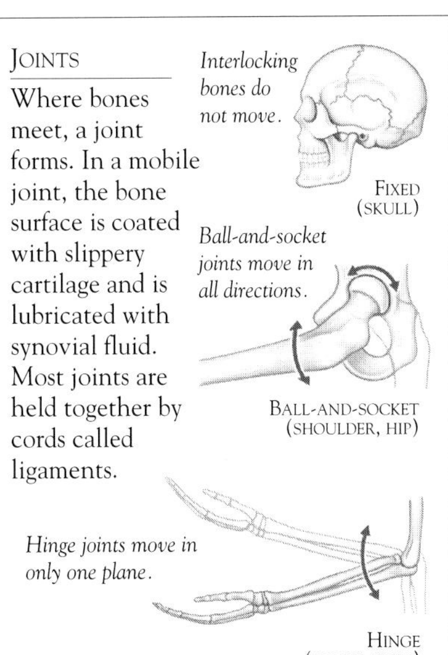
Interlocking bones do not move.
FIXED (SKULL)
Ball-and-socket joints move in all directions.
BALL-AND-SOCKET (SHOULDER, HIP)
Hinge joints move in only one plane.
HINGE (ELBOW, KNEE)

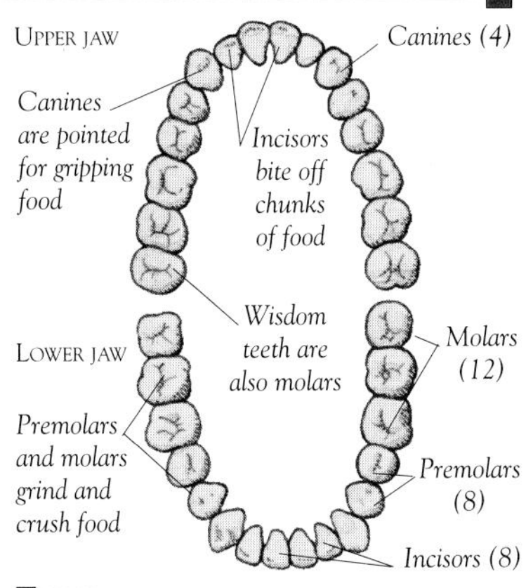
UPPER JAW
Canines (4)
Canines are pointed for gripping food
Incisors bite off chunks of food
Wisdom teeth are also molars
LOWER JAW
Molars (12)
Premolars and molars grind and crush food
Premolars (8)
Incisors (8)

TEETH

Humans have two sets of teeth. Children lose their first "baby" teeth when they are about six years old. These are gradually replaced by a second, permanent set of 32 teeth, each with a different job to do.

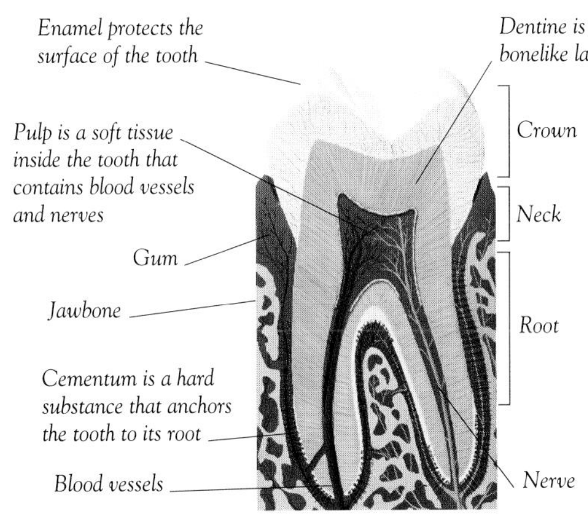
Enamel protects the surface of the tooth
Dentine is a bonelike layer
Pulp is a soft tissue inside the tooth that contains blood vessels and nerves
Crown
Neck
Gum
Jawbone
Root
Cementum is a hard substance that anchors the tooth to its root
Blood vessels
Nerve

TOOTH STRUCTURE

Teeth are harder than bone, and consist of several layers. The enamel is the hardest substance in the body, and forms the tough, nonliving exterior surface of the tooth. The dentine is the living tissue that gives the tooth its shape. The pulp contains vessels that bring blood to the tooth, enabling it to live and grow.

MUSCLES

TO MAKE A body part move, muscles convert chemical energy into motion and heat. We consciously control skeletal muscles, but all other muscle types work automatically.

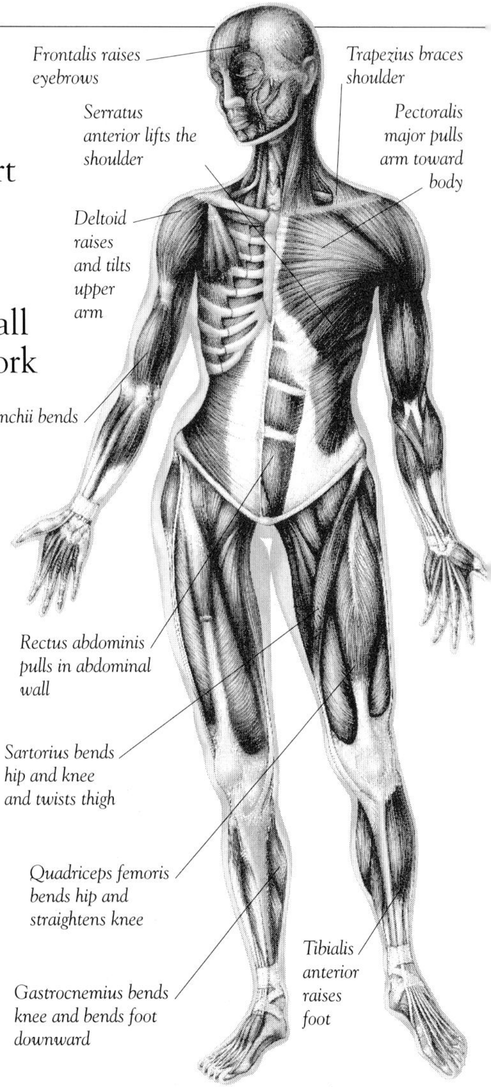

Frontalis raises eyebrows

Trapezius braces shoulder

Serratus anterior lifts the shoulder

Pectoralis major pulls arm toward body

Deltoid raises and tilts upper arm

Biceps branchii bends lower arm

Rectus abdominis pulls in abdominal wall

Sartorius bends hip and knee and twists thigh

Quadriceps femoris bends hip and straightens knee

Gastrocnemius bends knee and bends foot downward

Tibialis anterior raises foot

MUSCLE USE
When muscles are used, they provide the body with more than one-fifth of its heat. Regular exercise increases the flow of blood to the muscles, keeps them toned, and makes them grow in size.

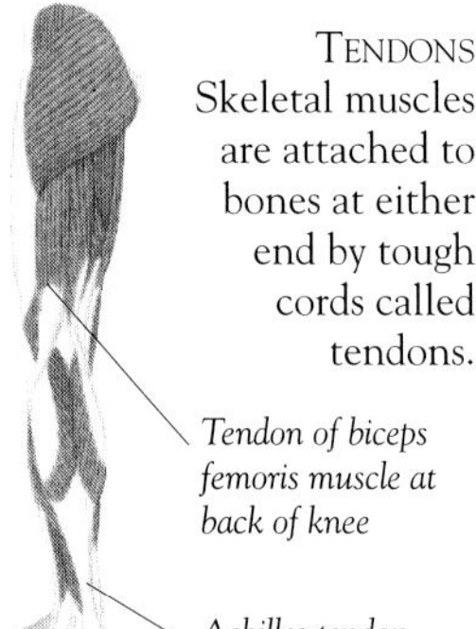

Tendon of biceps femoris muscle at back of knee

Achilles tendon

TENDONS
Skeletal muscles are attached to bones at either end by tough cords called tendons.

MUSCLE ACTION

A muscle can pull, but it cannot push, as it works by contracting. Muscles often work in pairs. A "flexor" muscle flexes, or bends a joint, and an "extensor" muscle straightens it again.

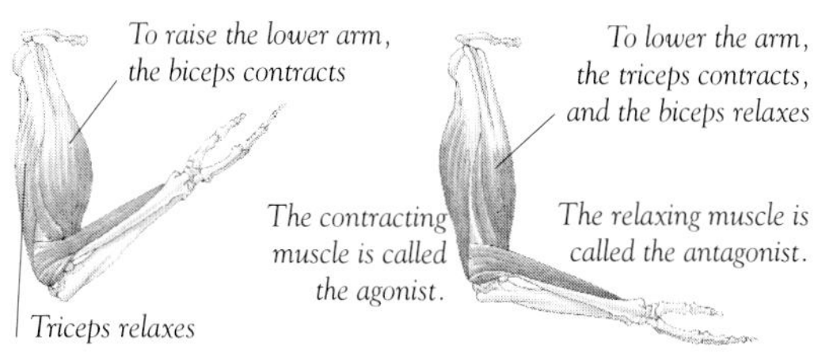
To raise the lower arm, the biceps contracts
Triceps relaxes
The contracting muscle is called the agonist.
To lower the arm, the triceps contracts, and the biceps relaxes
The relaxing muscle is called the antagonist.

MUSCLE STRUCTURE

Voluntary muscles consist of bundles of cells called fibers. Inside are strands of myofibrils containing the proteins actin and myosin. When a muscle contracts, the myosin pulls on the actin, making the muscle shorter.

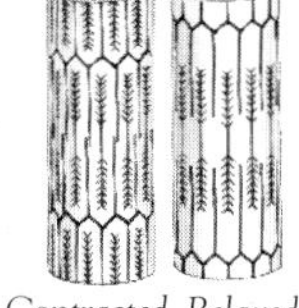
Contracted myofibril
Relaxed myofibril

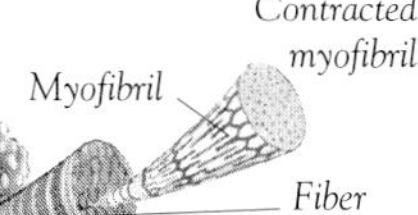
Myofibril
Fiber
Bundle of fibers

MUSCLE FACTS

- There are more than 600 different voluntary muscles in the body.
- Muscles make up 40 percent of a person's total weight.
- The largest muscle is the gluteus maximus, in the buttock.

TYPES OF MUSCLE

The three types of muscle are skeletal, cardiac, and smooth.

Skeletal muscles enable the body to move.

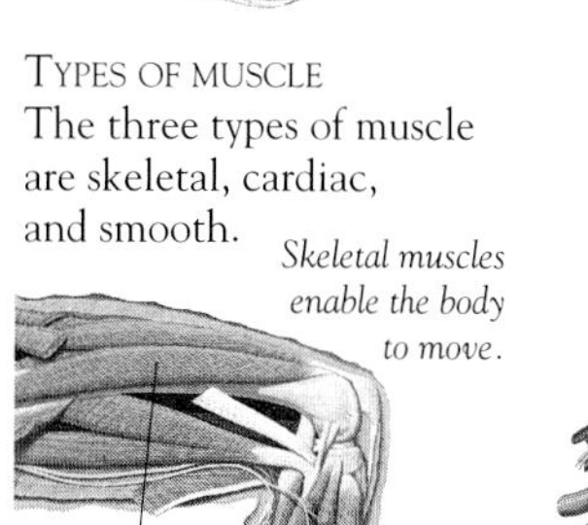
Skeletal muscle attached to bone

SKELETAL MUSCLES

Cardiac muscles are found only in the heart and cause it to contract rhythmically.

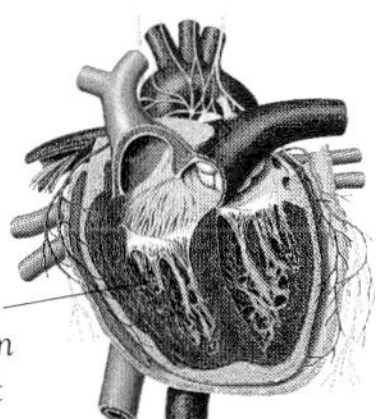
Cardiac muscle in the heart

CARDIAC MUSCLES

Smooth muscles perform automatic tasks such as propelling food through the stomach and gut.

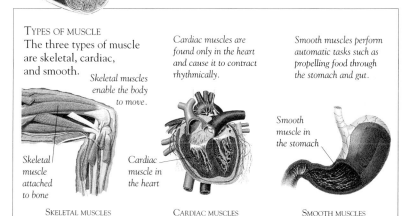

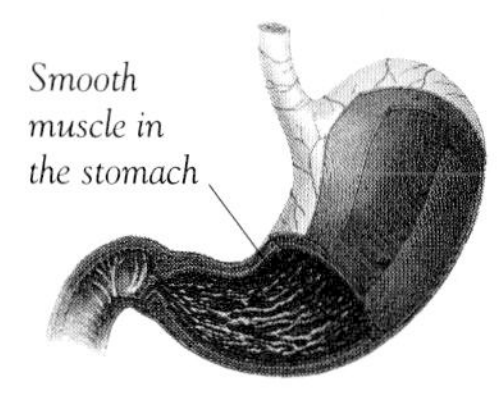
Smooth muscle in the stomach

SMOOTH MUSCLES

SKIN, NAILS, AND HAIR

THE SKIN is the body's waterproof coat, protecting it from the outside world and preventing it from drying out. It is also a sense organ, sensitive to touch, pressure, warmth, and pain. The skin produces nails, which shield the tips of fingers and toes, and hair to provide extra warmth and protection.

SKIN STRUCTURE

The skin has two main layers. The thin, tough, outer epidermis consists mostly of dead cells that are constantly shed and replaced by new skin cells. The thick, living inner dermis layer contains nerves, blood vessels, sense receptors, glands, and hair follicles.

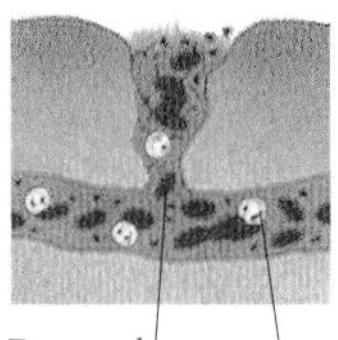
Damaged blood vessel
White blood cells attack germs

BLOOD CLOTTING

When the skin is cut, clotting stops bleeding. Small, sticky platelets form a plug, and fibrin threads bind red blood cells together into clot. White blood cells destroy invading germs.

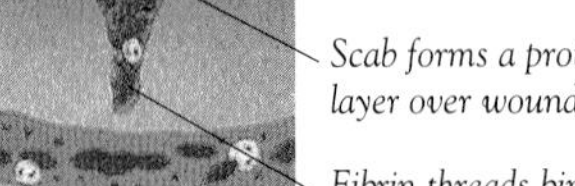
Scab forms a protective layer over wound
Fibrin threads bind cells together to stop bloodflow

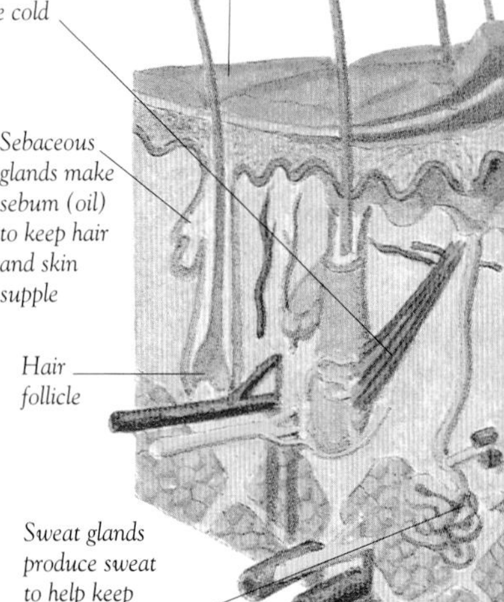
Each hair is a filament of dead cells
Outer layers of epidermis consist of dead cells filled with a tough, waterproof protein called keratin
Movement of hair gives sensation of touch
Hair erector muscle makes hair stand on end in the cold
Sebaceous glands make sebum (oil) to keep hair and skin supple
Hair follicle

Sweat glands produce sweat to help keep the skin cool

NAIL STRUCTURE

The dead tissue made from a tough protein called keratin forms our nails. Keratin is made by living cells at the base and side of each nail, which are protected by folds of skin called cuticles.

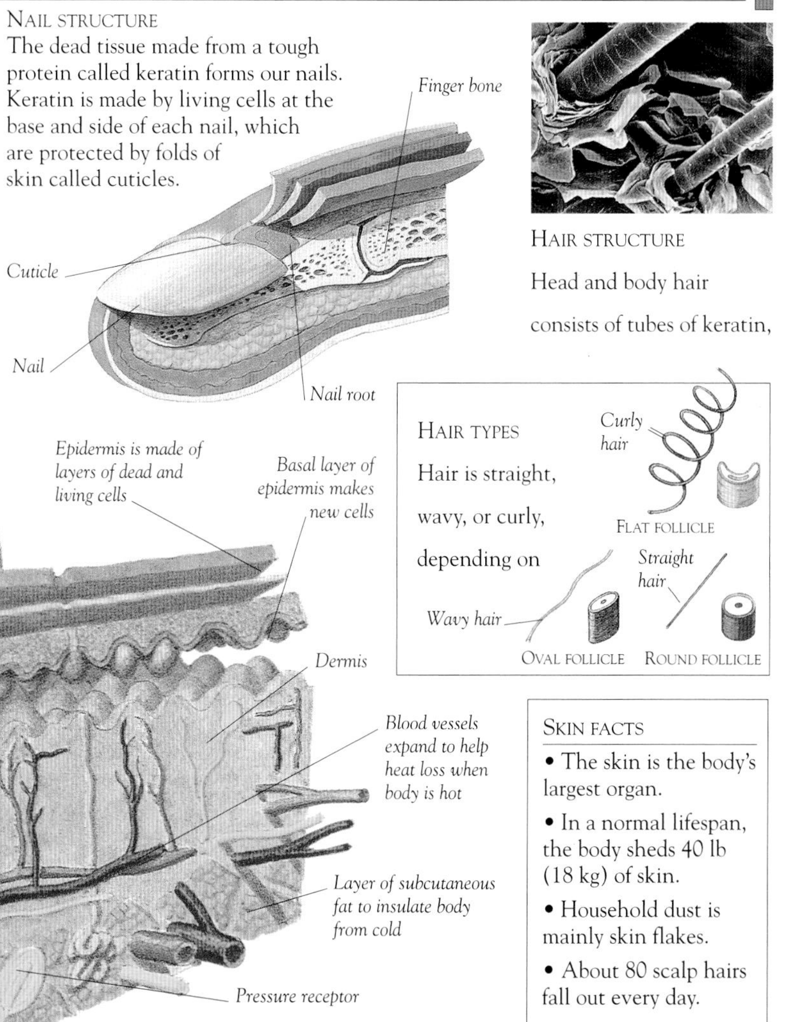
Finger bone
Cuticle
Nail
Nail root
Epidermis is made of layers of dead and living cells
Basal layer of epidermis makes new cells
Dermis
Blood vessels expand to help heat loss when body is hot
Layer of subcutaneous fat to insulate body from cold
Pressure receptor
Curly hair
FLAT FOLLICLE
Straight hair
Wavy hair
OVAL FOLLICLE
ROUND FOLLICLE

HAIR STRUCTURE

Head and body hair consists of tubes of keratin,

HAIR TYPES

Hair is straight, wavy, or curly, depending on

SKIN FACTS

- The skin is the body's largest organ.
- In a normal lifespan, the body sheds 40 lb (18 kg) of skin.
- Household dust is mainly skin flakes.
- About 80 scalp hairs fall out every day.

Brain and nerves

THE NERVOUS SYSTEM consists of billions of linked nerve cells. It controls most body actions and enables us to think and sense our surroundings.

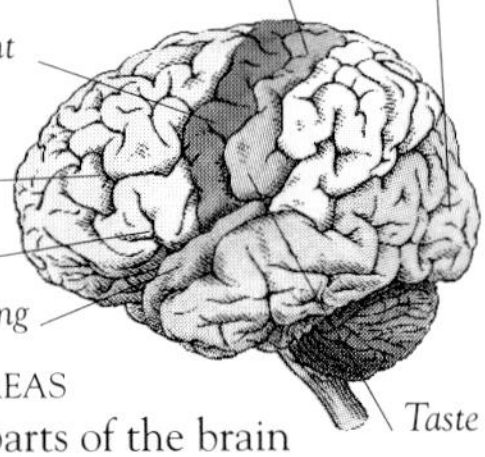

Touch
Vision
Movement
Behavior and emotion
Speech
Hearing
Taste

BRAIN AREAS
Certain parts of the brain have particular functions. "Sensory" areas receive information from sense organs; "motor" areas control voluntary muscles.

BRAIN STRUCTURE
The human brain is a complex network of nerve cells linked to the rest of the body via the cranial nerves and spinal cord. The brain has two halves, or hemispheres. Each controls the opposite side of the body.

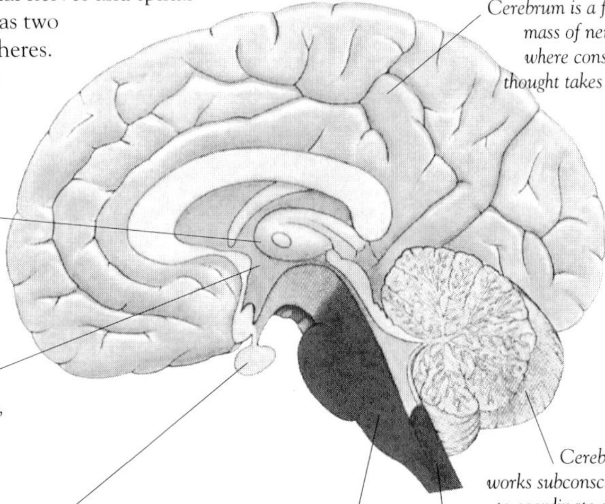

Cerebrum is a folded mass of neurons where conscious thought takes place

Thalamus relays nerve signals to and from cerebrum

Hypothalamus controls hunger, thirst, body temperature, sleeping, and waking

Pituitary gland sends out hormones (chemical messengers) that stimulate other glands to release hormones

Brain stem controls basic bodily functions such as breathing and heart rate

Spinal cord

Cerebellum works subconsciously to coordinate all our body movements

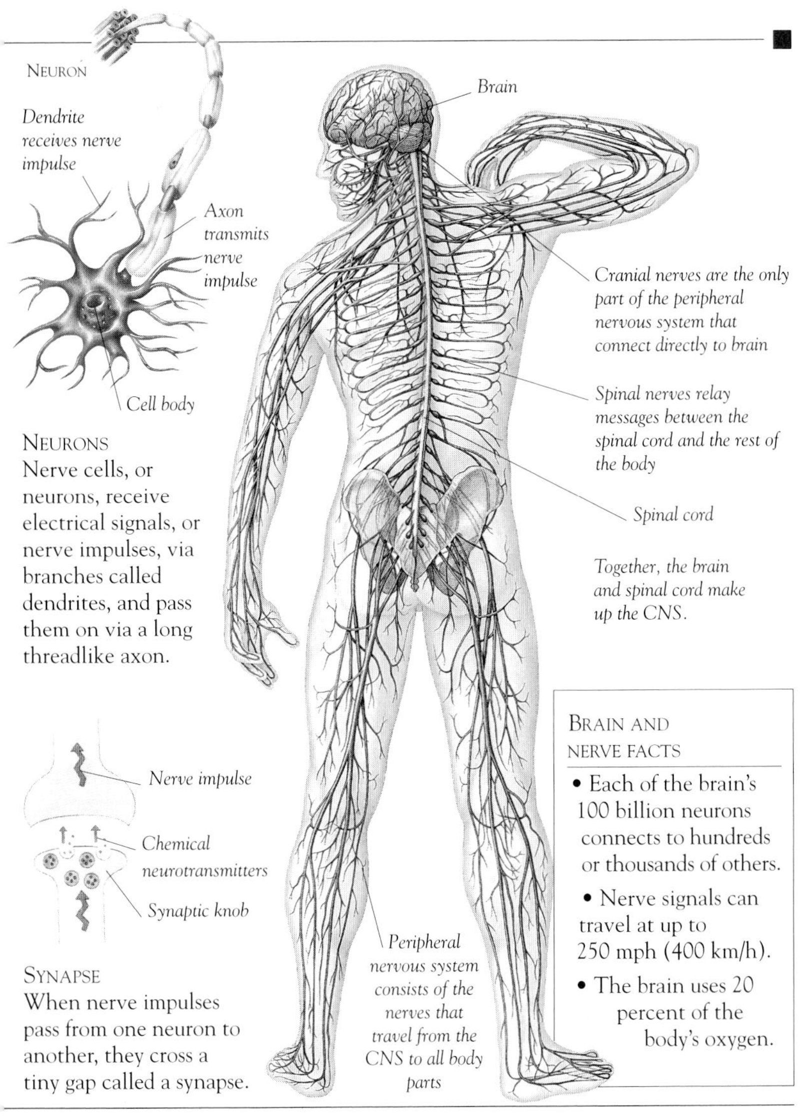
NEURON
Dendrite receives nerve impulse
Axon transmits nerve impulse
Cell body
Brain
Cranial nerves are the only part of the peripheral nervous system that connect directly to brain
Spinal nerves relay messages between the spinal cord and the rest of the body
Spinal cord
Together, the brain and spinal cord make up the CNS.
Nerve impulse
Chemical neurotransmitters
Synaptic knob
Peripheral nervous system consists of the nerves that travel from the CNS to all body parts

NEURONS

Nerve cells, or neurons, receive electrical signals, or nerve impulses, via branches called dendrites, and pass them on via a long threadlike axon.

SYNAPSE

When nerve impulses pass from one neuron to another, they cross a tiny gap called a synapse.

BRAIN AND NERVE FACTS

- Each of the brain's 100 billion neurons connects to hundreds or thousands of others.
- Nerve signals can travel at up to 250 mph (400 km/h).
- The brain uses 20 percent of the body's oxygen.

SIGHT

AT THE FRONT of each eye is a lens system that focuses an image onto the lining of the eye, called the retina. Millions of light-sensitive cells in the retina, called rods and cones, respond to the image and send signals to the brain.

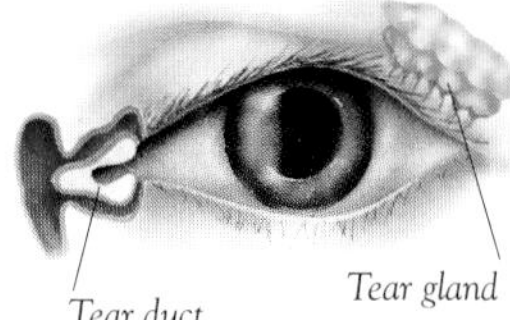
Tear duct
Tear gland

TEARS
The tear glands above each eye continually produce tears. Tears keep the eyes moist and clean. Excess tears are drained down into the nose via the tear ducts.

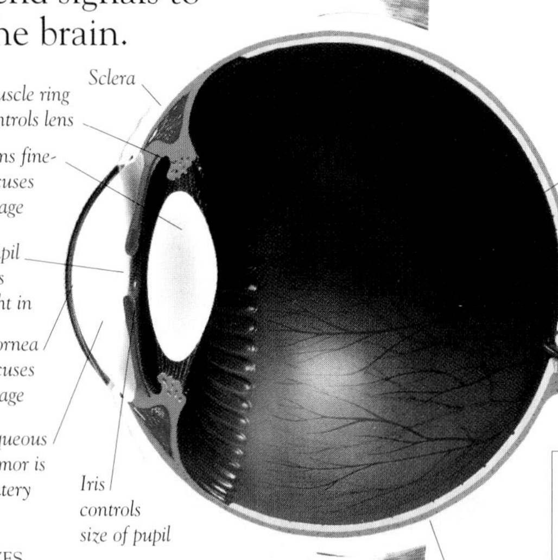
Sclera
Muscle ring controls lens
Lens fine-focuses image
Pupil lets light in
Cornea focuses image
Aqueous humor is watery
Iris controls size of pupil
Retina contains light-sensitive rods and cones
Vitreous humor is jellylike
Optic nerve leads to brain
Choroid consists of blood vessels

EYES
The eyeball is divided into two chambers on either side of the lens. One chamber is filled with aqueous humor, the other with vitreous humor. The casing consists of three layers: the sclera (the white of the eye), the choroid, and the retina.

EYE FACTS

- Rods respond to light but not color.
- Cones respond to color but not without light.
- Most people blink about 15 times a minute.

HEARING

SOUND CONSISTS of tiny vibrations in the air. We hear sound because the ear amplifies the vibrations, channeling them toward sensitive hairs in the inner ear. These hairs are stimulated by the vibrations and send signals to the brain.

EAR FACTS

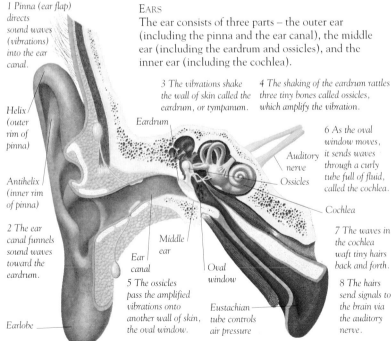

- The ear canal is about 1 in (2.5 cm) in length.
- Humans can detect 1,500 different tones.
- The sensation of ears "popping" is caused by air pressure equalized in the middle ear.

EARS

The ear consists of three parts – the outer ear (including the pinna and the ear canal), the middle ear (including the eardrum and ossicles), and the inner ear (including the cochlea).

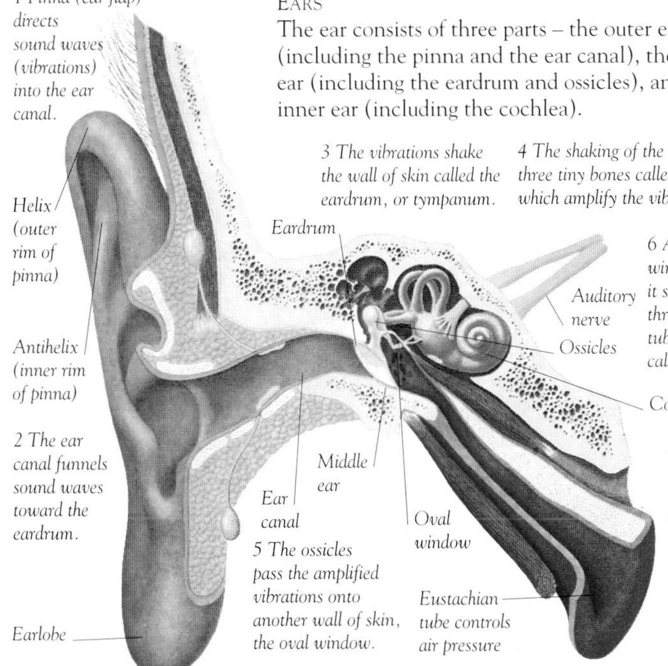
1 Pinna (ear flap) directs sound waves (vibrations) into the ear canal.
Helix (outer rim of pinna)
Antihelix (inner rim of pinna)
2 The ear canal funnels sound waves toward the eardrum.
Earlobe
3 The vibrations shake the wall of skin called the eardrum, or tympanum.
4 The shaking of the eardrum rattles three tiny bones called ossicles, which amplify the vibration.
Eardrum
Auditory nerve
Ossicles
6 As the oval window moves, it sends waves through a curly tube full of fluid, called the cochlea.
Cochlea
Middle ear
Ear canal
Oval window
5 The ossicles pass the amplified vibrations onto another wall of skin, the oval window.
Eustachian tube controls air pressure
7 The waves in the cochlea waft tiny hairs back and forth.
8 The hairs send signals to the brain via the auditory nerve.

TASTE

THE SENSES OF taste and smell are closely related, and work together to help us identify flavors. The microscopic chemical receptor cells on the tongue, called taste buds, are the main organs of taste.

TONGUE
This muscular structure is used in talking, eating, and tasting. It is covered with taste buds which can detect sweet, sour, bitter, and salty tastes.

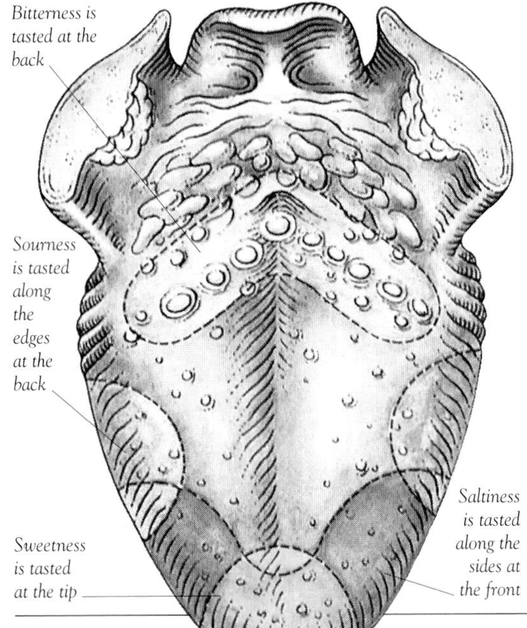
Bitterness is tasted at the back
Sourness is tasted along the edges at the back
Sweetness is tasted at the tip
Saltiness is tasted along the sides at the front

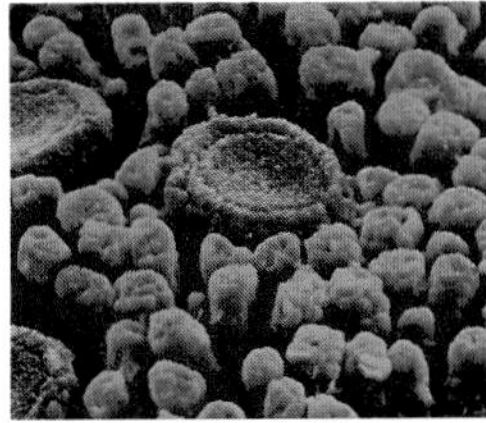

TONGUE SURFACE MAGNIFIED

Pore
Tongue tissue
Nerve fibers
Taste bud receptors

TASTE BUDS
There are about 10,000 taste buds on the tongue's surface. Each taste bud contains 10–20 receptors. Chemicals dissolved in saliva reach these taste receptors through pores.

TASTE FACTS

- Babies have taste buds all over the inside of their mouths.
- Taste bud cells last only a week before they are renewed.

SMELL

THE SENSE of smell detects chemicals in the air. These chemicals dissolve in the nasal mucus inside the nose and stimulate hairlike endings on the olfactory bulb. The fine hairs are so sensitive that they can detect even faint traces of chemicals.

Fine, hairlike cilia on each olfactory receptor are sensitive to the chemicals in mucus

There are 25 million receptors in the olfactory area

15,000 fibers in the olfactory nerve carry messages to the brain

NOSE
The septum divides the nose into two nostrils, each lined with hairs and membranes that secrete sticky mucus. Smell relies on the olfactory area at the top of the nose.

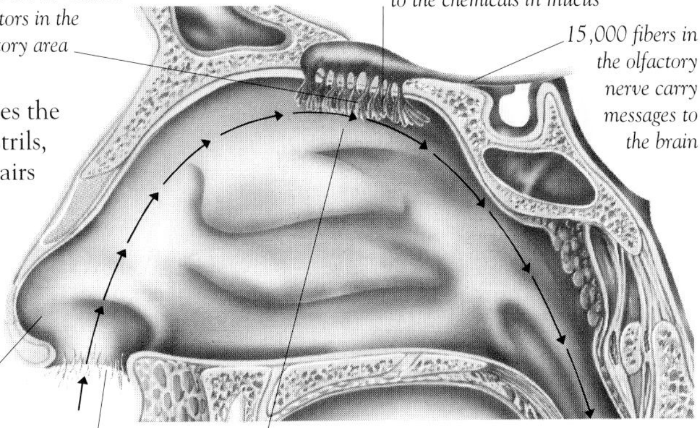

Nose warms and moistens air before it reaches the lungs

Nasal hairs filter out large particles as they are breathed in

Chemicals from the air dissolve in mucus

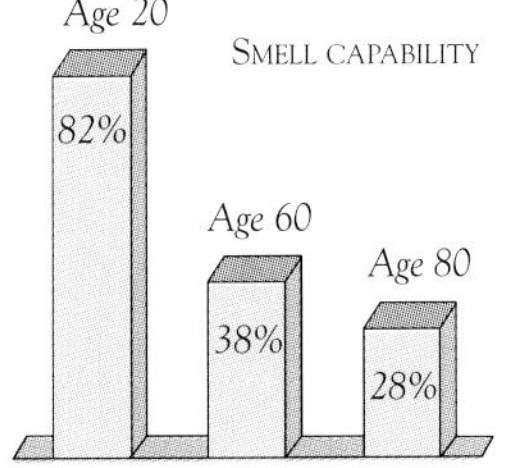
SMELL CAPABILITY
Age 20
82%
Age 60
38%
Age 80
28%

LOSS OF SENSITIVITY
Babies are very sensitive to smells, which may help them to identify their mother. But as we grow older, our sensitivity to smell diminishes, as this chart shows.

SMELL FACTS

- Humans can identify about 10,000 different smells.
- Smell is processed by the part of the brain that also deals with taste, memory, and emotions.

LUNGS AND BREATHING

LUNGS

OXYGEN IS NEEDED by body cells to release the energy that keeps them working and alive. To maintain a constant supply of oxygen, we breathe the air continuously into the lungs, from where oxygen enters the bloodstream.

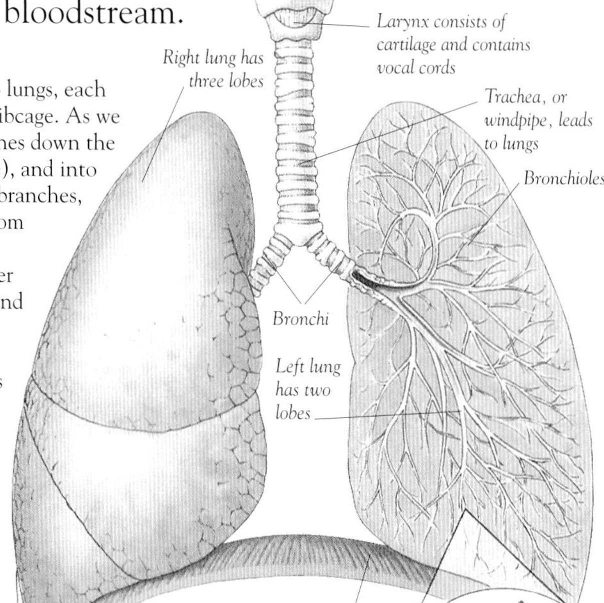

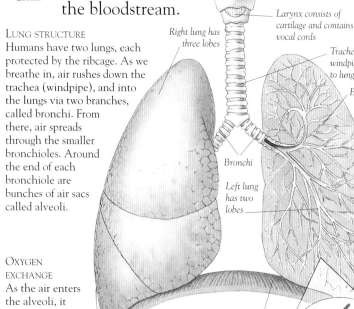

Larynx consists of cartilage and contains vocal cords
Right lung has three lobes
Trachea, or windpipe, leads to lungs
Bronchioles
Bronchi
Left lung has two lobes
The base of each lung rests on the muscular diaphragm
Network of tiny capillary blood vessels
Each lung has 150 million microscopic alveoli, or air sacs

LUNG STRUCTURE
Humans have two lungs, each protected by the ribcage. As we breathe in, air rushes down the trachea (windpipe), and into the lungs via two branches, called bronchi. From there, air spreads through the smaller bronchioles. Around the end of each bronchiole are bunches of air sacs called alveoli.

OXYGEN EXCHANGE
As the air enters the alveoli, it seeps through the thin walls into the blood-stream. At the same time, carbon dioxide seeps from the blood back into the lungs, to be breathed out.

Breathing

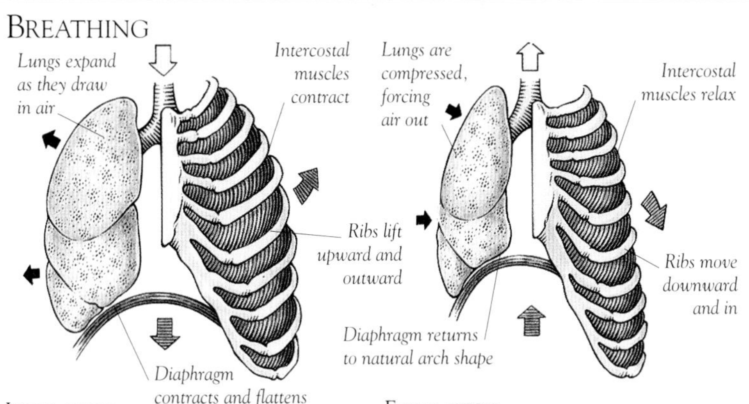
Lungs expand as they draw in air
Intercostal muscles contract
Ribs lift upward and outward
Diaphragm contracts and flattens
Lungs are compressed, forcing air out
Intercostal muscles relax
Ribs move downward and in
Diaphragm returns to natural arch shape

Inhalation

When we breathe in, the diaphragm contracts and the ribcage expands. Pressure in the chest cavity drops and draws air into the lungs.

Exhalation

When we breathe out, the diaphragm and the ribcage relax. Pressure in the chest cavity rises and pushes air out of the lungs.

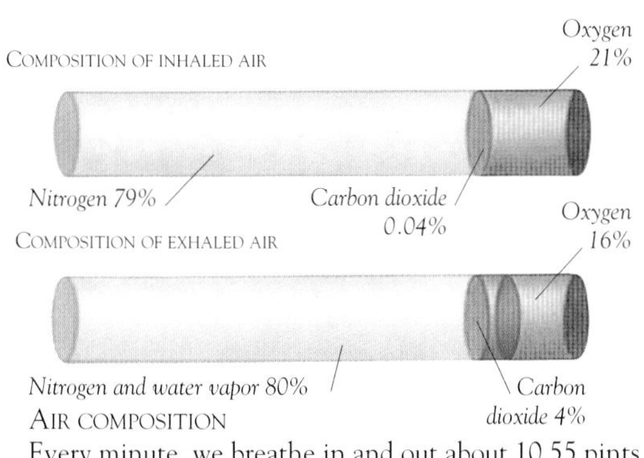
Composition of inhaled air
Oxygen 21%
Nitrogen 79%
Carbon dioxide 0.04%
Composition of exhaled air
Oxygen 16%
Nitrogen and water vapor 80%
Carbon dioxide 4%

Air composition

Every minute, we breathe in and out about 10.55 pints (6 litres) of air containing oxygen, nitrogen, and carbon dioxide. The air that we exhale contains about 100 times more carbon dioxide than the air we inhale.

Breathing facts

- The average human takes 600 million breaths in a 70-year lifetime.
- If the lungs were opened out and laid flat, they would cover a tennis court.
- The lungs contain 1,490 miles (2,400 km) of airways.
- Humans can survive with only one fully working lung.

HEART AND BLOOD

THE BODY'S transportation network, the heart, blood, and blood vessels, is called the cardiovascular system. Blood carries oxygen to cells and also transports food, hormones, waste, and warmth.

HEARTBEAT CYCLE

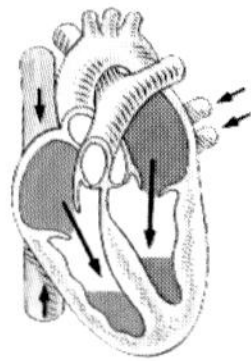

1 During diastole (resting), both atria fill with blood and some flows into the ventricles below.

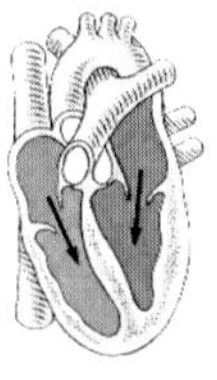

2 During atrial systole (pumping), the atria contract, forcing blood into the ventricles.

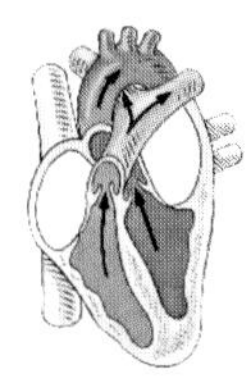

3 During ventricular systole, the ventricles contract, forcing blood out into the arteries.

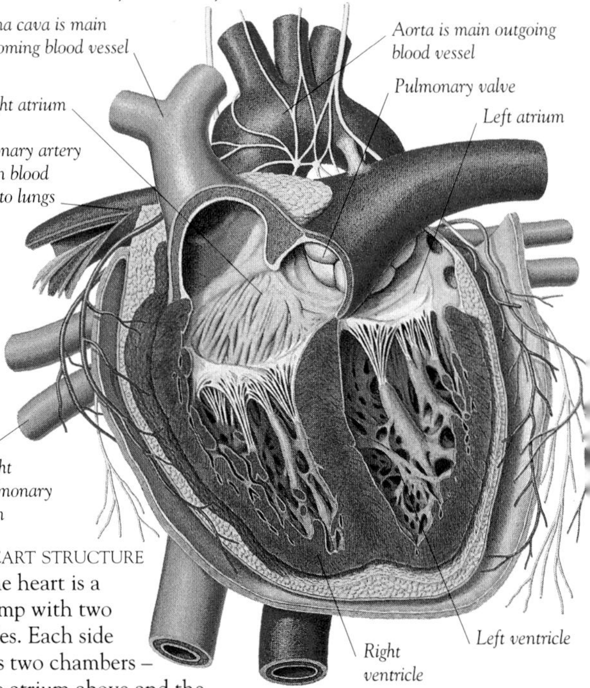

Vena cava is main incoming blood vessel

Aorta is main outgoing blood vessel

Pulmonary valve

Right atrium

Left atrium

Pulmonary artery is main blood vessel to lungs

Right pulmonary vein

Right ventricle

Left ventricle

HEART STRUCTURE

The heart is a pump with two sides. Each side has two chambers – the atrium above and the ventricle below. These contract and relax every 0.8 seconds to pump blood around the body.

Valves stop blood from flowing backward.

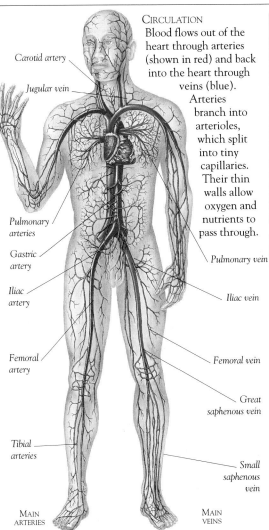

Carotid artery

Jugular vein

Pulmonary arteries

Gastric artery

Iliac artery

Femoral artery

Tibial arteries

MAIN ARTERIES

Pulmonary vein

Iliac vein

Femoral vein

Great saphenous vein

Small saphenous vein

MAIN VEINS

CIRCULATION

Blood flows out of the heart through arteries (shown in red) and back into the heart through veins (blue). Arteries branch into arterioles, which split into tiny capillaries. Their thin walls allow oxygen and nutrients to pass through.

HEART FACTS

- A human heart beats more than 30 million times a year.
- The heart rate increases with exercise to provide muscles with extra oxygen.
- With every heart beat, the heart pumps out about 2.8 fl oz (80 ml) of blood.

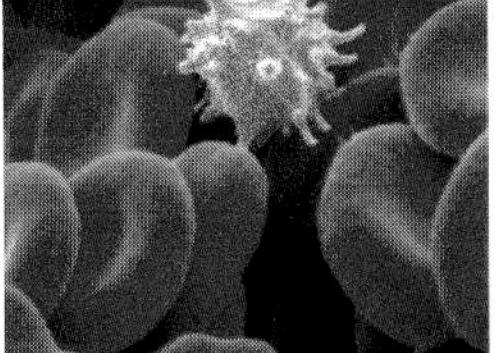

BLOOD

The liquid part of blood, called plasma, contains a rich mixture of blood cells, proteins, antibodies, hormones, and minerals. Red blood cells are button-shaped, and carry oxygen around the body. White cells, or leukocytes, fight infection. The tiny platelets help to plug leaks by forming blood clots.

Digestion

Food is broken down by a process called digestion as it passes along the alimentary canal, or gut. Digestion uses chemicals called enzymes to break down complex food molecules into simpler ones that can be absorbed into the blood and used by the body's cells for growth, repair, and to supply energy.

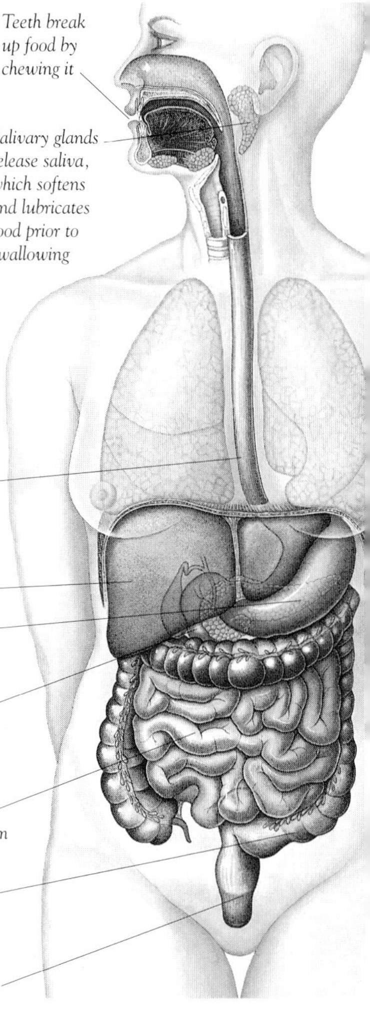
Teeth break up food by chewing it
Salivary glands release saliva, which softens and lubricates food prior to swallowing
Waves of muscular action push food down esophagus into stomach
Liver
Stomach breaks down food into semi-fluid chyme
Digestive enzymes in duodenum break down chyme
Ileum absorbs digested nutrients into bloodstream
Indigestible food passes on into colon where water is absorbed
Muscular rectum expels waste through anus

Alimentary canal

The digestive system runs from the mouth to the anus and is about 30 ft (9 m) long. Food passes from the mouth, down the oesophagus into the stomach. From here, it passes into the small intestines, made up of the duodenum, jejunum, and ileum, and into the large intestines, made up of the colon and rectum. Several organs and glands are connected to the tract to help digestion.

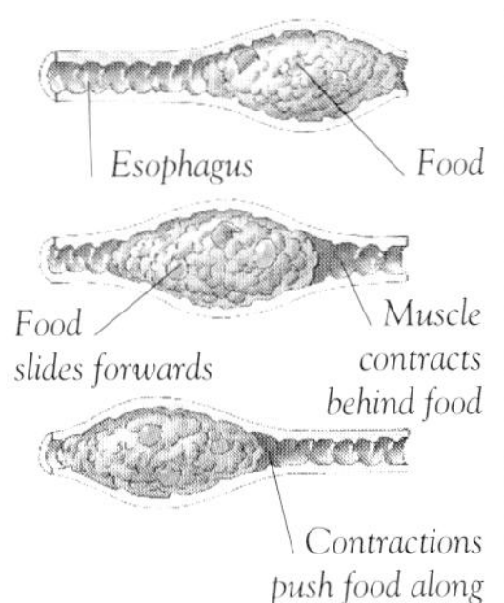
Esophagus
Food
Food slides forwards
Muscle contracts behind food
Contractions push food along

PERISTALSIS
The walls of the digestive tract contain smooth muscle fibers that produce wavelike contractions to propel food along. This process is called peristalsis.

STOMACH ACTION
The stomach is a bag-like chamber that stores food. As the stomach fills with food, its walls stretch. Powerful muscles churn up the food, and enzymes in gastric (stomach) juice part-digest it. The food passes from the stomach into the duodenum.

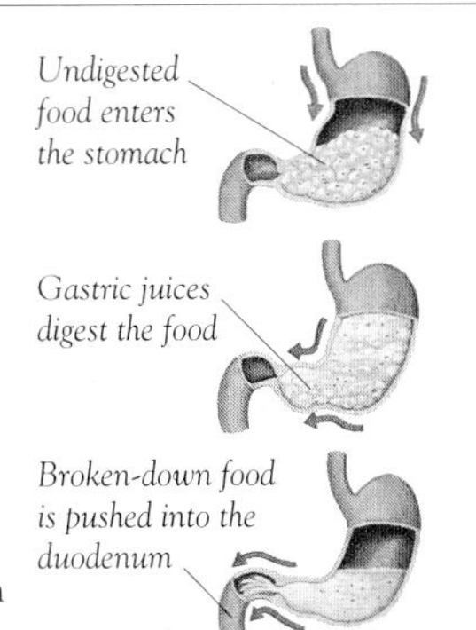
Undigested food enters the stomach
Gastric juices digest the food
Broken-down food is pushed into the duodenum

VILLI
The lining of the small intestine has millions of microscopic fingerlike villi that absorb nutrients.

Each villus measures 0.04 in (1 mm).

Capillaries

Smooth muscle layers

LIVER
The liver has many functions. It stores vitamins and minerals, makes blood proteins, and produces bile, which aids fat-digestion in the duodenum.

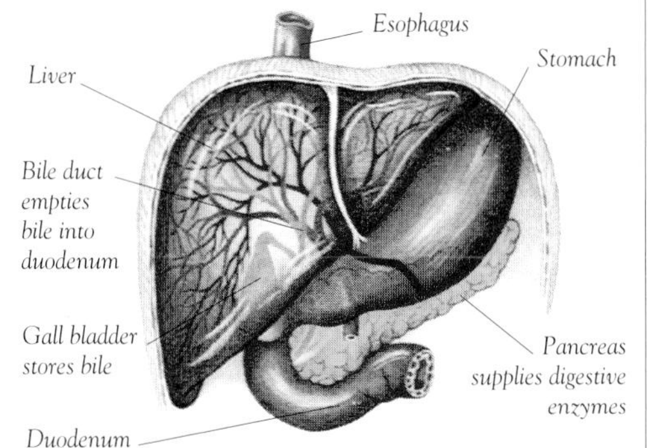
Esophagus
Stomach
Liver
Bile duct empties bile into duodenum
Gall bladder stores bile
Pancreas supplies digestive enzymes
Duodenum

DIGESTION FACTS

- Food stays in the stomach for up to five hours, and spends up to 20 hours in the colon.
- The wall of the stomach is protected by a lining of mucus so it cannot digest itself.
- The digestive process begins as soon as you take a bite of food.

URINARY SYSTEM

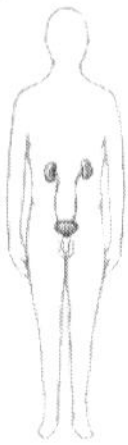

THE URINARY SYSTEM

AS BLOOD FLOWS through the kidneys, they filter out waste and drain off excess water. This is expelled from the body as urine, via the ureters, bladder, and urethra. In this way the urinary system clears the blood of waste and regulates its water content.

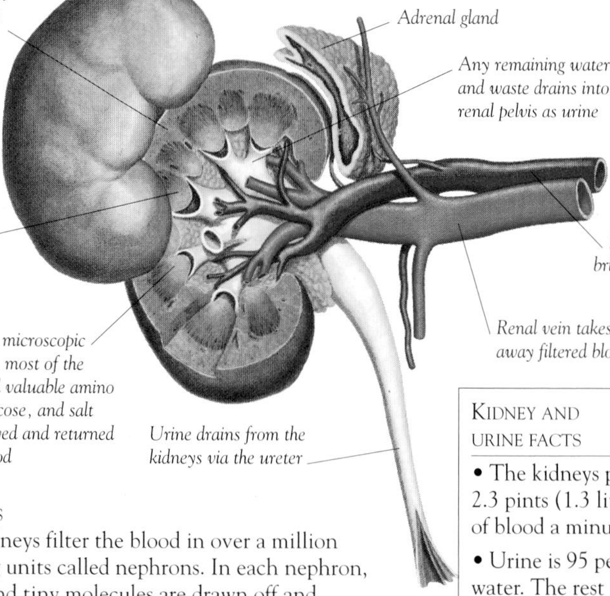

Cortex (outer part of kidney)

Adrenal gland

Any remaining water and waste drains into the renal pelvis as urine

Medulla (inner part of kidney)

Renal artery brings in blood for filtering

Renal vein takes away filtered blood

Inside the microscopic nephrons, most of the water and valuable amino acids, glucose, and salt are retrieved and returned to the blood

Urine drains from the kidneys via the ureter

KIDNEYS

The kidneys filter the blood in over a million filtering units called nephrons. In each nephron, water and tiny molecules are drawn off and channeled through little tubes called tubules. Inside these, valuable molecules and most of the water are retrieved and returned to the blood, leaving only a little water and waste to drain off as urine.

KIDNEY AND URINE FACTS

- The kidneys process 2.3 pints (1.3 liters) of blood a minute.
- Urine is 95 percent water. The rest is dissolved salts and the toxic waste urea, which is produced in the liver.

HORMONES

ENDOCRINE glands secrete chemical messengers called hormones into the blood. These stimulate, regulate, and coordinate a whole range of body processes.

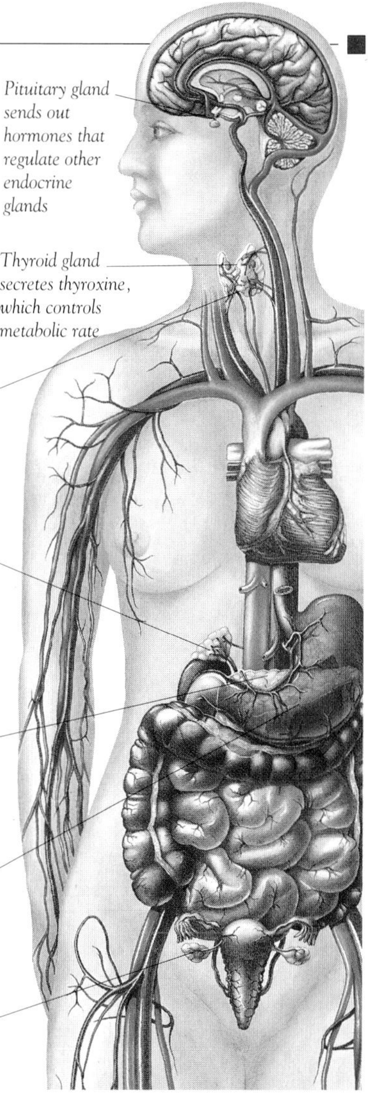

TESTOSTERONE

In men, the testes produce the hormone testosterone to control the development of sexual characteristics.

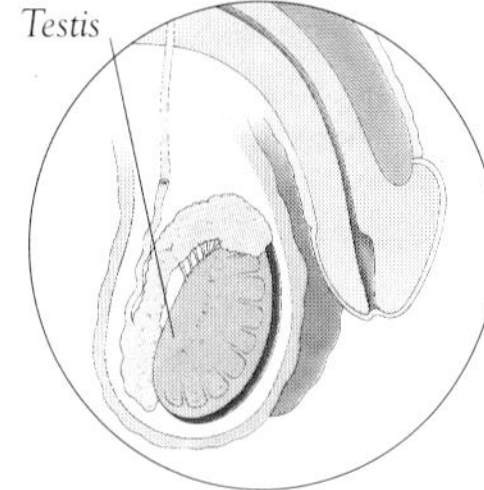
Testis

HORMONE FACTS

- Too much growth hormone can cause gigantism (excess growth); too little can cause slow growth.
- The hormone adrenalin can give short bursts of superhuman strength.

Pituitary gland sends out hormones that regulate other endocrine glands

Thyroid gland secretes thyroxine, which controls metabolic rate

Parathyroid glands secrete hormone that raises blood calcium levels

Adrenal glands secrete cortisone, which boosts metabolism, and adrenalin, which primes body for action

Pancreas secretes glucagon and insulin, which regulate blood sugar levels

Stomach and intestines secrete hormones that aid digestion

Ovaries in women make female sex hormones, estrogen and progesterone

REPRODUCTION

FROM PUBERTY ONWARD, the reproductive system in males and females is sufficiently developed for them to have sexual intercourse and potentially create new human beings. A new life begins when a man's sperm fertilizes, or joins with, a woman's ovum (egg).

THE MALE REPRODUCTIVE SYSTEM

MALE REPRODUCTIVE SYSTEM
Male sex cells, or sperm, are made inside each testis in tubes called seminiferous tubules. The sperm mature in a long, coiled tube called the epididymidis. When the penis is stimulated, muscles pump sperm from the epididymis along the vas deferens, where they mix with seminal fluid to make semen.

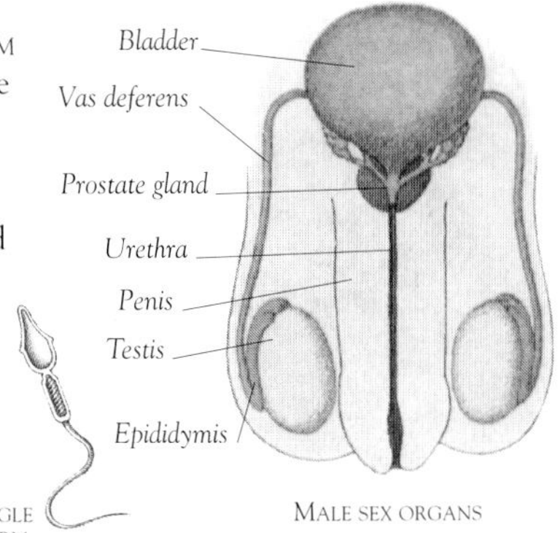
Bladder
Vas deferens
Prostate gland
Urethra
Penis
Testis
Epididymis

SINGLE SPERM

MALE SEX ORGANS

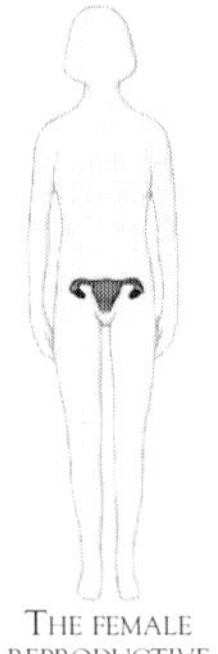

THE FEMALE REPRODUCTIVE SYSTEM

FEMALE REPRODUCTIVE SYSTEM
Female sex cells, or ova, are stored in the ovaries. Every 28 days or so, one ovum, or egg, is released during ovulation. The egg passes down one of two fallopian tubes to the uterus, or womb. If the ovum is fertilized, it is embedded in the womb lining. If not, both the ovum and lining are shed during menstruation.

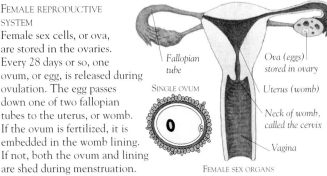

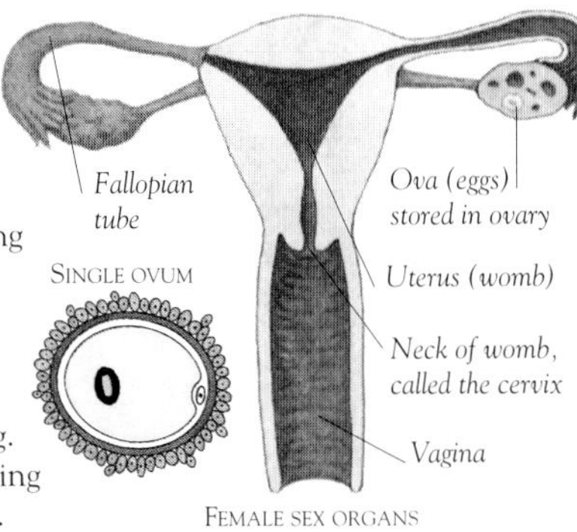
Fallopian tube
Ova (eggs) stored in ovary
Uterus (womb)
Neck of womb, called the cervix
Vagina

SINGLE OVUM

FEMALE SEX ORGANS

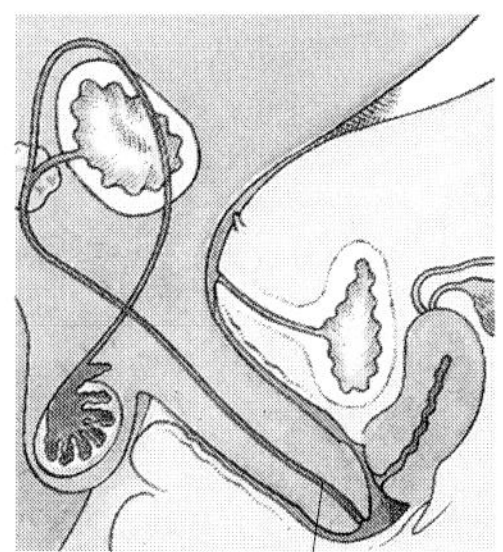
Penis inside vagina

SEXUAL INTERCOURSE
During sexual intercourse, the man's penis fills with blood, becoming hard and erect. It fits into the woman's vagina, where semen is released (ejaculated). If one of the 300 million sperm reaches the ovum, it may fertilize it.

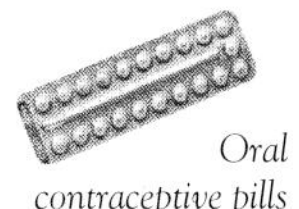
Oral contraceptive pills

Diaphragm

Condom

CONTRACEPTIVES
Condoms and other contraceptives are used to stop conception during intercourse. They prevent sperm fertilizing the egg.

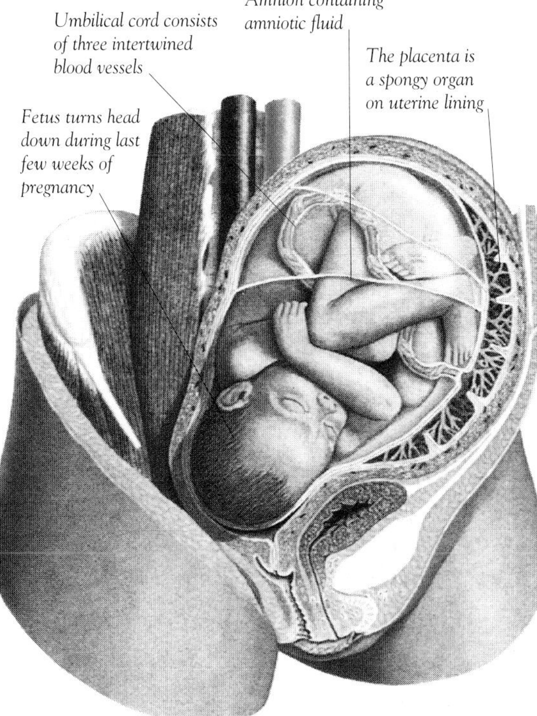
Amnion containing amniotic fluid

Umbilical cord consists of three intertwined blood vessels

The placenta is a spongy organ on uterine lining

Fetus turns head down during last few weeks of pregnancy

Pregnancy

Once the egg is fertilized, it becomes an embryo, which grows rapidly in the womb (uterus). After eight weeks, it is called a fetus, with recognizable features and all its internal organs. Fed through the umbilical cord with food and oxygen from the placenta, the fetus continues development. After 40 weeks, it is ready to be born.

GENES AND HEREDITY

STORED IN a cell's nucleus are packages called chromosomes, made up of long spirals of the molecule DNA. Each DNA molecule consists of genes, which are responsible for characteristics such as eye color.

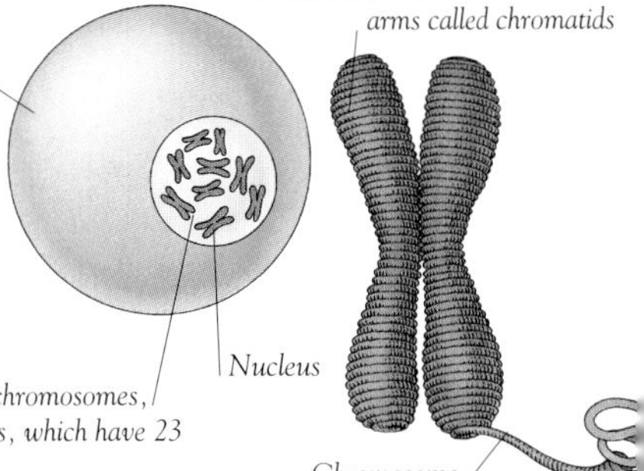

A chromosome has two identical arms called chromatids
Cell
Nucleus
Each cell has 46 chromosomes, except for sex cells, which have 23
Chromosome unwinds

GENES

Each chromosome contains hundreds or thousands of genes. Each gene provides instructions to make a single protein, used to build a new cell or to control a cell's activities. Genes are passed on to the next generation during sexual reproduction.

MITOSIS

As the body grows, or when worn-out cells need replacing, the cells divide into two by a process called mitosis. The normal number of chromosomes in each cell is 46. When the cells divide, each new cell has the same number of chromosomes – 46.

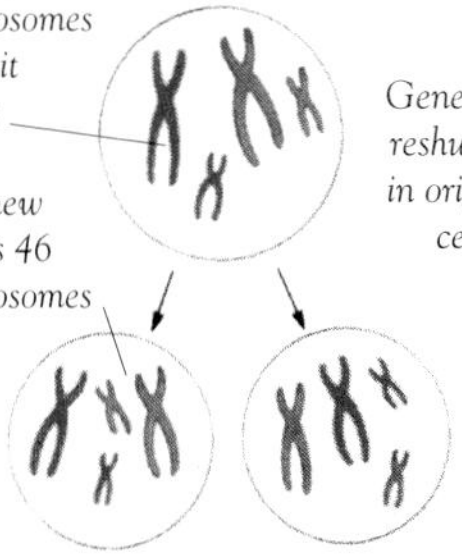

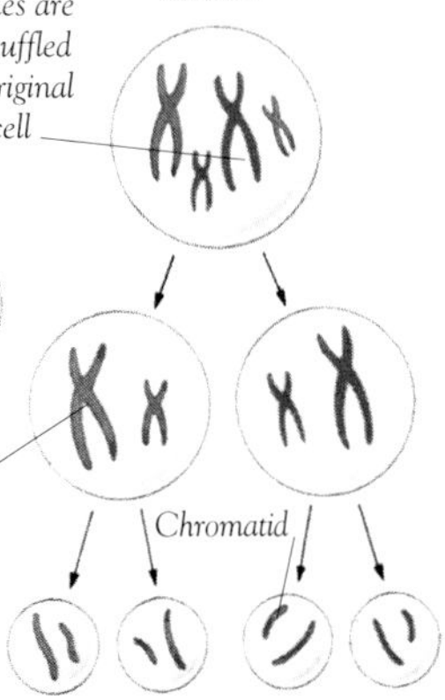

MITOSIS
Cell copies chromosomes before it divides
Each new cell has 46 chromosomes
MEIOSIS
Genes are reshuffled in original cell
Each pair of chromosomes splits in half and the two new cells receive half each
Chromatid

MEIOSIS

Sex cells are produced during the cell division called meiosis. The original cell's genes are mixed and recombined so that the new cells produced are genetically unique.

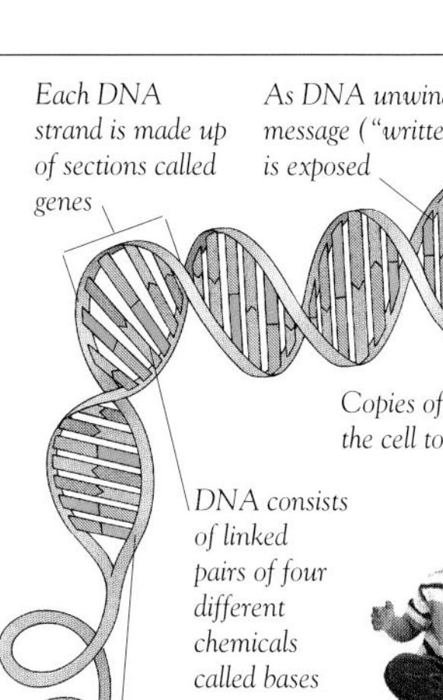
Each DNA strand is made up of sections called genes
DNA consists of linked pairs of four different chemicals called bases
Each DNA molecule is made up of two spiral strands

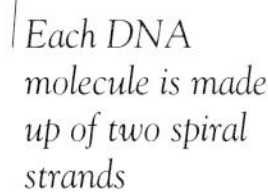

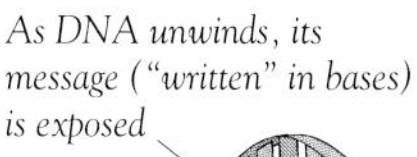
As DNA unwinds, its message ("written" in bases) is exposed

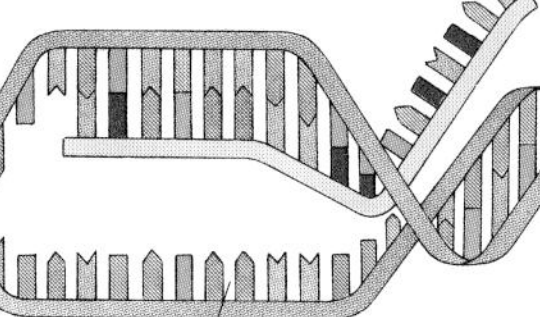
Copies of the gene are made and tell the cell to make a particular protein

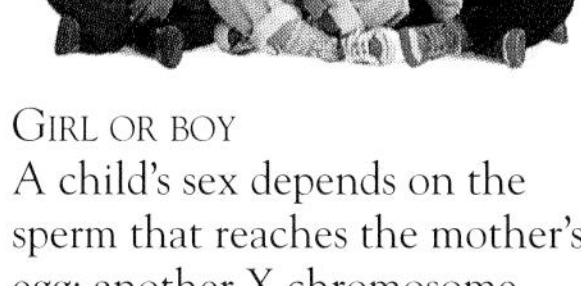

Girl or Boy

A child's sex depends on the sperm that reaches the mother's egg; another X chromosome means a girl; a Y means a boy.

Genetic Facts

- DNA stands for deoxyribonucleic acid.
- Red blood cells have no nucleus and do not contain genes.
- Women have two X chromosomes. Men have one X chromosome paired with a Y chromosome.

Heredity

The passing on of characteristics via the genes is called heredity. A baby inherits half its genes from its mother and half from its father. The reshuffling of genes means that brothers and sisters inherit different genes, but there may be a resemblance.

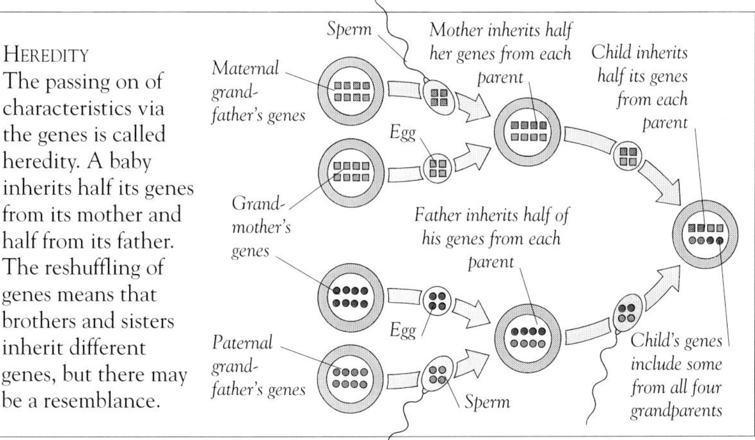
Sperm
Mother inherits half her genes from each parent
Child inherits half its genes from each parent
Maternal grand-father's genes
Egg
Grand-mother's genes
Father inherits half of his genes from each parent
Egg
Paternal grand-father's genes
Sperm
Child's genes include some from all four grandparents

FIGHTING INFECTION

IF BACTERIA or viruses enter the body and multiply, you can become ill. To fight infection, the body has a defense mechanism called the immune system.

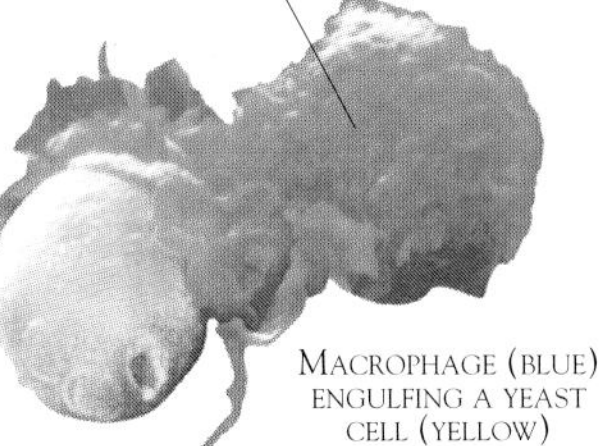
A single macrophage can ingest 100 bacteria

MACROPHAGE (BLUE) ENGULFING A YEAST CELL (YELLOW)

DEFENSE CELLS
Two types of white blood cell defend the body. Phagocytes, such as this macrophage, engulf germs, while lymphocytes release antibodies to destroy them.

IMMUNE FACTS

- A fever is caused when white blood cells release proteins called pyrogens, raising the body's temperature.
- Swollen lymph nodes are a sign of infection.

Tonsils contain lymphocytes that fight inhaled or ingested germs

Lymph enters bloodstream here

Spleen stores lymphocytes

Lymph nodes contain macrophages that ingest bacteria and other germs

Bone marrow produces lymphocytes and macrophages

Lymph vessels carry lymph from the tissues

LYMPHATIC SYSTEM
This system of tubes drains fluid called lymph from the body's tissues back into the blood. As the lymph passes through swellings called lymph nodes, lymphocytes and macrophages destroy any germs that it is carrying.

THE LYMPHATIC SYSTEM

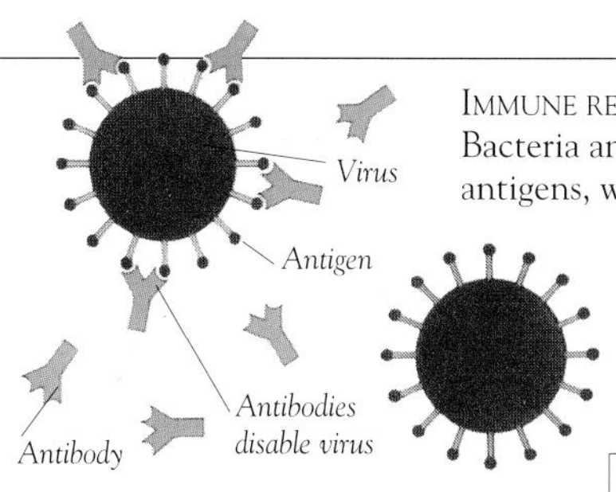
Virus
Antigen
Antibodies
disable virus
Antibody

IMMUNE RESPONSE
Bacteria and viruses carry molecules called antigens, which trigger the immune system into action. When the immune system detects an antigen, it produces antibodies to fight it. Lymphocytes called B-cells make these antibodies, and each one targets a specific antigen.

Medicine

The body's immune system is remarkably effective at dealing with infection, but sometimes it breaks down or takes a long time to work. Modern drugs and traditional forms of medicine such as herbalism can help the body to combat illness.

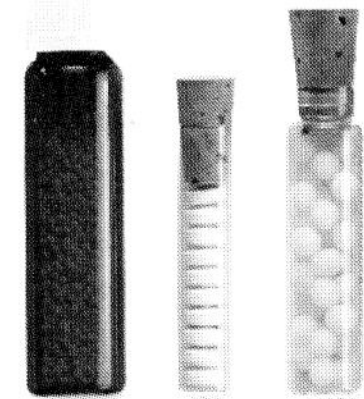

DRUGS
The drugs we use to treat illness and disease are made from plant extracts or from chemicals produced in a laboratory. They are commonly taken in the form of tablets, capsules, or liquid.

IMMUNIZATION
Active or passive immunization by injection provides the body with protection from certain diseases.

ACTIVE IMMUNIZATION

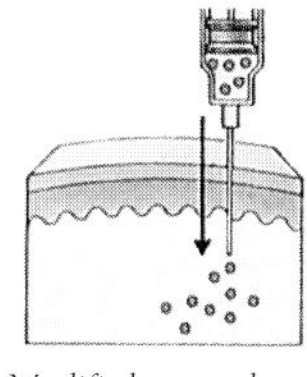

Modified germs that cannot cause disease are injected into the body.

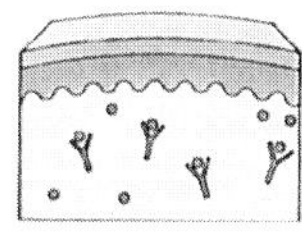

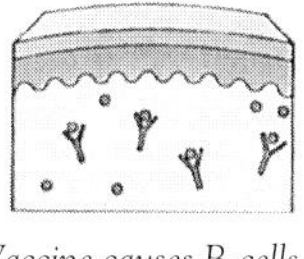

Vaccine causes B-cells to produce antibodies.

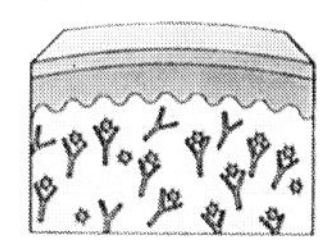

Immune system reacts rapidly to infection.

PASSIVE IMMUNIZATION

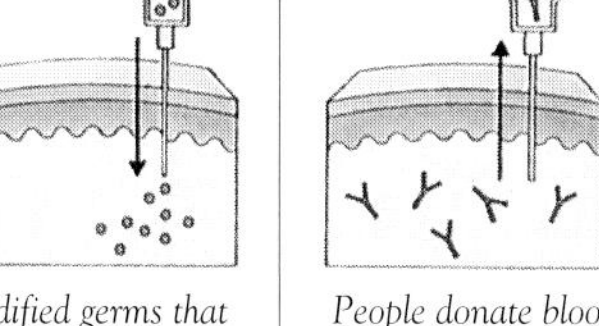

People donate blood that contains antibodies.

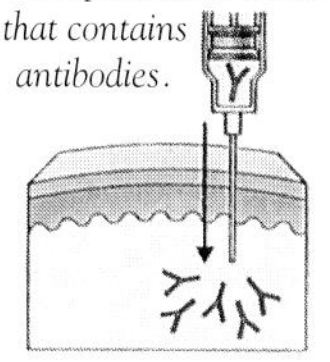

Antibodies to a disease are injected into patient.

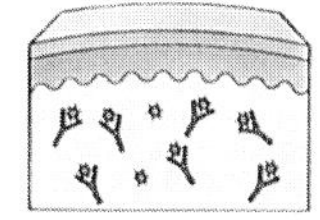

If disease attacks, the antibodies will fight it.

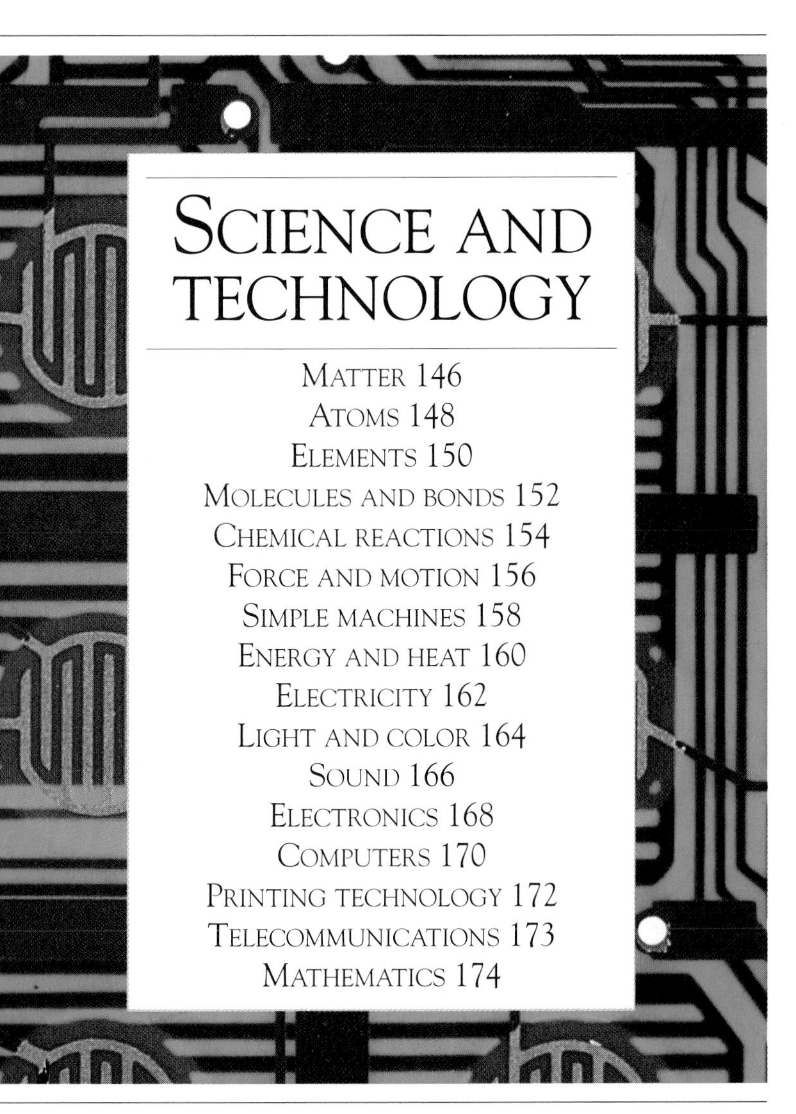

SCIENCE AND TECHNOLOGY

MATTER

FROM THE TINIEST speck of dust to giant stars, every object in the universe is made of matter. Matter consists of tiny particles, such as atoms, arranged in different ways. On Earth, matter usually occurs in one of three forms, or "states", called solid, liquid, or gas.

Electrode

Plasma streaks

PLASMA
A fourth state of matter called plasma forms when matter is so hot that electrons break away from atoms. Matter in a star is in the plasma state.

GAS
A gas has no fixed volume or shape. Gas particles are widely spaced, with the ability to move freely in all directions. A gas will expand to fill any container it is put in.

Gas dispersing from a chemical reaction

LIQUID
A liquid has a definite volume but no fixed shape. Liquid particles are more loosely bound than solid particles and can move over small distances. A liquid will flow and take the shape of its container.

Every liquid takes the shape of its container

Coins have a rigid shape

SOLID
A solid has a fixed shape and volume. Solid particles are tightly packed in regular patterns. Strong bonds allow the particles to vibrate, but prevent them moving far.

CHANGING STATE

The particles of a substance move more rapidly when heated. Eventually, they break the bonds that hold them together. Heat changes solids to liquids, and liquids to gases. When cooled, gases condense to liquids, and liquids freeze to solids as the bonds re-form.

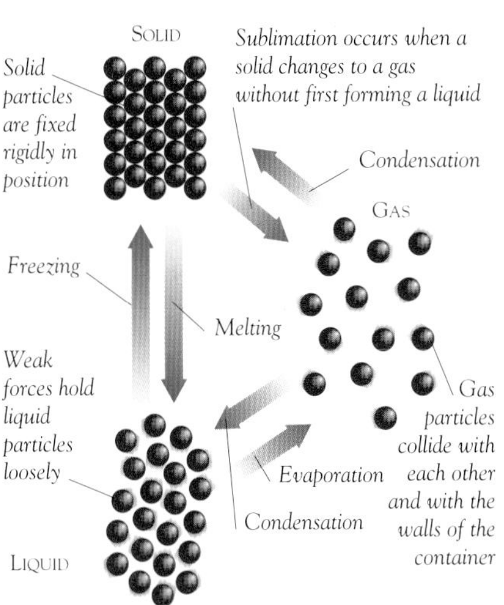
SOLID
Solid particles are fixed rigidly in position
Sublimation occurs when a solid changes to a gas without first forming a liquid
Condensation
GAS
Freezing
Melting
Weak forces hold liquid particles loosely
Gas particles collide with each other and with the walls of the container
Evaporation
Condensation
LIQUID

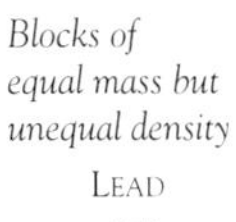
Blocks of equal mass but unequal density
LEAD
HIGH DENSITY

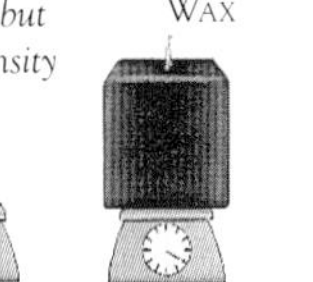
WAX
MEDIUM DENSITY

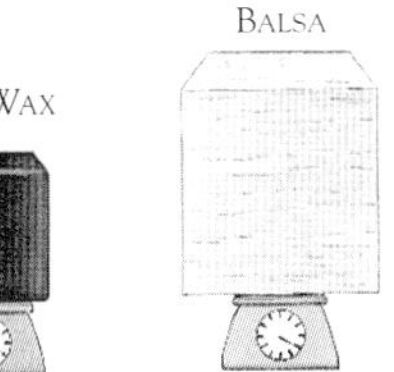
BALSA
LOW DENSITY

MASS, VOLUME, AND DENSITY

The amount of matter in an object is its mass. Volume is the space it occupies. The object's density is its mass divided by its volume.

GAS LAWS

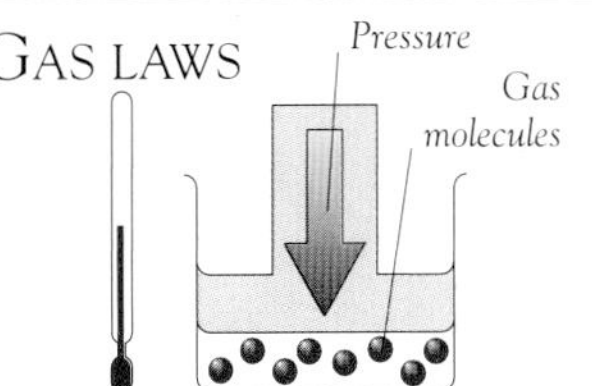
Pressure
Gas molecules

BOYLE'S LAW

At constant temperature (T), the volume of a gas (V) is inversely proportional to the pressure (P) (the gas contracts as the pressure rises): PV=constant.

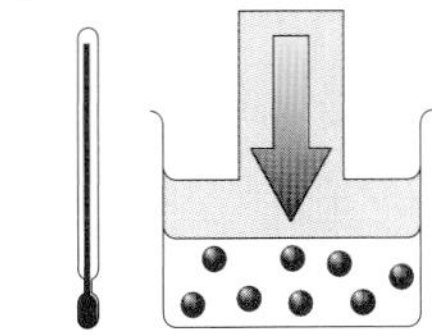

PRESSURE LAW

At constant volume, the pressure of a gas is proportional to the temperature (increasing the temperature raises the gas's pressure): P/T=constant.

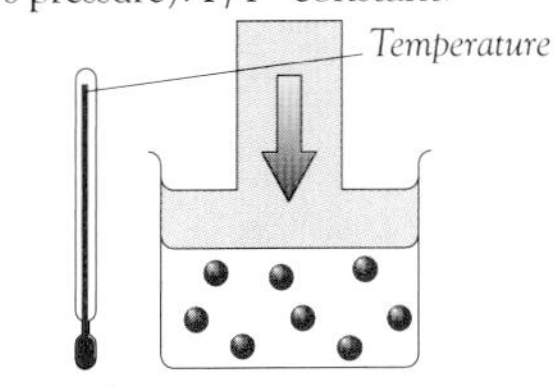
Temperature

CHARLES' LAW

At constant pressure, the gas's volume is proportional to the temperature (the gas expands if temperature rises): V/T=constant.

ATOMS

SOILDS, LIQUIDS, AND GASES are made up of tiny particles called atoms. Atoms are the building blocks for the materials that make up our world. There are just over a hundred types of atoms, which themselves consist of even smaller "subatomic" particles. Atoms and subatomic particles are not solid – they are clouds of energy.

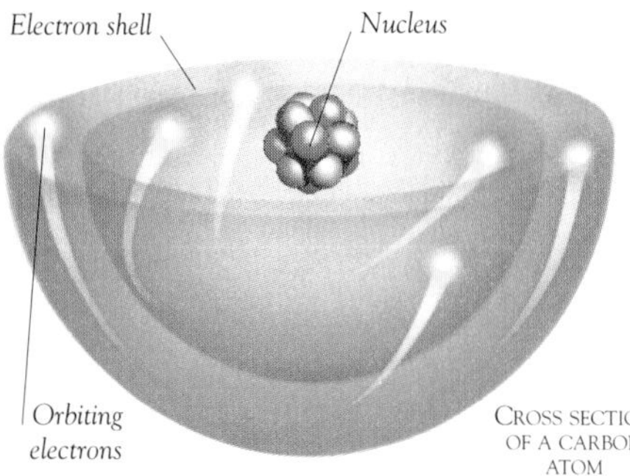
Electron shell
Nucleus
Orbiting electrons

CROSS SECTION OF A CARBON ATOM

INSIDE THE ATOM

The center, or nucleus, of an atom contains a number of protons (with a positive electrical charge) and neutrons (with no charge). The nucleus of a hydrogen atom consists of just a single proton. Negatively charged particles called electrons orbit the nucleus in layers or "shells."

NUCLEON NUMBER

The total number of protons and neutrons contained in the nucleus of an atom is called the nucleon number. The most common form of carbon is referred to as carbon–12, since it contains 6 protons and 6 neutrons.

CARBON–12 ATOM

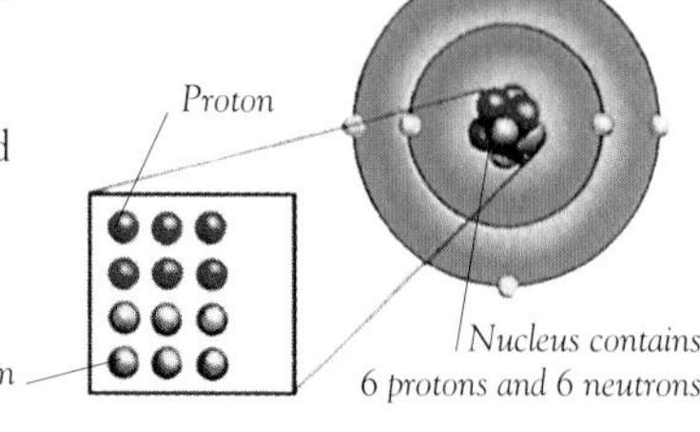
Proton
Neutron
Nucleus contains 6 protons and 6 neutrons

CARBON–14 ATOM

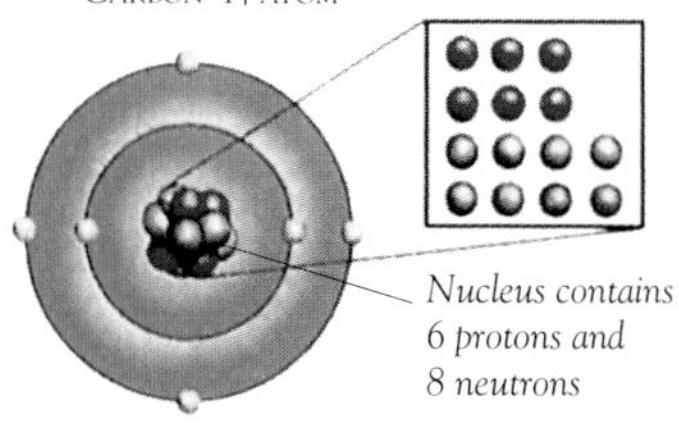
Nucleus contains 6 protons and 8 neutrons

ISOTOPES

All atoms of a particular element have the same number of protons, but some forms of the element may have different numbers of neutrons. These variations are called isotopes. The isotope carbon–14, for example, has two more neutrons than the isotope carbon–12.

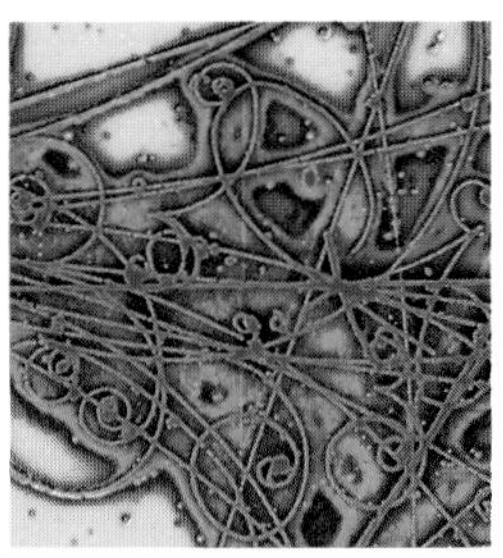
PATHS OF PARTICLES CREATED AFTER SUBATOMIC COLLISION

PARTICLE COLLISIONS
Scientists have discovered many new particles by smashing together subatomic particles at high speed. Most new particles exist for only a fraction of a second after the collision, but their movements can be recorded by computers.

ATOM FACTS

- An electron is 1,836 times lighter than a proton, and 1,839 times lighter than a neutron.
- Scientists know of more than 200 different subatomic particles.
- Specks of dust contain a trillion atoms.

QUARKS
Particles such as neutrons and protons are called hadrons. A hadron is made up of three smaller particles called quarks, held together by tiny particles called gluons. There are six types of quark, but only two types – "up" quarks and "down" quarks – make up protons and neutrons. An up quark has two-thirds of a unit of positive charge, while a down quark has one-third of a negative charge.

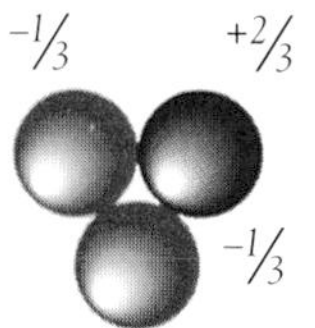
$-1/3$
$+2/3$
$-1/3$
QUARKS IN A NEUTRON
A neutron has 1 up quark and 2 down quarks, giving an overall neutral charge

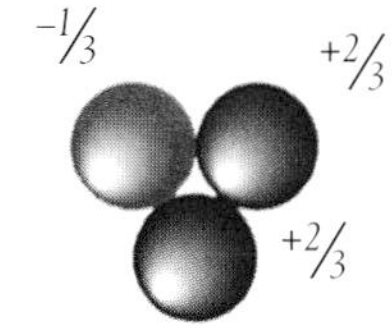
$-1/3$
$+2/3$
$+2/3$
QUARKS IN A PROTON
A proton has 2 up quarks and 1 down quark, giving an overall positive charge

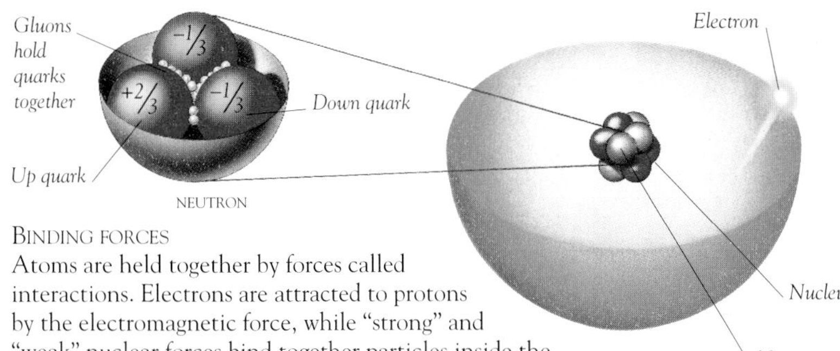
Gluons hold quarks together
$-1/3$
$+2/3$
$-1/3$
Down quark
Up quark
Electron
Nucleus
Neutron
NEUTRON

BINDING FORCES
Atoms are held together by forces called interactions. Electrons are attracted to protons by the electromagnetic force, while "strong" and "weak" nuclear forces bind together particles inside the nucleus. These forces, together with the force of gravity, make up the four fundamental forces that hold the entire universe together.

PERIODIC TABLE

CERTAIN ELEMENTS share similar chemical properties and atomic structures. These similarities become clear when all the known elements are set out in a chart called the periodic table. This chart arranges elements into "groups" (columns) and "periods" (rows).

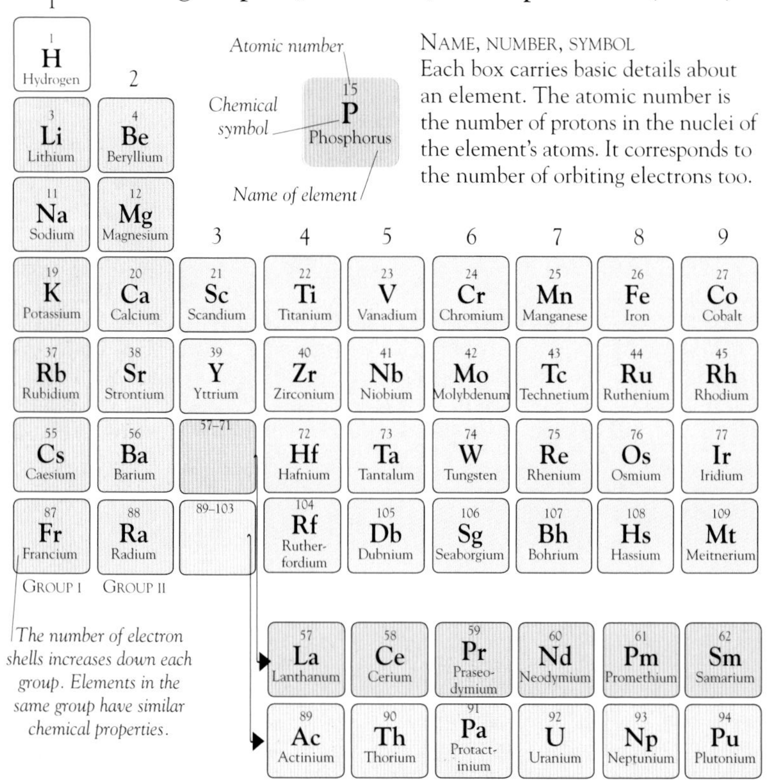

1
2
3
4
5
6
7
8
9
Atomic number
Chemical symbol
Name of element
15 P Phosphorus
1 H Hydrogen
3 Li Lithium
4 Be Beryllium
11 Na Sodium
12 Mg Magnesium
19 K Potassium
20 Ca Calcium
21 Sc Scandium
22 Ti Titanium
23 V Vanadium
24 Cr Chromium
25 Mn Manganese
26 Fe Iron
27 Co Cobalt
37 Rb Rubidium
38 Sr Strontium
39 Y Yttrium
40 Zr Zirconium
41 Nb Niobium
42 Mo Molybdenum
43 Tc Technetium
44 Ru Ruthenium
45 Rh Rhodium
55 Cs Caesium
56 Ba Barium
57–71
72 Hf Hafnium
73 Ta Tantalum
74 W Tungsten
75 Re Rhenium
76 Os Osmium
77 Ir Iridium
87 Fr Francium
88 Ra Radium
89–103
104 Rf Ruther-fordium
105 Db Dubnium
106 Sg Seaborgium
107 Bh Bohrium
108 Hs Hassium
109 Mt Meitnerium
GROUP I
GROUP II
57 La Lanthanum
58 Ce Cerium
59 Pr Praseo-dymium
60 Nd Neodymium
61 Pm Promethium
62 Sm Samarium
89 Ac Actinium
90 Th Thorium
91 Pa Protact-inium
92 U Uranium
93 Np Neptunium
94 Pu Plutonium

NAME, NUMBER, SYMBOL
Each box carries basic details about an element. The atomic number is the number of protons in the nuclei of the element's atoms. It corresponds to the number of orbiting electrons too.

The number of electron shells increases down each group. Elements in the same group have similar chemical properties.

GROUPS AND PERIODS

Each period starts on the left with a highly reactive alkali metal with an outer shell of one electron. It ends on the right with a stable noble gas in group 18 (0) with eight electrons in its outer shell. Elements in the same group have the same number of electrons in their outer shells.

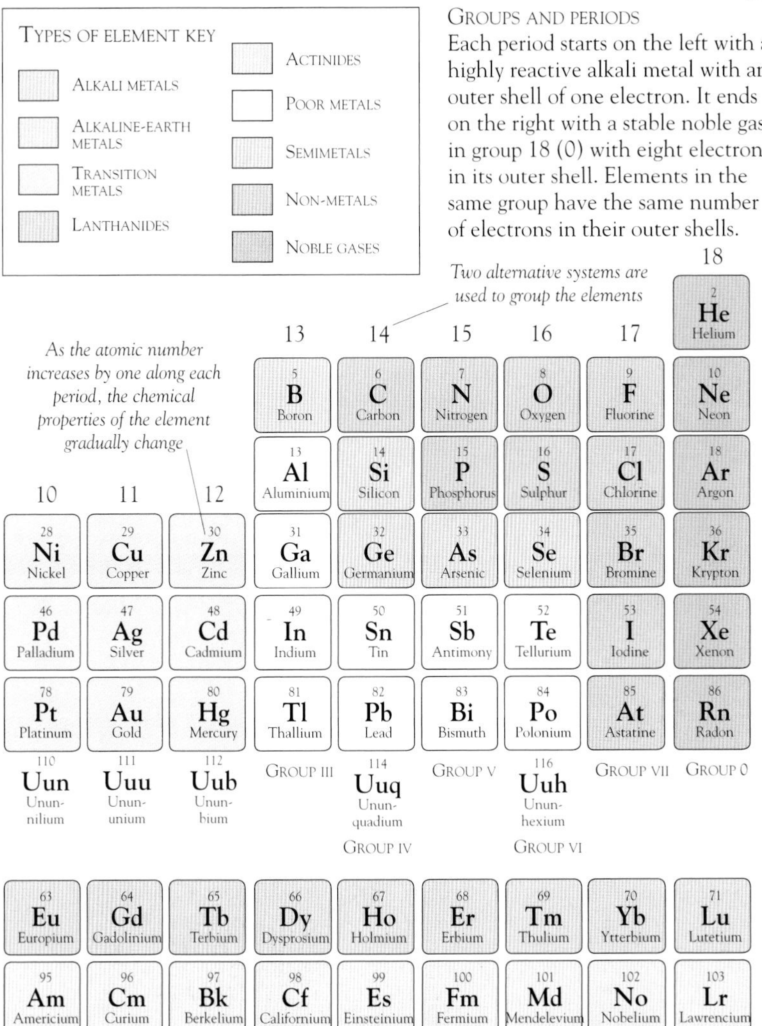

TYPES OF ELEMENT KEY
ALKALI METALS
ALKALINE-EARTH METALS
TRANSITION METALS
LANTHANIDES
ACTINIDES
POOR METALS
SEMIMETALS
NON-METALS
NOBLE GASES
Two alternative systems are used to group the elements
As the atomic number increases by one along each period, the chemical properties of the element gradually change
18
2 He Helium
13
14
15
16
17
5 B Boron
6 C Carbon
7 N Nitrogen
8 O Oxygen
9 F Fluorine
10 Ne Neon
13 Al Aluminium
14 Si Silicon
15 P Phosphorus
16 S Sulphur
17 Cl Chlorine
18 Ar Argon
10
11
12
28 Ni Nickel
29 Cu Copper
30 Zn Zinc
31 Ga Gallium
32 Ge Germanium
33 As Arsenic
34 Se Selenium
35 Br Bromine
36 Kr Krypton
46 Pd Palladium
47 Ag Silver
48 Cd Cadmium
49 In Indium
50 Sn Tin
51 Sb Antimony
52 Te Tellurium
53 I Iodine
54 Xe Xenon
78 Pt Platinum
79 Au Gold
80 Hg Mercury
81 Tl Thallium
82 Pb Lead
83 Bi Bismuth
84 Po Polonium
85 At Astatine
86 Rn Radon
110 Uun Ununnilium
111 Uuu Unununium
112 Uub Ununbium
GROUP III
114 Uuq Ununquadium
GROUP V
116 Uuh Ununhexium
GROUP VII
GROUP 0
GROUP IV
GROUP VI
63 Eu Europium
64 Gd Gadolinium
65 Tb Terbium
66 Dy Dysprosium
67 Ho Holmium
68 Er Erbium
69 Tm Thulium
70 Yb Ytterbium
71 Lu Lutetium
95 Am Americium
96 Cm Curium
97 Bk Berkelium
98 Cf Californium
99 Es Einsteinium
100 Fm Fermium
101 Md Mendelevium
102 No Nobelium
103 Lr Lawrencium

MOLECULES AND BONDS

A GROUP OF ATOMS that are linked together is called a molecule. A molecule may be made up of a few or very many atoms. Molecules are formed when the electrical forces created by electron movement "bond" atoms together. Electron transfer between atoms occurs because some atoms require extra electrons to fill their outer shell.

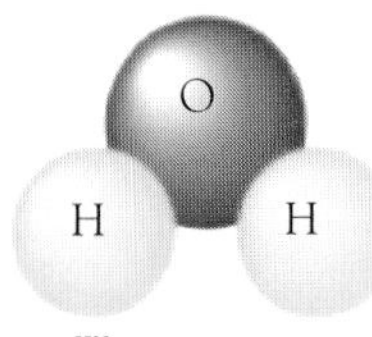
O
H
H

WATER MOLECULE

CHEMICAL FORMULAE

A chemical formula uses letters and numbers to show how elements combine in a compound. The formula for a water molecule is H_2O, as it is made up of two atoms of hydrogen linked to a single atom of oxygen.

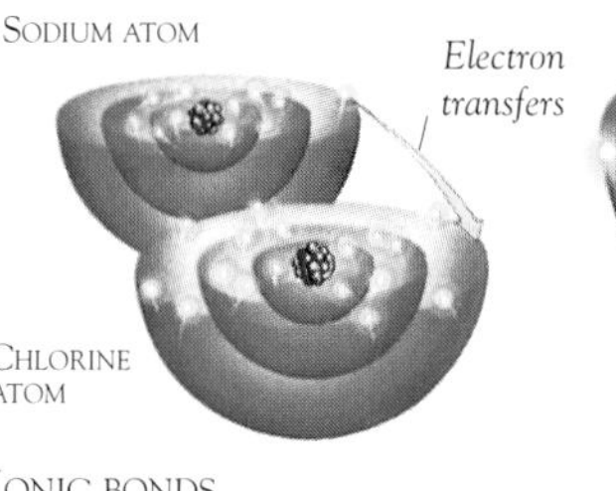
SODIUM ATOM
Electron transfers
CHLORINE ATOM

POSITIVELY CHARGED SODIUM ION

Both ions now have eight electrons in their outer shells

Ionic bond

IONIC BONDS

In ionic bonding, excess electrons transfer from the full outer shell of one atom to the outer shell of another that requires extra electrons to fill it. The transfer leaves both atoms as charged particles called ions. The atom losing the electron becomes a positively charged ion, or cation, and the atom gaining the electron becomes a negative ion, or anion. The force of attraction between the opposite charges binds the ions together.

NEGATIVELY CHARGED CHLORIDE ION

GIANT IONIC STRUCTURE

A crystal of salt (sodium chloride) contains sodium and chloride ions arranged in a regular, connected network that extends throughout the crystal. This network is called a giant ionic lattice.

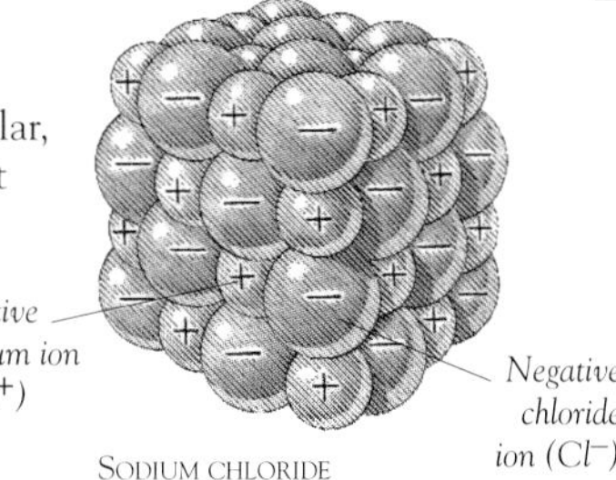
Positive sodium ion (Na^+)
Negative chloride ion (Cl^-)

SODIUM CHLORIDE

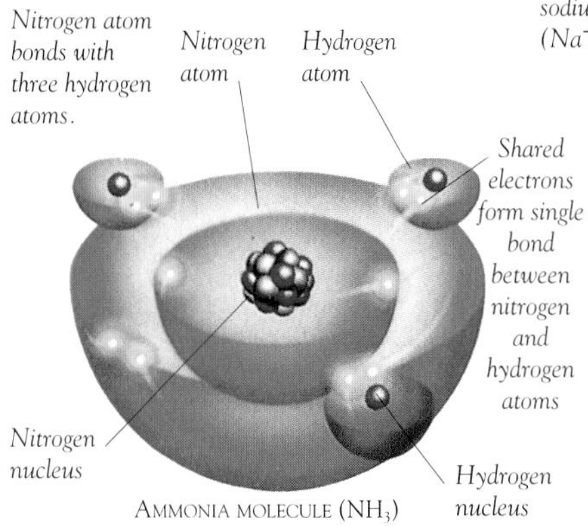
Nitrogen atom bonds with three hydrogen atoms.
Nitrogen atom
Hydrogen atom
Shared electrons form single bond between nitrogen and hydrogen atoms
Nitrogen nucleus
Hydrogen nucleus

AMMONIA MOLECULE (NH_3)

COVALENT BONDS

Ionic bonds are formed between metals and nonmetals. In covalent bonds, nonmetals bind together by sharing electrons. Two atoms each "donate" an electron, and the electrons form a pair that orbits both nuclei, holding the atoms together as a molecule. In a double bond, each atom donates two electrons.

ORGANIC CHEMISTRY

Carbon compounds are extremely common because carbon atoms link up easily with atoms of most other elements, and have the ability to form very stable bonds with other carbon atoms. All living things contain some compounds of carbon.The study of substances containing carbon is known as organic chemistry.

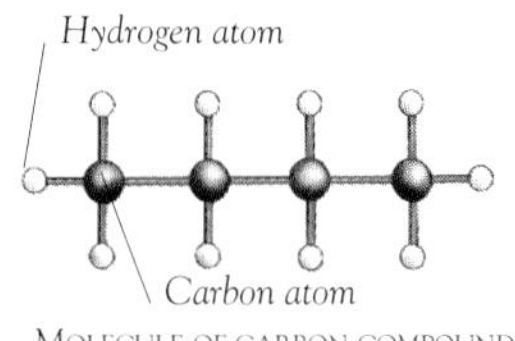
Hydrogen atom
Carbon atom

MOLECULE OF CARBON COMPOUND BUTANE (C_4H_{10})

MATERIALS CONTAINING CARBON COMPOUNDS

Plants
Fuels (butane, gas)
Foods
Textiles
Natural sponge
Plastics
Soaps

CHEMICAL REACTIONS

WHEN A CHEMICAL reaction occurs, new substances (called products) form from the original chemicals taking place in the reaction (called reactants). The atoms of the reactants rearrange themselves to form products.

Electron

ELECTRON TRANSFER
During the oxidation process, atoms lose electrons and are "oxidized." During reduction, atoms gain electrons and are "reduced."

EXOTHERMIC REACTIONS
A reaction that gives out more heat than it takes in, such as burning, is called an exothermic reaction. Burning is an example of an exothermic oxidation reaction. Oxidation occurs when a substance combines with oxygen. The reverse reaction, in which oxygen is lost, is called reduction.

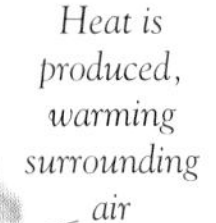

Heat is produced, warming surrounding air

Log burns, combining with oxygen in an oxidation reaction

Heat is absorbed during cooking

ACIDS
An acid is a compound that forms hydrogen ions when it dissolves in water. The greater the concentration of ions, the stronger the acid. Strong acids are corrosive and can burn skin and dissolve metals. The pH scale measures acidity; pH 1 is the strongest acid, pH 7 is neutral.

ENDOTHERMIC REACTIONS
Reactions that take in more heat than they give out, such as those during cooking, are endothermic.

UNIVERSAL INDICATOR COLOR/PH CHART OF ACIDS

DIGESTIVE JUICES	CAR BATTERY	LEMON JUICE	VINEGAR	ACID RAIN	TAP WATER	PURE WATER

Mixtures and compounds

Most substances are made of two or more elements, either mingled loosely as mixtures or, after chemical reactions, combined strongly as compounds.

Chlorine (gas)
+
Sodium (metal)
=
Sodium chloride or common salt

Compounds

A compound is a substance in which the atoms of two or more elements are combined together. Common salt (sodium chloride), for example, is a compound of sodium and chlorine atoms.

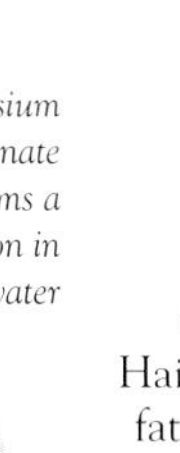

Potassium permanganate forms a solution in water

Colloids

In a colloid, tiny particles of one substance are dispersed evenly throughout another. Hair gel is a colloid of solid fat particles suspended in water.

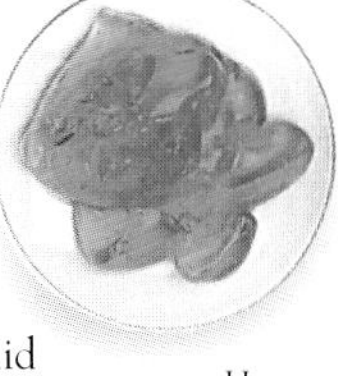

Hair gel

Solutions

A solution is a mixture of one substance (the solute) dissolved in another (the solvent). Many compounds dissolve in water, forming weak bonds with water molecules.

Bases and alkalis

A base is a compound that neutralizes acidity. Alkalis are bases that dissolve in water. The pH scale for bases ranges from neutral pure water (pH 7) to strongest alkali (pH 14).

Universal indicator color/pH chart of bases

Pure water	Soap	Bicarbonate of soda	Disinfectant	Household cleaner	Calcium hydroxide	Oven cleaner	Sodium hydroxide

FORCE AND MOTION

ALL MOVEMENT, or motion, is caused by forces. A force is invisible, but its effects are observable. Forces push or pull, causing objects to start or stop moving, change speed or direction, bend, twist, or change shape.

ATHLETES ACCELERATING UNDER FORCE FROM MUSCLES

Cue strikes white ball, transmitting momentum that overcomes ball's inertia
Ball accelerates away
White ball strikes red ball, transferring some of its momentum
Transferred momentum accelerates red ball away

INERTIA AND MOMENTUM

The tendency of all objects to resist efforts to change their state or motion, whether they are actually moving or at rest, is called inertia. Momentum is the transferable motion possessed by an object moving in a straight line, a circle, or back and forth. It is calculated by multiplying the object's mass by its velocity.

VELOCITY AND ACCELERATION

The speed of an object in a particular direction is called its velocity. A cornering motorcycle, for example, keeps a constant speed but changes velocity as the direction of motion shifts. An increase in the velocity of an object is called acceleration. As its velocity decreases, the object undergoes deceleration.

NEWTON'S LAWS OF MOTION

- **First Law**: An object will remain at rest or continue traveling at a uniform velocity unless a force acts on it.
- **Second Law:** An object's acceleration is equal to the force acting on it, divided by the object's mass.
- **Third Law:** When two objects act on each other, they experience equal forces in opposite directions.

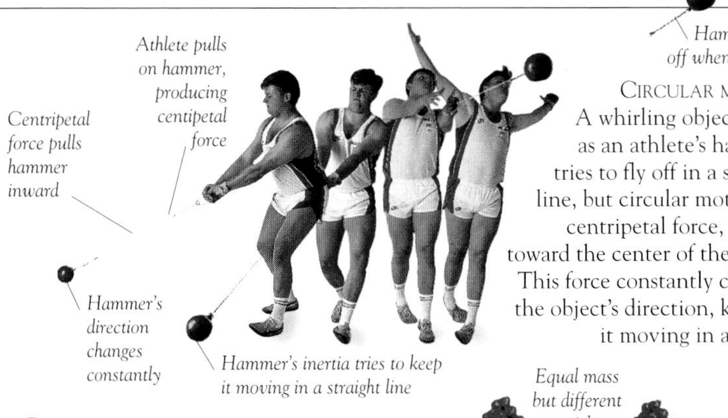
Athlete pulls on hammer, producing centipetal force
Centripetal force pulls hammer inward
Hammer's direction changes constantly
Hammer's inertia tries to keep it moving in a straight line
Hammer flies off when released

CIRCULAR MOTION
A whirling object, such as an athlete's hammer, tries to fly off in a straight line, but circular motion, or centripetal force, pulls it toward the center of the circle. This force constantly changes the object's direction, keeping it moving in a circle.

Gravity

A force of attraction between all objects is called gravity. The greater the object's mass, the stronger the pull. The large mass of Earth generates a strong gravitational pull, keeping us on the ground.

Equal mass but different weight
ON THE MOON
ON EARTH

WEIGHT AND MASS
The force exerted on an object by gravity is called weight. Mass is the amount of matter an object contains.

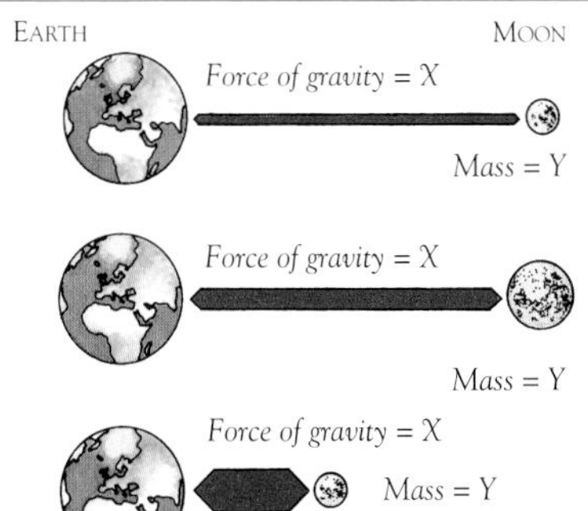
EARTH
MOON
Force of gravity = X
Mass = Y
Force of gravity = X
Mass = Y
Force of gravity = X
Mass = Y
Moon half as far

NEWTON'S LAW OF GRAVITATION
According to Newton's law, the force of gravity between two objects is calculated by multiplying their masses and dividing the result by the square of the distance between them. For example, if the Moon was half its actual distance from Earth, the force of gravity between them would be four times as strong. If the Moon had twice as much mass, the gravity between Earth and the Moon would be twice as great.

SIMPLE MACHINES

MACHINES can make tasks easier by changing the size or direction of a force. Many machines magnify effort, which is the level of force needed to overcome a resisting force, or load.

Axle turns with greater force

Effort applied to wheel rim magnified by axle

WHEEL AND AXLE
Effort applied to the wheel rim is magnified by the axle, which turns with greater force over a shorter distance. Applying effort to an axle turns the wheel rim with less force over a greater distance.

INCLINED PLANE
An inclined plane is an angled surface, or slope, that reduces the effort required to move an object. Moving a car by pulling it up a ramp, for example, is easier than lifting it vertically. The car must travel further, but less effort is needed to move it.

Force of tension in rope pulls car up slope

Car has to travel further than if lifted vertically

Weight of car pulls it downward

Ramp (inclined plane)

Winch magnifies force applied to a handle

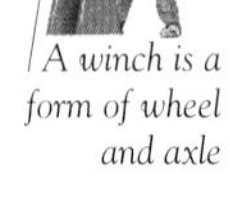

A winch is a form of wheel and axle

Force used to wield axe magnified and transferred into log, pushing it apart

WEDGE
A wedge is a moving inclined plane that pushes an object with more force than the effort needed to move the wedge. Cutting blades, such as axes, make use of the wedge.

Screw head

Screw thread

SCREW
A screw's spiral groove, or thread, is a type of inclined plane wrapped around a shaft. When the screw head is turned, the thread moves the whole screw forward with more force than the turning effort.

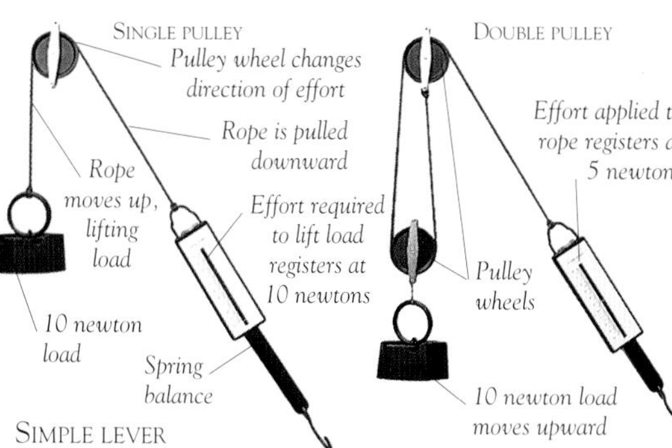
SINGLE PULLEY
Pulley wheel changes direction of effort
Rope is pulled downward
Rope moves up, lifting load
Effort required to lift load registers at 10 newtons
10 newton load
Spring balance
DOUBLE PULLEY
Effort applied to rope registers at 5 newtons
Pulley wheels
10 newton load moves upward

PULLEY

A pulley is a grooved wheel, or set of wheels, around which a rope passes in order to move a load. A single-wheeled pulley helps lift a load by changing the direction of effort applied to the rope. A double pulley halves the effort required to lift the same load.

SIMPLE LEVER

A lever is a bar that exerts a force by turning on a pivot, or "fulcrum". A small effort moved through a great distance at one end moves a larger load through a shorter distance at the other end.

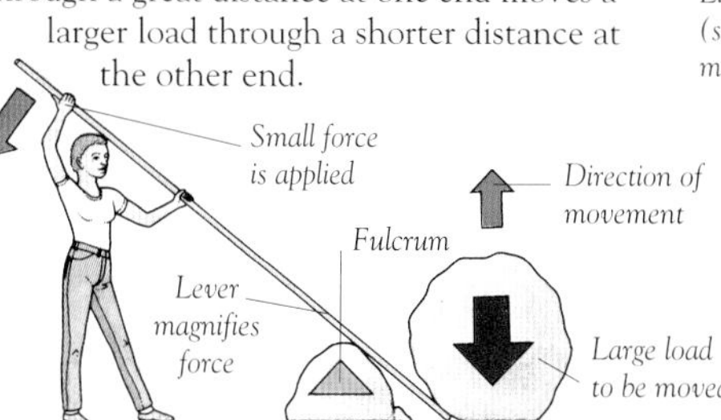
Small force is applied
Direction of movement
Fulcrum
Lever magnifies force
Large load to be moved

Rack

Linear (straight) motion

Pinion

Rotary (circular) motion

Worm gear (cog meshes with screw-threaded shaft)

Direction of motion

Spur gear

MACHINE FACTS

- A machine's force ratio (FR) shows how effective it is as a force magnifier. Force ratio is the force of the load divided by the effort needed to move it.
- A machine's velocity ratio (VR) shows how effective it is a distance magnifier. Velocity ratio is the distance moved by the effort divided by the distance moved by the load.
- Units of force are called newtons (N).

GEARS

Intermeshing toothed wheels, or cogs, that transmit and direct force and motion are called gears. A gear system uses large cogs to turn small cogs with less force but greater speed, and small cogs to turn large cogs with more force but less speed.

ENERGY AND HEAT

THE ABILITY to cause an action is called energy. Light, sound, heat, and electricity are forms of energy. Human energy comes from the chemical energy in food. Movement energy is also called kinetic energy.

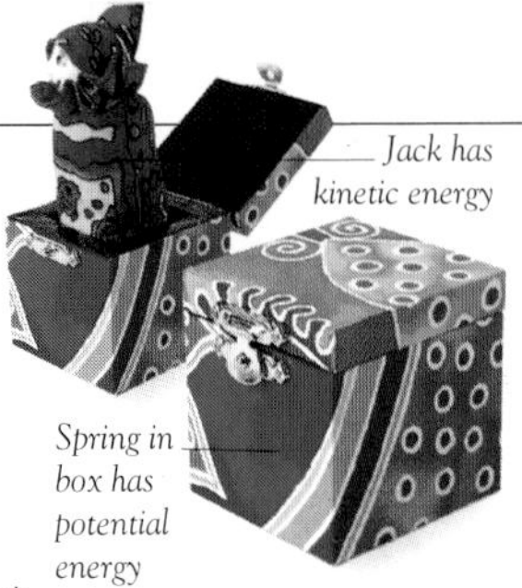
Jack has kinetic energy
Spring in box has potential energy

POTENTIAL ENERGY
Stored energy is called potential energy. Squeezing or stretching an object makes it gain potential energy, which is stored until the object is released. Dropping a raised object converts its potential to fall to Earth into kinetic energy.

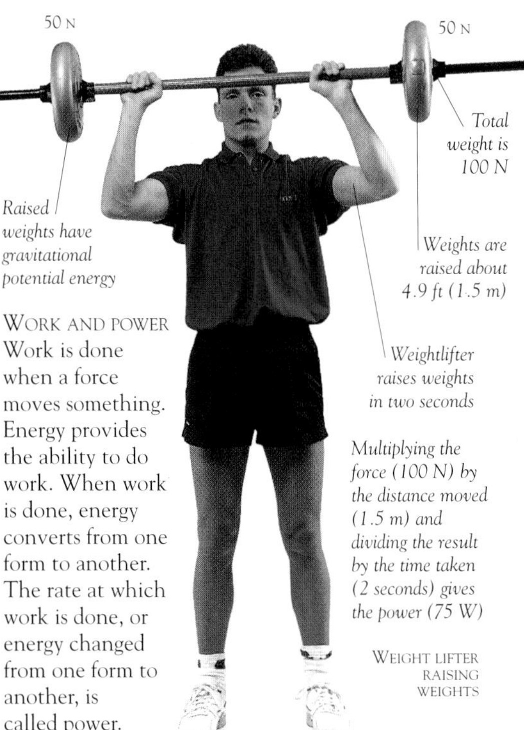
50 N
50 N
Total weight is 100 N
Raised weights have gravitational potential energy
Weights are raised about 4.9 ft (1.5 m)
Weightlifter raises weights in two seconds
Multiplying the force (100 N) by the distance moved (1.5 m) and dividing the result by the time taken (2 seconds) gives the power (75 W)

WEIGHT LIFTER RAISING WEIGHTS

WORK AND POWER
Work is done when a force moves something. Energy provides the ability to do work. When work is done, energy converts from one form to another. The rate at which work is done, or energy changed from one form to another, is called power.

WORK FACTS

- The **joule** (J) is the SI unit of energy and work: 1 J of energy is needed to move a force of 1 newton through a distance of 1 meter. A kilojoule (kJ) is 1,000 joules.
- The **watt** (W) is the SI unit of power: 1 W is the conversion of 1 joule of energy from one form to another in 1 second. A kilowatt (kW) is 1,000 watts.

Heat and temperature

When an object is heated, its particles jiggle around at random. Heat is the energy of this random movement.

Measuring temperature

Temperature is a measure of the average energy possessed by an object's particles because of their random movement. Most liquid and electronic thermometers measure temperature on the Celsius and Fahrenheit scales.

LIQUID THERMOMETER

Temperature

Column of mercury or alcohol expands as temperature rises

ELECTRONIC THERMOMETER

Liquid-crystal display

Heat-senstive tip

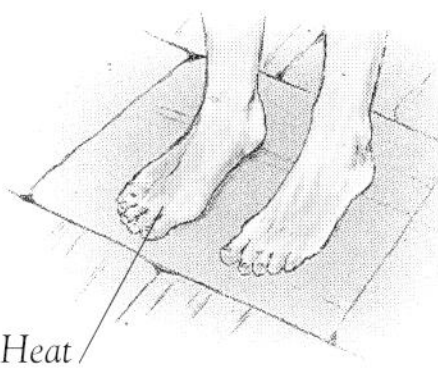

Heat from feet conducts into stone, leaving feet feeling cold

Conduction

Heat energy always passes from hot objects to cooler ones. Heat travels through solids by conduction. Particles in the heated part of the solid vibrate and excite neighboring particles.

Convection and radiation

Heat travels through liquids and gases by convection. Hot fluids are less dense than cold ones and float upward, sinking again as they cool. Matter can also lose or gain heat energy by radiation.

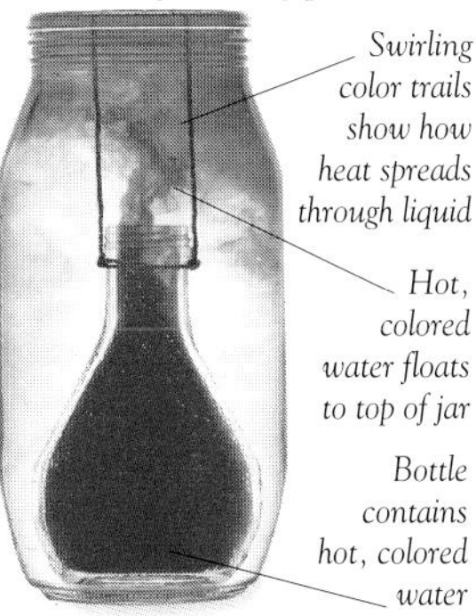

Swirling color trails show how heat spreads through liquid

Hot, colored water floats to top of jar

Bottle contains hot, colored water

Scale of temperature

Temperatures are measured in degrees on the Celsius (C) and Fahrenheit (F) scales, and in Kelvins (K).

482°F, 250°C, 523K
Burning point of wood

424°F, 218°C, 491K
Explosion point of nitroglycerine

230°F, 110°C, 383K
Sauna bath

212°F, 100°C, 373K
Boiling point of water

134°F, 56.7°C, 329.7K
Midday heat in Death Valley, California

98.6°F, 37°C, 310K
Human body temperature

71.6°F, 22°C, 295K
Body temperature of spiny anteater

32°F, 0°C, 273K
Freezing point of pure water

–38°F, –39°C, 234K
Freezing point of mercury

–459°F, –273°C, 0K
Absolute zero

ELECTRICITY

THE MOVEMENT OF electrons between atoms creates a form of energy called electricity. A flow of electrons is called a current. Electric currents and certain materials generate a force called magnetism.

BALLOON CHARGED BY RUBBING (FRICTION)

Negatively charged balloon repels electrons in pieces of paper, giving paper a positive static charge

Positively charged paper attracted to negatively charged balloon

ELECTROSTATIC INDUCTION

Electricity that does not flow in a current is called static electricity. A static charge can be produced by rubbing a balloon against an object such as a sweater. Friction causes electrons to transfer from the sweater's atoms to the balloon's atoms; the balloon gains a negative electric charge and the sweater a positive one. The charged balloon can also induce a static charge in other objects.

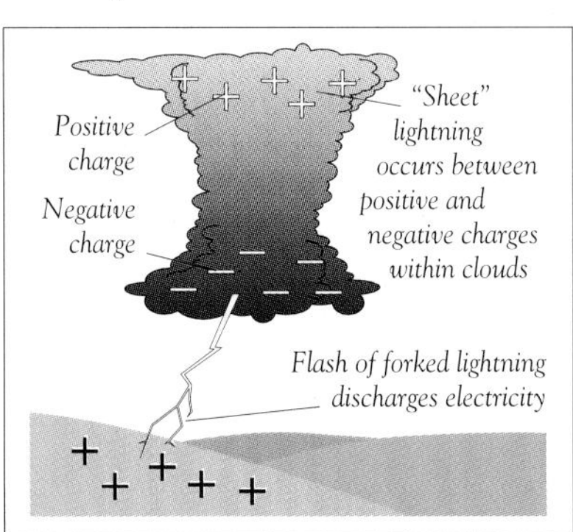
Positive charge
Negative charge
"Sheet" lightning occurs between positive and negative charges within clouds
Flash of forked lightning discharges electricity

LIGHTNING

Inside a thundercloud, positive and negative charges separate between the top and bottom of the cloud. The negative charge at the bottom of the cloud induces a positive charge to build up in the ground below. "Forked" lightning occurs when a strong pulse of electric current suddenly flows between the two opposite charges, discharging from the cloud's base to the ground and back again.

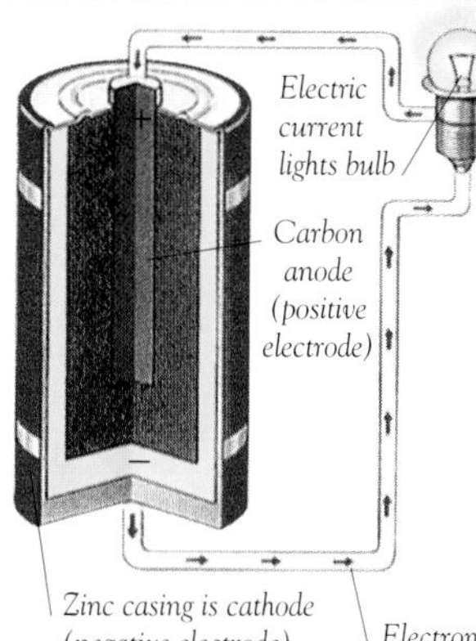
Electric current lights bulb
Carbon anode (positive electrode)
Zinc casing is cathode (negative electrode)
Electron flow

Battery

A battery is a device that produces and stores electric current. Many batteries produce current by using carbon and zinc conductors called electrodes and a chemical paste called an electrolyte. In a circuit, the current flows from the negative electrode (cathode) to the positive (anode). An electric current can be used to power anything from a light-bulb to a computer.

Battery

Current flows through wires

Electrical contacts

Opposing magnetic fields cause coil to rotate

Rotating coil can be attached to a driveshaft or flywheel

Electric motor

A current flows through a wire coil between the poles of a magnet. The current creates a magnetic field around the coil that interacts with the field produced by the magnet, forcing the coil to turn.

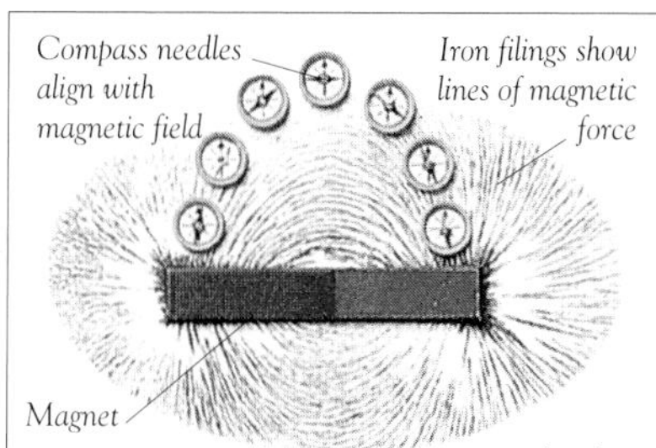
Compass needles align with magnetic field
Iron filings show lines of magnetic force
Magnet

Magnetism

A magnet exerts an invisible field of magnetic force that attracts objects made of iron, and a few other metals. Every magnet has two ends, called its north and south poles, where the forces it exerts are strongest. An electromagnet is a coil of wire that exerts magnetic force when a current is passed through it.

Unlike, or opposite, magnetic poles (a north pole and a south pole) attract each other. Like poles (two north or two south poles) repel each other. Iron filings scattered near the magnets show the lines of attraction and repulsion.

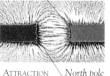

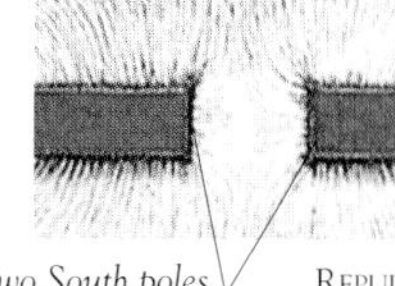
South pole
North pole

ATTRACTION

Two South poles

REPULSION

LIGHT AND COLOR

THE FASTEST-MOVING form of energy is light. It travels in waves that are part of a range of radiation called the electromagnetic spectrum. Visible "white light" is a mixture of many different colors of light, each with its own frequency and wavelength.

THE SUN

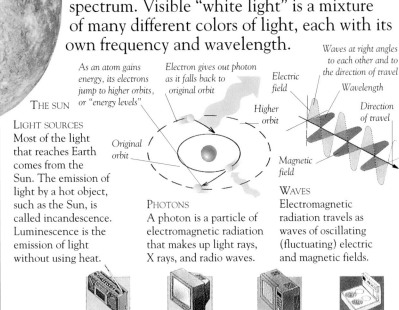

As an atom gains energy, its electrons jump to higher orbits, or "energy levels"

Electron gives out photon as it falls back to original orbit

Higher orbit

Original orbit

Waves at right angles to each other and to the direction of travel

Electric field

Wavelength

Direction of travel

Magnetic field

LIGHT SOURCES

Most of the light that reaches Earth comes from the Sun. The emission of light by a hot object, such as the Sun, is called incandescence. Luminescence is the emission of light without using heat.

PHOTONS

A photon is a particle of electromagnetic radiation that makes up light rays, X rays, and radio waves.

WAVES

Electromagnetic radiation travels as waves of oscillating (fluctuating) electric and magnetic fields.

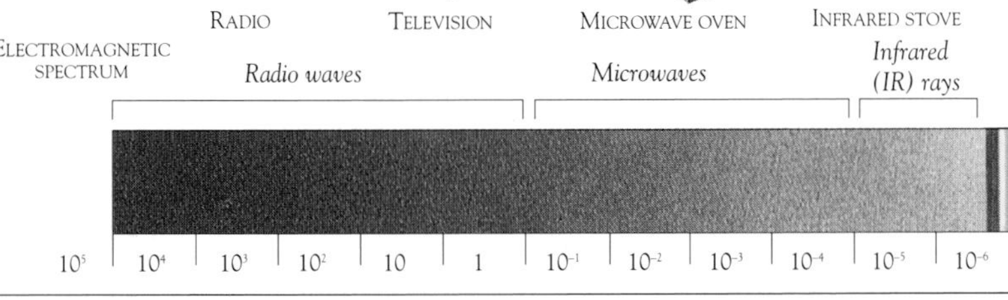
RADIO
TELEVISION
MICROWAVE OVEN
INFRARED STOVE
ELECTROMAGNETIC SPECTRUM
Radio waves
Microwaves
Infrared (IR) rays
10^5
10^4
10^3
10^2
10
1
10^{-1}
10^{-2}
10^{-3}
10^{-4}
10^{-5}
10^{-6}

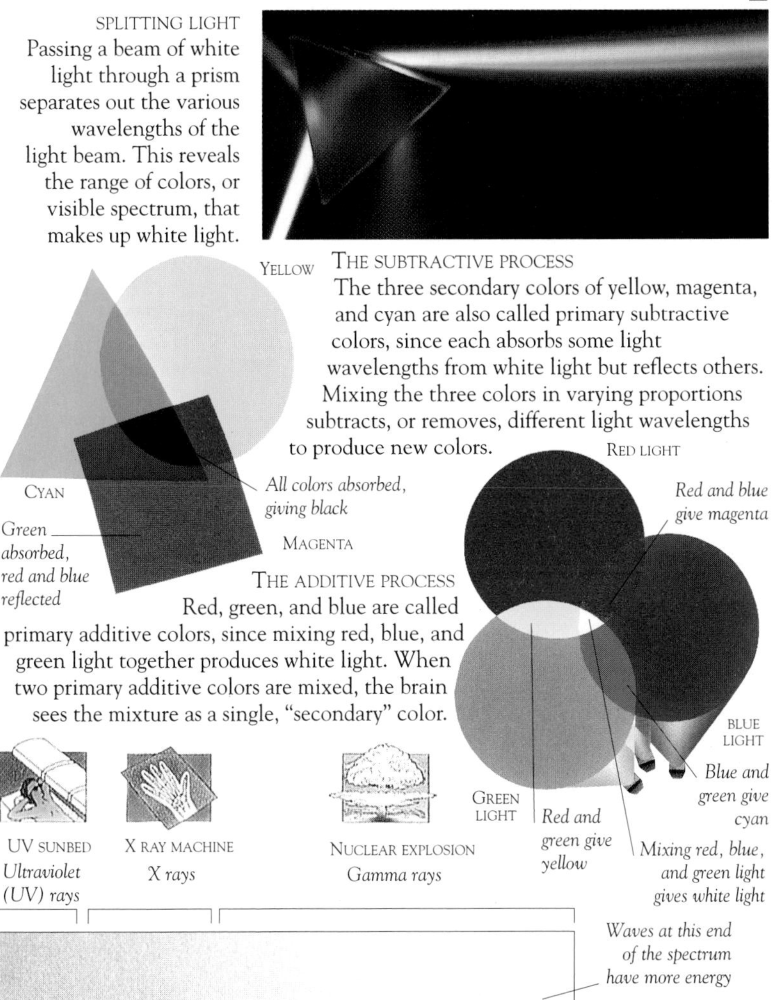
YELLOW
CYAN
MAGENTA
All colors absorbed, giving black
Green absorbed, red and blue reflected
RED LIGHT
Red and blue give magenta
BLUE LIGHT
Blue and green give cyan
GREEN LIGHT
Red and green give yellow
Mixing red, blue, and green light gives white light
UV SUNBED
Ultraviolet (UV) rays
X RAY MACHINE
X rays
NUCLEAR EXPLOSION
Gamma rays
Waves at this end of the spectrum have more energy
WAVELENGTH (IN METERS)
10⁻⁸ 10⁻⁹ 10⁻¹⁰ 10⁻¹¹ 10⁻¹² 10⁻¹³ 10⁻¹⁴ 10⁻¹⁵ 10⁻¹⁶ 10⁻¹⁷

SPLITTING LIGHT
Passing a beam of white light through a prism separates out the various wavelengths of the light beam. This reveals the range of colors, or visible spectrum, that makes up white light.

THE SUBTRACTIVE PROCESS
The three secondary colors of yellow, magenta, and cyan are also called primary subtractive colors, since each absorbs some light wavelengths from white light but reflects others. Mixing the three colors in varying proportions subtracts, or removes, different light wavelengths to produce new colors.

THE ADDITIVE PROCESS
Red, green, and blue are called primary additive colors, since mixing red, blue, and green light together produces white light. When two primary additive colors are mixed, the brain sees the mixture as a single, "secondary" color.

SOUND

A SOUND source generates vibrations that pass though a material in waves. Our ears pick up sound waves traveling in the air around us. Sound waves can travel through solids, liquids, and gases, but not through a vacuum, since there are no particles of matter to carry vibrations.

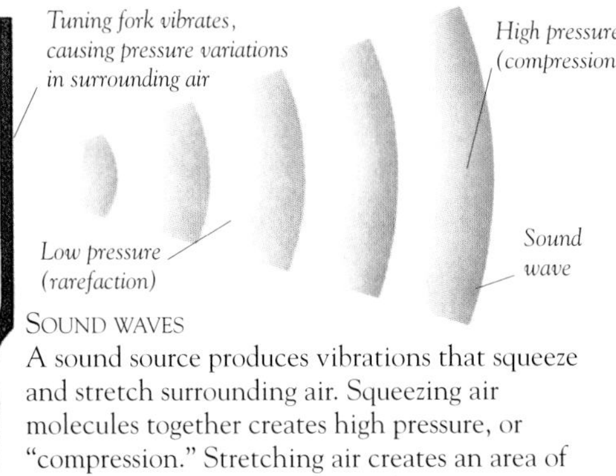

Tuning fork vibrates, causing pressure variations in surrounding air
High pressure (compression)
Low pressure (rarefaction)
Sound wave

SOUND WAVES
A sound source produces vibrations that squeeze and stretch surrounding air. Squeezing air molecules together creates high pressure, or "compression." Stretching air creates an area of low pressure, or "rarefaction." Alternating compressions and rarefactions travel through air as sound waves.

DECIBELS	
140	EAR DAMAGE *Rocket lifting off*
120	PAIN THRESHOLD *Jet plane taking off*
100	ROCK CONCERT
80	BUSY TRAFFIC
60	NORMAL CONVERSATION
	PEOPLE WHISPERING 18 FT (5 M) AWAY
30	
10	LEAVES FALLING 3.3 FT (1 M) AWAY
0	THRESHOLD OF HUMAN HEARING (SOUND JUST AUDIBLE)

LOUDNESS
The greater the pressure change between a sound wave's highest and average points (amplitude), the louder the sound. Loudness is measured in decibels (dB). A 10 dB increase means the sound is 10 times as loud.

HUMAN
HEARS: 20–20,000 Hz
MAKES: 85–1,100 Hz

PITCH AND FREQUENCY
Pitch (how high or low a sound is) depends on frequency – the number of vibrations per second, measured in hertz (Hz).

NUCLEAR EXPLOSION
MAKES: 0.01 Hz

ELEPHANT
HEARS: 1–20,000 H
MAKES: 12 Hz–?

RECORDING SOUND

COMPACT DISC

Pits pressed into CD surface store sound as a sequence of binary numbers

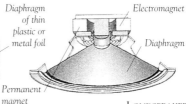

SOUND SYSTEMS

All sound recording systems store sound by making copies of sound waves, as spiral grooves on a vinyl record, magnetic patterns on tape, or tiny, laser-scanned pits on a compact disc.

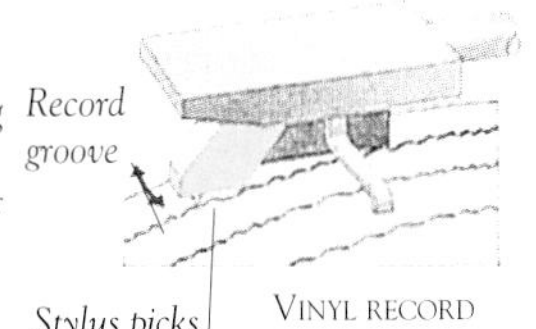
Record groove

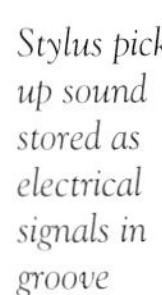
Stylus picks up sound stored as electrical signals in groove

VINYL RECORD

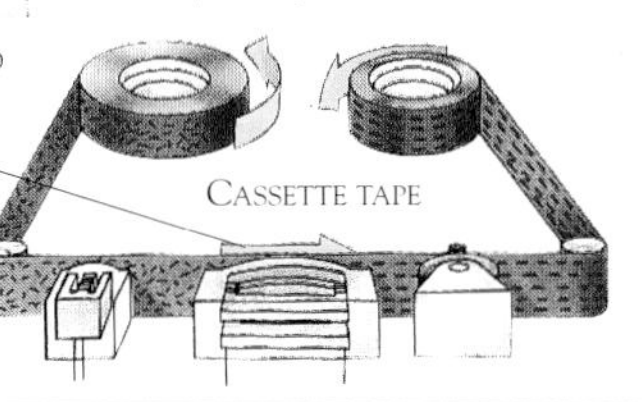
Magnetic field aligns particles on tape to reproduce sound

CASSETTE TAPE

MICROPHONE

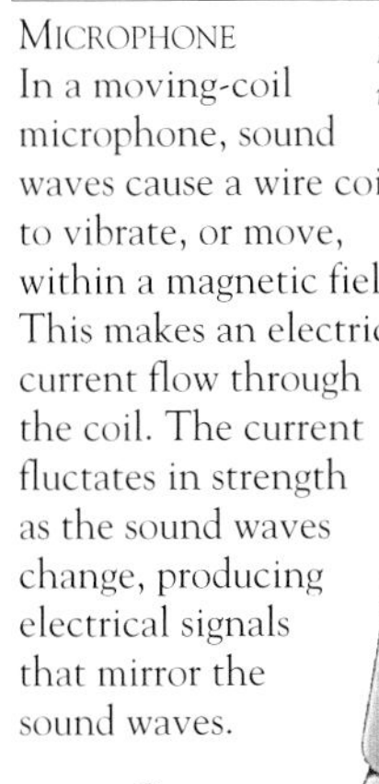

In a moving-coil microphone, sound waves cause a wire coil to vibrate, or move, within a magnetic field. This makes an electric current flow through the coil. The current fluctates in strength as the sound waves change, producing electrical signals that mirror the sound waves.

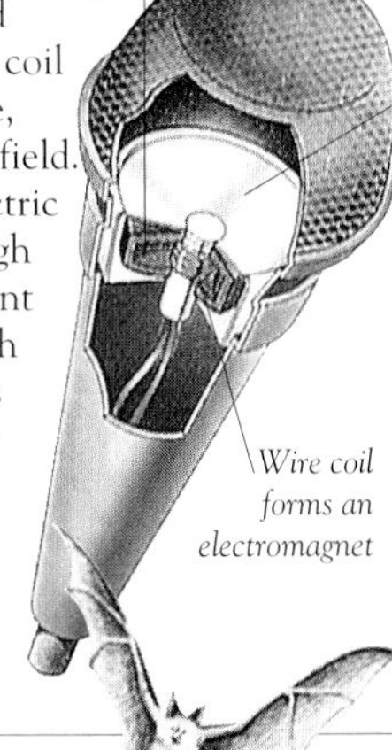
Permanent magnet
Diaphragm of thin plastic or metal foil
Wire coil forms an electromagnet

Electromagnet

Diaphragm

Permanent magnet

LOUDSPEAKER

Feeding electric signals to a loudspeaker generates a varying magnetic field around an electromagnet. The varying field causes a diaphragm to vibrate, producing sound waves.

DOG
HEARS: 15–50,000 Hz
MAKES: 450–1,080 Hz

ULTRASOUND SCANNER
MAKES AND RECEIVES: 3,500,000–7,500,000 Hz

BAT
HEARS: 1,000–120,000 Hz
MAKES: 10,000–120,000 Hz

PORPOISE
HEARS: 150–150,000 Hz
MAKES: 7,000–120,000 Hz

ELECTRONICS

THE SCIENCE OF electronics is concerned with controlling and directing the movement of electrons. The complex operation of machines such as computers and jet aircraft is dependent on electronic technology.

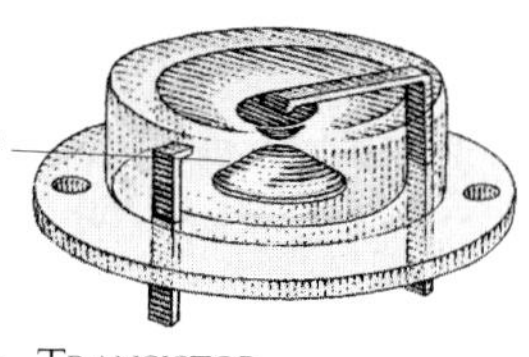
Three layer "sandwich" of n- and p-type silicon

TRANSISTOR
A transistor is a semiconducting component that boosts or switches current. In computers, transistors switch on and off many times each second, enabling rapid information processing.

SEMICONDUCTORS
A semiconductor is a material found in most electronic components that can vary its ability to conduct electricity. Adding impurities alters its electrical properties. Boron atoms in p-type silicon take up electrons from the outer shells of silicon atoms, leaving moving "holes" that carry current. In n-type silicon, extra electrons donated by added arsenic atoms carry current.

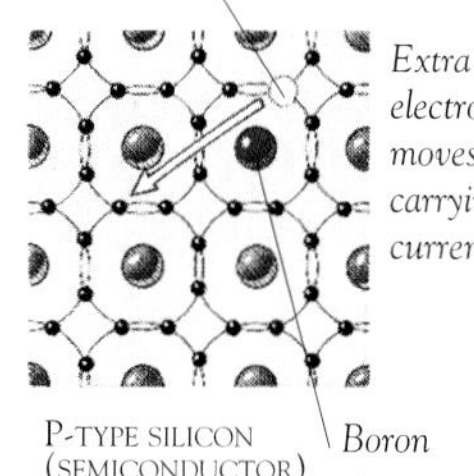
Hole in outer shell of atom moves, carrying current
Boron atom

P-TYPE SILICON (SEMICONDUCTOR)

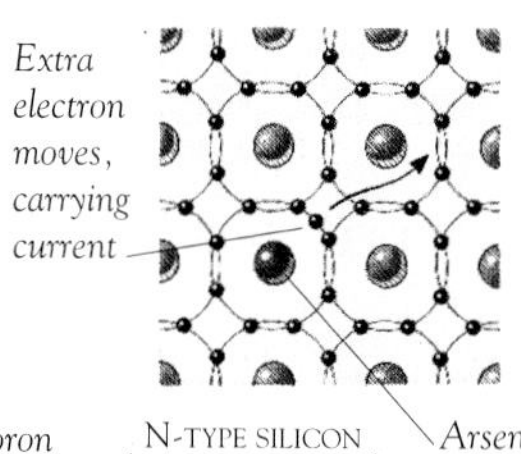
Extra electron moves, carrying current
Arsenic atom

N-TYPE SILICON (SEMICONDUCTOR)

INTERNATIONAL ELECTRICAL COMPONENT SYMBOLS

CAPACITOR
Stores charge

DIODE
Permits current to flow in one direction only; can also be used to convert ac signals to dc signals (a rectifier)

LIGHT-EMITTING DIODE
Emits light when current flows through it

MICROPHONE
Converts sound waves into ac signals

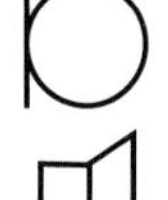

LOUDSPEAKER
Converts ac signals into sound waves

n-p-n TRANSISTOR
Amplifies electric current, and turns it on and off

p-n-p TRANSISTOR
Amplifies electric current, and turns it on and off

Integrated circuits

An integrated circuit, or "microchip," is a tiny piece, or "wafer," of silicon that contains a complete circuit of thousands of electronic components. Layers of n- and p-type semi-conductors and other materials are built up on the silicon wafer and linked by fine conducting wires.

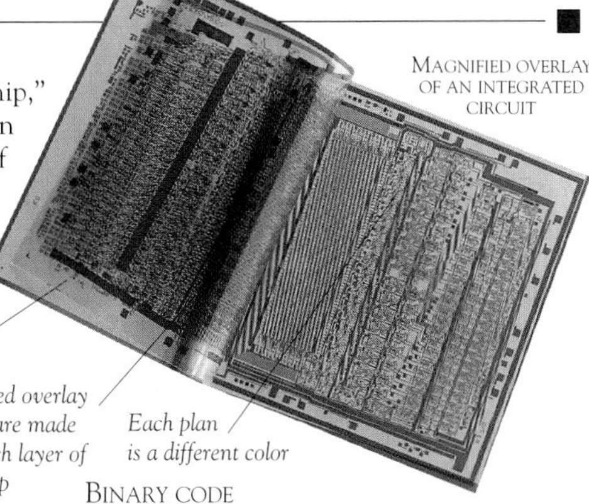

Magnified overlay of an integrated circuit

Circuits are "printed" onto wafer photographically through transparent overlay

Detailed overlay plans are made for each layer of the chip

Each plan is a different color

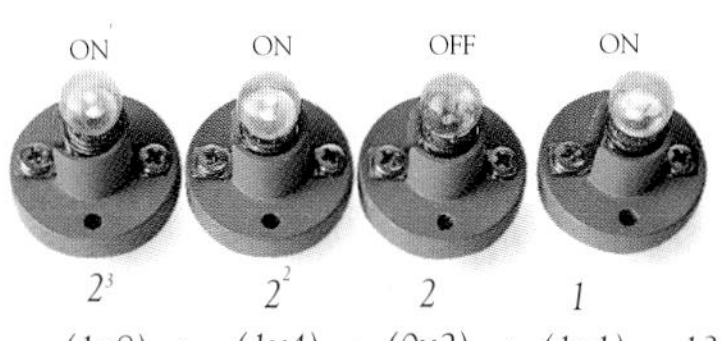
ON
ON
OFF
ON

2^3 2^2 2 1

$(1 \times 8) + (1 \times 4) + (0 \times 2) + (1 \times 1) = 13$

Binary code

Microchips store data as on/off electrical pulses called binary code. All information is broken down into sequences of ones (on) and zeros (off). The decimal number 13, for example, is 1101 in binary form.

Microchips, or "chips," are encased in a tough plastic or ceramic capsule

Encased integrated circuit

Conducting pins can be soldered or plugged into a circuit board

Encased chip

A microchip is housed in a protective casing that dwarfs the tiny chip itself. An encased chip stores data as electrical signals in binary code, and uses logic gates (see right) to process that data. A microprocessor is a chip that can store instructions in an electronic memory.

Logic gates

Microchips use transistor circuits called logic gates to process binary code. Different types of gates switch on (open) or off (close) depending on the type of input received.

Output / A B

AND gate
Gives an output signal when a signal is applied to one input AND to the other input.

Output / A B

OR gate
Gives an output signal when a signal is applied to one input OR to the other input, OR to both.

Output / Input

NOT gate
Gives an output signal when a signal does NOT arrive at its input.

COMPUTERS

A COMPUTER IS an electronic machine that can perform a wide variety of complex tasks quickly. Each task is reduced to a series of simple calculations, which enables rapid processing of data.

COMPUTER PROGRAMS
A program is a set of instructions that tells a computer to carry out a task. The instructions may be written as long sets of numbers called "machine code", or in a computer language such as BASIC or FORTRAN. Computer programs are also called "software".

PERSONAL COMPUTER
The most familiar type of computer is the personal computer (PC), which can only be used by one person at a time. The machinery that makes up a PC, such as the keyboard and mouse, disk drive, and monitor screen, is called "hardware".

Disk drive contains software programs
Monitor displays data
Keyboard and mouse for inputting data

CENTRAL PROCESSING UNIT
A computer is controlled by a central processing unit (CPU). In a PC, the CPU is a single microprocessor chip containing a large number of circuits. The CPU processes data from the keyboard, ROM, and RAM. It also sends information to the RAM, outputs data to the printer, and displays software on the monitor.

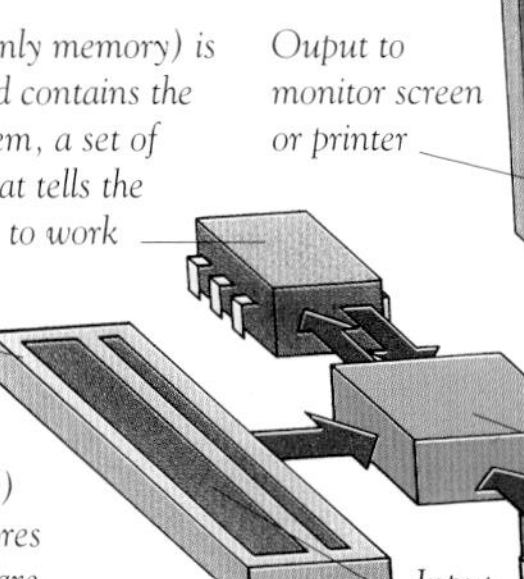
ROM (read-only memory) is permanent and contains the operating system, a set of instructions that tells the computer how to work
Ouput to monitor screen or printer
Keyboard
RAM (random-access memory) temporarily stores programs that are currently being run
CPU
Input

INTERNET

The Internet is a global web of interconnected computer networks. It enables people all over the world to exchange data and send electronic mail (email). The worldwide web is an Internet service that provides a wide range of information in the form of user-friendly websites. When a person needs to find out something specific on the web, software programs called search engines can be used to trawl through the millions of websites and very rapidly find the ones most likely to contain the required information. The Internet can be used for banking, shopping (e-commerce), listening to the radio, watching videos, or even playing chess with an opponent thousands of kilometers away.

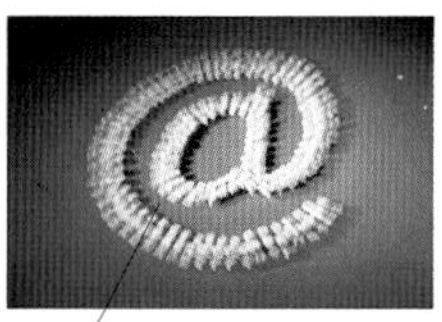

The alpha sign @ means "at", and is part of each email address; like sending letters via the post office, email is routed via companies and organizations called Internet service providers

COMPUTER-AIDED DESIGN

Designers and architects test new ideas by using computer-aided design (CAD) to create 3-D graphic models on screen.

COMPUTER FACTS

- Neural networks are computers designed to imitate the workings of the human brain.
- The world's largest computer manufacturer is US company IBM, which employs about 220,000 people.

CD-ROM AND DVD

Large amounts of data, such as pictures, sounds, text, and video, can be permanently stored on CD-ROM and DVD. A laser reads the data from the disc. The CD-R and DVD-R formats allow the user to record new data onto the discs.

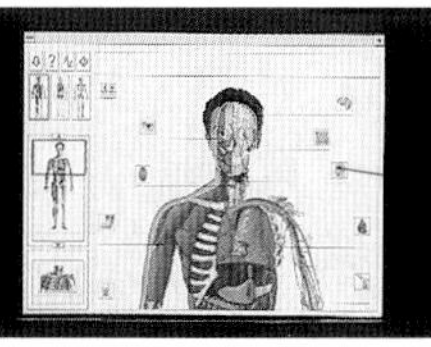

CD-ROM software page

VIRTUAL REALITY

A virtual-reality (VR) system enables the user to interact with a computer-generated "virtual" world. A headset supplies the user with 3-D images, while a "data glove" lets you "touch" what you see.

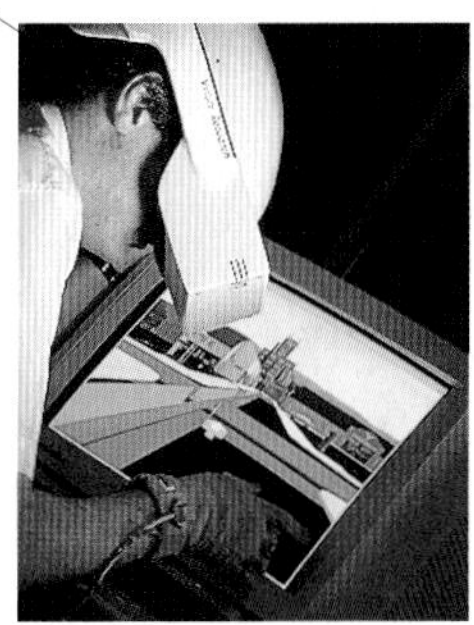

Virtual reality user moves hands to interact with 3-D world

Printing technology

THE PROCESS of reproducing words (text) and pictures (images) using ink is called printing. Printing presses enable numerous copies of text and images to be made very quickly. Modern print production uses computers at many stages in the printing process.

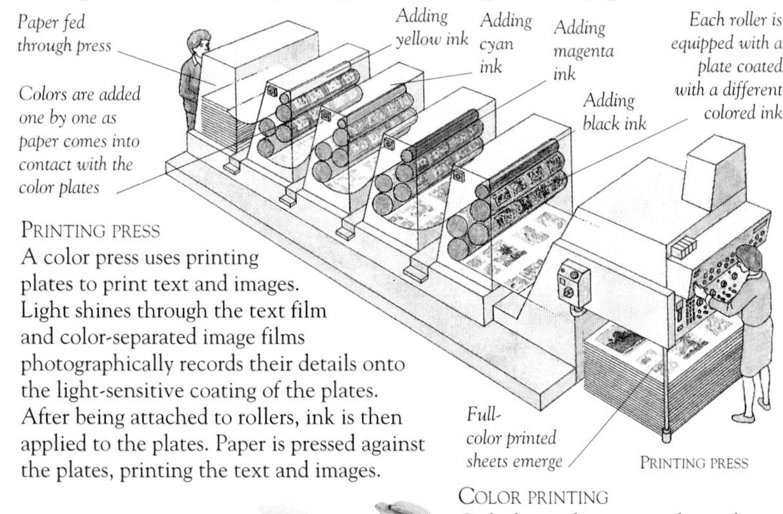
Paper fed through press
Colors are added one by one as paper comes into contact with the color plates
Adding yellow ink
Adding cyan ink
Adding magenta ink
Adding black ink
Each roller is equipped with a plate coated with a different colored ink
Full-color printed sheets emerge

PRINTING PRESS

PRINTING PRESS
A color press uses printing plates to print text and images. Light shines through the text film and color-separated image films photographically records their details onto the light-sensitive coating of the plates. After being attached to rollers, ink is then applied to the plates. Paper is pressed against the plates, printing the text and images.

PRINTED FULL-COLOR IMAGE

YELLOW

MAGENTA

CYAN

BLACK

COLOR PRINTING
Only four colors are used in color printing – yellow, magenta, cyan, and black. The image to be printed is scanned electronically, producing a separate piece of film for each color. The details of these "separations" are transferred onto color plates in the printing press. The separations are then printed on top of one another, reproducing the full-color image.

Telecommunications

The science of broadcasting sound and pictures over long distances is called telecommunications.

Wave modulation

Radio and television programs are broadcast by radio waves, which must first be modulated (coded) so that they can carry sound and picture signals. A steady radio wave is modulated by a sound signal in one of two ways. Its amplitude (strength) may be modulated (AM) or its frequency may change (FM).

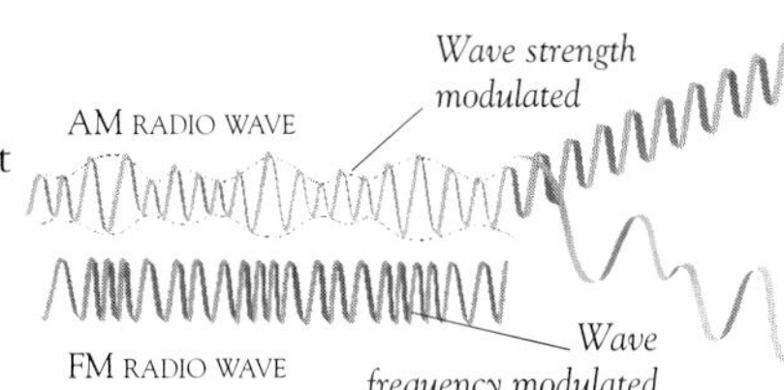

AM radio wave
Wave strength modulated
FM radio wave
Wave frequency modulated

How a television works

The antenna of a TV receives a modulated carrier wave (carrying sound and picture signals), which is then "demodulated" into electrical signals and sent to a cathode-ray tube. The tube contains three "electron guns" that fire beams of electrons at the phosphor-coated TV screen. Magnetic fields cause the beams to scan the screen. The picture builds as the electrons make the phosphors glow.

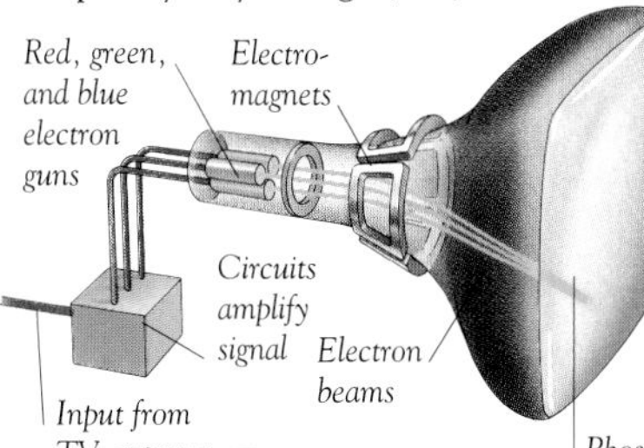

Red, green, and blue electron guns
Electro-magnets
Circuits amplify signal
Electron beams
Input from TV antenna
Phosphors glow red, blue, or green when hit by electron beams

Televsion set

Long-range communications

Low-frequency radio waves can be sent long distances by bouncing them between the ionosphere (an ion-rich region of the atmosphere) and the ground. High-frequency waves are transmitted through the ionosphere to orbiting communication satellites, which relay the radio waves to receiving stations on Earth.

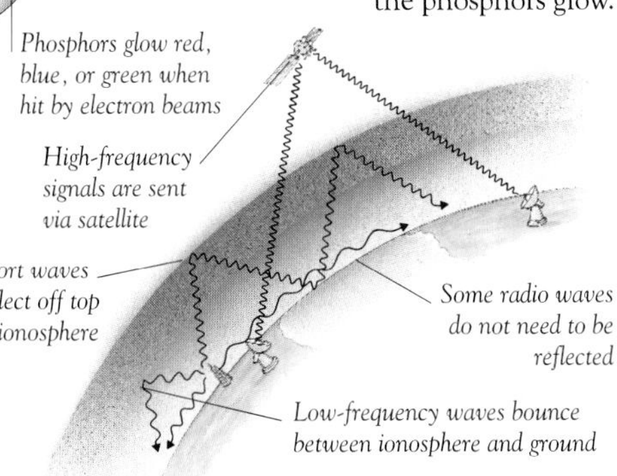

High-frequency signals are sent via satellite
Short waves reflect off top of ionosphere
Some radio waves do not need to be reflected
Low-frequency waves bounce between ionosphere and ground

Transmitting radio waves

MATHEMATICS

THE STUDY OF numbers and shapes is called mathematics. The different branches of mathematics enable us to create sophisticated machines, build structures, and run businesses. Algebra, for example, uses abstract symbols in place of numbers, while geometry deals with shapes and lines.

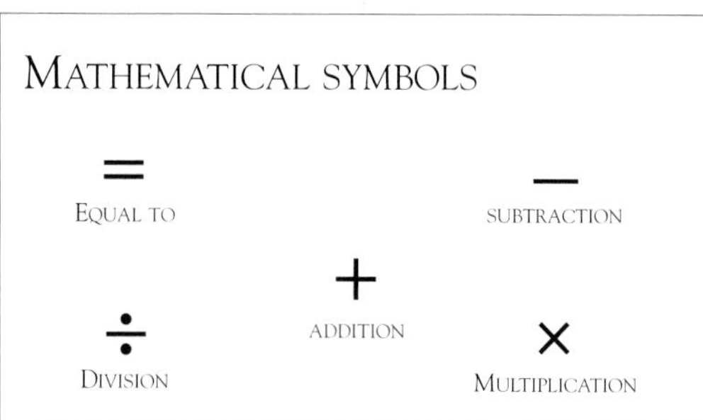
MATHEMATICAL SYMBOLS
=
EQUAL TO
—
SUBTRACTION
+
ADDITION
÷
DIVISION
×
MULTIPLICATION

TYPES OF NUMBERS
A written number consists of digits, or numerals; the number 313, for example, has 3 digits. A positive number is any number greater than zero, such as 6. A negative number is less than zero, such as –6. A prime number can only be divided by itself and 1.

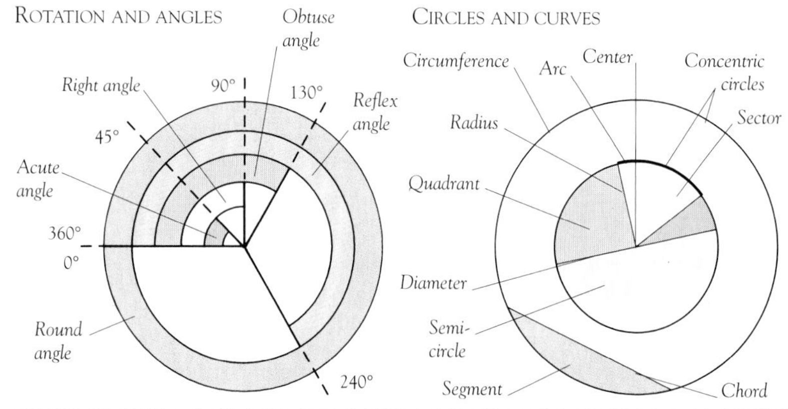
ROTATION AND ANGLES
Obtuse angle
Right angle
90°
130°
Reflex angle
45°
Acute angle
360°
0°
Round angle
240°
CIRCLES AND CURVES
Circumference
Arc
Center
Concentric circles
Sector
Radius
Quadrant
Diameter
Semi-circle
Segment
Chord

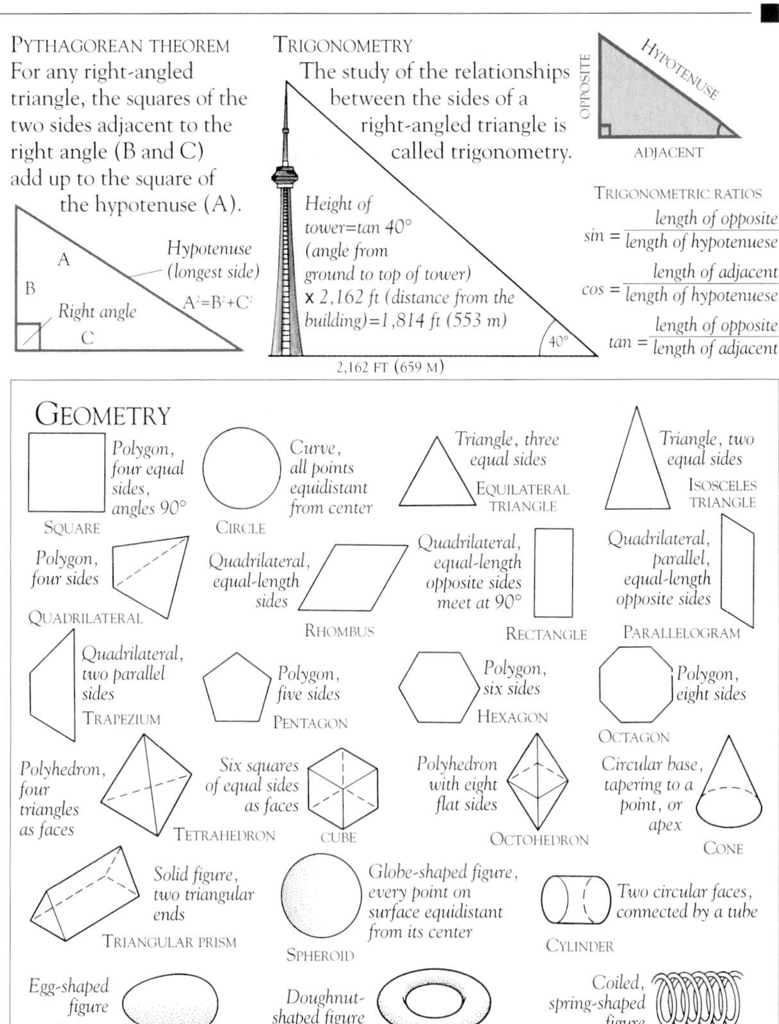
PYTHAGOREAN THEOREM
For any right-angled triangle, the squares of the two sides adjacent to the right angle (B and C) add up to the square of the hypotenuse (A).
A
B
C
Right angle
Hypotenuse (longest side)
$A^2=B^2+C^2$
TRIGONOMETRY
The study of the relationships between the sides of a right-angled triangle is called trigonometry.
Height of tower=tan 40° (angle from ground to top of tower) x 2,162 ft (distance from the building)=1,814 ft (553 m)
40°
2,162 FT (659 M)
OPPOSITE
HYPOTENUSE
ADJACENT
TRIGONOMETRIC RATIOS
sin = length of opposite / length of hypotenuese
cos = length of adjacent / length of hypotenuese
tan = length of opposite / length of adjacent
GEOMETRY
Polygon, four equal sides, angles 90°
SQUARE
Curve, all points equidistant from center
CIRCLE
Triangle, three equal sides
EQUILATERAL TRIANGLE
Triangle, two equal sides
ISOSCELES TRIANGLE
Polygon, four sides
QUADRILATERAL
Quadrilateral, equal-length sides
RHOMBUS
Quadrilateral, equal-length opposite sides meet at 90°
RECTANGLE
Quadrilateral, parallel, equal-length opposite sides
PARALLELOGRAM
Quadrilateral, two parallel sides
TRAPEZIUM
Polygon, five sides
PENTAGON
Polygon, six sides
HEXAGON
Polygon, eight sides
OCTAGON
Polyhedron, four triangles as faces
TETRAHEDRON
Six squares of equal sides as faces
CUBE
Polyhedron with eight flat sides
OCTOHEDRON
Circular base, tapering to a point, or apex
CONE
Solid figure, two triangular ends
TRIANGULAR PRISM
Globe-shaped figure, every point on surface equidistant from its center
SPHEROID
Two circular faces, connected by a tube
CYLINDER
Egg-shaped figure
SPHEROID
Doughnut-shaped figure
TORUS
Coiled, spring-shaped figure
HELIX

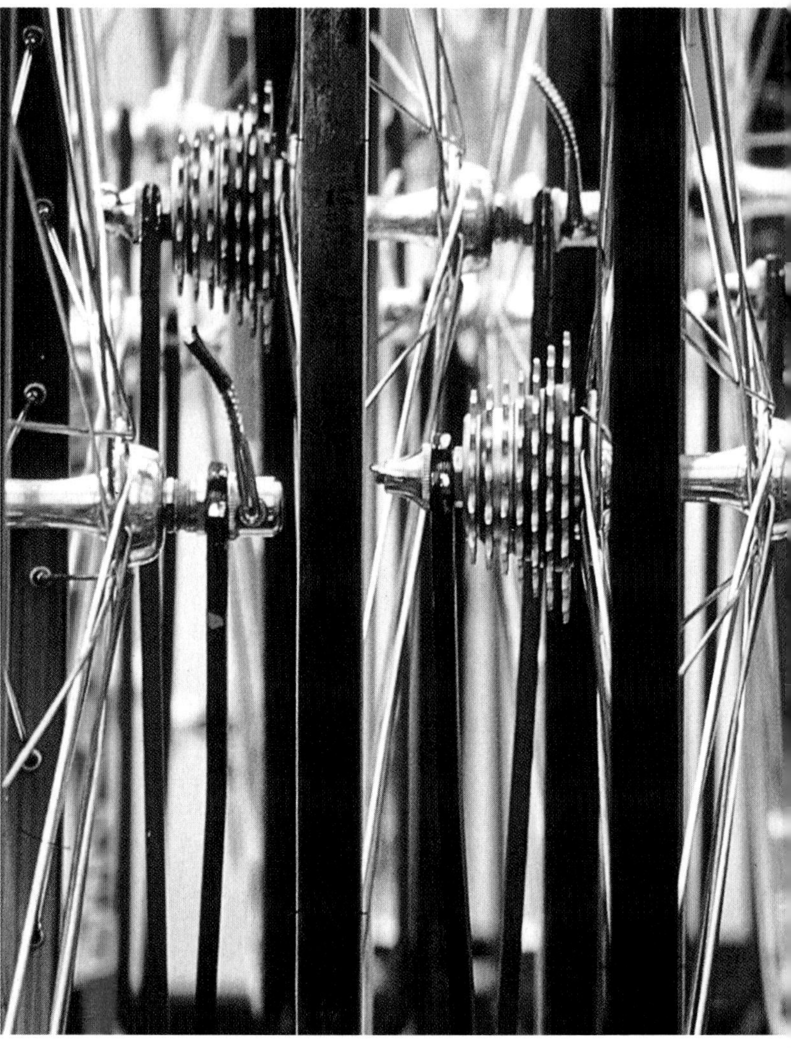

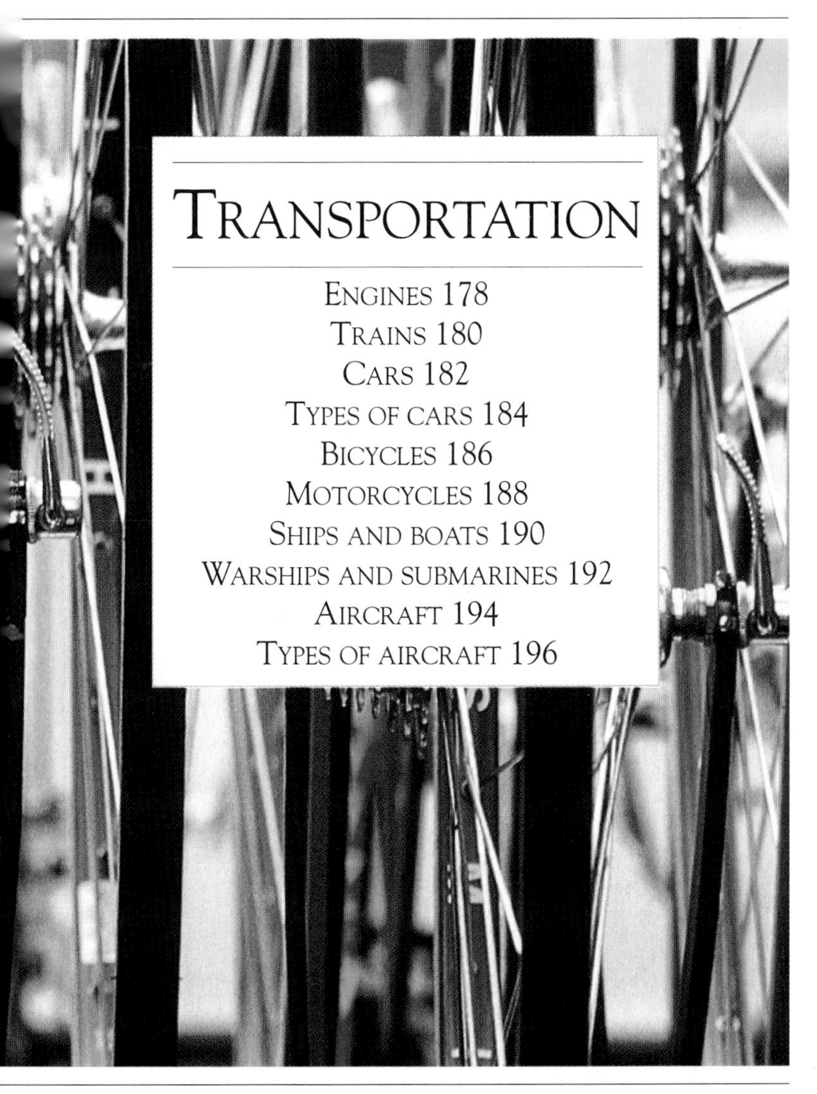

TRANSPORTATION

ENGINES

AN ENGINE harnesses one form of energy and converts it into motive force, or kinetic energy. Engines range in complexity from simple windmills to sophisticated turbofans.

WINDMILL
The sails of a windmill convert wind force into rotary motion, driving a central shaft that powers the milling machinery.

INTERNAL COMBUSTION
An internal combustion engine provides motive force by harnessing the energy released when a mix of fuel and air is burned (combusted) inside its cylinders. The stages of the combustion cycle are called strokes.

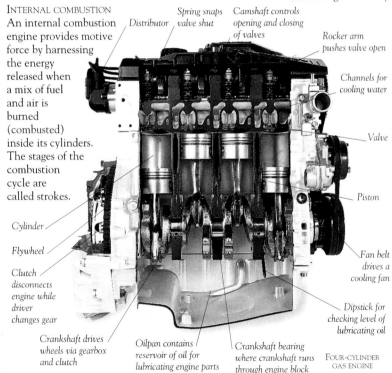

Distributor

Spring snaps valve shut

Camshaft controls opening and closing of valves

Rocker arm pushes valve open

Channels for cooling water

Valve

Piston

Fan belt drives a cooling fan

Dipstick for checking level of lubricating oil

Cylinder

Flywheel

Clutch disconnects engine while driver changes gear

Crankshaft drives wheels via gearbox and clutch

Oilpan contains reservoir of oil for lubricating engine parts

Crankshaft bearing where crankshaft runs through engine block

FOUR-CYLINDER GAS ENGINE

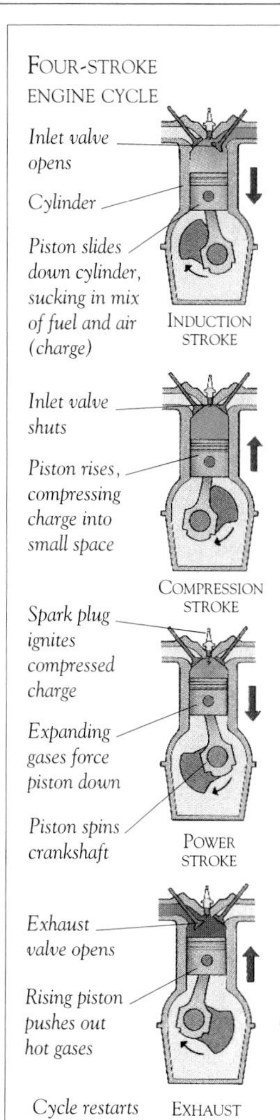
FOUR-STROKE ENGINE CYCLE
Inlet valve opens
Cylinder
Piston slides down cylinder, sucking in mix of fuel and air (charge)
INDUCTION STROKE
Inlet valve shuts
Piston rises, compressing charge into small space
COMPRESSION STROKE
Spark plug ignites compressed charge
Expanding gases force piston down
Piston spins crankshaft
POWER STROKE
Exhaust valve opens
Rising piston pushes out hot gases
Cycle restarts
EXHAUST STROKE

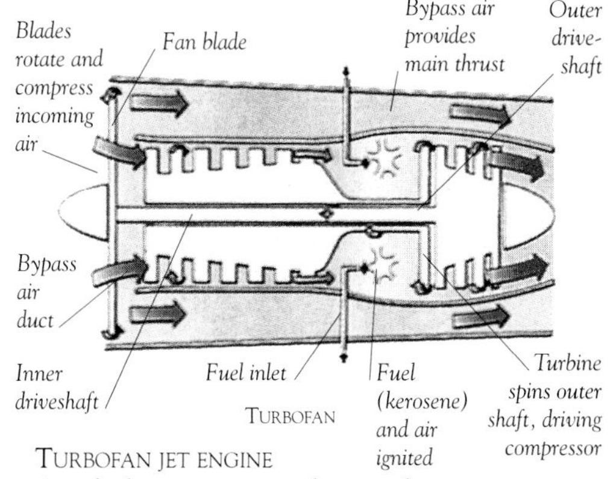
Blades rotate and compress incoming air
Fan blade
Bypass air provides main thrust
Outer drive-shaft
Bypass air duct
Inner driveshaft
Fuel inlet
Fuel (kerosene) and air ignited
Turbine spins outer shaft, driving compressor
TURBOFAN

TURBOFAN JET ENGINE

A turbofan jet engine sucks in and compresses air, which is then mixed with fuel and ignited. The hot gases produced create forward thrust and drive air-circulating turbines that cool the engine.

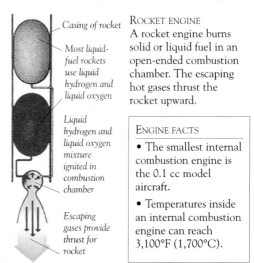

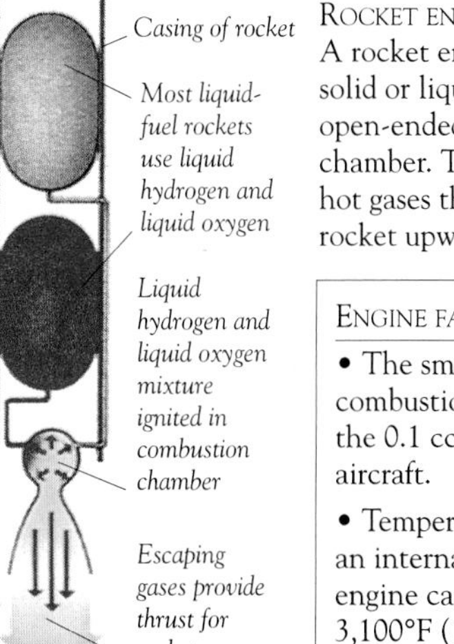
Casing of rocket
Most liquid-fuel rockets use liquid hydrogen and liquid oxygen
Liquid hydrogen and liquid oxygen mixture ignited in combustion chamber
Escaping gases provide thrust for rocket

ROCKET ENGINE

A rocket engine burns solid or liquid fuel in an open-ended combustion chamber. The escaping hot gases thrust the rocket upward.

ENGINE FACTS

- The smallest internal combustion engine is the 0.1 cc model aircraft.
- Temperatures inside an internal combustion engine can reach 3,100°F (1,700°C).

TRAINS

PEOPLE AND GOODS are transported along railroads in long trains of trucks and carriages. These trains are pulled by powerful engine units called locomotives.

STEAM TRAVEL

Water in a steam locomotive's boiler is heated by a coal fire in the firebox, making steam. Pressure from the steam moves a piston back and forth; a connecting rod and crank linked to the piston makes the wheels turn. Steam locomotives were used to pull the earliest trains, eventually being replaced by electric and diesel locomotives in the 1960s.

The tracks rests on concrete or wooden beams known as ties or sleepers

Rail

When a switch takes place, short sections of rail swing across to guide the train on to the new track

Switch (point)

TRACKS AND SWITCHES

Rails are often welded into one continuous track as they are laid, allowing trains to run smoothly. Trains change tracks at pivoting sections called switches, or points.

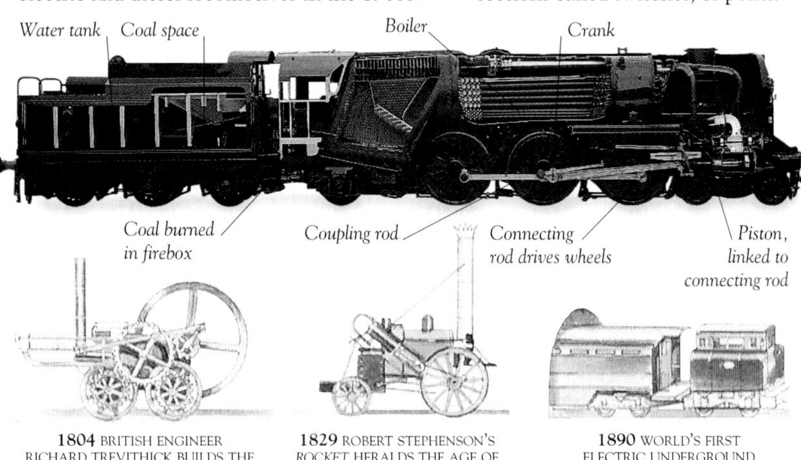
Water tank
Coal space
Boiler
Crank
Coal burned in firebox
Coupling rod
Connecting rod drives wheels
Piston, linked to connecting rod

1804 BRITISH ENGINEER RICHARD TREVITHICK BUILDS THE FIRST STEAM LOCOMOTIVE

1829 ROBERT STEPHENSON'S *ROCKET* HERALDS THE AGE OF THE PASSENGER TRAIN

1890 WORLD'S FIRST ELECTRIC UNDERGROUND RAILROAD OPENS IN UK

MONORAIL

Some trains run on or hang underneath a single (mono) electric rail. Monorails are fast and clean, and do not interfere with ground traffic.

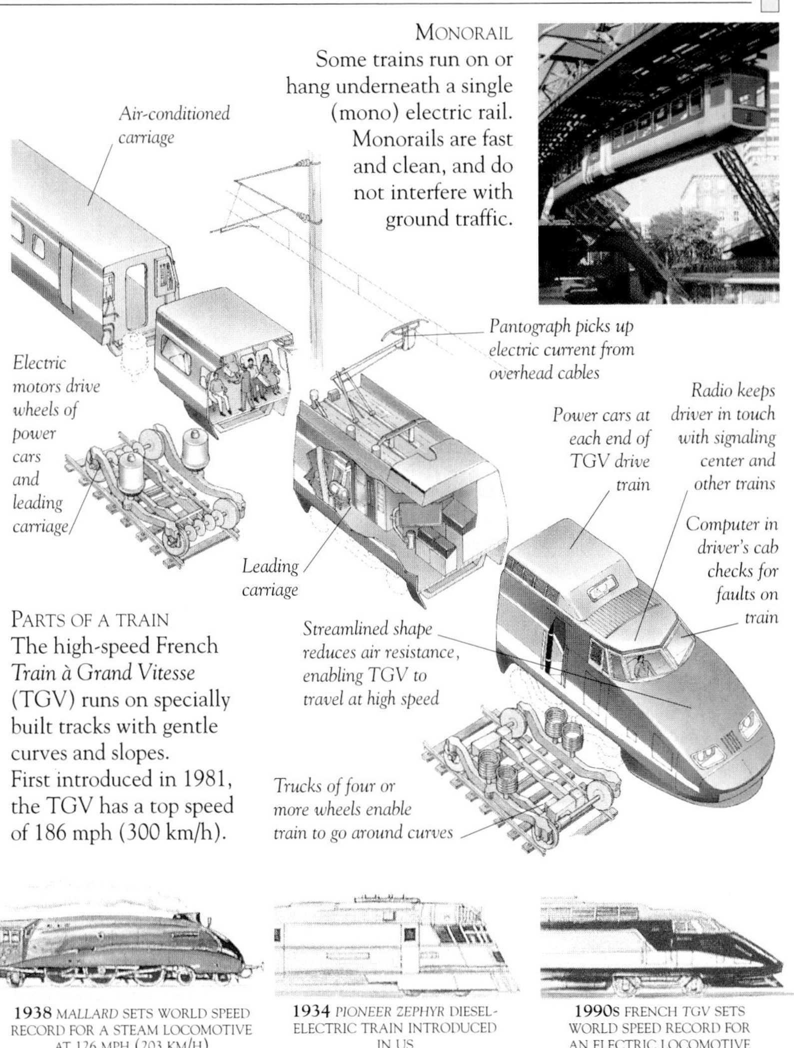
Air-conditioned carriage
Pantograph picks up electric current from overhead cables
Electric motors drive wheels of power cars and leading carriage
Radio keeps driver in touch with signaling center and other trains
Power cars at each end of TGV drive train
Computer in driver's cab checks for faults on train
Leading carriage
Streamlined shape reduces air resistance, enabling TGV to travel at high speed
Trucks of four or more wheels enable train to go around curves

PARTS OF A TRAIN

The high-speed French *Train à Grand Vitesse* (TGV) runs on specially built tracks with gentle curves and slopes. First introduced in 1981, the TGV has a top speed of 186 mph (300 km/h).

1938 *MALLARD* SETS WORLD SPEED RECORD FOR A STEAM LOCOMOTIVE AT 126 MPH (203 KM/H)

1934 *PIONEER ZEPHYR* DIESEL-ELECTRIC TRAIN INTRODUCED IN US

1990s FRENCH *TGV* SETS WORLD SPEED RECORD FOR AN ELECTRIC LOCOMOTIVE

CARS

MODERN CARS use a variety of mechanical and electrical systems to provide the transportation we take for granted. Car manufacturers are always looking for new ways to make cars safer and more efficient.

ENGINE LAYOUTS

Design features

FRONT ENGINE, REAR-WHEEL DRIVE

Compromise between traction (roadgrip), handling, and internal space requirements.

REAR ENGINE, REAR-WHEEL DRIVE

Provides maximum traction, but reduces amount of internal space.

FRONT ENGINE, FRONT-WHEEL DRIVE

Maximizes internal space, and provides good traction. Used by most family cars.

MIDENGINE, REAR-WHEEL DRIVE

Good handling and traction, but little internal space. Fast sports cars use this engine layout.

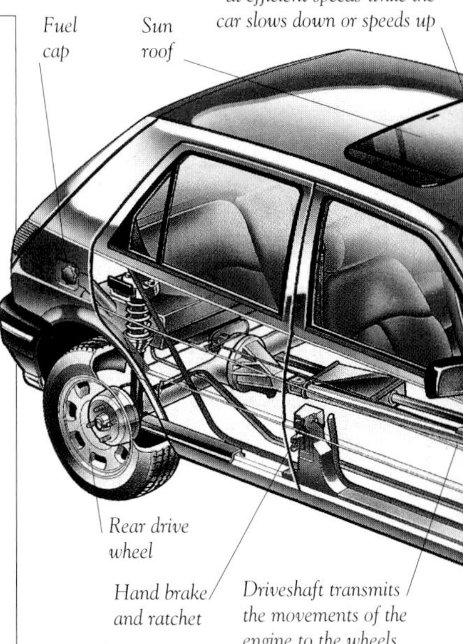
Gearshift changes gears, which enable the engine to run at efficient speeds while the car slows down or speeds up
Fuel cap
Sun roof
Rear drive wheel
Hand brake and ratchet
Driveshaft transmits the movements of the engine to the wheels

THE ANATOMY OF A CAR
Most cars have four wheels, an engine at the front, and room for at least two passengers. This illustration shows the main features of a rear-wheel drive hatchback.

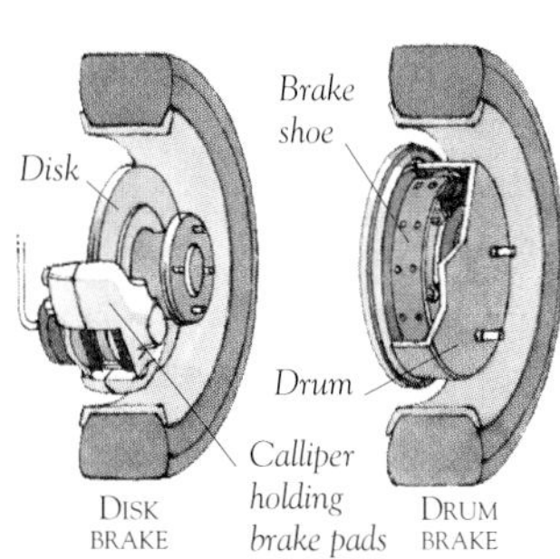
Disk
Brake shoe
Drum
Calliper holding brake pads
DISK BRAKE
DRUM BRAKE

TYPES OF BRAKES
Modern disk brakes use hydraulic pressure to squeeze a steel disk attached to the wheel between two brake pads, slowing the car. In older drum brakes, curved brake "shoes" push against the inside of a metal drum attached to the wheel.

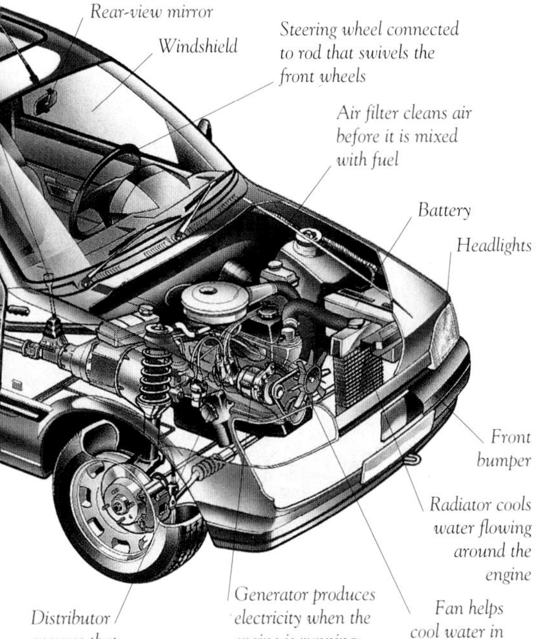
Rear-view mirror
Windshield
Steering wheel connected to rod that swivels the front wheels
Air filter cleans air before it is mixed with fuel
Battery
Headlights
Front bumper
Radiator cools water flowing around the engine
Fan helps cool water in the radiator
Generator produces electricity when the engine is running; this electricity is stored in the battery
Distributor ensures that spark plugs fire in sequence

SUSPENSION SYSTEMS

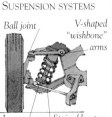

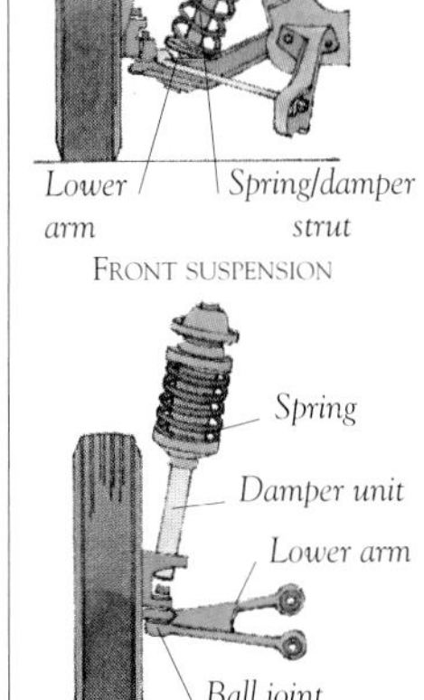
Ball joint
V-shaped "wishbone" arms
Lower arm
Spring/damper strut
FRONT SUSPENSION
Spring
Damper unit
Lower arm
Ball joint
MACPHERSON STRUT

Suspension isolates the wheels from the rest of the car, providing a smoother ride.
Front suspension uses hinged, swiveling V-shaped arms that enable the steered wheels to go up and down as well as swivel. A MacPherson Strut is a swiveling coil and damper unit that gives lighter suspension for front or rear wheels.

Types of car

Since 1901, when the Oldsmobile became the first mass-produced motor vehicle, car design has changed drastically. Today, there are many different designs to suit a wide variety of purposes, from driving to work to motor racing.

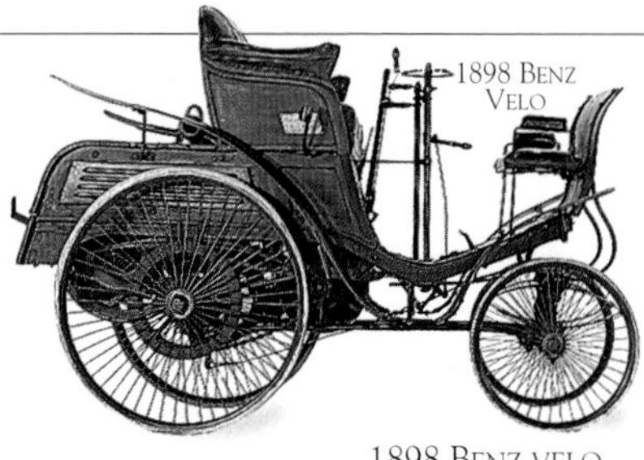
1898 BENZ VELO

1898 BENZ VELO
German engineer Karl Benz produced the first car to be sold to the public in 1885. The Benz Velo, introduced in 1894, was the first car to sell in significant numbers.

1903 DE DION BOUTON MODEL Q
Produced by the French De Dion Bouton company, the 698 cc Model Q is typical of the light, reliable cars popular in the early years of the 20th century.

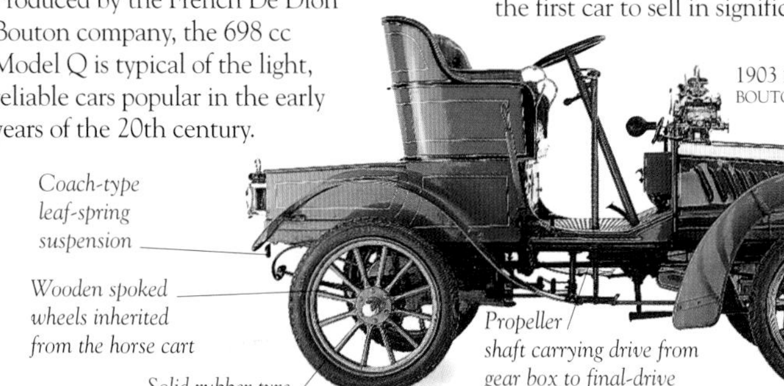
1903 DE DION BOUTON MODEL Q
Coach-type leaf-spring suspension
Wooden spoked wheels inherited from the horse cart
Solid rubber tyre
Propeller shaft carrying drive from gear box to final-drive

1909 ROLLS-ROYCE SILVER GHOST
Demand for more luxurious cars led to the manufacture of quality vehicles such as the Rolls-Royce Silver Ghost.

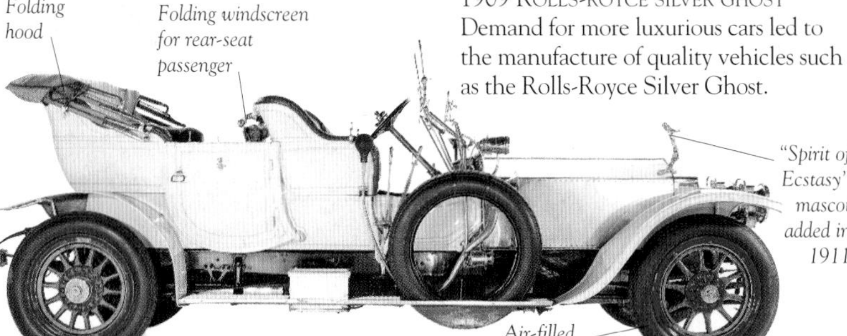
Folding hood
Folding windscreen for rear-seat passenger
"Spirit of Ecstasy" mascot added in 1911
Air-filled "pneumatic" tyres

1909 ROLLS-ROYCE SILVER GHOST

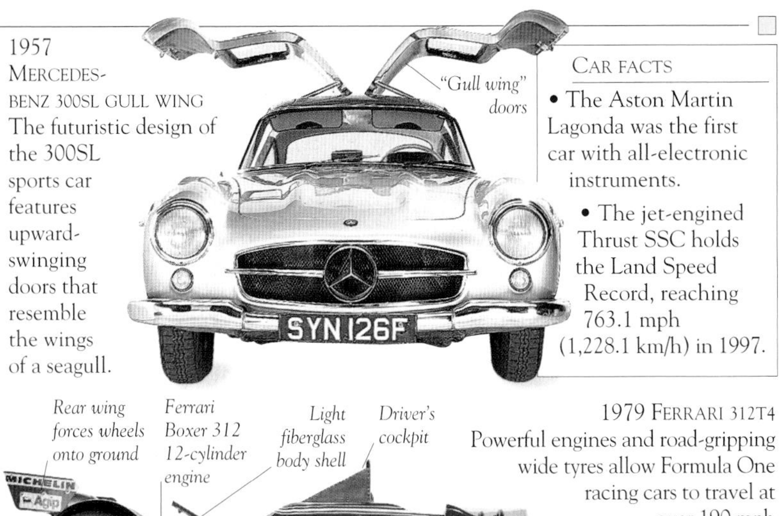
"Gull wing" doors
SYN 126F
Rear wing forces wheels onto ground
Ferrari Boxer 312 12-cylinder engine
Light fiberglass body shell
Driver's cockpit

1957 MERCEDES-BENZ 300SL GULL WING
The futuristic design of the 300SL sports car features upward-swinging doors that resemble the wings of a seagull.

CAR FACTS

- The Aston Martin Lagonda was the first car with all-electronic instruments.
- The jet-engined Thrust SSC holds the Land Speed Record, reaching 763.1 mph (1,228.1 km/h) in 1997.

1979 FERRARI 312T4
Powerful engines and road-gripping wide tyres allow Formula One racing cars to travel at over 190 mph (300 km/h).

CONTEMPORARY CARS

Modern cars are designed to cater to specific driving requirements.

COMPACT CITY CAR, SMART CAR

FOUR-WHEEL-DRIVE OFF-ROAD VEHICLE, MERCEDES M CLASS

MULTI-PURPOSE VEHICLE (MPV), FIAT MULTIPLA

FOUR-WHEEL DRIVE LUXURY SEDAN, BMW 745I

BICYCLES

APART FROM WALKING there is no simpler and cheaper way to travel than on a bicycle. Bicycles were invented in Europe little more than 200 years ago, but today they are popular worldwide for both transportation and leisure.

MODERN RACING BIKE
Air-filled tires, an efficient gearing system, and a cushioned saddle make modern bicycles more comfortable and easier to ride than their predecessors.

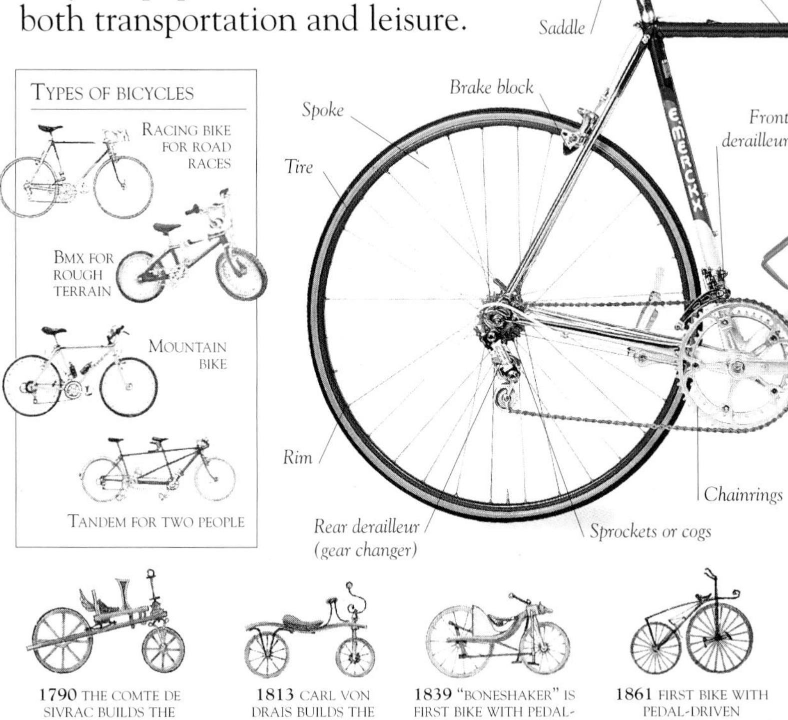
Crossbar
Saddle
Brake block
Spoke
Front derailleur
Tire
Rim
Chainrings
Rear derailleur (gear changer)
Sprockets or cogs

TYPES OF BICYCLES

RACING BIKE FOR ROAD RACES

BMX FOR ROUGH TERRAIN

MOUNTAIN BIKE

TANDEM FOR TWO PEOPLE

1790 THE COMTE DE SIVRAC BUILDS THE *CELERIFERE*

1813 CARL VON DRAIS BUILDS THE *DRAISIENNE*

1839 "BONESHAKER" IS FIRST BIKE WITH PEDAL-DRIVEN BACK WHEEL

1861 FIRST BIKE WITH PEDAL-DRIVEN FRONT WHEEL

TOUR DE FRANCE
Cycle races range from track sprints held over 1,094 yd (1,000 m) to multistage events lasting several weeks. One of the most famous road races is the 24-day Tour de France.

BICYCLE FACTS

- The longest bicycle, ridden by 40 people for 367 ft (112 m) in 1998, was 85.91 ft (25.88 m) long.
- There are 800 million bicycles in the world. They outnumber cars two to one.

Brake cable
Handlebar
Brake lever
Stem
Gearshift
Fork blade
Pedal
Hub axle or spindle
Valve

Pedal
Large cogs used for climbing uphill
Small cogs allow fast travel downhill or on flat ground
Chain

GEAR SYSTEMS
Many bicycles have gear systems that enable the cyclist to travel quickly or slowly while pedaling at a comfortable rate. By moving the gearshift, the cyclist lifts the chain from one cog to another.

C.1870 THE "PENNY FARTHING" FIRST APPEARS

1839 THE "BICYCLETTE" IS THE FIRST COMMERCIAL BICYCLE

1959 THE "MOULTON" IS FIRST NEW BIKE DESIGN FOR 50 YEARS

1990S "HPV" HUMAN-POWERED VEHICLE

MOTORCYCLES

THE SMALLEST and lightest form of motorized transportation, motorcycles range from small-engined commuter mopeds to racers that can reach speeds of more than 300 mph (500 km/h).

TYPES OF MOTORCYCLES

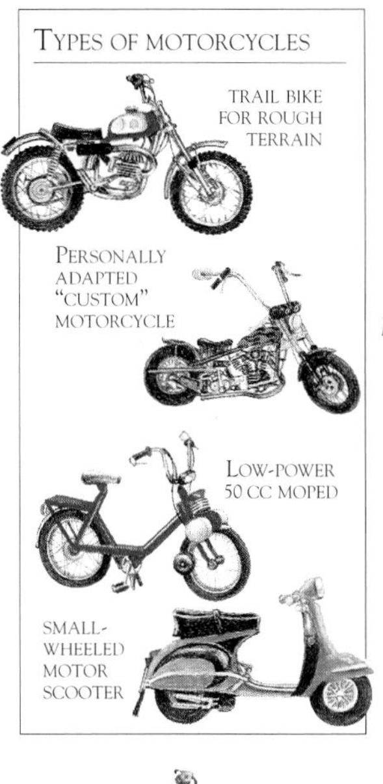

TRAIL BIKE FOR ROUGH TERRAIN

PERSONALLY ADAPTED "CUSTOM" MOTORCYCLE

LOW-POWER 50 CC MOPED

SMALL-WHEELED MOTOR SCOOTER

PARTS OF A MOTORCYCLE

A motorcycle is essentially a bicycle powered by an engine. Motorcycle engine sizes range from 50 cc (cubic capacity) to more than 1,000 cc.

FZR
GENESIS
Saddle
Exhaust
Brake disk
Drive chain
Four-cylinder 1,002 cc engine

1885 MAYBACH AND DAIMLER'S WOODEN MOTORCYCLE

1892 FIRST COMMERCIALLY PRODUCED MOTORCYCLE

1901 WERNER COMPANY PRODUCES ONE OF FIRST PRACTICAL MOTORCYCLES

1904 FIRST HARLEY-DAVIDSON MOTORCYCLE, THE *SILENT GRAY FELLOW*, PRODUCED

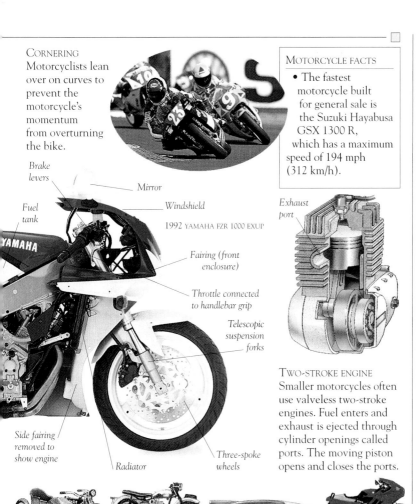

CORNERING
Motorcyclists lean over on curves to prevent the motorcycle's momentum from overturning the bike.

MOTORCYCLE FACTS

- The fastest motorcycle built for general sale is the Suzuki Hayabusa GSX 1300 R, which has a maximum speed of 194 mph (312 km/h).

Brake levers

Mirror

Fuel tank

Windshield

1992 YAMAHA FZR 1000 EXUP

Fairing (front enclosure)

Throttle connected to handlebar grip

Telescopic suspension forks

Side fairing removed to show engine

Radiator

Three-spoke wheels

Exhaust port

TWO-STROKE ENGINE
Smaller motorcycles often use valveless two-stroke engines. Fuel enters and exhaust is ejected through cylinder openings called ports. The moving piston opens and closes the ports.

1910 FIRST POPULAR MOTORCYCLE SIDECARS

1959 TRIUMPH COMPANY INTRODUCES THE HIGH PERFORMANCE *BONNEVILLE*

1978 MOTORCYCLE SPEED RECORD OF 318 MPH (512 KM/H) SET BY DONALD VESCO

1990S BMW COMPANY LAUNCHES COMPUTERIZED R1100

SHIPS AND BOATS

BOATS AND SHIPS have been used to transport people and goods across rivers, lakes, and oceans for thousands of years. From the first dugout canoes to ocean liners, boats have played a major role in world trade.

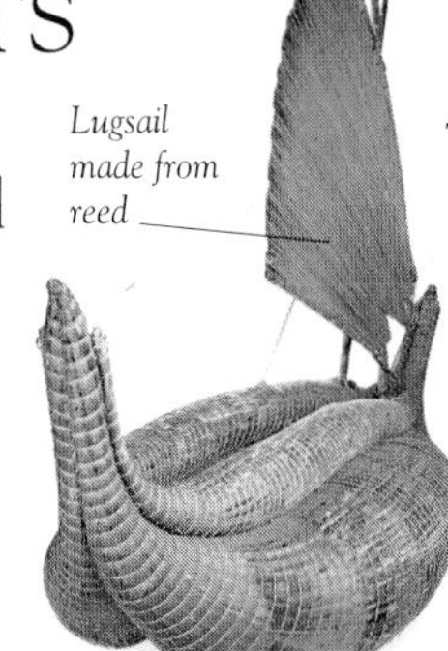
Bipod or "double" mast
Lugsail made from reed

TITICACA RAFT
The elegant rafts made by the people of Lake Titicaca in the Andes mountains are built from reeds that grow in the lake.

ALGONQUIN TRANSPORTATION
Birch bark canoes were used by the native Canadian Algonquins to traverse the St. Lawrence River, in what is now called Ontario. The boats ranged in length from 10 ft (3 m) vessels to 35 ft (10.5 m) war canoes.

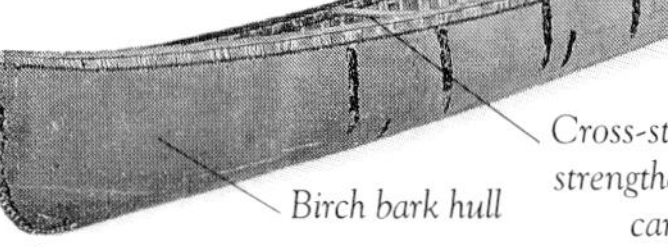
Cross-strut strengthens canoe
Birch bark hull

Yard
Mast
Battens keep sail straight
Four-sided sail

CHINESE JUNK
Traditional Chinese vessels, or "junks," have four-sided sails that hang from a yard that crosses the mast at an angle.

OCEAN LINER
From the early 1900s to the 1950s, huge, luxurious liners carried many passengers across the oceans. Cheap, fast air travel caused their popularity to decline.

Bridge
Funnels expel exhaust fumes from boiler rooms
Deck café

CUNARD LINE MAURETANIA

TACKING

A boat cannot sail straight into the wind, and so must cut a zigzag course when heading upwind. This is called tacking. Turning when the wind is behind the boat is called jibing.

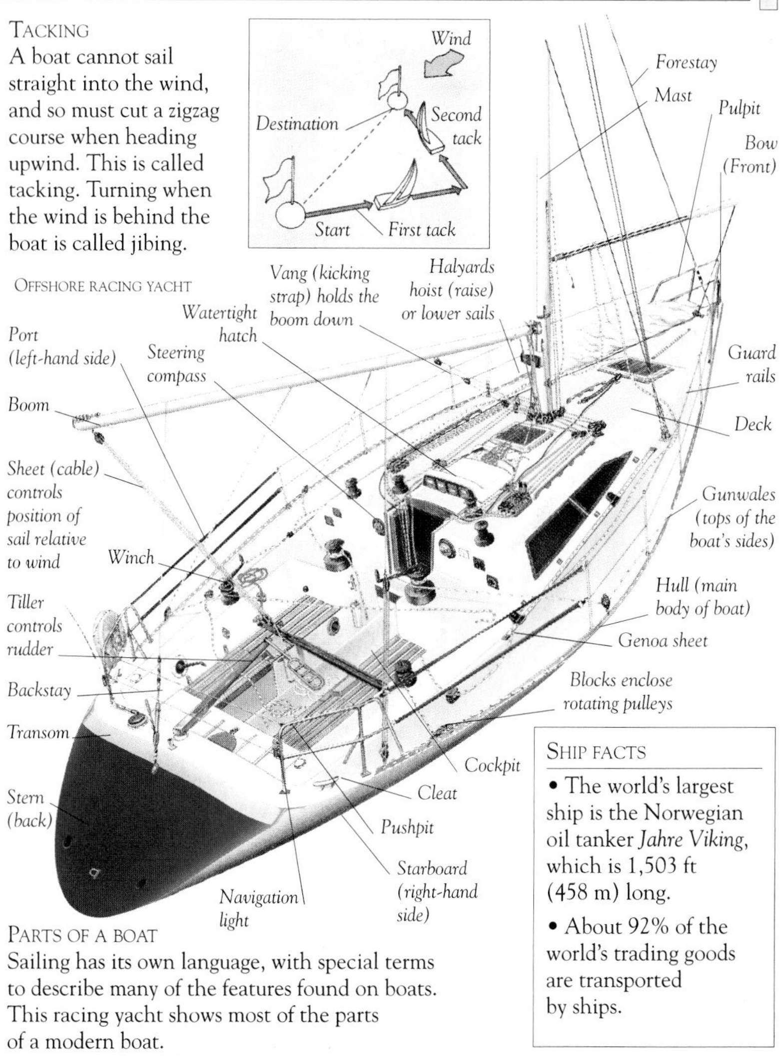

Wind
Destination
Second tack
Start
First tack
OFFSHORE RACING YACHT
Forestay
Mast
Pulpit
Bow (Front)
Vang (kicking strap) holds the boom down
Halyards hoist (raise) or lower sails
Watertight hatch
Port (left-hand side)
Steering compass
Guard rails
Deck
Boom
Sheet (cable) controls position of sail relative to wind
Gunwales (tops of the boat's sides)
Winch
Hull (main body of boat)
Tiller controls rudder
Genoa sheet
Backstay
Blocks enclose rotating pulleys
Transom
Cockpit
Cleat
Stern (back)
Pushpit
Starboard (right-hand side)
Navigation light

PARTS OF A BOAT

Sailing has its own language, with special terms to describe many of the features found on boats. This racing yacht shows most of the parts of a modern boat.

SHIP FACTS

- The world's largest ship is the Norwegian oil tanker *Jahre Viking*, which is 1,503 ft (458 m) long.
- About 92% of the world's trading goods are transported by ships.

WARSHIPS AND SUBMARINES

THERE ARE MANY types of fighting vessel, from light, speedy destroyers, to huge aircraft carriers and nuclear submarines.

1700S "MAN-OF-WAR"
By the 18th century, sailing ships had become floating fortresses. Rival northern European powers built heavily armed fighting ships called "men-of-war."

Mizzen topgallant sail
Main topgallant sail
Fore mast topgallant sail
Fore mast topsail
Fore topsail
Jib sail
Mizzen topsail
Sprit topsail
Gun ports
Main topsail

1700S 74-GUN SHIP

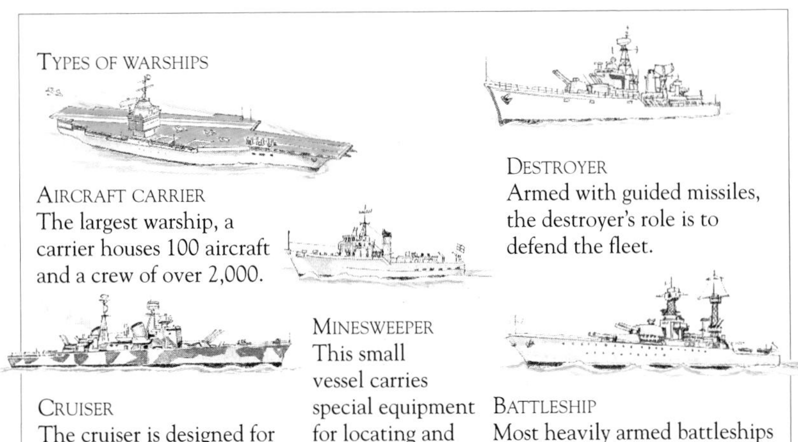

TYPES OF WARSHIPS

AIRCRAFT CARRIER
The largest warship, a carrier houses 100 aircraft and a crew of over 2,000.

DESTROYER
Armed with guided missiles, the destroyer's role is to defend the fleet.

MINESWEEPER
This small vessel carries special equipment for locating and destroying mines.

CRUISER
The cruiser is designed for speed and endurance at sea.

BATTLESHIP
Most heavily armed battleships have been replaced by carriers.

PARTS OF A WARSHIP

Modern warships are armed with guns and guided missiles for attack and defense. Most vessels are also equipped with advanced electronic equipment for tracking and hitting targets.

WARSHIP FACTS

- The first iron battleship, *Warrior*, was built in Britain in 1860.
- Russian Typhoon class submarines are the largest, measuring 558 ft (170 m) long.

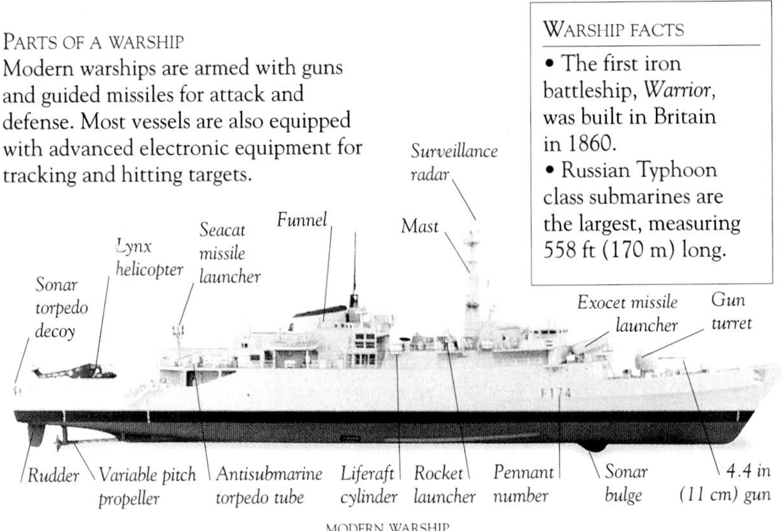
Surveillance radar
Mast
Funnel
Seacat missile launcher
Lynx helicopter
Sonar torpedo decoy
Exocet missile launcher
Gun turret
Rudder
Variable pitch propeller
Antisubmarine torpedo tube
Liferaft cylinder
Rocket launcher
Pennant number
Sonar bulge
4.4 in (11 cm) gun

MODERN WARSHIP

MILITARY SUBMARINES

There are two main types of underwater warships. Patrol submarines seek and destroy other vessels, while missile-carrying submarines are equipped with nuclear warheads aimed at enemy cities and military targets.

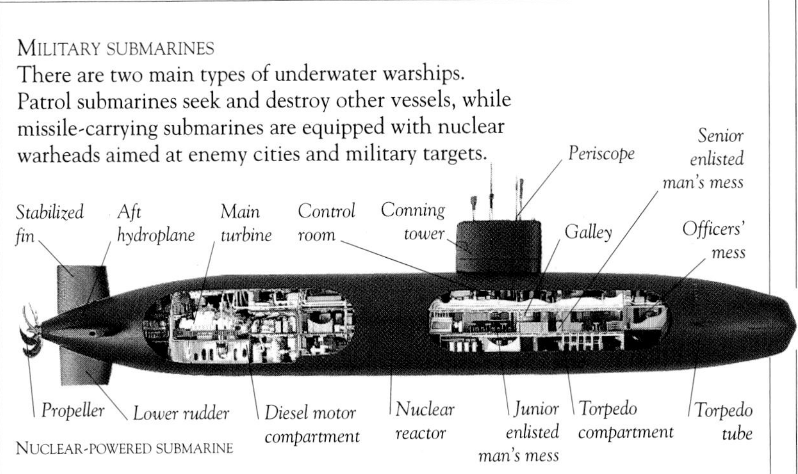
Periscope
Senior enlisted man's mess
Stabilized fin
Aft hydroplane
Main turbine
Control room
Conning tower
Galley
Officers' mess
Propeller
Lower rudder
Diesel motor compartment
Nuclear reactor
Junior enlisted man's mess
Torpedo compartment
Torpedo tube

NUCLEAR-POWERED SUBMARINE

AIRCRAFT

THE FIRST PLANE flew in only 1903, yet today millions of people fly each year. Airplanes are heavier-than-air aircraft with fixed wings, usually powered by propellers or jet turbines.

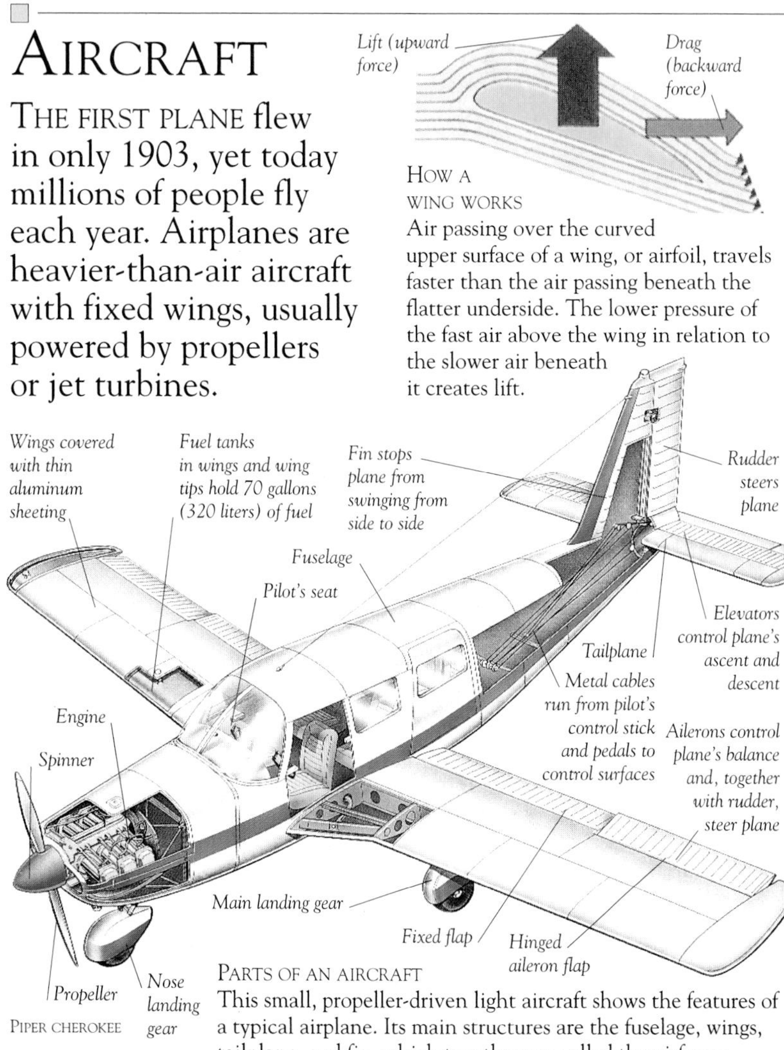

Lift (upward force)
Drag (backward force)
Wings covered with thin aluminum sheeting
Fuel tanks in wings and wing tips hold 70 gallons (320 liters) of fuel
Fin stops plane from swinging from side to side
Rudder steers plane
Fuselage
Pilot's seat
Elevators control plane's ascent and descent
Tailplane
Metal cables run from pilot's control stick and pedals to control surfaces
Engine
Spinner
Ailerons control plane's balance and, together with rudder, steer plane
Main landing gear
Fixed flap
Hinged aileron flap
Propeller
Nose landing gear

HOW A WING WORKS
Air passing over the curved upper surface of a wing, or airfoil, travels faster than the air passing beneath the flatter underside. The lower pressure of the fast air above the wing in relation to the slower air beneath it creates lift.

PIPER CHEROKEE

PARTS OF AN AIRCRAFT
This small, propeller-driven light aircraft shows the features of a typical airplane. Its main structures are the fuselage, wings, tailplane, and fin, which together are called the airframe.

Fuselage of an Airliner

The airframe of a jet airliner has to be capable of withstanding the stresses of high-speed flight and pressurization and depressurization of the passenger cabin. Airliners are built from light, strong materials such as aluminum alloys, titanium, and carbon fiber.

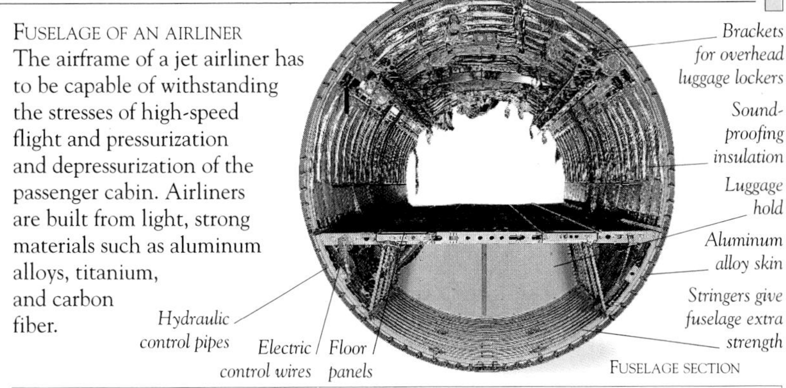
Brackets for overhead luggage lockers
Sound-proofing insulation
Luggage hold
Aluminum alloy skin
Stringers give fuselage extra strength
Hydraulic control pipes
Electric control wires
Floor panels

FUSELAGE SECTION

Controlling the Plane

The wings and tail of an airplane are equipped with hinged flaps, or control surfaces, that allow it to pitch up or down, roll from side to side, or yaw left and right. To turn, the plane is banked, rolling and yawing at the same time.

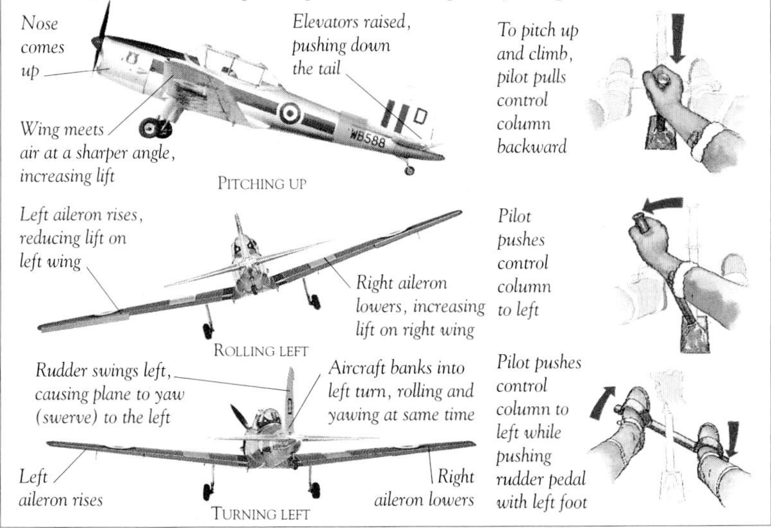
Nose comes up
Elevators raised, pushing down the tail
Wing meets air at a sharper angle, increasing lift
To pitch up and climb, pilot pulls control column backward
Left aileron rises, reducing lift on left wing
Right aileron lowers, increasing lift on right wing
Pilot pushes control column to left
Rudder swings left, causing plane to yaw (swerve) to the left
Aircraft banks into left turn, rolling and yawing at same time
Left aileron rises
Right aileron lowers
Pilot pushes control column to left while pushing rudder pedal with left foot

PITCHING UP

ROLLING LEFT

TURNING LEFT

Types of aircraft

An aircraft is essentially any machine that enables people to fly. Powered aeroplanes and helicopters, hot-air balloons, gas-filled airships, and unpowered gliders are all different types of aircraft. There are many different types of aircraft for different uses, including transport, warfare, and recreation.

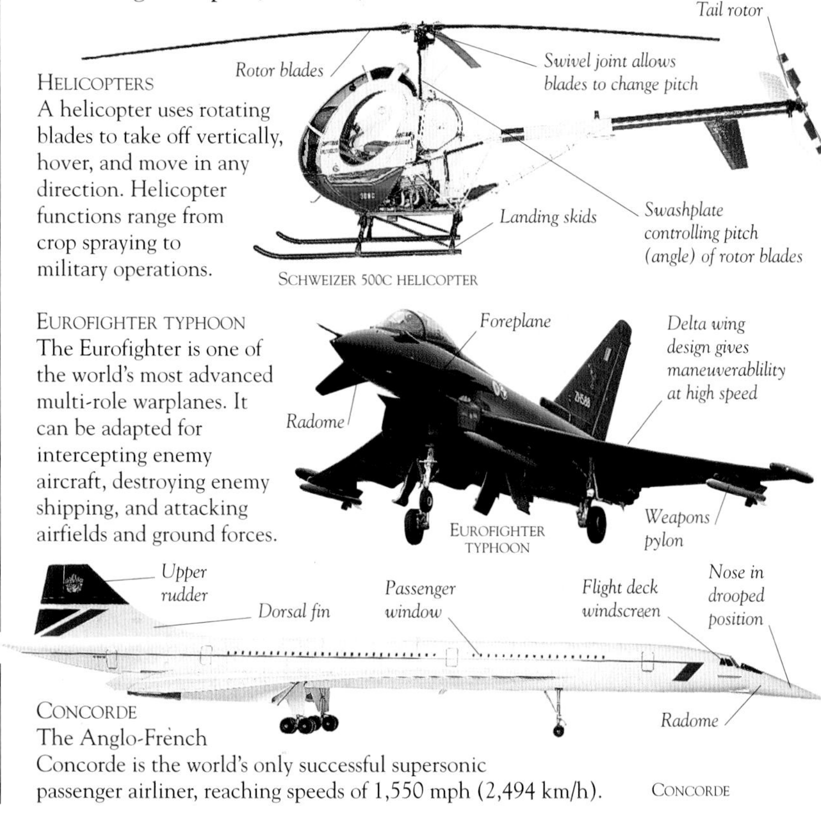
Tail rotor
Rotor blades
Swivel joint allows blades to change pitch
Landing skids
Swashplate controlling pitch (angle) of rotor blades
Foreplane
Delta wing design gives maneuverablility at high speed
Radome
Weapons pylon
Upper rudder
Dorsal fin
Passenger window
Flight deck windscreen
Nose in drooped position
Radome

SCHWEIZER 500C HELICOPTER

EUROFIGHTER TYPHOON

CONCORDE

HELICOPTERS

A helicopter uses rotating blades to take off vertically, hover, and move in any direction. Helicopter functions range from crop spraying to military operations.

EUROFIGHTER TYPHOON

The Eurofighter is one of the world's most advanced multi-role warplanes. It can be adapted for intercepting enemy aircraft, destroying enemy shipping, and attacking airfields and ground forces.

CONCORDE

The Anglo-French Concorde is the world's only successful supersonic passenger airliner, reaching speeds of 1,550 mph (2,494 km/h).

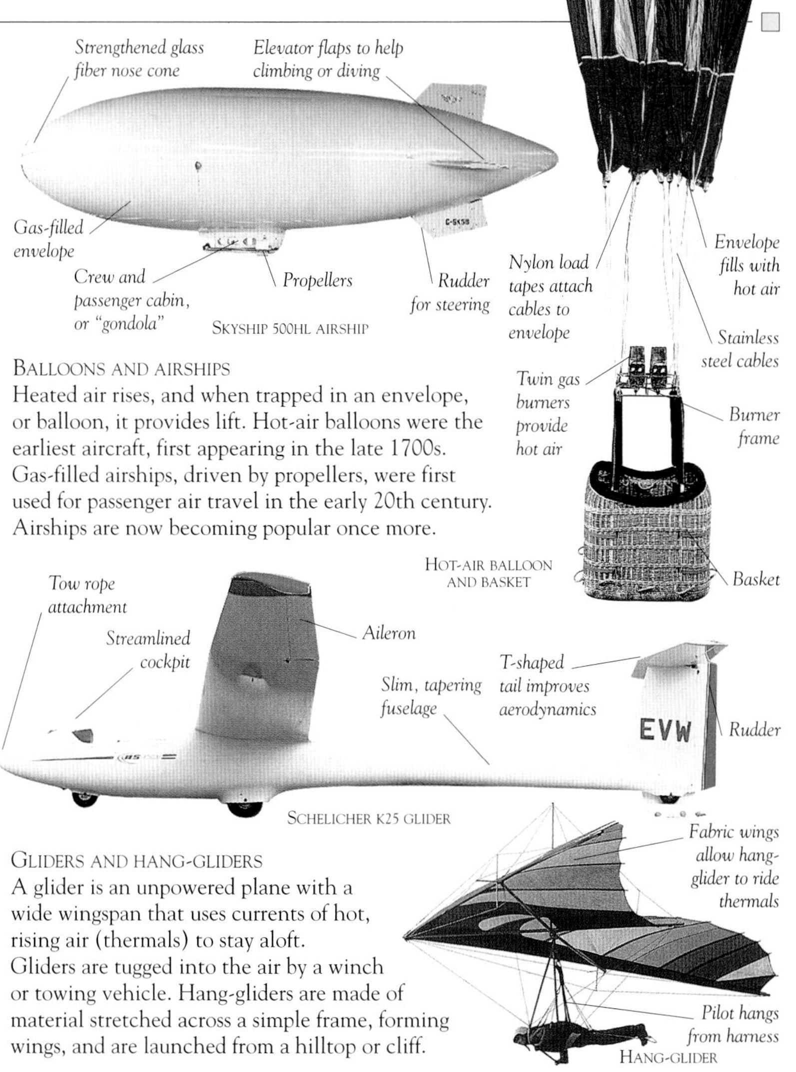
Strengthened glass fiber nose cone
Elevator flaps to help climbing or diving
Gas-filled envelope
Crew and passenger cabin, or "gondola"
Propellers
Rudder for steering
Nylon load tapes attach cables to envelope
Envelope fills with hot air
Stainless steel cables
Twin gas burners provide hot air
Burner frame
Basket
Tow rope attachment
Streamlined cockpit
Aileron
Slim, tapering fuselage
T-shaped tail improves aerodynamics
Rudder
EVW
Fabric wings allow hang-glider to ride thermals
Pilot hangs from harness

SKYSHIP 500HL AIRSHIP

HOT-AIR BALLOON AND BASKET

SCHELICHER K25 GLIDER

HANG-GLIDER

BALLOONS AND AIRSHIPS

Heated air rises, and when trapped in an envelope, or balloon, it provides lift. Hot-air balloons were the earliest aircraft, first appearing in the late 1700s. Gas-filled airships, driven by propellers, were first used for passenger air travel in the early 20th century. Airships are now becoming popular once more.

GLIDERS AND HANG-GLIDERS

A glider is an unpowered plane with a wide wingspan that uses currents of hot, rising air (thermals) to stay aloft. Gliders are tugged into the air by a winch or towing vehicle. Hang-gliders are made of material stretched across a simple frame, forming wings, and are launched from a hilltop or cliff.

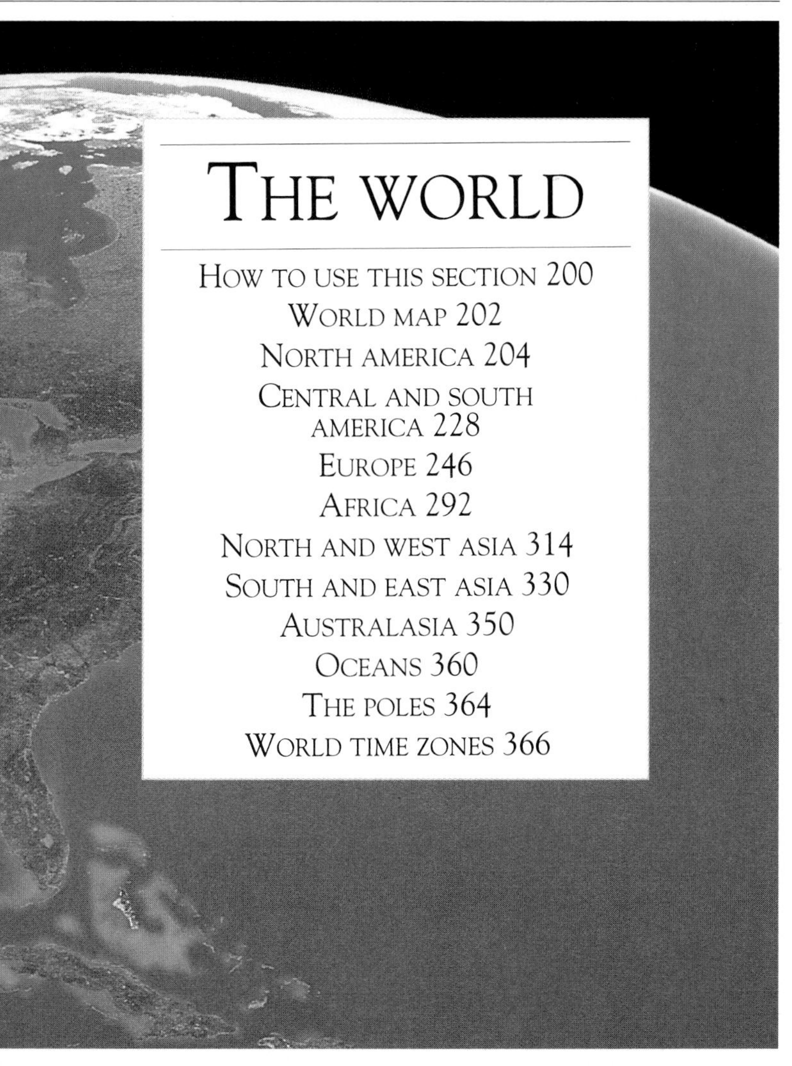

THE WORLD

How to use this section

THESE PAGES SHOW YOU how to use the World section of the encyclopedia. The maps are organized by continent: North America, Central and South America, Europe, Africa, North and West Asia, South and East Asia, and Australasia. Information-packed country fact pages separate the maps.

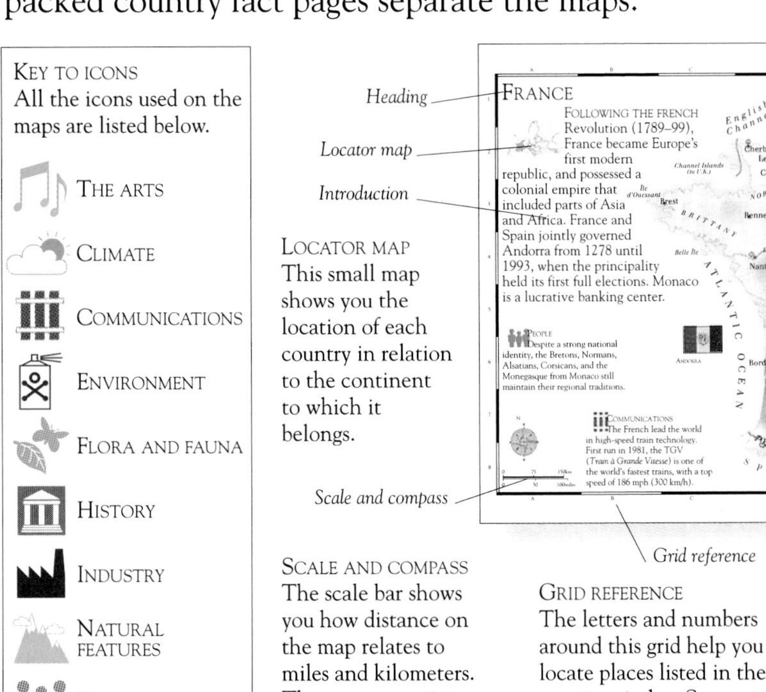
Heading
Locator map
Introduction
Scale and compass
Grid reference
FRANCE
FOLLOWING THE FRENCH Revolution (1789–99), France became Europe's first modern republic, and possessed a colonial empire that included parts of Asia and Africa. France and Spain jointly governed Andorra from 1278 until 1993, when the principality held its first full elections. Monaco is a lucrative banking center.
PEOPLE
Despite a strong national identity, the Bretons, Normans, Alsatians, Corsicans, and the Monegasque from Monaco still maintain their regional traditions.
ANDORRA
COMMUNICATIONS
The French lead the world in high-speed train technology. First run in 1981, the TGV (Train à Grande Vitesse) is one of the world's fastest trains, with a top speed of 186 mph (300 km/h).
English Channel
Channel Islands (to U.K.)
Cherbourg
Le Havre
Caen
NORMANDY
Ile d'Ouessant
Brest
BRITTANY
Rennes
Belle Ile
Nantes
Loire
ATLANTIC OCEAN
Bordeaux
PYRENEES
SPAIN

KEY TO ICONS
All the icons used on the maps are listed below.

- THE ARTS
- CLIMATE
- COMMUNICATIONS
- ENVIRONMENT
- FLORA AND FAUNA
- HISTORY
- INDUSTRY
- NATURAL FEATURES
- PEOPLE

LOCATOR MAP
This small map shows you the location of each country in relation to the continent to which it belongs.

SCALE AND COMPASS
The scale bar shows you how distance on the map relates to miles and kilometers. The compass points show you north, south, east, and west.

GRID REFERENCE
The letters and numbers around this grid help you locate places listed in the gazetteer index. See page 470 for an explanation on how to use this grid.

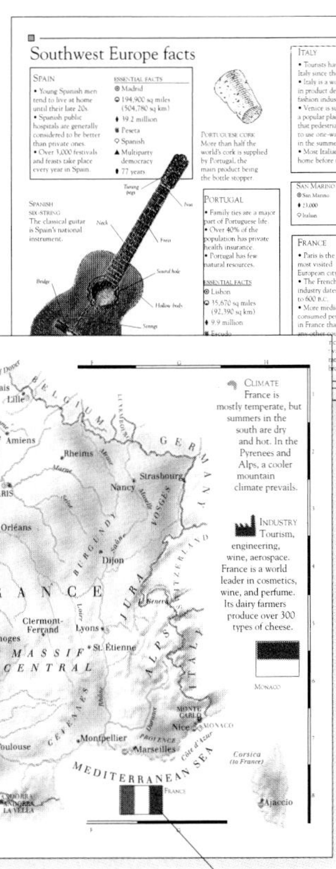

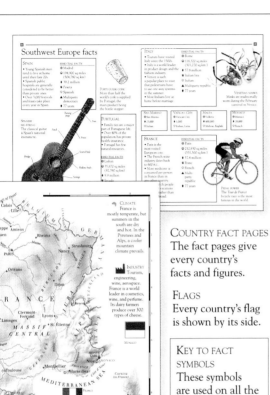

Southwest Europe facts
SPAIN
ESSENTIAL FACTS
• Young Spanish men tend to live at home until their late 20s.
• Spanish public hospitals are generally considered to be better than private ones.
• Over 3,000 festivals and feasts take place every year in Spain.
Madrid
194,900 sq miles (504,780 sq km)
39.2 million
Peseta
Spanish
Multiparty democracy
77 years
PORTUGUESE CORK
More than half the world's cork is supplied by Portugal, the main product being the bottle stopper.
SPANISH SIX-STRING
The classical guitar is Spain's national instrument.
PORTUGAL
• Family ties are a major part of Portuguese life.
• Over 40% of the population has private health insurance.
• Portugal has few natural resources.
ESSENTIAL FACTS
Lisbon
35,670 sq miles (92,390 sq km)
9.9 million
Escudo
ITALY
• Tourists have visited Italy since the 1500s.
• Italy is a world leader in product design and the fashion industry.
• Venice is such a popular place to visit that pedestrians have to use one-way systems in the summer.
• Most Italians live at home before marriage.
ESSENTIAL FACTS
Rome
116,320 sq miles (301,270 sq km)
57.8 million
Italian lira
Italian
Multiparty republic
77 years
VENETIAN MASKS
Masks are traditionally worn during the February carnival in Venice.
SAN MARINO
San Marino
25,000
Italian
VATICAN CITY
Vatican City
1,000
Italian, Latin
MALTA
Valletta
400,000
Maltese, English
MONACO
Monaco
28,000
French
FRANCE
• Paris is the most visited European city.
• The French wine industry dates back to 600 B.C.
• More medicine is consumed per person in France than in any other country.
ESSENTIAL FACTS
Paris
212,930 sq miles (551,500 sq km)
57.4 million
Franc
French
Multiparty republic
77 years
PEDAL POWER
The Tour de France bicycle race is the most famous in the world.
CLIMATE
France is mostly temperate, but summers in the south are dry and hot. In the Pyrenees and Alps, a cooler mountain climate prevails.
INDUSTRY
Tourism, engineering, wine, aerospace. France is a world leader in cosmetics, wine, and perfume. Its dairy farmers produce over 300 types of cheese.
MONACO
FRANCE
Strait of Dover
Calais
Lille
Dieppe
Amiens
Rouen
Rheims
PARIS
Nancy
Strasbourg
VOSGES
Orléans
BURGUNDY
Dijon
JURA
FRANCE
Clermont-Ferrand
Lyons
Limoges
St. Étienne
MASSIF CENTRAL
ALPS
Montpellier
Marseilles
Nice
MONTE CARLO
MONACO
Toulouse
Corsica (to France)
Ajaccio
MEDITERRANEAN SEA

Flag

COUNTRY FACT PAGES

The fact pages give every country's facts and figures.

FLAGS

Every country's flag is shown by its side.

KEY TO FACT SYMBOLS

These symbols are used on all the country fact pages.

- ⊙ CAPITAL CITY
- AREA
- POPULATION
- CURRENCY
- MAIN LANGUAGE
- ▲ GOVERNMENT
- LIFE EXPECTANCY

GAZETTEER INDEX

A gazetteer index at the back of the book lists major towns, cities, rivers, lakes, and mountain ranges that appear on the map pages.

KEY TO MAPS

INTERNATIONAL BORDER

DISPUTED BORDER

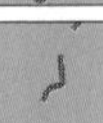

STATE BORDER

SHING' D.C.

CAPITAL CITY

LANTA

STATE OR ADMINISTRATIVE CAPITAL

arlesto

MAJOR TOWN

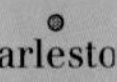

AIRPORT

SEAPORT

RIVER

CANAL

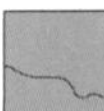

WADI

LAKE

SEASONAL LAKE

GUIDE TO MAP PAGES

EUROPE
pp. 246–289

NORTH AND
WEST ASIA
pp. 314–329

AFRICA
pp. 290–313

SOUTH AND
EAST ASIA
pp. 330–349

*INDIAN
OCEAN*
P. 362-363

AUSTRALASIA
AND OCEANIA
pp. 350–359

*ATLANTIC
OCEAN*
P. 360-361

*SOUTHERN
OCEAN*

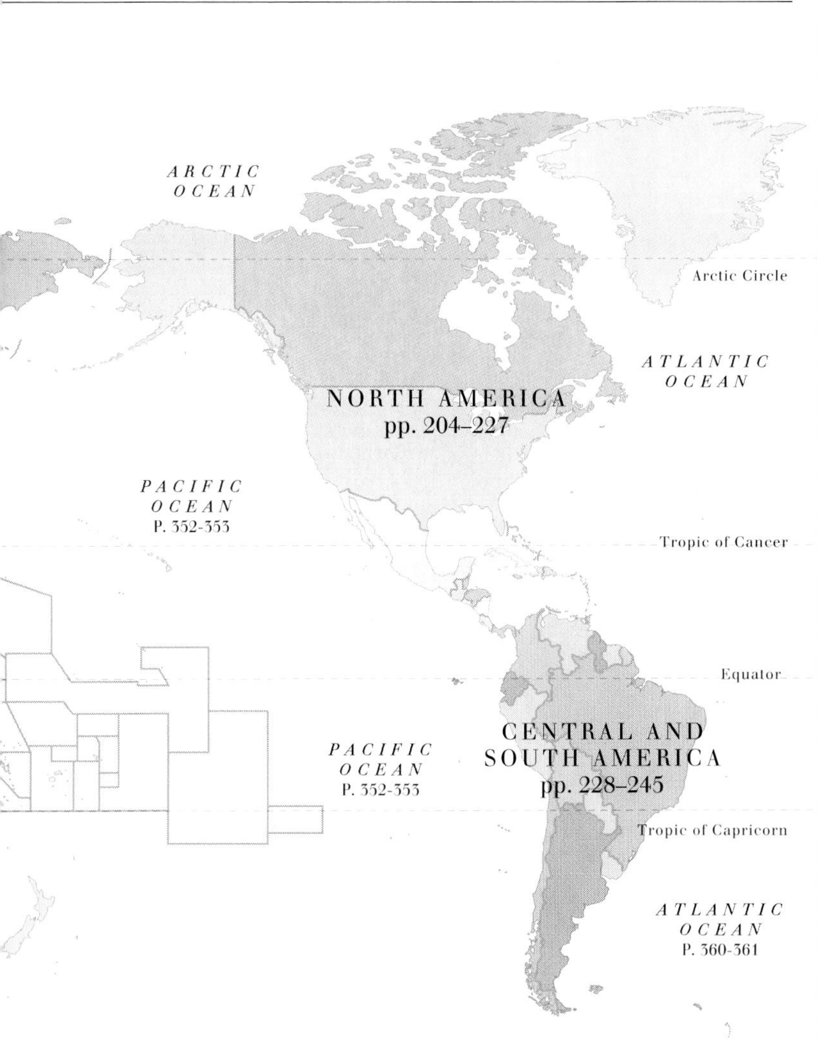
ARCTIC OCEAN
Arctic Circle
ATLANTIC OCEAN
NORTH AMERICA pp. 204–227
PACIFIC OCEAN P. 352-353
Tropic of Cancer
Equator
PACIFIC OCEAN P. 352-353
CENTRAL AND SOUTH AMERICA pp. 228–245
Tropic of Capricorn
ATLANTIC OCEAN P. 360-361

NORTH AMERICA

ARCTIC OCEAN
BEAUFORT SEA
Alaska
CANADA
GULF OF ALASKA
PACIFIC OCEAN
UNITED STATES
MEXICO
Hawaii

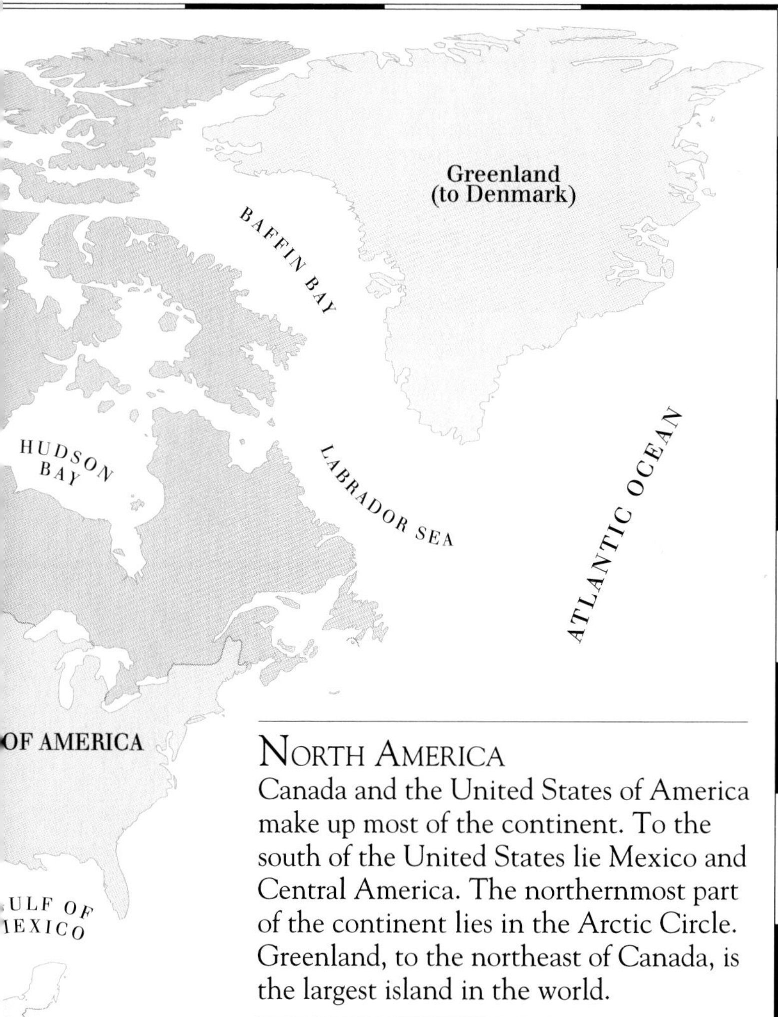
Greenland
(to Denmark)
BAFFIN BAY
HUDSON BAY
LABRADOR SEA
ATLANTIC OCEAN
OF AMERICA
ULF OF
IEXICO

North America

Canada and the United States of America make up most of the continent. To the south of the United States lie Mexico and Central America. The northernmost part of the continent lies in the Arctic Circle. Greenland, to the northeast of Canada, is the largest island in the world.

Alaska and Western Canada

At the end of the last ice age, people traveled from Asia into North America over the Bering landbridge, which connected the continents at present-day Alaska.

Alaska
634,892
English

Industry

Fishing, oil, minerals, timber. Railroads were the key to the development of farming in western Canada. The biggest oilfield in the US is at Prudhoe Bay, Alaska.

Climate

A polar climate prevails in the north; the south is warmer. The Pacific coast, near Vancouver, has the warmest winters, and temperatures rarely fall below freezing.

History

The US bought Alaska from Russia in 1867 for $7.2 million. Many Americans thought this was a waste of money until gold was discovered there in 1896 and oil in 1968.

ARCTIC OCEAN
Bering Strait
Prudhoe Bay
BROOKS RANGE
BEAUFORT
St. Lawrence I.
Aleutian Islands
Nunivak I.
St. Matthew I.
Yukon
BERING SEA
ALASKA (U.S.A.)
Porcupine
YUKON TERRITORY
Fairbanks
ALASKA RANGE
Umnak I.
Unalaska I.
Unimak I.
Bristol Bay
Dawson
Anchorage
ROCKY MOUNTAINS
Gulf of Alaska
Kodiak I.
WHITEHORSE
PACIFIC OCEAN
JUNEAU
Queen Charlotte Is.
BRITISH COLUMBIA
Vancouver I.
Vancouver
VICTORIA

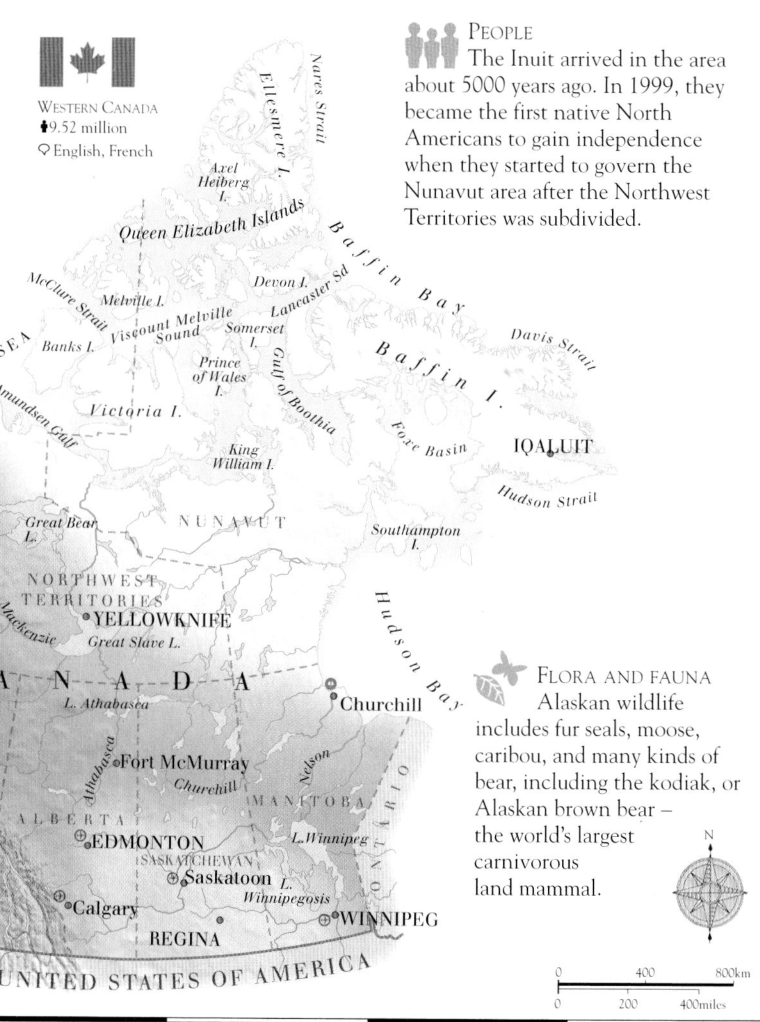
E
F
G
H
WESTERN CANADA
9.52 million
English, French
Nares Strait
Ellesmere I.
Axel Heiberg I.
Queen Elizabeth Islands
Baffin Bay
McClure Strait
Melville I.
Devon I.
Lancaster Sd
Viscount Melville Sound
Somerset I.
Davis Strait
SEA
Banks I.
Prince of Wales I.
Gulf of Boothia
Baffin I.
Amundsen Gulf
Victoria I.
Foxe Basin
IQALUIT
King William I.
Hudson Strait
Great Bear L.
NUNAVUT
Southampton I.
NORTHWEST TERRITORIES
YELLOWKNIFE
Mackenzie
Great Slave L.
Hudson Bay
CANADA
L. Athabasca
Churchill
Athabasca
Fort McMurray
Nelson
Churchill
MANITOBA
ONTARIO
ALBERTA
EDMONTON
L. Winnipeg
SASKATCHEWAN
Saskatoon
L. Winnipegosis
Calgary
WINNIPEG
REGINA
UNITED STATES OF AMERICA
N
0
400
800km
0
200
400miles
E
F
G
H
1
2
3
4
5
6
7
8

PEOPLE

The Inuit arrived in the area about 5000 years ago. In 1999, they became the first native North Americans to gain independence when they started to govern the Nunavut area after the Northwest Territories was subdivided.

FLORA AND FAUNA

Alaskan wildlife includes fur seals, moose, caribou, and many kinds of bear, including the kodiak, or Alaskan brown bear – the world's largest carnivorous land mammal.

EASTERN CANADA

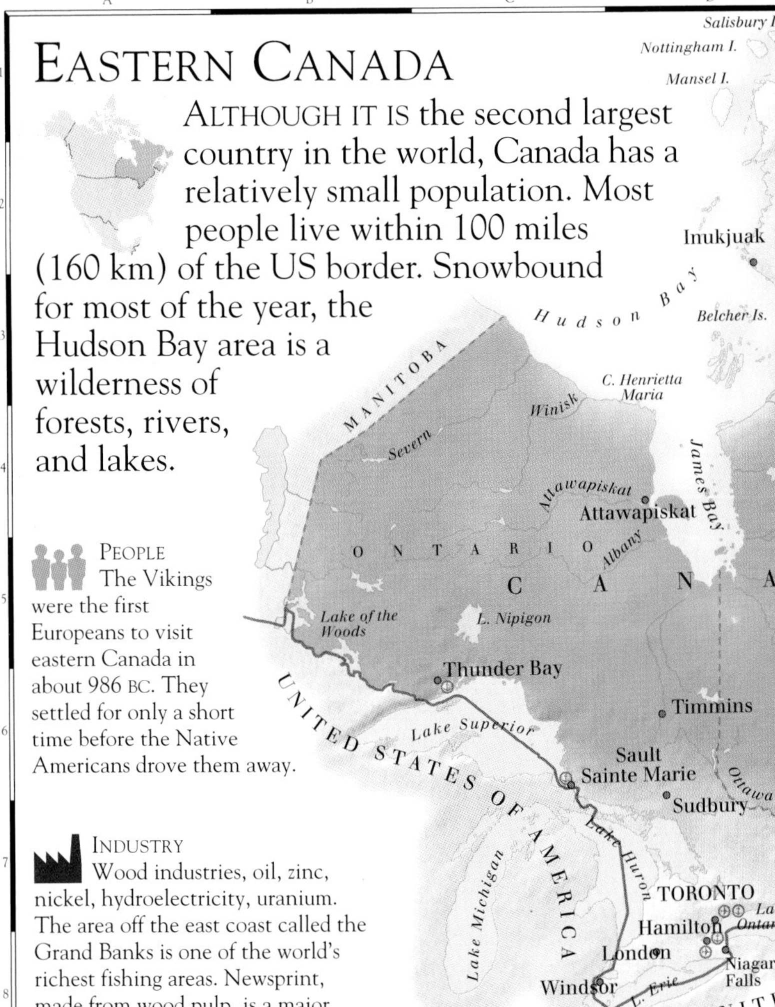
Salisbury I.
Nottingham I.
Mansel I.
Inukjuak
Hudson Bay
Belcher Is.
C. Henrietta Maria
MANITOBA
Winisk
Severn
James Bay
Attawapiskat
Attawapiskat
ONTARIO
Albany
CANADA
Lake of the Woods
L. Nipigon
Thunder Bay
Timmins
UNITED STATES OF AMERICA
Lake Superior
Sault Sainte Marie
Ottawa
Sudbury
Lake Huron
Lake Michigan
TORONTO
Lake Ontario
Hamilton
London
Niagara Falls
Windsor
L. Erie
UNITE

ALTHOUGH IT IS the second largest country in the world, Canada has a relatively small population. Most people live within 100 miles (160 km) of the US border. Snowbound for most of the year, the Hudson Bay area is a wilderness of forests, rivers, and lakes.

PEOPLE
The Vikings were the first Europeans to visit eastern Canada in about 986 BC. They settled for only a short time before the Native Americans drove them away.

INDUSTRY
Wood industries, oil, zinc, nickel, hydroelectricity, uranium. The area off the east coast called the Grand Banks is one of the world's richest fishing areas. Newsprint, made from wood pulp, is a major export from the Atlantic provinces.

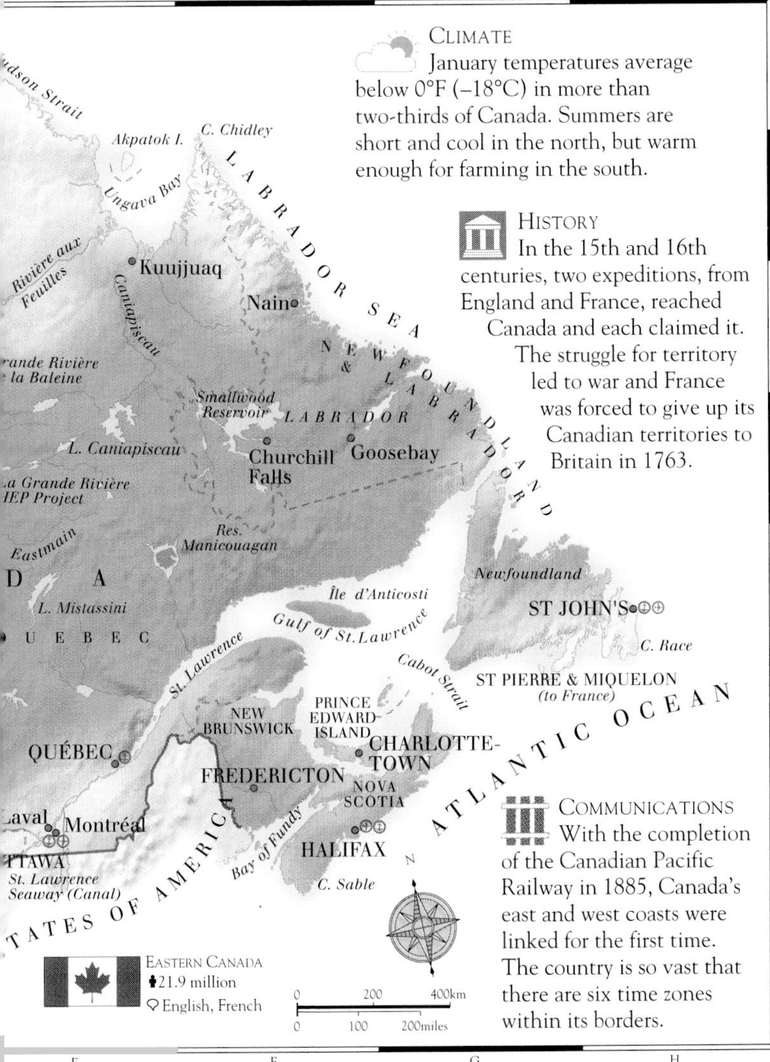
Hudson Strait
Akpatok I.
C. Chidley
Ungava Bay
LABRADOR SEA
Rivière aux Feuilles
Kuujjuaq
Caniapiscau
Nain
NEWFOUNDLAND & LABRADOR
Grande Rivière de la Baleine
Smallwood Reservoir
LABRADOR
L. Caniapiscau
Churchill Falls
Goosebay
La Grande Rivière HEP Project
Res. Manicouagan
Eastmain
L. Mistassini
QUEBEC
Newfoundland
Île d'Anticosti
Gulf of St. Lawrence
ST JOHN'S
C. Race
Cabot Strait
St. Lawrence
ST PIERRE & MIQUELON (to France)
ATLANTIC OCEAN
NEW BRUNSWICK
PRINCE EDWARD ISLAND
CHARLOTTETOWN
QUÉBEC
FREDERICTON
NOVA SCOTIA
Laval
Montréal
HALIFAX
Bay of Fundy
OTTAWA
St. Lawrence Seaway (Canal)
C. Sable
UNITED STATES OF AMERICA
N
EASTERN CANADA
21.9 million
English, French
0 200 400km
0 100 200miles

CLIMATE

January temperatures average below 0°F (–18°C) in more than two-thirds of Canada. Summers are short and cool in the north, but warm enough for farming in the south.

HISTORY

In the 15th and 16th centuries, two expeditions, from England and France, reached Canada and each claimed it. The struggle for territory led to war and France was forced to give up its Canadian territories to Britain in 1763.

COMMUNICATIONS

With the completion of the Canadian Pacific Railway in 1885, Canada's east and west coasts were linked for the first time. The country is so vast that there are six time zones within its borders.

NORTHEASTERN STATES

WITH ITS RICH MINERAL resources and safe harbors, northeast America was the first area on the continent to be colonized by Europeans. In 1620, English pilgrims sailed on the *Mayflower* to settle in a region that is still called New England. During the mid-19th century, European immigrants settled in New York and in other East Coast cities. Today, this region is the most densely populated and heavily industrialized area of the US.

CLIMATE

This area of the US has a temperate climate, with warm and humid summers. However, the northeastern region, in particular, can experience very heavy snowfall from November to April.

NORTHEASTERN STATES
54.6 million
English

PEOPLE

Northeastern Native American tribes, such as the Wampanoag, the Algonquin, and the tribes of the Iroquois League, were the first to come into contact with European settlers and explorers.

INDUSTRY

Oil, iron, steel, chemicals, maple sugar, blueberries, cranberries, fishing, tourism. Vermont is the main producer of maple syrup in the US. The stock exchange on Wall Street, New York City, is the largest in the world.

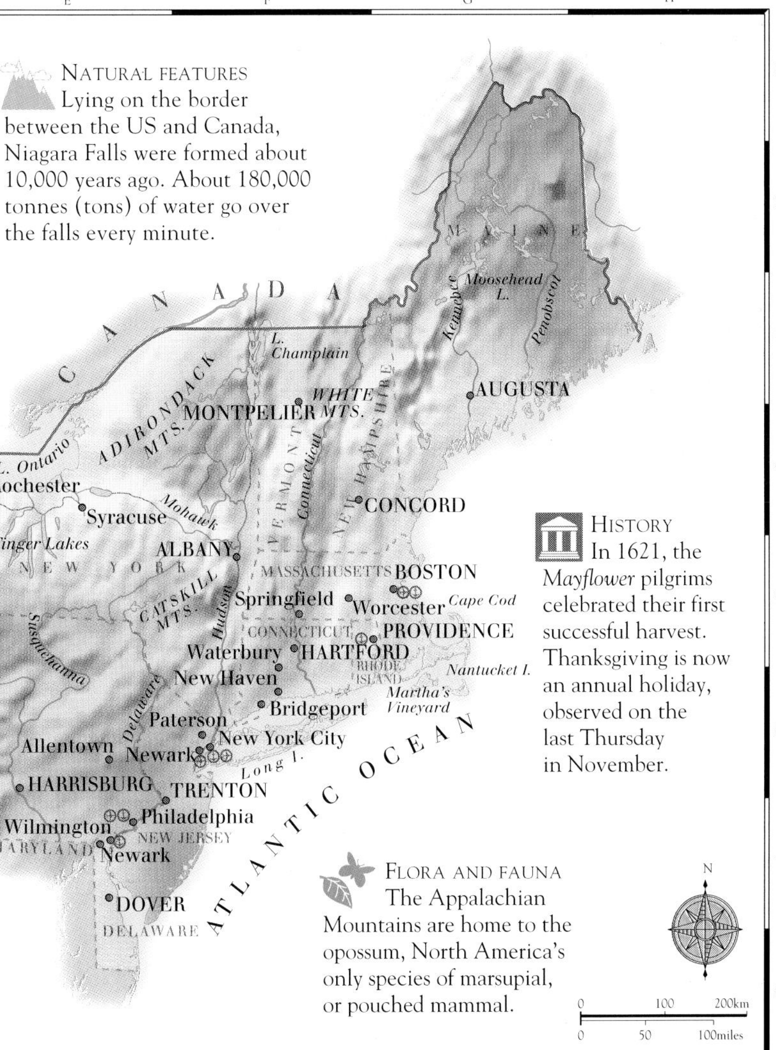
E
F
G
H
C A N A D A
MAINE
Moosehead L.
Kennebec
Penobscot
L. Champlain
AUGUSTA
WHITE MTS.
MONTPELIER
ADIRONDACK MTS.
VERMONT
Connecticut
NEW HAMPSHIRE
L. Ontario
Rochester
Syracuse
Mohawk
CONCORD
Finger Lakes
ALBANY
NEW YORK
MASSACHUSETTS
BOSTON
CATSKILL MTS.
Hudson
Springfield
Worcester
Cape Cod
Susquehanna
CONNECTICUT
PROVIDENCE
Waterbury
HARTFORD
RHODE ISLAND
Nantucket I.
New Haven
Martha's Vineyard
Delaware
Bridgeport
Paterson
New York City
Allentown
Newark
Long I.
ATLANTIC OCEAN
HARRISBURG
TRENTON
Philadelphia
Wilmington
NEW JERSEY
MARYLAND
Newark
DOVER
DELAWARE
N
0
100
200km
0
50
100miles
1
2
3
4
5
6
7
8

Natural features

Lying on the border between the US and Canada, Niagara Falls were formed about 10,000 years ago. About 180,000 tonnes (tons) of water go over the falls every minute.

History

In 1621, the *Mayflower* pilgrims celebrated their first successful harvest. Thanksgiving is now an annual holiday, observed on the last Thursday in November.

Flora and fauna

The Appalachian Mountains are home to the opossum, North America's only species of marsupial, or pouched mammal.

SOUTHERN STATES

BY THE 19TH CENTURY, the wealth of the South was based on crops like tobacco, indigo, rice, and especially cotton, which was grown on large plantations by African slaves. The area is known today for New Orleans' jazz, Florida's Disney World, and the Kentucky Derby. The city of Washington, in the District of Columbia, was made the US capital in 1800.

MISSOURI
OKLAHOMA
BOSTON MTS.
LITTLE ROCK
Memphis
ARKANSAS
Arkansas
Ouachita
Mississippi
Yazoo
Shreveport
Red R.
TEXAS
MISSISSIPPI
JACKSON
Tombigbe
LOUISIANA
Mississippi
BATON ROUGE
L. Pontchartrain
Mobile
New Orleans
Mississippi Delta

CLIMATE

Summers are long and hot; winters are mild, but temperatures are generally warmer on the coast than inland. Southern Florida is tropical.

INDUSTRY

Soybeans, coal, groundnuts, cotton, citrus fruits, tobacco, oil, tourism. Georgia grows half of the groundnuts in the US – most are used to make peanut butter.

THE ARTS

The French brought Mardi Gras to America in the early 1700s. Celebrated in many of the southern states, the most famous festival is held in New Orleans. Here parades last for a week before Mardi Gras Day, the day before Lent starts.

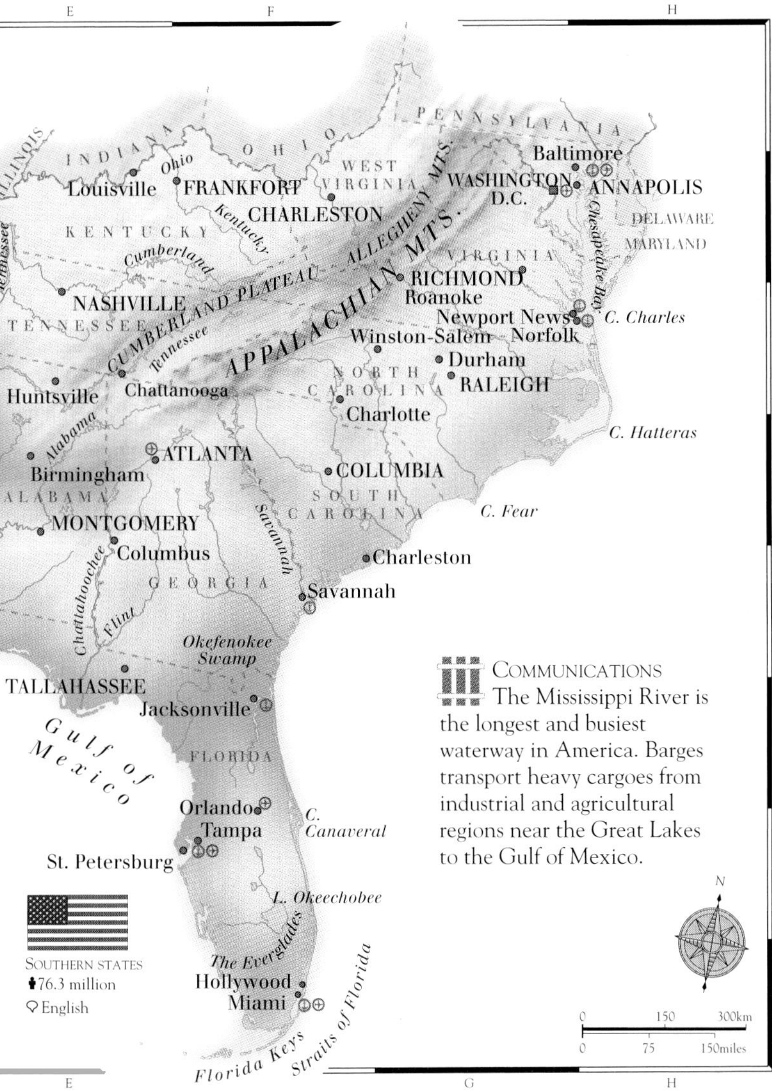
E
F
H
1
2
3
4
5
6
7
8
PENNSYLVANIA
ILLINOIS
INDIANA
OHIO
Ohio
WEST VIRGINIA
Baltimore
WASHINGTON D.C.
ANNAPOLIS
Louisville
FRANKFORT
CHARLESTON
Kentucky
KENTUCKY
DELAWARE
MARYLAND
Chesapeake Bay
Tennessee
Cumberland
ALLEGHENY MTS.
VIRGINIA
RICHMOND
Roanoke
NASHVILLE
CUMBERLAND PLATEAU
APPALACHIAN MTS.
Newport News
C. Charles
TENNESSEE
Tennessee
Winston-Salem
Norfolk
Durham
NORTH CAROLINA
RALEIGH
Huntsville
Chattanooga
Charlotte
Alabama
C. Hatteras
ATLANTA
Birmingham
COLUMBIA
ALABAMA
SOUTH CAROLINA
Savannah
C. Fear
MONTGOMERY
Columbus
Charleston
Chattahoochee
GEORGIA
Savannah
Flint
Okefenokee Swamp
TALLAHASSEE
Jacksonville
Gulf of Mexico
FLORIDA
Orlando
C. Canaveral
Tampa
St. Petersburg
L. Okeechobee
The Everglades
Hollywood
Miami
Straits of Florida
Florida Keys
N
0 150 300km
0 75 150miles
G

COMMUNICATIONS
The Mississippi River is the longest and busiest waterway in America. Barges transport heavy cargoes from industrial and agricultural regions near the Great Lakes to the Gulf of Mexico.

SOUTHERN STATES
76.3 million
English

GREAT LAKES

THE STATES OF Indiana, Illinois, Michigan, Ohio, Wisconsin, and Minnesota, which all border on one or more of the five Great Lakes, are often called the industrial and agricultural heartland of the United States. The region is rich in natural resources, with large areas of fertile farmland on flat plains called prairies.

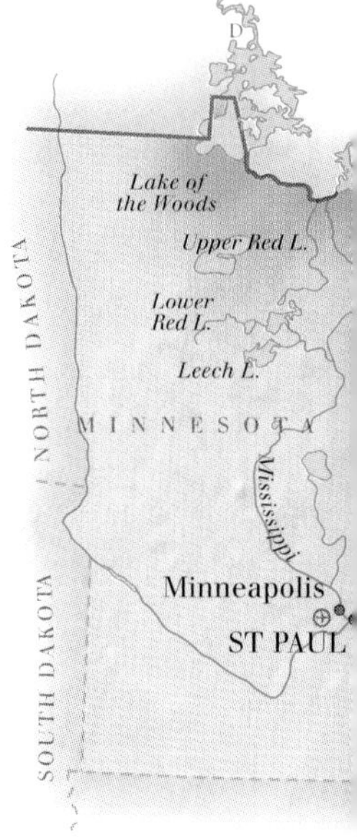
Lake of the Woods
Upper Red L.
Lower Red L.
Leech L.
NORTH DAKOTA
MINNESOTA
Mississippi
Minneapolis
ST PAUL
SOUTH DAKOTA

CLIMATE

The region around the Great Lakes has warm summers but quite severe winters, and parts of the lakes can freeze over. Minnesota, in particular, suffers from heavy snowstorms.

GREAT LAKES STATES
50.3 million
English

ENVIRONMENT

The Great Lakes – Ontario, Huron, Superior, Michigan, and Erie – together form the largest area of freshwater in the world. Heavy industry has caused severe water pollution, and in some areas it is dangerous to eat the fish or swim.

INDUSTRY

Vehicles, coal, iron, grain, corn, cherries.
Nearly half of the world's corn crop and a third of the cherry crop are grown in the Great Lakes region. Detroit is known as "motor city" because it is the center of the US auto industry.

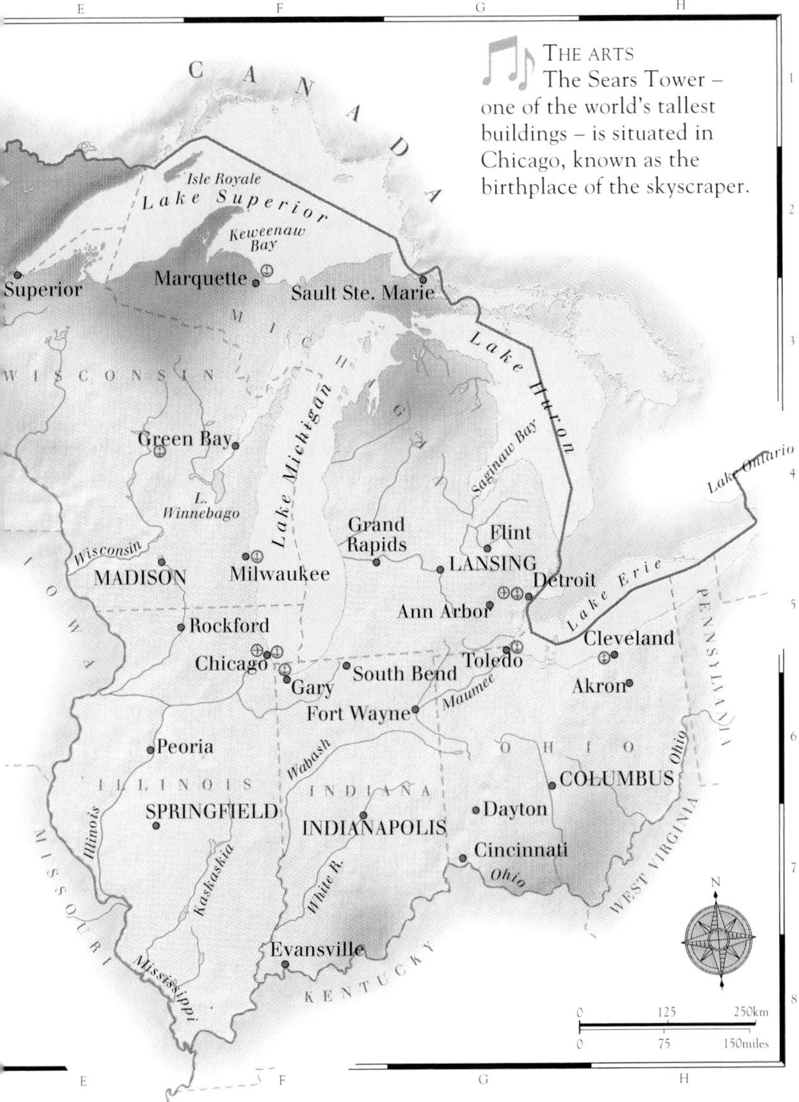

E
F
G
H
1
2
3
4
5
6
7
8
CANADA
Isle Royale
Lake Superior
Keweenaw Bay
Superior
Marquette
Sault Ste. Marie
MICHIGAN
Lake Huron
WISCONSIN
Lake Michigan
Saginaw Bay
Green Bay
L. Winnebago
Lake Ontario
Grand Rapids
Flint
Wisconsin
Milwaukee
LANSING
MADISON
Detroit
Lake Erie
IOWA
Ann Arbor
PENNSYLVANIA
Rockford
Cleveland
Chicago
Toledo
South Bend
Gary
Akron
Maumee
Fort Wayne
Peoria
OHIO
Wabash
Ohio
ILLINOIS
INDIANA
COLUMBUS
SPRINGFIELD
Dayton
INDIANAPOLIS
Illinois
MISSOURI
Cincinnati
Kaskaskia
White R.
Ohio
WEST VIRGINIA
N
Mississippi
Evansville
KENTUCKY
0
125
250km
0
75
150miles

THE ARTS
The Sears Tower – one of the world's tallest buildings – is situated in Chicago, known as the birthplace of the skyscraper.

Central and Mountain States

The great Plains, the Rocky Mountains, and the Mississippi lowlands dominate the landscape of the Midwest. Once home to Native Americans and herds of bison, the Great Plains were settled in the 19th century by Europeans, who forced the Native Americans onto reservations and slaughtered the bison to near extinction.

History

Pioneers traveling to the West had to cross the Great Plains, which were known as the "Great American Desert". The last area to be settled, it is now a wealthy agricultural region.

CENTRAL AND
MOUNTAIN STATES
20.5 million
English

Climate

West of the Rockies, the summers are cooler and the winters are warmer. States on the Great Plains have an extreme climate, which can change quite suddenly and violently – blizzards, hail, thunderstorms, and tornadoes may occur.

Natural features

The Rocky Mountains extend through Canada and the US for more than 3000 miles (4800 km). They divide North America and separate the rivers flowing west to the Pacific from those flowing east to the Atlantic.

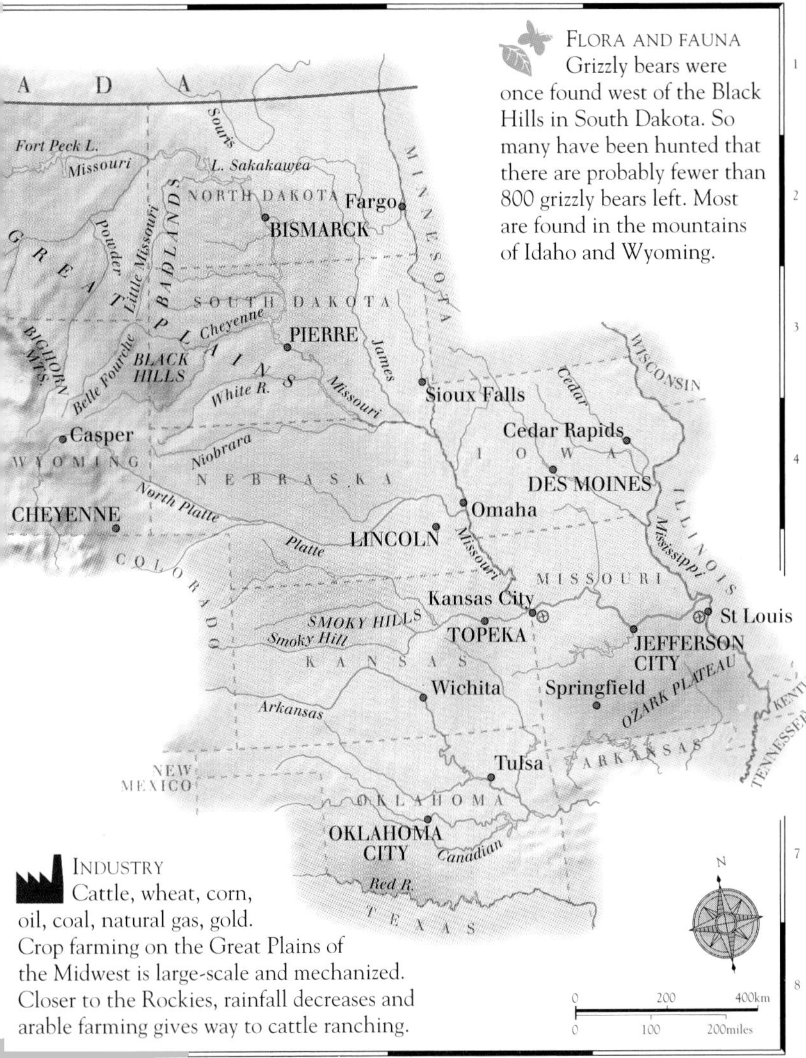
E
F
G
H
1
2
3
4
7
8
A D A
Fort Peck L.
Missouri
Souris
L. Sakakawea
NORTH DAKOTA
Fargo
BISMARCK
MINNESOTA
GREAT PLAINS
Powder
Little Missouri
BADLANDS
SOUTH DAKOTA
BIGHORN MTS.
Belle Fourche
BLACK HILLS
Cheyenne
PIERRE
James
White R.
Missouri
Sioux Falls
Casper
WYOMING
Niobrara
NEBRASKA
North Platte
CHEYENNE
Platte
LINCOLN
Omaha
Missouri
COLORADO
Cedar
WISCONSIN
Cedar Rapids
IOWA
DES MOINES
ILLINOIS
Mississippi
MISSOURI
Kansas City
St Louis
SMOKY HILLS
Smoky Hill
TOPEKA
JEFFERSON CITY
KANSAS
Wichita
Springfield
OZARK PLATEAU
KENTUCKY
Arkansas
TENNESSEE
Tulsa
ARKANSAS
NEW MEXICO
OKLAHOMA
OKLAHOMA CITY
Canadian
Red R.
TEXAS
N
0
200
400km
0
100
200miles

FLORA AND FAUNA
Grizzly bears were once found west of the Black Hills in South Dakota. So many have been hunted that there are probably fewer than 800 grizzly bears left. Most are found in the mountains of Idaho and Wyoming.

INDUSTRY
Cattle, wheat, corn, oil, coal, natural gas, gold. Crop farming on the Great Plains of the Midwest is large-scale and mechanized. Closer to the Rockies, rainfall decreases and arable farming gives way to cattle ranching.

SOUTHWESTERN STATES

THE FIRST Europeans in the Southwest were the Spanish, who traveled north from Mexico. This resulted in a mingling of Spanish and Native American cultures in the region. Gold and silver mining and cattle-ranching attracted other settlers in the late 19th century, when this area became part of the US after the Mexican War.

OREGON
IDAHO
BLACK ROCK DESERT
GREAT BASIN
Great Salt L.
Pyramid L.
Humboldt
GREAT SALT LAKE DESERT
Reno
SALT LAKE CITY
L. Tahoe
CARSON CITY
NEVADA
UT
Sevier L.
CALIFORNIA
Bryce Canyon
Las Vegas
L. Mead
Grand Canyon
COLORADO PLATEAU
ARIZONA
Colorado
PHOENIX
SONORAN DESERT
Mesa
Tucson

NATURAL FEATURES

The Colorado plateau has some unusual landforms, including natural bridges and arches of solid rock. Over the past million years, the Colorado River has cut away the plateau, forming the world's largest river gorge – the Grand Canyon.

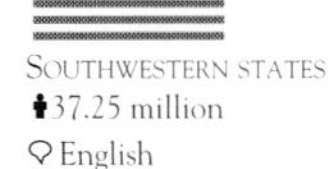

SOUTHWESTERN STATES
37.25 million
English

HISTORY

At the end of the Mexican War (1846–48), the US acquired Utah, Nevada, California, and parts of Arizona, New Mexico, Colorado, and Wyoming. One of the causes of the war was a border dispute between Texas and Mexico.

PEOPLE

Some of the earliest Native Americans lived in the Nevada area. Bones and ashes discovered near Las Vegas indicate that people may have lived there more than 20,000 years ago. Today, the region has the largest concentration of Native Americans in the country.

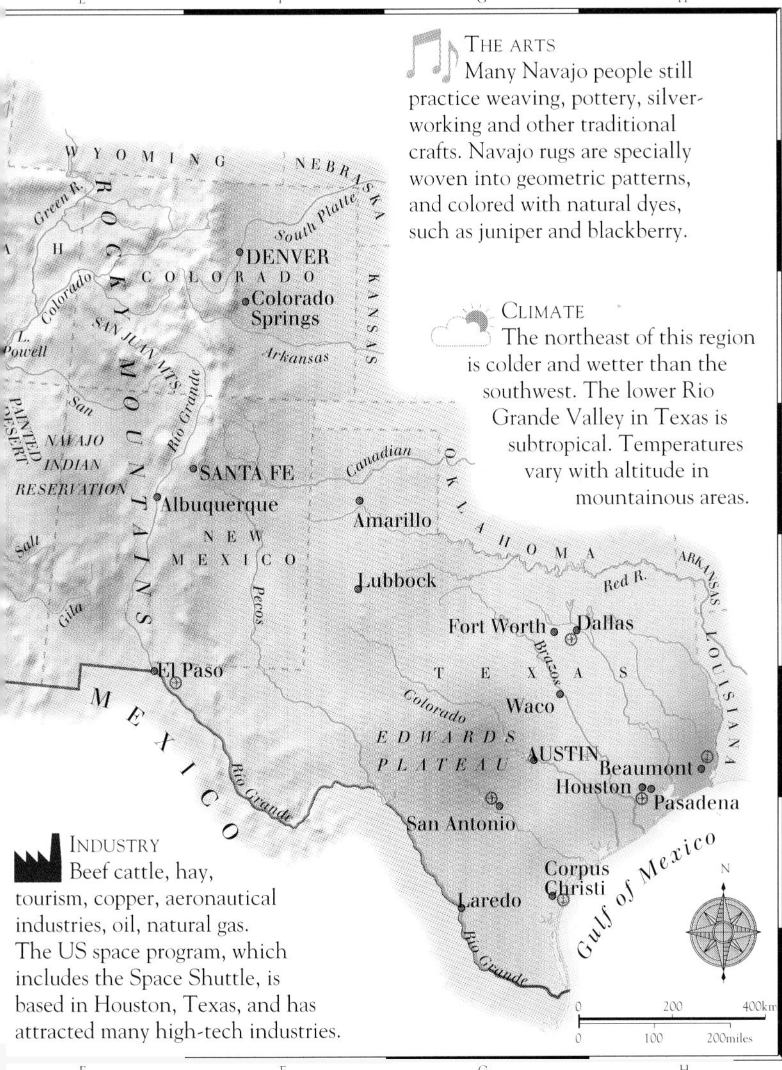
E
F
G
H
1
2
3
4
5
6
7
8
WYOMING
NEBRASKA
Green R.
South Platte
DENVER
COLORADO
Colorado
Colorado Springs
KANSAS
SAN JUAN MTS.
ROCKY MOUNTAINS
L. Powell
Arkansas
Rio Grande
San
PAINTED DESERT
NAVAJO INDIAN RESERVATION
SANTA FE
Albuquerque
Canadian
Amarillo
OKLAHOMA
NEW MEXICO
Salt
Pecos
Lubbock
Red R.
ARKANSAS
Gila
Fort Worth
Dallas
LOUISIANA
Brazos
El Paso
TEXAS
MEXICO
Colorado
Waco
EDWARDS PLATEAU
AUSTIN
Beaumont
Houston
Pasadena
Rio Grande
San Antonio
Gulf of Mexico
N
Corpus Christi
Laredo
Rio Grande
0
200
400km
0
100
200miles

THE ARTS

Many Navajo people still practice weaving, pottery, silver-working and other traditional crafts. Navajo rugs are specially woven into geometric patterns, and colored with natural dyes, such as juniper and blackberry.

CLIMATE

The northeast of this region is colder and wetter than the southwest. The lower Rio Grande Valley in Texas is subtropical. Temperatures vary with altitude in mountainous areas.

INDUSTRY

Beef cattle, hay, tourism, copper, aeronautical industries, oil, natural gas. The US space program, which includes the Space Shuttle, is based in Houston, Texas, and has attracted many high-tech industries.

Pacific States

All three states on the West Coast are major agricultural producers – Washington and Oregon supply one-third of the softwood timber in the US, and California produces half of the country's fruits and vegetables. Situated where two of the Earth's plates meet, the area suffers from earthquakes and volcanic activity. Mount St. Helens, dormant since 1857, erupted in 1980, losing 1300 ft (400 m) off its height.

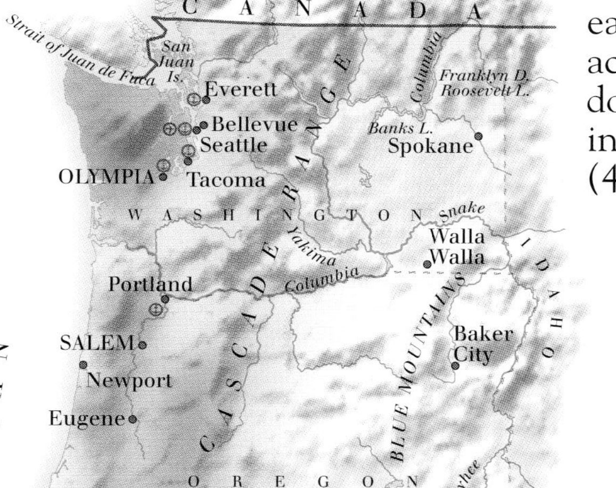

CANADA
Strait of Juan de Fuca
San Juan Is.
Everett
Bellevue
Seattle
OLYMPIA
Tacoma
Columbia
Franklyn D. Roosevelt L.
Banks L.
Spokane
WASHINGTON
Snake
Walla Walla
Yakima
Columbia
CASCADE RANGE
Portland
SALEM
Newport
Eugene
BLUE MOUNTAINS
Baker City
IDAHO
OREGON
Owyhee
OCEAN

Natural features
The lowest point in the western hemisphere is in Death Valley, 282 ft (86 m) below sea level. One of the driest, hottest places on Earth, the highest temperature, 135°F (57°C), was recorded there in 1913, and its average rainfall is only 1.5 in (38 mm) per year.

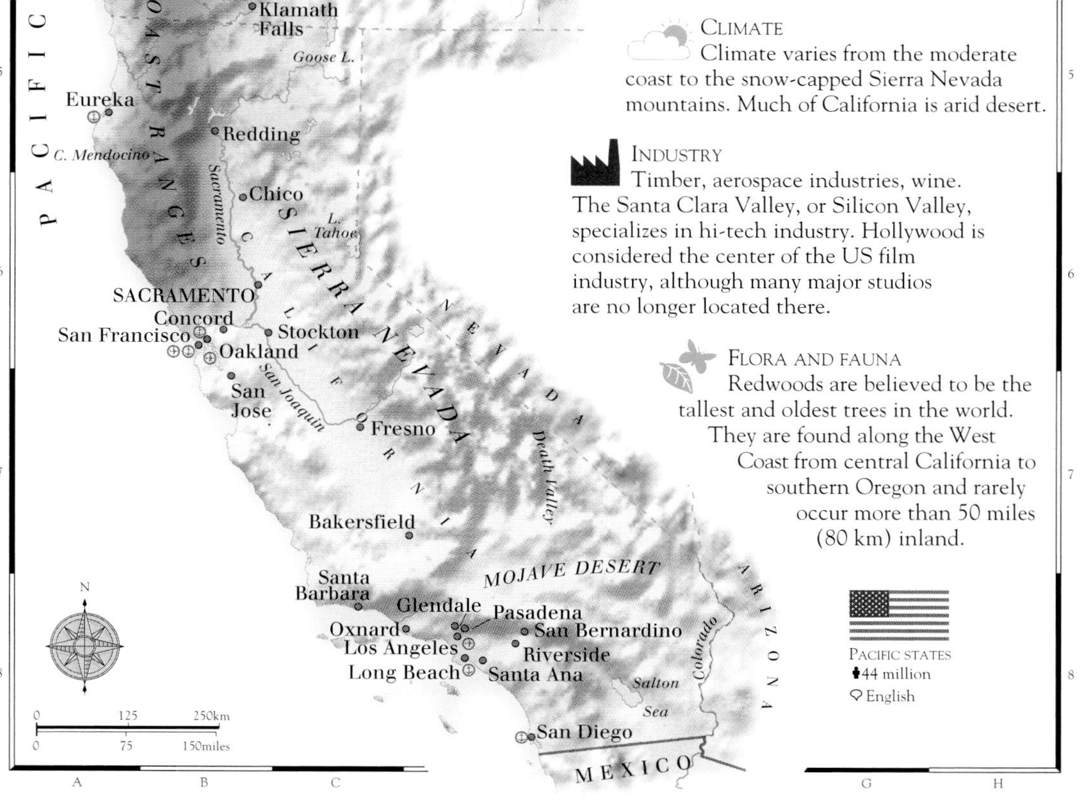
PACIFIC
COAST RANGES
Klamath Falls
Goose L.
Eureka
Redding
C. Mendocino
Sacramento
Chico
L. Tahoe
SIERRA NEVADA
CALIFORNIA
NEVADA
SACRAMENTO
Concord
San Francisco
Stockton
Oakland
San Jose
San Joaquin
Fresno
Death Valley
Bakersfield
MOJAVE DESERT
Santa Barbara
Glendale
Pasadena
Oxnard
San Bernardino
Los Angeles
Riverside
Long Beach
Santa Ana
Salton Sea
Colorado
ARIZONA
San Diego
MEXICO
N
0 125 250km
0 75 150miles
A
B
C
G
H
5
6
7
8

CLIMATE

Climate varies from the moderate coast to the snow-capped Sierra Nevada mountains. Much of California is arid desert.

INDUSTRY

Timber, aerospace industries, wine. The Santa Clara Valley, or Silicon Valley, specializes in hi-tech industry. Hollywood is considered the center of the US film industry, although many major studios are no longer located there.

FLORA AND FAUNA

Redwoods are believed to be the tallest and oldest trees in the world. They are found along the West Coast from central California to southern Oregon and rarely occur more than 50 miles (80 km) inland.

PACIFIC STATES
44 million
English

MEXICO

THE ANCIENT empires of the Maya and Aztec flourished for centuries before the Spanish invaded Mexico in 1519, lured there by legends of hoards of gold and silver. Mexico gained its independence in 1810, after 300 years of Spanish rule. Today, most Mexicans are *mestizo*, a mix of Spanish and Native American. Although Spanish is the official language, Native American languages such as Maya, Nahuatl, and Zapotec are also widely spoken.

UNITED STATES
Tijuana
Mexicali
Nogales
SIERRA MADRE
BAJA CALIFORNIA
Ángel de la Guarda I.
Hermosillo
Cedros I.
Tiburón I.
Gulf of California
Culiacán
La Paz

CLIMATE
The Mexican plateau and mountains are warm for most of the year. The Pacific coast has a tropical climate.

MEXICO

FLORA AND FAUNA
The Mexican beaded lizard and the gila monster are the only two poisonous lizards known. The largest of all cacti is the giant saguaro, which grows in the Sonora Desert to a height of more than 60 ft (18 m).

NATURAL FEATURES
The plateau of Mexico is enclosed to the west and east by the Sierra Madre mountain ranges, which occupy 75 percent of the total land area. Mexico is so mountainous and arid in parts that only 12 percent of the land is arable.

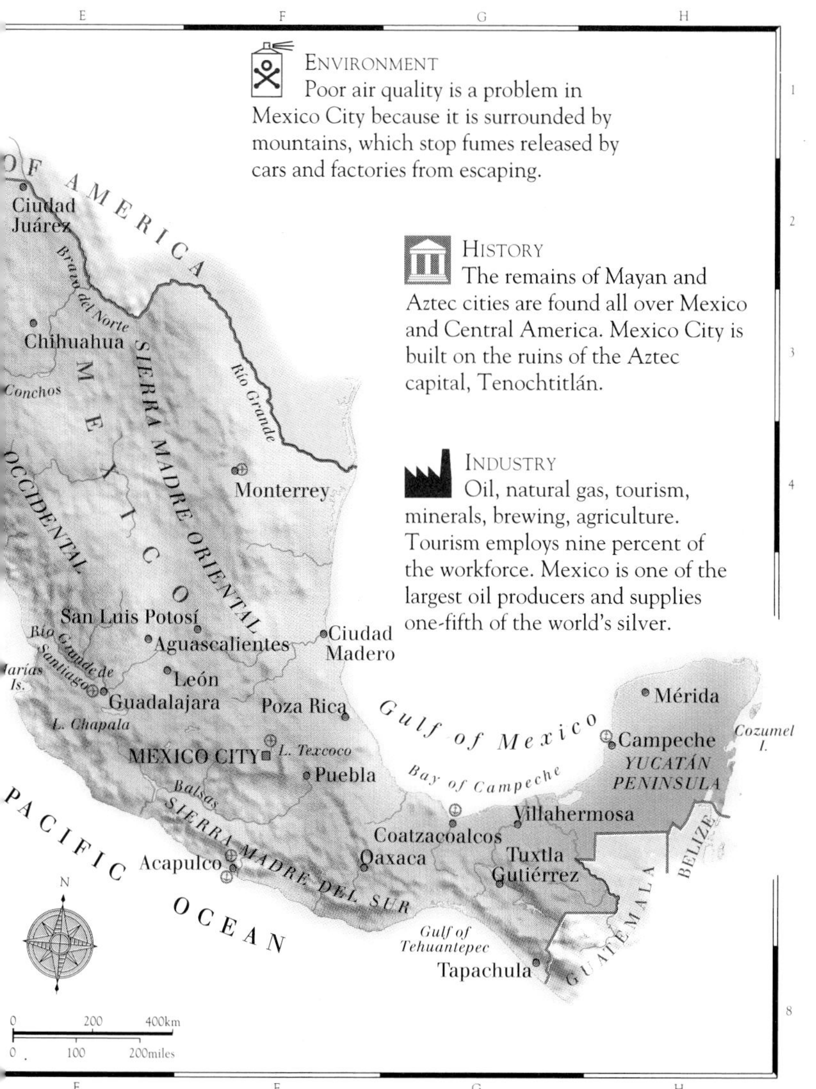
E
F
G
H
1
2
3
4
8
OF AMERICA
Ciudad Juárez
Bravo del Norte
Chihuahua
Conchos
MEXICO
SIERRA MADRE OCCIDENTAL
SIERRA MADRE ORIENTAL
Río Grande
Monterrey
San Luis Potosí
Aguascalientes
Ciudad Madero
Río Grande de Santiago
Marías Is.
León
Guadalajara
L. Chapala
Poza Rica
MEXICO CITY
L. Texcoco
Puebla
Balsas
SIERRA MADRE DEL SUR
Acapulco
PACIFIC OCEAN
N
Gulf of Mexico
Bay of Campeche
Mérida
Campeche
Cozumel I.
YUCATÁN PENINSULA
Villahermosa
Coatzacoalcos
Oaxaca
Tuxtla Gutiérrez
BELIZE
GUATEMALA
Gulf of Tehuantepec
Tapachula
0
200
400km
0
100
200miles

Environment

Poor air quality is a problem in Mexico City because it is surrounded by mountains, which stop fumes released by cars and factories from escaping.

History

The remains of Mayan and Aztec cities are found all over Mexico and Central America. Mexico City is built on the ruins of the Aztec capital, Tenochtitlán.

Industry

Oil, natural gas, tourism, minerals, brewing, agriculture. Tourism employs nine percent of the workforce. Mexico is one of the largest oil producers and supplies one-fifth of the world's silver.

North America facts

United States of America

- The US economy is the largest in the world.
- The nation is made up of 50 states plus the District of Columbia.
- The world's leading computer software is produced in the US.

ESSENTIAL FACTS

- ⊙ Washington, DC
- 3,717,792 sq miles (9,629,091 sq km)
- 284.8 million
- US dollar
- English
- ▲ Presidential democracy
- 77 years

WISE OLD BIRD
The national symbol of the US is the bald eagle.

WYOMING LANDSCAPE
The varied US scenery ranges from arid desert in Arizona through to mountainous lakeland in Wyoming.

Southwestern states

Arizona	Nevada	Texas
⊙ Phoenix	⊙ Carson City	⊙ Austin
5.3 million	2.1 million	21.3 million

Colorado	New Mexico	Utah
⊙ Denver	⊙ Santa Fe	⊙ Salt Lake City
4.4 million	1.8 million	2.3 million

COWBOYS
Cattle-ranching is still big business in Texas today.

Northeastern states

Connecticut
⊙ Hartford
🚹 3.4 million

Delaware
⊙ Dover
🚹 800,000

Maine
⊙ Augusta
🚹 1.3 million

Massachusetts
⊙ Boston
🚹 6.4 million

New Hampshire
⊙ Concord
🚹 1.3 million

New Jersey
⊙ Trenton
🚹 8.5 million

New York
⊙ Albany
🚹 19 million

Pennsylvania
⊙ Harrisburg
🚹 12.3 million

Rhode Island
⊙ Providence
🚹 1 million

Vermont
⊙ Montpelier
🚹 613,090

Pacific states

California
⊙ Sacramento
🚹 34.5 million

Oregon
⊙ Salem
🚹 3.5 million

Washington
⊙ Olympia
🚹 6 million

Baseball is the national sport of the US

THE STATUE OF LIBERTY New York's famous statue was given to the US by France in 1884.

Outlying states

Alaska
⊙ Juneau
🚹 634,892

Hawaii
⊙ Honolulu
🚹 1.2 million

North American moose

Great Lakes

Illinois
⊙ Springfield
🚹 12.5 million

Indiana
⊙ Indianapolis
🚹 6.1 million

Michigan
⊙ Lansing
🚹 10 milllion

Minnesota
⊙ St. Paul
🚹 5 million

Ohio
⊙ Columbus
🚹 11.4 million

Wisconsin
⊙ Madison
🚹 5.4 million

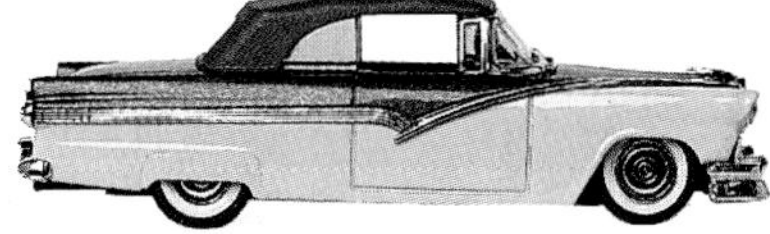

Detroit, Michigan, is the center of the US motor industry

Central and mountain states

Idaho
⊙ Boise
🚹 1.3 million

Iowa
⊙ Des Moines
🚹 2.9 million

Kansas
⊙ Topeka
🚹 2.7 million

Missouri
⊙ Jefferson City
🚹 5.6 million

Montana
⊙ Helena
🚹 900,000

Nebraska
⊙ Lincoln
🚹 1.7 million

North Dakota
⊙ Bismarck
🚹 640,000

Oklahoma
⊙ Oklahoma City
🚹 3.5 million

South Dakota
⊙ Pierre
🚹 760,000

Wyoming
⊙ Cheyenne
🚹 490,000

popcorn
POP CORN
pop
Popcorn is roasted, puffed-up maize

POPCORN
Corn products are an export of the midwestern states.

Southern states

Alabama
⊙ Montgomery
🚹 4.5 million

Arkansas
⊙ Little Rock
🚹 2.7 million

Florida
⊙ Tallahassee
🚹 16.4 million

Georgia
⊙ Atlanta
🚹 8.4 million

Kentucky
⊙ Frankfort
🚹 4 million

Louisiana
⊙ Baton Rouge
🚹 4.5 million

Maryland
⊙ Annapolis
🚹 5.4 million

Mississippi
⊙ Jackson
🚹 2.9 million

North Carolina
⊙ Raleigh
🚹 8.1 million

Tennessee
⊙ Nashville
🚹 5.7 million

South Carolina
⊙ Columbia
🚹 4 million

Virginia
⊙ Richmond
🚹 7.2 million

West Virginia
⊙ Charleston
🚹 1.8 million

Peanut butter
Peanut

GEORGIA GROWS NEARLY HALF THE TOTAL PEANUT CROP OF THE USA

CANADA

- The CN Tower in Toronto is the tallest free-standing structure in the world.
- French-speaking Québec's claim for independence from the rest of the country is a key constitutional issue.
- Forests and lakes cover 40% of Canada.

ESSENTIAL FACTS

⊙ Ottawa

3,851,788 sq miles (9,976,140 sq km)

31.4 million

Canadian dollar

English, French

▲ Presidential democracy

79 years

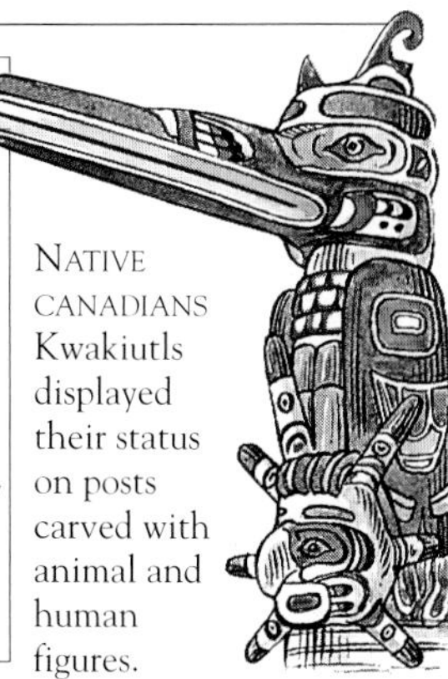

NATIVE CANADIANS Kwakiutls displayed their status on posts carved with animal and human figures.

SPOOKY FESTIVAL Celebrating skeletons are seen everywhere during Mexico's Day of the Dead.

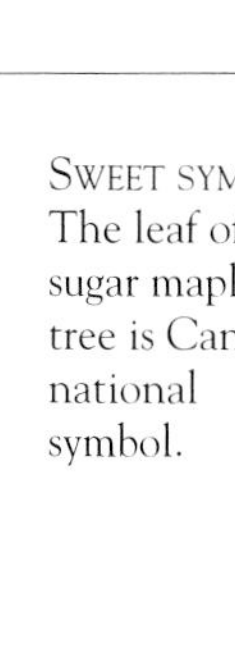

SWEET SYMBOL The leaf of the sugar maple tree is Canada's national symbol.

MEXICO

- The Mexican landscape ranges from snow-capped mountains to tropical rain forests.
- Mexico City is the world's largest city.
- More people emigrate from Mexico than any other country in the world.

ESSENTIAL FACTS

⊙ Mexico City

761,602 sq miles (1,972,550 sq km)

100.4 million

Mexican peso

Spanish

▲ Presidential democracy

73 years

CENTRAL AND SOUTH AMERICA

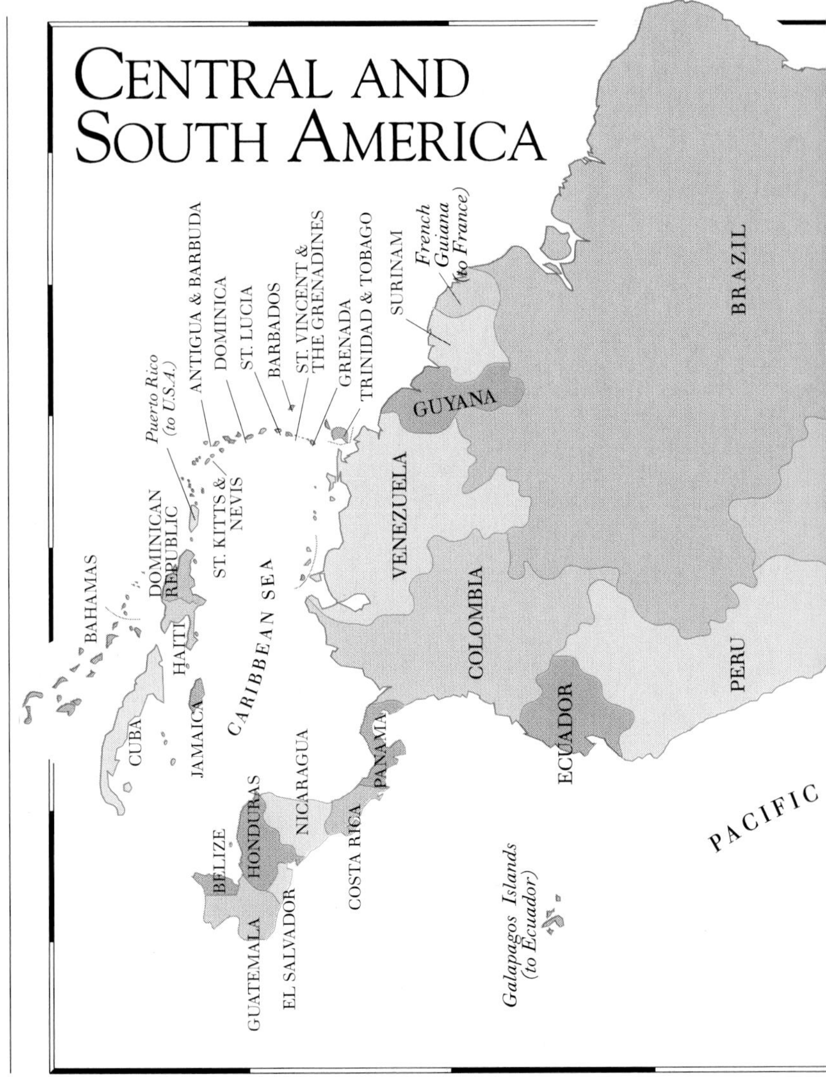
ANTIGUA & BARBUDA
DOMINICA
ST. LUCIA
BARBADOS
ST. VINCENT & THE GRENADINES
GRENADA
TRINIDAD & TOBAGO
SURINAM
French Guiana (to France)
BRAZIL
Puerto Rico (to U.S.A.)
GUYANA
ST. KITTS & NEVIS
DOMINICAN REPUBLIC
VENEZUELA
BAHAMAS
CARIBBEAN SEA
COLOMBIA
HAITI
PERU
CUBA
JAMAICA
ECUADOR
NICARAGUA
PANAMA
HONDURAS
PACIFIC
BELIZE
COSTA RICA
Galapagos Islands (to Ecuador)
GUATEMALA
EL SALVADOR

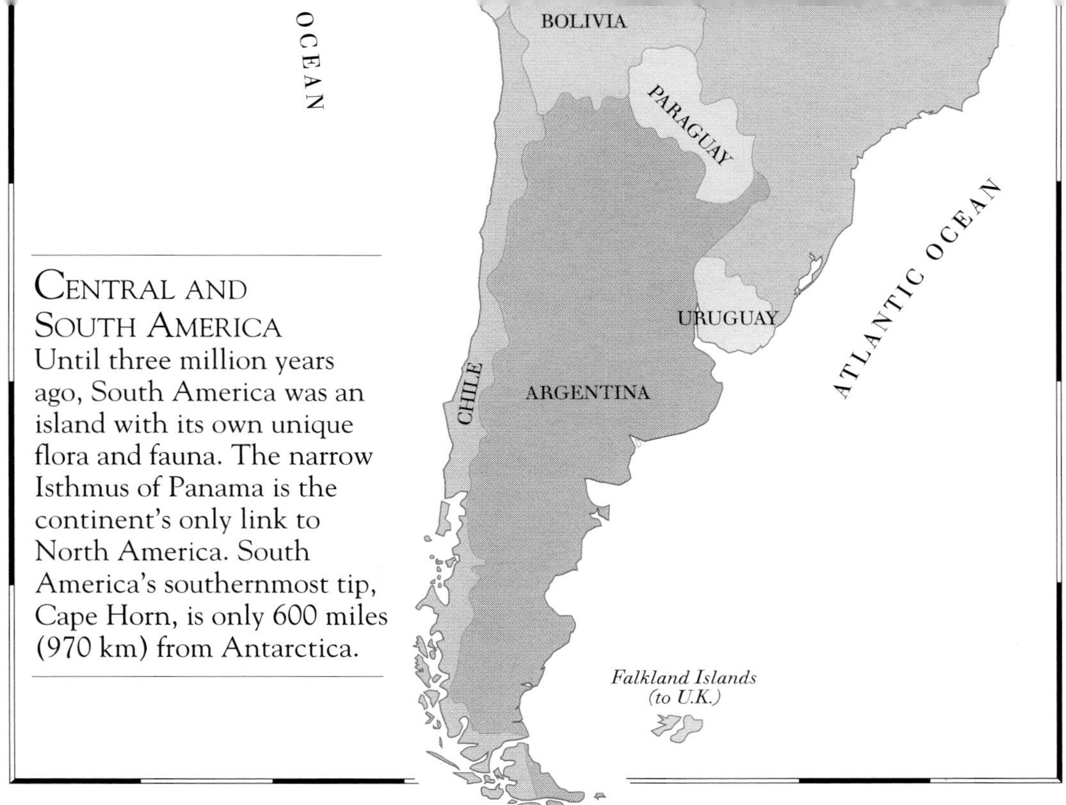
OCEAN
BOLIVIA
PARAGUAY
URUGUAY
ARGENTINA
CHILE
ATLANTIC OCEAN
Falkland Islands
(to U.K.)

Central and South America

Until three million years ago, South America was an island with its own unique flora and fauna. The narrow Isthmus of Panama is the continent's only link to North America. South America's southernmost tip, Cape Horn, is only 600 miles (970 km) from Antarctica.

CENTRAL AMERICA AND THE CARIBBEAN

CENTRAL AMERICA FORMS a narrow land bridge joining North and South America. To the east lie the Caribbean islands, many of which are uninhabited.

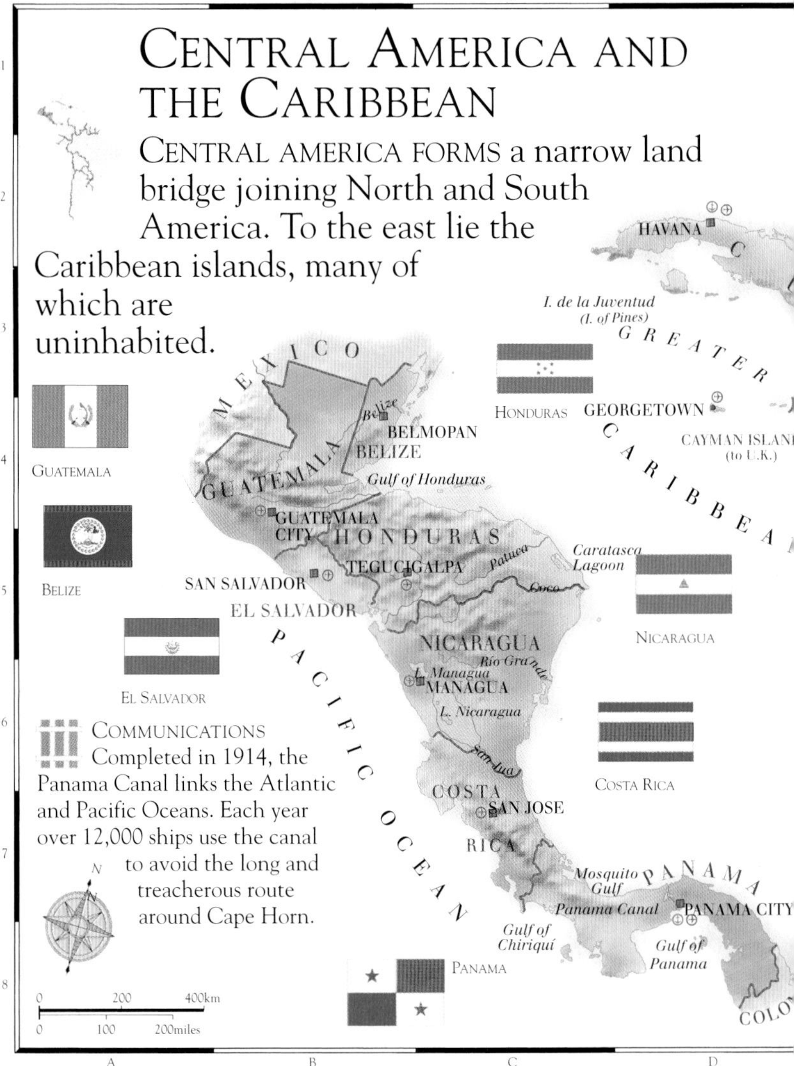
A
B
C
D
1
2
3
4
5
6
7
8
HAVANA
I. de la Juventud
(I. of Pines)
GREATER
MEXICO
HONDURAS
GEORGETOWN
CAYMAN ISLANDS
(to U.K.)
GUATEMALA
Belize
BELMOPAN
BELIZE
CARIBBEAN
Gulf of Honduras
GUATEMALA
GUATEMALA CITY
HONDURAS
Patuca
Caratasca Lagoon
BELIZE
SAN SALVADOR
TEGUCIGALPA
Coco
EL SALVADOR
NICARAGUA
Río Grande
L. Managua
MANAGUA
EL SALVADOR
PACIFIC OCEAN
L. Nicaragua
San Juan
COSTA RICA
SAN JOSE
COSTA RICA
Mosquito Gulf
PANAMA
Panama Canal
PANAMA CITY
Gulf of Chiriquí
Gulf of Panama
PANAMA
0
200
400km
0
100
200miles
N

COMMUNICATIONS Completed in 1914, the Panama Canal links the Atlantic and Pacific Oceans. Each year over 12,000 ships use the canal to avoid the long and treacherous route around Cape Horn.

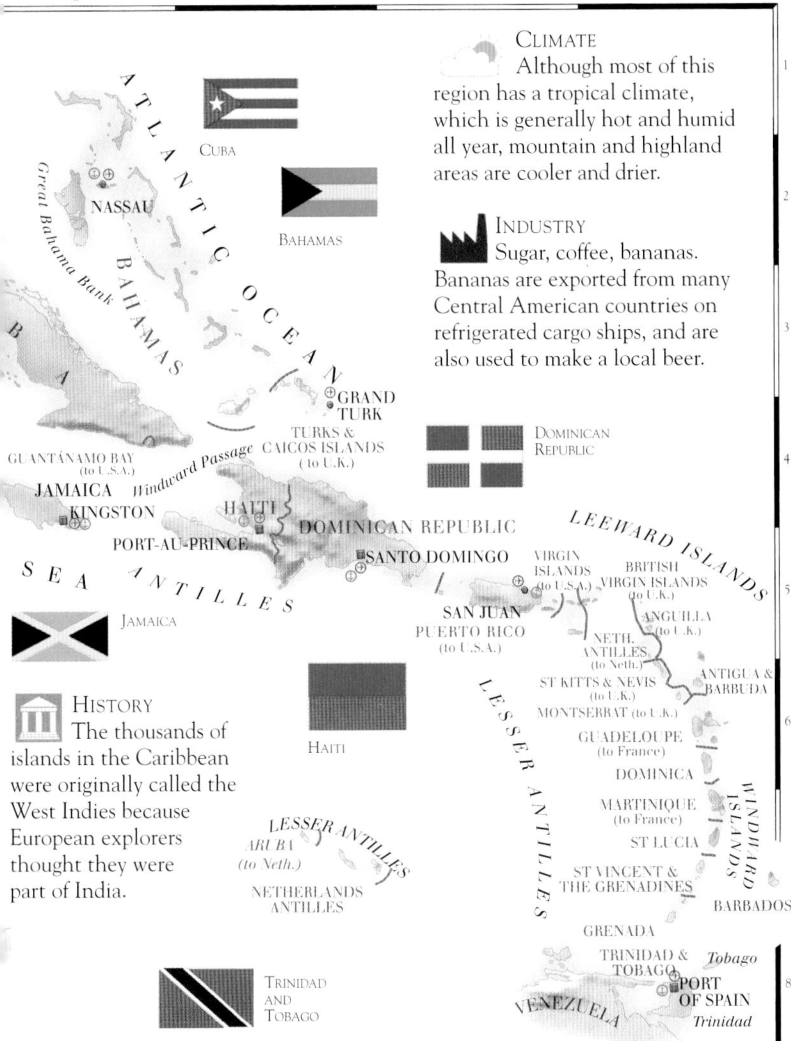
E
F
G
H
1
2
3
4
5
6
8
ATLANTIC OCEAN
Great Bahama Bank
BAHAMAS
NASSAU
CUBA
BAHAMAS
GRAND TURK
TURKS & CAICOS ISLANDS (to U.K.)
DOMINICAN REPUBLIC
GUANTÁNAMO BAY (to U.S.A.)
Windward Passage
JAMAICA
KINGSTON
HAITI
DOMINICAN REPUBLIC
PORT-AU-PRINCE
SANTO DOMINGO
SEA
ANTILLES
LEEWARD ISLANDS
VIRGIN ISLANDS (to U.S.A.)
BRITISH VIRGIN ISLANDS (to U.K.)
SAN JUAN
PUERTO RICO (to U.S.A.)
ANGUILLA (to U.K.)
NETH. ANTILLES (to Neth.)
JAMAICA
ST KITTS & NEVIS (to U.K.)
ANTIGUA & BARBUDA
LESSER ANTILLES
MONTSERRAT (to U.K.)
HAITI
GUADELOUPE (to France)
DOMINICA
MARTINIQUE (to France)
WINDWARD ISLANDS
LESSER ANTILLES
ARUBA (to Neth.)
ST LUCIA
ST VINCENT & THE GRENADINES
NETHERLANDS ANTILLES
BARBADOS
GRENADA
TRINIDAD & TOBAGO
Tobago
PORT OF SPAIN
TRINIDAD AND TOBAGO
VENEZUELA
Trinidad
E
F

Climate

Although most of this region has a tropical climate, which is generally hot and humid all year, mountain and highland areas are cooler and drier.

Industry

Sugar, coffee, bananas. Bananas are exported from many Central American countries on refrigerated cargo ships, and are also used to make a local beer.

History

The thousands of islands in the Caribbean were originally called the West Indies because European explorers thought they were part of India.

Central America facts

Nicaragua

• Lake Nicaragua is the only freshwater lake in the world to contain ocean animals.

ESSENTIAL FACTS

- Managua
- 49,998 sq miles (129,494 sq km)
- 5.2 million
- Córdoba
- Spanish

Honduras

• The swampy Caribbean shoreline of Honduras is known as the Mosquito Coast.

ESSENTIAL FACTS

- Tegucigalpa
- 43,278 sq miles (112,090 sq km)
- 6.6 million
- Lempira
- Spanish

QUETZAL
Inca headdresses were decorated with the colorful tail feathers of the quetzal bird.

COTTON
The export of cotton is a major Nicaraguan industry.

BANANAS
Honduras has huge banana plantations. The work is hard and the pay is low.

Guatemala

• The ruined remains of temples and pyramids built by the ancient Mayans can still be seen in the forests of Guatemala.

ESSENTIAL FACTS

- Guatemala City
- 42,043 sq miles (108,890 sq km)
- 11.7 million
- Quetzal
- Spanish

El Salvador

• Coffee accounts for 90% of the country's exported goods.
• El Salvador means "the saviour", referring to Christ.

ESSENTIAL FACTS

- San Salvador
- 21,040 sq km (8,124 sq miles)
- 6.4 million
- Salvadorean colón
- Spanish

Costa Rica

- The constitution of Costa Rica is the only one in the world to ban National Armies.
- The name Costa Rica means "rich coast" in Spanish.

ESSENTIAL FACTS

⊙ San José

19,730 sq miles (51,100 sq km)

4.1 million

Costa Rican colón

Spanish

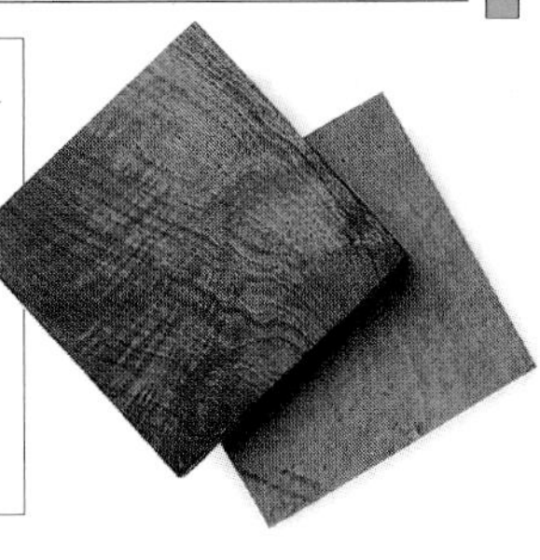

MAHOGANY
Costa Rica's forests have been devastated by excessive felling of trees, such as mahogany and cedar, for timber. Today, much forestland is protected.

CUBAN BEE HUMMINGBIRD

Cuba

- As a result of fuel shortages, the main form of public transportation is the bicycle.
- Cuba is the only communist country in the Americas.

ESSENTIAL FACTS

⊙ Havana

42,803 sq miles (110,860 sq km)

11.2 million

Cuban peso

Spanish

Panama

- Many rare bird and animal species are threatened by the wholesale destruction of Panama's rain forests.

ESSENTIAL FACTS

⊙ Panama City

30,193 sq miles (78,200 sq km)

2.9 million

Balboa

Spanish

EXPORTS
Belize exports grapefruit. Sugar is made from cane, which grows in Panama.

Belize

- The Belizean barrier reef is the second largest in the world.
- Belize was formerly known as British Honduras, gaining independence in 1981.

ESSENTIAL FACTS

⊙ Belmopan

8867 sq miles (22,966 sq km)

200,000

Belizean dollar

English

Caribbean facts

Dominican Republic

• Founded in 1496 by Christopher Columbus' brother, Santo Domingo is the oldest American city.

ESSENTIAL FACTS

⊙ Santo Domingo

18,815 sq miles (48,730 sq km)

8.5 million

Dominican Republic peso

Spanish

Haiti

• Many Haitians still practice the folk religion of voodoo.

• Haiti became the first independent black republic in 1804.

ESSENTIAL FACTS

⊙ Port-au-Prince

10,714 sq miles (27,750 sq km)

8.3 million

Gourde

French, Creole

Molasses
Rum, made from cane juice
Sugarcane

CANE PRODUCTS Sugarcane thrives in the tropical Caribbean.

Jamaica

• Reggae music originated in Jamaica.

• The Rastafarians of Jamaica worship Haile Selassie, the late emperor of Ethiopia.

• Large areas of Kingston are ruled by gang leaders, or *Dons*.

ESSENTIAL FACTS

⊙ Kingston

4243 sq miles (10,990 sq km)

2.6 million

Jamaican dollar

English

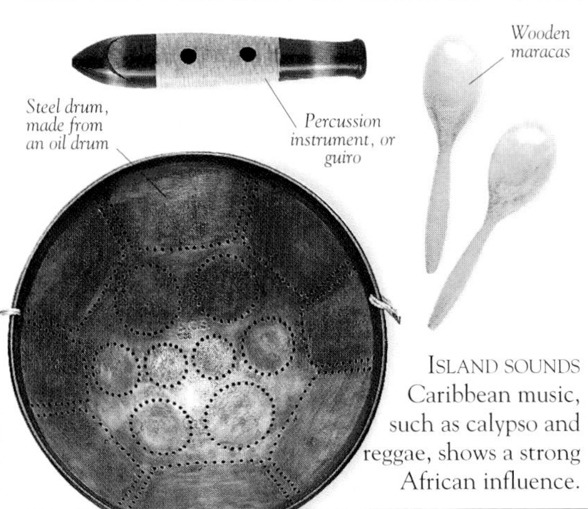
Steel drum, made from an oil drum
Percussion instrument, or guiro
Wooden maracas

ISLAND SOUNDS Caribbean music, such as calypso and reggae, shows a strong African influence.

GRENADA
⊙ St. George's
🚹 98,000
🗨 English

ST. LUCIA
⊙ Castries
🚹 156, 300
🗨 English

THE BAHAMAS
⊙ Nassau
🚹 308,000
🗨 English

DOMINICA
⊙ Roseau
🚹 73,000
🗨 English

ISLE OF SPICES Many varieties of spice are grown on the island of Grenada.

Mace
Cloves
Bay leaf
Saffron
Cinnamon stick
Ground cinnamon

BARBADOS
⊙ Bridgetown
🚹 268,000
🗨 English

ST. KITTS & NEVIS
⊙ Basseterre
🚹 41,000
🗨 English

ST. VINCENT & THE GRENADINES
⊙ Kingstown
🚹 115,500
🗨 English

TRINIDAD & TOBAGO
⊙ Port-of-Spain
🚹 1.3 million
🗨 English

ANTIGUA & BARBUDA
⊙ St. John's
🚹 66,400
🗨 English

STORMY WEATHER The Caribbean islands are often subject to extreme weather, such as hurricanes and typhoons.

Northern South America

The Incas ruled much of this area in the 15th century, and today large numbers of their descendants live in Peru, Ecuador, and Bolivia. In 1533, the last Incan emperor was executed by the Spanish, who colonized this region. The French, Dutch, and British later settled in the countries east of Venezuela, although all but French Guiana are now independent.

Venezuela
Guyana
Surinam
CARIBBEAN SEA
Gulf of Venezuela
Margarita I.
Santa Marta
Barranquilla
Cartagena
PANAMA
Gulf of Darien
Maracaibo
CARACAS
Cumaná
Barquisimeto
Valencia
Maturín
L. Maracaibo
Barinas
Mérida
Apure
Ciudad Bolívar
Orinoco
Ciudad Guayana
Arauca
Cauca
Magdalen
VENEZUELA
Medellín
BOGOTA
Meta
ANDES
Buenaventura
Cali
Villavicencio
Guaviare
COLOMBIA
GEORGETOWN
New Amsterdam
PARAMARIBO
GUYANA
Berbice
Essequibo
Courantyne
SURINAME
Marowijne
CAYENNE
FRENCH GUIANA (to France)

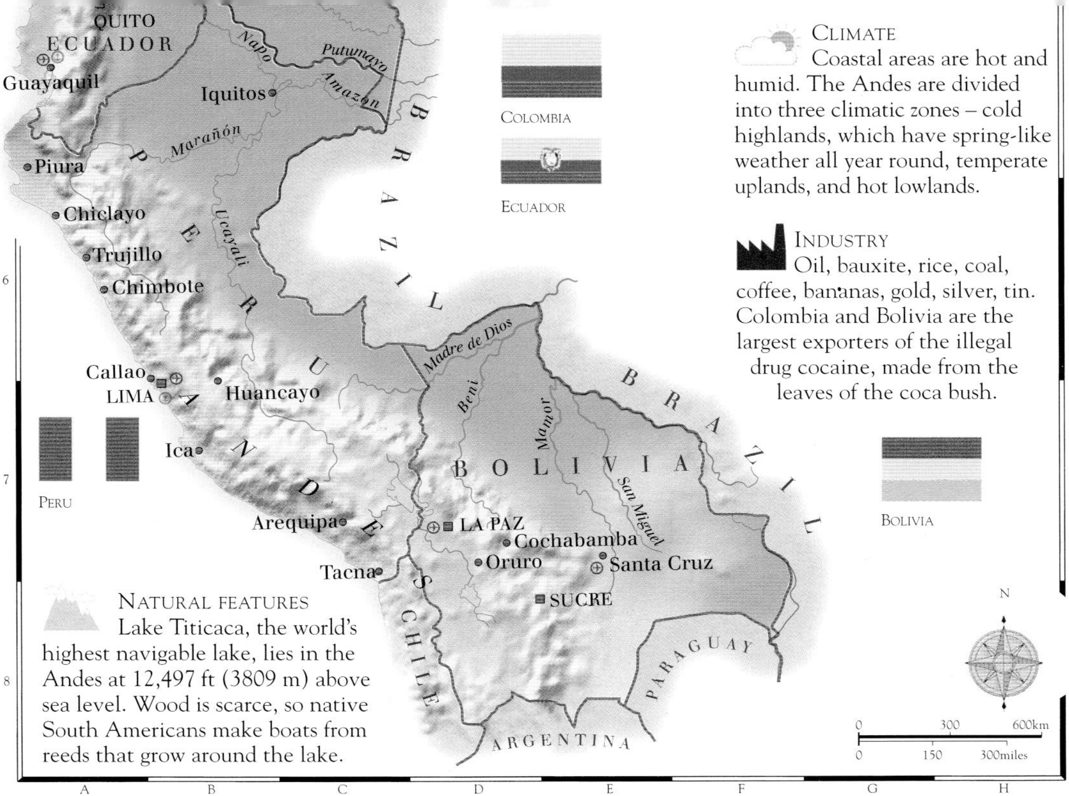

COLOMBIA

ECUADOR

CLIMATE

Coastal areas are hot and humid. The Andes are divided into three climatic zones – cold highlands, which have spring-like weather all year round, temperate uplands, and hot lowlands.

INDUSTRY

Oil, bauxite, rice, coal, coffee, bananas, gold, silver, tin. Colombia and Bolivia are the largest exporters of the illegal drug cocaine, made from the leaves of the coca bush.

BOLIVIA

PERU

NATURAL FEATURES

Lake Titicaca, the world's highest navigable lake, lies in the Andes at 12,497 ft (3809 m) above sea level. Wood is scarce, so native South Americans make boats from reeds that grow around the lake.

QUITO
ECUADOR
Guayaquil
Iquitos
Napo
Putumayo
Amazon
Marañón
Piura
Chiclayo
Trujillo
Chimbote
Ucayali
PERU
BRAZIL
Callao
LIMA
Huancayo
Ica
ANDES
Arequipa
Tacna
CHILE
Madre de Dios
Beni
Mamor
BOLIVIA
San Miguel
LA PAZ
Cochabamba
Oruro
Santa Cruz
SUCRE
PARAGUAY
ARGENTINA
N
0 300 600km
0 150 300miles
A B C D E F G H
5 6 7 8

Northern South America facts

SURINAME

• Jaguars, pumas, ocelots, and iguanas live wild in Suriname.

ESSENTIAL FACTS

⊙ Paramaribo

63,039 sq miles (163,270 sq km)

419,000

Suriname guilder

Dutch

COLOMBIA

• The country of Colombia produces two-thirds of the world's emeralds.

ESSENTIAL FACTS

⊙ Bogotá

439,733 sq miles (1,138,910 sq km)

42.8 million

Colombian peso

Spanish

▲ Multiparty republic

71 years

PERU

• The Morochocha railroad in Peru has the world's highest section of railroad track.
• Peru is a strongly patriarchal, or male-dominated, society.

ESSENTIAL FACTS

⊙ Lima

496,223 sq miles (1,285,220 sq km)

26.1 million

New sol

Spanish, Quechua

Uncut gem
Rock
COLOMBIAN EMERALD

ECUADOR AND THE GALÁPAGOS

• Charles Darwin's studies on the Galápagos Islands in 1856 helped formulate his theories on the evolution of species.
• Ecuador's landscape features low coastal regions, high Andean peaks, and dense jungle.

ESSENTIAL FACTS

⊙ Quito

109,483 sq miles (283,560 sq km)

12.9 million

Sucre

Spanish, Quechua

▲ Presidential democracy

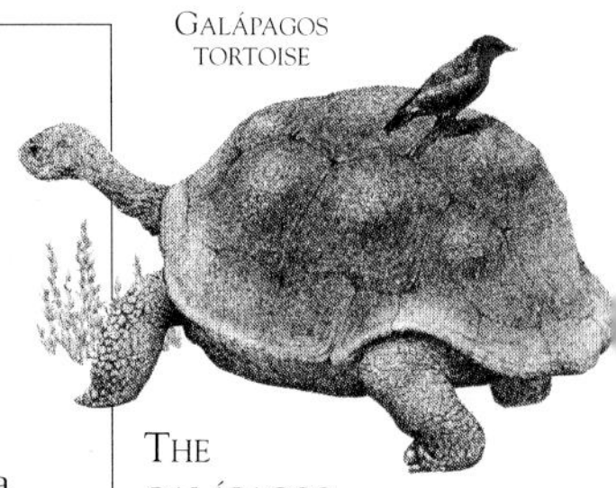
GALÁPAGOS TORTOISE

THE GALÁPAGOS
These islands lie 603 miles (970 km) west of Ecuador. Many of the islands' animals are unique.

ANDEAN CONDOR
The heaviest bird of prey in the world, the condor lives in the highest parts of the Andes.

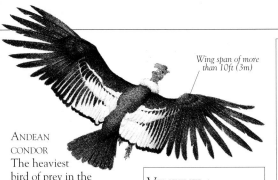

Wing span of more than 10ft (3m)

BOLIVIA

- La Paz is the highest capital city in the world.
- Many Bolivian farmers are very poor, growing just enough food for their families to live on.
- Bolivia has the world's highest golf course and ski run.

ESSENTIAL FACTS

⊙ La Paz, Sucre

424,162 sq miles (1,098,580 sq km)

8.5 million

Boliviano

Spanish, Quechua, and Aymará

VENEZUELA

- Many Venezuelan people live in poverty.
- Venezuela is the most urbanized country in South America.
- Angel Falls, the highest waterfall in the world, lies in southern Venezuela.

ESSENTIAL FACTS

⊙ Caracas

352,143 sq miles (912,050 sq km)

24.6 million

Bolivár

Spanish

CAYENNE PEPPER
Crushed South American chilis are used to make cayenne pepper.

GUYANA

- The Guyanese nation is the only English-speaking country in South America.
- Guyana means "land of many waters."

ESSENTIAL FACTS

⊙ Georgetown

83,000 sq miles (214,970 sq km)

763,000

Guyana dollar

English

FRENCH GUIANA

- The European Space Agency conducts its rocket launches from French Guiana.
- The territory of French Guiana is the last remaining colony in South America.

ESSENTIAL FACTS

⊙ Cayenne

86,303 sq km (33,313 sq miles)

172,605

French franc

French

BRAZIL

OCCUPYING NEARLY HALF of South America, Brazil has the largest river basin in the world. Many Brazilians are descendants of Portuguese, who colonized Brazil in the 16th century, and Africans, who were brought to work on sugar plantations. Brazil's Native American tribes have little contact with the outside world. In 1992, the United Nations held its first Earth Summit in Rio, partly to highlight the destruction of the Amazon rain forest, the largest rain forest in the world.

PEOPLE

There were once about two million indigenous people living in Amazonia. Today only 50,000 remain. The survival of many tribes and their way of life is threatened by the destruction of the Amazon rain forest.

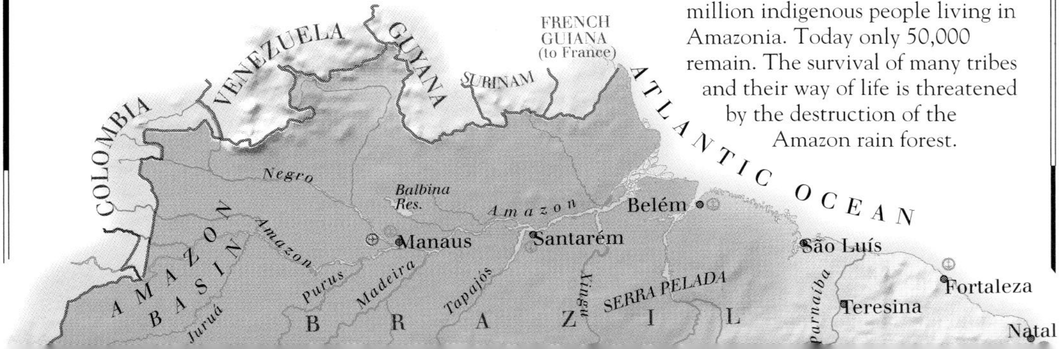

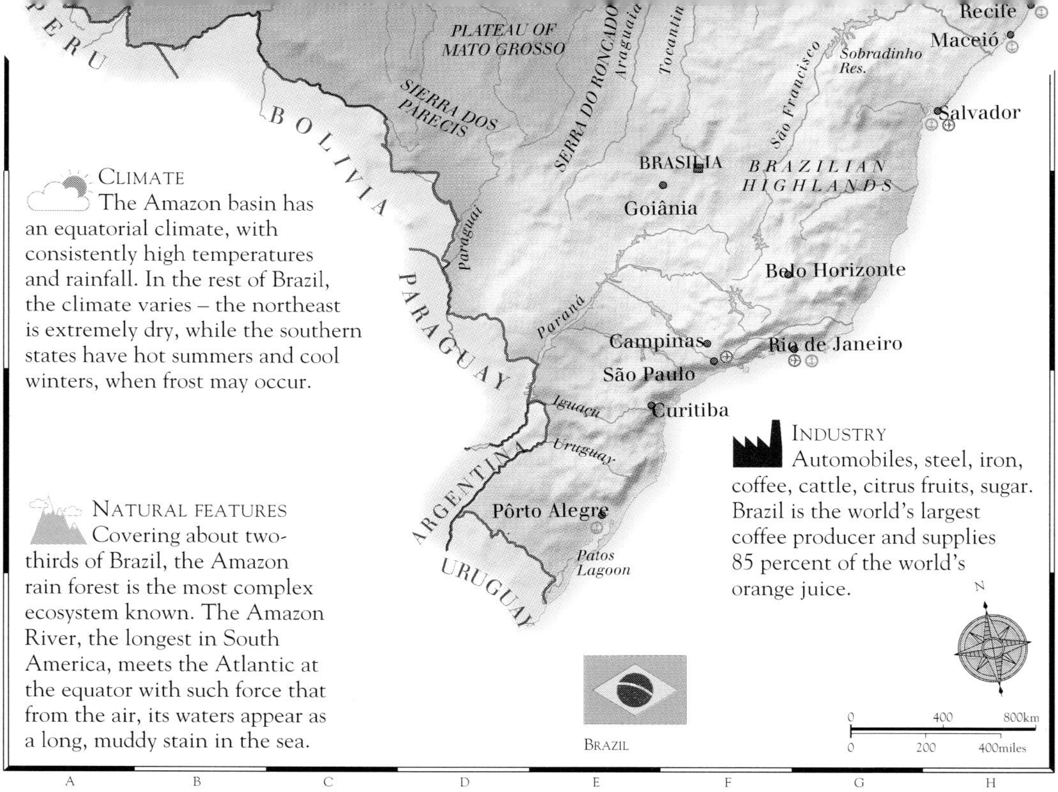

CLIMATE

The Amazon basin has an equatorial climate, with consistently high temperatures and rainfall. In the rest of Brazil, the climate varies – the northeast is extremely dry, while the southern states have hot summers and cool winters, when frost may occur.

NATURAL FEATURES

Covering about two-thirds of Brazil, the Amazon rain forest is the most complex ecosystem known. The Amazon River, the longest in South America, meets the Atlantic at the equator with such force that from the air, its waters appear as a long, muddy stain in the sea.

INDUSTRY

Automobiles, steel, iron, coffee, cattle, citrus fruits, sugar. Brazil is the world's largest coffee producer and supplies 85 percent of the world's orange juice.

BRAZIL

Southern South America

The landscape of this region of South America varies from snow-capped volcanoes in the Andes to the wastelands of Patagonia. In the heart of Argentina lie the Pampas, fertile grasslands where vast herds of cattle graze. In parts, grasses grow up to 10 ft (3 m) high. Chile is separated from the rest of the region by the Andes, which run the length of the continent.

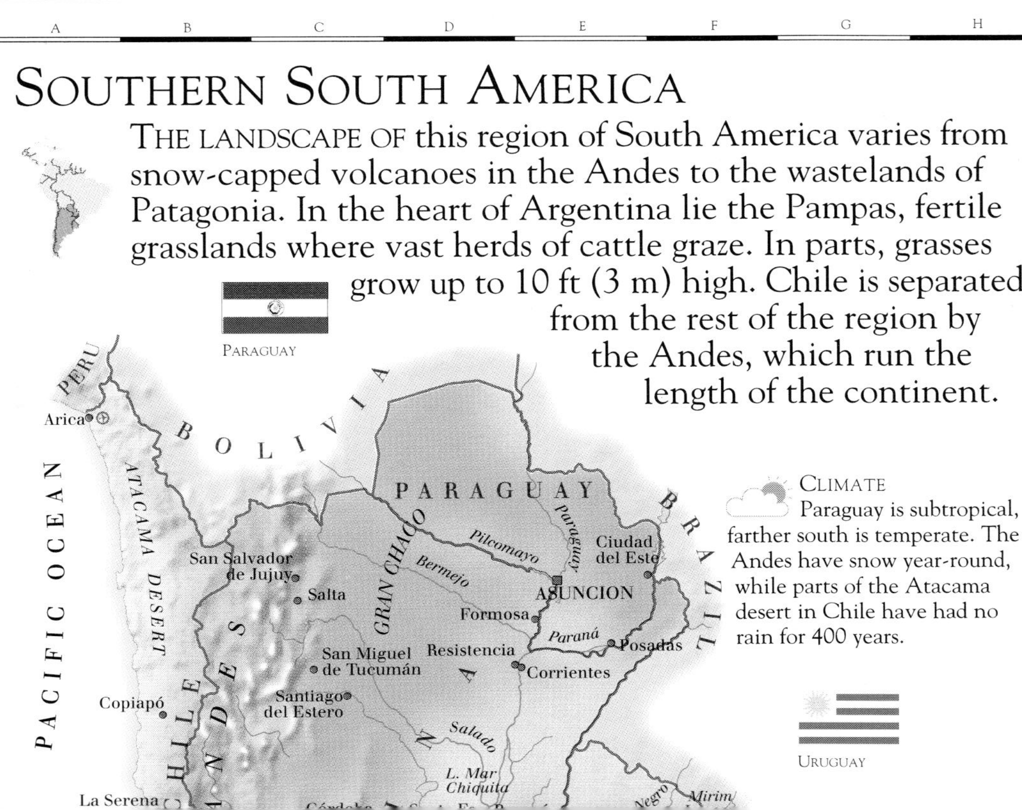

A
B
C
D
E
F
G
H
1
2
3
4
PARAGUAY
URUGUAY
PERU
BOLIVIA
PARAGUAY
BRAZIL
PACIFIC OCEAN
ATACAMA DESERT
GRAN CHACO
ANDES
CHILE
Arica
San Salvador de Jujuy
Salta
San Miguel de Tucumán
Santiago del Estero
Copiapó
La Serena
Pilcomayo
Bermejo
Paraguay
Paraná
Salado
Negro
Mirim
L. Mar Chiquita
ASUNCION
Ciudad del Este
Formosa
Resistencia
Corrientes
Posadas

Climate
Paraguay is subtropical, farther south is temperate. The Andes have snow year-round, while parts of the Atacama desert in Chile have had no rain for 400 years.

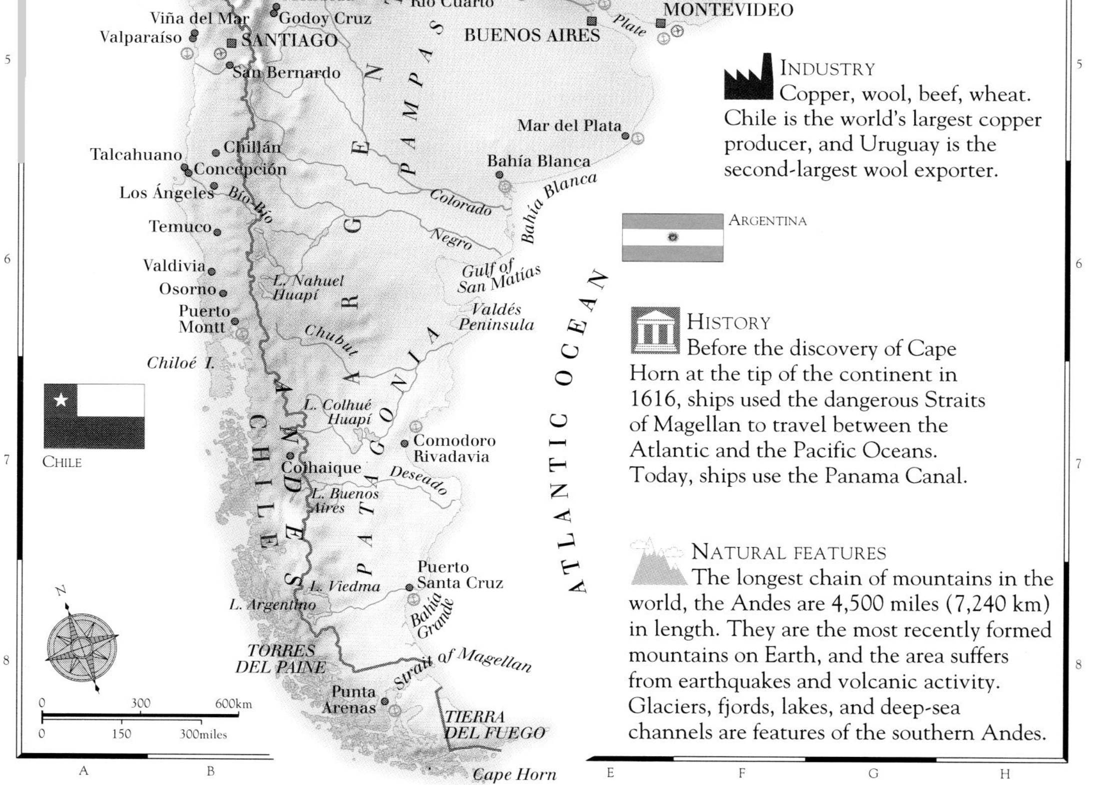
Mendoza
Río Cuarto
Viña del Mar
Godoy Cruz
Valparaíso
SANTIAGO
BUENOS AIRES
Plate
MONTEVIDEO
San Bernardo
PAMPAS
ARGENTINA
Mar del Plata
Talcahuano
Chillán
Concepción
Bahía Blanca
Los Ángeles
Bío-Bío
Colorado
Bahía Blanca
Temuco
Negro
Valdivia
Osorno
L. Nahuel Huapí
Gulf of San Matías
Puerto Montt
Valdés Peninsula
Chubut
Chiloé I.
PATAGONIA
L. Colhué Huapí
ANDES
CHILE
Comodoro Rivadavia
Coihaique
Deseado
L. Buenos Aires
ATLANTIC OCEAN
Puerto Santa Cruz
L. Viedma
L. Argentino
Bahía Grande
TORRES DEL PAINE
Strait of Magellan
Punta Arenas
TIERRA DEL FUEGO
Cape Horn
N
0
300
600km
0
150
300miles
5
6
7
8
A
B
E
F
G
H

CHILE

ARGENTINA

INDUSTRY

Copper, wool, beef, wheat. Chile is the world's largest copper producer, and Uruguay is the second-largest wool exporter.

HISTORY

Before the discovery of Cape Horn at the tip of the continent in 1616, ships used the dangerous Straits of Magellan to travel between the Atlantic and the Pacific Oceans. Today, ships use the Panama Canal.

NATURAL FEATURES

The longest chain of mountains in the world, the Andes are 4,500 miles (7,240 km) in length. They are the most recently formed mountains on Earth, and the area suffers from earthquakes and volcanic activity. Glaciers, fjords, lakes, and deep-sea channels are features of the southern Andes.

Southern South America Facts

CHILE

• Democracy was restored in Chile in 1989 after 12 years of military rule under General Pinochet.
• The Atacama Desert in northern Chile is the driest place on Earth.

ESSENTIAL FACTS

⊙ Santiago
292,258 sq miles (756,950 sq km)
15.4 million
Chilean peso
Spanish
▲ Presidential democracy
75 years

TREE OF MYSTERY
The Chile pine, also known as the monkey puzzle tree, is native to the Andes, the world's longest mountain range.

URUGUAY

• The country of Uruguay is the smallest in South America.
• Almost half of the population lives in Montevideo.
• Hydroelectric power generates 86% of the country's electricity.
• Uruguay is tolerant of all forms of religion.

ESSENTIAL FACTS

⊙ Montevideo
68,039 sq miles (176,220 sq km)
3.4 million
Uruguayan peso
Spanish

PARAGUAY

• The majority of Paraguayans are *mestizo* – a mixture of native Guaraní Indian and Spanish blood.
• Half the workforce is employed in agriculture.

ESSENTIAL FACTS

⊙ Asunción
157,046 sq miles (406,750 sq km)
5.6 million
Guaraní
Spanish, Guaraní

WOOLEN SCARF

TEXTILES
Uruguay is a major exporter of handmade wool products.

GAUCHO
Argentinian cowboys are known as gauchos.

ARGENTINA

- Crop production and cattle and sheep rearing produces three-quarters of the nation's income.
- The Argentinian daily drink is a tea called *maté*.
- The tango dance originated in Buenos Aires in the late 19th century.

ESSENTIAL FACTS

- Buenos Aires
- 1,068,296 sq miles (2,766,890 sq km)
- 37.5 million
- Argentine peso
- Spanish
- ▲ Presidential democracy
- 73 years

PUDU
Southern Argentina's Patagonia region is home to the pudu, the world's smallest deer.

BRAZILIAN SOCCER
Soccer is Brazil's favorite sport, with more than 20,000 soccer teams.

BRAZIL

- São Paulo is the world's second largest city, with 17 million inhabitants.
- Rio de Janeiro's *Mardi Gras* carnival is a major tourist attraction.
- Brazil has rich gold and diamond reserves.
- Many Brazilians live in poverty, despite the country's resources.

ESSENTIAL FACTS

- Brasília
- 3,286,470 sq miles (8,511,965 sq km)
- 172.6 million
- Reál
- Portuguese
- ▲ Presidential democracy
- 68 years

EUROPE

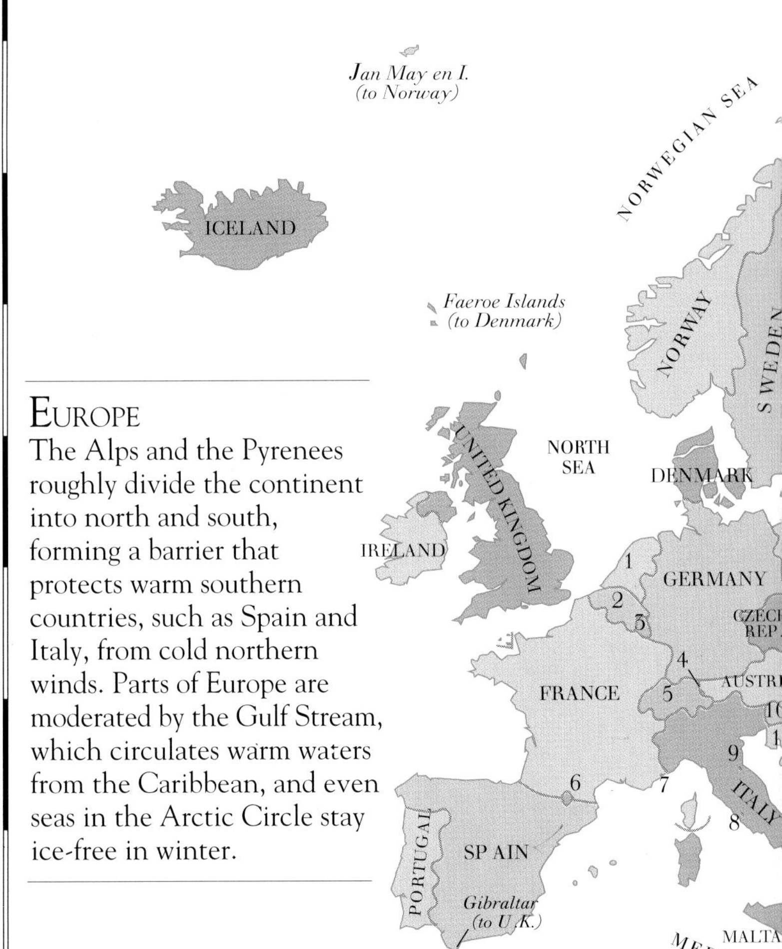
Jan Mayen I.
(to Norway)
NORWEGIAN SEA
ICELAND
Faeroe Islands
(to Denmark)
NORWAY
SWEDEN
UNITED KINGDOM
NORTH
SEA
DENMARK
IRELAND
1
GERMANY
2
3
CZECH
REP.
4
AUSTRIA
FRANCE
5
9
ITALY
6
7
8
PORTUGAL
SPAIN
Gibraltar
(to U.K.)
MALTA
MEDITERR

EUROPE

The Alps and the Pyrenees roughly divide the continent into north and south, forming a barrier that protects warm southern countries, such as Spain and Italy, from cold northern winds. Parts of Europe are moderated by the Gulf Stream, which circulates warm waters from the Caribbean, and even seas in the Arctic Circle stay ice-free in winter.

BARENTS SEA
FINLAND
BALTIC SEA
ESTONIA
LATVIA
LITHUANIA
RUSSIAN FEDERATION
BELARUS
OLAND
UKRAINE
LOVAKIA
UNGARY
16
ROMANIA
2
13
BLACK SEA
BULGARIA
14
15
GEORGIA
AZERBAIJAN
ARMENIA
GREECE
ANEAN SEA
1 Netherlands
2 Belgium
3 Luxembourg
4 Liechtenstein
5 Switzerland
6 Andorra
7 Monaco
8 Vatican City
9 San Marino
10 Slovenia
11 Croatia
12 Bosnia/Herzegovina
13 Serbia & Montenegro
14 Macedonia
15 Albania
16 Moldova

Scandinavia and Finland

DURING PAST ICE AGES, much of Scandinavia and Finland were covered in glaciers that carved out the land, leaving steep-sided valleys, fjords, and lakes. The Finnish, originally from the east via Russia, differ from Scandinavians in culture and language.

CLIMATE
Norway's west coast is warmed by the Gulf Stream. Northern temperatures fall to –22°F (–30°C) during the six-month winter; the south is milder.

INDUSTRY
Fishing, timber, wood-pulp, paper, oil, gas, auto manufacture. Norway is western Europe's largest producer of oil.

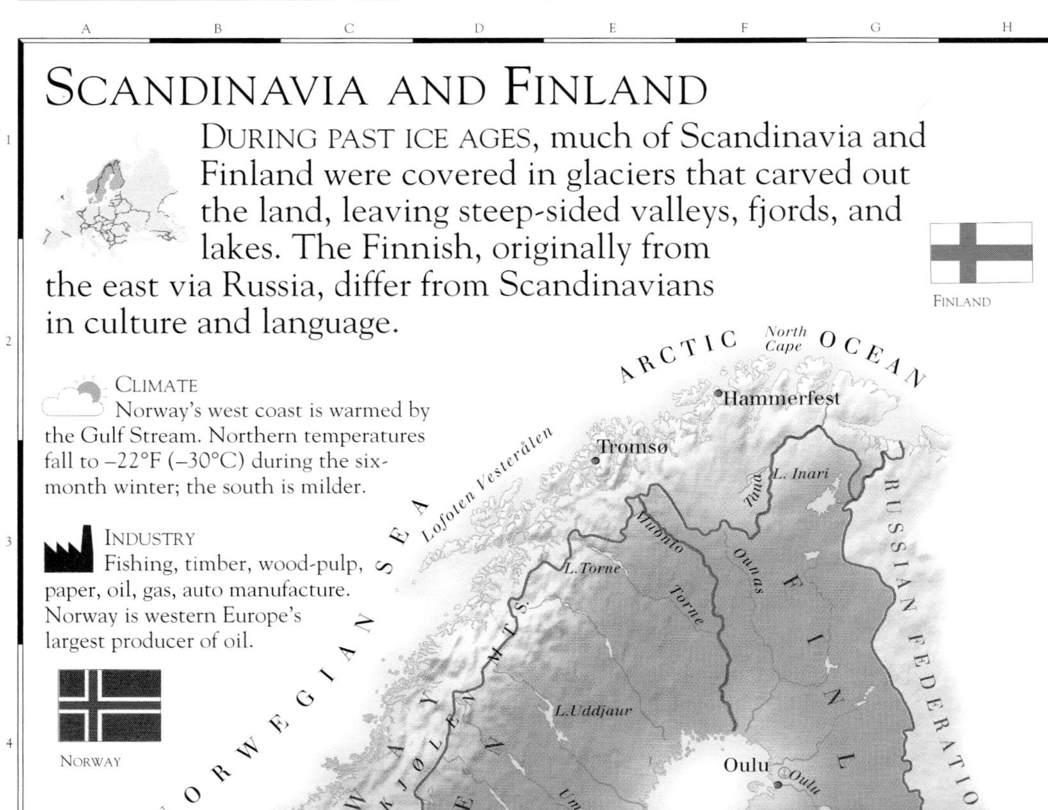

A B C D E F G H
1 2 3 4
FINLAND
NORWAY
ARCTIC OCEAN
North Cape
Hammerfest
Tromsø
Lofoten Vesterålen
NORWEGIAN SEA
RUSSIAN FEDERATION
FINL
L. Inari
Tana
Ounas
Muonio
Torne
L. Torne
L.Uddjaur
KJØLEN MTS.
Oulu
Ume

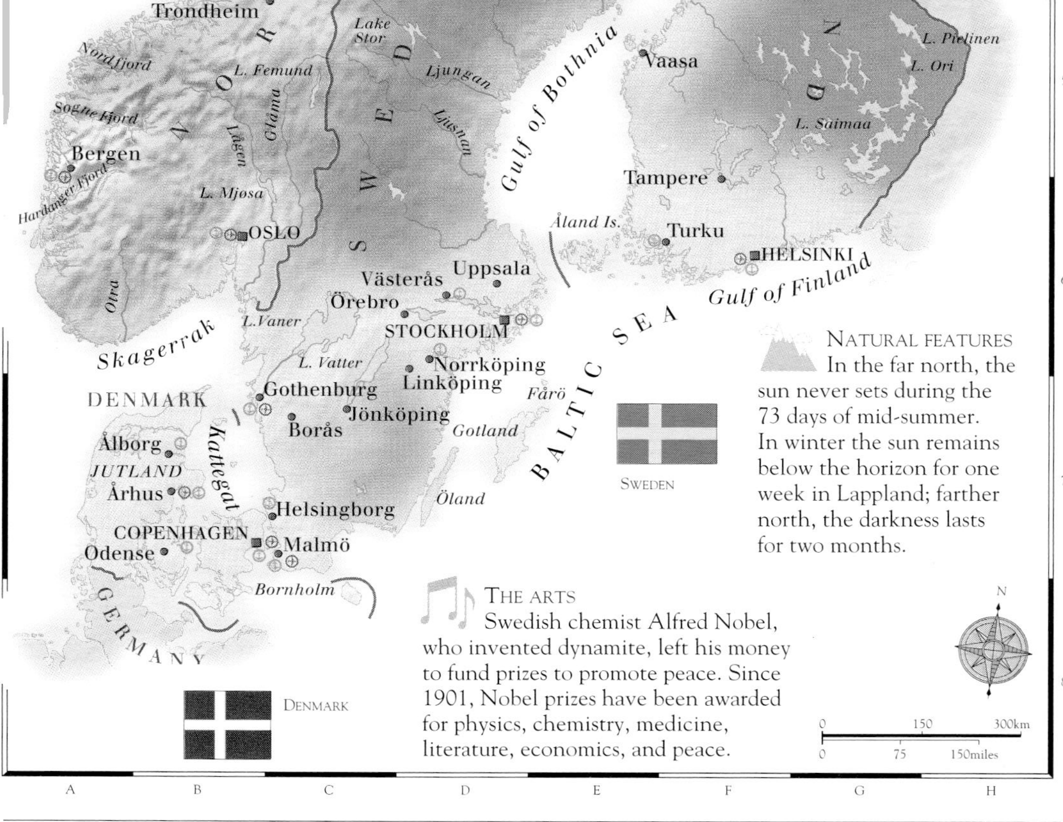
Trondheim
Nordfjord
Sogne Fjord
Bergen
Hardanger Fjord
N O R
L. Femund
Glåma
Lågen
L. Mjøsa
OSLO
Otra
Skagerrak
Lake Stor
S W E D
Ljungan
Ljusnan
Gulf of Bothnia
Vaasa
N D
L. Pielinen
L. Ori
L. Saimaa
Tampere
Åland Is.
Turku
HELSINKI
Gulf of Finland
Uppsala
Västerås
Örebro
STOCKHOLM
L. Vaner
L. Vatter
Norrköping
Linköping
Gothenburg
Jönköping
Borås
Fårö
Gotland
Öland
BALTIC SEA
DENMARK
Ålborg
JUTLAND
Århus
Kattegat
Helsingborg
COPENHAGEN
Malmö
Odense
Bornholm
GERMANY
SWEDEN
DENMARK
N
0 150 300km
0 75 150miles
A B C D E F G H
5 6 7 8

NATURAL FEATURES
In the far north, the sun never sets during the 73 days of mid-summer. In winter the sun remains below the horizon for one week in Lappland; farther north, the darkness lasts for two months.

THE ARTS
Swedish chemist Alfred Nobel, who invented dynamite, left his money to fund prizes to promote peace. Since 1901, Nobel prizes have been awarded for physics, chemistry, medicine, literature, economics, and peace.

Northern Europe facts

ICELAND

• The remote interior of Iceland can only be reached by special vehicle, pony, or small plane.
• Iceland has the lowest population in Europe.
• Heating is provided by geothermal power.

ESSENTIAL FACTS

⊙ Reykjavik
◒ 39,770 sq miles (103,000 sq km)
† 281,000
$ New Icelandic krona
♡ Icelandic
▲ Multiparty democracy
● 79 years

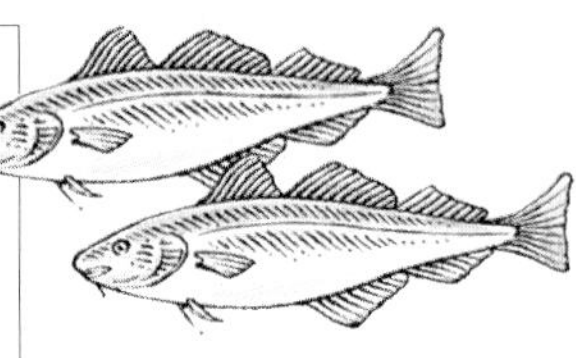

ICELANDIC COD
More than a third of the world's cod-liver oil is produced in Iceland.

NORWAY

• According to Norway's constitution, the government's duty is to create conditions enabling every person to find work.

ESSENTIAL FACTS

⊙ Oslo
◒ 125,181 sq miles (324,220 sq km)
† 4.5 million
$ Norwegian krone
♡ Norwegian
▲ Parliamentary democracy
● 79 years

GRASS ROOFS
Some Norwegian vacation homes have turf-covered roofs.

LAND OF LEGO
Lego building bricks, known by children worldwide, were invented in Denmark.

DENMARK

• Single parents and cohabiting couples raise 40% of Danish children.
• Denmark is Europe's oldest monarchy, dating back to the 1100s.

ESSENTIAL FACTS

⊙ Copenhagen
◒ 16,629 sq miles (43,069 sq km)
† 5.2 million
$ Danish krone
♡ Danish
▲ Parliamentary democracy
● 76 years

Sweden

- Over 50% of Swedish women go out to work.
- Sweden has maintained a position of armed neutrality since 1815.
- Swedish law requires cars to travel with their headlights on at all times.
- Many Swedes invest in overseas property.

ESSENTIAL FACTS

- Stockholm
- 173,730 sq miles (449,960 sq km)
- 8.8 million
- Swedish krona
- Swedish
- Parliamentary democracy
- 80 years

SMÖRGÅSBORD
A Swedish smörgåsbord, meaning "sandwich table", is a spread of local delicacies served cold.

Greenland

Dependency of Denmark
(*Atlantic Ocean*, pp.360–361)

- Nuuk
- 56,569
- Inuit, Danish

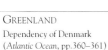

FINNISH TIMBER
Most of Finland's wealth is provided by its timber exports.

Ladle
Sauna bucket

STEAM CLEANING
The Finns invented the steam bath, or sauna, over 1000 years ago.

Finland

- Over half of Finland's population lives in the five districts around Helsinki.
- Finland was the first country to allow women to run for parliament.
- Finland's inland waterway system is the largest in Europe.

ESSENTIAL FACTS

- Helsinki
- 130,127 sq miles (337,030 sq km)
- 5.2 million
- Euro
- Finnish, Swedish
- Parliamentary democracy
- 78 years

British Isles

Lying off the coast of mainland Europe, the British Isles consist of two main islands, Ireland and Great Britain, and many smaller islands. England, Scotland, Wales, and Northern Ireland form the United Kingdom (UK). The Republic of Ireland became independent of the UK in 1921.

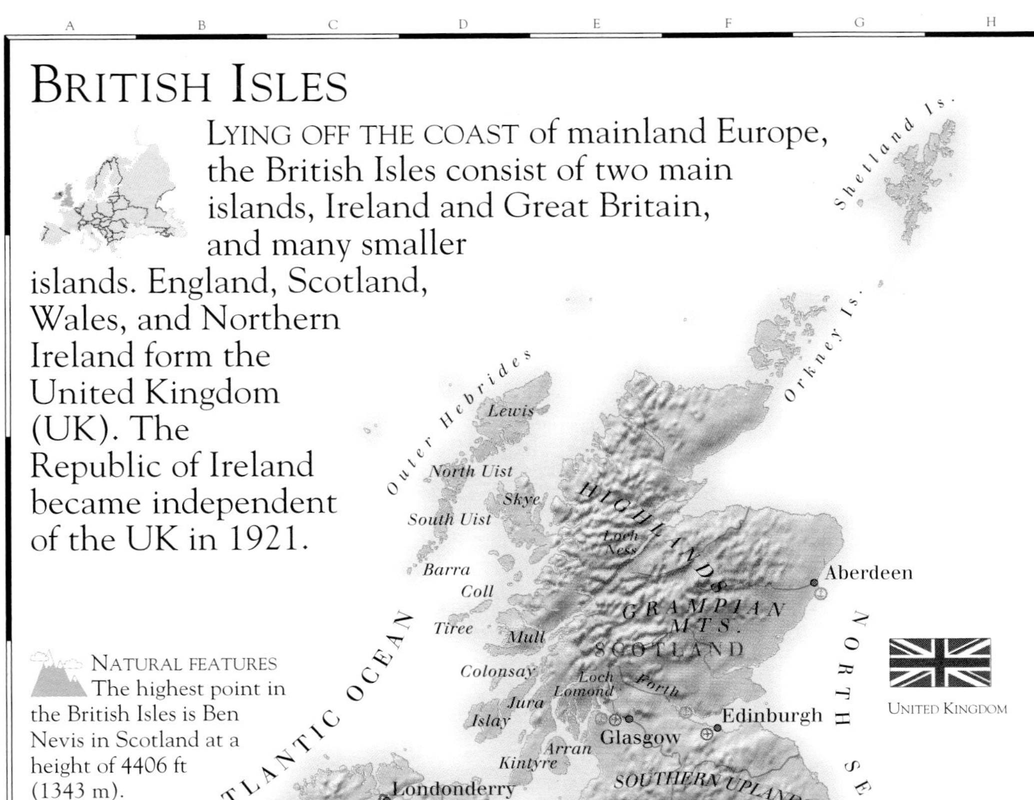
Shetland Is.
Orkney Is.
Outer Hebrides
Lewis
North Uist
Skye
South Uist
Barra
Coll
Tiree
Mull
Colonsay
Jura
Islay
Arran
Kintyre
HIGHLANDS
Loch Ness
GRAMPIAN MTS.
SCOTLAND
Loch Lomond
Forth
Aberdeen
Edinburgh
Glasgow
Londonderry
SOUTHERN UPLANDS
ATLANTIC OCEAN
NORTH SEA
United Kingdom

Natural features
The highest point in the British Isles is Ben Nevis in Scotland at a height of 4406 ft (1343 m).

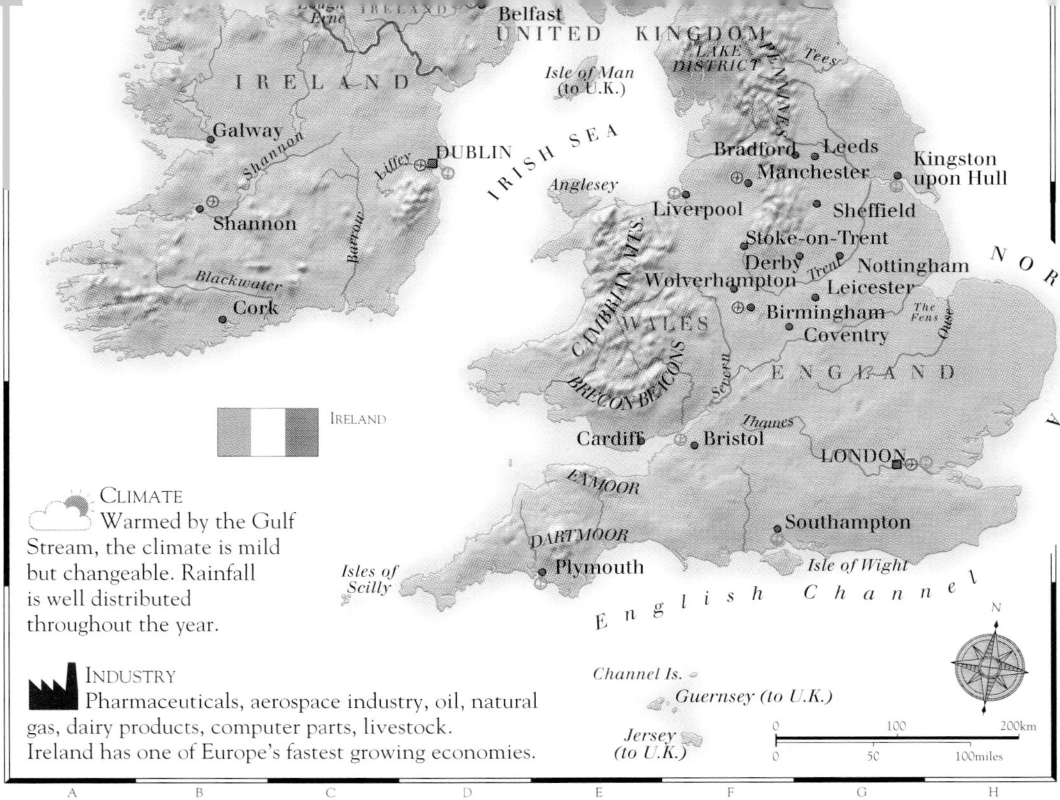

Belfast
UNITED KINGDOM
IRELAND
LAKE DISTRICT
PENNINES
Tees
Isle of Man (to U.K.)
Galway
Shannon
DUBLIN
Liffey
IRISH SEA
Anglesey
Bradford
Leeds
Manchester
Kingston upon Hull
Shannon
Barrow
Liverpool
Sheffield
Stoke-on-Trent
Derby
Trent
Nottingham
NORTH SEA
Blackwater
Wolverhampton
Leicester
CAMBRIAN MTS.
The Fens
Ouse
Cork
Birmingham
WALES
Coventry
ENGLAND
BRECON BEACONS
Severn
IRELAND
Thames
Cardiff
Bristol
LONDON
EXMOOR
Southampton
DARTMOOR
Isles of Scilly
Plymouth
Isle of Wight
English Channel
N
Channel Is.
Guernsey (to U.K.)
Jersey (to U.K.)
0 100 200km
0 50 100miles

CLIMATE

Warmed by the Gulf Stream, the climate is mild but changeable. Rainfall is well distributed throughout the year.

INDUSTRY

Pharmaceuticals, aerospace industry, oil, natural gas, dairy products, computer parts, livestock. Ireland has one of Europe's fastest growing economies.

THE LOW COUNTRIES

BELGIUM, THE NETHERLANDS, and Luxembourg are known as the "Low Countries" because they are flat and low-lying. Much of the Netherlands lies below sea level and has been reclaimed from the sea. The Low Countries, also called "Benelux," are Europe's most densely populated countries.

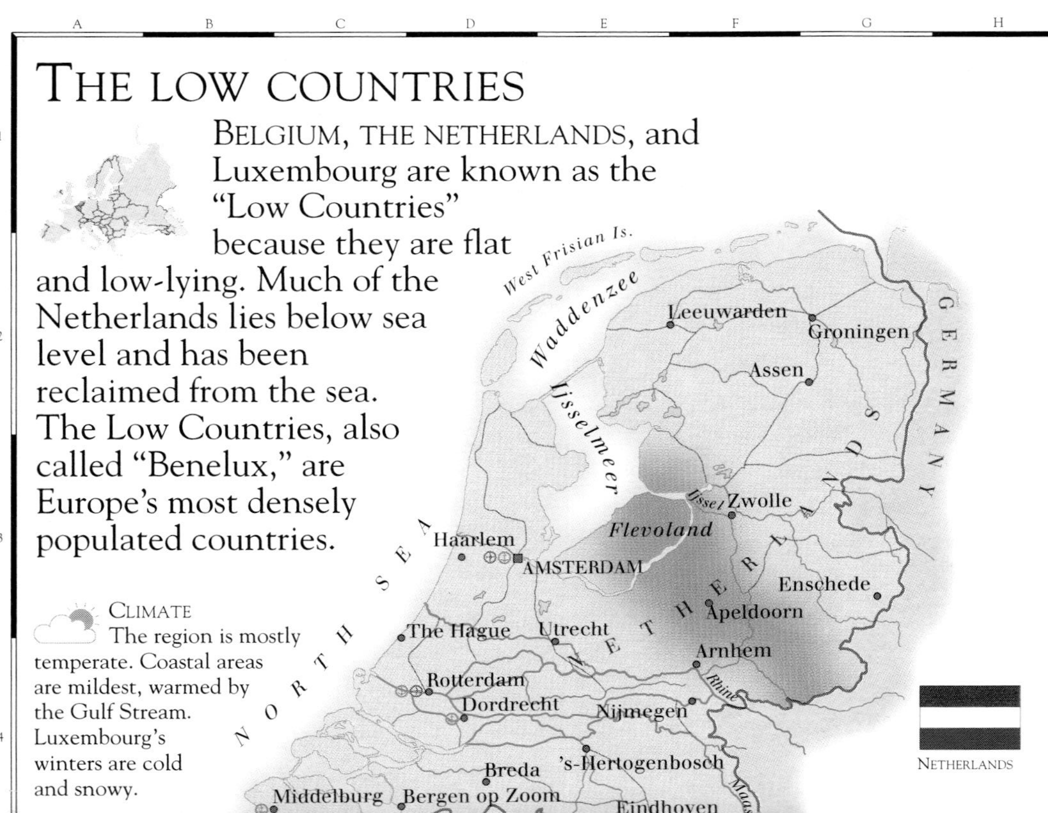
A
B
C
D
E
F
G
H
1
2
3
4
West Frisian Is.
Waddenzee
Ijsselmeer
NORTH SEA
NETHERLANDS
GERMANY
Leeuwarden
Groningen
Assen
Ijssel
Zwolle
Flevoland
Haarlem
AMSTERDAM
Enschede
Apeldoorn
The Hague
Utrecht
Arnhem
Rhine
Rotterdam
Dordrecht
Nijmegen
's-Hertogenbosch
Breda
Middelburg
Bergen op Zoom
Eindhoven
Maas
NETHERLANDS

CLIMATE
The region is mostly temperate. Coastal areas are mildest, warmed by the Gulf Stream. Luxembourg's winters are cold and snowy.

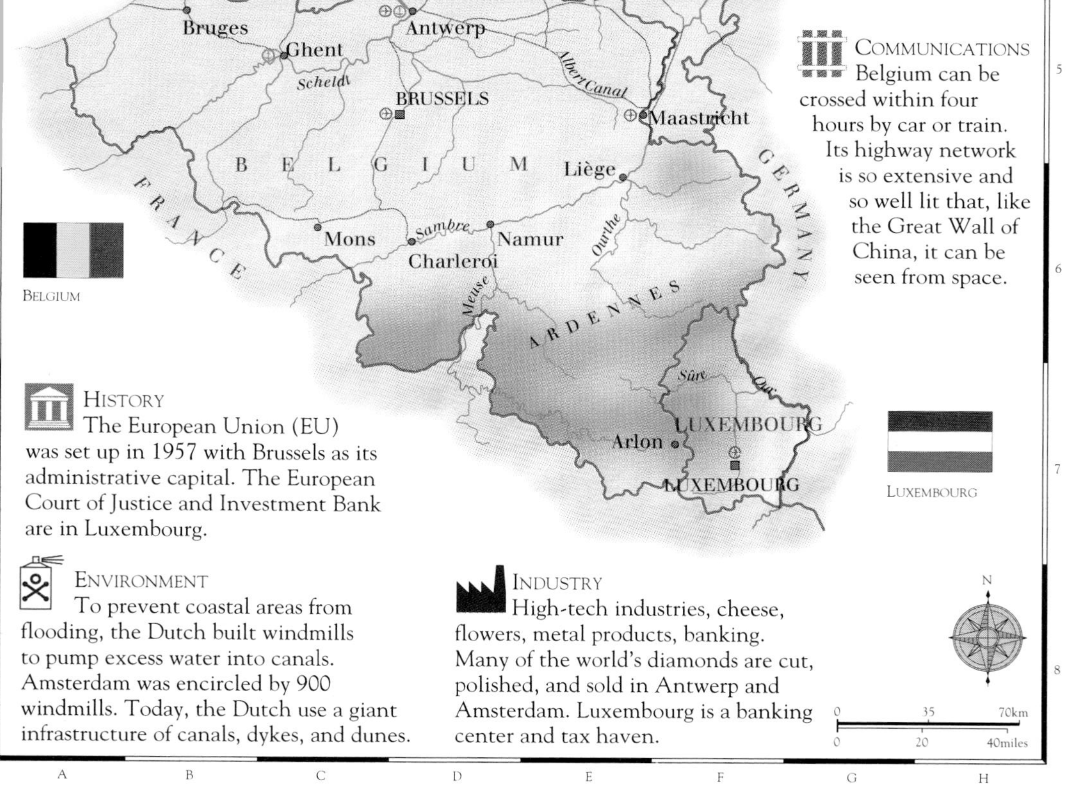
Bruges
Ghent
Scheldt
Antwerp
BRUSSELS
Albert Canal
Maastricht
B E L G I U M
Liège
FRANCE
GERMANY
Mons
Sambre
Namur
Charleroi
Ourthe
Meuse
ARDENNES
Sûre
Our
LUXEMBOURG
Arlon
LUXEMBOURG
Belgium
Luxembourg
N
0
35
70km
0
20
40miles
A
B
C
D
E
F
G
H
5
6
7
8

Communications

Belgium can be crossed within four hours by car or train. Its highway network is so extensive and so well lit that, like the Great Wall of China, it can be seen from space.

History

The European Union (EU) was set up in 1957 with Brussels as its administrative capital. The European Court of Justice and Investment Bank are in Luxembourg.

Environment

To prevent coastal areas from flooding, the Dutch built windmills to pump excess water into canals. Amsterdam was encircled by 900 windmills. Today, the Dutch use a giant infrastructure of canals, dykes, and dunes.

Industry

High-tech industries, cheese, flowers, metal products, banking. Many of the world's diamonds are cut, polished, and sold in Antwerp and Amsterdam. Luxembourg is a banking center and tax haven.

Northwest Europe facts

United Kingdom

- London's theaters, art galleries, and historical buildings are a major tourist attraction.
- British people meet to talk and drink in public houses (pubs).
- Scotland retains a distinct educational and legal system that differs from the rest of the UK.

ESSENTIAL FACTS

- ⊙ London
- 94,550 sq miles (244,880 sq km)
- 59.5 million
- Pound sterling
- English
- ▲ Parliamentary democracy
- 78 years

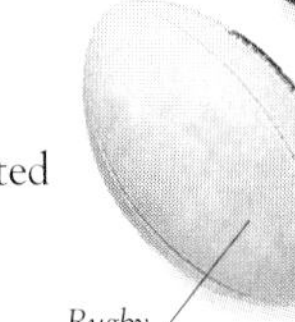
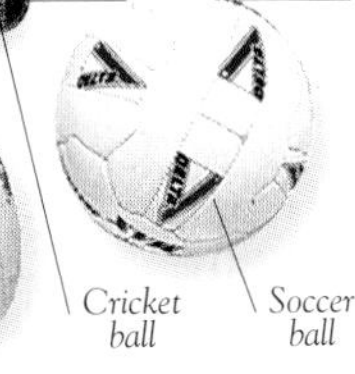

Rugby ball

Cricket ball

Soccer ball

SPORTING EXPORTS
Many sports invented in the UK are now played worldwide.

TALL BOY
Big Ben, the Houses of Parliament's clock, is one of London's major landmarks.

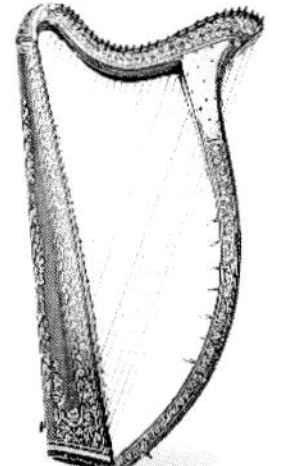

IRISH HARP
An instrument used in traditional Irish music, the harp has been played in Ireland since the 1100s.

Ireland

- The nation gained full sovereignty from the UK in 1937.
- Ireland has the lowest consumption of alcohol per person in the European Union.
- Irish Gaelic is used as an everyday language by around 20,000 people.

ESSENTIAL FACTS

- ⊙ Dublin
- 27,135 sq miles (70,280 sq km)
- 3.8 million
- Euro
- Irish, English
- ▲ Parliamentary democracy
- 77 years

BELGIUM

- The cultural mix of French-speaking Walloons and Flemings forms the national identity of Belgium.
- Belgium's highway network is so extensive and well lit that it can be seen from space.
- The country is the world's third largest producer of chocolate.

ESSENTIAL FACTS

⊙ Brussels

11,780 sq miles (30,510 sq km)

10.3 million

Euro

French, Dutch, German

▲ Parliamentary democracy

78 years

SPACE-AGE STRUCTURE
The design of Belgium's futuristic Atomium building is based on the molecular structure of an iron crystal.

DUTCH TULIPS
The Netherlands is Europe's largest producer of flowers. The cultivation of bulbs such as daffodils and tulips is a specialty.

NETHERLANDS

- Dutch laws on sexuality and drugs are less strict than in other parts of Europe.
- Rotterdam is the world's largest port.

ESSENTIAL FACTS

⊙ Amsterdam, The Hague

41,526 sq km (16,033 sq miles)

16.2 million

Euro

Dutch

▲ Parliamentary democracy

78 years

LUXEMBOURG

⊙ Luxembourg Ville

442,000

Letzeburgish, French, German

LUXEMBOURG BANKING
The nation of Luxembourg is a center of international banking and finance.

SPAIN AND PORTUGAL

SUPREME SKILL IN shipbuilding and navigation enabled both Spain and Portugal to become the most powerful empires of the 16th century. Both have a seafaring history; Christopher Columbus sailed to America in 1492, and Vasco da Gama, the Portuguese explorer, was the first to sail around Africa to India in 1497.

ATLANTIC OCEAN
Oviedo
Santiago
Galicia
Minh
Esla Res.
Porto
Douro
Coimbra
PORTUGAL
Tagus
Alcántara Res.
LISBON (LISBOA)
Setúbal
Guadiana
Beja
SIERRA
Sevilla
Lagos
Faro
Gibraltar
Strait of

INDUSTRY

Fishing, auto manufacture, olives, cork, shipbuilding, citrus fruits, tourism. Spain and Portugal are famous for fortified wines. Sherry is named after Jerez de la Frontera, Spain, and Port after Porto, Portugal.

CLIMATE

Spain's coastal areas are milder than the central plateau, which has a more extreme temperature range. Almeria, Spain, contains Europe's only desert. Portugal's Mediterranean climate is moderated by the Atlantic.

PORTUGAL

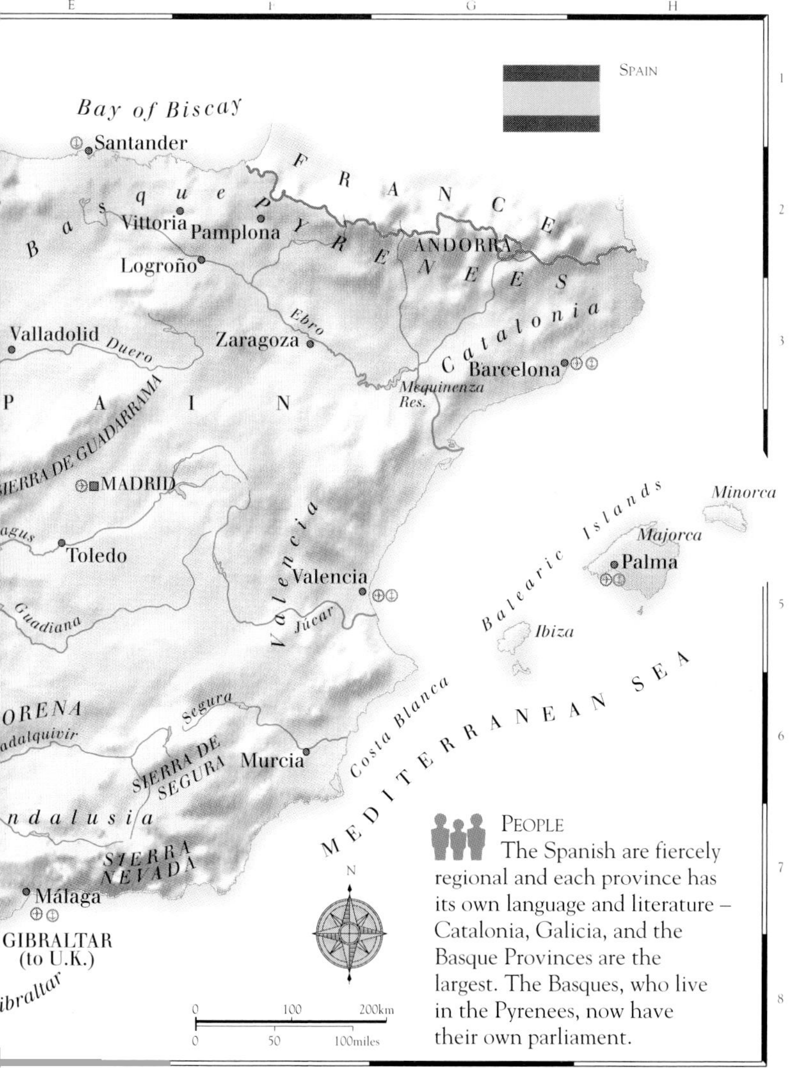

E
F
G
H
1
2
3
5
6
7
8
SPAIN
Bay of Biscay
Santander
FRANCE
Basque
Vittoria
Pamplona
PYRENEES
ANDORRA
Logroño
Ebro
Catalonia
Valladolid
Duero
Zaragoza
Barcelona
Mequinenza Res.
SPAIN
SIERRA DE GUADARRAMA
MADRID
Minorca
Balearic Islands
Majorca
Palma
Tagus
Toledo
Valencia
Valencia
Guadiana
Júcar
Ibiza
MEDITERRANEAN SEA
Costa Blanca
MORENA
Segura
Guadalquivir
SIERRA DE SEGURA
Murcia
Andalusia
SIERRA NEVADA
Málaga
GIBRALTAR (to U.K.)
Gibraltar
N
0
100
200km
0
50
100miles

PEOPLE

The Spanish are fiercely regional and each province has its own language and literature – Catalonia, Galicia, and the Basque Provinces are the largest. The Basques, who live in the Pyrenees, now have their own parliament.

FRANCE

FOLLOWING THE FRENCH Revolution (1789–99), France became Europe's first modern republic, and possessed a colonial empire that included parts of Asia and Africa. France and Spain jointly governed Andorra from 1278 until 1993, when the principality held its first full elections. Monaco is a lucrative banking center.

English Channel
Cherbourg
Le Havre
Channel Islands (to U.K.)
Caen
NORMANDY
Île d'Ouessant
Brest
BRITTANY
Rennes
Le Mans
Belle Île
Loire
Nantes
ATLANTIC OCEAN
Poitiers
Bordeaux
Garonne
PYRENEES
SPAIN

PEOPLE

Despite a strong national identity, the Bretons, Normans, Alsatians, Corsicans, and the Monegasque from Monaco still maintain their regional traditions.

ANDORRA

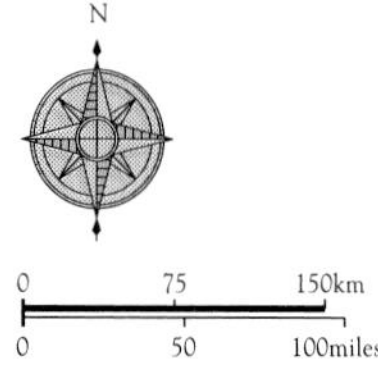
N
0 75 150km
0 50 100miles

COMMUNICATIONS

The French lead the world in high-speed train technology. First run in 1981, the TGV (*Train à Grande Vitesse*) is one of the world's fastest trains, with a top speed of 186 mph (300 km/h).

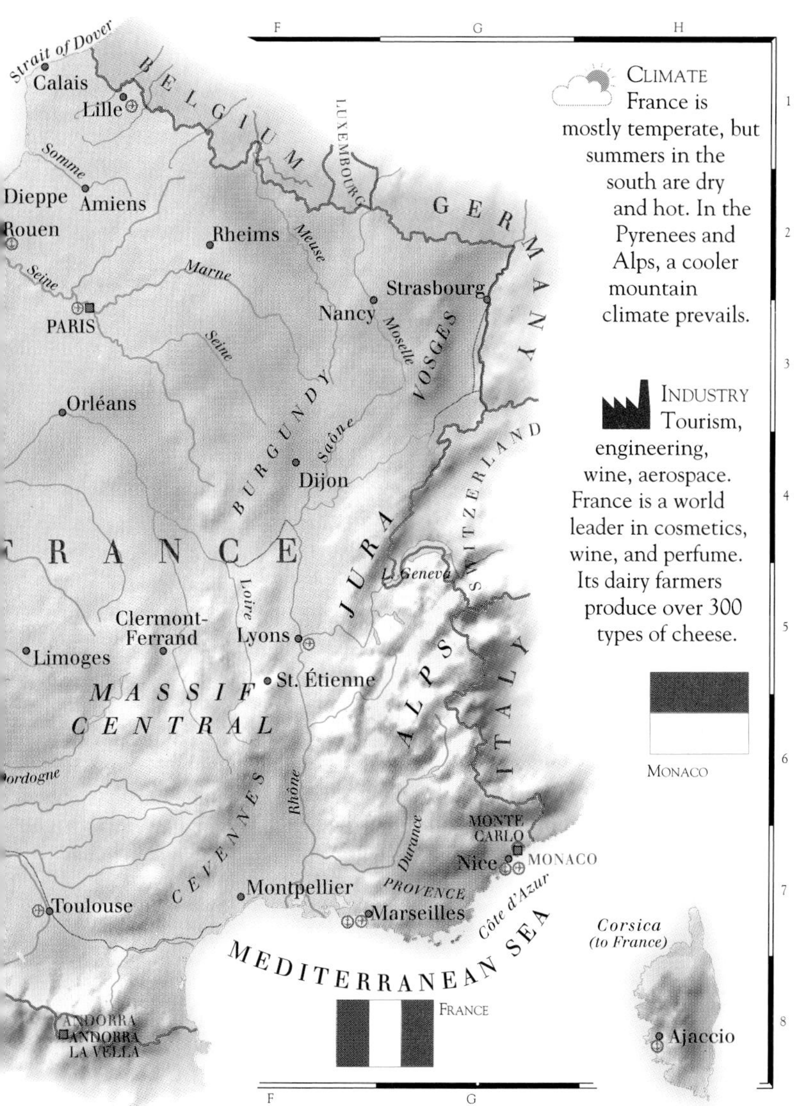
F
G
H
Strait of Dover
Calais
Lille
BELGIUM
LUXEMBOURG
Somme
Dieppe
Amiens
Rouen
Rheims
Meuse
GERMANY
Seine
Marne
Strasbourg
PARIS
Nancy
Moselle
VOSGES
Seine
Orléans
BURGUNDY
Saône
Dijon
SWITZERLAND
FRANCE
JURA
L. Geneva
Loire
Clermont-Ferrand
Lyons
Limoges
St. Étienne
MASSIF CENTRAL
ALPS
ITALY
Dordogne
Rhône
CEVENNES
Durance
MONTE CARLO
Nice
MONACO
Montpellier
PROVENCE
Toulouse
Marseilles
Côte d'Azur
Corsica
(to France)
MEDITERRANEAN SEA
ANDORRA
ANDORRA LA VELLA
Ajaccio
FRANCE
MONACO
1
2
3
4
5
6
7
8

CLIMATE France is mostly temperate, but summers in the south are dry and hot. In the Pyrenees and Alps, a cooler mountain climate prevails.

INDUSTRY Tourism, engineering, wine, aerospace. France is a world leader in cosmetics, wine, and perfume. Its dairy farmers produce over 300 types of cheese.

Italy and Malta

THE BOOT-SHAPED PENINSULA of Italy stretches from the Alps to the Ionian Sea and includes Sardinia, Sicily, and other small, offshore islands. Italy also contains two independent enclaves – the Vatican City in Rome and the Republic of San Marino near Rimini. The Romans, Arabs, French, Turks, Spanish, and British have all fought for or colonized Malta, which has been independent since 1964.

AUSTRIA
SWITZERLAND
ALPS
L. Como
LOMBARDY
DOLOMITES
SLOVENIA
L. Maggiore
L. Garda
Piave
Trieste
Milan
Mestre
Verona
Padua
Venice
Turin
Po
Gulf of Venice
Comacchio Lagoon
FRANCE
Genoa
APENNINES
Reno
Bologna
SAN MARINO
ADRIATIC
Gulf of Genoa
Florence
SAN MARINO
Arno
LIGURIAN SEA

PEOPLE
Venetians were a seafaring people, whose ships carried silks and spices from Asia. The Venetian trader and explorer Marco Polo is said to have brought the recipe for pasta from China.

HISTORY
Italy was once a collection of small kingdoms and city-states, which were vulnerable to internal wars. It was united in 1870, through the efforts of the soldier Guiseppe Garibaldi and the politician Count Camillo di Cavour.

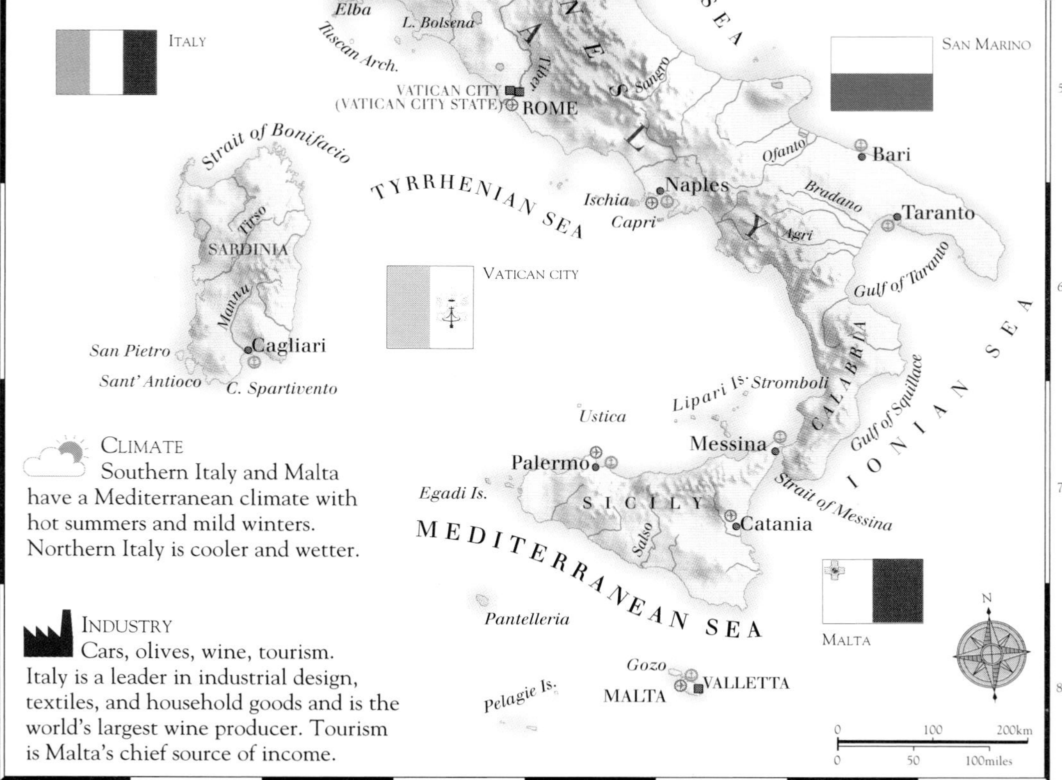

ITALY
SAN MARINO
VATICAN CITY
MALTA
Elba
L. Bolsena
Tuscan Arch.
VATICAN CITY
(VATICAN CITY STATE)
ROME
Tiber
Sangro
Ofanto
Bari
Bradano
Taranto
Agri
Naples
Ischia
Capri
TYRRHENIAN SEA
Strait of Bonifacio
Tirso
SARDINIA
Mannu
Cagliari
San Pietro
Sant' Antioco
C. Spartivento
Gulf of Taranto
CALABRIA
IONIAN SEA
Lipari Is.
Stromboli
Gulf of Squillace
Ustica
Messina
Palermo
Egadi Is.
SICILY
Salso
Catania
Strait of Messina
MEDITERRANEAN SEA
Pantelleria
Gozo
VALLETTA
MALTA
Pelagie Is.
N
0
100
200km
0
50
100miles
A
B
C
D
E
F
G
H
5
6
7
8

CLIMATE

Southern Italy and Malta have a Mediterranean climate with hot summers and mild winters. Northern Italy is cooler and wetter.

INDUSTRY

Cars, olives, wine, tourism. Italy is a leader in industrial design, textiles, and household goods and is the world's largest wine producer. Tourism is Malta's chief source of income.

Southwest Europe facts

Spain

- Young Spanish men tend to live at home until their late 20s.
- Spanish public hospitals are generally considered to be better than private ones.
- Over 3000 festivals and feasts take place every year in Spain.

ESSENTIAL FACTS

- Madrid
- 194,896 sq miles (504,782 sq km)
- 39.9 million
- Euro
- Spanish
- Parliamentary democracy
- 79 years

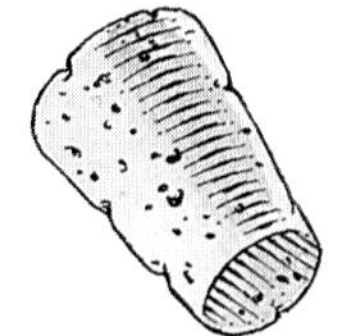

PORTUGUESE CORK
More than half the world's cork is supplied by Portugal, the main product being the bottle stopper.

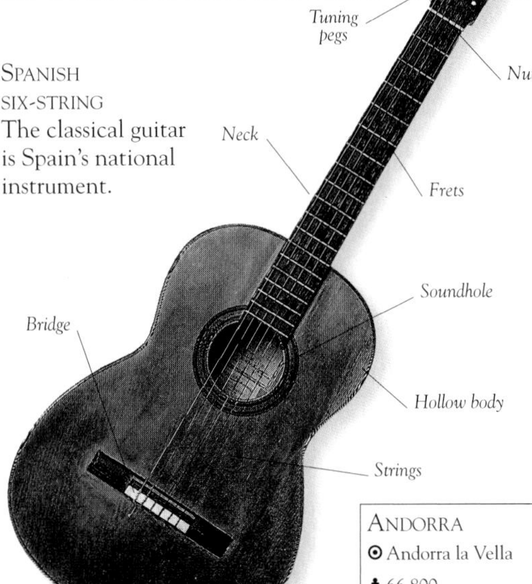
Tuning pegs
Nut
Neck
Frets
Soundhole
Bridge
Hollow body
Strings

SPANISH SIX-STRING
The classical guitar is Spain's national instrument.

Portugal

- Family ties are a major part of Portuguese life.
- Over 40% of the population have private health insurance.
- Portugal has few natural resources.

ESSENTIAL FACTS

- Lisbon
- 35,672 sq miles (92,391 sq km)
- 10 million
- Euro
- Portuguese
- Multiparty democracy
- 76 years

Andorra

- Andorra la Vella
- 66,800
- Catalan

ITALY

- Tourists have visited Italy since the 1500s.
- Italy is a world leader in product design and the fashion industry.
- Venice is such a popular place to visit that pedestrians have to use one-way systems in the summer.
- Most Italians live at home before marriage.

ESSENTIAL FACTS

⊙ Rome

116,305 sq miles (301,230 sq km)

57.5 million

Euro

Italian

▲ Parliamentary democracy

79 years

VENETIAN MASKS
Masks are traditionally worn during the February carnival in Venice.

SAN MARINO

⊙ San Marino

26,900

Italian

VATICAN CITY

⊙ Vatican City

524

Italian, Latin

MALTA

⊙ Valletta

392,000

Maltese, English

MONACO

⊙ Monaco

31,700

French

FRANCE

- Paris is the most visited European city.
- The French wine industry dates back to 600 BC.
- More medicine is consumed per person in France than in any other country.
- Most French people spend their holidays in France, rather than traveling abroad.

ESSENTIAL FACTS

⊙ Paris

547,030 sq km (211,208 sq miles)

59.5 million

Euro

French

▲ Multiparty republic

79 years

PEDAL POWER
The *Tour de France* bicycle race is the most famous in the world.

CENTRAL EUROPE

HISTORICALLY AN unstable part of the continent, central Europe became part of the Eastern Bloc after World War II. Czechoslovakia and Poland had governments with strong ties to the former USSR. In 1989, they broke away from Communism, and in 1993 Czechoslovakia split into the Czech Republic and Slovakia. Poland is still moving slowly towards a market economy.

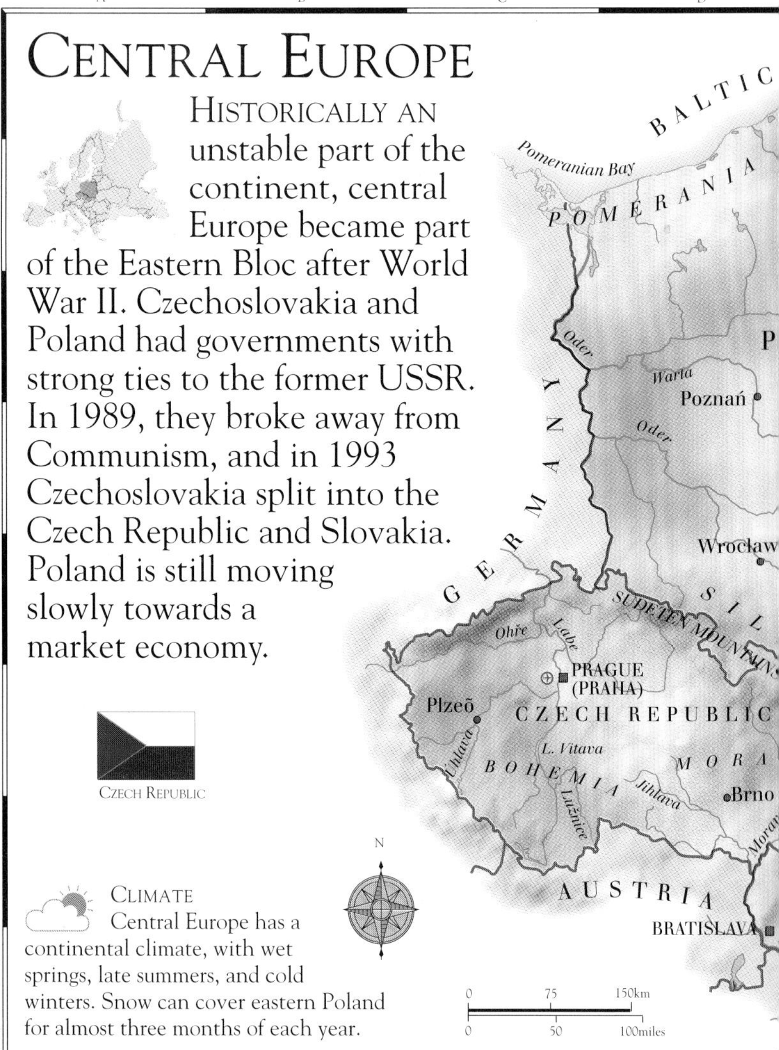
BALTIC
Pomeranian Bay
POMERANIA
Oder
Warta
Poznań
Oder
GERMANY
Wrocław
SUDETEN MOUNTAINS
Ohře
Labe
PRAGUE
(PRAHA)
Plzeõ
CZECH REPUBLIC
Úhlava
L. Vitava
BOHEMIA
Lužnice
Jihlava
Brno
AUSTRIA
BRATISLAVA
N
0 75 150km
0 50 100miles

CZECH REPUBLIC

CLIMATE
Central Europe has a continental climate, with wet springs, late summers, and cold winters. Snow can cover eastern Poland for almost three months of each year.

SEA
RUSSIAN FEDERATION (KALININGRAD OBLAST)
LITHUANIA
Gdańsk
L. Mamry
L. Śniardwy
L. Jeziorak
Bydgoszcz
Narew
PODLASIE
BELARUS
POLAND
Bug
L. Włocławskie
WARSAW (WARSZAWA)
Krzna
Prosna
Vistula
Łódź
Warta
Lublin
Sosnowiec
Vistula
MALOPOLSKA
San
Katowice
Wisłoka
Kraków
WYZYNA
Ostrava
GALICIA
BESKID MTS.
UKRAINE
CARPATHIANS
Váh
SLOVAKIA
Torysa
Košice
Banská Bystrica
Hron
Slaná
Váh
Danube
HUNGARY

POLAND

INDUSTRY

Wood industries, coal, sulfur, iron, steel, copper, fruits. Beer, made from barley grown locally, is one of the best-known products to come out of the Czech Republic. Mining and metal production has a long history in Slovakia, and Poland is a major world exporter of coal.

ENVIRONMENT

After 1945, the central European states industrialized rapidly. Today, only four percent of Poland's rivers have water fit for consumption, and half of its cities have no sewage treatment facilities. In central Europe acid rain has harmed trees and eroded buildings across the region.

SLOVAKIA

GERMANY

IT WAS NOT UNTIL 1871 that many small independent states were united under Prussia to form Germany. After 1945, the country was divided again, into a democratic West Germany and a Soviet-dominated East Germany. Reunified in 1990, Germany is, like France, a leading member of the European Union and is currently Europe's strongest economic power.

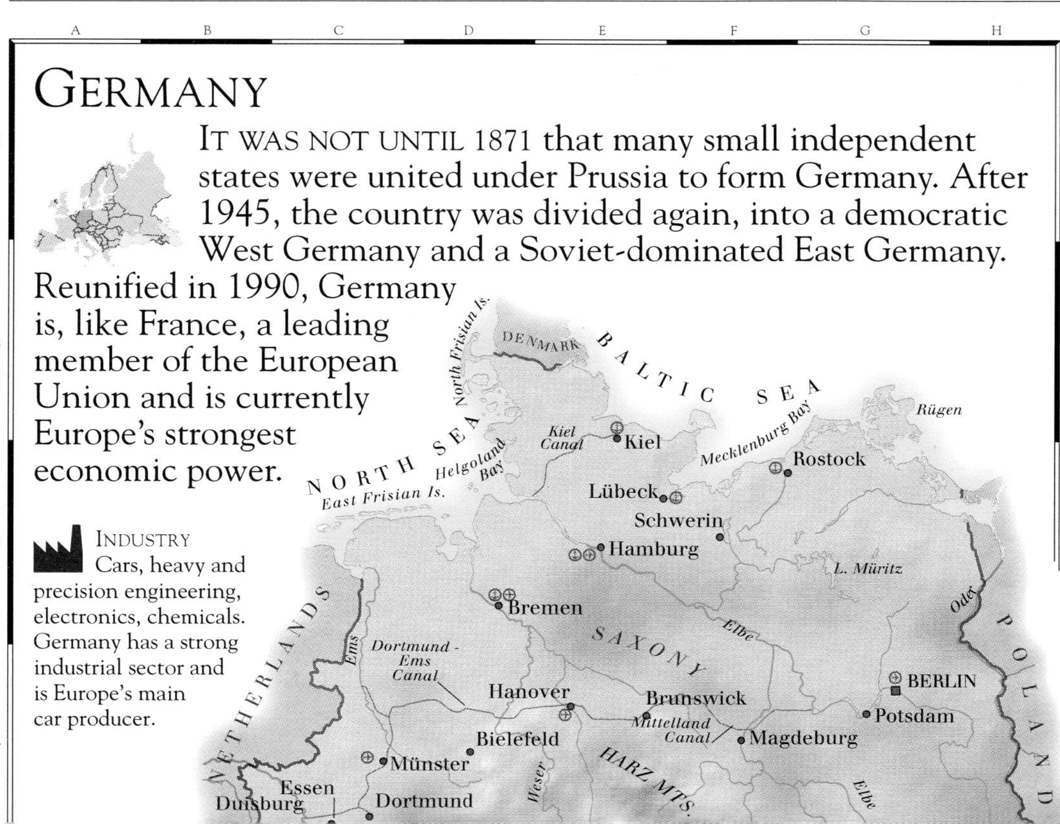
A B C D E F G H
1 2 3 4
NORTH SEA
BALTIC SEA
North Frisian Is.
East Frisian Is.
DENMARK
Helgoland Bay
Kiel Canal
Kiel
Mecklenburg Bay
Rostock
Rügen
Lübeck
Schwerin
Hamburg
L. Müritz
Bremen
SAXONY
Elbe
Oder
POLAND
NETHERLANDS
Ems
Dortmund - Ems Canal
Hanover
Brunswick
Mittelland Canal
Magdeburg
BERLIN
Potsdam
Bielefeld
Münster
HARZ MTS.
Weser
Essen
Duisburg
Dortmund

INDUSTRY
Cars, heavy and precision engineering, electronics, chemicals. Germany has a strong industrial sector and is Europe's main car producer.

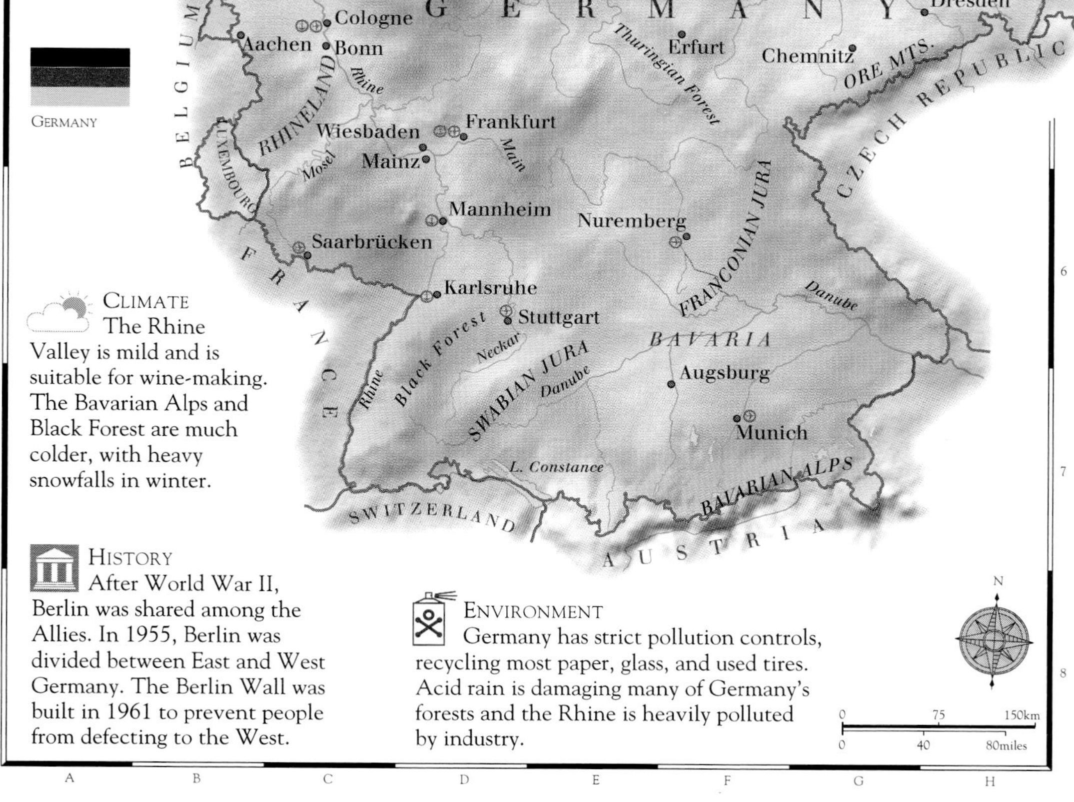

GERMANY
G E R M A N Y
Dresden
Cologne
Aachen
Bonn
Erfurt
Chemnitz
ORE MTS.
CZECH REPUBLIC
BELGIUM
LUXEMBOURG
RHINELAND
Rhine
Thuringian Forest
Wiesbaden
Frankfurt
Mainz
Main
Mosel
Mannheim
Nuremberg
FRANCONIAN JURA
Saarbrücken
FRANCE
Karlsruhe
Stuttgart
Danube
Black Forest
Neckar
BAVARIA
SWABIAN JURA
Augsburg
Munich
L. Constance
BAVARIAN ALPS
SWITZERLAND
AUSTRIA
N
0
75
150km
40
80miles
A
B
C
D
E
F
G
H
5
6
7
8

Climate

The Rhine Valley is mild and is suitable for wine-making. The Bavarian Alps and Black Forest are much colder, with heavy snowfalls in winter.

History

After World War II, Berlin was shared among the Allies. In 1955, Berlin was divided between East and West Germany. The Berlin Wall was built in 1961 to prevent people from defecting to the West.

Environment

Germany has strict pollution controls, recycling most paper, glass, and used tires. Acid rain is damaging many of Germany's forests and the Rhine is heavily polluted by industry.

Switzerland and Austria

ONCE THE CENTER OF the vast Hapsburg Empire, the Republic of Austria was created after World War I. Switzerland has been a neutral country since 1815, and many international organizations such as the Red Cross have their headquarters there. Liechtenstein is closely allied to Switzerland, which handles its foreign relations.

LIECHTENSTEIN

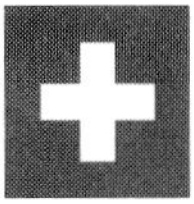

SWITZERLAND

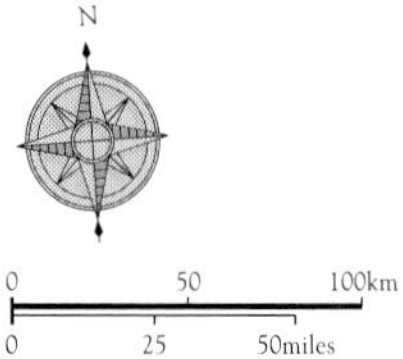

GERMANY
FRANCE
ITALY
SWITZERLAND
ALPS
L. Constance
Winterthur
Bregenz
St. Gallen
Basle
Rhine
Zurich
L. Zurich
LIECHTENSTEIN
VADUZ
Aare
L. Biel
L. Lucerne
BERN
ÖTZTAL ALPS
RHAETIAN ALPS
L. Neuchâtel
L. Thun
Lausanne
L. Geneva
BERNESE ALPS
Geneva
Rhône
PENNINE ALPS
L. Maggiore
L. Lugano
N
0 50 100km
0 25 50miles

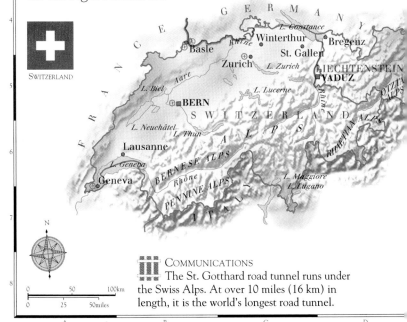

COMMUNICATIONS

The St. Gotthard road tunnel runs under the Swiss Alps. At over 10 miles (16 km) in length, it is the world's longest road tunnel.

E F G H

CLIMATE
Altitude determines climate, with alpine areas experiencing colder temperatures and more rainfall. South of the Alps is considerably warmer and sunnier.

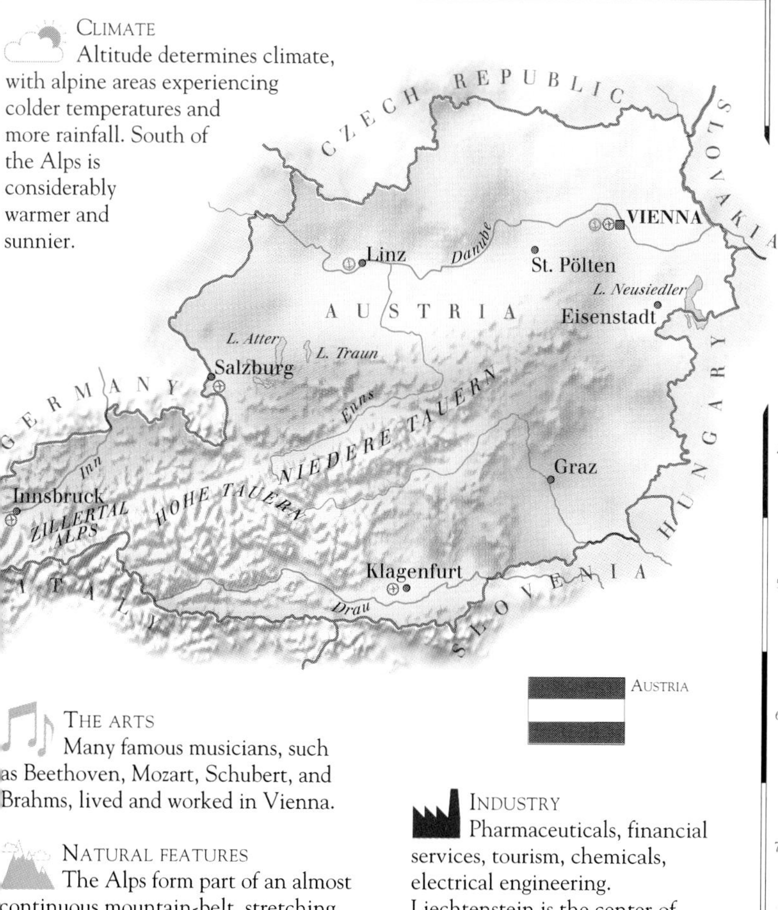
CZECH REPUBLIC
SLOVAKIA
VIENNA
Linz
Danube
St. Pölten
L. Neusiedler
AUSTRIA
Eisenstadt
L. Atter
L. Traun
Salzburg
GERMANY
Enns
NIEDERE TAUERN
HUNGARY
Graz
Inn
Innsbruck
HOHE TAUERN
ZILLERTAL ALPS
Klagenfurt
SLOVENIA
ITALY
Drau
1
4
5

AUSTRIA

THE ARTS
Many famous musicians, such as Beethoven, Mozart, Schubert, and Brahms, lived and worked in Vienna.

NATURAL FEATURES
The Alps form part of an almost continuous mountain-belt, stretching from the Pyrenees in France to the Himalayas in Asia. They are also the source of Europe's largest rivers – the Rhine, Rhône, and Danube.

INDUSTRY
Pharmaceuticals, financial services, tourism, chemicals, electrical engineering. Liechtenstein is the center of world dental manufacture. False teeth and dental materials are exported to over 100 countries.

6 7 8

E F G H

Central Europe facts

SWITZERLAND

- Three-quarters of Switzerland consists of mountains, forests, and ice.
- Swiss inventions include baby food and condensed milk.
- The banks of Switzerland attract investors worldwide.

ESSENTIAL FACTS

⊙ Bern

15,942 sq miles (41,290 sq km)

7.2 million

Swiss franc

German, French, Italian

▲ Multiparty republic

79 years

QUALITY TIME
Swiss watchmakers are famous for the quality and craftmanship of their products.

GERMANY

- The rivers and canals of Germany carry as much freight as its roads.
- The best-known beer festival in Europe, the *Oktoberfest*, is held annually in the city of Munich.

ESSENTIAL FACTS

⊙ Berlin

137,846 sq miles (357,021 sq km)

82 million

Euro

German

▲ Parliamentary democracy

78 years

GERMAN BEER STEIN

AUSTRIA

- University degrees take six years or more to complete in Austria.
- Salzburg's summer music festival is a major tourist attraction.

ESSENTIAL FACTS

⊙ Vienna

32,378 sq miles (83,858 sq km)

8.1 million

Euro

German

▲ Parliamentary democracy

78 years

VIENNESE WHIRL
Austrian composer Johann Strauss (1825–1899) composed the famous Viennese *Blue Danube* waltz.

Czech Republic

• The Czech homeland was originally called Bohemia.
• Prague's gilded church roofs gave the city the name *zlata Praha*, or "golden Prague."
• The Czech Republic is the most polluted country in Europe.

ESSENTIAL FACTS

- ⊙ Prague
- 30,450 sq miles (78,866 sq km)
- 10.3 million
- Czech koruna
- Czech
- ▲ Multiparty republic
- 75 years

Slovakia

• Separation from the Czech Republic in 1993 resulted in full independence for Slovakia for the first time in over 1000 years.

ESSENTIAL FACTS

- ⊙ Bratislava
- 18,859 sq miles (48,845 sq km)
- 5.4 million
- Slovak koruna
- Slovak

Liechtenstein

- ⊙ Vaduz
- 32,200
- German

Poland

• The largest remaining herds of European bison are found in the eastern forests of Poland.
• Poland has seven international borders.
• Polish women hold prominent policy-making posts in politics and business.

ESSENTIAL FACTS

- ⊙ Warsaw
- 120,728 sq miles (312,685 sq km)
- 38.6 million
- Zloty
- Polish
- ▲ Multiparty democracy
- 73 years

PRAGUE, CZECH REPUBLIC
Dating from medieval times, the beautiful capital city of Prague is now a popular tourist destination. The city lies on both banks of the River Vltava and is connected by a series of bridges. It is often called "city of a hundred spires" because it has so many churches.

SOUTH CENTRAL EUROPE

FOR CENTURIES the countries of this region have had strong ties with Europe. In the early 1990s Slovenia, Croatia, and Bosnia and Herzegovina declared their independence from Yugoslavia, to which they had been annexed after World War I. This area boasts the snow-capped Alps, the sunny Adriatic Sea in the south, as well as Hungary's fertile plain.

SLOVENIA

CROATIA

Pag
Zadar
DALM
ADRIATIC SEA
Split
C.Ploâa
Braâ
Hvar
N
0
75
150km
0
50
100miles

CLIMATE

The climate in the region is just as varied as its geography. The interior has a continental climate, with warm summers and bitterly cold winters. Coastal areas in Croatia benefit from Mediterranean temperatures suitable for growing plums, apricots, and grapes.

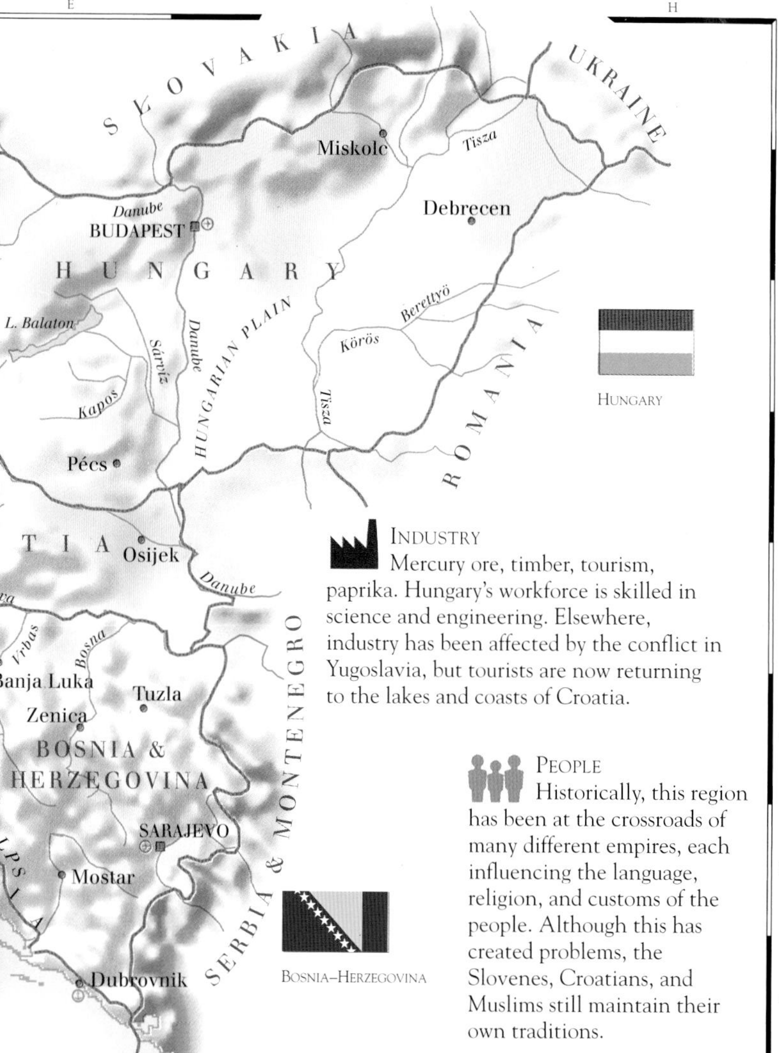
SLOVAKIA
UKRAINE
Miskolc
Tisza
Danube
BUDAPEST
Debrecen
HUNGARY
L. Balaton
HUNGARIAN PLAIN
Berettyó
Danube
Sárviz
Körös
Kapos
Tisza
ROMANIA
Pécs
TIA
Osijek
Danube
Vrbas
Bosna
Banja Luka
Tuzla
Zenica
BOSNIA & HERZEGOVINA
SARAJEVO
SERBIA & MONTENEGRO
Mostar
Dubrovnik

HUNGARY

BOSNIA–HERZEGOVINA

INDUSTRY
Mercury ore, timber, tourism, paprika. Hungary's workforce is skilled in science and engineering. Elsewhere, industry has been affected by the conflict in Yugoslavia, but tourists are now returning to the lakes and coasts of Croatia.

PEOPLE
Historically, this region has been at the crossroads of many different empires, each influencing the language, religion, and customs of the people. Although this has created problems, the Slovenes, Croatians, and Muslims still maintain their own traditions.

SOUTHEAST EUROPE

THIS REGION IS often referred to as the Balkans, from the Turkish word for "mountain." It is made up of countries that have a long history of invasion and occupation. From its source in the Alps, the mighty Danube River flows eastward through Romania and Bulgaria, before pouring into the Black Sea.

A
B
C
D
E
F
G
H
1
2
3
4
ROMANIA
SERBIA & MONTENEGRO
UKRAINE
MOLDOVA
HUNGARY
ROMANIA
CROATIA
CARPATHIANS
TRANSYLVANIAN ALPS
Satu Mare
Baia Mare
Someș
Suceava
Botoșani
Siret
Bistrița
Iași
Cluj-Napoca
Piatra-Neamț
Bacău
Prut
Arad
Târgu Mureș
Mureș
Sibiu
Brașov
Focșani
Zrenjanin
Novi Sad
Danube
Reșița
Timiș
Buzău
Galați
Brăila
Danube Delta
Panâevo
Drobeta-Turnu-Severin
Râmnicu Vâlcea
Târgoviște
Ploiești
Ialomița
BELGRADE (BEOGRAD)
Sava
Smederevo
Jiu
Pitești
Argeș
Olt
BUCHAREST (BUCURESTI)
L. Razim
L. Sinoe
Kraljevo
Serbia
Craiova
Constanța

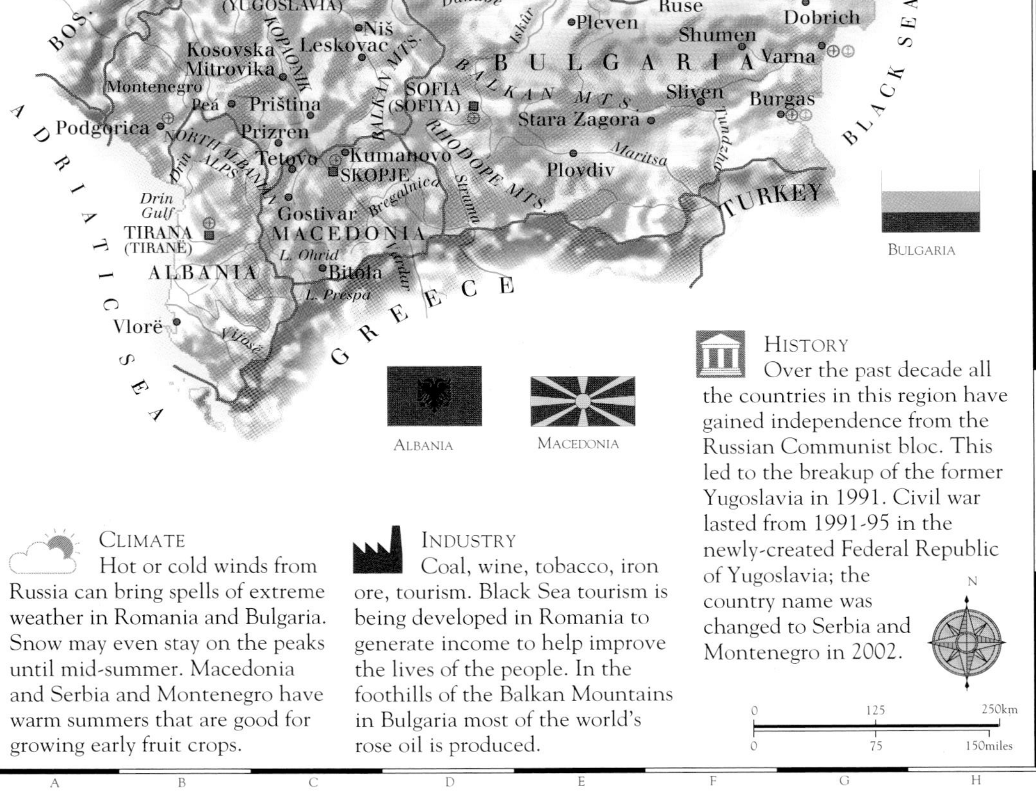

(YUGOSLAVIA)
BOS.
Danube
Iskŭr
Ruse
Pleven
Dobrich
Shumen
Varna
Niš
Leskovac
Kosovska
Mitrovika
KOPAONIK
BALKAN MTS.
B U L G A R I A
BALKAN MTS.
Montenegro
Peá
Priština
SOFIA
(SOFIYA)
Sliven
Burgas
Stara Zagora
Tundzha
BLACK SEA
Podgorica
NORTH ALBANIAN ALPS
Drin
Prizren
Tetovo
Kumanovo
SKOPJE
RHODOPE MTS.
Struma
Maritsa
Plovdiv
TURKEY
ADRIATIC SEA
Drin
Gulf
Gostivar
Bregalnica
TIRANA
(TIRANË)
MACEDONIA
L. Ohrid
Vardar
ALBANIA
Bitola
L. Prespa
GREECE
Vlorë
Vijosë
BULGARIA
ALBANIA
MACEDONIA
N
0
125
250km
0
75
150miles

Climate

Hot or cold winds from Russia can bring spells of extreme weather in Romania and Bulgaria. Snow may even stay on the peaks until mid-summer. Macedonia and Serbia and Montenegro have warm summers that are good for growing early fruit crops.

Industry

Coal, wine, tobacco, iron ore, tourism. Black Sea tourism is being developed in Romania to generate income to help improve the lives of the people. In the foothills of the Balkan Mountains in Bulgaria most of the world's rose oil is produced.

History

Over the past decade all the countries in this region have gained independence from the Russian Communist bloc. This led to the breakup of the former Yugoslavia in 1991. Civil war lasted from 1991-95 in the newly-created Federal Republic of Yugoslavia; the country name was changed to Serbia and Montenegro in 2002.

GREECE

SURROUNDED BY THE Aegean, Ionian, and Cretan seas, no part of Greece is more than 85 miles (137 km) from the coast. Its territory includes the mainland on the Balkan peninsula, and more than 1400 islands. The country is mountainous and less than one-third of the land is cultivated. Greece gained its independence in 1830 after a long and fierce war, ending 400 years of Turkish rule.

CLIMATE

Northwestern Greece is alpine, while parts of Crete are almost subtropical. The islands and the large central plain of the mainland have a Mediterranean climate, with high summer temperatures and mild winters.

GREECE

ENVIRONMENT

Athens suffers from smog, known as *nefos*, which damages its ancient monuments. The Parthenon, part of the Acropolis, has suffered more erosion in the previous two decades than in the past two thousand years.

HISTORY

Regarded as the founders of democracy, the ancient Greeks were advanced for their time. They were the first to study medicine, geometry, and physics (on a scientific basis), and Greece was home to great thinkers such as Plato, Aristotle, and Socrates.

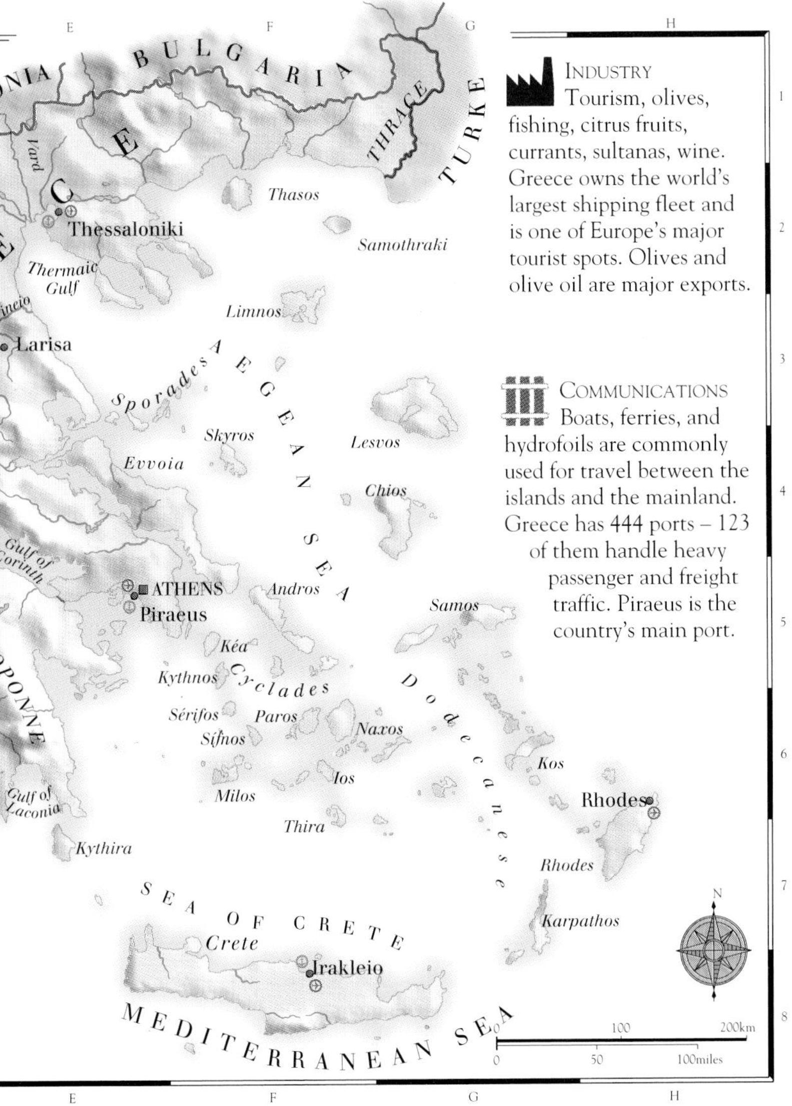

BULGARIA
THRACE
TURKEY
Thasos
Samothraki
Thessaloniki
Thermaic Gulf
Limnos
Larisa
Sporades
AEGEAN SEA
Skyros
Lesvos
Evvoia
Chios
Gulf of Corinth
ATHENS
Piraeus
Andros
Samos
Kéa
Kythnos
Cyclades
Dodecanese
Sérifos
Paros
Naxos
Sífnos
Kos
Ios
Milos
Rhodes
Gulf of Laconia
Thira
Kythira
Rhodes
Karpathos
SEA OF CRETE
Crete
Irakleio
MEDITERRANEAN SEA
0
100
200km
0
50
100miles
N

INDUSTRY
Tourism, olives, fishing, citrus fruits, currants, sultanas, wine. Greece owns the world's largest shipping fleet and is one of Europe's major tourist spots. Olives and olive oil are major exports.

COMMUNICATIONS
Boats, ferries, and hydrofoils are commonly used for travel between the islands and the mainland. Greece has 444 ports – 123 of them handle heavy passenger and freight traffic. Piraeus is the country's main port.

Southern Europe facts

Croatia

- One-third of Croatia is held by the Serbs.
- The Adriatic coastline of Croatia was a popular tourist destination before the recent civil war.

ESSENTIAL FACTS

- ⊙ Zagreb
- 21,830 sq miles (56,540 sq km)
- 4.7 million
- Kuna
- Croatian

DALMATIANS
The Dalmatian dog is named after its first known home, the Dalmatian coastal region of Croatia.

Serbia & Montenegro (Yugoslavia)

- Settlers have lived on the site of present-day Belgrade for 7000 years.

ESSENTIAL FACTS

- ⊙ Belgrade
- 39,517 sq miles (102,350 sq km)
- 10.5 million
- Dinar
- Serbo-Croatian

Bosnia and Herzegovina

- The Bosnian civil war made over two million people homeless by the year 1995.

ESSENTIAL FACTS

- ⊙ Sarajevo
- 19,741 sq miles (51,130 sq km)
- 4.1 million
- Marka
- Serbo-Croat

Albania

- The Albanian's name for their nation is *Shqipërisë*, which means "land of the eagle."

ESSENTIAL FACTS

- ⊙ Tirana
- 11,100 sq miles (28,750 sq km)
- 3.1 million
- Lek
- Albanian

Slovenia

- The average wage in Slovenia is the highest among the former Yugoslav republics.

ESSENTIAL FACTS

- ⊙ Ljubljana
- 7820 sq miles (20,250 sq km)
- 2 million
- Tolar
- Slovene

SLOVENIA IS A MAJOR PRODUCER OF MERCURY, WHICH IS USED IN THERMOMETERS

ROMANIA

- The tuberculosis rate in Romania is the highest in Europe.
- The Romanian Danube delta is to be used as a site for a biosphere reserve.

ESSENTIAL FACTS

⊙ Bucharest

◒ 91,700 sq miles (237,500 sq km)

† 21.7 million

Romanian Leu

♡ Romanian

BULGARIA

- In Bulgaria there is a national museum devoted entirely to humor and satire.
- Bulgarians nod for "no" and shake their heads for "yes."
- People in Sofia travel by trolleybuses that get their power from overhead electric cables.

ESSENTIAL FACTS

⊙ Sofia

◒ 42,822 sq miles (110,910 sq km)

† 7.9 million

Lev

♡ Bulgarian

▲ Multiparty republic

71 years

GREECE

- People throughout the Greek Islands use the flat roofs of their houses to dry fruit in summer and collect rain in winter.

ESSENTIAL FACTS

⊙ Athens

◒ 50,942 sq miles (131,940 sq km)

† 10.6 million

Euro

♡ Greek

▲ Presidential democracy

78 years

MACEDONIA

- Lake Ohrid in Macedonia is the deepest lake in Europe.

MACEDONIA FACTS

⊙ Skopje

◒ 9781 sq miles (25,333 sq km)

† 2 million

Macedonian denar

♡ Macedonian

GREEK MUSIC
The bouzouki is a traditional Greek stringed instrument.

HUNGARY

- The Hungarian language has features not found in any other western language.
- The city of Budapest was originally Buda and Pest, two towns located on each side of the Danube River.

ESSENTIAL FACTS

⊙ Budapest

◒ 35,919 sq miles (93,030 sq km)

† 9.9 million

Forint

♡ Hungarian

▲ Multiparty republic

71 years

THE BALTIC STATES AND BELARUS

LITHUANIA, ESTONIA, AND LATVIA – the three Baltic States – were the first republics to declare their independence from the Soviet Union in 1990-91. Economic reform has been slow and problems such as food shortages still remain. The Chernobyl nuclear disaster in Ukraine in 1986 has had lasting effects on the environment and economy, as well as the health of Belarussians.

PEOPLE

Russians, Belarussians, and Ukrainians resettled in Latvia when it was part of the USSR. Today Latvians make up only about half of the whole population, and they are a minority in the capital.

Gulf of Finland
TALLINN
ESTONIA
Narva
Hiiumaa
Saaremaa
Pärnu
L. Peipus
Võrtsjärv
Tartu
BALTIC SEA
Gulf of Riga
RUSSIAN
Venta
RIGA
W. Dvina
LATVIA
Liepāja

LITHUANIA

ESTONIA

LATVIA

BELARUS

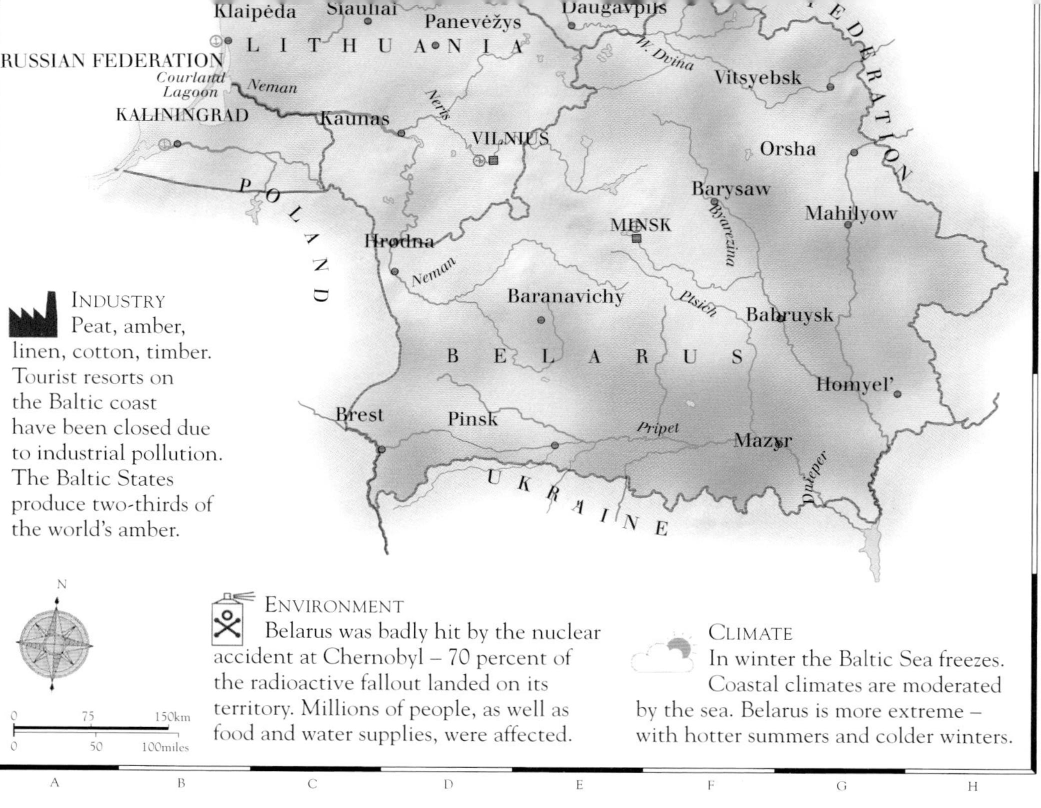
Klaipėda
Šiauliai
Panevėžys
Daugavpils
LITHUANIA
RUSSIAN FEDERATION
Courland Lagoon
Neman
KALININGRAD
Kaunas
Neris
VILNIUS
W. Dvina
Vitsyebsk
Orsha
FEDERATION
Barysaw
Byarezina
Mahilyow
MINSK
POLAND
Hrodna
Neman
Baranavichy
Ptsich
Babruysk
BELARUS
Homyel'
Brest
Pinsk
Pripet
Mazyr
Dnieper
UKRAINE
N
0 75 150km
0 50 100miles
A B C D E F G H
5 6 7 8

INDUSTRY
Peat, amber, linen, cotton, timber. Tourist resorts on the Baltic coast have been closed due to industrial pollution. The Baltic States produce two-thirds of the world's amber.

ENVIRONMENT
Belarus was badly hit by the nuclear accident at Chernobyl – 70 percent of the radioactive fallout landed on its territory. Millions of people, as well as food and water supplies, were affected.

CLIMATE
In winter the Baltic Sea freezes. Coastal climates are moderated by the sea. Belarus is more extreme – with hotter summers and colder winters.

EUROPEAN RUSSIA

SPANNING THE TWO continents of Europe and Asia, the Russian Federation is the world's largest country. In 1917, the world's first communist government took power and in 1923, Russia became the USSR, which included many territories that were once part of the Russian Empire. Economic reforms in the 1980s led to changes resulting in the fall of communism in 1991.

INDUSTRY

Oil, gas, gold, diamonds, hydrocarbons, precious metals. Russia has large reserves of iron, coal, and nickel. Huge factories, which have grown without environmental controls, are causing pollution problems.

Novaya Zemlya
KARA SEA
Murmansk
L. Umbozero
BARENTS SEA
Kara Strait
Vaygach I.
L. Pyaozero
KOLA PENINSULA
L. Topozero
Kolguyev I.
FINLAND
WHITE SEA
L. Segozero
Arkhangel'sk
Pechora
L. Ladoga
Vorkuta
ESTONIA
L. Onega
Onega
Usa
St. Petersburg
LATVIA
RUSSIAN
Izhma

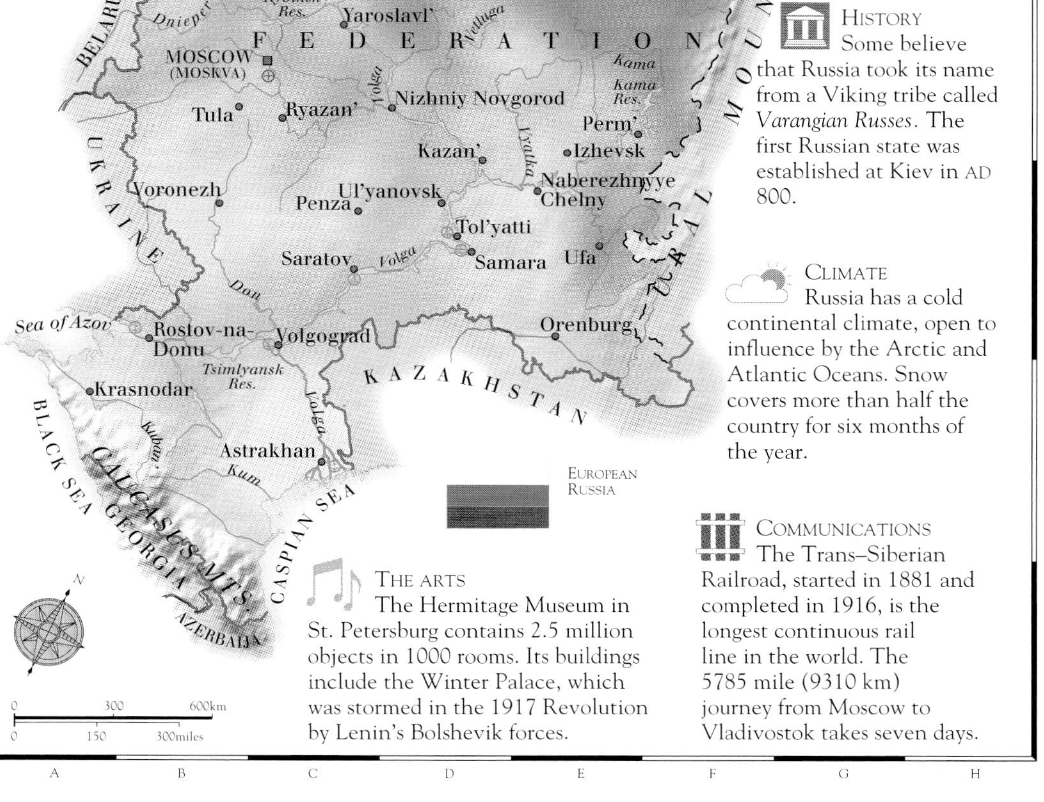
FEDERATION
URAL MOUN
KAZAKHSTAN
UKRAINE
BELARUS
GEORGIA
AZERBAIJAN
CAUCASUS MTS.
BLACK SEA
CASPIAN SEA
Sea of Azov
MOSCOW (MOSKVA)
Tula
Ryazan'
Yaroslavl'
Nizhniy Novgorod
Kazan'
Perm'
Izhevsk
Naberezhnyye Chelny
Voronezh
Penza
Ul'yanovsk
Tol'yatti
Samara
Ufa
Saratov
Orenburg
Rostov-na-Donu
Volgograd
Krasnodar
Astrakhan
Rybinsk Res.
Kama Res.
Tsimlyansk Res.
Dnieper
Vetluga
Volga
Kama
Vyatka
Don
Kuban'
Kum
N
0 300 600km
0 150 300miles
EUROPEAN RUSSIA
A B C D E F G H
5 6 7 8

HISTORY

Some believe that Russia took its name from a Viking tribe called *Varangian Russes*. The first Russian state was established at Kiev in AD 800.

CLIMATE

Russia has a cold continental climate, open to influence by the Arctic and Atlantic Oceans. Snow covers more than half the country for six months of the year.

COMMUNICATIONS

The Trans–Siberian Railroad, started in 1881 and completed in 1916, is the longest continuous rail line in the world. The 5785 mile (9310 km) journey from Moscow to Vladivostok takes seven days.

THE ARTS

The Hermitage Museum in St. Petersburg contains 2.5 million objects in 1000 rooms. Its buildings include the Winter Palace, which was stormed in the 1917 Revolution by Lenin's Bolshevik forces.

UKRAINE AND THE CAUCASUS

SEPARATED FROM the Russian Federation by the Caucasus mountains, the newly independent Caucasian Republics – Armenia, Azerbaijan, and Georgia – are rich in natural resources. The Ukraine, Europe's largest country, is dominated by a flat and fertile plain.

BELARUS
POLAND
SLOVAKIA
HUNGARY
MOLDOVA
ROMANIA
UKRA
Styr
Sluch
Dniester
Luts'k
Rivne
L'viv
Ternopil'
Zhytomyr
Chernobyl
Chernihiv
Kiev Res.
KIEV (KIYIV)
Bila Tserkva
Khmel'nyts'kyy
Ivano-Frankivs'k
Vinnytsya
Chernivtsi
CHISINAU (KISHINEV)
Odesa

ENVIRONMENT

As a result of the 1986 Chernobyl nuclear disaster, 4 million Ukrainians live in radioactive areas. In 1994, reactors from the Chernobyl plant were still being used to provide nuclear power.

MOLDOVA

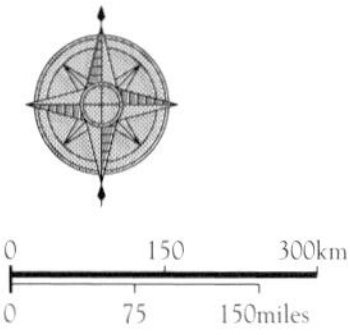

N
0 150 300km
0 75 150miles

CLIMATE

Ukraine and Moldova have a continental climate, with distinctive seasons. Armenia, Azerbaijan, and Georgia are protected from cold air from the north by the Caucasus mountains.

INDUSTRY

Coal, iron, automobiles, wine, citrus fruits, cotton, minerals. The Ukraine was known as the "breadbasket" of the Soviet Union as its steppes were extensively cultivated. Georgia's known oil reserves are as yet unexploited.

PEOPLE

There are about 40 languages and 150 dialects spoken in the Caucasian republics. No relationship has yet been established between languages spoken within the Caucasus and those outside it.

NATURAL FEATURES

The Caucasus mountains extend for 750 miles (1200 km). They form a natural boundary between Europe and Asia, and separate temperate climate zones from warmer climate zones.

FLORA AND FAUNA

The Russian sturgeon fish grows up to 23 ft (7 m) long. Its eggs, called caviar, are a delicacy, but numbers of sturgeon are falling due to polluted water.

HISTORY

With its strategic position, the Crimean peninsula has had a troubled history. It was part of Greece until 100 BC, Turkey from 1475, and Russia from 1783, and was the scene of the Crimean War in 1853-56.

UKRAINE

GEORGIA

AZERBAIJAN

ARMENIA

RUSSIAN FEDERATION
Desna
Sumy
Sula
Kharkiv
Kremenchuk Res.
Donets
UKRAINE
Dnipropetrovs'k
Kramators'k
DONBASS
Horlivka
Luhans'k
Kryvyy Rih
Donets'k
Makiyivka
Dnieper
Zaporizhzhya
Kakhovka Res.
Mykolayiv
Mariupol'
Kherson
SEA OF AZOV
Kerch Strait
CRIMEA
Simferopol'
Sevastopol'
BLACK SEA
RUSSIAN FEDERATION
CAUCASUS MTS.
GEORGIA
K'ut'aisi
TBILISI (T'BILISI)
Mingäçevir Res.
AZERBAIJAN
CASPIAN SEA
Vanadzor
Gyumri
BAKU (BAKI)
Kura
Gäncä
ARMENIA
TURKEY
YEREVAN
AZERBAIJAN
IRAN

Northeast Europe facts

European Russia

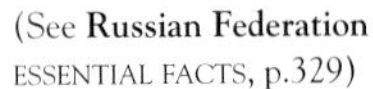
(See **Russian Federation** ESSENTIAL FACTS, p.329)

- Many Russians now have satellite dishes and tune in to Western TV channels for news and entertainment.
- Hospital food is normally provided by patients' families due to lack of funds.

ST. BASIL'S CATHEDRAL This 16th-century Russian building, with its nine great domes, is situated within Moscow's Kremlin fortress.

Latvia

- The national flag is said to represent a sheet stained with the blood of a 13th-century Latvian hero.
- Latvia is the most built-up Baltic State.

ESSENTIAL FACTS

⊙ Riga

24,938 sq miles (64,589 sq km)

2.4 million

Lats

Latvian

Estonia

- The standard of living in Estonia is higher than in any former Soviet republic.

ESSENTIAL FACTS

⊙ Tallinn

17,462 sq miles (45,226 sq km)

1.4 million

Kroon

Estonian

Lithuania

- Most of the Baltic States' amber is found on Lithuania's Amber Coast.

ESSENTIAL FACTS

⊙ Vilnius

25,174 sq miles (65,200 sq km)

3.7 million

Litas

Lithuanian

Belarus

- Cancer cases have increased dramatically since the Chernobyl nuclear disaster in 1986.

ESSENTIAL FACTS

⊙ Minsk

80,154 sq miles (207,600 sq km)

10.1 million

Belorussian rouble

Belorussian, Russian

GEORGIA

- Most Georgians live in poverty.
- In Greek mythology, the legendary Golden Fleece was found in Western Georgia.

ESSENTIAL FACTS

⊙ Tbilisi

26,911 sq miles (69,700 sq km)

5.2 million

Lari

Georgian

ARMENIA

- In the fourth century, Armenia became the first country in the world to adopt Christianity as its state religion.

ESSENTIAL FACTS

⊙ Yerevan

11,505 sq miles (29,800 sq km)

3.8 million

Armenian dram

Armenian

AZERBAIJAN

- The nation of Azerbaijan became the first of the former Soviet republics to declare independence from Moscow in 1991.

ESSENTIAL FACTS

⊙ Baku

33,436 sq miles (86,600 sq km)

8.1 million

Manat

Azeri

UKRAINE

- Western Ukrainians oppose their eastern counterparts' proposed closer ties with Russia.
- The name Ukraine means "frontier."

ESSENTIAL FACTS

⊙ Kiev

233,090 sq miles (603,700 sq km)

48.4 million

Hyrvna

Ukrainian

▲ Multiparty republic

68 years

Sour cream

Borscht

Piroshki (savory pastries)

BORSCHT
Russia's famous beetroot soup, *borscht*, comes from the Ukraine.

MOLDOVA

- The underground wine vaults of Moldova contain entire "streets" of bottles built into rock quarries.
- Moldova was part of Romania until Soviet incorporation in 1940.

ESSENTIAL FACTS

⊙ Chişinâu

13,067 sq miles (33,843 sq km)

4.3 million

Moldovan leu

Moldovan

AFRICA

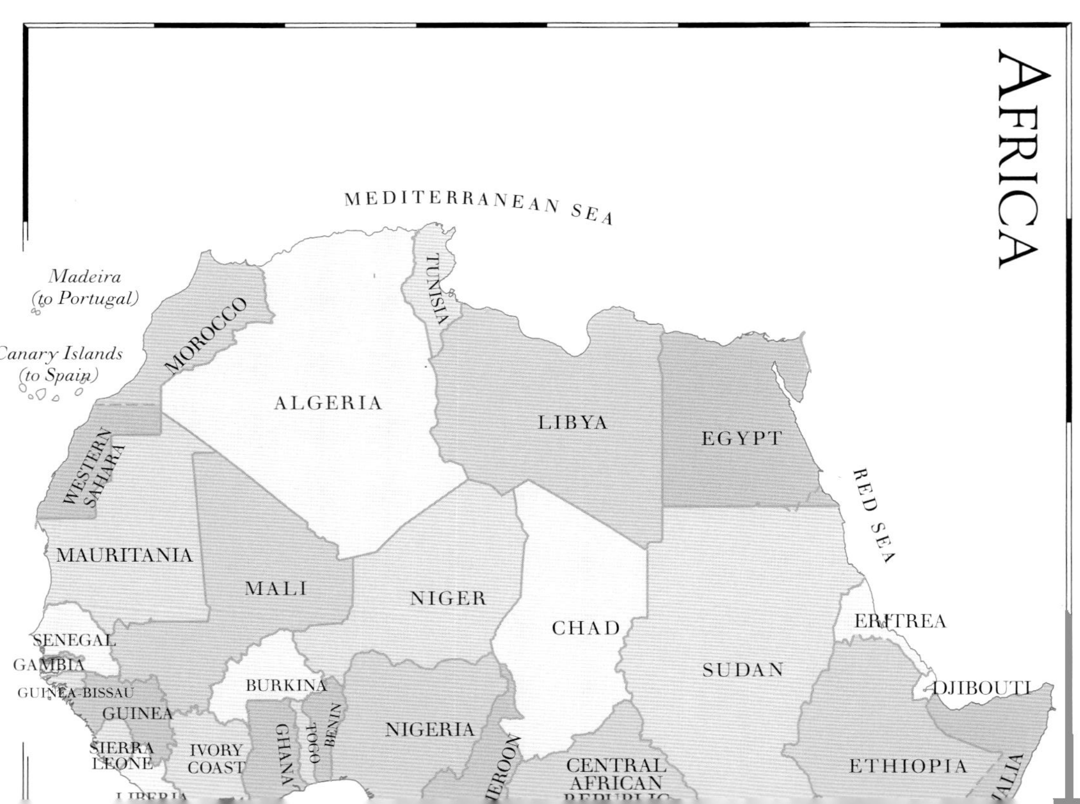
MEDITERRANEAN SEA
Madeira (to Portugal)
Canary Islands (to Spain)
MOROCCO
TUNISIA
ALGERIA
LIBYA
EGYPT
RED SEA
WESTERN SAHARA
MAURITANIA
MALI
NIGER
CHAD
SUDAN
ERITREA
DJIBOUTI
SENEGAL
GAMBIA
GUINEA-BISSAU
GUINEA
BURKINA
SIERRA LEONE
IVORY COAST
GHANA
TOGO
BENIN
NIGERIA
CENTRAL AFRICAN
ETHIOPIA

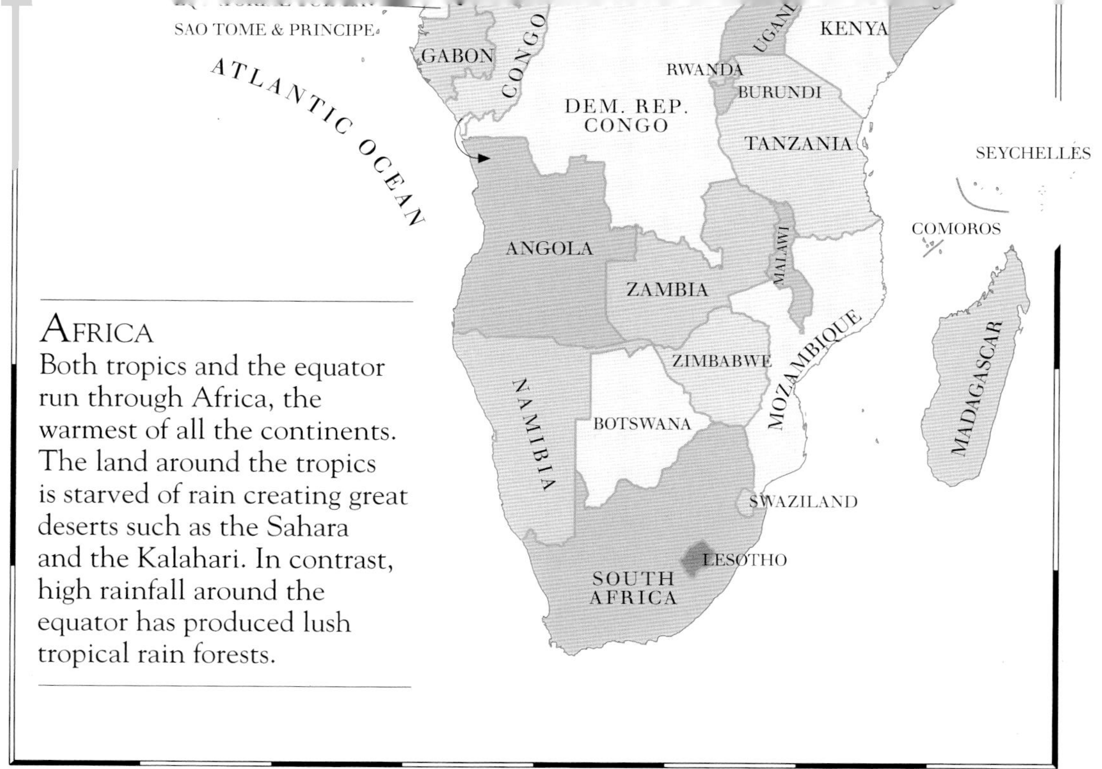

SAO TOME & PRINCIPE
ATLANTIC OCEAN
GABON
CONGO
DEM. REP. CONGO
RWANDA
BURUNDI
KENYA
TANZANIA
SEYCHELLES
COMOROS
ANGOLA
ZAMBIA
MALAWI
ZIMBABWE
MOZAMBIQUE
NAMIBIA
BOTSWANA
MADAGASCAR
SWAZILAND
LESOTHO
SOUTH AFRICA

AFRICA

Both tropics and the equator run through Africa, the warmest of all the continents. The land around the tropics is starved of rain creating great deserts such as the Sahara and the Kalahari. In contrast, high rainfall around the equator has produced lush tropical rain forests.

West Africa

By 1914, many European countries, such as France, Britain, and Portugal, had divided up most of Africa between them. Despite independence, foreign companies still own many of the coffee and cocoa plantations in the region.

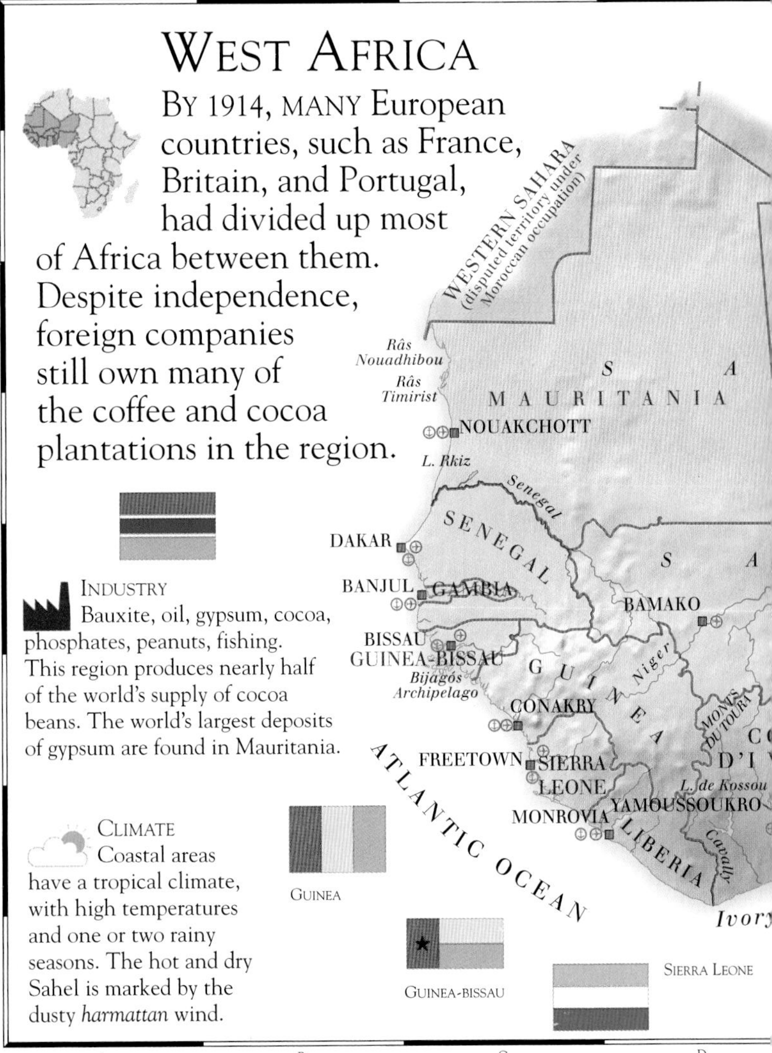

WESTERN SAHARA
(disputed territory under Moroccan occupation)
Râs Nouadhibou
Râs Timirist
MAURITANIA
NOUAKCHOTT
L. Rkiz
Senegal
SENEGAL
DAKAR
BANJUL
GAMBIA
BAMAKO
BISSAU
GUINEA-BISSAU
Bijagós Archipelago
GUINEA
Niger
CONAKRY
MONTS DU TOURA
FREETOWN
SIERRA LEONE
L. de Kossou
YAMOUSSOUKRO
MONROVIA
LIBERIA
Cavally
ATLANTIC OCEAN

Industry

Bauxite, oil, gypsum, cocoa, phosphates, peanuts, fishing. This region produces nearly half of the world's supply of cocoa beans. The world's largest deposits of gypsum are found in Mauritania.

Climate

Coastal areas have a tropical climate, with high temperatures and one or two rainy seasons. The hot and dry Sahel is marked by the dusty *harmattan* wind.

Guinea

Guinea-Bissau

Sierra Leone

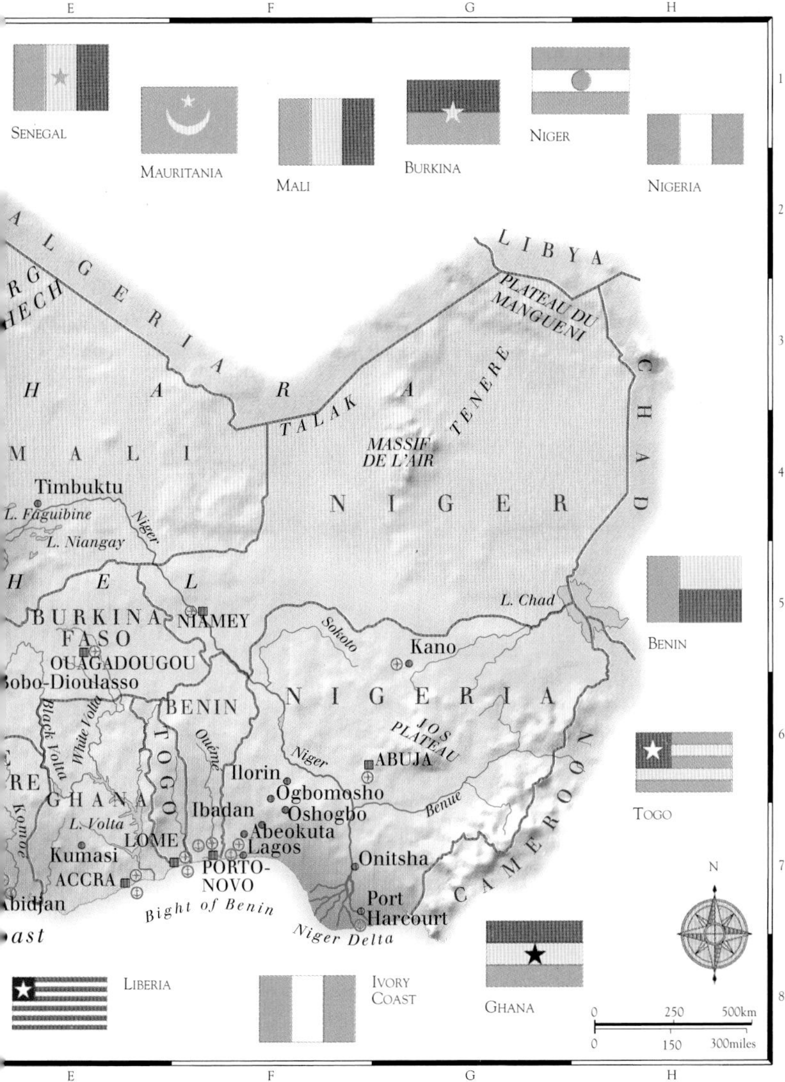

E
F
G
H
SENEGAL
MAURITANIA
MALI
BURKINA
NIGER
NIGERIA
1
2
3
4
5
6
7
8
LIBYA
ALGERIA
PLATEAU DU MANGUENI
TALAK
TENERE
MASSIF DE L'AIR
SAHARA
MALI
NIGER
CHAD
Timbuktu
L. Faguibine
L. Niangay
Niger
SAHEL
L. Chad
BURKINA FASO
NIAMEY
OUAGADOUGOU
Bobo-Dioulasso
Sokoto
Kano
NIGERIA
BENIN
Black Volta
White Volta
TOGO
Ouémé
JOS PLATEAU
Niger
ABUJA
Ilorin
Ogbomosho
Oshogbo
GHANA
Ibadan
Benue
L. Volta
Abeokuta
LOME
Lagos
Kumasi
Onitsha
ACCRA
PORTO-NOVO
Abidjan
Bight of Benin
Port Harcourt
Niger Delta
CAMEROON
BENIN
TOGO
GHANA
LIBERIA
IVORY COAST
N
0
250
500km
0
150
300miles

NORTHWEST AFRICA

SPANNING THE continent of Africa, from the Atlantic to the Red Sea, the Sahara covers 3.5 million sq miles (9 million sq km) and is the world's largest desert. Droughts and the over-use of land for farming are causing the Sahara to spread into the Sahel (semi-arid grasslands). Italy, the UK, Spain, and France have all had colonies in this region.

Strait of Gibraltar
Ceuta (to Spain)
Melilla (to Spain)
Tangier (Tanger)
RABAT
Casablanca
Fez
MOROCCO
Marrakesh
Agadir
ATLAS
Béch
ATLANTIC OCEAN
LAÂYOUNE
Dakhla
WESTERN SAHARA
MAURITANIA

Morocco occupied the whole of Western Sahara in 1979.

INDUSTRY

Oil, gas, phosphates, tourism, olives, dates, fruit. Morocco and Tunisia attract millions of tourists every year. They are also leading phosphate producers. Algeria and Libya have significant oil reserves.

MOROCCO

CLIMATE

Coastal areas have a temperate climate with hot, dry summers and wet winters. Mountain areas are cooler. Most areas are affected by the many different kinds of Sahara wind, such as the *sirocco*, the *chergui*, and the *chili*.

NATURAL FEATURES

The Atlas Mountains exter over 1500 miles (2410 km) from the Canary Islands in the Atlantic to Tunisia. Like the Alps, the Atlas Mountains were formed when the continental plates of Europe and Africa pushed together.

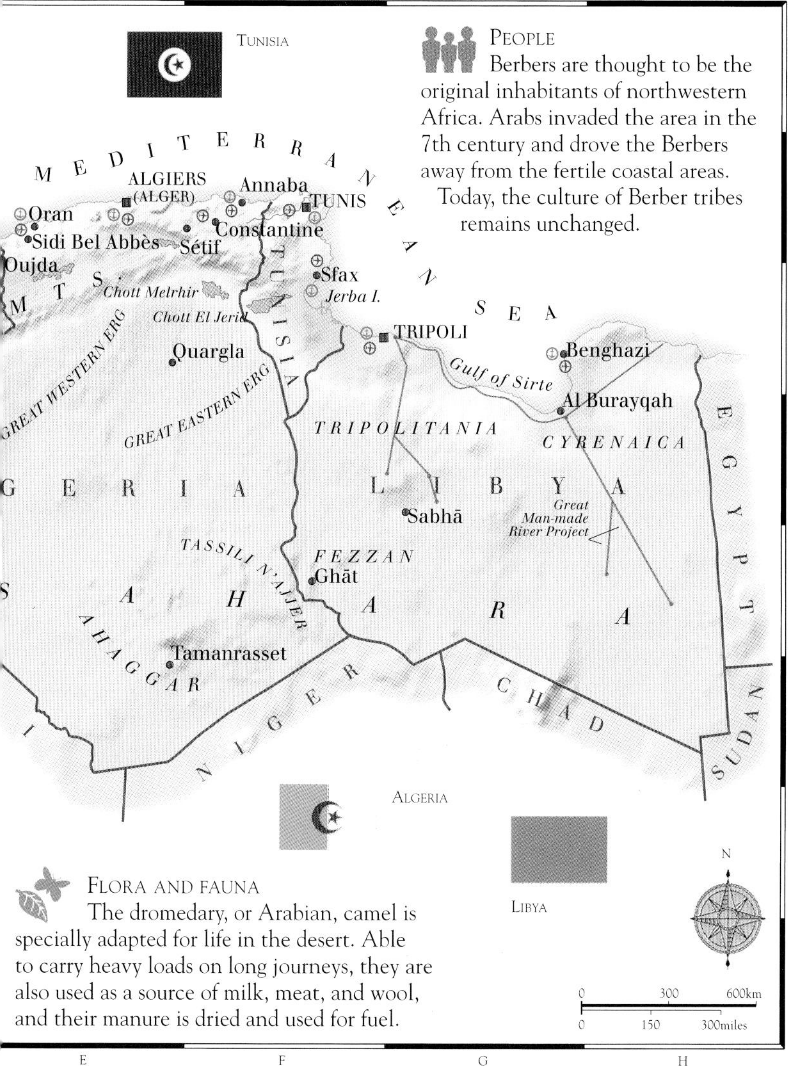

Tunisia
MEDITERRANEAN SEA
ALGIERS (ALGER)
Annaba
TUNIS
Oran
Sidi Bel Abbès
Constantine
Sétif
Oujda
Sfax
Chott Melrhir
Jerba I.
Chott El Jerid
TUNISIA
TRIPOLI
Benghazi
Quargla
GREAT WESTERN ERG
GREAT EASTERN ERG
Gulf of Sirte
Al Burayqah
TRIPOLITANIA
CYRENAICA
EGYPT
LIBYA
Sabhā
Great Man-made River Project
TASSILI N'AJJER
FEZZAN
Ghāt
AHAGGAR
Tamanrasset
NIGER
CHAD
SUDAN
Algeria
Libya
N
0 300 600km
0 150 300miles

People

Berbers are thought to be the original inhabitants of northwestern Africa. Arabs invaded the area in the 7th century and drove the Berbers away from the fertile coastal areas. Today, the culture of Berber tribes remains unchanged.

Flora and fauna

The dromedary, or Arabian, camel is specially adapted for life in the desert. Able to carry heavy loads on long journeys, they are also used as a source of milk, meat, and wool, and their manure is dried and used for fuel.

West Africa facts

Ivory Coast

• Yamoussoukro's giant Christian basilica is the second largest church in the world.
• The Ivory Coast is home to 66 different West African tribes.
• Most people live on the sandy coastal strip.

ESSENTIAL FACTS

⊙ Yamoussoukro

124,502 sq miles (322,460 sq km)

16.3 million

CFA franc

French

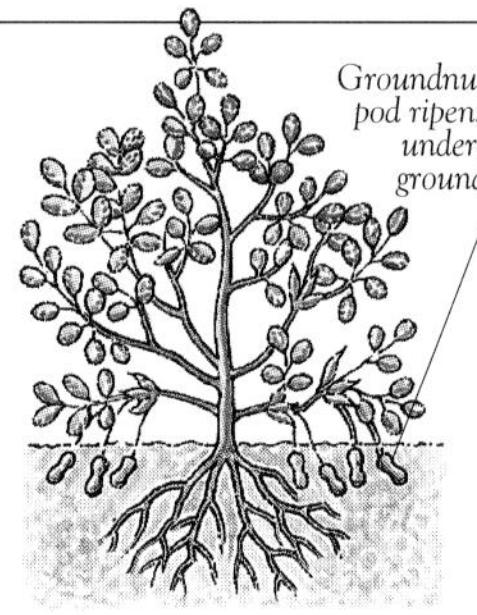
Groundnut pod ripens underground

GROUNDNUT PLANT
Groundnuts, or peanuts, are a major crop in West Africa.

Liberia

• The country of Liberia was founded in 1847 as a home for freed slaves from the US.
• Human rights have have frequently been abused in Liberia, with citizens being massacred or forced to flee to neighboring states.

ESSENTIAL FACTS

⊙ Monrovia

43,000 sq miles (111,370 sq km)

3.1 million

Liberian dollar

English

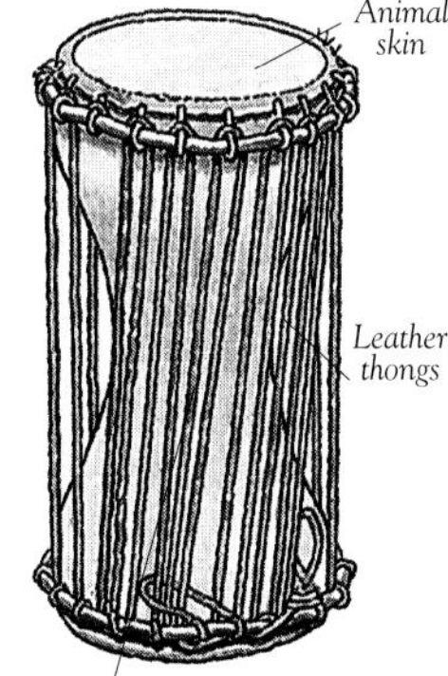
Animal skin
Leather thongs
Squeezing the "waist" changes the drum's sound

WEST AFRICAN KALUNGU, OR "TALKING DRUM"

Western Sahara

⊙ No capital

200,000

Varied Arab dialects

Senegal

• The name Senegal comes from the Islamic Zenegar Berbers, who invaded the region in the 1300s.
• Senegal produced the first satirical journal in Africa with the founding of the publication *Le Politicien* in 1978.

ESSENTIAL FACTS

⊙ Dakar

75,749 sq miles (196,190 sq km)

9.7 million

CFA franc

French

Ghana

• Mining has polluted the environment and destroyed areas of land.
• Ghana was the first British colony in Africa to gain independence.

ESSENTIAL FACTS

⊙ Accra

92,100 sq miles (238,540 sq km)

19.7 million

Cedi

English

Sierra Leone

• The citizens of Freetown are largely descended from slaves freed from Britain and the US.
• Sierra Leone is one of the world's poorest nations.

ESSENTIAL FACTS

⊙ Freetown

27,699 sq miles (71,740 sq km)

4.6 million

Leone

English

Benin

• Positions of power in Benin's retail trade are often held by women.

ESSENTIAL FACTS

⊙ Porto-Novo

43,480 sq miles (112,620 sq km)

6.4 million

CFA franc

French

Mauritania

• Slavery, although officially illegal, still persists in Mauritania.

ESSENTIAL FACTS

⊙ Nouakchott

397,953 sq miles (1,030,700 sq km)

2.7 million

Ouguiya

Arabic

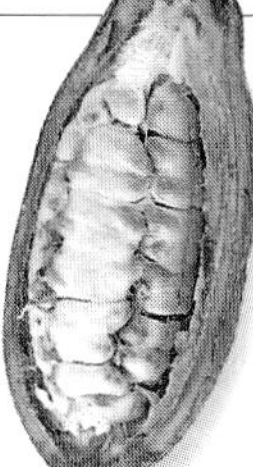

COCOA West Africa grows half the world's cocoa.

Burkina

• Poor soils and droughts in Burkina force many men to migrate seasonally to Ghana and the Ivory Coast for work.

ESSENTIAL FACTS

⊙ Ouagadougou

105,870 sq miles (274,200 sq km)

11.9 million

CFA franc

French

Mali

• The Malian town of Timbuktu was the center of the huge Malinke empire in the 14th century.
• Malians strongly disapprove of flaunted wealth.

ESSENTIAL FACTS

⊙ Bamako

478,764 sq miles (1,240,000 sq km)

11.7 million

CFA franc

French

West Africa facts

NIGER

• The threat of drought and desertification is Niger's primary concern.

ESSENTIAL FACTS

⊙ Niamey

489,188 sq miles (1,267,000 sq km)

11.2 million

CFA franc

French

CAPE VERDE

(*Atlantic Ocean*, pp.360–361)

⊙ Praia

437,000

Portuguese

GAMBIA

⊙ Banjul

1.3 million

English

GUINEA

• The three bright colors of Guinea's flag represent the national motto of "work, justice, solidarity".

ESSENTIAL FACTS

⊙ Conakry

94,925 sq miles (245,857 sq km)

8.3 million

Guinea franc

French

TOGO

• The retail trade in Togo is dominated by the "Nana Benz," or market-women, of Lomé.

ESSENTIAL FACTS

⊙ Lomé

21,925 sq miles (56,785 sq km)

4.7 million

CFA franc

French

GUINEA-BISSAU

⊙ Bissau

1.2 million

Portuguese

NIGERIA

• Modern medicine is not available in rural Nigeria as the health service is concentrated in urban areas.

• Nigeria is the most heavily populated country in Africa.

ESSENTIAL FACTS

⊙ Abuja

356,667 sq miles (923,768 sq km)

116.9 million

Naira

English

▲ Military republic

52 years

NIGERIAN TWINS
All twins in Nigeria, boys and girls, are given the same names. The firstborn is called Taiwo, the second Kehinde.

Northwest Africa facts

TUNISIA

- The Berber village of Matmata was a location for the planet Tatooine in the 1977 film *Star Wars*.
- Esparto grass grown on the plains of Tunisia is used to make quality paper.
- Tunisians use falcons to hunt partridge, quail, and hare in the summer.

ESSENTIAL FACTS

⊙ Tunis

63,170 sq miles (163,610 sq km)

9.6 million

Tunisian dinar

Arabic

ALGERIA

- The Algerian population is mainly Arab, under 30 years of age, and urban-based.
- The highest sand dunes in the world are found in east central Algeria.
- More than 80% of Algeria lies within the Sahara desert.

ESSENTIAL FACTS

⊙ Algiers

919,590 sq miles (2,381,740 sq km)

30.8 million

Algerian dinar

Arabic

PATTERNED LEATHER BAG

LEATHER GOODS Morocco and Tunisia produce quality leather goods for tourists to buy.

LIBYA

- The West has ignored Libya due to its past links with terrorist groups.
- Libyan oil contains no sulfur, resulting in little pollution when it is burned.

ESSENTIAL FACTS

⊙ Tripoli

679,358 sq miles (1,759,540 sq km)

5.4 million

Libyan dinar

Arabic

MOROCCO

- The Karueein University at Fès, which was founded in AD 859, is the world's oldest existing educational institution.

ESSENTIAL FACTS

⊙ Rabat

172,316 sq miles (446,300 sq km)

30.4 million

Moroccan dirham

Arabic

NORTHEAST AFRICA

THE NILE, THE LONGEST river in the world, carries rich mud from the highlands of Sudan into Egypt, creating some of the most fertile land in the world. About 99 percent of Egypt's population live on the river's banks. Ethiopia, Somalia, and Sudan have been beset by drought, famine, and war and about half of Africa's 4.5 million refugees come from this area.

MEDITERRANEAN SEA
El Mansûra
Port Said
Alexandria
CAIRO (EL QAHIRA)
Qattâra Depression
Ismâ'ilîya
Suez
SINAI
ISRAEL
Giza
Helwân
El Faiyûm
El Minya
Asyût
Nile
Sohâg
Valley of the Kings
Qena
Gulf of Aqaba
Gulf of Suez
Luxor
EGYPT
Aswân
Philae
L. Nasser
Abu Simbel
LIBYA
LIBYAN DESERT
NUBIAN DESERT
RED SEA

EGYPT

HISTORY

Hieroglyphs were a set of mysterious symbols until the discovery of the Rosetta Stone in 1799. The Stone is inscribed in three different scripts: ancient Greek, demotic, and hieroglyphs. By comparing the royal names in the scripts, hieroglyphs were finally deciphered 25 years later.

ERITREA

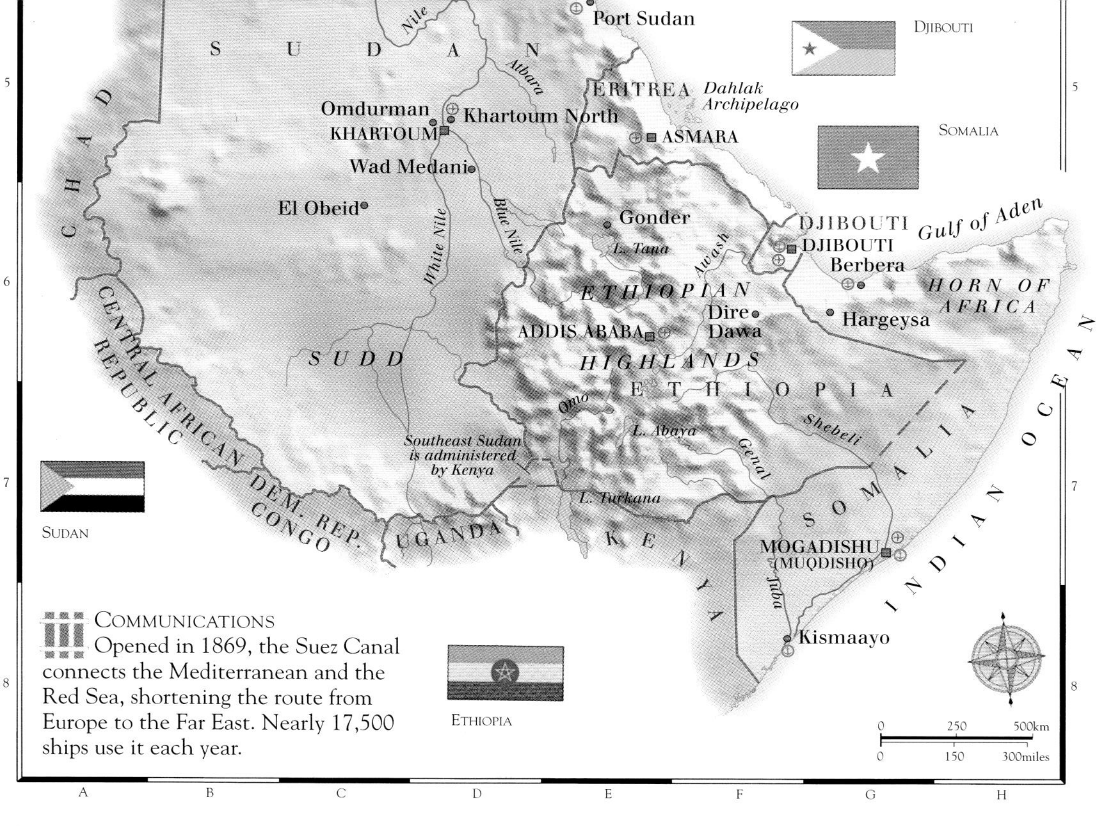
SUDAN
Port Sudan
Nile
Atbara
ERITREA
Dahlak Archipelago
Omdurman
Khartoum North
KHARTOUM
ASMARA
Wad Medani
El Obeid
Blue Nile
White Nile
CHAD
Gonder
L. Tana
Awash
DJIBOUTI
DJIBOUTI
Gulf of Aden
Berbera
HORN OF AFRICA
Hargeysa
ETHIOPIAN HIGHLANDS
Dire Dawa
ADDIS ABABA
SUDD
ETHIOPIA
Omo
L. Abaya
Shebeli
Genal
CENTRAL AFRICAN REPUBLIC
Southeast Sudan is administered by Kenya
DEM. REP. CONGO
UGANDA
L. Turkana
KENYA
SOMALIA
MOGADISHU (MUQDISHO)
Juba
Kismaayo
INDIAN OCEAN
Djibouti
Somalia
Sudan
Ethiopia
0 250 500km
0 150 300miles
A B C D E F G H
5 6 7 8

COMMUNICATIONS
Opened in 1869, the Suez Canal connects the Mediterranean and the Red Sea, shortening the route from Europe to the Far East. Nearly 17,500 ships use it each year.

Central Africa

MUCH OF THIS region is covered in dense tropical rain forest, drained by the Congo (Zaire) River, which forms a huge arc on its way to the Atlantic. In the 16th century Portugal and Spain set up trading posts on the west coast as part of the slave trade. Millions of Africans from this region were sent as slaves to the New World. Many people in coastal areas still speak Spanish and Portuguese.

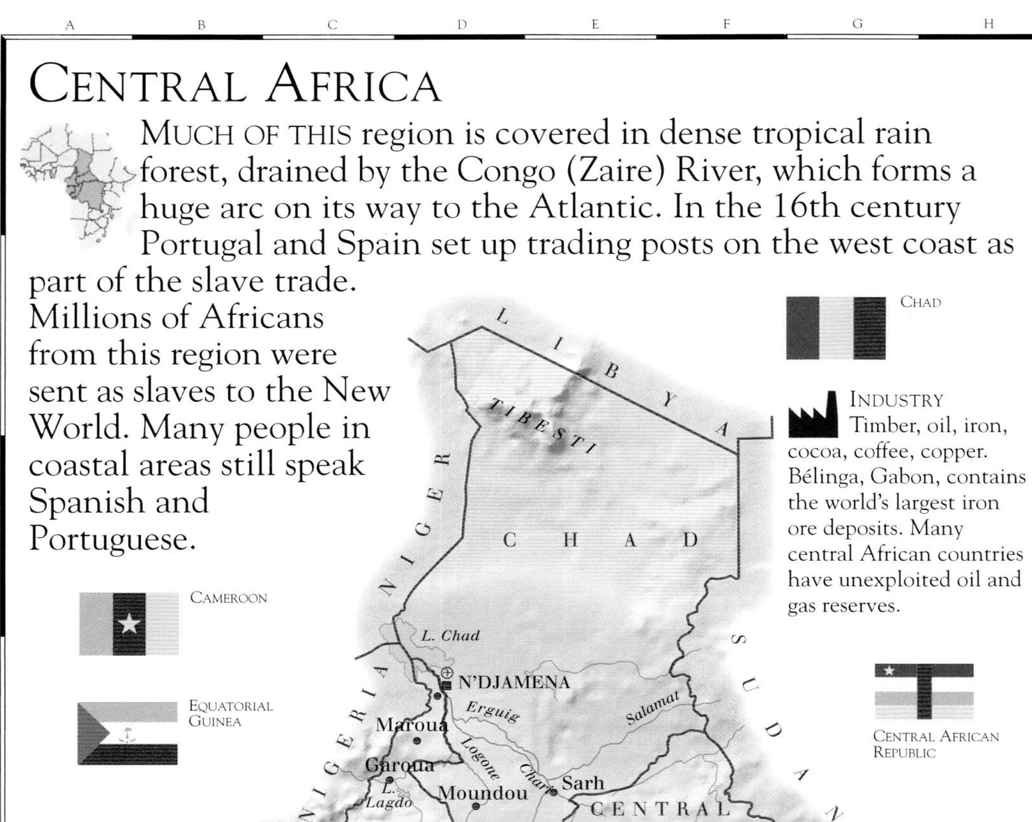
A B C D E F G H
1 2 3 4
LIBYA
TIBESTI
CHAD
NIGER
SUDAN
NIGERIA
CENTRAL
L. Chad
N'DJAMENA
Erguig
Salamat
Maroua
Logone
Chari
Garoua
Sarh
L. Lagdo
Moundou
CHAD
CAMEROON
EQUATORIAL GUINEA
CENTRAL AFRICAN REPUBLIC

INDUSTRY
Timber, oil, iron, cocoa, coffee, copper. Bélinga, Gabon, contains the world's largest iron ore deposits. Many central African countries have unexploited oil and gas reserves.

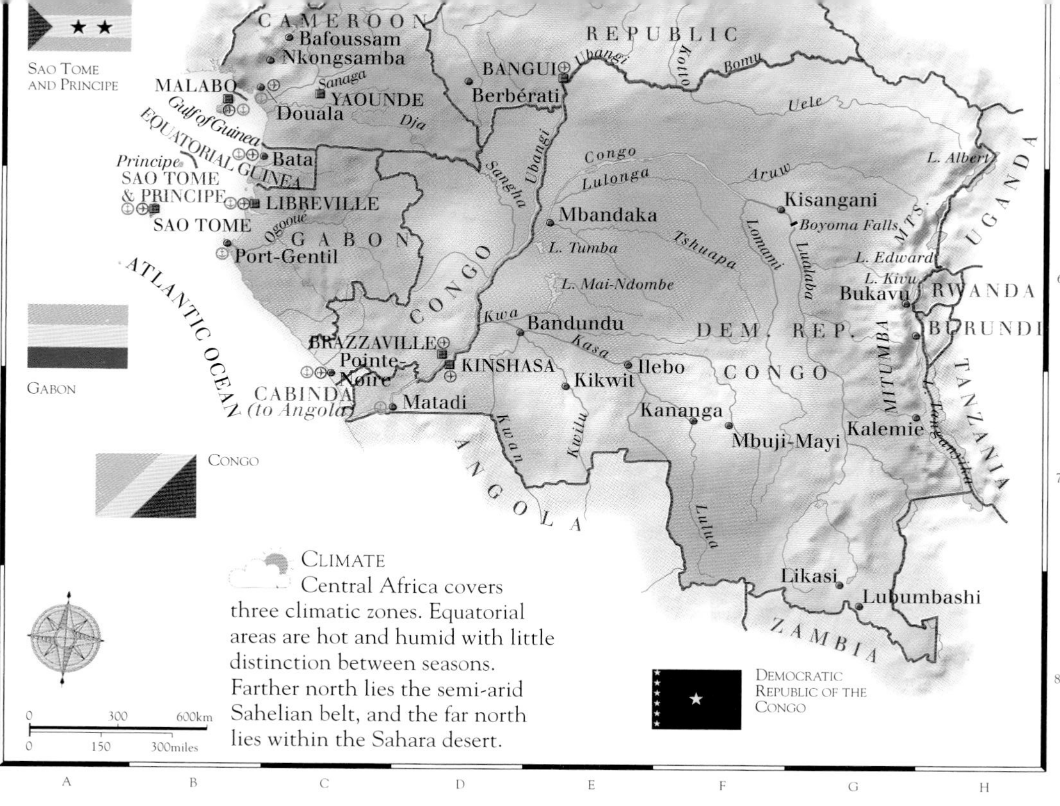
CAMEROON
Bafoussam
Nkongsamba
MALABO
Sanaga
YAOUNDE
Douala
Dja
Gulf of Guinea
EQUATORIAL GUINEA
Bata
Principe
SAO TOME & PRINCIPE
LIBREVILLE
SAO TOME
Ogooué
GABON
Port-Gentil
ATLANTIC OCEAN
CONGO
BRAZZAVILLE
Pointe-Noire
CABINDA (to Angola)
Matadi
KINSHASA
REPUBLIC
BANGUI
Berbérati
Ubangi
Kotto
Bomu
Uele
Sangha
Congo
Lulonga
Aruw
Mbandaka
L. Tumba
L. Mai-Ndombe
Tshuapa
Lomami
Kisangani
Boyoma Falls
Lualaba
MTS.
L. Albert
UGANDA
L. Edward
L. Kivu
Bukavu
RWANDA
BURUNDI
Kwa
Bandundu
Kasa
Ilebo
Kikwit
Kwilu
Kwan
DEM. REP. CONGO
Kananga
Mbuji-Mayi
MITUMBA
Kalemie
L. Tanganyika
TANZANIA
ANGOLA
Lulua
Likasi
Lubumbashi
ZAMBIA
SAO TOME AND PRINCIPE
GABON
CONGO
DEMOCRATIC REPUBLIC OF THE CONGO
0 300 600km
0 150 300miles
A B C D E F G H
5 6 7 8

CLIMATE

Central Africa covers three climatic zones. Equatorial areas are hot and humid with little distinction between seasons. Farther north lies the semi-arid Sahelian belt, and the far north lies within the Sahara desert.

CENTRAL EAST AFRICA

LARGE AREAS OF savannah, or grassland, in central Africa provide grazing for both domestic and wild animals. Industry is poorly developed in the region – Zambia, Rwanda, Burundi, and Uganda suffer from having no seaports. Lake Victoria is the largest lake in Africa, and a source of the River Nile.

UGANDA

KENYA

RWANDA

FLORA AND FAUNA Poaching remains a major problem in this area. To combat this, all the countries in this region have set up wildlife parks to protect animals such as elephants and zebra.

INDUSTRY Tobacco, coffee, tea, tourism, cloves, copper. Zambia is the world's fifth-largest producer of copper. Wildlife parks in this region attract thousands of tourists.

ETHIOPIA
SUDAN
Southeast Sudan is administered by Kenya
L. Turkana
CHALBI DESERT
SOMALIA
Albert Nile
Victoria Nile
L. Kyoga
L. Albert
UGANDA
KENYA
RUWENZORI MTS.
KAMPALA
Great Rift Valley
ABERDARE RANGE
Tana
L. Edward
Lake Victoria
NAIROBI
DEM. REP. CONGO
KIGALI
RWANDA
Mwanza
BUJUMBURA
L. Eyasi
L. Manyara
Galana
Mombasa

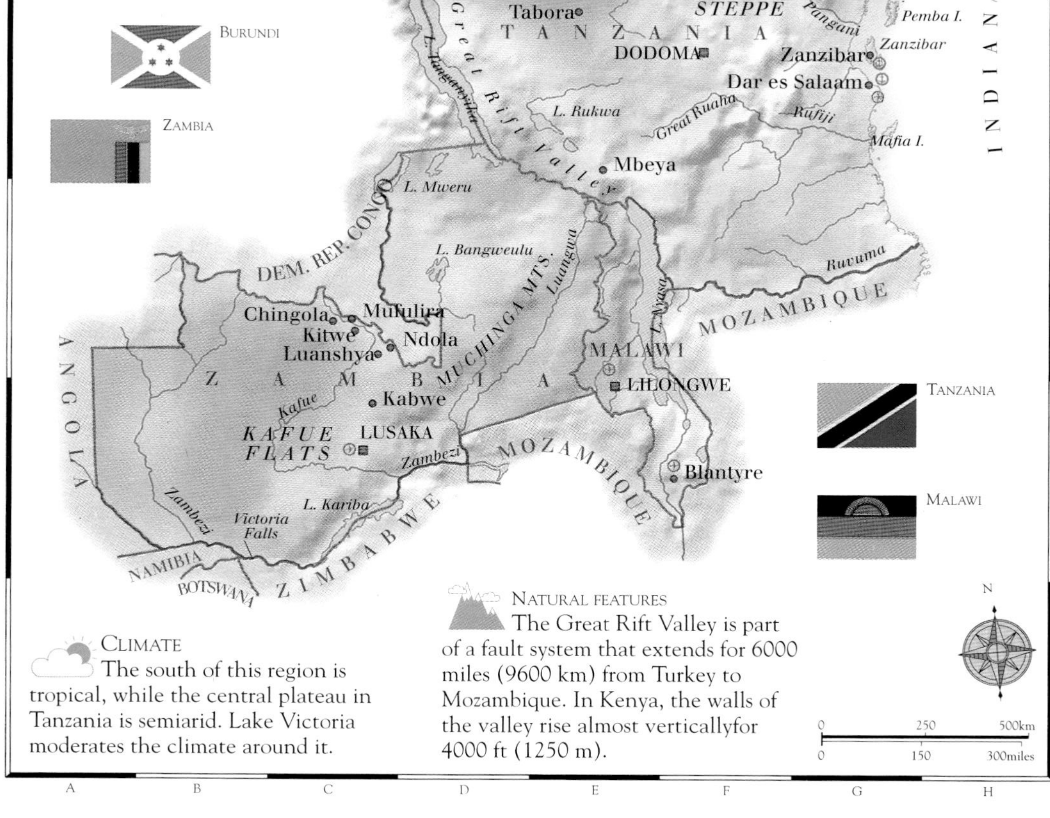
BURUNDI
ZAMBIA
TANZANIA
MALAWI
Tabora
STEPPE
TANZANIA
DODOMA
Zanzibar
Dar es Salaam
Pangani
Pemba I.
Zanzibar
Mafia I.
Rufiji
Great Ruaha
L. Rukwa
L. Tanganyika
Great Rift Valley
Mbeya
INDIAN
L. Mweru
DEM. REP. CONGO
L. Bangweulu
MUCHINGA MTS.
Luangwa
L. Nyasa
Ruvuma
MOZAMBIQUE
MALAWI
LILONGWE
Chingola
Mufulira
Kitwe
Ndola
Luanshya
ZAMBIA
Kabwe
Kafue
KAFUE FLATS
LUSAKA
Zambezi
MOZAMBIQUE
Blantyre
ANGOLA
Zambezi
Victoria Falls
L. Kariba
ZIMBABWE
NAMIBIA
BOTSWANA
N
0
250
500km
0
150
300miles
A
B
C
D
E
F
G
H
5
6
7
8

CLIMATE
The south of this region is tropical, while the central plateau in Tanzania is semiarid. Lake Victoria moderates the climate around it.

NATURAL FEATURES
The Great Rift Valley is part of a fault system that extends for 6000 miles (9600 km) from Turkey to Mozambique. In Kenya, the walls of the valley rise almost verticallyfor 4000 ft (1250 m).

Northeast Africa facts

Egypt

• Overpopulation is a major problem in Eygpt, where it is estimated a baby is born every 24 seconds.
• The ancient pyramids were built to house the mummified bodies of Egyptian kings.

ESSENTIAL FACTS

⊙ Cairo

386,660 sq miles (1,001,450 sq km)

69.1 million

Egyptian pound

Arabic

▲ Presidential democracy

GREAT PYRAMIDS AT GIZA, EGYPT

Ethiopia

• Famines are a regular occurrence in Ethiopia.

ESSENTIAL FACTS

⊙ Addis Ababa

435,184 sq miles (1,127,127 sq km)

64.5 million

Ethiopian birr

Amharic

Djibouti

⊙ Djibouti

644,000

Arabic, French

Sudan

• The Sudd plain in Sudan contains the world's largest swamp.

ESSENTIAL FACTS

⊙ Khartoum

967,493 sq miles (2,505,810 sq km)

31.8 million

Sudanese dinar

Arabic

Eritrea

• Three-quarters of Eritrea's people are dependent on food aid.

ESSENTIAL FACTS

⊙ Asmara

46,842 sq miles (121,320 sq km)

3.8 million

Nakfa

Tigrinya

Somalia

• In 1992, civil war in Somalia led to the UN's worst refugee crisis.

ESSENTIAL FACTS

⊙ Mogadishu

246,199 sq miles (637,657 sq km)

9.2 million

Somali shilling

Somali, Arabic

Central East Africa facts

KENYA

• Ethnic violence is the main political issue.
• Kenya has over 40 national parks and game reserves, and two marine parks in the Indian Ocean.

ESSENTIAL FACTS

- Nairobi
- 224, 081 sq miles (580,370 sq km)
- 26.1 million
- Kenya shilling
- Kiswahili

RWANDA

- Kigali
- 7.5 million
- Kinyarwanda, French

GORILLAS OF RWANDA
Rwanda is one of the last remaining sanctuaries of the mountain gorilla.

MASAI WARRIORS
The Masai are a tribe of nomadic herders who live on the borders of Kenya and Tanzania.

BURUNDI

- Bujumbura
- 6.5 million
- Kirundi, French

UGANDA

• The Ruwenzori mountain range of Uganda is also known as the "Mountains of the Moon."

ESSENTIAL FACTS

- Kampala
- 91,135 sq miles (236,040 sq km)
- 24 million
- New Uganda shilling
- English

TANZANIA

• One-third of Tanzania is national park or game reserve.
• The use of Kiswahili as a universal language has reduced ethnic rivalries.

ESSENTIAL FACTS

- Dodoma
- 364,898 sq miles (945,087 sq km)
- 36 million
- Tanzanian shilling
- English, Kiswahili

Central Africa facts

ZAMBIA

• Victoria Falls in Zambia is called *Musi-o-Tunyi* by African people, which means "the smoke that thunders."

ESSENTIAL FACTS

⊙ Lusaka

290,584 sq miles (752,614 sq km)

10.6 million

Zambian kwacha

English

CHAD

• The tropical, cotton-producing south is Chad's most heavily populated region.
• The Tibesti plateau is a site of prehistoric rock painting.

ESSENTIAL FACTS

⊙ N'Djamena

495,752 sq miles (1,284,000 sq km)

8.1 million

CFA franc

French, Arabic

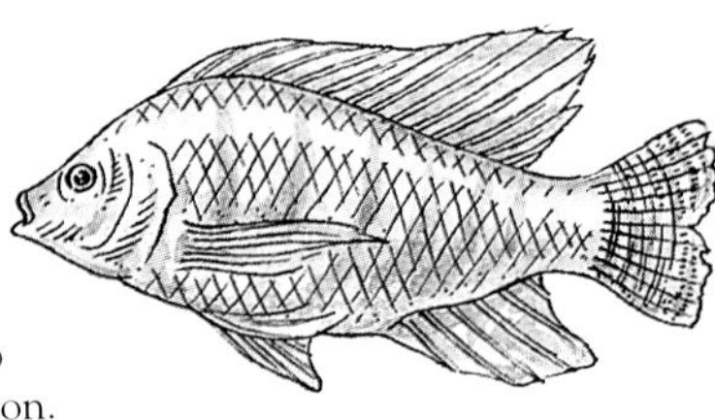

FISH FOOD
Lake Chad's fish, such as this *tilapia*, are a major source of food for people who live in the region.

EQUATORIAL GUINEA

⊙ Malabo

470,000

Spanish, Fang

Alluvial diamond

LITTLE GEMS
Congo (Zaire) is the world's largest producer of diamonds used in industry.

DEM. REP. CONGO

• The rain forests of Dem. Rep. Congo comprise almost 50% of Africa's remaining woodlands.

ESSENTIAL FACTS

⊙ Kinshasa

905,563 sq miles (2,345,410 sq km)

41.2 million

Congolese Franc

French

CENTRAL AFRICAN REPUBLIC

• Hunting of elephants in the CAR was finally banned in 1985.

ESSENTIAL FACTS

⊙ Bangui

240,534 sq miles (622,984 sq km)

3.8 million

CFA franc

French

Congo

• In 1970, Congo became the first declared communist state in Africa.
• Congo has been used in the past as a dump for Western toxic waste.

ESSENTIAL FACTS

⊙ Brazzaville
◒ 132,046 sq miles (342,000 sq km)
🕴 3.1 million
💰 CFA franc
💬 French

Cameroon

• The Portuguese explorers who colonized Cameroon fished for prawns called *camaroes*, from which the country derived its name.

ESSENTIAL FACTS

⊙ Yaoundé
◒ 183,567 sq miles (475,440 sq km)
🕴 15.2 million
💰 CFA franc
💬 English, French

RESPECT FOR THE DEAD
This wooden figure from Cameroon was made to honor an ancestor.

São Tomé & Príncipe

⊙ São Tomé
🕴 159,900
💬 Portuguese

SPIRITED FIGURE
Central African folk religions believe fetish figures like this are inhabited by spirits.

Gabon

• Libreville was founded as a settlement for freed French slaves in 1849.
• Menial jobs in Gabon are done by immigrant workers.

ESSENTIAL FACTS

⊙ Libreville
◒ 103,346 sq miles (267,667 sq km)
🕴 1.3 million
💰 CFA franc
💬 French

Malawi

• Lake Malawi contains at least 500 species of fish.
• Malawi's name means "the land where the sun is reflected in the water like fire."

ESSENTIAL FACTS

⊙ Lilongwe
◒ 45,745 sq miles (118,480 sq km)
🕴 11.6 million
💰 Milawi kwacha
💬 English

SOUTHERN AFRICA

THE RICHEST DEPOSITS of valuable minerals in Africa, such as gold and diamonds, are found in its southern region. Many surrounding countries rely on South Africa for work and trade. Racial segregation under apartheid operated from 1948 until 1994 when South Africa's first multiracial elections were held. Namibia won its independence from South Africa in 1990, but neighboring Angola has been in a state of civil war since 1975.

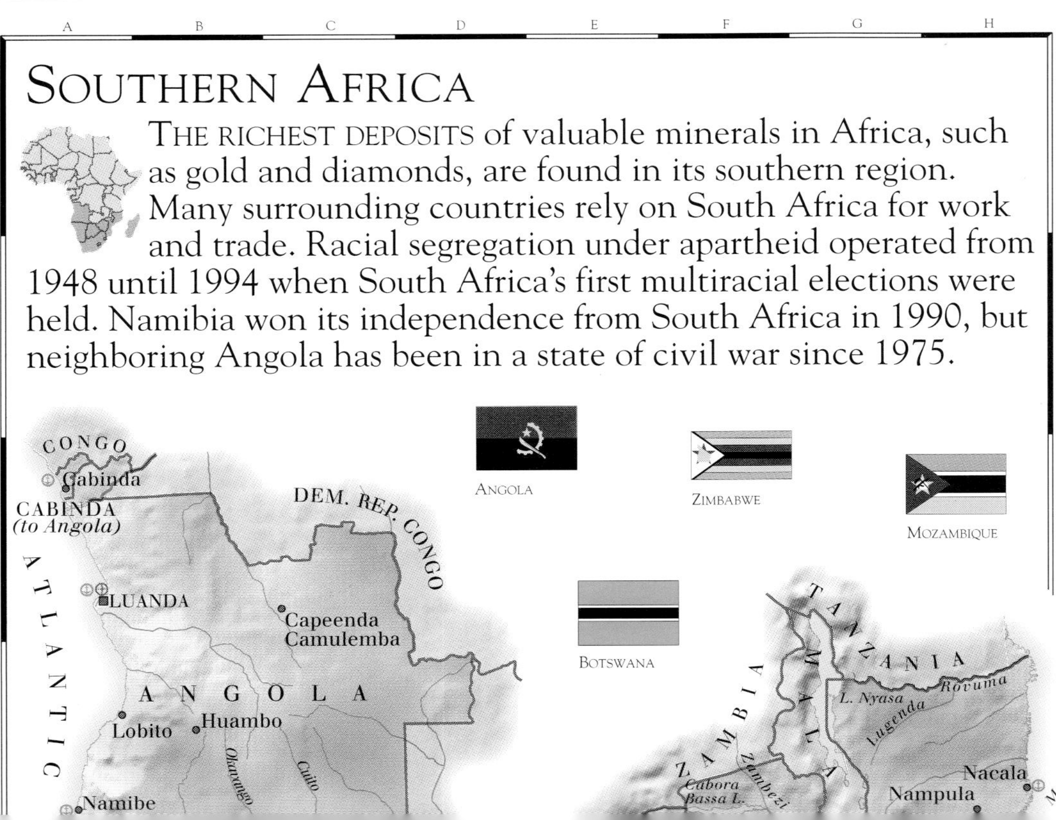

A
B
C
D
E
F
G
H
1
2
3
4
ANGOLA
ZIMBABWE
MOZAMBIQUE
BOTSWANA
CONGO
Cabinda
CABINDA
(to Angola)
DEM. REP. CONGO
ATLANTIC
LUANDA
Capeenda
Camulemba
ANGOLA
Lobito
Huambo
Okavango
Cuito
Namibe
TANZANIA
ZAMBIA
MALAWI
L. Nyasa
Lugenda
Rovuma
Zambezi
Cabora
Bassa L.
Nacala
Nampula
Mozambique
Channel

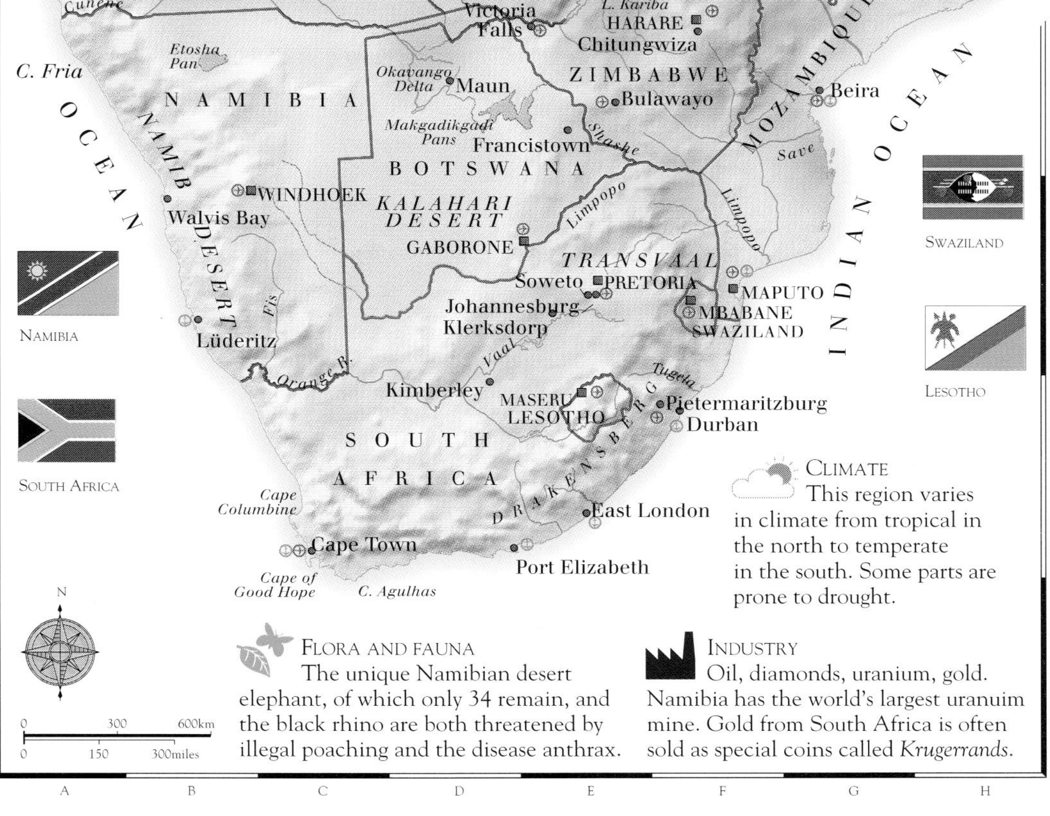
C. Fria
OCEAN
NAMIB
DESERT
Etosha Pan
NAMIBIA
Cunene
Walvis Bay
WINDHOEK
Lüderitz
Fis
Orange R.
Okavango Delta
Maun
Makgadikgadi Pans
Francistown
BOTSWANA
KALAHARI DESERT
GABORONE
Victoria Falls
L. Kariba
HARARE
Chitungwiza
ZIMBABWE
Bulawayo
Shashe
Limpopo
MOZAMBIQUE
Beira
Save
INDIAN OCEAN
TRANSVAAL
Soweto
PRETORIA
Johannesburg
Klerksdorp
Vaal
MAPUTO
MBABANE
SWAZILAND
Kimberley
MASERU
LESOTHO
Tugela
Pietermaritzburg
Durban
DRAKENSBERG
SOUTH AFRICA
Cape Columbine
Cape Town
Cape of Good Hope
C. Agulhas
East London
Port Elizabeth
N
0
300
600km
0
150
300miles
A
B
C
D
E
F
G
H
5
6
7
8
NAMIBIA
SOUTH AFRICA
SWAZILAND
LESOTHO

CLIMATE

This region varies in climate from tropical in the north to temperate in the south. Some parts are prone to drought.

FLORA AND FAUNA

The unique Namibian desert elephant, of which only 34 remain, and the black rhino are both threatened by illegal poaching and the disease anthrax.

INDUSTRY

Oil, diamonds, uranium, gold. Namibia has the world's largest uranuim mine. Gold from South Africa is often sold as special coins called *Krugerrands*.

Southern Africa facts

ZIMBABWE

- Most people in Zimbabwe belong to the Shona or Ndebele tribes.
- Zimbabwe was formerly known as Southern Rhodesia.

ESSENTIAL FACTS

⊙ Harare

150,803 sq miles (390,580 sq km)

12.9 million

Zimbabwe dollar

English

COLORFUL DECOR
Ndebele women decorate their homes with bright geometric patterns.

MOZAMBIQUE

- Over 90% of the citizens of Mozambique live in poverty.
- Polygamous marriages are common among those wealthy enough to take second wives.

ESSENTIAL FACTS

⊙ Maputo

309,494 sq miles (801,590 sq km)

18.6 million

Metical

Portuguese

BOTSWANA

- The people of Botswana place such value on rain as a resource that their currency, the pula, is named in its honor.

ESSENTIAL FACTS

⊙ Gaborone

231,803 sq miles (600,370 sq km)

1.6 million

Pula

English

SWAZILAND

⊙ Mbabane

938,000

Siswati, English

ANGOLA

- Injuries caused by exploding mines have led to the nation of Angola having the highest number of amputees in the world.

ESSENTIAL FACTS

⊙ Luanda

481,351 sq miles (1,246,700 sq km)

13.5 million

Readjusted kwanza

Portuguese

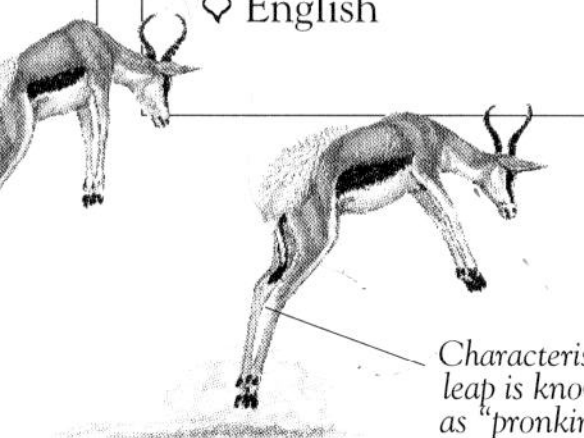

SPRINGBOKS
These small antelopes live in the grasslands of South Africa

Characteristic leap is known as "pronking"

MADAGASCAR

(*Indian Ocean*, pp.362–363)

• This country is the world's largest producer of vanilla.
• Madagascar is a unique environment; 80% of its plants and animal species are found nowhere else.

ESSENTIAL FACTS

⊙ Antananarivo
226,656 sq miles (587,040 sq km)
16.4 million
Malagasy franc
Malagasy, French

LESOTHO

⊙ Maseru
2.1 million
English, Sesotho

COMOROS

⊙ Moroni
727,000
Arabic, French, Comoran

LARGEST LEMUR
Madagascar is home to the Indri, the largest of the world's lemurs.

NAMIBIA

• The Namib is the Earth's oldest, and one of its driest, deserts.

ESSENTIAL FACTS

⊙ Windhoek
318,260 sq miles (824,290 sq km)
1.8 million
Nambian dollar
English

SOUTH AFRICA

• President Nelson Mandela and former president F. W. De Klerk were awarded the Nobel Peace Prize in 1994 for their work dismantling apartheid.
• Tourists are increasingly attracted to South Africa's beaches, stunning scenery, and prize-winning vineyards.

ESSENTIAL FACTS

⊙ Pretoria, Cape Town, Bloemfontein
471,008 sq miles (1,219,912 sq km)
43.8 million
Rand
Afrikaans, English, 9 African languages
▲ Multiparty republic
52 years

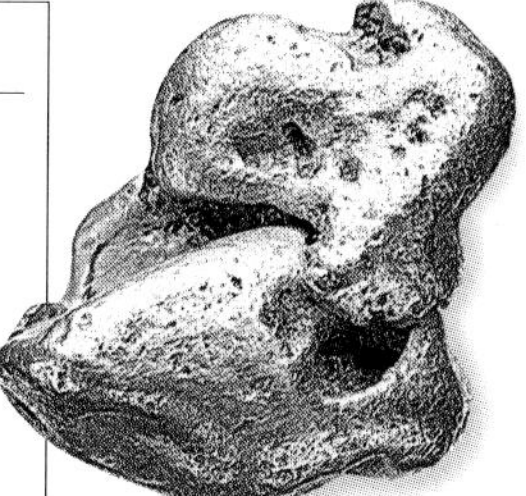

BURIED TREASURE
South Africa has the world's deepest goldmine, descending 12,392 ft (3777 m) underground.

North and West Asia

BARENTS SEA
KARA SEA
RUSSIAN FEDERATION
(EUROPEAN RUSSIA)
KAZAKHSTAN
CASPIAN SEA
BLACK SEA
GEORGIA
ARMENIA
AZERBAIJAN
UZBEKISTAN
KYRGYZSTAN
TURKEY
TURKMENISTAN
TAJIKISTAN
CYPRUS
LEBANON
SYRIA
ISRAEL
IRAQ
IRAN
AFGHANISTAN
JORDAN
KUWAIT
BAHRAIN
QATAR
UNITED ARAB EMIRATES
RED SEA
SAUDI ARABIA
OMAN
ARABIAN SEA
YEMEN

ARCTIC OCEAN
LAPTEV SEA
EAST SIBERIAN SEA
BERING SEA
SEA OF OKHOTSK

North and West Asia

Asia is the largest continent in the world, occupying nearly one-third of the world's total land area. In the south, the Arabian Peninsula is mostly hot, dry desert. In the north lie cold deserts, treeless plains called steppes, and the largest needleleaf forest in the world, which stretches from Siberia to northern Europe.

NEAR EAST

AT THE JUNCTION of Africa, Asia, and Europe, the Near East is a mosaic of deserts, mountains, and fertile valleys. After centuries of conflict, the end of the 20th century gave high hopes of peace in the region, with Lebanon beginning to emerge from a 25 year civil war. However, a "land for peace" deal to end the Israeli–Palestinian conflict was mired in a cycle of violence by 2002.

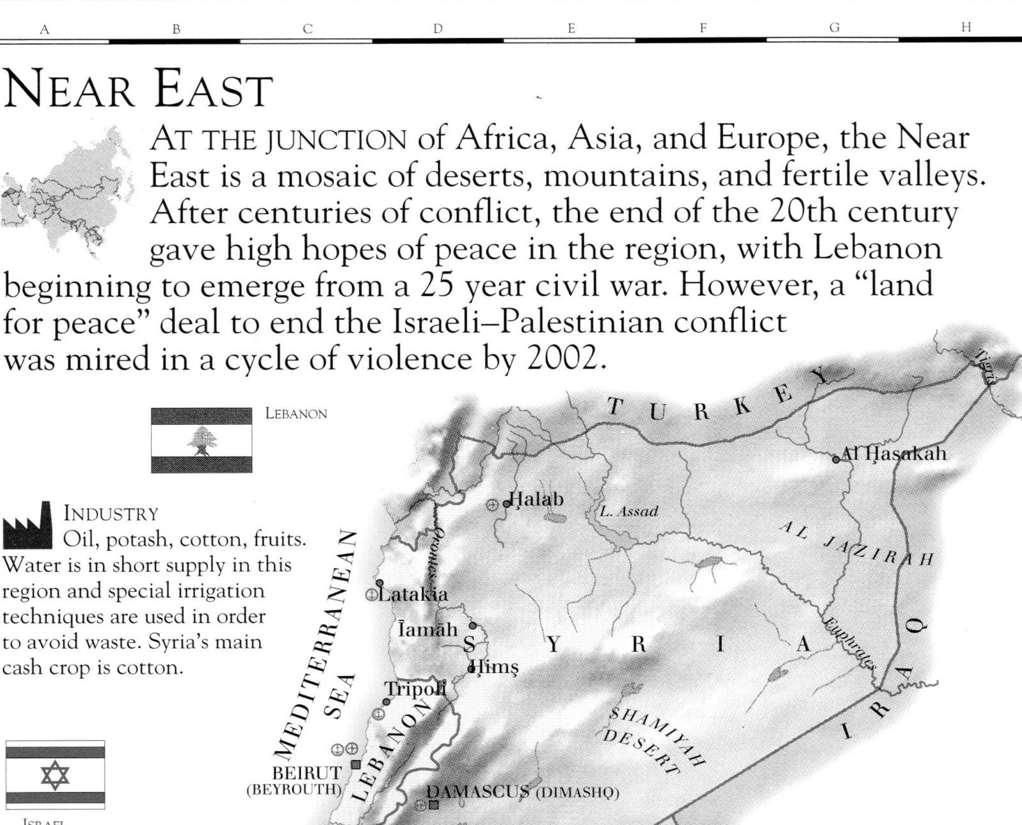

LEBANON
TURKEY
Al Ḥasakah
Ḥalab
L. Assad
AL JAZIRAH
Orontes
Latakia
Īamāh
SYRIA
Ḥimṣ
Euphrates
IRAQ
Tripoli
MEDITERRANEAN SEA
SHAMIYAH DESERT
LEBANON
BEIRUT (BEYROUTH)
DAMASCUS (DIMASHQ)
Tigris
ISRAEL

INDUSTRY

Oil, potash, cotton, fruits. Water is in short supply in this region and special irrigation techniques are used in order to avoid waste. Syria's main cash crop is cotton.

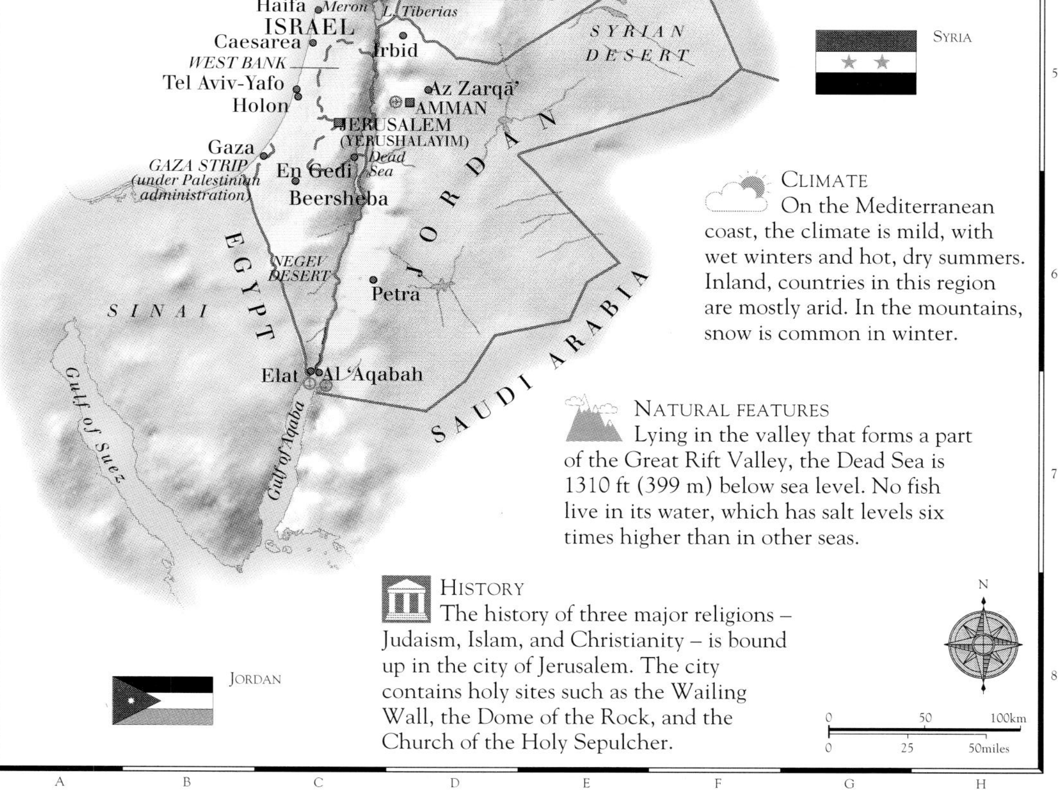
Haifa
Mt. Meron
GOLAN HEIGHTS
L. Tiberias
ISRAEL
Caesarea
Irbid
SYRIAN DESERT
WEST BANK
Tel Aviv-Yafo
Holon
Az Zarqā'
AMMAN
JERUSALEM (YERUSHALAYIM)
Gaza
GAZA STRIP (under Palestinian administration)
En Gedi
Dead Sea
Beersheba
JORDAN
EGYPT
NEGEV DESERT
Petra
SINAI
SAUDI ARABIA
Elat
Al 'Aqabah
Gulf of Suez
Gulf of Aqaba
Syria
Jordan
N
0 50 100km
0 25 50miles
A B C D E F G H
5 6 7 8

Climate

On the Mediterranean coast, the climate is mild, with wet winters and hot, dry summers. Inland, countries in this region are mostly arid. In the mountains, snow is common in winter.

Natural features

Lying in the valley that forms a part of the Great Rift Valley, the Dead Sea is 1310 ft (399 m) below sea level. No fish live in its water, which has salt levels six times higher than in other seas.

History

The history of three major religions – Judaism, Islam, and Christianity – is bound up in the city of Jerusalem. The city contains holy sites such as the Wailing Wall, the Dome of the Rock, and the Church of the Holy Sepulcher.

TURKEY AND CYPRUS

BRIDGING THE CONTINENTS of Europe and Asia, Turkey was once the center of the Ottoman Empire, which controlled a quarter of Europe. Cyprus became independent from the UK in 1960, but was invaded by Turkey in 1974. The northern half of the island, the "Turkish Republic of Northern Cyprus," is a state recognised only by Turkey.

TURKEY

BULGARIA
GREECE
Bosporus
Zonguldak
Istanbul
Izmit
Sea of Marmara
Adapazari
Dardanelles
Gallipoli
Bursa
Sakarya
Balikesir
Eskişehir
Kütahya
AEGEAN SEA
T
U
Manisa
Izmir
Ephesus
Pamukkale
L. Eğridir
Kuşadasi
Isparta
Denizli
L. Beyşehir
Antalya
MEDITERRANEAN

INDUSTRY

Wheat, grain, sugar beets, nuts, fruits, cotton, tobacco, tourism. Carpetweaving is a centuries-old tradition. Figs and peaches are grown on the coast of the Mediterranean.

ENVIRONMENT

Turkey's dam building projects on the Tigris and Euphrates Rivers have met with disapproval from Syria and Iraq, whose own rivers have a reduced flow as a result.

PEOPLE

The Kurds are Turkey's main minority group and one of the largest groups of stateless people in the world. Their homeland, Kurdistan, straddles three countries: Turkey, Iraq, and Iran. There are some 500,000 speakers of Arabic within Turkey.

Natural features

Turkey lies within the Alpine-Himalayan mountain belt. The Arabian, African, Eurasian, Aegean, and Turkish plates all converge within its borders, resulting in severe seismic activity.

Climate

Coastal regions of Turkey and Cyprus have a Mediterranean climate. The Turkish interior has cold, snowy winters and hot, dry summers.

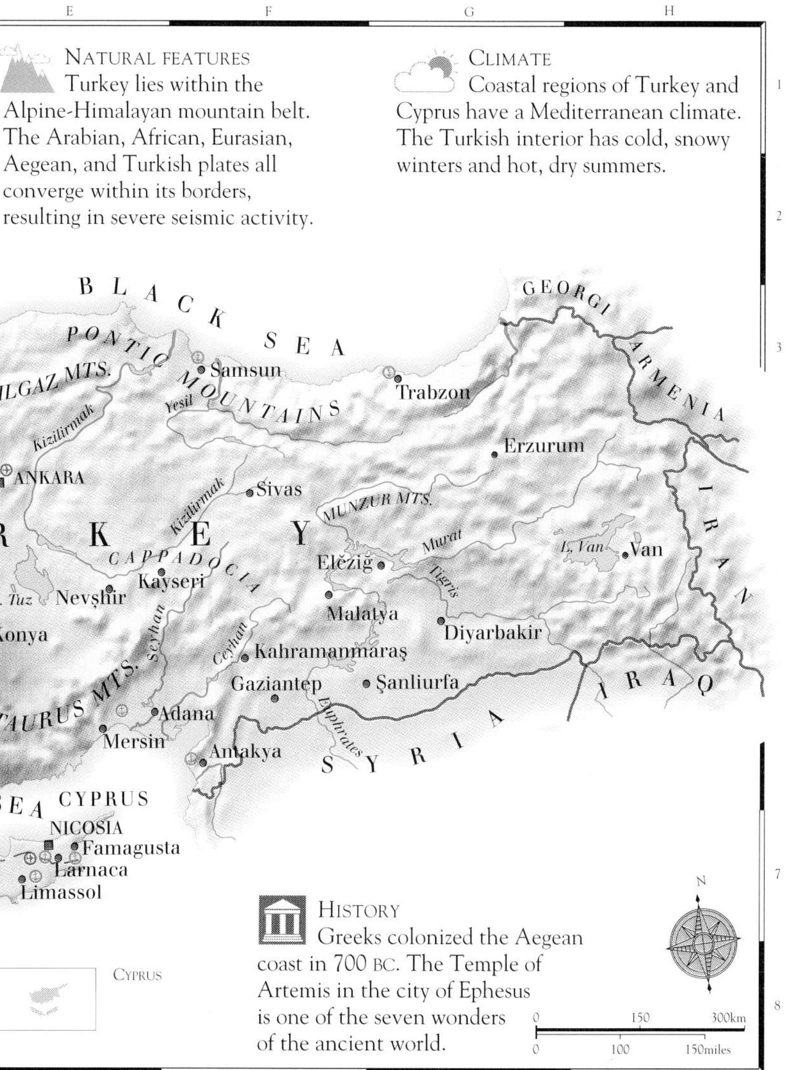
E
F
G
H
1
2
3
7
8
BLACK SEA
GEORGI
ARMENIA
IRAN
IRAQ
SYRIA
PONTIC MOUNTAINS
ILGAZ MTS.
Samsun
Trabzon
Yesil
Kizilirmak
Erzurum
ANKARA
Sivas
MUNZUR MTS.
K E Y
CAPPADOCIA
Elâzig
Murat
L. Van
Van
Tigris
Kayseri
Tuz
Nevşhir
Malatya
Diyarbakir
Konya
Seyhan
Ceyhan
Kahramanmaraş
TAURUS MTS.
Gaziantep
Şanliurfa
Adana
Euphrates
Mersin
Antakya
SEA
CYPRUS
NICOSIA
Famagusta
Larnaca
Limassol
Cyprus
N
0
150
300km
0
100
150miles

History

Greeks colonized the Aegean coast in 700 BC. The Temple of Artemis in the city of Ephesus is one of the seven wonders of the ancient world.

Middle East

ISLAM WAS FOUNDED in AD 570 in Mecca, Saudi Arabia, and spread throughout the Middle East, where today it is the main religion. Oil has brought wealth to the region but in 1991, the area was devastated by the Gulf War.

IRAQ

Industry

Oil, natural gas, fishing, carpet-weaving, offshore banking. Saudi Arabia has the world's largest oil reserves. Over 60 percent of the world's desalination plants are used in this region to make sea water drinkable.

SAUDI ARABIA

KUWAIT

BAHRAIN

Mecca
Jedda

Climate

Most of the countries in this region are semi-arid, with low rainfall. Inland, summer temperatures can reach 119°F (48°C) with winter temperatures falling to freezing.

QATAR

History

Ancient civilizations developed about 5500 years ago in Mesopotamia, between the Tigris and Euphrates Rivers. The Sumerian civilization had advanced methods of irrigation, sophisticated architecture, and a form of writing called cuneiform.

UNITED ARAB EMIRATES

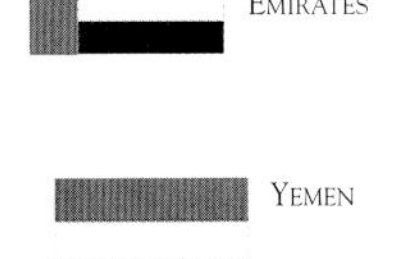

YEMEN

Hodeida
Al Mukhā
Bab el Mandeb

EGYPT JORDAN Gulf of Aqaba HEJAZ RED SEA Abh

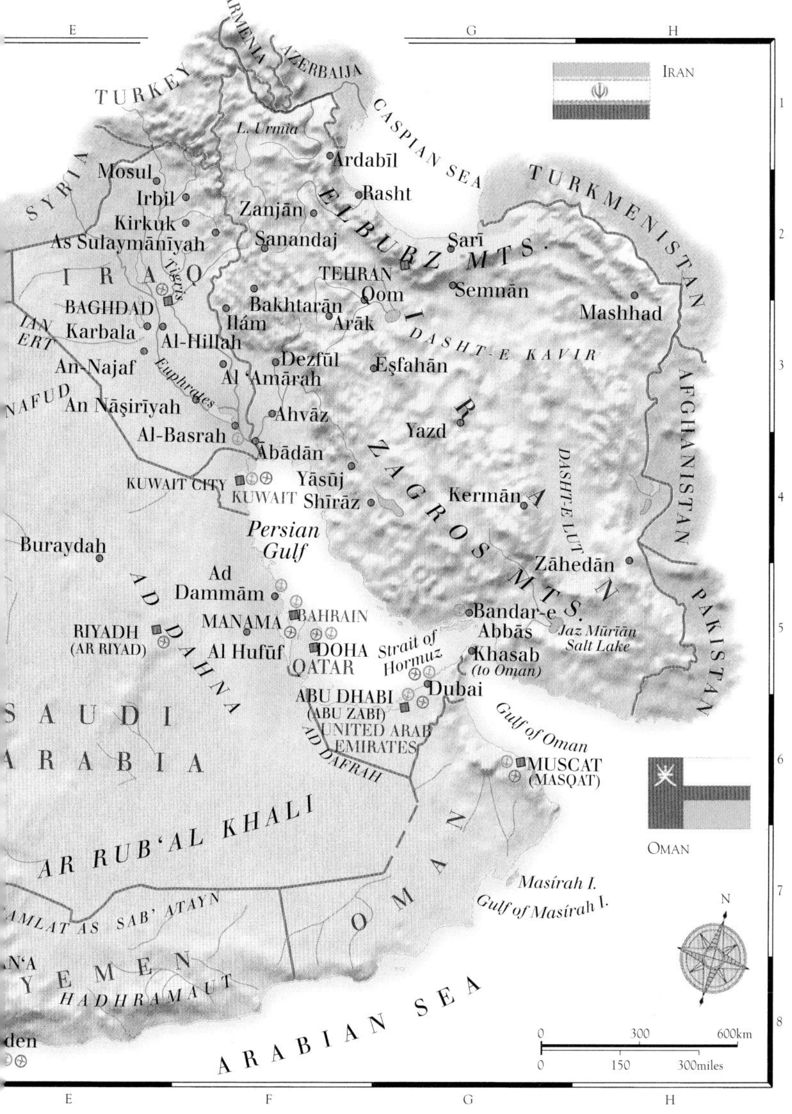
E
G
H
IRAN
1
2
3
4
5
6
7
8
ARMENIA
AZERBAIJAN
TURKEY
CASPIAN SEA
L. Urmia
Ardabīl
SYRIA
Mosul
Irbil
Rasht
Zanjān
Kirkuk
ELBURZ MTS.
Sarī
As Sulaymānīyah
Sanandaj
TURKMENISTAN
IRAQ
Tigris
TEHRAN
Qom
Semnān
BAGHDAD
Bakhtarān
Mashhad
Karbala
Ilám
Arāk
Al-Hillah
DASHT-E KAVIR
An-Najaf
Dezfūl
Eşfahān
Al 'Amārah
Euphrates
AFGHANISTAN
IRAN
An Nāşirīyah
Ahvāz
Al-Basrah
Yazd
Ābādān
ZAGROS MTS.
DASHT-E LUT
KUWAIT CITY
Yāsūj
KUWAIT
Shīrāz
Kermān
Persian Gulf
Buraydah
Zāhedān
Ad Dammām
AD DAHNA
MANAMA
BAHRAIN
Bandar-e Abbās
PAKISTAN
RIYADH (AR RIYAD)
Al Hufūf
DOHA
QATAR
Strait of Hormuz
Jaz Mūrīān Salt Lake
Khasab (to Oman)
Dubai
ABU DHABI (ABU ZABI)
UNITED ARAB EMIRATES
SAUDI ARABIA
Gulf of Oman
AD DAFRAH
MUSCAT (MASQAT)
AR RUB'AL KHALI
OMAN
Masírah I.
Gulf of Masírah I.
N
YEMEN
HADHRAMAUT
ARABIAN SEA
0
300
600km
0
150
300miles
den
E
F
G
H

Near East facts

Israel

• The average age in Israel is only 25.6 years.
• Israeli citizenship is the right of all Jews.

ESSENTIAL FACTS

- ⊙ Jerusalem
- 7992 sq miles (20,700 sq km)
- 6.2 million
- Shekel
- Hebrew, Arabic
- ▲ Multiparty republic
- 79 years

WAILING WALL, JERUSALEM

Cyprus

- ⊙ Nicosia
- 790,000
- Greek, Turkish

Jordan

• King Hussein, the longest-reigning Arab ruler, has led Jordan since 1952.

ESSENTIAL FACTS

- ⊙ Amman
- 35,637 sq miles (92,300 sq km)
- 5.1 million
- Jordanian dinar
- Arabic

Lebanon

• The press has greater freedom in Lebanon than in any other Arab country.

ESSENTIAL FACTS

- ⊙ Beirut
- 4015 sq miles (10,400 sq km)
- 3.6 million
- Lebanese pound
- Arabic

Syria

• The world's first alphabet was found in the ancient Syrian city of Ugarit.

ESSENTIAL FACTS

- ⊙ Damascus
- 71,498 sq miles (185,180 sq km)
- 16.6 million
- Syrian pound
- Arabic

Turkey

• Grapes, one of the world's oldest crops, were first grown in Anatolia, Turkey.

ESSENTIAL FACTS

- ⊙ Ankara
- 301,382 sq miles (780,580 sq km)
- 67.6 million
- Turkish lira
- Turkish
- ▲ Multiparty republic
- 70 years

Middle East facts

Iran

ESSENTIAL FACTS

- ⊙ Tehran
- 636,406 sq miles (1,648,293 sq km)
- 71.4 million
- Iranian rial
- Farsi
- ▲ Islamic theocracy
- 69 years

Saudi Arabia

ESSENTIAL FACTS

- ⊙ Riyadh
- 756,981 sq miles (1,960,582 sq km)
- 21 million
- Saudi riyal
- Arabic
- ▲ Monarchy
- 69 years

Qatar

- ⊙ Doha
- 575,000
- Arabic

Bahrain

- ⊙ Manama
- 625,000
- Arabic

Iraq

ESSENTIAL FACTS

- ⊙ Baghdad
- 168,753 sq miles (437,072 sq km)
- 23.6 million
- Iraqi dinar
- Arabic
- ▲ Single-party republic
- 61 years

ARAB HEADDRESSES
Men and women wear headcloths to protect them from the sun.

United Arab Emirates

ESSENTIAL FACTS

- ⊙ Abu Dhabi
- 32,000 sq miles (82,880 sq km)
- 2.7 million
- UAE dirham
- Arabic

Kuwait

ESSENTIAL FACTS

- ⊙ Kuwait City
- 6880 sq miles (17,820 sq km)
- 2 million
- Kuwaiti dinar
- Arabic

Oman

ESSENTIAL FACTS

- ⊙ Muscat
- 82,030 sq miles (212,460 sq km)
- 2.6 million
- Omani rial
- Arabic

Yemen

ESSENTIAL FACTS

- ⊙ Sana
- 203,849 sq miles (527,970 sq km)
- 19.1 million
- Yemen rial
- Arabic

Central Asia

For centuries, many people in central Asia lived in mountains as nomads, or in cities that sprang up along the Silk Road. When the region came under Soviet rule, industry was developed and irrigation schemes made farming possible.

Turkmenistan

Industry

Cotton, gold, gas, sulfur, mercury, opium, hydroelectricity. Uzbekistan has the largest single gold mine in the world. Tajikistan has 14 percent of the world's known uranium resources.

Environment

Crop irrigation draws water from the Amu Darya River, reducing the amount of water flowing into the Aral Sea. By the year 2000 the Sea will have shrunk to a third of its original size.

History

In the early 1900s, most of this region, except for Afghanistan, came under Soviet rule, which restricted the use of local languages and Islam. Today, these newly independent countries are resuming the religions, languages, and traditions of their past.

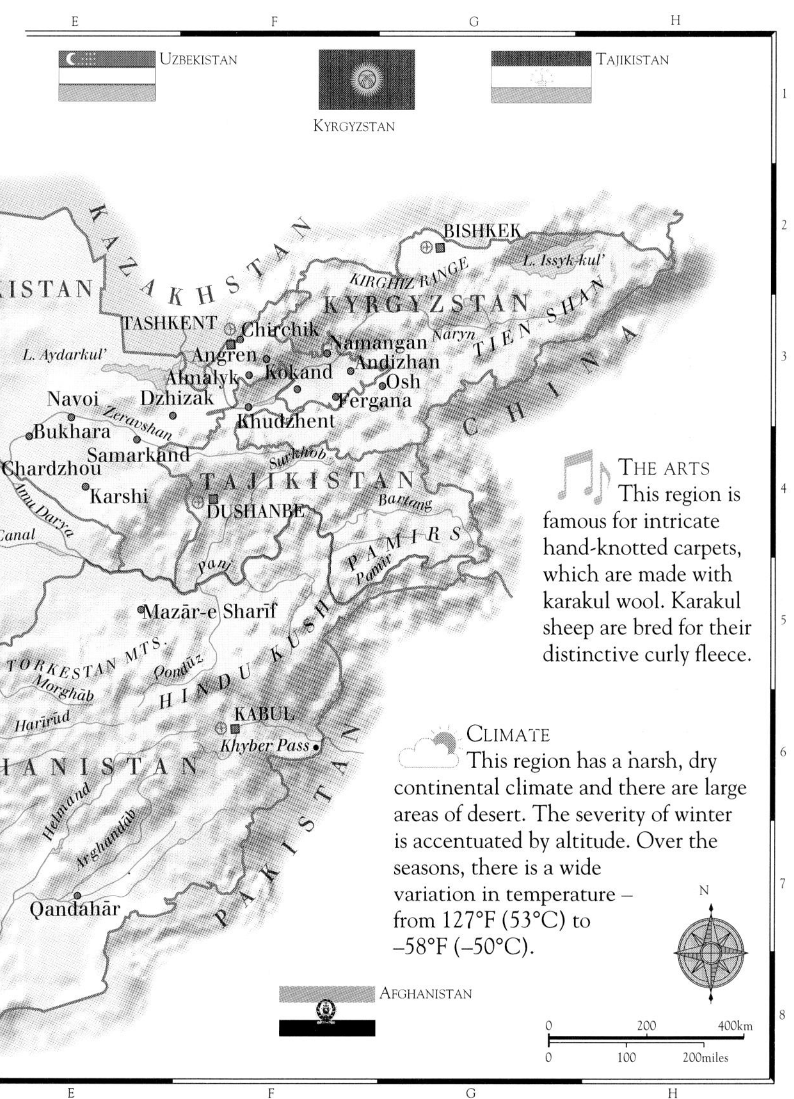
E
F
G
H
1
2
3
4
5
6
7
8
UZBEKISTAN
KYRGYZSTAN
TAJIKISTAN
KAZAKHSTAN
BISHKEK
L. Issyk-kul'
KIRGHIZ RANGE
KYRGYZSTAN
TIEN SHAN
TASHKENT
Chirchik
Namangan
Naryn
L. Aydarkul'
Angren
Andizhan
Almalyk
Kokand
Osh
Navoi
Dzhizak
Fergana
Zeravshan
Khudzhent
CHINA
Bukhara
Samarkand
Surkhob
Chardzhou
TAJIKISTAN
Karshi
DUSHANBE
Bartang
Amu Darya
Canal
PAMIRS
Panj
Pamir
Mazār-e Sharīf
HINDU KUSH
TORKESTAN MTS.
Qondūz
Morghāb
Harīrūd
KABUL
Khyber Pass
AFGHANISTAN
Helmand
Arghandāb
PAKISTAN
Qandahār
AFGHANISTAN
N
0
200
400km
0
100
200miles

THE ARTS

This region is famous for intricate hand-knotted carpets, which are made with karakul wool. Karakul sheep are bred for their distinctive curly fleece.

CLIMATE

This region has a harsh, dry continental climate and there are large areas of desert. The severity of winter is accentuated by altitude. Over the seasons, there is a wide variation in temperature – from 127°F (53°C) to –58°F (–50°C).

RUSSIAN FEDERATION AND KAZAKHSTAN

THE URAL mountains separate European and Asian Russia, which extends from the frozen Arctic lands in the north to the central Asian deserts in the south. In 1991, Kazakhstan became the last Soviet republic to gain independence.

FINLAND
Murmansk
BARENTS SEA
ESTONIA
LATVIA
St. Petersburg
Pskov
Novgorod
Arkhangel'sk
BELARUS
Smolensk
MOSCOW
Yaroslavl'
URAL MOUNTAINS
Ob
UKRAINE
Tula
Ryazan'
Kirov
Voronezh
Irtysh
Penza
Kazan'
Izhevsk
Perm'
Rostov-na-Donu
Ul'yanovsk
Naberezhnyye Chelny
Saratov
Samara
Yekaterinburg
Tol'yatti
Krasnodar
Volgograd
Ural'sk
Ufa
Chelyabinsk
KIRGHIZ STEPPE
Orenburg
GEORGIA
Astrakhan
Ural
Kostanay
Omsk
Atyrau
Aktobe
Groznyy
CASPIAN SEA
Emba
Ishim
Tselinograd
L. Tengiz
ASTANA
AZERBAIJAN
Karaganda
ARAL SEA
KAZAKHSTAN
Syr Darya
Kyzylorda
Chu
L. Balkhash
TURKMENISTAN
UZBEKISTAN
Ili
Shymkent
Almaty
KYRGYZSTAN

CLIMATE
Kazakhstan has a continental climate. Winter temperatures in Russia vary little from north to south, but fall sharply in the east, especially in Siberia.

PEOPLE
There are 57 nationalities with their own territories within the Russian Federation. A further 95 groups have no territories of their own, although these groups make up only six percent of the population.

KAZAKHSTAN

History

Kazakhstan was absorbed by Russia in the 19th century, when Russians began to settle the land used by nomadic Kazakhs. Settlement and industrial development increased after 1917.

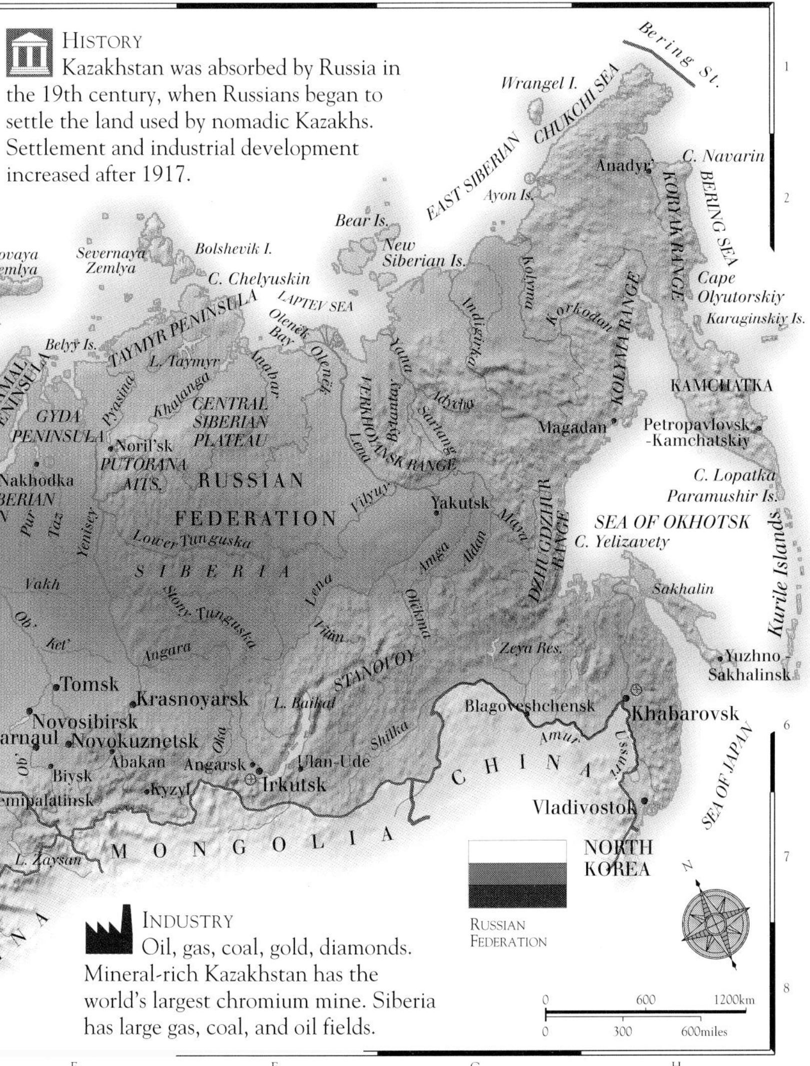

Bering St.
Wrangel I.
CHUKCHI SEA
EAST SIBERIAN
Anadyr'
C. Navarin
KORYAK RANGE
BERING SEA
Ayon Is.
Bear Is.
New Siberian Is.
Novaya Zemlya
Severnaya Zemlya
Bolshevik I.
C. Chelyuskin
LAPTEV SEA
Olenek Bay
Olenek
Kolyma
Indigirka
Korkodon
KOLYMA RANGE
Cape Olyutorskiy
Karaginskiy Is.
TAYMYR PENINSULA
Belyy Is.
YAMAL PENINSULA
L. Taymyr
Anabar
Yana
VERKHOYANSK RANGE
Bytantay
Adycha
Sartang
KAMCHATKA
Magadan
Petropavlovsk-Kamchatskiy
GYDA PENINSULA
Pyasina
Khatanga
CENTRAL SIBERIAN PLATEAU
Noril'sk
PUTORANA MTS.
Lena
Nakhodka
RUSSIAN FEDERATION
Vilyuy
Yakutsk
Maya
DZHUGDZHUR RANGE
C. Lopatka
Paramushir Is.
SEA OF OKHOTSK
C. Yelizavety
Kurile Islands
Pur
Taz
Yenisey
Lower Tunguska
SIBERIA
Amga
Aldan
Vakh
Ob'
Stony Tunguska
Olëkma
Vitim
Sakhalin
Ket'
Angara
STANOVOY
Zeya Res.
Yuzhno-Sakhalinsk
Tomsk
Krasnoyarsk
L. Baikal
Blagoveshchensk
Khabarovsk
Novosibirsk
Barnaul
Novokuznetsk
Oka
Amur
Shilka
Ussuri
Biysk
Abakan
Angarsk
Ulan-Ude
CHINA
SEA OF JAPAN
Semipalatinsk
Kyzyl
Irkutsk
Vladivostok
MONGOLIA
L. Zaysan
NORTH KOREA
N
0 600 1200km
0 300 600miles

Industry

Oil, gas, coal, gold, diamonds. Mineral-rich Kazakhstan has the world's largest chromium mine. Siberia has large gas, coal, and oil fields.

RUSSIAN FEDERATION

Central Asia facts

Uzbekistan

- Many young Uzbeks are sent to Turkey to study business practice.
- Arranged marriages are still the custom in rural areas.

ESSENTIAL FACTS

- Tashkent
- 172,741 sq miles (447,400 sq km)
- 25.3 million
- Som
- Uzbek

UZBEK HEADWEAR Velvet hats like this one are commonly worn in Uzbekistan.

Kyrgyzstan

- The nation of Kyrgyzstan is the most rural ex-Soviet republic.

ESSENTIAL FACTS

- Bishkek
- 76,641 sq miles (198,500 sq km)
- 5 million
- Som
- Kyrgyz, Russian

Turkmenistan

- Ashgabat is a breeding center for the Akhal-Teke, a breed of racehorse able to maintain its speed in desert conditions.
- Most Turkmen live around desert oases.

ESSENTIAL FACTS

- Ashgabat
- 188,455 sq miles (488,100 sq km)
- 4.8 million
- Manat
- Turkmen

Tajikistan

- The traditions and language of Tajikistan are similar to those of Iran.
- Violence perpetrated by armed gangs is a major problem in all but the most remote areas.

ESSENTIAL FACTS

- Dushanbe
- 55,251 sq miles (143,100 sq km)
- 6.1 million
- Somoni
- Tajik

Afghanistan

- Most Afghans live in extreme poverty.

ESSENTIAL FACTS

- Kabul
- 250,000 sq miles (647,500 sq km)
- 22.5 million
- Afghani
- Dari, Pashtu

CARROTS WERE FIRST GROWN FOR FOOD IN AFGHANISTAN

Russian Federation and Kazakhstan facts

Russian Federation

• Moscow and St. Petersburg are the most popular tourist destinations in the Commonwealth of Independent States (CIS).
• Russia still maintains a military presence in most of the former USSR.
• Organized crime bosses are Russia's wealthiest group.

Essential facts

⊙ Moscow
◒ 6,592,735 sq miles (17,075,200 sq km)
🚹 144.7 million
💰 Russian rouble
🗨 Russian
▲ Multiparty republic
● 66 years

(See also **European Russia**, p.288)

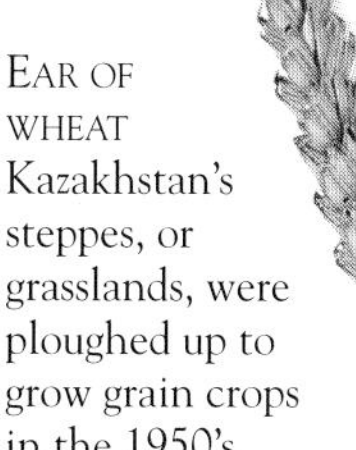

Ear of wheat
Kazakhstan's steppes, or grasslands, were ploughed up to grow grain crops in the 1950's.

Kazakhstan

• A large community of foreign business people now lives in Almaty.
• Kazakhstan joined the International Monetary Fund (IMF) in 1992.
• The Kazakhs remain committed to Islam and loyal to the three clan federations, or Hordes.

Essential facts

⊙ Astana
◒ 1,049,150 sq miles (2,717,300 sq km)
🚹 16.1 million
💰 Tenge
🗨 Kazakh
▲ Multiparty republic
● 65 years

Siberian huskies
The husky is used for pulling sledges and hunting.

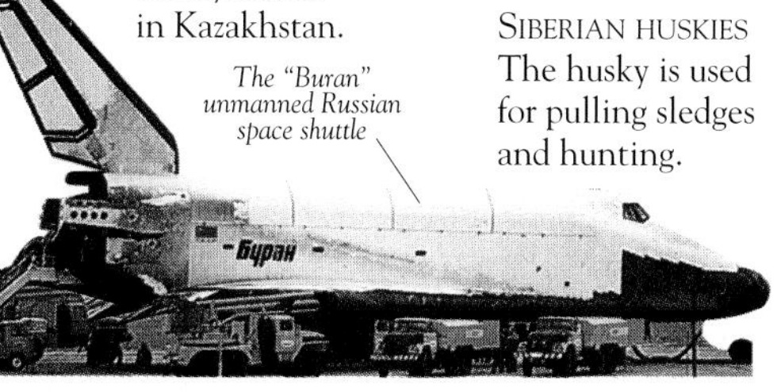
Буран

Kazakhstan space center
The Russian space program is based at Baykonour in Kazakhstan.

The "Buran" unmanned Russian space shuttle

SOUTH AND EAST ASIA

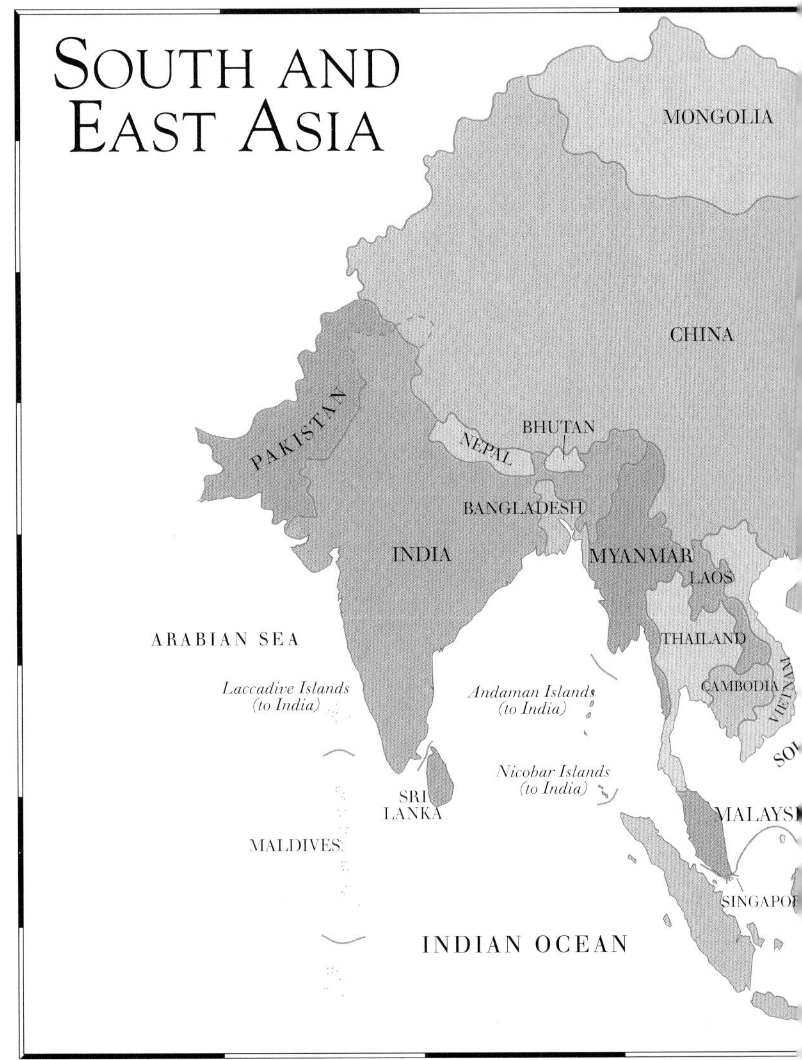

MONGOLIA
CHINA
PAKISTAN
NEPAL
BHUTAN
BANGLADESH
INDIA
MYANMAR
LAOS
THAILAND
CAMBODIA
ARABIAN SEA
Laccadive Islands
(to India)
Andaman Islands
(to India)
Nicobar Islands
(to India)
SRI
LANKA
MALDIVES
INDIAN OCEAN

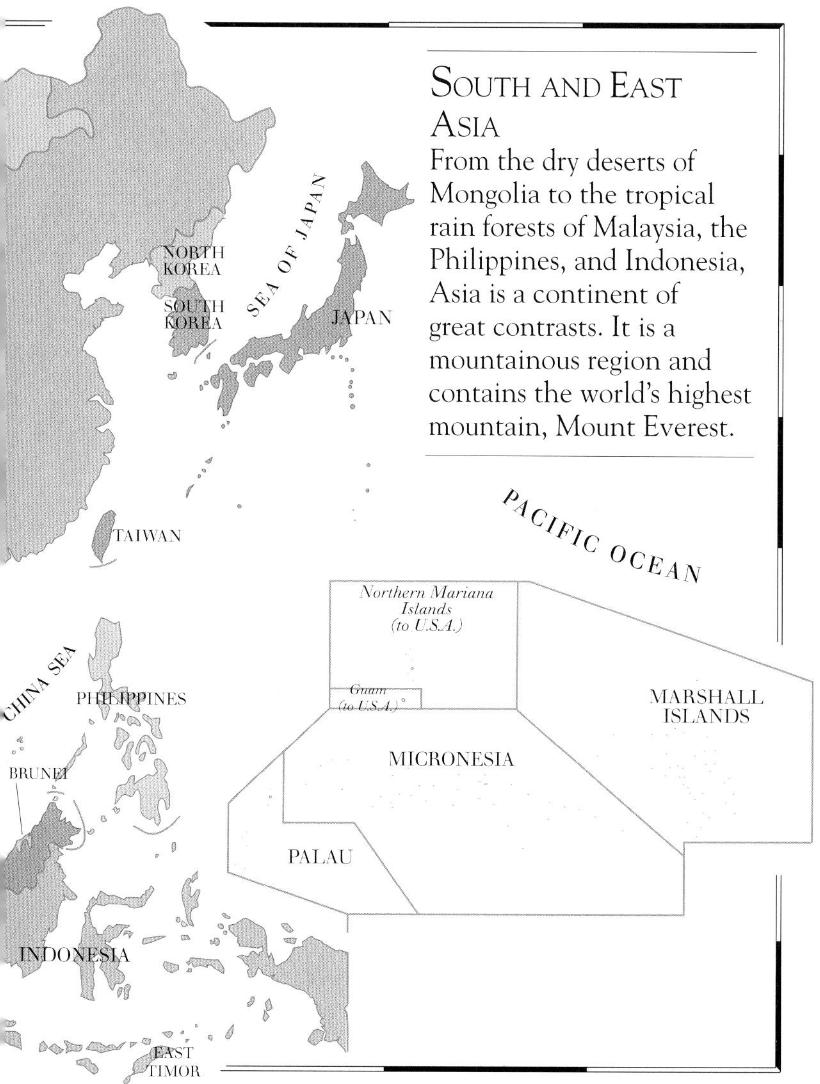
NORTH KOREA
SOUTH KOREA
SEA OF JAPAN
JAPAN
TAIWAN
PACIFIC OCEAN
Northern Mariana Islands (to U.S.A.)
Guam (to U.S.A.)
MARSHALL ISLANDS
MICRONESIA
PALAU
CHINA SEA
PHILIPPINES
BRUNEI
INDONESIA
EAST TIMOR

South and East Asia

From the dry deserts of Mongolia to the tropical rain forests of Malaysia, the Philippines, and Indonesia, Asia is a continent of great contrasts. It is a mountainous region and contains the world's highest mountain, Mount Everest.

INDIAN SUBCONTINENT

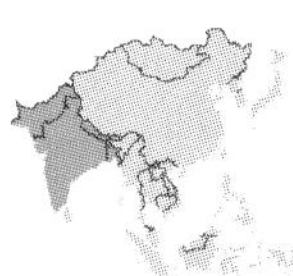

SEPARATED FROM THE rest of Asia by the Himalayas, India is the second most populated country after China. It is estimated that India's population will overtake that of China by 2030. To the north, Nepal and Bhutan lie nestled in the Himalayas between China and India. To the south lies Sri Lanka, once known as Ceylon.

AFGHANISTAN
TOBA KAKAR RANGE
IRAN
CHAGAI HILLS
PAKISTAN
THAR
Indus
MAKRAN
Hyderabad
Karachi
ARABIAN SEA
Gulf of
Rajkot
Gulf of Khambhat
INDIA
N
0 350 700km
0 200 400miles

INDUSTRY

Tea, jute, iron, cut diamonds, cotton, rice, sugarcane, textiles. Bangladesh exports 80 percent of the world's jute fiber. Sri Lanka is the largest tea exporter in the world. Pakistan is a major exporter of rice.

HISTORY

In 1947, when India gained independence, religious differences led to the creation of two countries – Hindu India and Muslim Pakistan. Border conflicts between the two states over the disputed areas of Jammu and Kashmir are ongoing.

NATURAL FEATURES

The Himalayas were formed as a result of a violent crumpling of the Earth's crust. Frequent earthquakes indicate that the process is continuing. The highest peaks in the world, including Mount Everest, are in this mountain system.

INDIAN SUBCONTINENT

PAKISTAN

NEPAL

BHUTAN

BANGLADESH

SRI LANKA

CLIMATE

Sri Lanka and southern India are tropical, with little seasonal variation in temperature. The north has a cold alpine climate. Cyclones regularly build up in the Bay of Bengal, and Bangladesh is often flooded during the monsoon.

Indian Subcontinent facts

INDIA

- The Bombay film industry is the world's biggest producer of feature films.
- Nearly half of India's adults are illiterate.
- Cultural and religious pressures in India encourage people to have large families.

ESSENTIAL FACTS

⊙ New Delhi

1,289,338 sq miles (3,287,590 sq km)

1 billion

Indian rupee

Hindi, English

▲ Multiparty republic

63 years

REGAL BEAST
The national symbol of India is the Royal Bengal tiger, which is a protected species.

THE SPICE OF LIFE
Indian cooking uses highly flavored seasonings and subtle combinations of spices to flavor each dish.

Fresh coriander

Ground coriander

Cardamom pods

Ground turmeric

Fresh ginger

SRI LANKA

- In 1960, Sri Lanka became the first country in the world to elect a woman prime minister.
- Ethnic tension between the minority Tamils and majority Sinhalese led to civil war in 1983.

ESSENTIAL FACTS

⊙ Columbo

25,332 sq miles (65,610 sq km)

19.1 million

Sri Lanka rupee

Sinhalese, Tamil

BANGLADESH

- Most transportation in Bangladesh is via rivers and waterways.
- Destruction of crops by cyclones and flooding is a frequent problem.

ESSENTIAL FACTS

⊙ Dhaka

55,598 sq miles (144,000 sq km)

140.4 million

Taka

Bengali

PAKISTAN

• The first woman ever to lead a Muslim country was Benazir Bhutto, elected prime minister of Pakistan in 1988.
• The Punjabi majority controls Pakistan's army and bureaucracy.

ESSENTIAL FACTS

⊙ Islamabad

310,401 sq miles (803,940 sq km)

145 million

Pakistani rupee

Urdu, Punjabi

▲ Multiparty republic

60 years

TOP TEAM
The nation of Pakistan has one of the world's best cricket teams.

EYES OF BUDDHA
The all-seeing eyes of Buddha adorn the walls of many temples in Nepal.

NEPAL

• Prince Siddhartha Gautama, the founder of Buddhism, was born in southern Nepal in 563 BC.
• Nepal's divorce laws are biased in favor of the male partner.

ESSENTIAL FACTS

⊙ Kathmandu

54,363 sq miles (140,800 sq km)

23.6 million

Nepalese rupee

Nepali

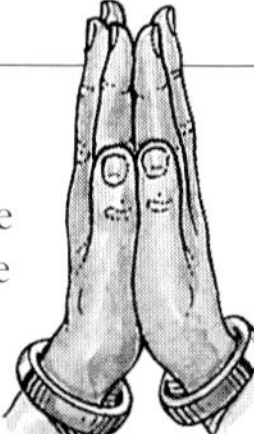

NEPALESE WELCOME
A prayer-like gesture is the traditional greeting in Nepal.

SEYCHELLES

(*Indian Ocean*, pp.362–363)

⊙ Victoria

29,300

Seselwa (French creole)

BHUTANESE SPORT
Archery is the national sport of Bhutan.

BHUTAN

⊙ Thimphu

2.1 million

Dzongkha

MALDIVES

(*Indian Ocean*, pp.362–363)

⊙ Male'

300,000

Dhivehi

MAURITIUS

(*Indian Ocean*, pp.362–363)

⊙ Port Louis

1.2 million

English

CHINA AND MONGOLIA

ISOLATED FROM THE western world for centuries, the Chinese were the first to develop the compass, paper, gunpowder, porcelain, and silk. Three autonomous regions lie within western China – Inner Mongolia, Xinjiang, and Tibet. The Gobi desert, in vast Mongolia, is the world's most northern desert.

PEOPLE

Han Chinese make up 93 percent of China's population. China has relaxed its 1979 one-child policy for minority groups, such as the Mongolians, Tibetans, and Muslim Uygurs, after some groups faced near extinction.

HISTORY

Tibet was invaded by China in 1950. The Chinese have destroyed Tibet's traditional agricultural society and Buddhist monasteries. In 1959 there were more than 6,000 monasteries – by 1980, only 179 remained.

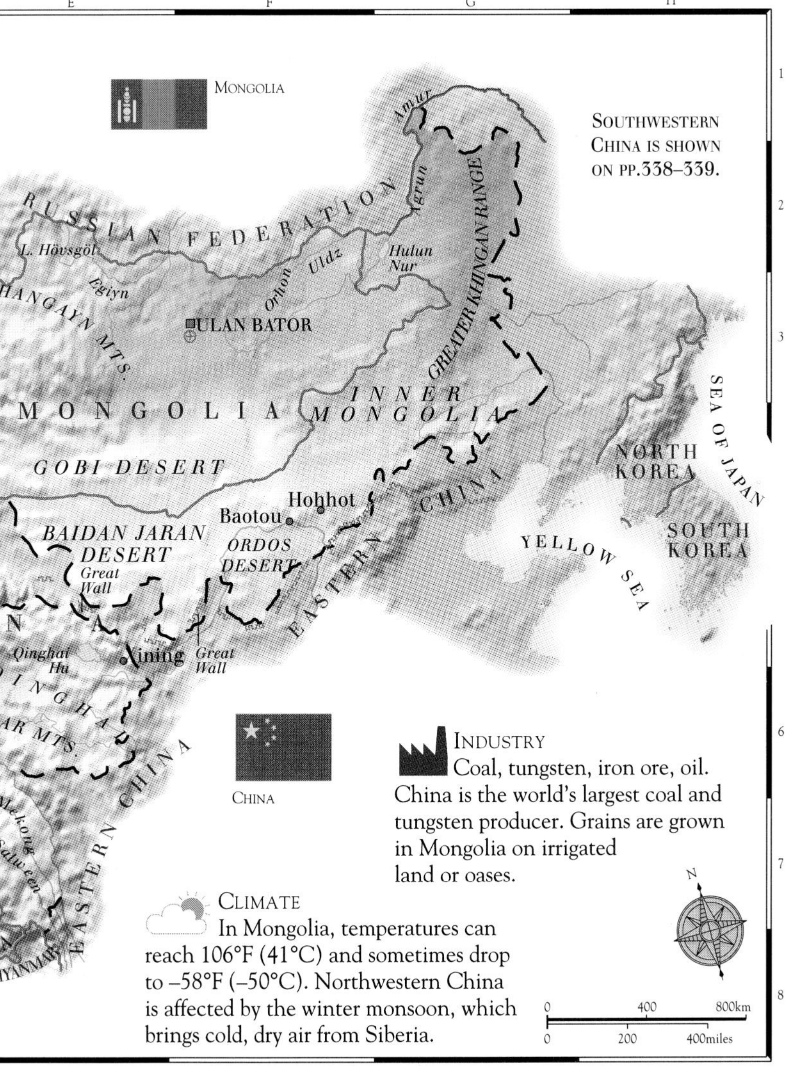
E
F
G
H
1
2
3
6
7
8
RUSSIAN FEDERATION
L. Hövsgöl
Egiyn
HANGAYN MTS.
Orhon
Uldz
Hulun Nur
Argun
Amur
GREATER KHINGAN RANGE
ULAN BATOR
MONGOLIA
INNER MONGOLIA
GOBI DESERT
Hohhot
Baotou
BAIDAN JARAN DESERT
ORDOS DESERT
Great Wall
Qinghai Hu
Xining
Great Wall
EASTERN CHINA
NORTH KOREA
SOUTH KOREA
SEA OF JAPAN
YELLOW SEA
Mekong
Salween
N
0
400
800km
0
200
400miles

MONGOLIA

SOUTHWESTERN CHINA IS SHOWN ON PP.338–339.

CHINA

INDUSTRY

Coal, tungsten, iron ore, oil. China is the world's largest coal and tungsten producer. Grains are grown in Mongolia on irrigated land or oases.

CLIMATE

In Mongolia, temperatures can reach 106°F (41°C) and sometimes drop to –58°F (–50°C). Northwestern China is affected by the winter monsoon, which brings cold, dry air from Siberia.

China and Korea

One-fifth of the world's population lives in China – mostly in the eastern part of the country. Annexed to Japan in 1910, Korea was divided between the US and Communist Russia after World War II. North and South Korea were formed in 1948.

North-western China is shown on pp.118-119.

RUSSIAN FEDERATION
LESSER KHINGAN MTS.
Amur
Qiqihar
Harbin
MANCHURIA
Jilin
Changchun
Fushun
Ch'ôngjin
NORTH KOREA
Shenyang
Anshan
Sinûiju
P'YONGYANG
MONGOLIA
WESTERN CHINA
Great Wall
Datong
Tiajin
BEIJING
Bo Hai
Dalian
Namp'o
Tianjin
YELLOW SEA
SEOUL
Inch'ôn
Taegu
Pusan
SOUTH KOREA
Shijiazhuang
Shandong Pen.
Taiyuan
NINGXIA AUTONOMOUS REGION
Zibo
Handan
Jinan
Qingdao
Lanzhou
Zhengzhou
Grand Canal
Zaozhuang
Korea Strait
Xi'an
Luoyang
QIN LING
CHINA
Cheju
Huainan
Nanjing
Hefei
Wuxi
Shanghai
Chengdu
Yangtze
Wuhan
Hangzhou
Ningbo
Chongqing
Shaoxing
Jinsha
Dadu He
CHINA SEA
A
B
C
D
E
F
G
H
1
2
3
4

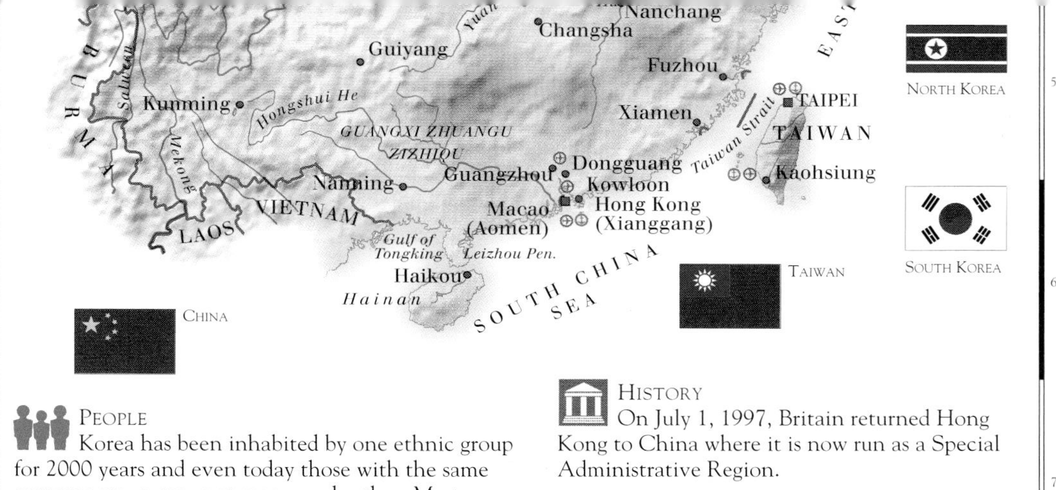
BURMA
Salween
Kunming
Mekong
LAOS
VIETNAM
Nanning
Hongshui He
GUANGXI ZHUANGU ZIZHIQU
Guiyang
Yuan
Changsha
Nanchang
Fuzhou
Xiamen
Guangzhou
Dongguang
Kowloon
Hong Kong (Xianggang)
Macao (Aomen)
Gulf of Tongking
Leizhou Pen.
Haikou
Hainan
SOUTH CHINA SEA
Taiwan Strait
TAIPEI
TAIWAN
Kaohsiung
EAST
CHINA
TAIWAN
NORTH KOREA
SOUTH KOREA
N
0 300 600km
0 150 300miles

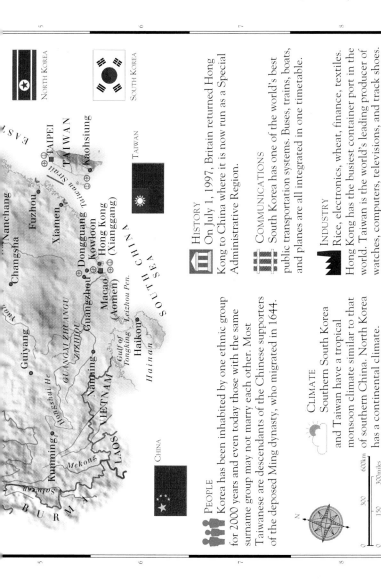

People

Korea has been inhabited by one ethnic group for 2000 years and even today those with the same surname group may not marry each other. Most Taiwanese are descendants of the Chinese supporters of the deposed Ming dynasty, who migrated in 1644.

Climate

Southern South Korea and Taiwan have a tropical monsoon climate similar to that of southern China. North Korea has a continental climate.

History

On July 1, 1997, Britain returned Hong Kong to China where it is now run as a Special Administrative Region.

Communications

South Korea has one of the world's best public transportation systems. Buses, trains, boats, and planes are all integrated in one timetable.

Industry

Rice, electronics, wheat, finance, textiles. Hong Kong has the busiest container port in the world. Taiwan is the world's leading producer of watches, computers, televisions, and track shoes.

JAPAN

CONSISTING OF FOUR main islands and 4000 smaller ones, Japan is the world's leading industrial nation. Since two-thirds of the land is mountainous, the majority of people live on the coast. Japan has about 1500 minor earthquakes a year, but severe earthquakes, such as the one in Kobe in 1994, occur every few years. Underwater earthquakes sometimes cause huge surge waves, or *tsunami*, along Japan's Pacific coast.

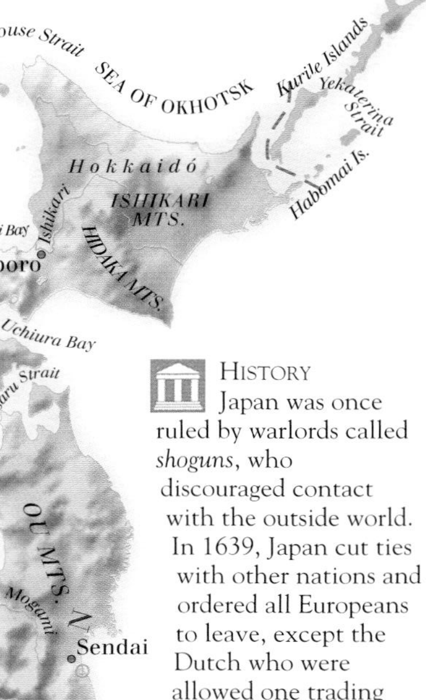
La Perouse Strait
SEA OF OKHOTSK
Kurile Islands
Yekaterina Strait
Habomai Is.
Hokkaidó
ISHIKARI MTS.
HIDAKA MTS.
Ishikari Bay
Ishikari
Sapporo
Uchiura Bay
Tsugaru Strait
OU MTS.
Mogami
Sendai
SEA OF JAPAN
Toyama Bay
Shinano
Honshú

INDUSTRY
Fishing, shipbuilding, motor vehicles, computers, televisions, high-tech electronics. Motor vehicles are Japan's biggest export, and its stock exchange ranks second in the world. Japan excels at producing miniature electronic goods.

HISTORY
Japan was once ruled by warlords called *shoguns*, who discouraged contact with the outside world. In 1639, Japan cut ties with other nations and ordered all Europeans to leave, except the Dutch who were allowed one trading ship per year.

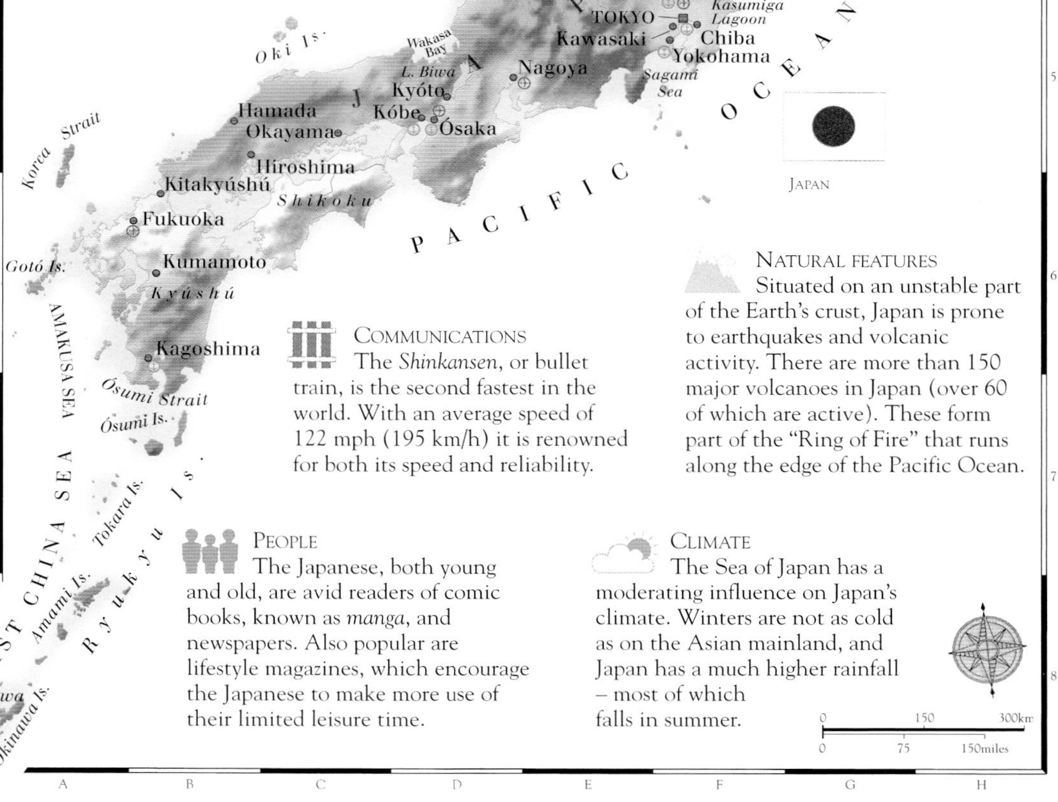
Oki Is.
Korea Strait
Wakasa Bay
L. Biwa
TOKYO
Kasumiga Lagoon
Kawasaki
Chiba
Yokohama
Sagami Sea
Nagoya
Kyóto
Kóbe
Ósaka
Hamada
Okayama
Hiroshima
Kitakyúshú
Shikoku
Fukuoka
Gotó Is.
Kumamoto
Kyúshú
Kagoshima
AMAKUSA SEA
Ósumi Strait
Ósumi Is.
Tokara Is.
Ryukyu Is.
Amami Is.
EAST CHINA SEA
Okinawa
Okinawa Is.
PACIFIC OCEAN
JAPAN
0 150 300km
0 75 150miles

NATURAL FEATURES

Situated on an unstable part of the Earth's crust, Japan is prone to earthquakes and volcanic activity. There are more than 150 major volcanoes in Japan (over 60 of which are active). These form part of the "Ring of Fire" that runs along the edge of the Pacific Ocean.

COMMUNICATIONS

The *Shinkansen*, or bullet train, is the second fastest in the world. With an average speed of 122 mph (195 km/h) it is renowned for both its speed and reliability.

PEOPLE

The Japanese, both young and old, are avid readers of comic books, known as *manga*, and newspapers. Also popular are lifestyle magazines, which encourage the Japanese to make more use of their limited leisure time.

CLIMATE

The Sea of Japan has a moderating influence on Japan's climate. Winters are not as cold as on the Asian mainland, and Japan has a much higher rainfall – most of which falls in summer.

Eastern Asia facts

CHINA

• China has the world's oldest continuous civilization; recorded history began 4000 years ago.
• Mao Tse-tung founded and dominated communist China from 1949 until his death in 1976.

ESSENTIAL FACTS

⊙ Beijing
3,705,386 sq miles (9,596,960 sq km)
1.3 billion
Renminbi
Mandarin
▲ One-party state
71 years

WONDERWALL
The Great Wall of China is the longest manmade structure in the world.

BAMBOO LUNCH
Pandas living in the forests of China's Sichuan mountains feed on bamboo shoots.

MONGOLIA

• The Mongolian press is strongly outspoken, with no slander or libel laws.
• Most Mongolians are nomadic, but some now live on state-run farms.
• The poorest people in Mongolia cannot even afford to buy bread.

ESSENTIAL FACTS

⊙ Ulan Bator
604,247 sq miles (1,565,000 sq km)
2.6 million
Tughrik (tögrög)
Khalkha Mongol

MACAO

Chinese territory under Portuguese administration until 1999.

⊙ Macao
477,850
Chinese, Portuguese

HONG KONG

Territory reverted to Chinese administration in 1997.

⊙ Victoria
5.8 million
English, Cantonese

MONGOLIAN YAK
Yaks provide Mongolian herders with milk, butter, meat, wool, and leather.

South Korea

- Over 60% of South Koreans are named Kim, Lee, or Pak.
- It is not considered respectable for married women to have jobs in South Korea.

ESSENTIAL FACTS

⊙ Seoul

38,232 sq miles (99,020 sq km)

47.1 million

South Korean Won

Korean

▲ Presidential democracy

75 years

North Korea

- The Korean Worker's Party is the only legal political party.
- Private telephones and cars are forbidden.

ESSENTIAL FACTS

⊙ Pyongyang

46,540 sq miles (120,540 sq km)

22.4 million

North Korean Won

Korean

KOREAN GINSENG ROOT IS WIDELY USED IN TRADITIONAL ASIAN MEDICINE

TAIWAN PRODUCES ABOUT 10% OF THE WORLD'S COMPUTERS

Taiwan

- Taiwan is the world's biggest bicycle producer.
- China regards Taiwan as a province of the Chinese mainland.

ESSENTIAL FACTS

⊙ Taipei

13,892 sq miles (35,980 sq km)

20.8 million

New Taiwan dollar

Mandarin, Chinese

Japan

- People in Japan define themselves by the company they work for, not the job they do.
- Japan is Hollywood's biggest export market.
- The Japanese constitution forbids the use of troops abroad except in self-defense.

ESSENTIAL FACTS

⊙ Tokyo

145,882 sq miles (377,835 sq km)

127.3 million

Yen

Japanese

▲ Multiparty democracy

81 years

HEAVYWEIGHTS Japanese sumo wrestlers eat a daily stew called *chanko-nabe*, made of seafood, meat, vegetables, and tofu, to maintain their bulk.

MAINLAND SOUTHEAST ASIA

FOR MOST OF its history, Thailand has been an independent kingdom. Malaysia includes 11 states on the mainland (Malaya), as well as Sabah and Sarawak in Borneo. Cambodia, Laos, and Vietnam have suffered from years of civil war. Burma has become more and more isolated from the world by its repressive government.

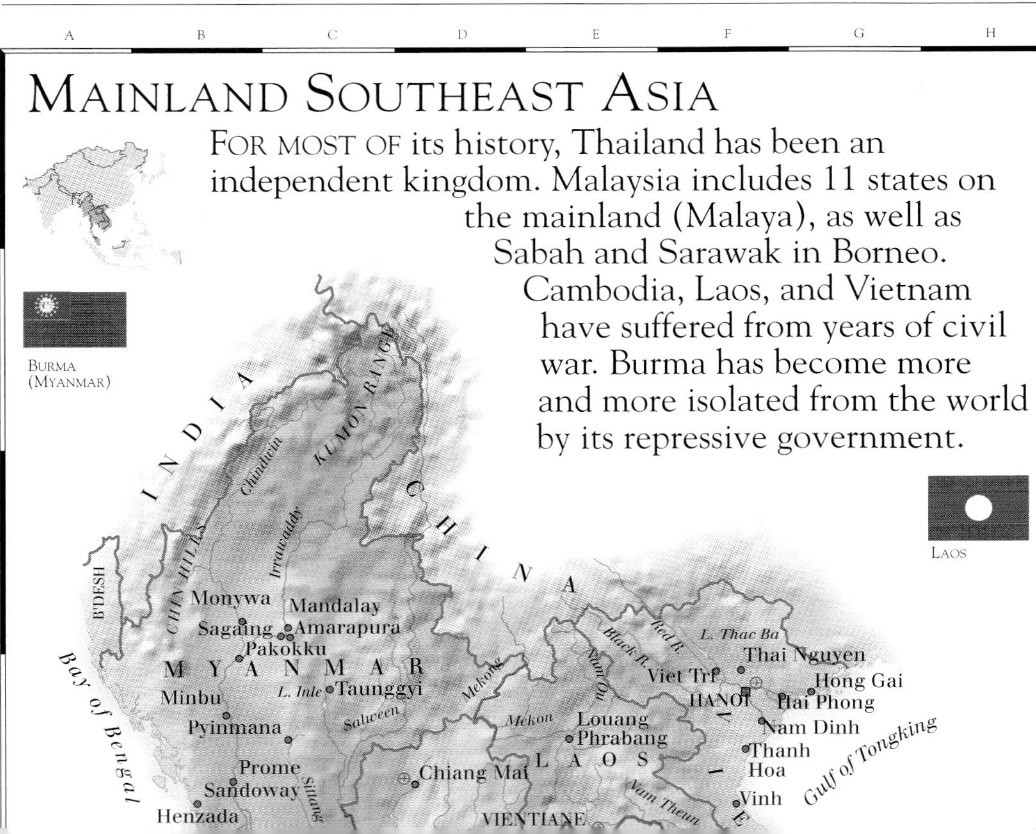
BURMA (MYANMAR)
LAOS
INDIA
CHINA
B'DESH
CHIN HILLS
KUMON RANGE
Chindwin
Irrawaddy
Bay of Bengal
MYANMAR
Monywa
Mandalay
Sagaing
Amarapura
Pakokku
Minbu
L. Inle
Taunggyi
Pyinmana
Salween
Prome
Sandoway
Sittang
Henzada
Mekong
Mekon
Chiang Mai
VIENTIANE
LAOS
Louang Phrabang
Nam Ou
Black R.
Red R.
L. Thac Ba
Thai Nguyen
Viet Tri
HANOI
Hong Gai
Hai Phong
Nam Dinh
Thanh Hoa
Vinh
Nam Theun
Gulf of Tongking

Pegu
RANGOON
C. Negrais
Moulmein
Kyaikkami
Gulf of Martaban
ANDAMAN SEA
Phitsanulok
Khon Kaen
THAILAND
Nakhon Sawan
Mae Nam Mun
Nakhon Ratchasima
Tavoy
Ayutthaya
BANGKOK
Natchaburi
Chon Buri
Mergui Archipelago
Gulf of Thailand
ISTHMUS OF KRA
Phangan I.
Samui I.
Phuket I.
Nakhon Si Thammarat
Songkhla
Hat Yai
Langkawi
George Town
Taiping
Ipoh
CAMERON HIGHLANDS
Kota Baharu
Kuala Terengganu
Kuantan
Pahang
KUALA LUMPUR
Klang
MALAYSIA
Seremban
Melaka
Johor Baharu
SINGAPORE
Singapore Strait
Khanthabouli
Mekong
Hue
Da Nang
Ubon Ratchathani
Pakxé
Sên
San
Bătdâmbâng
CAMBODIA
Tônlé Sap
PHNOM PENH
Kâmpóng Cham
Quy Nhon
Ban Me Thuot
Nha Trang
Da Lat
Bien Hoa
Ho Chi Minh City
Long Xuyen
Rach Gia
Can Tho
SOUTH CHINA SEA
VIETNAM
THAILAND
CAMBODIA
MALAYSIA (WEST)
SINGAPORE
N
0 200 400km
0 100 200miles
A B C D F G H
5 6 7 8

CLIMATE
Most of Southeast Asia has a tropical climate, with consistently high temperatures and one or two rainy seasons that can last up to six months.

INDUSTRY
Palm oil, timber, tin, gems, rice, rubber, tourism. Singapore controls the shipping route between the Indian and Pacific Oceans. Thailand is a leading exporter of pineapples and prawns.

MARITIME SOUTHEAST ASIA

SCATTERED BETWEEN the Indian and Pacific Oceans are thousands of tropical mountainous islands. Once called the East Indies, Indonesia was ruled by the Dutch for 350 years. More than half of its 13,677 islands are still uninhabited. The Philippines lie on the "Ring of Fire," and are subject to earthquakes and volcanic activity. East Timor, the world's newest state, gained independence in 2002.

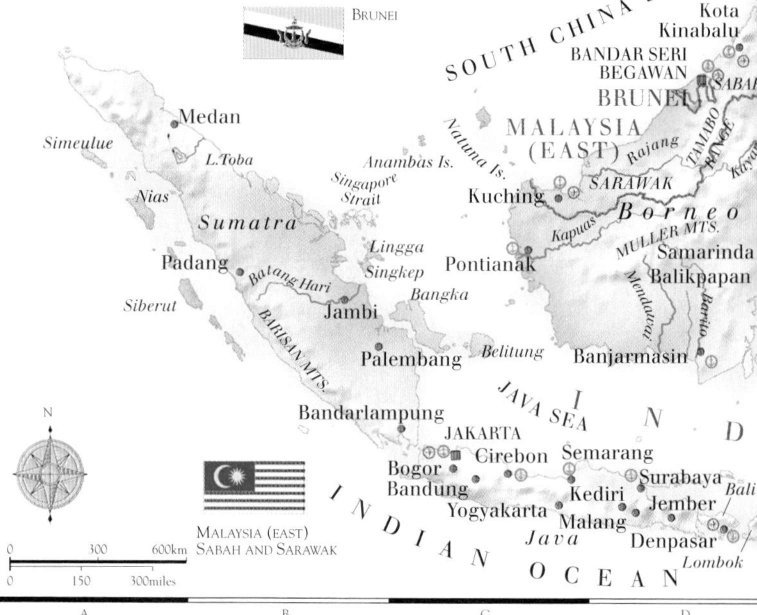
PHILI
Balabac Strait
SOUTH CHINA SEA
BRUNEI
Kota Kinabalu
BANDAR SERI BEGAWAN
SABAH
BRUNEI
MALAYSIA (EAST)
Rajang
TAMABO RANGE
Kayan
Medan
Simeulue
L. Toba
Anambas Is.
Natuna Is.
Singapore Strait
Kuching
SARAWAK
Nias
Sumatra
Borneo
Kapuas
MULLER MTS.
Samarinda
Lingga
Singkep
Pontianak
Padang
Batang Hari
Balikpapan
Mendawai
Barito
Siberut
Jambi
Bangka
BARISAN MTS.
Palembang
Belitung
Banjarmasin
JAVA SEA
Bandarlampung
I N D
JAKARTA
Cirebon
Semarang
Bogor
Bandung
Surabaya
Bali
Kediri
Jember
Yogyakarta
Malang
INDIAN OCEAN
Java
Denpasar
Lombok
N
0 300 600km
0 150 300miles
MALAYSIA (EAST)
SABAH AND SARAWAK

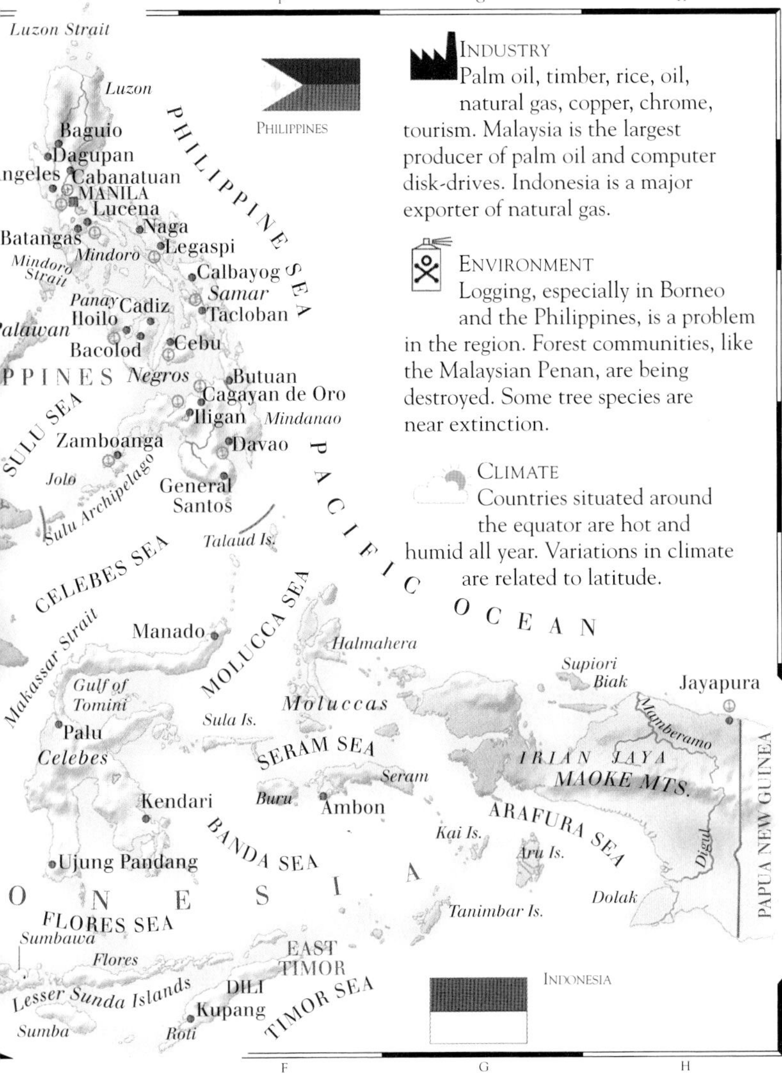
F
G
H
Luzon Strait
Luzon
PHILIPPINES
Baguio
Dagupan
ngeles
Cabanatuan
MANILA
Lucena
Batangas
Naga
Legaspi
Mindoro
Mindoro Strait
PHILIPPINE SEA
Calbayog
Samar
Panay
Cadiz
Iloilo
Tacloban
alawan
Bacolod
Cebu
PPINES
Negros
Butuan
Cagayan de Oro
SULU SEA
Iligan
Mindanao
Zamboanga
Davao
Jolo
Sulu Archipelago
General Santos
PACIFIC OCEAN
Talaud Is.
CELEBES SEA
MOLUCCA SEA
Manado
Halmahera
Makassar Strait
Supiori
Biak
Jayapura
Gulf of Tomini
Moluccas
Mamberamo
Sula Is.
Palu
SERAM SEA
Celebes
IRIAN JAYA
Seram
MAOKE MTS.
Buru
Ambon
Kendari
ARAFURA SEA
Kai Is.
BANDA SEA
Aru Is.
Digul
PAPUA NEW GUINEA
Ujung Pandang
O N E S I A
Dolak
Tanimbar Is.
FLORES SEA
Sumbawa
Flores
EAST TIMOR
DILI
Lesser Sunda Islands
Kupang
TIMOR SEA
Sumba
Roti
INDONESIA
1
2
3
4
5
8
F
G
H

INDUSTRY

Palm oil, timber, rice, oil, natural gas, copper, chrome, tourism. Malaysia is the largest producer of palm oil and computer disk-drives. Indonesia is a major exporter of natural gas.

ENVIRONMENT

Logging, especially in Borneo and the Philippines, is a problem in the region. Forest communities, like the Malaysian Penan, are being destroyed. Some tree species are near extinction.

CLIMATE

Countries situated around the equator are hot and humid all year. Variations in climate are related to latitude.

Southeast Asia facts

BURMA

• The country of Burma is also called Myanmar.
• Burma is the world's biggest exporter of teak.

ESSENTIAL FACTS

⊙ Rangoon
261,969 sq miles (678,500 sq km)
48.4 million
Kyat
Burmese (Myanmar)

LAOS

• In 1994, the Mekong River's "Friendship Bridge" became the first Thai–Laos road link.

LAOS FACTS

⊙ Vientiane
91,428 sq miles (236,800 sq km)
5.4 million
Kip
Lao

SINGAPORE

• The nation is the world leader in new biotechnologies.
• Chewing gum is banned by law in Singapore.

SINGAPORE FACTS

⊙ Singapore
250 sq miles (648 sq km)
4.1 million
Singapore dollar
Malay, Mandarin, Tamil, English

THAILAND

• Criticism of the Thai king, who is head of state, is not allowed.
• Thailand, meaning "land of the free," is the only Southeast Asian nation never to be colonized.

THAILAND FACTS

⊙ Bangkok
198,455 sq miles (514,000 sq km)
63.6 million
Baht
Thai
▲ Parliamentary democracy
70 years

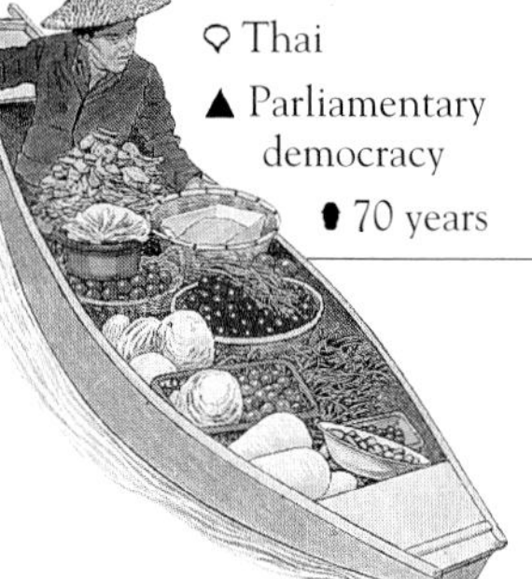

MOBILE SHOP
Floating markets are a common sight on the waterways of Southeast Asia.

VIETNAM

• A new species of mammal, the Vu Quang Ox, was recently discovered in the forests of north Vietnam.
• The Vietnam war cost two million lives.

VIETNAM FACTS

⊙ Hanoi
127,243 sq miles (329,560 sq km)
70.9 million
New dong
Vietnamese

KOMODO DRAGON
The "dragon" of Komodo in Indonesia is the world's largest lizard.

INDONESIA

• The world's biggest island chain, Indonesia is made up of 13,677 islands spread over 3000 miles (4830 km) and three time zones.
• Indonesia was formerly known as the Dutch East Indies.
• Forest survival is threatened by logging.

INDONESIA FACTS

- ⊙ Jakarta
- 741,096 sq miles (1,919,440 sq km)
- 214 million
- Rupiah
- Bahasa Indonesia
- ▲ Multiparty republic
- 66 years

BRUNEI

- ⊙ Bandar Seri Begawan
- 335,000
- Malay

EAST TIMOR

- ⊙ Dili
- 750,000
- Tetum, Bahasa Malay

MALAYSIA

• The nation is the world's leading producer of natural rubber.

ESSENTIAL FACTS

- ⊙ Kuala Lumpur
- 127,316 sq miles (329,750 sq km)
- 22.6 million
- Ringgit
- Bahasa Malaysia

PHILIPPINES

• The Filipino nation is the only Christian country in Asia.

PHILIPPINES FACTS

- ⊙ Manila
- 115,830 sq miles (300,000 sq km)
- 66.5 million
- Philippine peso
- Filipino, English
- ▲ Multiparty republic
- 69 years

CAMBODIA

• Cambodians are descended from the Khmers, who arrived in Southeast Asia in around 2000 BC.

CAMBODIA FACTS

- ⊙ Phnom Penh
- 69,000 sq miles (181,040 sq km)
- 13.4 million
- Riel
- Khmer

MALAYSIAN RUBBER
Workers extract latex by cutting rubber trees and collecting the sap that oozes from the cut.

Australasia and Oceania

PAPUA NEW GUINEA
NAURU
SOLOMON ISLANDS
Coral Sea Islands (to Australia)
VANUATU
New Caledonia (to France)
AUSTRALIA
TASMAN SEA
NEW ZEALAN
SOUTHERN OCEAN
Auckland Islands (to N.Z.)

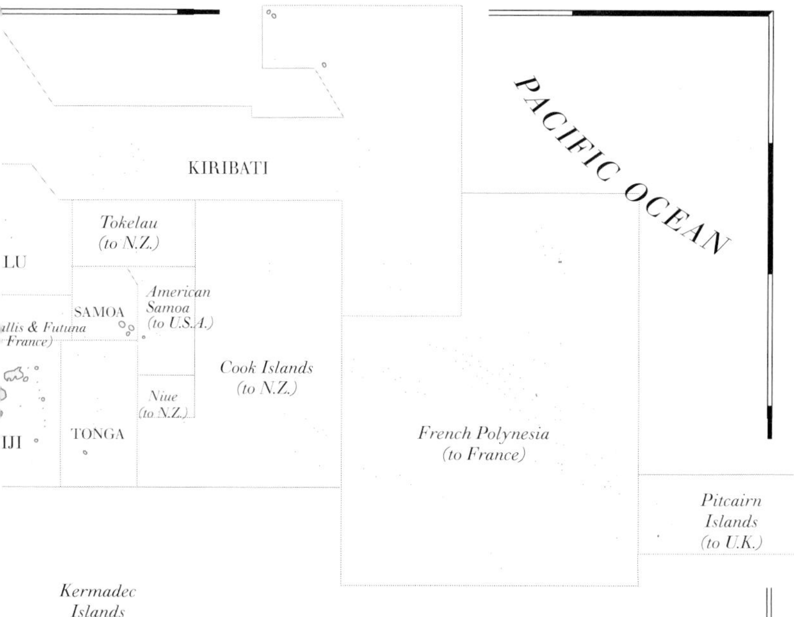
PACIFIC OCEAN
KIRIBATI
Tokelau
(to N.Z.)
LU
SAMOA
American
Samoa
(to U.S.A.)
allis & Futuna
France)
Cook Islands
(to N.Z.)
Niue
(to N.Z.)
IJI
TONGA
French Polynesia
(to France)
Pitcairn
Islands
(to U.K.)

Kermadec Islands (to N.Z.)

Chatham Island (to N.Z.)

Australasia and Oceania

Millions of years ago, the continent of Australia and the islands of New Guinea and New Zealand split away from the other southern continents. These island countries have many unique plants and animals, such as Australia's marsupials, or pouched mammals. The thousands of islands scattered in the Pacific are either volcanic islands or coral atolls.

PACIFIC OCEAN

THE LARGEST AND deepest ocean, the Pacific covers a greater area of the Earth's surface than all the land areas together. Its deepest point – 36,197ft (11,033 m) – is deep enough to cover Mount Everest. Melanesia, Micronesia, and Polynesia are the main inner Pacific island groups.

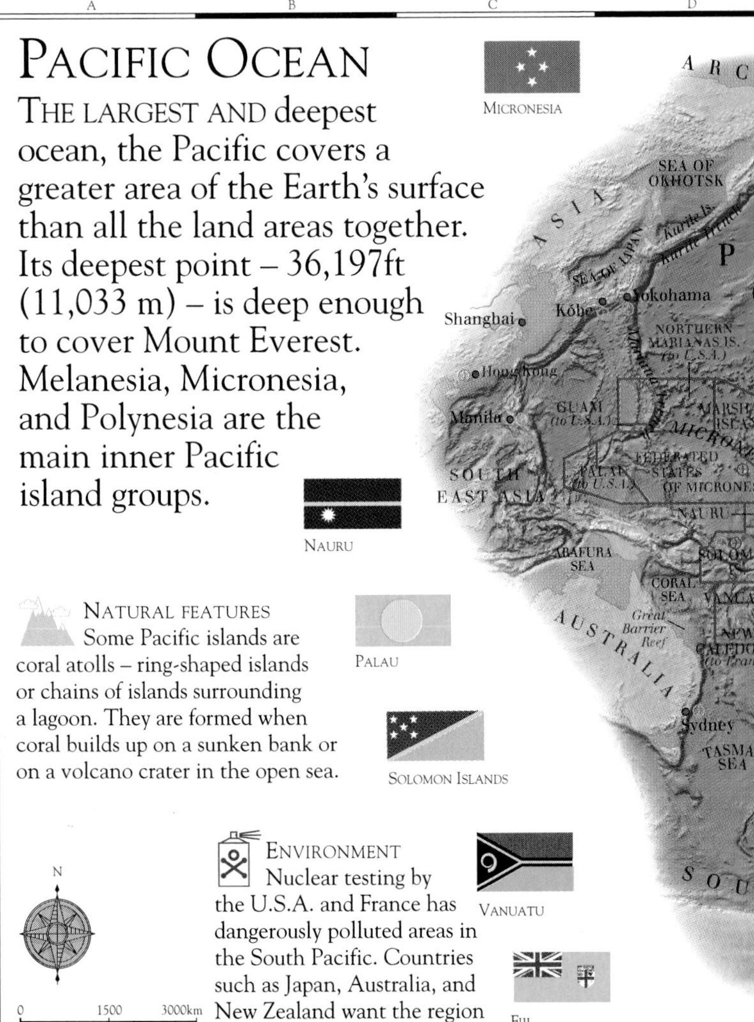
MICRONESIA
NAURU
PALAU
SOLOMON ISLANDS
VANUATU
FIJI
ASIA
SEA OF OKHOTSK
SEA OF JAPAN
Kurile Is.
Kurile Trench
Shanghai
Kōbe
Yokohama
NORTHERN MARIANAS IS. (to U.S.A.)
Hong Kong
Manila
GUAM (to U.S.A.)
FEDERATED STATES OF MICRONESIA
SOUTH EAST ASIA
PALAU (to U.S.A.)
NAURU
ARAFURA SEA
CORAL SEA
Great Barrier Reef
AUSTRALIA
Sydney
TASMAN SEA
N
0 1500 3000km
0 750 1500miles

NATURAL FEATURES

Some Pacific islands are coral atolls – ring-shaped islands or chains of islands surrounding a lagoon. They are formed when coral builds up on a sunken bank or on a volcano crater in the open sea.

ENVIRONMENT

Nuclear testing by the U.S.A. and France has dangerously polluted areas in the South Pacific. Countries such as Japan, Australia, and New Zealand want the region made into a nuclear-free zone.

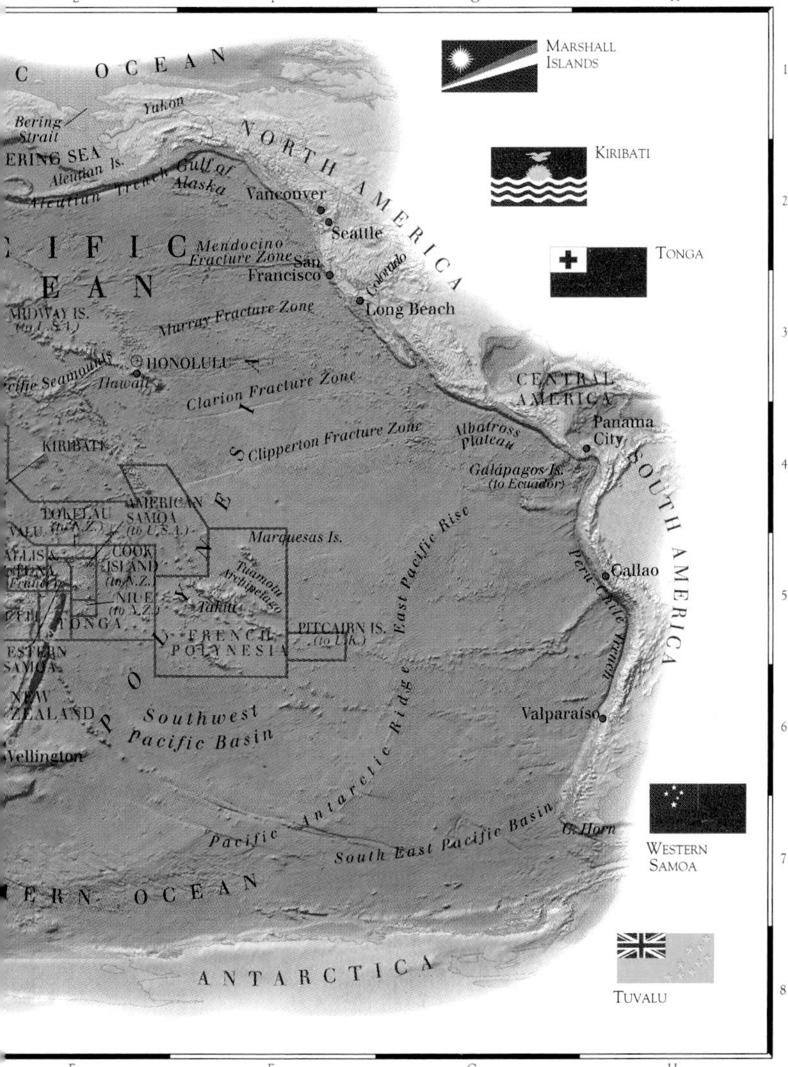
MARSHALL ISLANDS
KIRIBATI
TONGA
WESTERN SAMOA
TUVALU
OCEAN
Yukon
Bering Strait
BERING SEA
Aleutian Is.
Aleutian Trench
Gulf of Alaska
NORTH AMERICA
Vancouver
Seattle
Mendocino Fracture Zone
San Francisco
Colorado
Long Beach
PACIFIC OCEAN
MIDWAY IS.
Murray Fracture Zone
HONOLULU
Hawaii
Clarion Fracture Zone
CENTRAL AMERICA
Panama City
Clipperton Fracture Zone
Albatross Plateau
Galápagos Is. (to Ecuador)
SOUTH AMERICA
KIRIBATI
AMERICAN SAMOA (to U.S.A.)
TOKELAU (to N.Z.)
Marquesas Is.
COOK ISLAND (to N.Z.)
Tuamotu Archipelago
NIUE (to N.Z.)
Tahiti
TONGA
FRENCH POLYNESIA
PITCAIRN IS. (to U.K.)
East Pacific Rise
Peru-Chile Trench
Callao
WESTERN SAMOA
NEW ZEALAND
POLYNESIA
Southwest Pacific Basin
Valparaíso
Wellington
Pacific Antarctic Ridge
South East Pacific Basin
C. Horn
SOUTHERN OCEAN
ANTARCTICA
E
F
G
H
1
2
3
4
5
6
7
8

Australia and Papua New Guinea

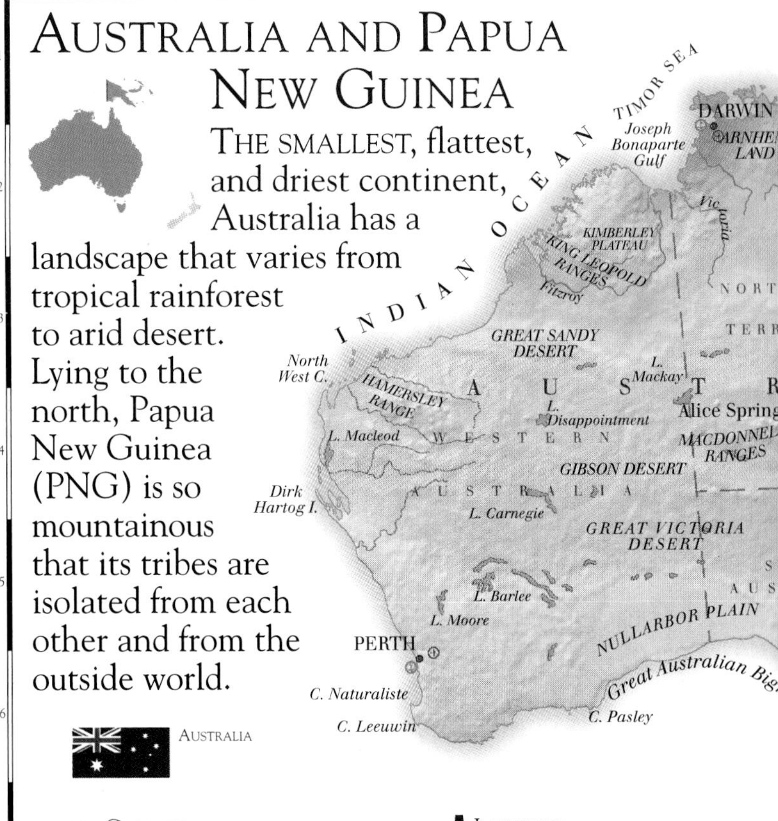
TIMOR SEA
DARWIN
Joseph Bonaparte Gulf
INDIAN OCEAN
KIMBERLEY PLATEAU
KING LEOPOLD RANGES
Fitzroy
GREAT SANDY DESERT
North West C.
HAMERSLEY RANGE
L. Mackay
A U S T R
Alice Spring
L. Disappointment
L. Macleod
W E S T E R N
MACDONNELL RANGES
GIBSON DESERT
Dirk Hartog I.
A U S T R A L I A
L. Carnegie
GREAT VICTORIA DESERT
L. Barlee
L. Moore
NULLARBOR PLAIN
PERTH
C. Naturaliste
C. Leeuwin
C. Pasley

The smallest, flattest, and driest continent, Australia has a landscape that varies from tropical rainforest to arid desert. Lying to the north, Papua New Guinea (PNG) is so mountainous that its tribes are isolated from each other and from the outside world.

Australia

Climate

Most people live in temperate zones that occur within 250 miles (400 km) of the coast in the east and southeast, and around Perth in the west. The interior, west, and south are arid; the north is tropical. PNG is tropical, yet snow falls on its highest mountains.

Industry

Coal, gold, uranium, cattle, tourism, wool, wine- and beer-making. Australia is a leading exporter of coal, iron ore, gold, bauxite, and copper, and has the largest known diamond deposits. PNG has the largest copper mine in the world and one of the largest gold mines.

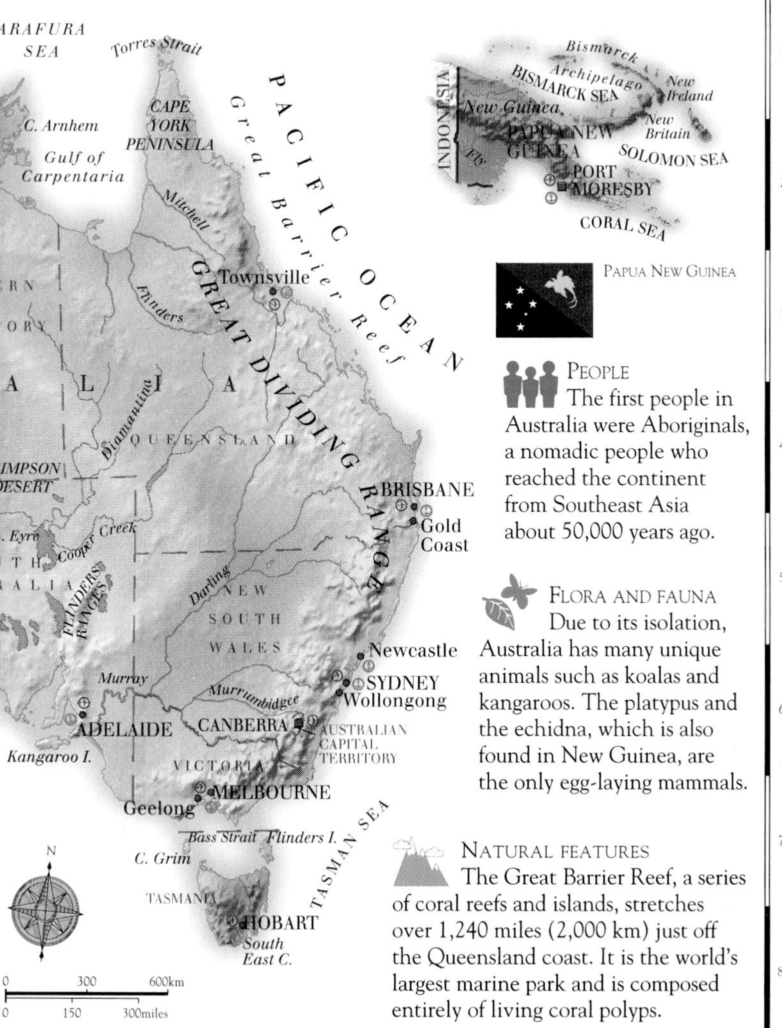
E
F
G
H
ARAFURA SEA
Torres Strait
C. Arnhem
CAPE YORK PENINSULA
Gulf of Carpentaria
PACIFIC OCEAN
Great Barrier Reef
Mitchell
Townsville
Flinders
GREAT DIVIDING RANGE
Diamantina
QUEENSLAND
SIMPSON DESERT
BRISBANE
Gold Coast
Eyre
Cooper Creek
FLINDERS RANGES
Darling
NEW SOUTH WALES
Newcastle
SYDNEY
Wollongong
Murray
Murrumbidgee
ADELAIDE
CANBERRA
AUSTRALIAN CAPITAL TERRITORY
Kangaroo I.
VICTORIA
MELBOURNE
Geelong
Bass Strait
Flinders I.
TASMAN SEA
C. Grim
TASMANIA
HOBART
South East C.
N
0 300 600km
0 150 300miles
Bismarck Archipelago
BISMARCK SEA
New Ireland
INDONESIA
New Guinea
New Britain
PAPUA NEW GUINEA
Fly
SOLOMON SEA
PORT MORESBY
CORAL SEA
PAPUA NEW GUINEA
1
2
3
4
5
6
7
8

PEOPLE

The first people in Australia were Aboriginals, a nomadic people who reached the continent from Southeast Asia about 50,000 years ago.

FLORA AND FAUNA

Due to its isolation, Australia has many unique animals such as koalas and kangaroos. The platypus and the echidna, which is also found in New Guinea, are the only egg-laying mammals.

NATURAL FEATURES

The Great Barrier Reef, a series of coral reefs and islands, stretches over 1,240 miles (2,000 km) just off the Queensland coast. It is the world's largest marine park and is composed entirely of living coral polyps.

New Zealand

One of the last places on Earth to be inhabited by people, New Zealand lies about halfway between the equator and the South Pole. It is made up of the main North and South Islands, separated by the Cook Strait, and numerous smaller islands. The first settlers were Maoris, who came from the Polynesian islands about 1,200 years ago.

Natural features

New Zealand lies on the "Ring of Fire," a band of volcanic activity that almost encircles the Pacific Ocean. New Zealand has about 400 earthquakes each year, although only about 100 are strong enough to be felt.

People

In recent years, Maoris have protested the lack of observance of the Treaty of Waitangi, which protected their rights. About 10 percent of the total population are Maori.

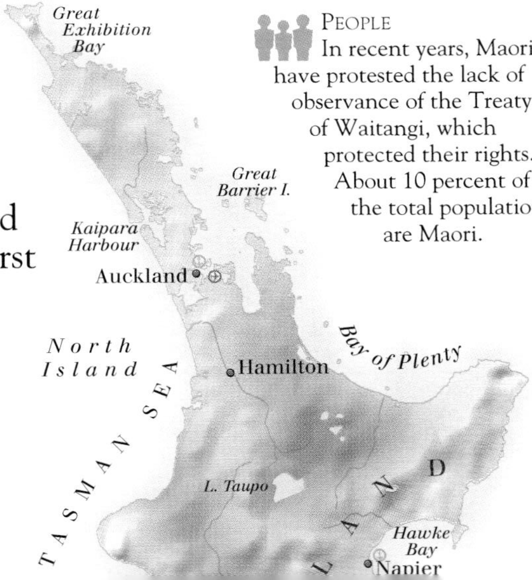

Flora and fauna

Many of New Zealand's animals have been introduced – two species of bat are the only native land mammals. New Zealand has no snakes.

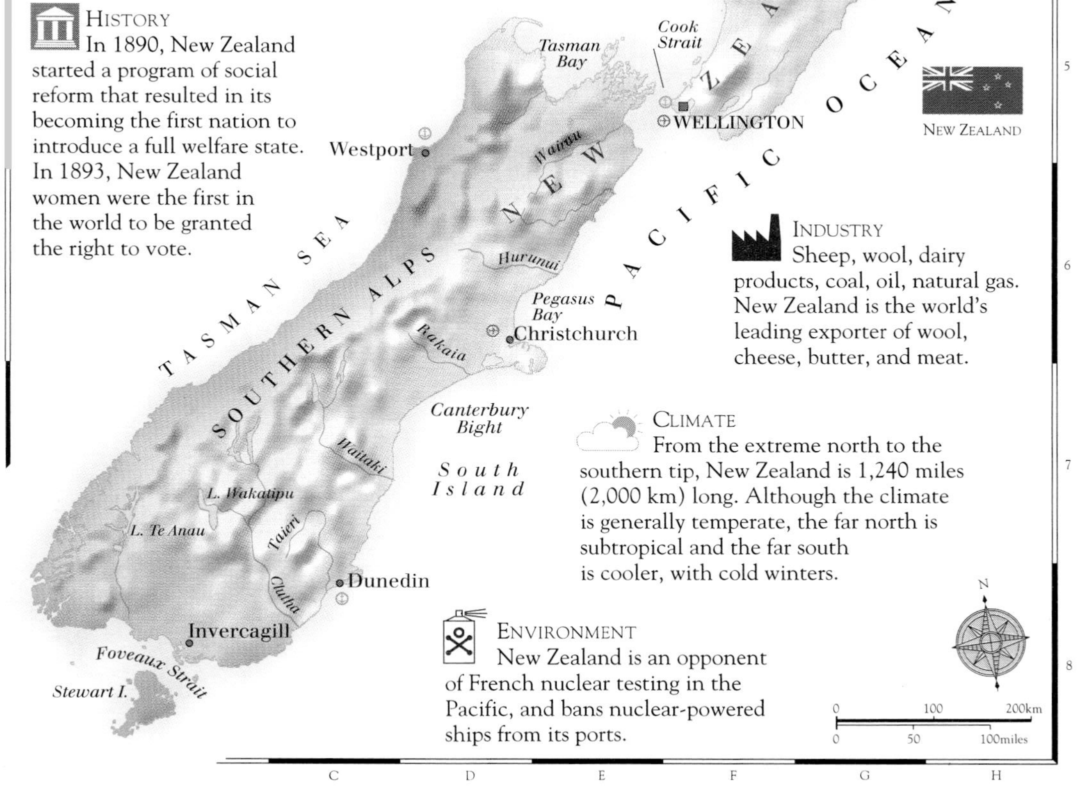
Tasman Bay
Cook Strait
WELLINGTON
NEW ZEALAND
PACIFIC OCEAN
Westport
TASMAN SEA
SOUTHERN ALPS
Wairau
Hurunui
Pegasus Bay
Christchurch
Rakaia
Canterbury Bight
Waitaki
South Island
L. Wakatipu
L. Te Anau
Taieri
Clutha
Dunedin
Invercagill
Foveaux Strait
Stewart I.
N
0
100
200km
0
50
100miles
C
D
E
F
G
H
5
6
7
8

HISTORY

In 1890, New Zealand started a program of social reform that resulted in its becoming the first nation to introduce a full welfare state. In 1893, New Zealand women were the first in the world to be granted the right to vote.

INDUSTRY

Sheep, wool, dairy products, coal, oil, natural gas. New Zealand is the world's leading exporter of wool, cheese, butter, and meat.

CLIMATE

From the extreme north to the southern tip, New Zealand is 1,240 miles (2,000 km) long. Although the climate is generally temperate, the far north is subtropical and the far south is cooler, with cold winters.

ENVIRONMENT

New Zealand is an opponent of French nuclear testing in the Pacific, and bans nuclear-powered ships from its ports.

Australasia and Oceania facts

Australia

• The suburban area of the city of Sydney is the largest in the world; it is twice as large as Beijing and six times the size of Rome.
• Aboriginal land and civil rights claims are an increasingly important item on the political agenda.

ESSENTIAL FACTS

- Canberra
- 2,967,893 sq miles (7,686,850 sq km)
- 19.3 million
- Australian dollar
- English
- Parliamentary democracy
- 79 years

LIFE'S A BEACH
Surfing and watersports are popular Australian leisure activities.

New Zealand

• The landscape of New Zealand is the most varied in the world relative to its size, offering mountains, fjords, lakes, glaciers, rain forests, beaches, mud pools, and geysers.
• Many of New Zealand's top jobs in business and politics are held by women.

ESSENTIAL FACTS

- Wellington
- 103,737 sq miles (268,680 sq km)
- 3.8 million
- New Zealand dollar
- English and Maori
- Parliamentary democracy
- 78 years

KIWI BIRD
The flightless kiwi is the most famous of New Zealand's creatures.

Papua New Guinea

• The feathers of certain unique bird species in Papua New Guinea produce a poison that causes painful blisters on contact with human skin.

ESSENTIAL FACTS

- Port Moresby
- 178,703 sq miles (462,840 sq km)
- 5.2 million
- Kina
- English

Vanuatu
Port-Vila

200,000

Bislama, English, French

Fiji
Suva

823,000

English

Palau
Koror

19,100

Palauan, English

Kiribati
Bairiki

92,000

English

Tonga
Nuku'alofa

102,200

Tongan, English

Tuvalu
Fingafale

10,800

English

Western Samoa
Apia

159,000

Samoan, English

Nauru
No official capital

11,800

Nauruan, English

Marshall Islands
Majuro

68,100

English, Marshallese

Solomon Islands
Honiara

463,000

English

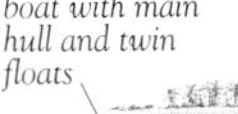

Thatched roof made of palm fronds
Simple house
Wooden outrigger boat with main hull and twin floats
Home-grown food

Micronesia
Palikir

133,000

English

Island Life
On the more remote islands of the Pacific, people live much as their ancestors did, fishing, keeping animals, and growing fruits and vegetables.

Atlantic Ocean

BENEATH THE WATERS OF the Atlantic Ocean lies the Mid-Atlantic Ridge, one of the world's longest mountain chains. Some of its peaks are so high they form islands, such as the Azores. Apart from a wide rift-valley in the center of the ridge, the ocean consists of vast featureless plains and is 5 miles (8 km) at its deepest point.

Iceland

Cape Verde

ARCTIC OCEAN
GREENLAND
(to Denmark)
GREENLAND SEA
Baffin Bay
Davis Strait
Denmark Strait
ICELAND
REYKJAVIK
Murmansk
Hudson Bay
LABRADOR SEA
C. Farewell
Faeroe Islands
(to Denmark)
NORTH SEA
Bergen
BALTIC SEA
EUROPE
NORTH AMERICA
Aberdeen
Rotterdam
Newfoundland
Mid-Atlantic Ridge
St. Lawrence
Grand Banks
New York City
Azores
(to Portugal)
BLACK SEA
MEDITERRANEAN SEA
Madeira
(to Portugal)
GIBRALTAR
Mississippi
Bermuda
(to U.K.)
New Orleans
SARGASSO SEA
Canary Islands
(to Spain)
Port Said

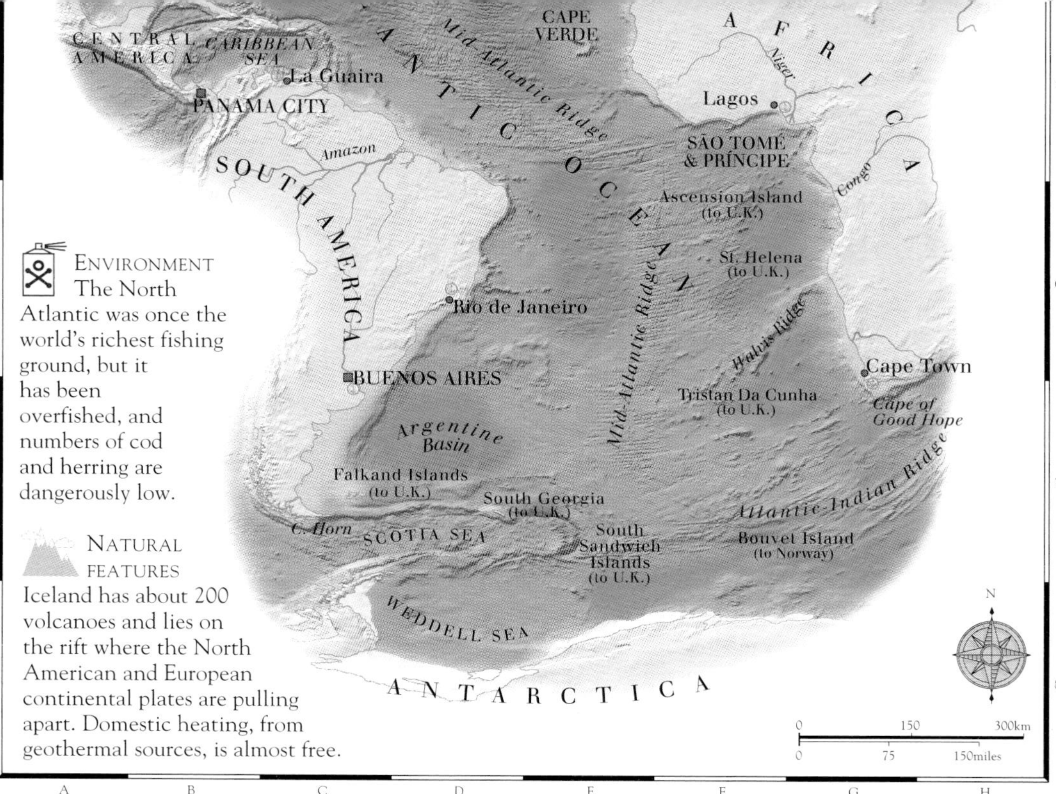
CENTRAL AMERICA
CARIBBEAN SEA
La Guaira
PANAMA CITY
CAPE VERDE
Mid-Atlantic Ridge
ATLANTIC OCEAN
AFRICA
Niger
Lagos
SÃO TOMÉ & PRÍNCIPE
Congo
Amazon
SOUTH AMERICA
Ascension Island (to U.K.)
St. Helena (to U.K.)
Rio de Janeiro
Walvis Ridge
Cape Town
BUENOS AIRES
Tristan Da Cunha (to U.K.)
Cape of Good Hope
Argentine Basin
Falkand Islands (to U.K.)
South Georgia (to U.K.)
Atlantic-Indian Ridge
C. Horn
SCOTIA SEA
South Sandwich Islands (to U.K.)
Bouvet Island (to Norway)
N
WEDDELL SEA
ANTARCTICA
0 150 300km
0 75 150miles
A B C D E F G H
5 6 7 8

ENVIRONMENT
The North Atlantic was once the world's richest fishing ground, but it has been overfished, and numbers of cod and herring are dangerously low.

NATURAL FEATURES
Iceland has about 200 volcanoes and lies on the rift where the North American and European continental plates are pulling apart. Domestic heating, from geothermal sources, is almost free.

Indian Ocean

THE SMALLEST OF the world's oceans, the Indian Ocean has some 5000 islands scattered across its area. Beneath its surface, three great mountain ranges converge towards the ocean's center – an area of strong seismic and volcanic activity. The ocean's greatest depth, 24,400 ft (7440 m), is in the Java Trench.

Flora and Fauna

Owing to its position off the African coast, Madagascar is home to many unique animals, such as tenrecs, lemurs, and fossas.

Environment

The Indian Ocean is at risk of oil pollution by tankers carrying oil from the Persian Gulf.

Climate

The monsoon winds blow over the Indian Ocean – from the southwest or from the northeast according to the season. The southwesterly monsoon brings heavy rains to southern Asia.

Maldives

Seychelles

Port Said
Suez
Suez Canal
Nile
Kuwait City
Persian Gulf
RED SEA
ARABIA
Aden
Gulf of Aden
Djibouti
Socotra (to Yemen)
C. Xaafuun
Somali Basin
Ra's al Iadd
ARABIAN SEA
Laccadive Is. (to India)
MALDIVES
MALE
Indus
Karachi
ASIA
Ganges
Calcutta (Kolkata)
Mumbai (Bombay)
Chennai (Madras)
Cochin
Sri Lanka
Bay of Bengal
Andaman Is. (to India)
Nicobar Is. (to India)
Irrawaddy
Mekong
Rangoon
ANDAMAN SEA
Gulf of Thailand
SOUTH CHINA

Comoros

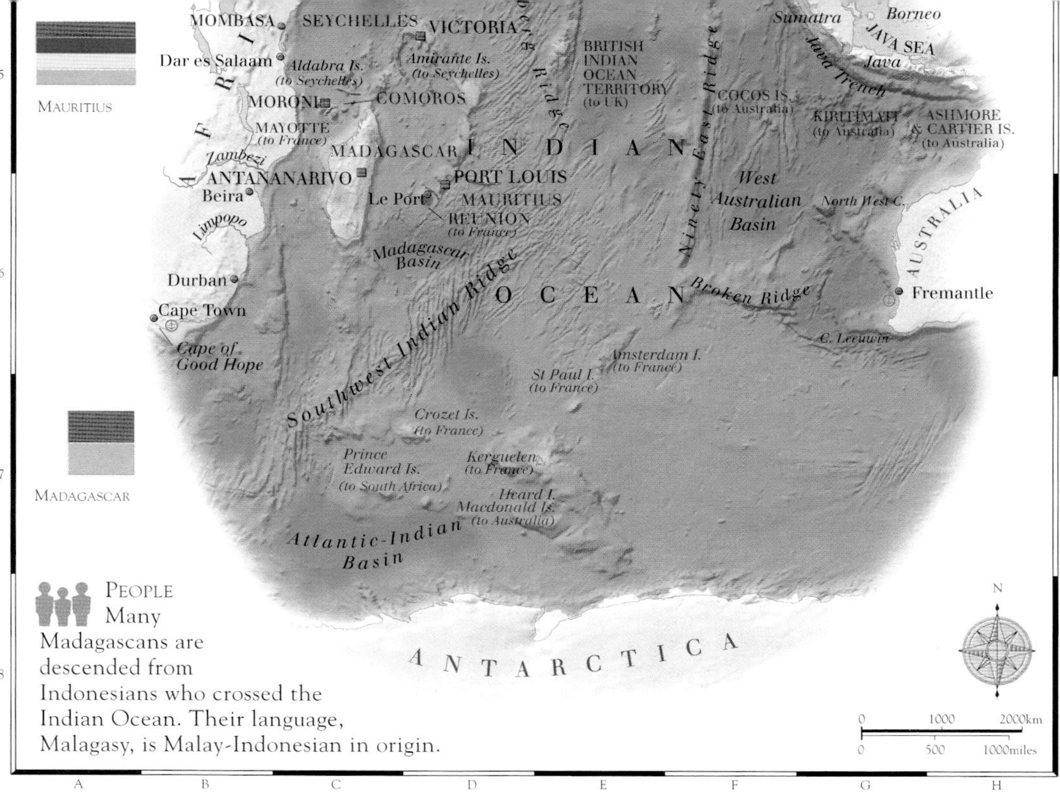

MOMBASA
SEYCHELLES
VICTORIA
Dar es Salaam
Aldabra Is. (to Seychelles)
Amirante Is. (to Seychelles)
BRITISH INDIAN OCEAN TERRITORY (to UK)
MORONI
COMOROS
MAYOTTE (to France)
MADAGASCAR
Zambezi
ANTANANARIVO
Beira
Limpopo
PORT LOUIS
MAURITIUS
Le Port
RÉUNION (to France)
Madagascar Basin
Durban
Cape Town
Cape of Good Hope
Southwest Indian Ridge
INDIAN OCEAN
Ninety East Ridge
COCOS IS. (to Australia)
Sumatra
Borneo
JAVA SEA
Java
Java Trench
KIRITIMATI (to Australia)
ASHMORE & CARTIER IS. (to Australia)
West Australian Basin
North West C.
AUSTRALIA
Fremantle
Broken Ridge
C. Leeuwin
Amsterdam I. (to France)
St Paul I. (to France)
Crozet Is. (to France)
Prince Edward Is. (to South Africa)
Kerguelen (to France)
Heard I. Macdonald Is. (to Australia)
Atlantic-Indian Basin
ANTARCTICA
MAURITIUS
MADAGASCAR
N
0 1000 2000km
0 500 1000miles
A B C D E F G H
5 6 7 8

PEOPLE

Many Madagascans are descended from Indonesians who crossed the Indian Ocean. Their language, Malagasy, is Malay-Indonesian in origin.

THE ANTARCTIC

CONTAINING 80 PERCENT of the world's freshwater, the continent of Antarctica lies buried under ice more than 1.2 miles (2 km) thick. The surrounding seas are partly frozen, and icebergs barricade over 90 percent of the coastline.

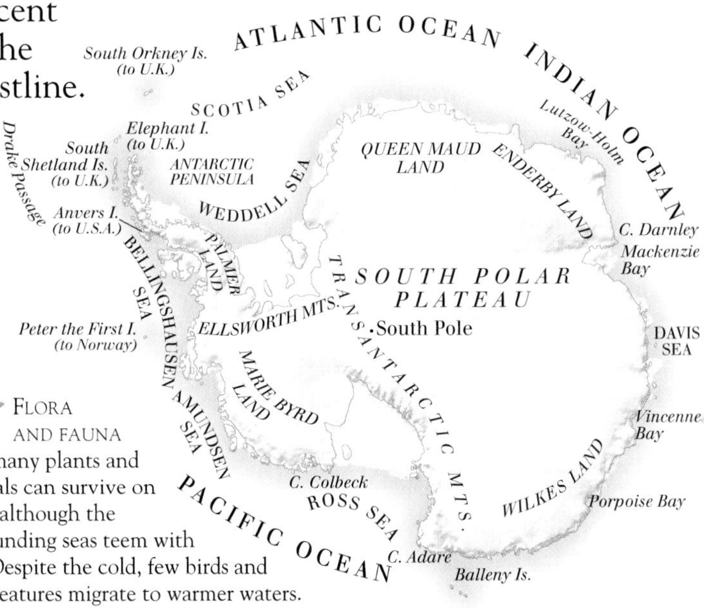

ATLANTIC OCEAN
INDIAN OCEAN
PACIFIC OCEAN
South Orkney Is. (to U.K.)
SCOTIA SEA
Elephant I. (to U.K.)
South Shetland Is. (to U.K.)
Drake Passage
ANTARCTIC PENINSULA
WEDDELL SEA
Anvers I. (to U.S.A.)
PALMER LAND
BELLINGSHAUSEN SEA
Peter the First I. (to Norway)
ELLSWORTH MTS.
QUEEN MAUD LAND
Lutzow-Holm Bay
ENDERBY LAND
C. Darnley
Mackenzie Bay
SOUTH POLAR PLATEAU
South Pole
TRANSANTARCTIC MTS.
DAVIS SEA
MARIE BYRD LAND
AMUNDSEN SEA
Vincennes Bay
WILKES LAND
Porpoise Bay
C. Colbeck
ROSS SEA
C. Adare
Balleny Is.

FLORA AND FAUNA

Not many plants and animals can survive on land, although the surrounding seas teem with life. Despite the cold, few birds and sea creatures migrate to warmer waters.

CLIMATE

Powerful winds form a narrow storm belt that creates severe blizzards. Summer temperatures barely reach over freezing, and in winter, the temperature can plummet to –112°F (–80°C).

ENVIRONMENT

Scientists estimate that the ozone hole emerged over Antarctica in 1980. Each spring, increased sunshine activates CFCs, leading to rapid ozone depletion.

The Arctic

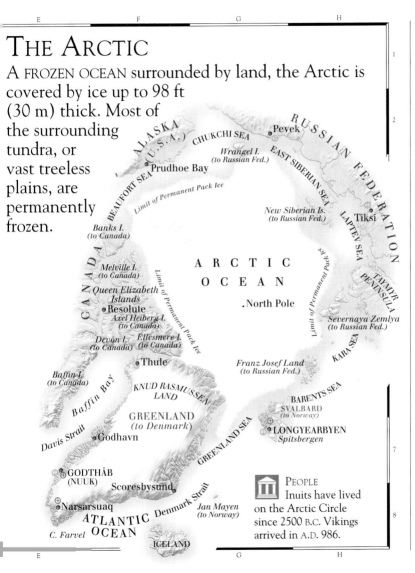

A FROZEN OCEAN surrounded by land, the Arctic is covered by ice up to 98 ft (30 m) thick. Most of the surrounding tundra, or vast treeless plains, are permanently frozen.

ALASKA (U.S.A.)
Prudhoe Bay
BEAUFORT SEA
CHUKCHI SEA
Wrangel I. (to Russian Fed.)
Pevek
RUSSIAN FEDERATION
EAST SIBERIAN SEA
New Siberian Is. (to Russian Fed.)
Tiksi
LAPTEV SEA
TAYMYR PENINSULA
Severnaya Zemlya (to Russian Fed.)
KARA SEA
Limit of Permanent Pack Ice
Banks I. (to Canada)
CANADA
Melville I. (to Canada)
Queen Elizabeth Islands
Resolute
Axel Heiberg I. (to Canada)
Devon I. (to Canada)
Ellesmere I. (to Canada)
ARCTIC OCEAN
.North Pole
Franz Josef Land (to Russian Fed.)
Thule
Baffin I. (to Canada)
Baffin Bay
KNUD RASMUSSEN LAND
GREENLAND (to Denmark)
BARENTS SEA
SVALBARD (to Norway)
LONGYEARBYEN
Spitsbergen
GREENLAND SEA
Davis Strait
Godhavn
GODTHÅB (NUUK)
Scoresbysund
Narsarsuaq
Denmark Strait
Jan Mayen (to Norway)
ATLANTIC OCEAN
C. Farvel
ICELAND

PEOPLE
Inuits have lived on the Arctic Circle since 2500 B.C. Vikings arrived in A.D. 986.

ANTARCTICA • ARCTIC

WORLD TIME ZONES

IMAGINARY LINES are drawn around the globe, either parallel to the equator (latitude) or from pole to pole (longitude, or meridians). The Earth is divided into 24 time zones, one for each hour of the day. Greenwich is on 0° meridian and time advances by one hour for every 15° of longitude east of Greenwich.

–1
0
ATLANTIC OCEAN
INDIAN OCEAN
Greenwich Meridian
+1
+2
+3
+3½
+4
+4½
+5
+5½
+5¾
+6
+6½
+7
+8

TIME ZONES

The numbers on the map indicate the number of hours that must be subtracted or added to reach GMT. When it is noon at Greenwich, for example, it is 11 p.m. in Sydney, Australia. Time zones are adjusted to regional administrative boundaries.

KEY TO MAP

- MINUS HOURS
- PLUS HOURS
- GREENWICH MEAN TIME
- DATE LINE
- TIME ZONES

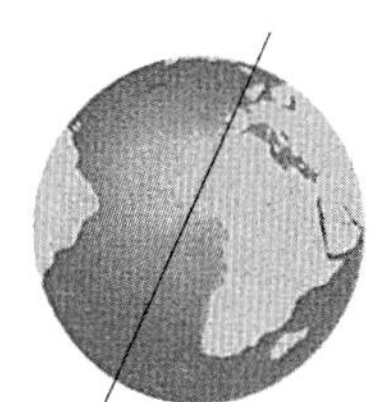

GMT

Greenwich Mean Time (GMT) is the time in Greenwich, England. Clocks are set depending on whether they are east or west of Greenwich.

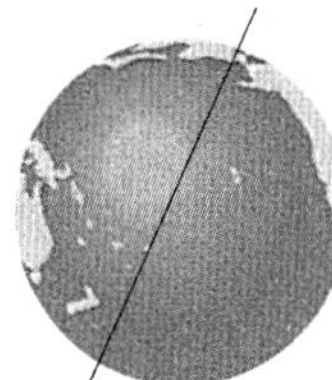

INTERNATIONAL DATE LINE

The International Date Line is an imaginary line that runs along the 180° meridian but deviates around countries.

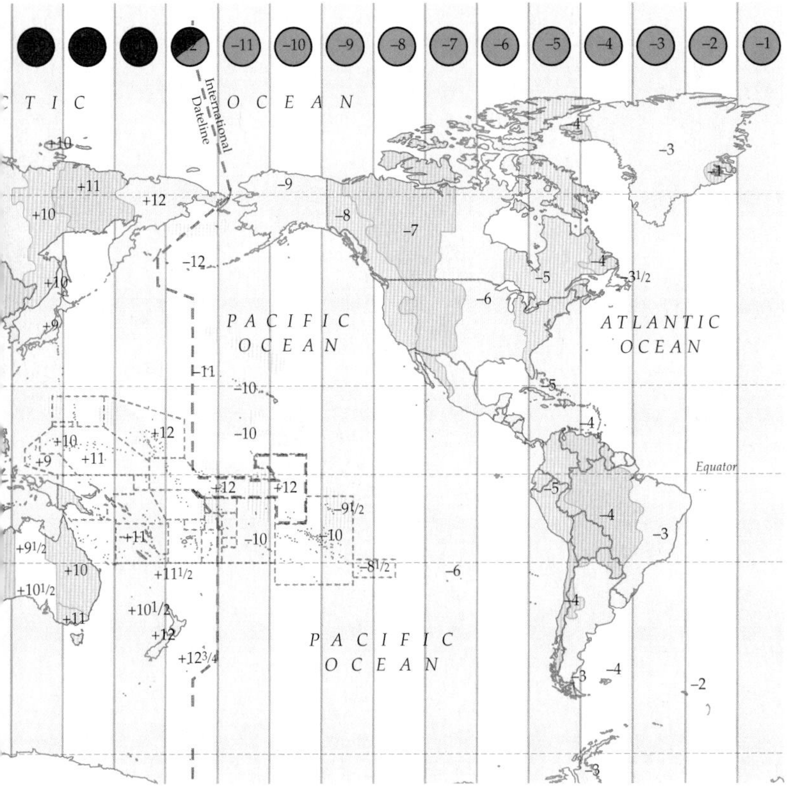

–11
–10
–9
–8
–7
–6
–5
–4
–3
–2
–1
International Dateline
PACIFIC OCEAN
ATLANTIC OCEAN
PACIFIC OCEAN
Equator

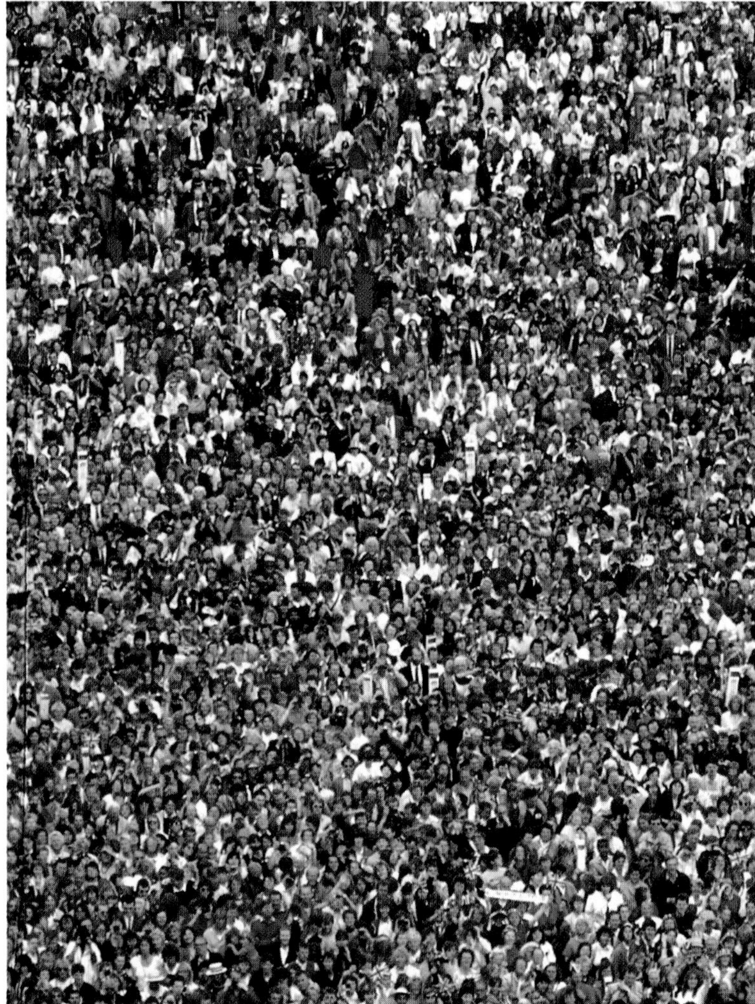

People and Society

MYTHS AND LEGENDS

ALMOST EVERY culture has stories, or myths, to explain the world around them. Legends are tales which have some basis in real events.

DRAGON'S BREATH

MYTHICAL BEASTS

Many myths are about fantastic beasts, such as the unicorn (a single-horned horse) and the phoenix (a bird that rises from its own ashes). The dragon is a winged serpent that breathes fire. It is an important symbol in cultures as far apart as Wales and China.

KING ARTHUR

One of Britain's most famous legendary figures is the hero King Arthur, who is thought to be based on a real 5th-century Celtic chieftain. One of the many stories about King Arthur tells how he was given the magic sword Excalibur by the Lady of the Lake, as shown in the above picture.

SACRED SITES

- Mt. Shasta in California is sacred to Native Americans.
- Uluru (Ayers Rock) in Australia is sacred to the Aboriginals.
- The Tor (mound) at Glastonbury, England, is said to be the resting place of the Holy Grail, the cup Christ drank from at the Last Supper.

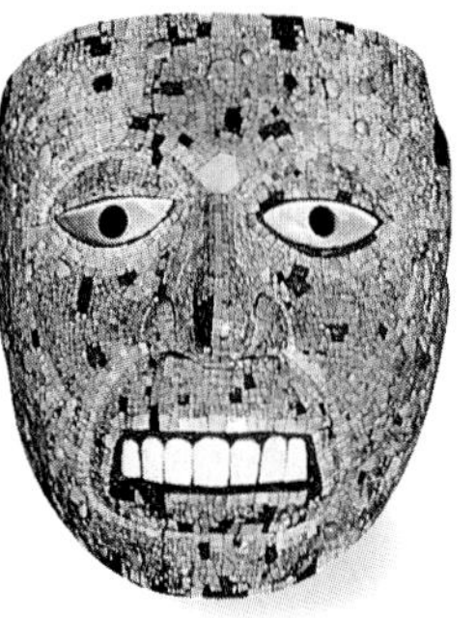

This mask, made of turquoise mosaic, represents Quetzalcoatl, the chief god of the Aztecs.

AZTEC MYTHS

The mythical world of the Aztec people of central Mexico, North America, was dominated by the figure of Quetzalcoatl. He was the chief god of the Aztecs, and took the form of a feathered serpent. According to myth, Quetzalcoatl created humans and gave them knowledge, then sailed away on a raft of serpents.

Greek myths

Many stories are told about ancient Greece. Legendary tales, such as those surrounding the Trojan War, have a basis in historical fact, while myths about figures like Perseus and Medusa are more fantastic.

Theseus

Minotaur

THESEUS AND THE MINOTAUR
The Minotaur was a mythical creature, half-man and half-bull, that lived in a labyrinth (maze) on the island of Crete. It was eventually slain by a Theban prince called Theseus.

Perseus

Gorgons have a head of snakes instead of hair

PERSEUS AND MEDUSA
One Greek myth tells the story of Perseus, who beheaded a gorgon called Medusa. The gorgon's head had the power to turn people to stone.

MASK OF KING AGAMEMNON

TROJAN WARS
In *The Iliad*, which Homer wrote around 1200 B.C., the legend tells how Agamemnon, King of Mycenae, Greece, led an army against the Trojans to rescue his brother's captured wife, Helen.

Greek soldiers hid inside the huge wooden horse

TROJAN HORSE
According to legend, when the Greeks were fighting the Trojans, they beat them by a trick. They built a wooden horse, then hid in it, outside the gates of Troy. The Trojans dragged the wooden horse into the city to see what it was. At night, the Greek soldiers crept out and opened the city gates to let their army in.

Religions

MOST PEOPLE HAVE some kind of belief or faith that helps to explain life and death. Many worship either one or several gods. The four major world religions are Christianity, Islam, Hinduism, and Buddhism.

Christianity

Christians believe that Jesus Christ is the Son of God, through whose life, death, and resurrection believers are freed from their sinful state. Christianity has more followers than any other religion.

The cross is the symbol of Christianity.

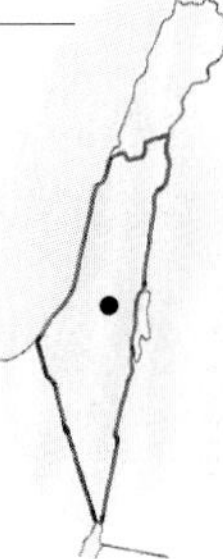

ORIGIN
Christianity began in about A.D. 30 in Jerusalem, then part of the Roman Empire.

The Bible

This Christian holy book is made up of two parts called the Old and New Testaments. In the Old Testament are the sacred writings of the Jews. The New Testament tells the story of Christ's life and the origin of Christianity.

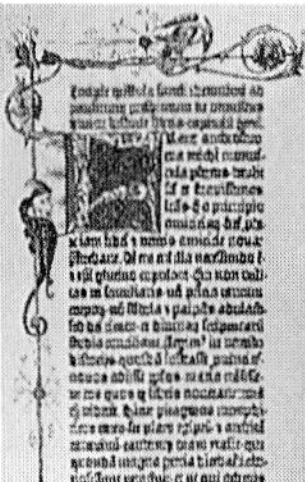

The first printed Bible was produced in 1455 by Gutenberg.

Ten commandments

Christians try to obey ten rules, which are adapted from the Jewish scriptures.

1 Worship one God.
2 Make no image of God.
3 Respect God's name.
4 Keep Sunday holy.
5 Honor your parents.
6 Do not kill.
7 Do not commit adultery.
8 Do not steal.
9 Do not tell lies.
10 Do not be envious.

Jesus Christ

Jesus lived in the Holy Land (present-day Israel) about 2,000 years ago. From the age of about 30, he began to preach and heal the sick. He was tried and put to death by the Roman authorities.

ISLAM

A star and a crescent moon symbolize Islam.

The followers of Islam are Muslims, who believe in Allah. Islam means "submission," and Muslims believe they must obey Allah and live by the five pillars (rules) set out in their holy book, the *Koran*.

ORIGIN

Islam began in about A.D. 600 in Mecca, in present-day Saudi Arabia. It is now practiced all over the world.

THE KORAN

In Islam's holy book, Allah shows the prophet Muhammad how people should live. Muslims treat this book with great respect, and must wash before touching it.

KORAN *(Qur'an)*

MUHAMMAD

Born in Mecca, Muhammad (c. 570–632) was the last and the greatest of the 26 Islamic prophets.

Muhammad is Allah's messenger.

HINDUISM

The symbol of Hinduism is the sound "Om."

Hindus worship many gods, and believe in *dharma*, the correct way to live. Like Buddhists, Hindus believe we have all lived before, as animals as well as people. By following the *dharma*, we may achieve a perfect state of *Moksha* and need never be reborn again.

ORIGIN

Hinduism began in India, around 1750 B.C. It has spread through much of Asia.

VEDAS

About 1400 B.C., Hindu beliefs were written as songs and chants in the *Vedas*.

The Rig Veda *is the most important book of the Vedas.*

FOUNDERS

Hinduism has no single founder. The Aryans, who invaded India nearly 4,000 years ago, brought early Hindu gods, such as Shiva.

SHIVA

BUDDHISM

The symbol of Buddhism is an eight-spoked wheel.

The Buddhist faith is based on the teachings of Buddha, who believed that we must rid ourselves of desire in order to free ourselves from suffering. Buddhists believe that life is a sequence of birth, death, and rebirth, and that by following the Eightfold path of Buddhism, we can reach a state of peace called *Nirvana*.

Extracts from the Pali Canon

THE *PALI*

The collected teachings of Buddha are called the *Pali Canon*. The best-known is the *Dhammapada*.

ORIGINS

Buddhism began in India in around 500 B.C. It is now the religion of around 300 million people.

BUDDHA

Prince Siddhartha Gautama (Buddha) lived about 563–483 B.C. He gave up his riches to preach and meditate.

Buddha means "enlightened one."

SIKHISM

The Khanda is the symbol of Sikhism.

This faith began in northern India. It is based on the worship of one God, the eternal Guru, and on the cycle of rebirth.

ORIGINS

Sikhism began in north India and Pakistan around 1500. It has spread to North America and Britain.

GURU GRANTH SAHIB

This book is treated with great respect

GURU GRANTH

This sacred book contains hymns and poems written by the Gurus.

THE FIVE K'S

Sikhs must wear these five items: *Kesh* (uncut hair, under a turban, if a man); *Kara* (a steel bracelet); *Kangha* (a hair comb); *Kirpan* (a sword); and *Kaccha* (short pants as an undergarment).

Sikh men wear a turban

JUDAISM

The Jewish symbol is the Star of David.

Followers of Judaism are called Jews. They believe in one God whose law is written in the *Tanach*. Judaism began about 4,000 years ago in Canaan. Today this area is mainly Israel.

ORIGINS

Judaism originated around 2000 B.C. in Canaan, "the Promised Land." Today, Judaism has spread to most parts of the world.

Tallit, or prayer shawl

Menorah, or branched candlestick

Yarmulke, or skull cap

The Tanach

TANACH

The Jewish Bible, or *Tanach*, tells the history of the Jewish people. The *Torah* is the most important part, since it contains the laws that God revealed to Moses.

SHINTOISM

In Japan, Shintoists worship gods of nature, and there are Shinto shrines in parks, gardens, and on mountains. Shintoists worship alone, and their symbol is the outline of a temple gate.

According to Shinto faith, Mount Fuji is a Shinto god. People come to pray at a shrine on its summit.

CONFUCIANISM

This faith is based on the teachings of K'ung-Fu tzu (551–479 B.C.), or Confucius, who was known for his wise sayings. In the *Analects*, Confucius taught the wisdom of living in harmony with nature. He said "Never do to others what you would not like them to do to you."

K'UNG-FU-TZU

TAOISM

YIN YANG

Lao-Tze founded the faith of Taoism in China 2,400 years ago. Taoists believe in many gods. Their symbol of *Yin Yang* represents the balance and harmony of opposites.

The name Lao-Tze means "Old Master."

LAO-TZE

GODS AND GODDESSES

MANY OF THE ANCIENT civilizations, such as those in Greece, Rome, and Egypt, worshipped several gods and goddesses.

Ancient Egypt

The gods and goddesses of ancient Egypt often had the body of a human and the head of an animal, which represented that creature's power. The chief of the gods was the Sun god Re, who had different names at different times of the day.

BASTET, THE CAT GODDESS

HORUS' EYE

The symbol of the "wadjet" eye represents the vengeful eye of Horus, torn out in the struggle for Egypt.

"WADJET" EYE

BASTET

The goddess Bastet was the daughter of Re, the Sun god. She represented the power of the sun to ripen crops, and she took the form of a cat.

OSIRIS

The god of the underworld and judge of the dead was called Osiris. People believed he ruled over a world below ground that looked like Egypt. Osiris took the form of a mummified man.

OSIRIS

ANUBIS

The son of Osiris was the god Anubis, who had the head of a jackal. Anubis was said to guide the souls of the dead to Osiris for their judgment.

ANUBIS

Ancient Greece

The Greeks believed that all the gods were the descendants of Gaia (the earth) and Uranos (the sky), and that they behaved in the same way as humans.

ZEUS
The King of the gods was Zeus, who is represented as a strong, middle-aged man. He was noble, but easily angered.

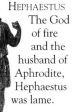

HEPHAESTUS
The God of fire and the husband of Aphrodite, Hephaestus was lame.

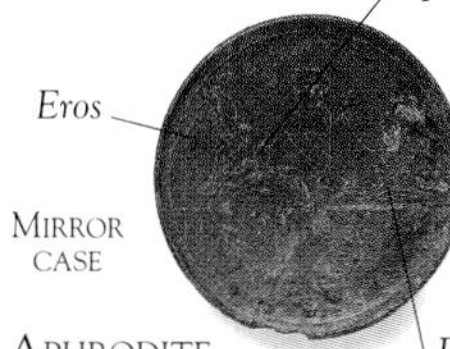
Aphrodite
Eros
Pan

MIRROR CASE

APHRODITE
The Greek goddess of love was called Aphrodite.

APOLLO
The young god of the sun and of medicine was Apollo.

Ancient Rome

The Romans adopted many Greek gods and gave them new names. Aphrodite became Venus, Zeus became Jupiter, and Ares, the god of war, became Mars.

TEMPLES
Many emperors were made gods after their death. Temples such as this were built in their honor.

TEMPLE OF AUGUSTUS AND LIVIA

JUPITER
The king of the Roman gods, Jupiter was a sky-god whose symbols were the eagle and the thunderbolt. Jupiter was much like the Greek god Zeus.

MONEY AND TRADE

THE METAL COINS and paper banknotes that we use to buy things are called money, or currency. Money also comes in the form of credit cards, checks, and the computer records of a bank account.

Cowrie shells were used as money

EARLY MONEY

Before coins were invented, people used to exchange stones, shells, beads, and furs for food and other goods.

EARLY LYDIAN COIN

THE FIRST COINS

The earliest known coins were made in the kingdom of Lydia (now Turkey) more than 2,700 years ago. These coins were weighed lumps of electrum (a mix of silver and gold), which were stamped, or "minted," to guarantee their weight.

14TH-CENTURY CHINESE PAPER MONEY

THE FIRST PAPER MONEY

In 10th-century China, people began to leave their coins with merchants, in exchange for a handwritten paper receipt. In the 11th century, the Chinese government fixed the value of these receipts. This became the first paper money.

Burnisher for smoothing

Sharp "burins" for engraving the design

The design for the banknote is hand engraved back-to-front on to a steel plate

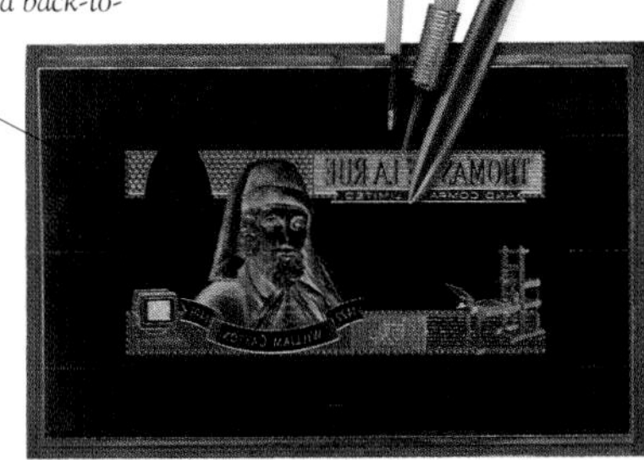

PRINTING PLATE

MAKING BANKNOTES

Banknotes have to be printed in a very elaborate and secret way to reduce the chances of forgery. The four stages of making a banknote are designing, paper-making, ink-mixing, and printing. The design is engraved on a steel plate by hand. This is called "intaglio" engraving.

PROOF FOR BACKGROUND

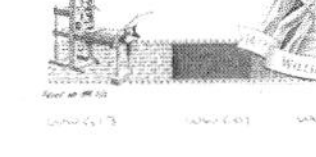

PROOF FOR MAIN DESIGN

This design uses eight inks, printed in reds, yellows, blues, and buffs.

Every note is individually numbered

NUMBERING MACHINE

The finished specimen banknote is shown to customers all over the world.

THOMAS DE LA RUE
AND COMPANY LIMITED
1422
WILLIAM CAXTON
1491

FINISHED BANKNOTE

BALANCE OF TRADE

Countries measure their success at trading by their "balance of payments," which is the difference between the amount they sell abroad (exports) and the amount they buy (imports).

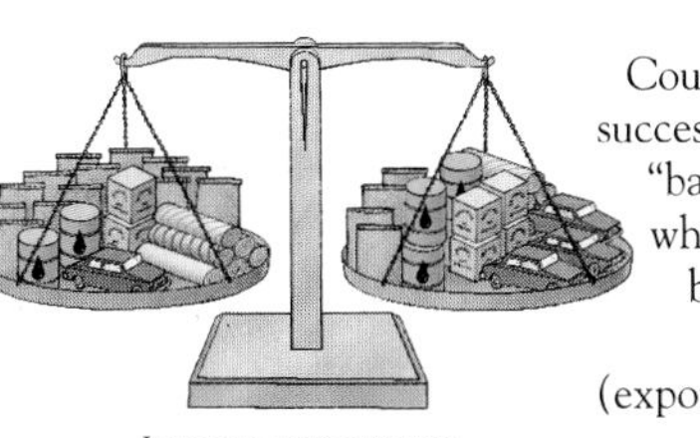

IMPORTS AND EXPORTS

THE STOCK MARKET

People often raise money to start a business by selling "shares" in it. If the business make a profit, the shareholders receive a dividend (payment). The stock market is where shares, or stocks, are bought and sold by "stockbrokers."

TOKYO STOCK EXCHANGE, JAPAN

KEY STOCK EXCHANGES

Country	City	Index
Japan	Tokyo	Nikkei Average
United States	New York	Dow-Jones
United Kingdom	London	FTSE-100 *
Germany	Frankfurt	DAX **

* *Financial Times Stock Exchange 100*
** *Deutsche Aktien Index*

GOVERNMENT AND LAW

ALL COUNTRIES are run by a government. Some are harsh dictatorships, and others are liberal democracies. Every government implements policies that affect the everyday lives of the nation's people. The business of government is called politics.

DEMOCRACY
This system, in which a country is ruled by the people, or their elected representatives, began in Athens, Greece, 2,500 years ago. Many other countries are now governed in this way.

Pericles was leader of democratic Athens at the height of its power

POLITICAL SYSTEMS
Most countries are "capitalist," and the land and businesses are owned by individuals or small groups. In "communist" countries, all businesses are state-run. "Socialists" believe that governments should grant everyone equal rights, a fair share of money, education, health, and housing.

КОММУНИСТИЧЕСКИЙ
ИНТЕРНАЦИОНАЛ
№
Москва
Петроград
18
COMMUNIST MAGAZINE

Abraham Lincoln was US president 1861–65.

PARLIAMENT
In many countries, government policy is debated and the laws are agreed upon in an assembly called parliament. People elect members of parliament to act as their representatives.

HOUSE OF COMMONS, UK

REPUBLIC
Most countries are republics, which have no king or queen. The "head of state" in a republic is usually a president. In democracies, the president is elected by the people. A country with a king or queen is called a monarchy. Kings were once thought to rule by God's will. Their power is now usually limited by a set of rules called a constitution.

Branches of Government

THE CAPITOL, HOME OF THE US CONGRESS, WASHINGTON, D.C.

LEGISLATURE
The legislature is an elected assembly, or "house," that amends and makes laws. In the US, it is called Congress.

EXECUTIVE
The executive puts laws into effect and administers the country. It is headed by a president or a prime minister who appoints heads of different departments.

JUDICIARY
The judiciary makes sure that laws are applied fairly. In the US, the highest legal body is the Supreme Court.

Law

Every country has rules, or laws, to help people live together and to keep them in order. Laws are decided by governments or religious leaders and they are enforced by the police and the courts.

COURT ROOM
Judge helps jury on points of law, and passes sentence if verdict is "guilty"
Lawyer
A person on trial is "the accused"
In Britain, a jury must consist of 12 men and women over 18 years old

CRIMINAL LAW
Criminal law covers crimes such as murder and theft.

CIVIL LAW
This kind of law deals with disputes, rather than crimes. Civil law also deals with day-to-day events such as buying a house and making a will.

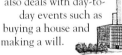

TRIAL
People accused of crimes are usually taken to court to be "tried." Typically, trials are "adversarial" – one set of lawyers (the prosecution) tries to prove that the accused is guilty, while another (the defense) tries to prove that he or she is innocent. A judge or a jury (a group of ordinary men and women) decides who is right.

Buildings

Houses, churches, and offices are all buildings. The design and construction of buildings is called architecture.

In Oceania, "longhouses" are built on stilts in case of flooding.

Traditional homes

People around the world build their homes from the materials they have available. From houses of timber or stone, to huts of mud or woven reeds, every country has its own style.

In South Africa, the dome-shaped kraals have grass roofs.

Swiss chalets are built from wooden timbers.

Some Asian nomads live in canvas or felt "yurts."

Algerian houses are close together to keep out the sun.

Japanese houses have sliding doors.

North American houses have wooden "clapboards."

Classical architecture

There are three styles, or orders, of classical Greek architecture: Doric, Ionic, and Corinthian. The columns of Greek temples often have a decorative head, or capital, on the top. Across the columns is a broad lintel called the entablature. This consists of an architrave, a frieze, and a cornice.

Entablature
Frieze
Decorative capital

Classical Greek temple

Orders

These three orders were used in three different periods of history.

Doric was used from 700 B.C.

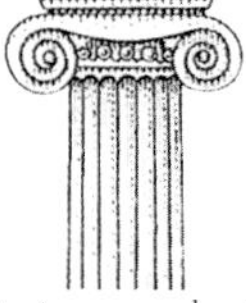

Ionic was used from 600 B.C.

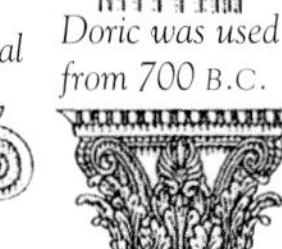

Corinthian was used from 500 B.C.

DOMES

Curved roofs, or domes, are a feature of many religious and state buildings around the world.

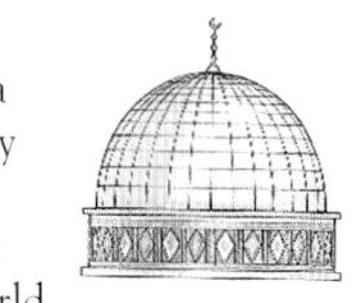
HEMISPHERICAL DOME

ONION DOME

POLYHEDRAL DOME

SAUCER DOME

VAULTS

Vaults are arched roofs or ceilings. The four main types of vaults are shown here.

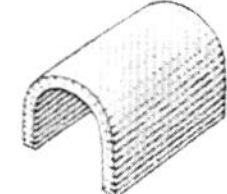
BARREL VAULT

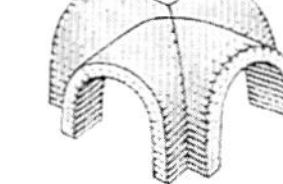
GROIN VAULT

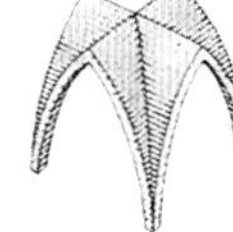
RIB VAULT

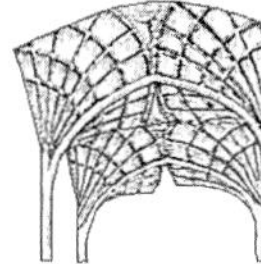
FAN VAULT

ARCHES

An arch is an opening that is curved or pointed at the top. These features are often used in large buildings to span openings and carry weight.

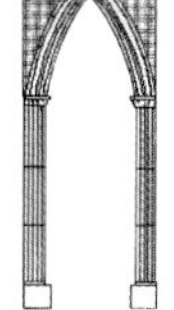
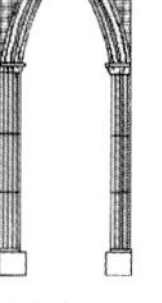
POINTED ARCH

HORSESHOE ARCH

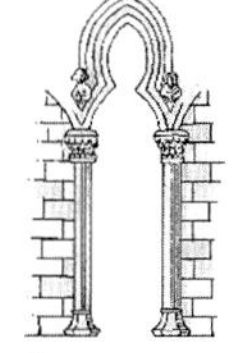
LOBED ARCH

SKYSCRAPERS

The invention of reinforced concrete, plate glass, and steel in the mid 1800s enabled architects to design and build extremely tall constructions, or "skyscrapers." The first skyscrapers were built in Chicago. Giant buildings are now found in most major cities. At 1,482 ft (452 m), the Petronas Tower, in Kuala Lumpur, Malaysia, is the world's tallest building.

NEW YORK SKYSCRAPERS

Many of the workers who built the New York skyscrapers were Iroquois and Mohawk people, who showed no fear of heights.

Cathedral-like spire
WOOLWORTH BUILDING 1913

Art Deco crown
GENERAL ELECTRIC BUILDING 1930s

6500 B.C.–301 B.C.	300 B.C.–A.D. 850

c. 6500 B.C. One the first known towns, Çatal Hüyük, is built in present-day Turkey, using rectangular mud bricks.
c. 2650–2150 B.C. Pyramids are built in the lower Nile valley, in Egypt. The Step Pyramid at Saqqara is designed by a High Priest called Imhotep, who is the first known architect.

Massive stones arranged in a huge circle

STONEHENGE, ENGLAND

c. 2200 B.C. Stonehenge is built in England, using massive stones. It was probably built as a religious monument.
c. 2112–2095 B.C. The Sumerians build stepped temples called ziggurats in Mesopotamia, using mud bricks.
c. 1700–1200 B.C. Beehive tombs, or tholos, are built by the Mycenaean civilization on the Greek mainland.
c. 1500 B.C. The Minoan Palace of Knossos is rebuilt on the Greek island of Crete.
800–200 B.C. Etruscans use arches in the construction of their buildings in what is now called Italy.
700–400 B.C. The ancient Greeks build temples of such perfect proportions that their style of building becomes known as "classical." This classical style of architecture is copied many times throughout history.

THE PARTHENON, ATHENS, GREECE

c. 300 B.C. Buddhists build stupas (mounds) in India and southeastern Asia to symbolize the dome of heaven.
c. 200 B.C.–A.D. 500 Roman architecture takes over the classical Greek style and the Etruscan arch. The Romans introduce concrete, which enables them to build huge vaults and arches.
A.D. 300–1540 Pre-Columbian civilizations in the Americas build stepped pyramids crowned with temples. One of these is the pyramid known as Giant Jaguar, at Tikal in Guatemala.
330–1453 The Byzantine style of architecture develops when the Roman Empire moves its capital to Byzantium, renaming it Constantinople (now Istanbul, Turkey) The largest dome of its time, the Hagia Sophia, is built there in A.D. 537.
607–670 The oldest surviving wooden building, the Horyuji Buddhist monastery, is built at Nara, in Japan.
618–782 The earliest Chinese timber building, the Nanchan Buddhist temple, is built on a holy mountain in Shaanxi province.
690–850 Early Islamic mosques and palaces are designed around courtyards.

900–1839

900–1150 The Romanesque style of architecture spreads across western Europe, featuring round-headed arches on top of cylindrical columns.
1100–1500 The Gothic style is used in Christian churches in northern Europe. It has pointed arches and flying buttresses, allowing very tall, light structures.
1113–1150 Angkor Wat, a vast stone city, is built by the Khmers in what is now Cambodia.
c. 1420 The Renaissance begins in Italy, reviving Roman and Greek building methods. Brunelleschi (1377–1446) and Alberti (1404–72) are key figures.

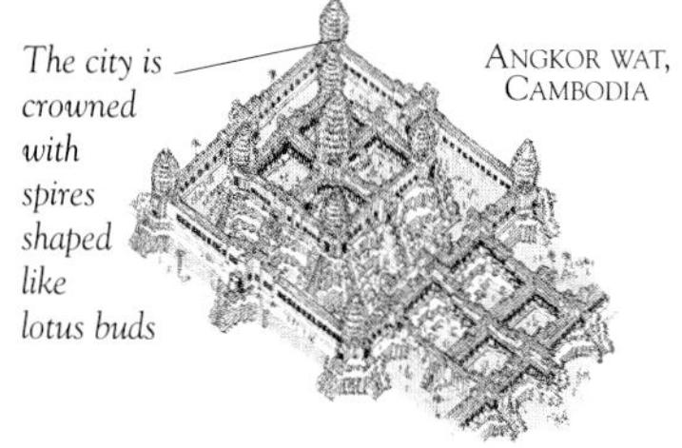
The city is crowned with spires shaped like lotus buds
ANGKOR WAT, CAMBODIA

c. 1650 The Baroque style is developed. Architects are commissioned by the Catholic Church to build very grand, ornate churches and palaces.
1750–1840 Neoclassical architects return to plain, elegant Roman and Greek styles of building.
1830–1930s During a Gothic revival, architects build churches, public buildings, and even train stations, trying to recapture the style of medieval cathedrals.

1840–TODAY

1840–90 The Industrial Revolution provides new materials, such as plate glass, steel, and reinforced concrete, which transform traditional building methods.
1890 After the elevator is invented, the first skyscrapers are built in Chicago.
1900–40s American architect Frank Lloyd Wright (1867–1959) promotes "organic" architecture, designing buildings that blend in with nature.
1919–33 Walter Gropius (1883–1969) leads a design team in Weimar, Germany (the Bauhaus school), creating designs based on modern industrial technology.
1920s The Swiss architect Le Corbusier (1887–1965) leads the new style of International Modernism in building design.
1970s A "hi-tech" style, with much steel, glass, and exposed pipes, is led by Richard Rogers (b. 1933) and Norman Foster (b. 1935).
Late 1970s Postmodern design develops. New designs blend elements from the architectural styles of different eras and cultures.
1980s–2000s Architects increasingly take note of environmental concerns, such as recycling and saving energy. Some new buildings use solar power.

EMPIRE STATE BUILDING, NEW YORK CITY

ARTISTS' MATERIALS

ARTISTS paint pictures and create sculptures. The main materials that an artist needs for painting are sketching materials (for an initial drawing or a finished work), paint and paintbrushes, and a surface to paint on. This surface may be paper for watercolor painting, canvas for oils, or wood for acrylics.

SCULPTURE

A sculptor can use almost any material for sculpting, but bronze, marble, and clay are the most popular for figurative work (based on the human body).

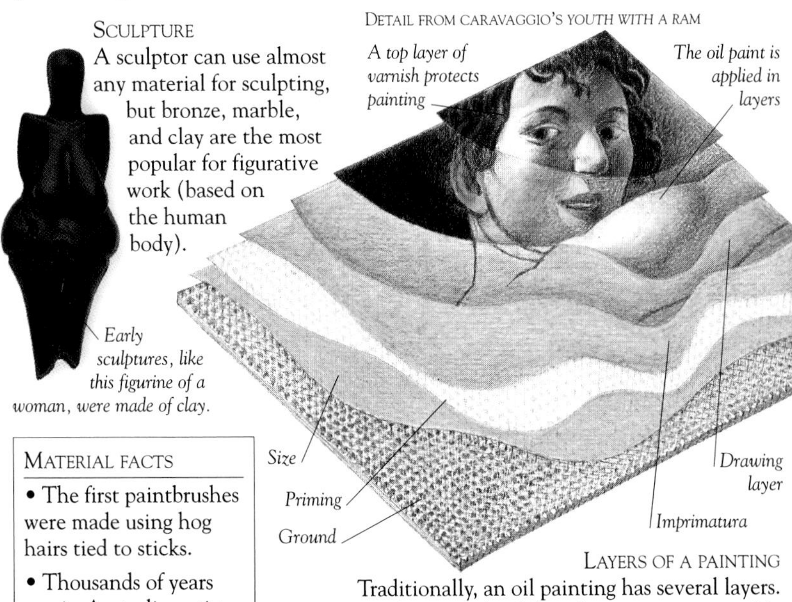
DETAIL FROM CARAVAGGIO'S YOUTH WITH A RAM
A top layer of varnish protects painting
The oil paint is applied in layers
Size
Priming
Ground
Drawing layer
Imprimatura

Early sculptures, like this figurine of a woman, were made of clay.

MATERIAL FACTS

- The first paintbrushes were made using hog hairs tied to sticks.
- Thousands of years ago in Australia, artists mixed natural pigments in their mouths to paint cave walls.

LAYERS OF A PAINTING

Traditionally, an oil painting has several layers. By analyzing each of these layers, experts are able to date a picture accurately, and they can also tell if it is a fake. This artwork, showing a section of Caravaggio's *Youth with a Ram*, shows the layers that were used in paintings of the 17th century.

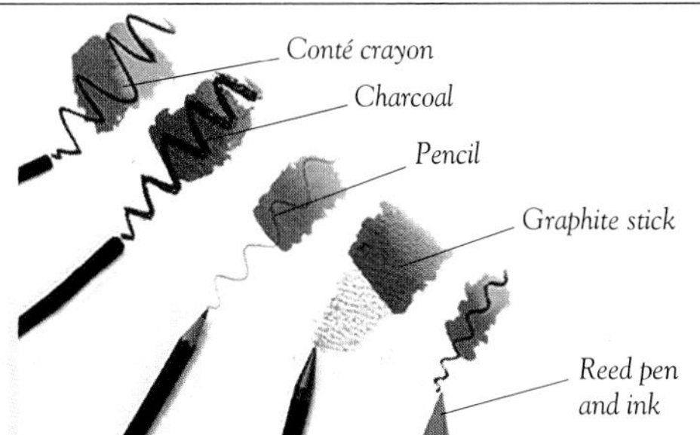
Conté crayon
Charcoal
Pencil
Graphite stick
Reed pen and ink

Drawing tools

Most drawings are sketches (quick drawings) done as a preparation for a finished work. But a drawing can also be a finished picture in itself. Artists usually draw with dry materials such as pencils, crayons, or charcoal.

Paints

The three main kinds of paint are oils, which were first used in the 1400s; watercolors, popular with 18th-century landscape artists; and acrylics, popular in the 1960s.

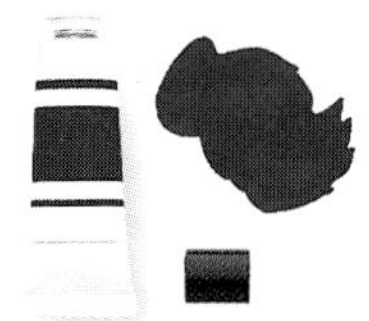

Oil paints are a mixture of dry pigment and an oil such as linseed.

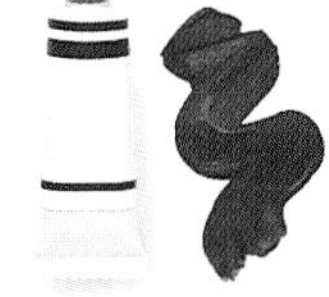

Watercolor paints are pigments bound with gum arabic. They are diluted with water.

Acrylic paints are either applied with a knife or diluted and used with a paintbrush.

Round Flat Filbert

Paintbrushes

The two main kinds of paintbrushes are soft-hair brushes for watercolors, and bristle brushes for oil paintings and acrylics. The length and shape of the hairs on a brush may be round, flat, or "filbert."

Mona Lisa

The most famous painting is Leonardo da Vinci's *Mona Lisa*, painted in 1503. It is a portrait of Lisa, the wife of a nobleman named Francesco del Gioconda. That is why the painting is sometimes called *La Gioconda*.

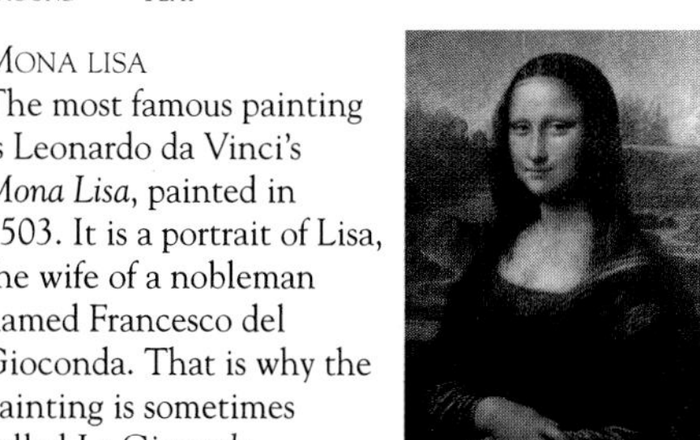

MONA *LISA*, THE LOUVRE, PARIS

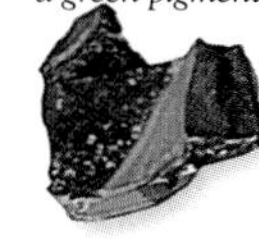

Malachite makes a green pigment.

Lapis lazuli makes a blue pigment.

Pigments

Paint is made from powdered colors called pigments. These were originally natural colors from plants and rocks, but today most are made using chemicals.

2700 B.C.–A.D. 599

c. 27,000 B.C. Small clay statues of pregnant women, known as "Venus figurines" appear across Europe.
c. 15,000 B.C. Early artists use fingers, brushes and hollow reeds to paint animals on the walls of the Lascaux caves, France.
c, 4000–1000 B.C. Egyptian art includes wall and scroll paintings, gold jewelry, and painted statues sculpted from limestone.

VENUS FIGURINE, FRANCE C. 27,000 BC

2000–1100 B.C. Minoans on the island of Crete, Greece, decorate their palace walls with colored murals.
1600–1027 B.C. The Shang dynasty in China discovers how to cast bronze and create bowls and urns for food and wine.
c. 500 B.C. The Nok culture in Nigeria, West Africa, produces lifelike terra cotta figurines of humans.
c. 500–323 B.C. Greek sculptors produce statues of gods and athletes made of marble, bronze, and clay.
A.D. 100–400 Gandharan sculpture develops in the Indus valley, Pakistan. It is influenced by Greek art, and shows scenes from the life of Buddha.
100–1000 Mayan carvings are created in Central America, combining ornate figures with hieroglyphs (picture writing).
400–1110 Medieval monks in Europe create illuminated manuscripts.

600–1839

600–1185 Icons (religious portraits) are painted in Eastern Europe.
618–907 Chinese artists of the T'ang dynasty paint stunning landscapes.
1000–1200 The Romanesque style develops in the church sculptures and murals of Europe.
1000–1600 Huge stone figures are made on Easter Island, Polynesia.
1368–1644 The Ming dynasty in China is famous for its blue-glazed porcelain bowls and vases.
1400–1500 The Renaissance begins in Florence, Italy. Masaccio (1401–28) uses perspective in his paintings.
Late 1400s Islamic miniature painting flourishes in Persia.
1490–1520 The High Renaissance, exemplified in works by Leonardo da Vinci (1452–1519), Michelangelo (1475–1564), and Raphael (1483–1520).

THE ANNUNCIATION, LEONARDO DA VINCI

1600s The golden age of Dutch painting, with pictures by Rembrandt (1606–69) and Vermeer (1632–75).
Late 1700s–mid 1800s The Romantic school, notably Turner (1775–1851) and Friedrich (1774–1840) focuses on human emotions and nature.

1840–1899	1900–TODAY

1840s Realism develops in France, with painters such as Courbet (1819–77) depicting people in a more lifelike way.

THE WINNOWERS, GUSTAVE COURBET 1855

1850s–70s In England, Pre-Raphaelites such as Millais (1829–96), Burne-Jones (1833–98), and Rossetti (1828–82) are influenced by artists before Raphael, but develop their own style of painting.
1860s–90s Impressionism begins in France as painters try to capture their impressions of fleeting moments, especially Monet (1840–1926) and Manet (1832–83).
1880–1905 Postimpressionist artists such as Cézanne (1839–1906), van Gogh (1853–90), and Gauguin (1848–1903) develop their own style, using strong colors and shapes.
1880s–1890s Expressionism develops in Europe as artists such as Kirchner (1880–1938) use intense color and free brush strokes to express their feelings.
1880s–90s Symbolist artists such as Moreau (1826–98) create images based on symbolic inner meanings.

1907–1920s Cubism develops in Paris with Picasso (1881–1973) and Braque (1882–1963) using bold geometric shapes.
1910–50 Artists of the Abstract movement, led by Kandinsky (1866–1944) begin to paint and sculpt ideas instead of realistic objects.
1916 The Dada movement, originally a protest against World War I, rejects traditional forms of art.
1920s Surrealist painters such as Dali (1904–89) and Ernst (1891–1976) explore their dreams and Freud's psychoanalytic ideas in their painting.
1940s Abstract Expressionism appears in New York, where artists such as Jackson Pollock (1912–56) experiment with the physical properties of paint.
1950s–60s Pop Art develops in the US and Britain as artists such as Warhol (1928–87) begin to use consumer goods and images from the media in their art.
1960s–90s Performance artists such as Gilbert (b. 1943) & George (b. 1942) combine music, theater, film, and video in their work.
1970s–90s Video artists such as Korean-born Nam Jun-Paik (b. 1932) feature video projection and computer technology in their exhibitions.

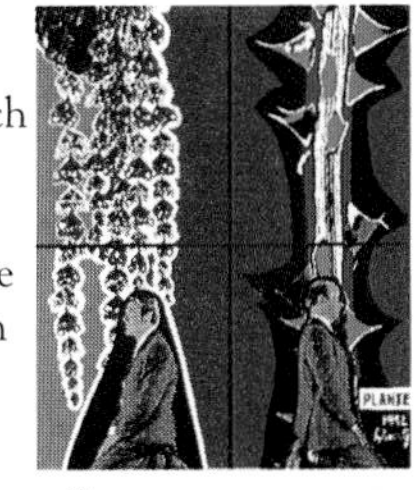

PLANTED, GILBERT AND GEORGE, 1992

MUSICAL INSTRUMENTS

THERE ARE THOUSANDS of musical instruments, each making its own distinctive sound. They are usually grouped into percussion, strings, woodwinds, brasses, and keyboards.

HARP
Harps date back at least 6,000 years. Strings stretched over a frame are finger-plucked to give a beautiful rippling sound. This harp is for traditional Irish music.

IRISH HARP

Strings

All stringed instruments consist of a series of stretched strings connected to a hollow box that amplifies (makes louder) the string's vibrations. The string is set in motion by being plucked, as with a harp; by the friction of a bow, as with a violin, or by being struck, as with a piano.

Strands of horse hair

Screw for tightening bow

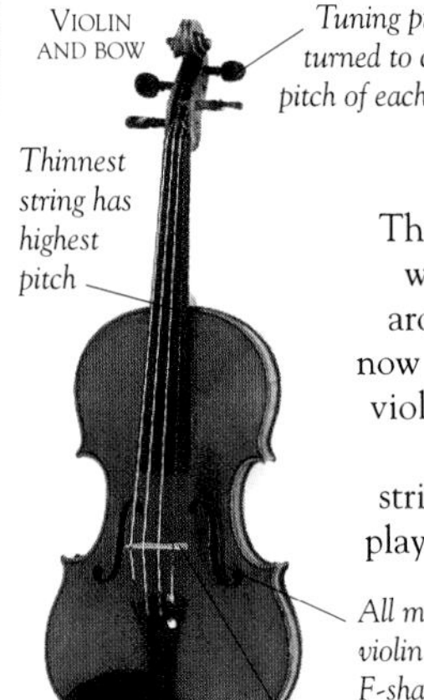
Tuning pins are turned to change pitch of each string
Thinnest string has highest pitch
All members of the violin family have an F-shaped sound hole
Bridge supports strings

VIOLIN AND BOW

VIOLIN
The violin family was invented in around 1550 and now consists of the violin, viola, cello and bass. The strings are usually played with a bow.

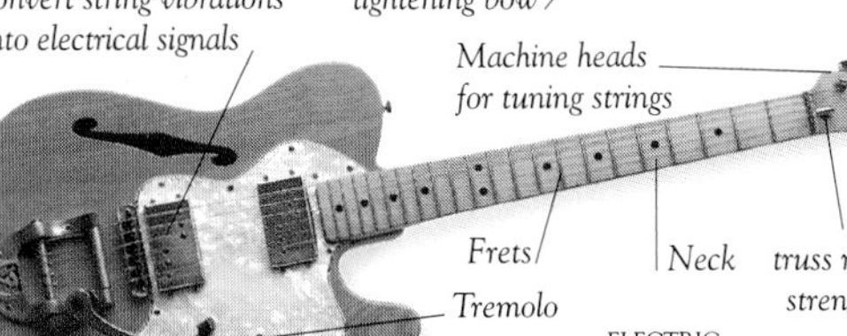
Magnetic pick-ups convert string vibrations into electrical signals
Machine heads for tuning strings
Frets
Neck
Steel truss rod to strengthen neck
Tremolo arm

ELECTRIC GUITAR

GUITAR
The electric guitar is a key instrument in rock and pop music. On an electric guitar, plucked strings are amplified electronically.

Crash cymbal
Tom-tom drums
Ride cymbal
Snare drum
Bass drum

DRUM KIT

PERCUSSION

Instruments that are played by striking them are called percussion. They include drums, cymbals, xylophones, gongs, and much more. Percussion underlines the rhythm of the music.

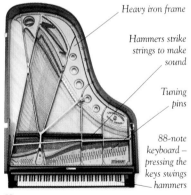

Heavy iron frame

Hammers strike strings to make sound

Tuning pins

88-note keyboard – pressing the keys swings hammers

KEYBOARD

Keyboards, including harpsichord, piano, organ, and synthesizer, are among the most versatile of all instruments. They are played by pressing levers or keys with the fingers.

WIND INSTRUMENTS

WOODWINDS

Flutes, clarinets, oboes, and bassoons all have a reed in the mouthpiece to set up the vibrations that make the sound. They are called woodwinds even though they are often made of brass.

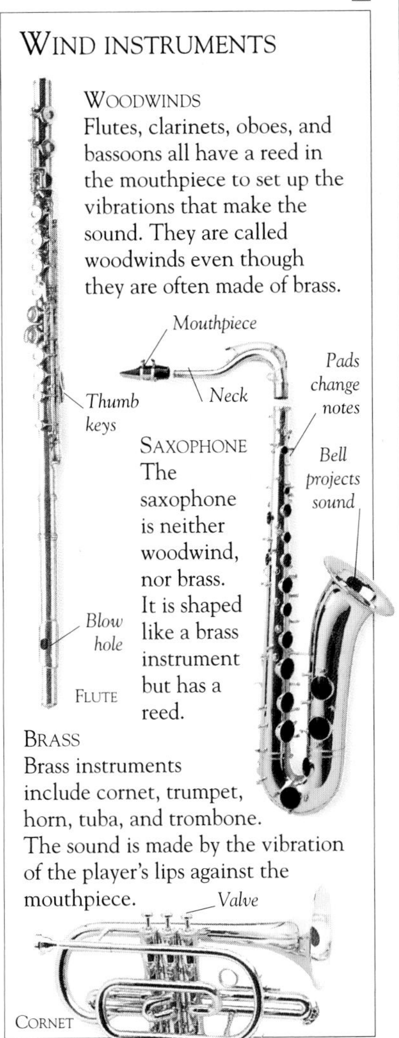
Mouthpiece
Neck
Pads change notes
Thumb keys
Bell projects sound
Blow hole
Valve

FLUTE

SAXOPHONE

The saxophone is neither woodwind, nor brass. It is shaped like a brass instrument but has a reed.

BRASS

Brass instruments include cornet, trumpet, horn, tuba, and trombone. The sound is made by the vibration of the player's lips against the mouthpiece.

CORNET

MUSIC

ROCK, JAZZ, AND FOLK MUSIC are often played from memory by small groups of talented musicians. Some types of music, such as classical music, is written down for soloists or groups of musicians.

THE ORCHESTRA
Orchestras range from small string orchestras to huge symphony orchestras. Similar instruments are grouped together.

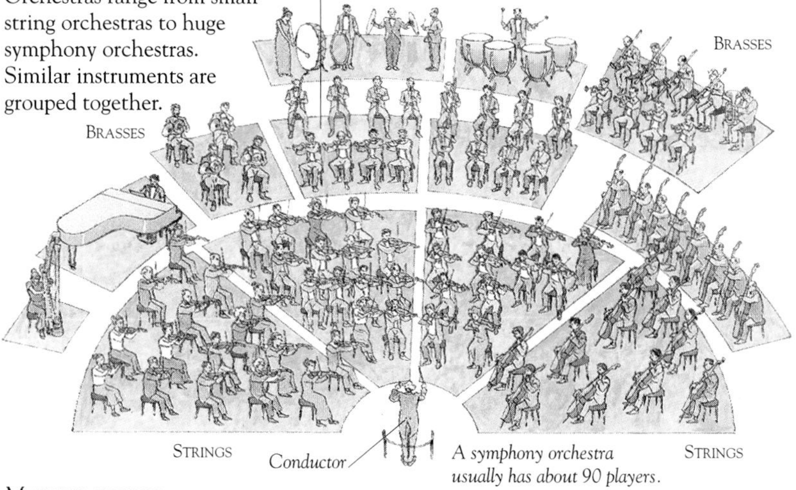

WOODWINDS

PERCUSSION

BRASSES

BRASSES

STRINGS

Conductor

A symphony orchestra usually has about 90 players.

STRINGS

MUSICAL GROUPS
Musical groups range from duos with two performers to symphony orchestras with up to 120.

A jazz quartet includes drums and bass; a string quartet is two violins, viola, and cello.

A quintet usually has five wind or five brass instruments.

CELLO AND PIANO DUO

Violin
Viola
Cello

STRING TRIO

JAZZ QUARTET

MIXED QUINTET

Pitch

The pitch of each note is shown by how high it sits on the staff. Musical pitch is grouped into eight notes called an octave. The notes of each octave are named from low to high using the letters A to G, plus the A that begins the next octave.

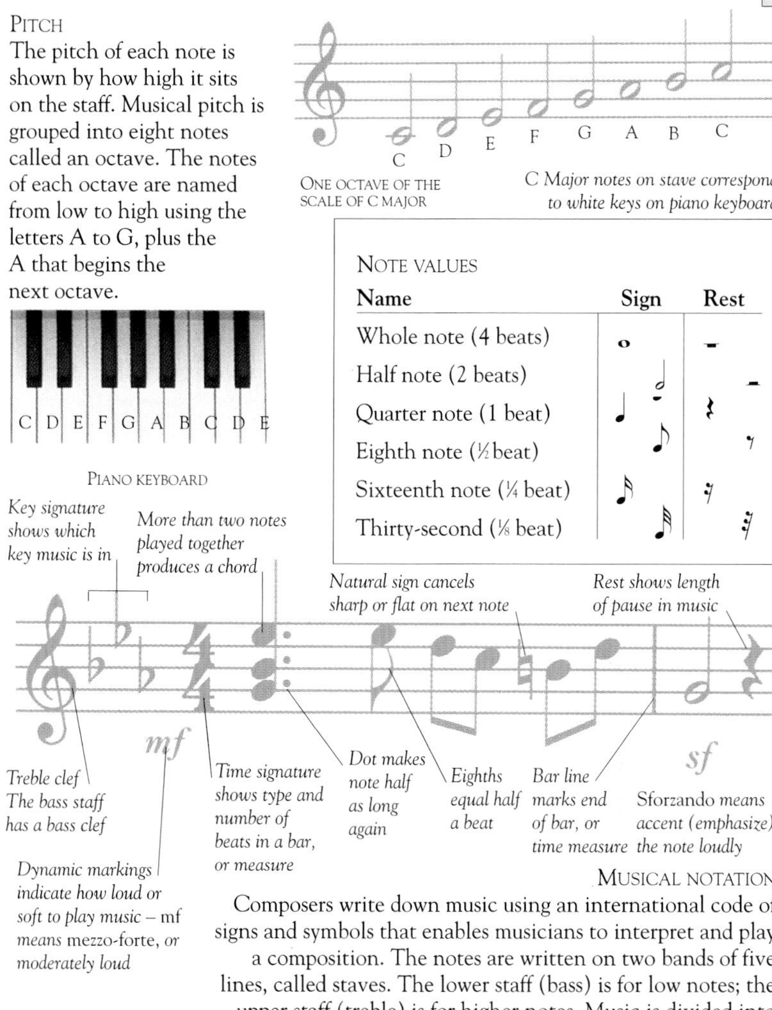
C D E F G A B C
C D E F G A B C D E
Key signature shows which key music is in
More than two notes played together produces a chord
Natural sign cancels sharp or flat on next note
Rest shows length of pause in music
mf
sf
Treble clef The bass staff has a bass clef
Time signature shows type and number of beats in a bar, or measure
Dot makes note half as long again
Eighths equal half a beat
Bar line marks end of bar, or time measure
Sforzando means accent (emphasize) the note loudly
Dynamic markings indicate how loud or soft to play music – mf means mezzo-forte, or moderately loud

ONE OCTAVE OF THE SCALE OF C MAJOR

C Major notes on stave correspond to white keys on piano keyboard

PIANO KEYBOARD

Note values

Name	Sign	Rest
Whole note (4 beats)		
Half note (2 beats)		
Quarter note (1 beat)		
Eighth note (½ beat)		
Sixteenth note (¼ beat)		
Thirty-second (⅛ beat)		

MUSICAL NOTATION

Composers write down music using an international code of signs and symbols that enables musicians to interpret and play a composition. The notes are written on two bands of five lines, called staves. The lower staff (bass) is for low notes; the upper staff (treble) is for higher notes. Music is divided into measures called bars, each with the same number of beats.

15,000 B.C.–A.D. 650

Before 15,000 B.C. Stone Age people play bone flutes.
c. 3000 B.C. Harps and lyres appear in Sumerian writing.
2600 B.C. Pa-Pab-Bi-gagir-gal of Ur in Mesopotamia is the first musician whose name is known.
c. 2500 B.C. Oldest known harp placed in Queen Puabi's tomb at Ur.

EGYPTIAN TOMB PAINTINGS

2200 B.C. Groups of musicians appear in Egyptian tomb paintings.
605 B.C. King Nebuchadnezzar of Babylon has an orchestra play at the dedication ceremony of an image of himself made in gold.
c. 550 B.C. The ancient Greek philosopher Pythagoras (580–500 B.C.) creates the first mathematical theory of musical harmony.
408 B.C. The oldest fragment of written music is a chorus for a play called *Orestes*, by ancient Greek dramatist Euripides (c. 484–406 B.C.).
A.D. 650 School for church music founded in Rome by Pope Gregory (c. A.D 540–604) develops Gregorian style of singing.

770–1750

700s Orchestras play *gamelan* (gongs) in Indonesia, to accompany traditional puppet shows and dance.
750 The Court of Caliph Harun al-Rashid in Persia becomes famous for its music, played by musicians like Ishaq al-Mausili (767–850).
1100s Monks add a second or third tune to the simple "plainsong" of the Gregorian chant to create the first polyphonic music.
1300s Paris becomes focus of polyphonic music, and early French composer Guillaume de Machaut (1300–77) writes ballads (songs) in this form.
1480 First printed music in Europe.
1500s Palestrina (1525–94) and Monteverdi (1567–1643) write polyphonic vocal masses for church.

FIRST PRINTED MUSIC IN EUROPE

1500s Polyphonic music played on instruments such as viola and lutes, especially for dances such as the pavane.
1600s Opera developed by the Camerata, a group of poets and musicians in Florence, Italy.
1600–1750 Baroque-era composers write in harmony, creating melody by combining notes from the major and minor scales. Baroque pieces contrast loud and soft, fast and slow musical passages.

1650–1889	1890–TODAY

J.S. BACH

1650–1700 Composers like J.S. Bach (1685–1750), Vivaldi (1678–1741), and Handel (1685–1759) write elaborate instrumental works called sonatas and concerto grossos.
1750–1820 In the classical era, composers produce elegant, clearly structured instumental pieces.
Late 1700s Classical music is brought to a peak by Mozart (1756–91) and Beethoven (1770–1827).
Early 1800s Beethoven writes emotional, passionate pieces on a grand scale, ushering in the romantic era.
1820–1900 The Romantic Era features composers such as Schubert (1797–1828), Berlioz (1803–1869), and Schumann (1810–1856), who write great piano and orchestral works.
1830s–1850s Liszt (1811–86) and Chopin (1810–49) compose dazzling, virtuoso piano music.
1870s–1880s Verdi (1813–1901) and Wagner (1813–1883) take opera to new heights.
1860s–1890s Composers including Dvorák (1841–1904), Grieg (1843–1907), and Tchaikovsky (1840–1893), are inspired by the folk music of their countries.

Late 1800s Blues played by black Americans.
c. 1900 Jazz music appears in New Orleans, US, combining African rhythms and Western harmony.
Early 1900s Composers, like Stravinsky (1882–1971) and Bartók (1881–1945), begin to write music in which dissonance (clashing notes) creates a thrilling sound.
1910s onward Schoenberg (1874–1951) creates "atonal" music, which is not based on any key or scale.
1930s Gershwin (1898–1937) mixes jazz and classical music, for example in *Rhapsody in Blue*.
1950s Black Americans play rock and roll, later taken up by white singers, such as Buddy Holly and Elvis Presley.
1960s Rock and roll develops into rock, with bands such as The Who and The Rolling Stones, and pop, with groups like The Beatles and The Beach Boys.
1970s Groups such as The Bee Gees and Chic make disco music popular.
1980s Electronic dance music emerges from black American neighborhoods into mainstream music.
1990s Energetic dance beats, such as house, techno, and jungle, are popular. Emergence of guitar-based "alternative" rock.

SINGER CHUCK BERRY

DANCE

DANCE TIMELINE

TANZANIAN ROCK PAINTING

15,000 B.C. Stone Age rock paintings show people dancing.
3000–1000 B.C. Ancient Egyptians use ritual dance to worship gods such as Isis.
A.D. 400 First Kagura dances are performed at Shinto shrines in Japan.
1300–1500 Mass dances in Europe cause frenzy.
Late 1400s *Ballo*, Italian dance with a story line, is the earliest form of ballet.
c. 1600 Kathakali dance emerges in India.
1830s–1840s Romantic ballet flourishes.
c. 1900 Isadora Duncan (1877–1927) develops freer forms of modern dance.
1930s Fred Astaire popularizes tap dancing.
1950s Rock-and-roll dancing.
1980s Break dancing and slam dancing are born.
1990s Companies design dances for TV and stage.

FRED ASTAIRE

OVER THOUSANDS of years, varied styles of dance have developed all over the world.

FIVE BASIC ARM POSITIONS

FIRST

SECOND

THIRD

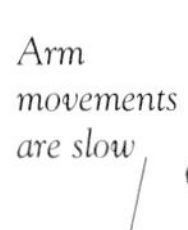
FOURTH

FIFTH

BALLET

The three main ballet styles are romantic, classical, and modern, distinguished mainly by differences in clothing and music. All ballet dancers learn five basic positions for the arms and feet.

FIVE BASIC FEET POSITIONS

FIRST

SECOND

THIRD

FOURTH

FIFTH

TRADITIONAL DANCE

Nearly every country in the world has its own traditional form of dance. These dances have often developed from simple religious or tribal rituals into complex dance forms with set movements.

Hand movements are complex
Arm movements are slow
Traditional costume
THAI CLASSICAL DANCER

THEATER

MODERN THEATER originated in ancient Greece, where actors wearing masks were used to tell a story or demonstrate a theme.

THEATER BUILDING
The ancient Greeks saw theater in vast open-air stadiums; modern theaters are smaller and indoors, and take many forms.

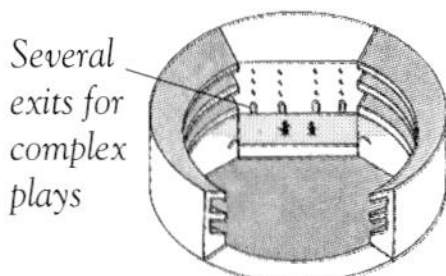
Several exits for complex plays

ENGLISH 16TH-CENTURY THEATER

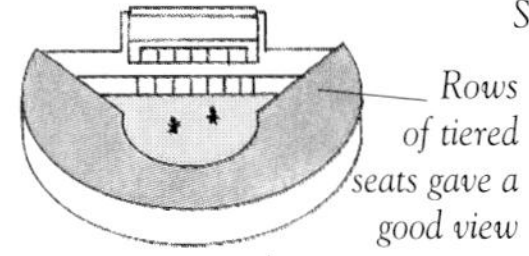
Rows of tiered seats gave a good view

ANCIENT GREEK AMPHITHEATER

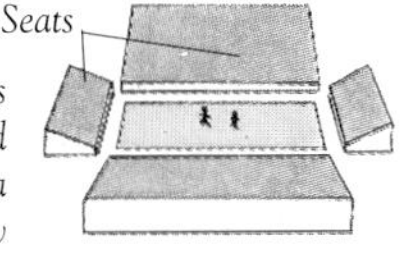
Seats

MODERN THEATER

SHAKESPEARE
William Shakespeare (1564–1616) was born in Stratford-upon-Avon, England. In about 1590, he moved to London, where he wrote at least 37 plays, including *Hamlet* and *Romeo and Juliet*.

KABUKI THEATER
The performers of Kabuki theater are men who wear elaborate makeup to play a particular role.

WICKED MALE

CRAB

NOBLE MALE

THEATER TIMELINE

c. 3000 B.C. Religious rituals involve music and drama.
c. 1000 B.C. Chinese and Indian dance-dramas become formalized.
c. 500 B.C. Ancient Greeks see dramas by Aeschylus (525–456 B.C.), Sophocles (496–406 B.C.), and Euripides (484–406 B.C.).
A.D. 1–100 "Pantomimus" popular in Rome.
c. 1500 Commedia dell'Arte, mimed comedy, spreads from Italy.
1603 Okuni, a young Japanese woman, creates Kabuki theater.
Early 1600s Theater flourishes in England and Spain with writers like Shakespeare and Lope de Vega (1562–1635).
c. 1800 Peking Opera begins in China.
1870s–90s New forms of drama created by Ibsen (1828–1906) and Chekhov (1860–1904).

COMMEDIA DELL'ARTE

PEKING OPERA

3500 B.C.–A.D. 1380	1380–1840s

c. 3500 B.C. The oldest known writing, marks on clay tablets, are made at the Sumerian city of Uruk.
3300 B.C. Egyptians write in hieroglyphs (picture writing).
c. 2000 B.C. The Sumerian epic *Gilgamesh* is recorded on clay tablets.
c. 800 B.C. The Greek writer Homer writes *The Iliad.*
600 B.C. The Greek writer Aesop writes his fables, which include the story of *The Boy Who Cried Wolf* and *The Crow and Pitcher.*

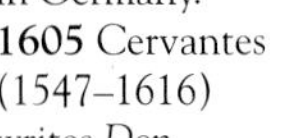
AESOP'S FABLES

500 B.C. Hindu *Bhagavadgita* written.
200 B.C. Greeks invent parchment.
c. 30–19 B.C. Roman writer Virgil writes *The Aeneid.*
A.D. 105 Chinese invent paper.
868 Earliest printed book, the Chinese *Diamond Sutra.*
1007 In Japan, Murasaki Shikibu (973–1014) writes *The Tale of Genji,* the world's first novel.
1048–1123 Persian poet Omar Khayyam writes *The Rubáiyát.*
1190–1320 Icelandic saga (oral tales) written down.
1321 Dante (1265–1321) writes his *Divine Comedy* in Ravenna, Italy.
c. 1350 Boccaccio (1313–75) writes *The Decameron* in Florence.

c. 1387 Chaucer (1343–1400) writes *The Canterbury Tales* in Windsor Castle.
c. 1450 Johann Gutenberg (1390–1468) invents printing by movable type in Germany.

GUTENBERG'S BIBLE

1605 Cervantes (1547–1616) writes *Don Quixote,* a satire about an elderly Spanish knight.
1667 English poet Milton (1608–74) writes *Paradise Lost.*
1697 French author Charles Perrault (1628–1703) writes *Tales of Mother Goose.*
1719 English writer Daniel Defoe (1660–1731) writes *Robinson Crusoe.*
1808 German poet Goethe (1749–1832) writes *Faust.*
1811–1817 Jane Austen (1775–1817) writes *Pride and Prejudice, Emma,* and other novels.
1818 Mary Shelley (1797–1851) writes *Frankenstein.*
1830s French novelist Balzac (1799–1850) writes *Père Goriot.*
1841 American writer Edgar Allen Poe (1809–49) writes *Murders in the Rue Morgue,* the first detective story.
1840–70 Charles Dickens (1812–70) writes *Great Expectations, Oliver Twist,* and other novels, often in parts that were serialized in magazines of the time.

1840s–1869	1900–TODAY

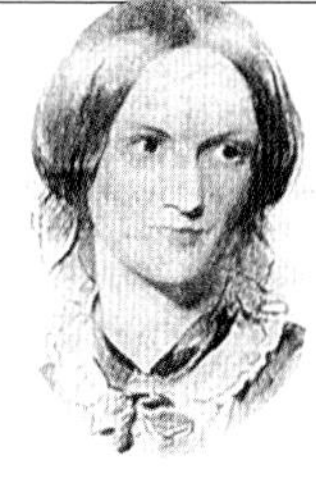
CHARLOTTE BRONTË

1840s Charlotte Brontë (1816–1855) writes *Jane Eyre*, her sister Emily (1818–1848) *Wuthering Heights*.
1851 American writer Herman Melville (1819–1891) writes *Moby Dick*.
1852 American writer Harriet Beecher Stowe (1811–1896) writes *Uncle Tom's Cabin* about the injustice of slavery.
1857 French author Gustave Flaubert (1821–1880) writes *Madame Bovary*.
1862 French author Victor Hugo (1802–1885) writes *Les Misérables*.
1864 French author Jules Verne (1828–1905) writes *Journey to the Center of the Earth*.
1865–72 Russian writer Tolstoy (1828–1910) writes *War and Peace*.
1866 Russian writer Dostoyevsky (1821–1881) writes *Crime and Punishment*.
1867 French writer Émile Zola (1840–1902) writes *Thérèse Raquin*.
1873 The first typewriter is made in the US by the Remington company.
1881 American author Henry James (1843–1916) writes *Portrait of a Lady*.
1883 Robert Louis Stevenson (1850–1894) writes *Treasure Island*.
1894 Rudyard Kipling (1865–1936) writes *The Jungle Book*.
1926 A.A. Milne (1882–1956) writes *Winnie-the-Pooh*.
1870–1900 Thomas Hardy (1840–1928) writes many novels and poems.
1913 Indian poet Rabindranath Tagore (1861–1941) writes *Gitanjali*.
1913 D. H. Lawrence (1885–1930) writes *Sons and Lovers*.
1917 Czech writer Franz Kafka (1883–1924) writes *The Trial*.
1922 Publication of French writer Marcel Proust's (1871–1922) *Remembrance of Things Past*; Irish writer James Joyce's (1882–1941) writes *Ulysses*.
1925 American writer F. Scott Fitzgerald (1896–1940) writes *The Great Gatsby*.
1929 Ernest Hemingway (1899–1961) writes *A Farewell to Arms*.
1935 Paperback books go on sale.
1943 Dutch Jewish girl Anne Frank (1929–1945) writes her diary.
1954 J. R. R. Tolkein (1892–1973) writes *The Lord of the Rings*.

EARLY PAPERBACKS

1967 Colombian author Gabriel García Marquez (b. 1928) writes *One Hundred Years of solitude*.
1970s Desktop publishing arrives.
1986 First CD-ROM book.
1997 J. K. Rowling (b. 1958) writes *Harry Potter and the Sorcerer's Stone*.

J. K. ROWLING

PHOTOGRAPHY

MILLIONS OF TIMES a day, a camera shutter clicks somewhere in the world to take a photograph, making an instant visual record of a scene, whether it is just a family snapshot or a dramatic news picture.

35MM ROLL FILM

FILM FORMATS

Cameras are built to suit particular film formats (sizes). The most popular format is 35mm, which is used in most compacts and SLRs. Studio photographers often use a medium format for extra quality.

INSIDE AN SLR CAMERA

The type of camera most popular with serious amateurs and many professional photographers is the SLR, or Single Lens Reflex. The SLR has a prism that reflects light from the lens to the eyepiece, allowing the photographer to see directly through the camera lens. It also has interchangeable lenses.

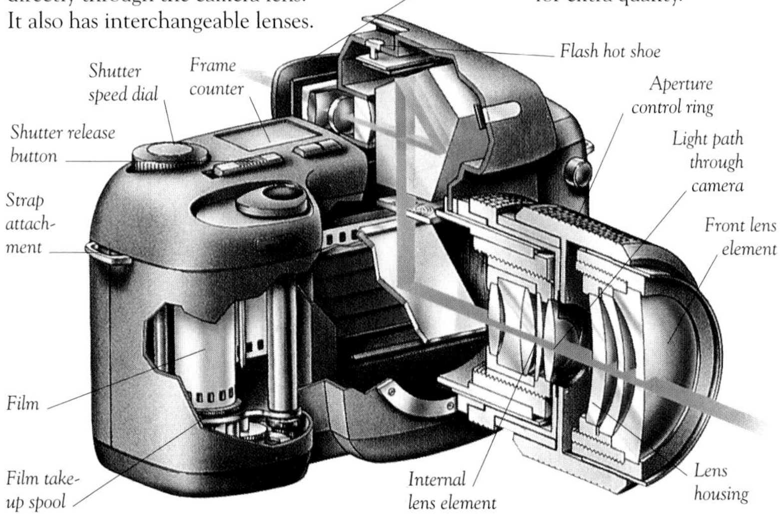
Rear viewfinder
Flash hot shoe
Shutter speed dial
Frame counter
Aperture control ring
Shutter release button
Light path through camera
Strap attachment
Front lens element
Film
Film take-up spool
Internal lens element
Lens housing

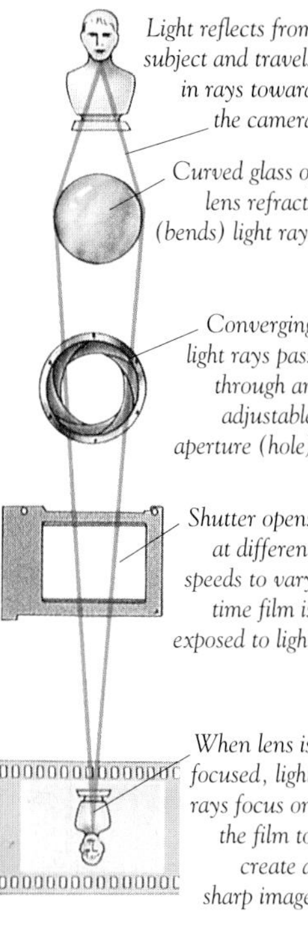
Light reflects from subject and travels in rays toward the camera
Curved glass of lens refracts (bends) light rays
Converging light rays pass through an adjustable aperture (hole)
Shutter opens at different speeds to vary time film is exposed to light
When lens is focused, light rays focus on the film to create a sharp image

LIGHT INSIDE A CAMERA

A camera is essentially a lightproof box with a hole at the front holding a glass lens. The lens projects a bright, sharp picture of the world into the camera where it is recorded on film, or, in electronic cameras (such as videos), on light-sensitive cells.

PHOTOGRAPHY TIMELINE

18TH-CENTURY CAMERA OBSCURA

400 B.C. Chinese scholar uses a pinhole in silk to project an image in a darkened room.

A.D. 1020 Arab scholar Alhazen describes how a pinhole in a camera obscura (dark room) can be used to view solar eclipses.

1558 Battista della Porta puts a lens in the pinhole to sharpen the image.

1560–1860 Camera obscuras become common in public buildings.

1700s Portable camera obscuras made for artists.

1727 Johann Schulze (1687–1744) shows how silver nitrate darkens when exposed to light.

c. 1800 Tom Wedgwood makes images by exposing paper coated with silver salts to the light.

1826 First photo made by Joseph Niepce (1765–1833) on a pewter plate in a camera obscura.

1839 Daguerreotype, first practical photographic process, invented by Frenchman Louis Daguerre (1800–1877).

1839 Fox Talbot (1800–1877) creates negatives using Calotype process, enabling copies of photos to be made.

1851 Archer's (1813–1857) Collodion allows paper prints to be made from glass negatives.

1861 Maxwell (1831–1879) makes first color photo.

1888 First Kodak camera, using roll film.

1906 First practical color photo process invented by French Lumière brothers.

1913 35-mm film invented.

1924 The Leica, the first successful 35-mm camera.

EARLY COLOR FILM

1935 Kodachrome color transparency film.

1947 Fist instant camera invented by Land (1909–1991) marketed as Polaroid.

1994 First electronic still and video camera launched.

2000 Digital cameras become popular.

CINEMA

ARNOLD SCHWARZENEGGER IN *TERMINATOR 2*

MOVIES ARE now a multimillion-dollar business, with people all over the world going to the movies to see feature films. Many high-budget films use complex special effects as well as "movie stars" to attract audiences.

FILM

Most movies are now recorded on 35mm film. All the pictures on the film are still, but they are run through the projector so quickly – eight frames, or pictures, a second – that we see only continuous movement on the screen. One full-length feature movie uses 1.5 miles (2.5 km) of film.

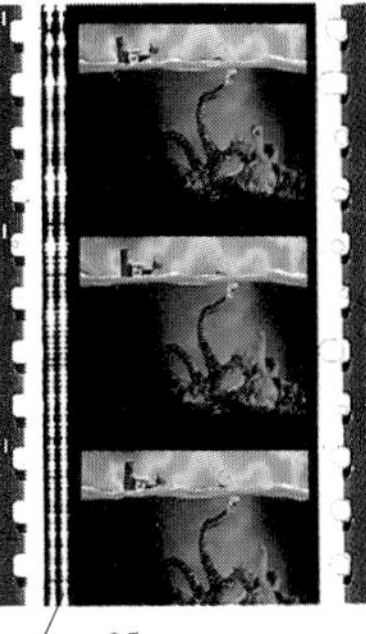

9.5-mm film introduced by French Pathé company in 1922 for amateur films

Sound track

35MM FILM

FILM GENRES

Most feature films fall into one of several categories or "genres," including romantic comedy (*Notting Hill*), fantasy (*Lord of the Rings*), science fiction (*The Matrix*), action (*Saving Private Ryan*), or horror (*Interview with the Vampire*).

SPECIAL EFFECTS

Computer technology has dramatically increased the scope of special effects, allowing techniques such as morphing.

The points of both the hand and the spider are plotted on the computer. When the two sets of points coincide, the transformation is complete.

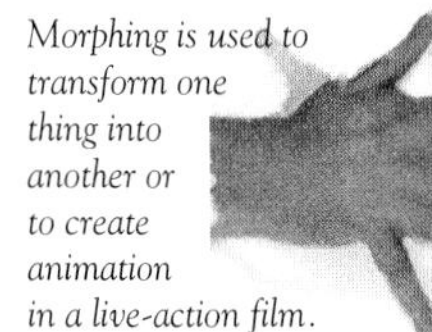

Morphing is used to transform one thing into another or to create animation in a live-action film.

The outline of the spider is just visible.

The midpoint of the morphing process.

The spider is almost complete.

ANIMATION

By filming drawings or models in different positions, animators can bring them to life. Computer-generated animation can produce very sophisticated animation sequences, such as those seen in *Toy Story*.

Bugs Bunny is one of the oldest cartoon characters.

Plasticine models can be moved to animate them, like this gorilla from Creature Comforts.

MOVIE TIMELINE

1879 The Zoogyroscope is developed by English photographer Eadweard Muybridge (1830–1914). It projects images of photographic sequences onto a screen in quick succession, creating an illusion of movement.

1881 Frenchman Étienne Marey (1830–1904) invents a camera that takes pictures on a revolving plate.

1894 Kinetograph (film camera) and Kinetoscope (film viewer) marketed by Americans Thomas Edison (1847–1931) and W.K. Dickson (1860–1933).

1895 French Lumière brothers show the first real movie in a movie theater in Paris.

1895 The world's first cinema opens in Atlanta, Georgia.

1913 Hollywood's first feature film, *Squaw Man*, made by Jesse Lasky (1880–1958), Cecil B. de Mille (1881–1959), and Samuel Goldwyn (1882–1974). Early films are in black and white and silent.

1920–1930s Picture palaces at the peak of their popularity.

1927 *The Jazz Singer* is the first movie with sound.

JAZZ SINGER POSTER

1929 The first Oscars.

1932 Technicolor invented.

1953 Wide-screen image created by Cinemascope.

1970 Steadycam allows camera operator to move while holding camera steady.

1990s–2000s Movies are increasingly dominated by computer-generated animations and special effects.

OSCAR

THE OLYMPIC GAMES

HELD EVERY FOUR YEARS, the modern Games began in 1896 as the brainchild of French scholar Pierre de Coubertin, who was inspired by stories of the ancient Greek games. Separate Winter Olympics have been staged since 1924, and Special Oympics for the disabled since 1960.

OLYMPIC FLAME
Following ancient Greek tradition, the Olympics are still started by a torch, which is lit on Mount Olympus in Greece and carried by runners in relays to the Olympic stadium.

OLYMPIC SYMBOL
The five Olympic rings represent the five continents of the world. Some 200 nations send more than 10,000 entrants to compete in nearly 30 different sports.

OLIVE WREATH
In the ancient Greek games, 2,000 years ago, winners were crowned with a sacred olive wreath.

PARALYMPICS
Like the Olympics, the Special Olympics for disabled people are held every four years.

OLYMPIC MEDALS
In the modern Olympics, individuals and teams compete for gold (first), silver (second), and bronze (third) medals.

GOLD MEDAL FROM THE 1984 GAMES

WINTER OLYMPICS
The Winter Games, held two years after the Summer Olympics include skiing, figure and speed skating, and ice hockey.

Classification of sports

The many different types of sports can be classified into three basic groups, which can then be subdivided further.

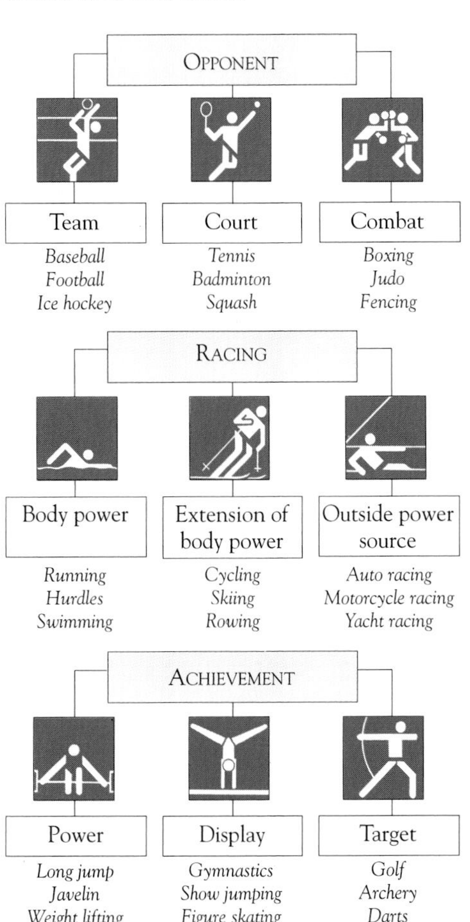

Opponent
Team
Baseball
Football
Ice hockey
Court
Tennis
Badminton
Squash
Combat
Boxing
Judo
Fencing
Racing
Body power
Running
Hurdles
Swimming
Extension of body power
Cycling
Skiing
Rowing
Outside power source
Auto racing
Motorcycle racing
Yacht racing
Achievement
Power
Long jump
Javelin
Weight lifting
Display
Gymnastics
Show jumping
Figure skating
Target
Golf
Archery
Darts

Summer Olympic venues

Year	Venue
1896	Athens, Greece
1900	Paris, France
1904	St. Louis, US
1908	London, UK
1912	Stockholm, Sweden
1920	Antwerp, Belgium
1924	Paris, France
1928	Amsterdam, Holland
1932	Los Angeles, CA
1936	Berlin, Germany
1948	London, UK
1952	Helsinki, Finland
1956	Melbourne, Australia
1960	Rome, Italy
1964	Tokyo, Japan
1968	Mexico City, Mexico
1972	Munich, Germany
1976	Montreal, Canada
1980	Moscow, USSR
1984	Los Angeles, CA
1988	Seoul, South Korea
1992	Barcelona, Spain
1996	Atlanta, GA
2000	Sydney, Australia
2004	Athens, Greece
2008	Beijing, China

BALL GAMES

MANY TEAM GAMES are played with a large, inflated ball. Soccer, volleyball, and basketball are played with a round ball, American football and rugby with an oval ball.

FOOTBALL

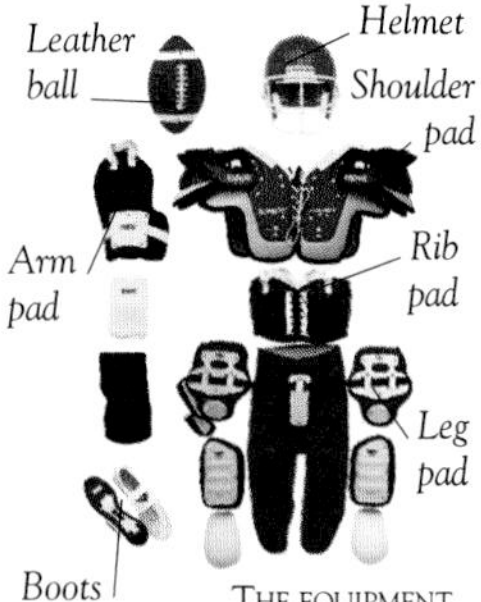
Leather ball
Helmet
Shoulder pad
Arm pad
Rib pad
Leg pad
Boots
THE EQUIPMENT

THE GAME

American football is a tough game of running, passing, and body-tackling. The field is divided into strips. When a team has the ball, it tries to advance the ball strip by strip in a series of "downs."

THE SNAP

Each down starts with a snap, as the center passes the ball back to the quarterback, who sets up a play by throwing a pass or slipping the ball to a running back.

SOCCER

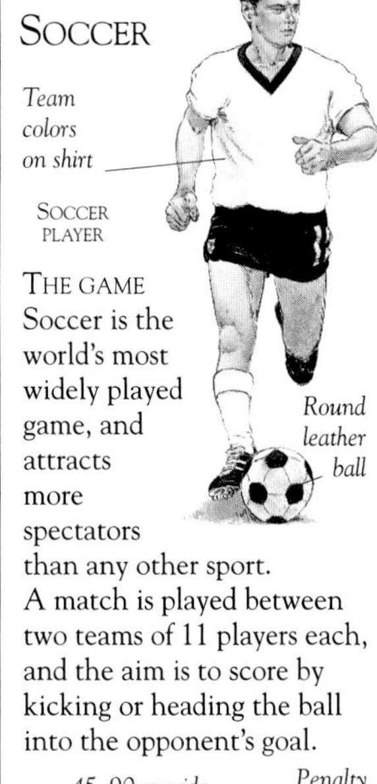
Team colors on shirt
Round leather ball
SOCCER PLAYER

THE GAME

Soccer is the world's most widely played game, and attracts more spectators than any other sport. A match is played between two teams of 11 players each, and the aim is to score by kicking or heading the ball into the opponent's goal.

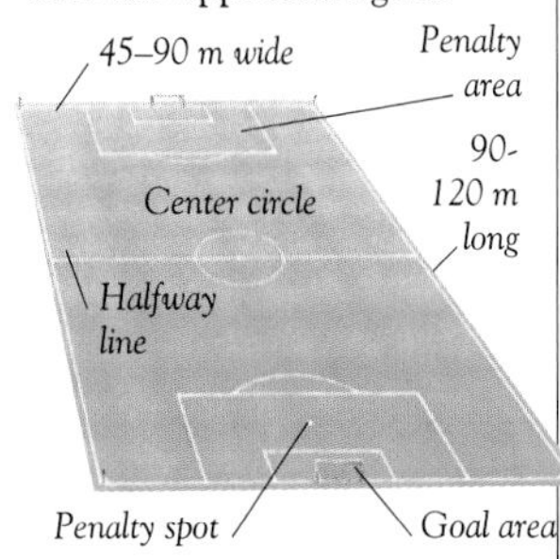
45–90 m wide
Penalty area
90-120 m long
Center circle
Halfway line
Penalty spot
Goal area

THE FIELD

Soccer fields are almost always of grass and vary in size, but penalty areas are always the same.

Volleyball

Two teams of six players use their hands and arms to knock a ball over a net. A point is won if the ball lands in the opposition's court or if they fail to return it. The high net means players must jump high.

OVERHAND SERVE
Forearms or fingers are used to knock the ball up, ready for the spike.
UNDERHAND SERVE
PREPARING TO SPIKE (SMASH)
A team may touch the ball up to three times before returning it.
FOREARM PASS (DIG)

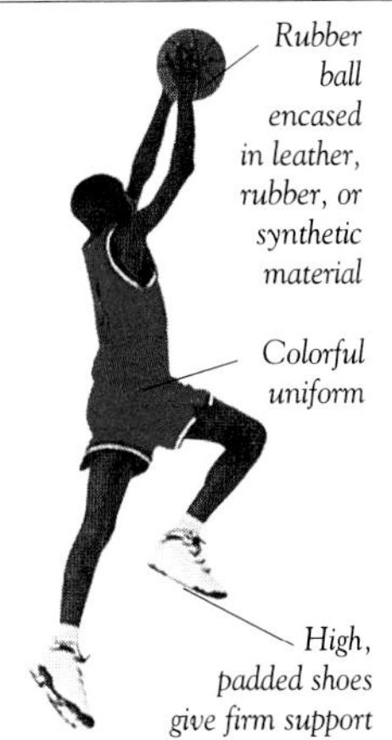
Rubber ball encased in leather, rubber, or synthetic material
Colorful uniform
High, padded shoes give firm support

Basketball

In this fast, popular game, teams of five dribble the ball with their hands or pass and compete to throw the ball into the opponents' net.

Rugby

Rugby Union has teams of 15 players; Rugby League has 13. Both games involve running, passing, and body-tackling. In Union, play often restarts with a scrum in which forwards interlock and try to push each other over the ball.

Scrum breaks when ball is cleared

RUGBY UNION SCRUM

Australian Rules

This 18-a-side game, developed in Melbourne c. 1858, is played on an oval field in four quarters of 25 minutes each. Players kick, handpass, and run with the oval ball.

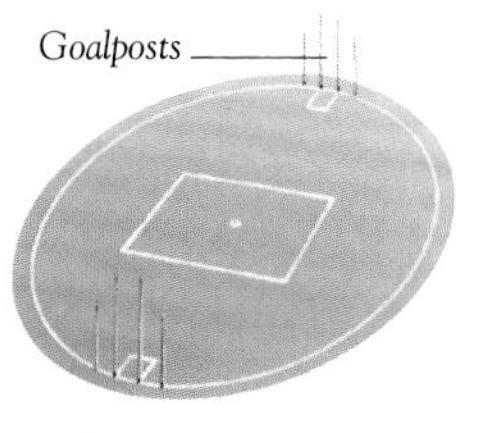
Goalposts

AUSTRALIAN RULES FIELD

STICK AND BALL GAMES

MANY OF THE WORLD'S most popular games involve hitting a small ball with a stick, a bat, or a racket.

BASEBALL

PITCH AND STRIKE

Two teams of nine take it in turns batting and fielding. The batter has three attempts to hit the ball thrown by the pitcher, then run around all the bases before the ball is fielded.

THE FIELD

The batter can only run if the ball lands within "fair territory," which consists of the infield (inside the bases) and the outfield.

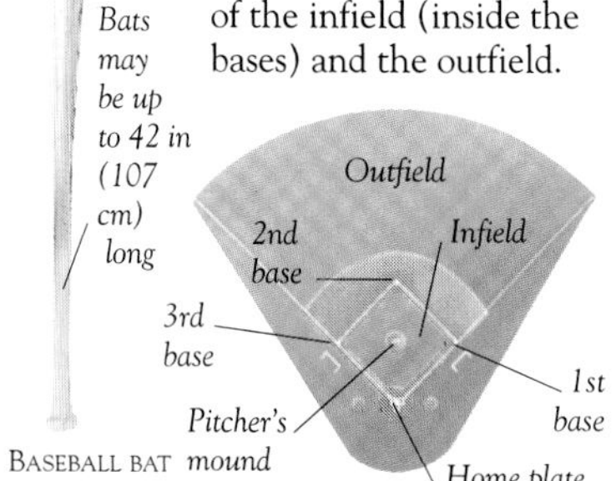
Outfield
2nd base
Infield
3rd base
Pitcher's mound
1st base
Home plate

Bats may be up to 42 in (107 cm) long

BASEBALL BAT

CRICKET

BATTING

Cricket is an 11-a-side game. Two batsmen are in at any one time. The batsman stands at the crease and defends the wicket with the bat as the ball is bowled. He must try to hit the ball to score runs.

DISMISSING THE BATSMAN

BOWLED

The ball hits the wicket. If the batsman blocks a ball with his body he is "leg before wicket."

Wicket

Crease

RUN OUT

The fielders team hit a wicket before the batsmen return.

STUMPED

The batsman leaves the crease, and the fielders hit the wicket.

Batsman tries to hit ball

Hockey and lacrosse

Hockey

Two teams of 11 use a stick to drive the ball into their opponent's goal. Goalkeepers have to be protected from the ball, which can travel at 100 mph (160 km/h).

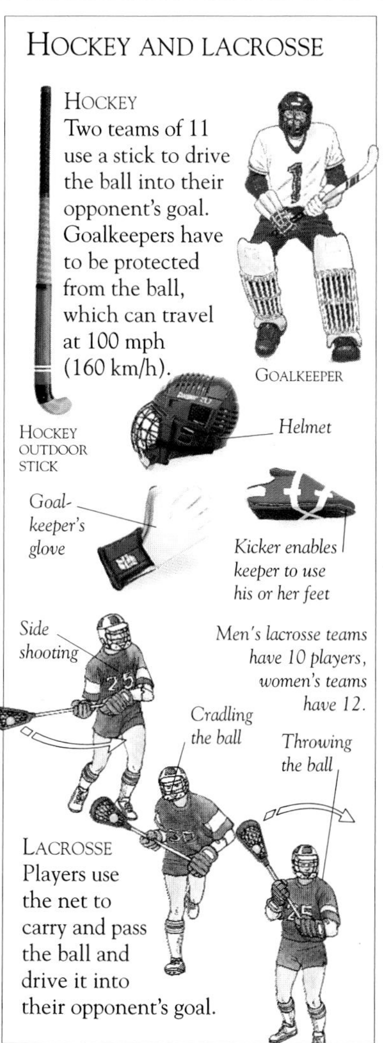

Helmet
Goal-keeper's glove
Kicker enables keeper to use his or her feet
Side shooting
Cradling the ball
Throwing the ball

GOALKEEPER

HOCKEY OUTDOOR STICK

Men's lacrosse teams have 10 players, women's teams have 12.

Lacrosse

Players use the net to carry and pass the ball and drive it into their opponent's goal.

Racket games

Tennis

Players use a racket to hit a ball over a net so that the ball lands in the opposite court and cannot be returned. Matches are played in sets of games, with a maximum of five sets for men and three for women. The court may be grass or clay. A doubles court is bigger than a singles court.

TENNIS RACKET

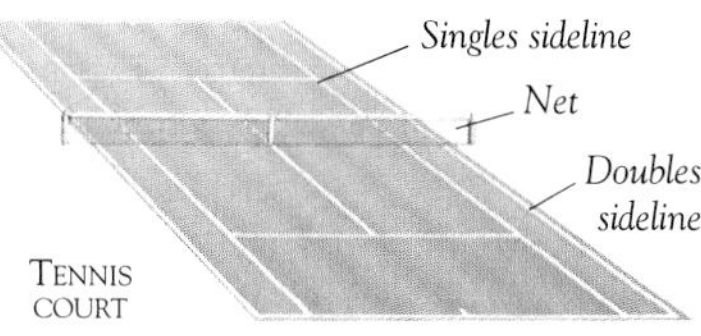

Singles sideline
Net
Doubles sideline

TENNIS COURT

Squash

A squash game is played in an enclosed court. Players aim to hit the ball onto one or more walls so their opponent cannot hit it before it bounces twice on the floor. Games are played to nine points, matches to the best of three or five games.

SQUASH

COMPETITION SPORTS

ATHLETICS AND sports like gymnastics and weight lifting are based on individual prowess.

TRACK EVENTS
Most running events take place on the track.

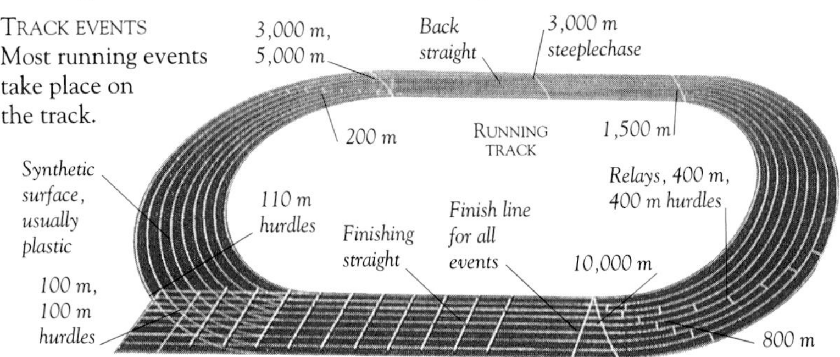
3,000 m,
5,000 m
Back straight
3,000 m steeplechase
200 m
RUNNING TRACK
1,500 m
Synthetic surface, usually plastic
110 m hurdles
Finishing straight
Finish line for all events
Relays, 400 m, 400 m hurdles
10,000 m
100 m, 100 m hurdles
800 m

FIELD EVENTS

These include jumping events, such as long jump, triple jump, high jump, and pole vault, and throwing events, such as the shot, discus, hammer, and javelin. Women do not take part in the pole vault or hammer in the Olympics.

THE SHOT
The athlete puts (throws) from the shoulder and must not step out of the circle.

THE DISCUS
Usually thrown after a couple of wind-up swings and a full turn.

THE JAVELIN
The throw is measured to where the point first touches the ground.

THE HAMMER
This metal ball on a wire is hurled after 3 or 4 full turns.

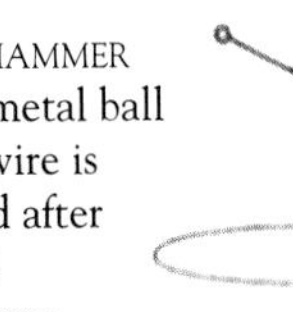

TRIPLE JUMP
This consists of a hop, step, and jump, starting with a run-up and ending in a sandpit.

HOP

Combined events

First day	Second day
Decathlon (men)	
100 m race	110 m hurdle
Long jump	Discus
Shot put	Pole vault
High jump	Javelin
400 m race	1500 m race
Heptathlon (women)	
100 m hurdle	Long jump
High jump	Javelin
Shot put	800 m race
200 m race	

Weight lifting

There are two categories: snatch, and clean and jerk.

Gymnastics

Gymnastics consists of exercises on the floor, beam, rings, uneven, parallel, and horizontal bars, vaulting horse, and pommel horse. Judges award marks out of ten for the gymnast's performance at the exercise. Rhythmic gymnastics for women is performed to music with ribbons, balls, ropes, clubs, or hoops.

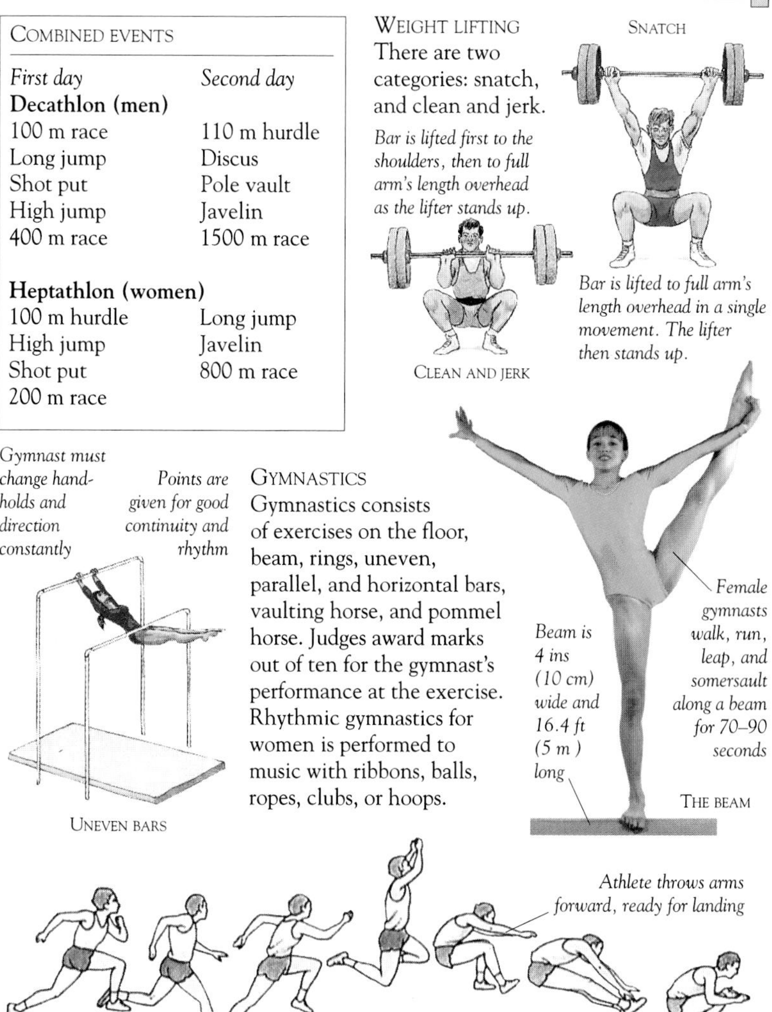
Snatch
Bar is lifted first to the shoulders, then to full arm's length overhead as the lifter stands up.
Clean and jerk
Bar is lifted to full arm's length overhead in a single movement. The lifter then stands up.
Gymnast must change hand-holds and direction constantly
Points are given for good continuity and rhythm
Uneven bars
Beam is 4 ins (10 cm) wide and 16.4 ft (5 m) long
Female gymnasts walk, run, leap, and somersault along a beam for 70–90 seconds
The beam
Athlete throws arms forward, ready for landing
Step
Jump

WINTER SPORTS

THE SLIPPERINESS of snow and ice has inspired a range of winter sports, from the grace of figure skating to the thrill of downhill skiing.

SPEED SKATING
In long-track racing, two skaters race against the clock on an outdoor 400 m track. In short-track racing, four or six skaters race each other round a 111.12 m indoor track.

SPEED SKATER

ICE HOCKEY PLAYER

ICE HOCKEY
Ice hockey is a fast and furious six-a-side game in three 20-minute periods. The aim is to shoot the hard rubber puck into the opposition's goal.

FIGURE SKATING
Marks out of six are given for artistic and technical merit. In spins, the skater should stay exactly on the spot. Names of jumps depend on take off and landing: axel, salchow, loop, and lutz.

One leg lifted behind and held parallel to ice
Skater spins once or twice in the air.

CAMEL SPIN

LUTZ JUMP

Blocking pad
Catch glove
Leg pad

THE GOALKEEPER
Goalkeepers need a lot of extra protection from the puck, which travels at high speed.

Jumpers speed down a ramp and leap into the air for a distance of 70–90 m.

SKI JUMPER

Skier adopts a streamlined shape for speed and distance through the air

Points are awarded for style as well as distance.

NORDIC SKIING

This includes ski-jumping and cross-country skiing, which involves short uphill sections. The biathlon involves cross-country skiing and rifle shooting at targets.

CROSS-COUNTRY SKIER

Skiers use freestyle (like a skater) or classical (diagonal stride).

Bindings allow heel to lift off ski

Narrower, shorter ski than Alpine skis

ALPINE SKIING

This type of skiing involves slalom and downhill races, which are all run against the clock, and freestyle, which is judged on style and technique. In downhill racing, each skier races once; slalom and giant slalom are decided on the combined time for two runs.

In downhill, skiers hurtle down a set route at speeds of up to 86 mph (140 km/h).

In slalom, skiers zigzag between red and blue flags without knocking them down.

Freestyle skiers perform acrobatics by jumping off "moguls" (snow bumps) and ramps.

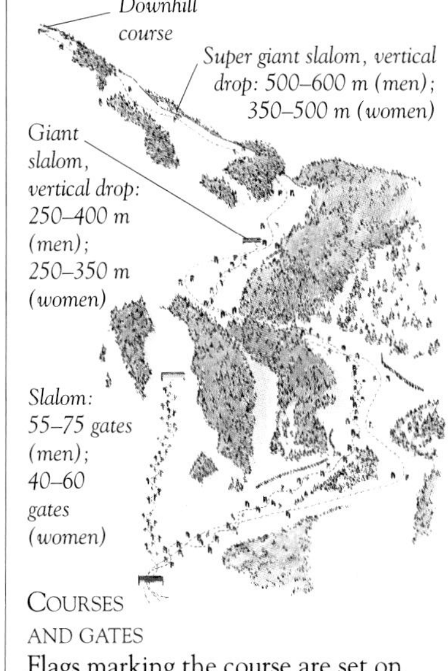

Downhill course

Super giant slalom, vertical drop: 500–600 m (men); 350–500 m (women)

Giant slalom, vertical drop: 250–400 m (men); 250–350 m (women)

Slalom: 55–75 gates (men); 40–60 gates (women)

COURSES AND GATES

Flags marking the course are set on single poles for slalom gates, double poles for giant, and super giant slalom.

WATER SPORTS

THE POPULARITY of water sports, both indoors in pools and outdoors on rivers, lakes, and the sea, has increased greatly in recent years.

WINDSURFING
Also called board-sailing, windsurfing uses a sailboard with a swiveling sail that propels and steers the board. The windsurfer holds the boom which surrounds and supports the sail.

Mast

Sail

Window

Boom

Board

Universal joint swivels in all directions

Wet suits protect against cold
Boards are usually made of fiberglass

SURFING
Surfing is a spectacular sport in which surfers paddle out to sea on boards and ride big breakers back to shore. In competition, surfers are judged for style, grace, and timing.

YACHT TYPES

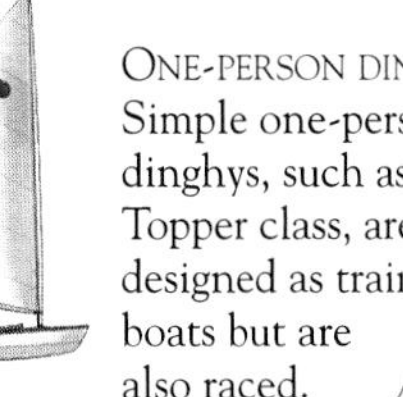

ONE-PERSON DINGHY
Simple one-person dinghys, such as the Topper class, are designed as training boats but are also raced.

TWO-PERSON BOAT WITH TRAPEZE
A two-person boat, such as the 470 class, is used in Olympic racing.

CATAMARAN
Twin-hulled, two-person catamarans , such as the Tornado class, also sail in Olympic races.

TWO-PERSON DINGHY
A two-person dinghy, such as the Flying Dutchman class, is used for training and racing.

OCEAN-GOING YACHT
An ocean-going yacht, such as the12 m class, sail heavy seas in offshore racing.

SWIMMING STROKES

FRONT CRAWL

This is the fastest stroke and is used in freestyle races.

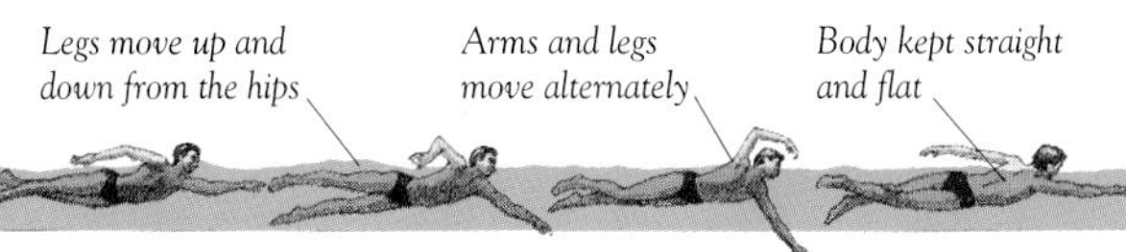
Legs move up and down from the hips
Arms and legs move alternately
Body kept straight and flat

BREASTSTROKE

This is the slowest stroke. Arms and legs stay underwater.

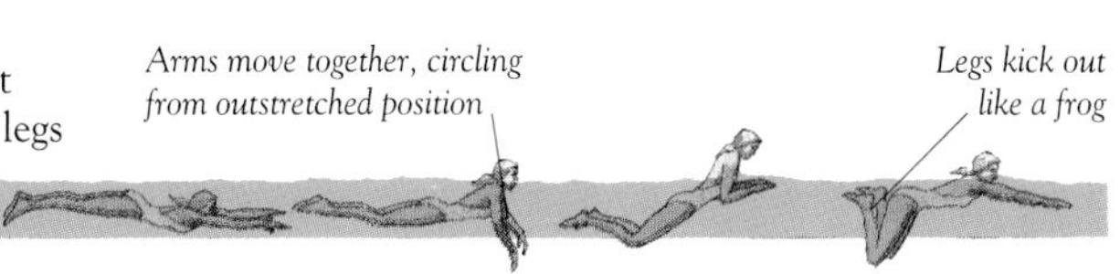
Arms move together, circling from outstretched position
Legs kick out like a frog

BACKSTROKE

This is the only stroke that swimmers start in the water.

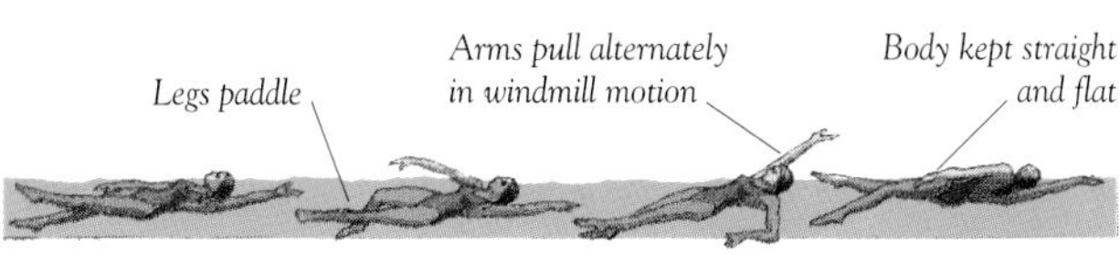
Legs paddle
Arms pull alternately in windmill motion
Body kept straight and flat

BUTTERFLY

Like the breaststroke, this is a symmetrical stroke, but it is very energetic.

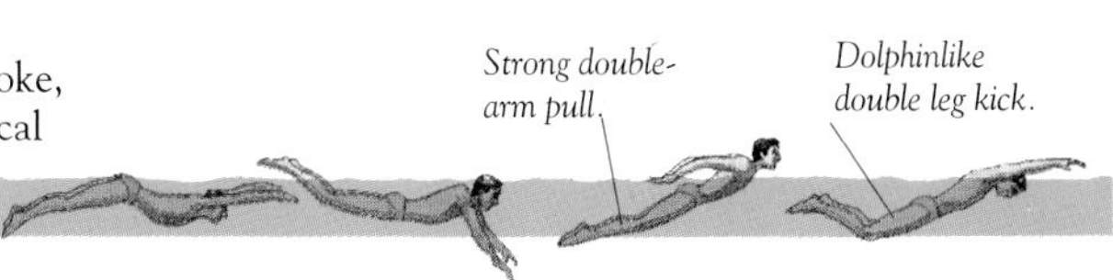
Strong double-arm pull
Dolphinlike double leg kick.

DIVING TYPES

In diving, marks are awarded for springboard (10 ft above the water) and highboard (33 ft). There are over 80 standard dives. Shown here are three of the best known dives.

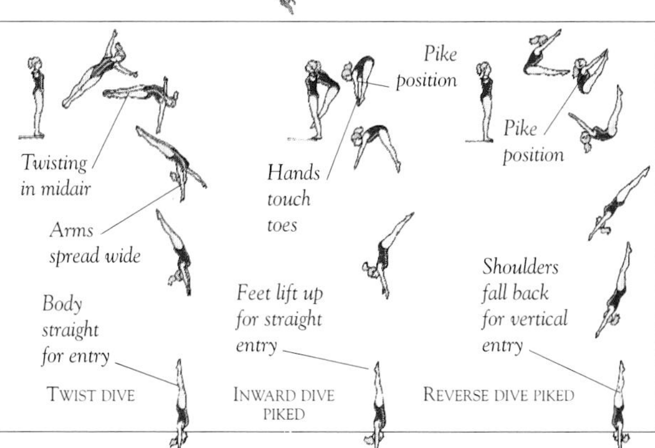
Twisting in midair
Arms spread wide
Body straight for entry
TWIST DIVE
Pike position
Hands touch toes
Feet lift up for straight entry
INWARD DIVE PIKED
Pike position
Shoulders fall back for vertical entry
REVERSE DIVE PIKED

COMBAT SPORTS

BOXING AND WRESTLING are combat sports, as are fencing, archery, and shooting, and the martial arts of East Asia.

MARTIAL ARTS

KARATE

Strikes and kicks are used in karate, which means "empty hands."

AIKIDO

Meaning "the way of all harmony," aikido uses only defensive techniques.

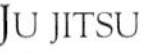

JU JITSU

This is the ancient Japanese fighting art from which judo and aikido developed.

KENDO

Japanese sword-fighting, or kendo, is practised in armour.

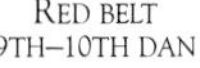

RED BELT
9TH–10TH DAN

BLACK BELT
1ST–5TH DAN

BROWN BELT
1ST KYU

BLUE BELT
2ND KYU

GREEN BELT
3RD KYU

ORANGE BELT
4TH KYU

YELLOW BELT
5TH KYU

JUDO

Competitors in the martial art of Judo, which means "the gentle way", use throws and holds to defeat their opponent. Grades or "belts" range from "kyu" (student) to "dan" (advanced).

BOXING

Governed by strict protective rules, competitors wear gloves. Professional fights are up to 12 three-minute rounds. Amateurs go three rounds.

BOXING WEIGHTS	PROFESSIONAL	AMATEUR
Flyweight	108–112 lb	106–112 lb
Featherweight	122–126 lb	119–126 lb
Lightweight	130–135 lb	126–132 lb
Middleweight	154–160 lb	157–165 lb
Heavyweight	Over 190 lb	179–201 lb

Archery

Archers fire "rounds" of arrows at a target. The number varies with the event. The aim is to hit the center of the target, worth ten points.

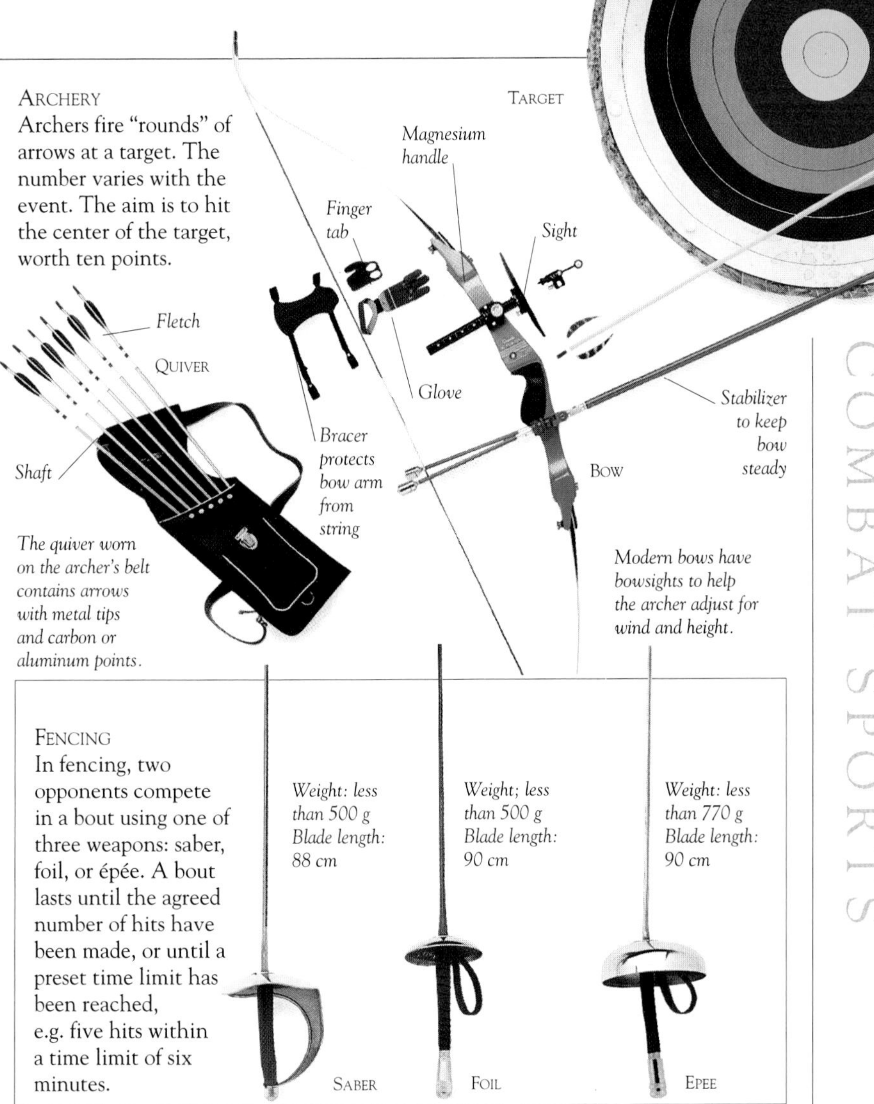

Target
Magnesium handle
Finger tab
Sight
Fletch
Quiver
Glove
Stabilizer to keep bow steady
Bracer protects bow arm from string
Shaft
Bow
Saber
Foil
Epee

The quiver worn on the archer's belt contains arrows with metal tips and carbon or aluminum points.

Modern bows have bowsights to help the archer adjust for wind and height.

Fencing

In fencing, two opponents compete in a bout using one of three weapons: saber, foil, or épée. A bout lasts until the agreed number of hits have been made, or until a preset time limit has been reached, e.g. five hits within a time limit of six minutes.

Weight: less than 500 g Blade length: 88 cm

Weight; less than 500 g Blade length: 90 cm

Weight: less than 770 g Blade length: 90 cm

EQUESTRIAN EVENTS

COMPETITIONS ON HORSEBACK are known as equestrian events. They include racing, show jumping, and eventing. In eventing, the riders' skill is tested as they take their horses through three disciplines over three days: show jumping, speed and endurance, and dressage.

THREE BASIC DRESSAGE PACES

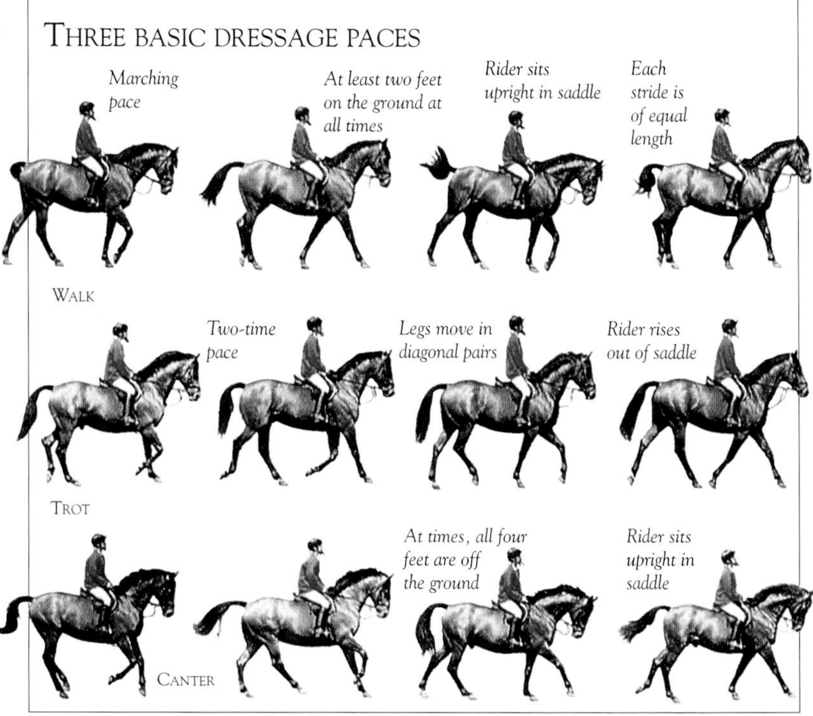
Marching pace
At least two feet on the ground at all times
Rider sits upright in saddle
Each stride is of equal length
WALK
Two-time pace
Legs move in diagonal pairs
Rider rises out of saddle
TROT
At times, all four feet are off the ground
Rider sits upright in saddle
CANTER

SHOW JUMPING
If the horse clips an obstacle, the rider incurs a fault. Riders with fewest faults compete against each other against the clock.

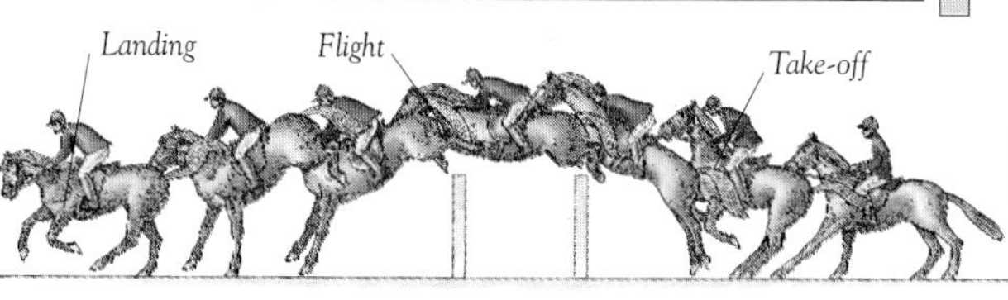
Landing
Flight
Take-off

Rider bends forwards from the hip and straightens on landing.

SHOW JUMPING COURSE

Start *Gate* *Triple bars* *Wall* *Finish*

OBSTACLES
Obstacles must be jumped in a set order between start and finish.

SHOW JUMPING FAULTS

ERROR	FAULT
Fence (or part of) down	4
Foot in water	4
Refusal	3
2nd refusal	6
3rd refusal	Elimination
Fall (horse or rider)	8
Exceeding time allowance	¼ per sec
Jumps taken out of sequence	Elimination

HORSE RACING
There are two kinds of horse racing. A steeplechase, is a race over jumps, such as fences, ditches, and water; other races are over hurdles. Racehorses also race on the Flat. The horses are almost always Thoroughbreds.

JOCKEY'S HELMET
A jockey wears a crash helmet under his or her cap, and carries a whip.

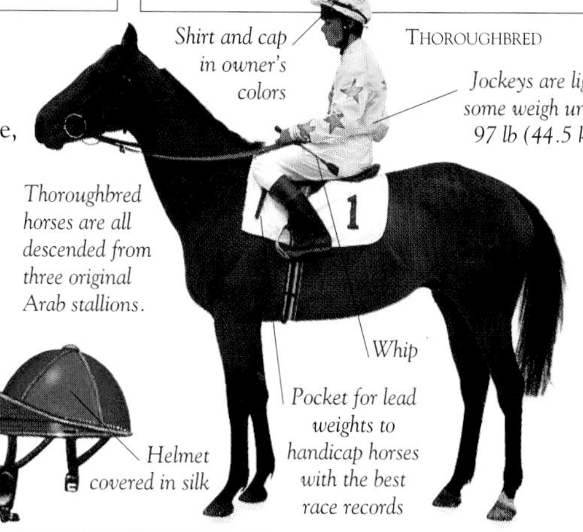
Shirt and cap in owner's colors
THOROUGHBRED
Jockeys are light; some weigh under 97 lb (44.5 kg).
Thoroughbred horses are all descended from three original Arab stallions.
1
Whip
Pocket for lead weights to handicap horses with the best race records
Helmet covered in silk

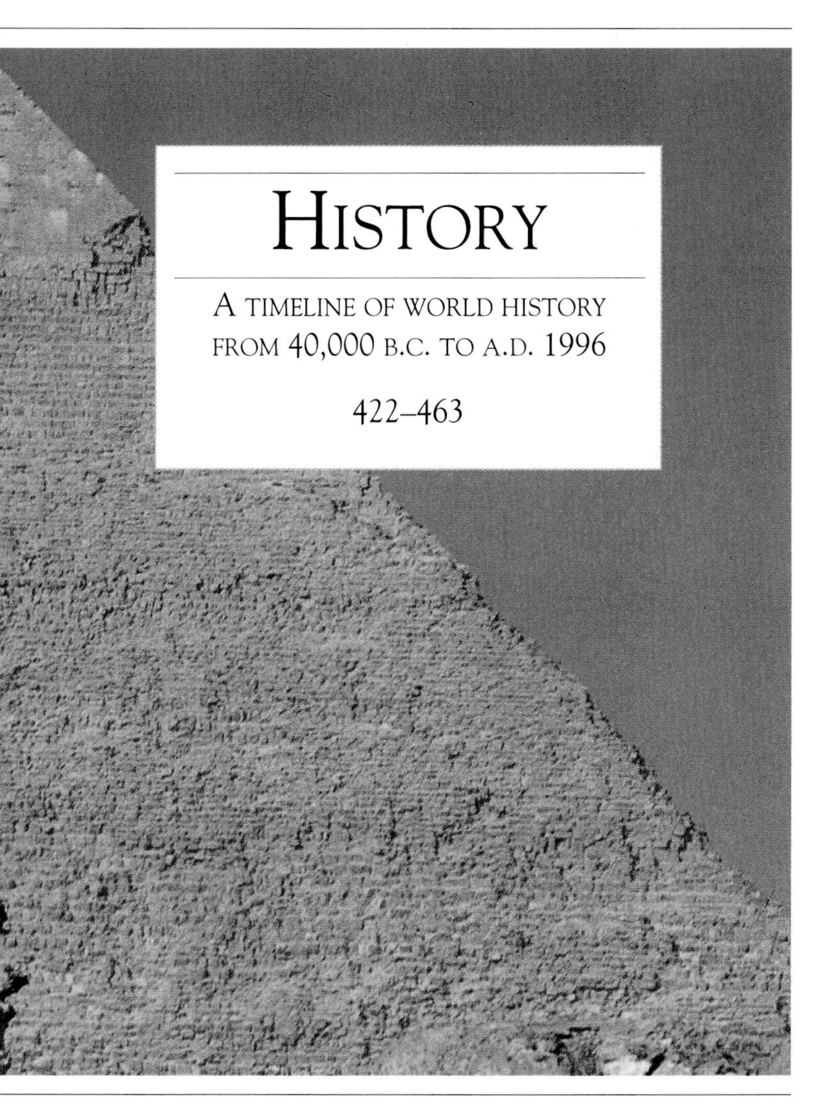

HISTORY

A TIMELINE OF WORLD HISTORY FROM 40,000 B.C. TO A.D. 1996

422–463

	40,000–32,501 B.C.	32,500–25,001 B.C.
AFRICA	**c. 34,000** Hunter-gatherers occupy areas of present-day Lesotho and Zambia.	**30,000** Disappearance of Neanderthals.
ASIA	**40,000** Cro-Magnon humans live in Palestine at Skhül and Kafzel.	**27,000–19,000** Female statuettes called "Venus" figurines, thought to have been used in worship, are made at various sites in Russia, France, and Italy.
EUROPE	**40,000** Neanderthals active in France, at La Chapelle-Aux-Saints, La Ferassie, and La Quina. Cro-Magnons start to spread to Europe. **35,000** Start of Upper Paleolithic Period. Use of flaked stone tools, and bone and horn implements.	**27,000–19,000** Probable date of earliest figurative art in Dordogne, France.
AMERICAS	**35,000** First humans arrive in North America from Asia.	
OCEANIA	**40,000** Probable arrival of Aboriginals in Australia.	

Ostrich
Wild ostriches formed part of the ancient African diet.

"Venus" figurines
These rounded statuettes of female figures may have been symbols of fertility.

Early flint tool

25,000–17,501 B.C.

20,000 The Ice Age causes the world's average temperature to drop and sea levels to lower. Humans have to adapt and work together to survive.

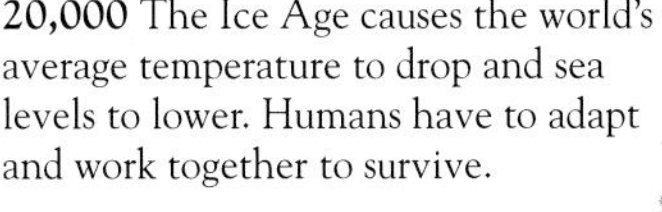

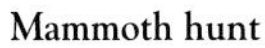

Mammoth hunt
Ice Age people hunted in groups and shared the kill.

17,500–10,001 B.C.

15,000 Last rainy period in northern Africa.

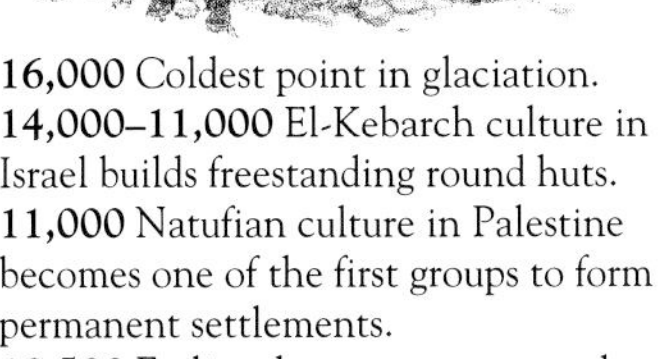

16,000 Coldest point in glaciation.
14,000–11,000 El-Kebarch culture in Israel builds freestanding round huts.
11,000 Natufian culture in Palestine becomes one of the first groups to form permanent settlements.
10,500 Earliest-known pottery produced, Fukui cave, Japan.

Natufian huts
The mud, reed, and timber huts of the Natufians were often used to store grain.

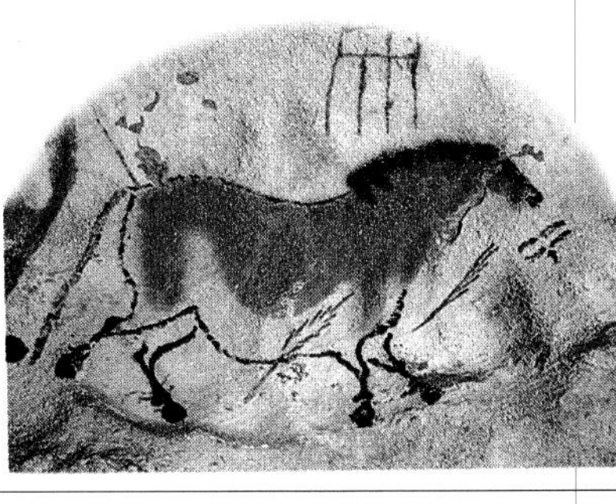

15,000 Wall paintings made in caves at Lascaux, France.
15,000–10,000 High point of art produced by Magdalenian culture.
12,500 Magdalenian toolmakers make the first bone and antler harpoons and fishing spears.
11,000 Cave paintings created at Altamira, Spain.

The origins of art
Early artists painted images of animals and humans on the walls of caves.

25,000–17,501 B.C.	17,500–10,001 B.C.
25,000 Cave dwellers present in Brazil.	**15,000** First Brazilian cave art.
24,000 Earliest-known cremation at Lake Mungo, New South Wales, Australia.	**16,000** Cave art, north coast of Australia.

	10,000–8501 B.C.	8500–7001 B.C.
AFRICA	**10,000** Hunting camps established in Sahara region after Ice Age ends.	**8500** Earliest Saharan rock paintings. **8000** Pottery made in Sahara region.
ASIA	**9000–8000** Wheat and barley grown in Jordan and Syria. Pottery produced at Mureybet, Syria. Goats and sheep domesticated in Iran and Jordan.	**8000** Jericho, the first town, appears. Ice Age ends in Far East. **7500** Pigs domesticated in Crimea.
EUROPE	**10,000** Ice cap retreats.	**8300** Retreat of glaciers.
AMERICAS	**10,000** First people reach southern tip of South America. **9000** Clovis hunter-gatherers in the Great Plains of North America begin to hunt bison.	**8500** Wild grasses and beans cultivated in Peru. **8000** Semipermanent settlements established in North America.
OCEANIA	**10,000** Tasmania separated from Australia as sea level rises.	

Early farming *Grain crops were first cultivated in the Middle East in 8000 B.C.*

Domesticated pig *The modern pig evolved from the wild boar, domesticated by early farmers.*

Jericho Tower *The ancient town of Jericho was strongly built to last, with a stone wall, tower, and defensive ditch.*

North American bison

7000–5501 **B.C.**	5500–4001 **B.C.**
6500 Cattle domesticated. **7000–6000** Discovery that heating certain rocks (ores) releases pure metal that can then be shaped or molded occurs. 	 **Early metal-workers**
7000–6500 Oxen domesticated in eastern Mediterranean. **6500–5700** Important early town forms at Çatal Hüyuk, Turkey. Its houses are built of mud brick and share walls. **6200** Copper smelted in Turkey. 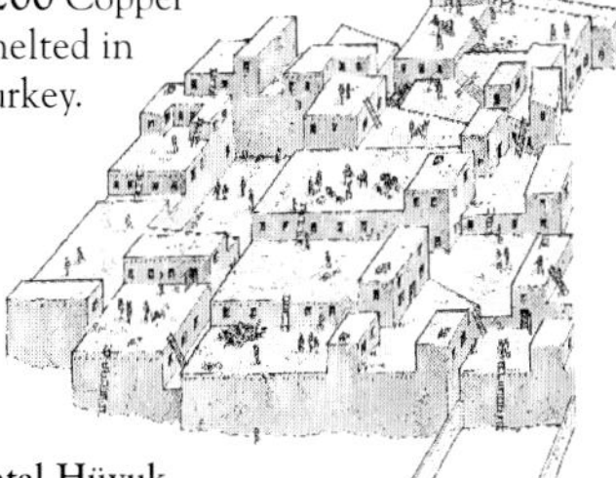 **Çatal Hüyuk**	**5000** Irrigation in Mesopotamia. Rice farming in China. Ubaid culture in Mesopotamia. **4500** Farming around Ganges River in India. **4400** Horses domesticated in Russia.
6500 Britain separated from mainland as ice melts. **6500** First farming communities established in southeastern Europe.	**5000** Farming begins in western Europe. Gold and copper used in Balkans. **4500** First megalithic chamber tombs built in Portugal and in Brittany, France. Their remains (dolmens) show a great knowledge of engineering. **Dolmens at Carnac** *Upright stones placed in a row and roofed to form a covered walk can be seen at Carnac, Brittany.* 
6500 Potatoes cultivated in Peru.	**c. 5000–4000** First settlements form at Anåhuac, Mexico. Corn grown in Mexico. Pyramid temples built in Peru.
6000 New Guinea separated from Australia.	

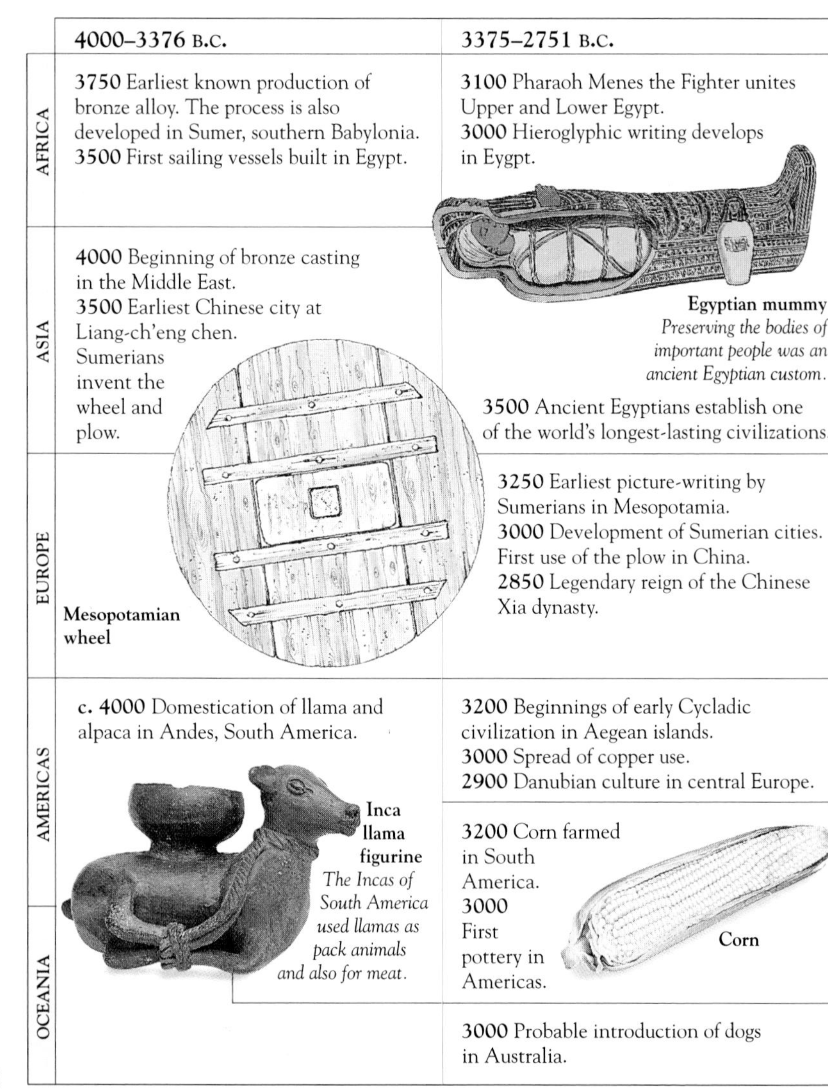

	4000–3376 B.C.	3375–2751 B.C.
AFRICA	**3750** Earliest known production of bronze alloy. The process is also developed in Sumer, southern Babylonia. **3500** First sailing vessels built in Egypt.	**3100** Pharaoh Menes the Fighter unites Upper and Lower Egypt. **3000** Hieroglyphic writing develops in Eygpt. **3500** Ancient Egyptians establish one of the world's longest-lasting civilizations.
ASIA	**4000** Beginning of bronze casting in the Middle East. **3500** Earliest Chinese city at Liang-ch'eng chen. Sumerians invent the wheel and plow.	**3250** Earliest picture-writing by Sumerians in Mesopotamia. **3000** Development of Sumerian cities. First use of the plow in China. **2850** Legendary reign of the Chinese Xia dynasty.
EUROPE		**3200** Beginnings of early Cycladic civilization in Aegean islands. **3000** Spread of copper use. **2900** Danubian culture in central Europe.
AMERICAS	**c. 4000** Domestication of llama and alpaca in Andes, South America.	**3200** Corn farmed in South America. **3000** First pottery in Americas.
OCEANIA		**3000** Probable introduction of dogs in Australia.

Egyptian mummy
Preserving the bodies of important people was an ancient Egyptian custom.

Mesopotamian wheel

Inca llama figurine
The Incas of South America used llamas as pack animals and also for meat.

Corn

2750–2126 B.C.	2125–1501 B.C.
2686 Beginning of ancient Egyptian Old Kingdom. **2646** Pyramid of Zoser built at Saqqara. **2590** Building of Great Pyramid of Khufu at Giza begins. **2500** Sahara region begins to dry out. **2150** Decline of ancient Egyptian Old Kingdom. **2133** Rise of ancient Egyptian Middle Kingdom.	**1786** Egyptian Middle Kingdom ends. **1652** War between Egypt and Asian Hyksos people. **1550** Rise of Egyptian New Kingdom.
2750 The legendary King Gilgamesh reigns in Uruk, Mesopotamia. **2500** Birth of Indus Valley civilization in Pakistan. Horse domesticated in Central Asia. **2371** Semite people establish Mesopotamia's greatest empire.	**2000** Hittites begin invasions of Anatolia. **1900** Fall of Indus civilization. **1800** Beginnings of Assyrian Empire. **1792** Birth of Hammurabi, founder of Babylonian Empire.
	2000 Rise of the prosperous Minoan sea-trading civilization in Crete. **1600** Origins of Mycenean civilization. **1500** Linear B script in use on Crete.
2500 Earliest barrow burials in Britain. Beginnings of Dolmen period of Scandinavian Neolithic age. **2200** The first Stonehenge is built in England.	
2500 First large settlements and building of temple mounds in Andes area.	**2000** Earliest Peruvian metalworking. Inuits reach northern Greenland.
	2000 Beginnings of settlement of Melanesia in the South Pacific.

Lotus-design tile
This tile dates from the reign of King Akhenaten in the Egyptian New Kingdom.

Indus Valley sculpture
This sculpture of a priest or divine king was made by people in the Indus Valley city of Mohenjo-Daro.

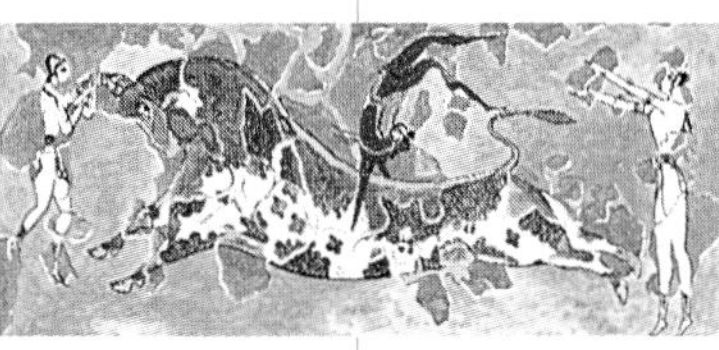

Minoan wall painting
The wealthy Minoan people decorated the walls of their palaces with colorful murals.

	1500–1276 B.C.	1275–1051 B.C.
AFRICA	**1300** Temple of Abu Simbel built in Nubia for Rameses II. **Hittite soldier**	**1218** Egypt invaded by Sea Peoples from the Aegean. **1182** Second invasion of Egypt by Aegean Sea Peoples.
ASIA	**1500** Phrygia established by people moving from Thrace in the Balkans to Asia Minor. Composition of hymns of Rig Veda. **1400** Chinese capital moved to Anyang, in present-day South Korea.	**c. 1375** First alphabet script devised by Phoenicians. **1294** Egyptians fight Hittites at Qadesh for control of Palestine. **1200** Collapse of Hittite Empire. Jews settle in Palestine. **1100** Phoenician traders begin to spread out from eastern Mediterranean.
EUROPE	**1500** Beginning of Bronze Age in Scandinavia. **1450** Decline of Minoan civilization in Crete.	**1200** Decline of Mycenean culture in Greece. **c. 1120** City of Mycenae destroyed.
AMERICAS	**1300** Rise of Olmec civilization in Mexico. **Olmec stone carving** *This colossal stone head of an Olmec king was carved from basalt.*	 **Mycenean bull's head** *This clay bull's head has small holes in its mouth and was used as a ritual sprinkler at religious ceremonies.*
OCEANIA	**1300** Settlers from Indonesia and Philippines reach Western Polynesia (Fiji).	

1050–826 B.C.	825–601 B.C.
900 Foundation of kingdom of Kushin Nubia.	**814** Phoenicians found the city-state of Carthage in northern Africa.
1027 Zhou warriors overthrow the Shang dynasty in China. **1000** Kingdom of Israel under King David.  **Shang Fang Ding** *This four-legged food vessel was made in China during the Shang dynasty (c. 1600–1027 BC).*	**800** Aryans from present-day Iran spread into southern India. **771** Zhou dynasty collapses in China. **721–05** Assyrian Empire at height of its powers. **660** Reign of Jimmu, legendary first Japanese emperor. **650** Chinese begin to use iron. **612** Decline of Assyrian power. **c. 604–562** Nebuchadnezzar II rules Neo-Babylonian (Chaldean) Empire. Hanging Gardens built in city of Babylon, Mesopotamia. 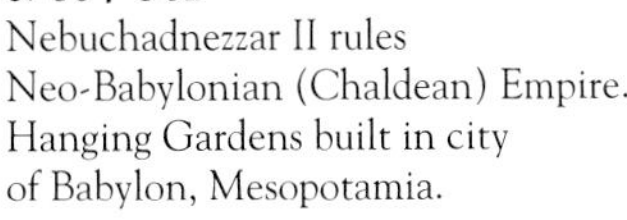 **Sentry at the Ishtar Gate, Babylon**
1000 Etruscans arrive in Italy and begin building a loosely connected alliance of city-states.  **Etruscan warrior figurine** *The Etruscans produced unique, high-quality sculpture and bronze work.*	
900 Height of Chavin farming civilization in Andes, South America. **800** Zapotec civilization of Central America produces first writing in Americas.	**776** First recorded Olympic Games in Greece. **753** Foundation of Rome. **750** Greek city-states establish settlements around Mediterranean. **700** Iron Age culture of Halstatt, Austria, spreads through central and western Europe. **650** Earliest surviving Latin inscriptions. **621** The Laws of Dracon become the first written laws of Athens, Greece.
1000 Most of Polynesian Islands settled.	

	600–451 B.C.	450–301 B.C.
AFRICA	**600** Phoenicians sail around Africa. **600** Building of Temple of the Sun at Meroë, Sudan. **500** Ironworking Nok culture begins in Nigeria.	**304** Egypt independent under Ptolemy I.
ASIA	**560** Lao–Tze writes his philosophical work, Tao Te Ching, in China. **550** King Cyrus II of Persia founds Persian Empire. **486** Death of Siddhartha Gautama, founder of Buddhist religion.	**403** Start of "Warring States" period in China. **334–26** Alexander the Great conquers Asia Minor, Persia, and parts of India. **323** Death of Alexander the Great and division of his empire. **322** Chandragupta founds Mauryan Empire in India.
EUROPE	**510** Origins of Roman Republic. **505** Establishment of democracy in Athens. **500** Celtic people flourish in central Europe. **490** Greeks defeat Persians at Battle of Marathon.	**450** Iron Age culture firmly established in central and western Europe. **431–04** Sparta defeats Athens in Peloponnesian Wars. **338** Macedonians gain control of Greece at Battle of Chaeronea.
AMERICAS		**400** Decline of Olmec civilization.
OCEANIA	**500** Trading contacts established in South Pacific islands.	

Alexander the Great
The Macedonian warrior-king Alexander the Great built an empire that helped spread Greek culture over western Asia.

Buddhist stupa at Sanchi, India
Mauryan emperor Asoka became a Buddhist and set up thousands of monuments (stupas) around the empire. Each is said to contain a part of the Buddha's body.

Decorative Celtic horned helmet

300–151 B.C.	150–1 B.C.
290 Foundation of library at Alexandria, Egypt.	**149–6** Rome destroys Carthage in Third Punic War and founds province of Africa. **100** Camels introduced into Sahara region. **30** Egypt becomes Roman province on death of Mark Antony and Cleopatra.
262 Mauryan Emperor Asoka converts to Buddhism. **240** Beginning of Parthian dynasty in northern Persia. **221** Chinese unity brought about by the first emperor, Qin Shi Huangdi. **207** Disintegration of unity in China. **202** China reunited under Han dynasty.	**112** Opening up of "Silk Road" trade route gives the West some access to China. **64** Roman general Pompey conquers Syria. **53** Parthia halts eastward expansion of Rome.
290 Rome gains control of central Italy. **264–41** Rome victorious against Carthage in First Punic War and wins control of Sicily. **218–01** Carthaginians, led by Hannibal, defeated in Second Punic War by Roman general Scipio. **Roman sword**	**49** Rome under Julius Caesar invades Gaul. **45** Julius Caesar becomes sole ruler of Rome after civil war. **31** Battle of Actium gives Octavian power over Rome. **27** Roman Empire replaces Republic. Octavian becomes Augustus, the first emperor.
300 Mound-building cultures flourish in North America. Beginning of early Mayan civilization in Central America. **200** Rise of Nazca civilization in Peru, South America. 	**100** Emergence of Anasazi, Hohokam, and Mogollon peoples as they begin farming in southwestern North America. Okvik hunters settle in northern Alaska. **Nazca pottery** *The Nazca produced decorative textiles, metalworks, and pottery.*

	A.D. 1–149	A.D. 150–299
AFRICA	**c. 17–24** Tacfarinas leads Numidian people in revolt against Roman government in northern Africa. **50** Kingdom of Axum begins to expand in Ethiopia. **61–63** Roman forces move into Sudan.	**150** Berber and Mandingo barbarians start to dominate Sudan area. **250** Axum (Ethiopia) controls trade in Red Sea.
ASIA	**9** Overthrow of Han dynasty in China. **25** Han dynasty restored. **c. 33** Jesus Christ crucified in Jerusalem. **60** Beginning of Kushan Empire in India. **70** Romans seize control of Jerusalem in Israel and destroy Jewish temple. **105** Paper first used in China. **132** Jewish revolt against Roman rule.	**Circular Sassanian city at Firuzbad, Persia (Iraq)**
EUROPE	**43** Romans invade Britain. **79** Mount Vesuvius erupts and destroys the town of Pompeii in southern Italy. **117** Height of Roman Empire.	**200** Mishnah, the book of Jewish law, completed. Indian epics of Ramayana and Mahabharata composed. Creation of the Hindu scripture, Bhagavad Gita.
AMERICAS	**1** Beginning of Moche civilization in northern Peru. **50** Nazca people create vast lines and patterns in the desert.	**The four tetrarchs** *In A.D. 293, Emperor Diocletian divided the Roman Empire in two, appointing an emperor and deputy to rule each half. This sculpture represents the Empire's four leaders (tetrarchs).*
OCEANIA	**1–100** Hindu-Buddhists from Southeast Asia colonize Sumatra and Java in Indonesia.	

Bust of Augustus, the first Roman emperor

A.D. 300–449	A.D. 450–599
325 Axum destroys kingdom of Meroë. **400** Adoption of Christianity in Axum. **439** Vandals establish kingdom in northern Africa.	**533** Emperor Justinian wins back northern Africa for Rome.
304 Invasion of Huns creates further division of China. **320** Chandragupta I founds Gupta Empire in northern India.	**480** End of Indian Gupta Empire. **520** Rise of mathematics in India with invention of decimal number system. **531** Height of Sassanian Empire in Persia. **550** Buddhism introduced into Japan. **589** Reunification of China under Sui dynasty. **Japanese carving of a sleeping Buddha**
The symbol of Christianity *The teachings of the Jewish preacher Jesus Christ, who was crucified c. A.D. 33, spread around the world after his death. The faith gained widespread acceptance after the Roman emperor Constantine converted to Christianity in A.D. 313. Christ's death on the cross led to its use as a symbol of the faith.* **313** Edict of Milan leads to toleration of Christianity throughout Roman Empire. **330** Emperor Constantine moves capital of Roman Empire to Constantinople, at site of present-day Istanbul, Turkey. **410** Invading Visigoths sack Rome.	**450** Angles, Jutes, and Saxons settle in Britain. **476** Overthrow of Romulus Augustulus, the last western Roman emperor. **486** Clovis people establish Frankish kingdom in present-day northern France, Belgium, and parts of western Germany. **493** Ostrogoths gain power in Italy. **552** Emperor Justinian restores Italy to Roman control. **568** Lombards take over northern Italy.
300 Rise of great Monte Alban and Teotihuacán civilizations in Mexico.	**c. 450–600** Population of city of Tiahuanaco in Bolivia reaches 50,000.
300 Eastern Polynesia settled.	

	A.D. 600–724	A.D. 725–849
AFRICA	**c.700** Trans-Saharan trade brings prosperity to Kingdom of Ghana. Bantu Africans cross Limpopo River and take ironworking technology to the south.	**751** Muslims defeat Mongols at Samarkand in central Asia. **794** Kyoto, ancient capital of Japan, established. **802** Khmers found empire in Cambodia and Laos.
ASIA	**618** Reunification of China under T'ang dynasty. **622** Year One of the Islamic calendar. **637** Followers of Islam (Muslims) seize Jerusalem.	
EUROPE	**c. 675** Nomadic Bulgar people settle in lands south of the Danube. **711** Islamic Moors invade Spain.	**732** Defeat of Moors by Frankish leader Charles Martel halts advance of Muslims through Europe. **768** Charlemagne crowned King of the Franks. **844** Defeat of Picts unites Scotland.
AMERICAS	**600** Mayan civilization in Central America flourishes. Mayans build great pyramidal temples and develop writing and advanced mathematics.	
OCEANIA		

Muslim at prayer *The Arab merchant Muhammad founded the Islamic religion in A.D. 610. His teachings inspired the Arab peoples, and by A.D. 750 Muslims had gained control of land stretching from Spain to Afghanistan.*

King Charlemagne *The Holy Roman Empire was founded by King Charlemagne of the Franks in A.D. 800 after he conquered most of the Christian lands of western Europe.*

Temple at Palenque *This Mayan temple contained the funeral chamber of the lord Pacol, who died in A.D. 683 after ruling for 68 years.*

A.D. 850–974	A.D. 975–1099
900 Hausa kingdom of Daura founded in northern Nigeria. **920** The Kingdom of Ghana in western Africa begins a prosperous golden age.	**980** Arab traders settle on eastern coast of Africa. **1054** Ghana conquered by Muslim Almoravid dynasty.
888 Chola dynasty of Tamil kings replaces the Pallavas in southern India and Sri Lanka. **935–41** Civil war in Japan. **960** Sung dynasty begins rule in China. **1007** Japanese noblewoman Murasaki Shikubu writes the first novel.	 **Japanese literature** *More than 600,000 words long, The Tale of Genji, a prince in search of love and wisdom, was the first novel.* **1044** Gunpowder invented in China.
911 The Viking leader Rollo is granted land in Normandy by the King of France. **930** Córdoba becomes the seat of Arab learning in Spain. **966** Conversion of Poles to Christianity. **Viking longship** *Late in the eighth century the Viking people of present-day Scandinavia went in search of treasure to plunder and new lands to settle. Their golden age of trade, exploration, and colonization lasted until A.D. 1100.*	**982** The Viking warrior Erik the Red settles in Greenland. **1000** Leif Eriksson, son of Erik the Red, sails down North American coast and names it "Vinland." **1066** William of Normandy defeats King Harold of England at Battle of Hastings. **1096** First Crusades begin.
900 Beginnings of Mixtec civilization in Mexico.	**980** Toltec people build their capital city at Tula in Mexico. **1000** Foundation of Chima civilization in Peru.
950 Polynesian navigator Kupe discovers New Zealand, and Maori settlers arrive.	**Maori hek tiki** *This hek tiki, or neck pendant, was worn by the first Maori settlers to bring good luck or ward off evil spirits.*

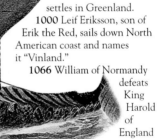

	1100–1149	1150–1199
AFRICA	**c. 1100** First Iron Age settlement in Zimbabwe, Southern Africa.	**1169** Saladin, a Muslim warrior and commander in the Egyptian army, becomes ruler of Egypt. **1190** Lalibela rules as Emperor of Ethiopia.
ASIA	**1104** Acre in Israel captured by Crusaders. Their name comes from the Latin *crux*, or cross, the symbol of Christ.	**1156** Civil war between rival clans in Japan leads to domination of the country by its Samurai warlords. **1187** Saladin captures Jerusalem from Crusaders. **1191** Zen Buddhism introduced to Japan.
EUROPE	**1115** French philosopher Peter Abelard begins teaching in Paris, France. St. Bernard establishes important monastery at Clairvaux, France. **1119** Foundation of Bologna University in Italy. **1142** Alfonso Henriques becomes first King of Portugal.	**1170** Murder of Thomas à Becket, Archbishop of Canterbury, England. **1174** Building of Old London Bridge in England and the "Leaning Tower" in Pisa, Italy.
AMERICAS	**c. 1100** Chimu civilization flourishes in Peru on northwest coast.	**1170s** Chichimec nomads overthrow Toltec capital city of Tula in Mexico, leading to fall of Toltec Empire.
OCEANIA	**1100s** Giant statues built on Easter Island, South Pacific.	

Knights of Christ *European Christians sent armed expeditions called Crusades to recapture the holy lands from Saracen Muslims.*

Zen Buddhist monks in meditation *The practice of Zen Buddhism is unlike other faiths in its belief that the path to self-knowledge lies in personal instruction by a master rather than the study of scriptures.*

"Leaning Tower" of Pisa

Chimu ear ornament

1200–1249

1234 Sun Diata founds the Mali Empire in West Africa.

1206 Genghis Khan establishes the Mongol Empire. The Islamic faith takes root in new Kingdom of Delhi, India.
1229 Sixth Crusaders recapture Jerusalem.
1232 Explosive rockets used in war between Chinese and Mongols.
1237 Mongol army begins conquest of Russia.
1244 Egyptians retake Jerusalem.

Genghis Khan
The Mongol chieftain Temujin was proclaimed Genghis Khan, or "Universal Ruler."

1204 Constantinople sacked and looted by Fourth Crusaders.
1209 Franciscan order founded by St. Francis of Assisi, Italy.
1215 St. Dominic establishes Dominican Order in Spain. King John of England grants political rights to barons by signing the Magna Carta.
1240s Foundations laid in Germany for commercial and defensive Hanseatic League of northern European trade towns.

c.1200 Incas in Peru centered around settlement at Cuzco. First corn farmers by Mississippi River in North America.

1250–1299

1250 Mamluk rebel slave-soldiers become the rulers of Egypt.

1250 The Japanese monk Nicherin proclaims *Lotus Sutra* the supreme Buddhist scripture.
1260 Mamluks halt Mongol advance at Battle of Ain Jalut in Palestine.
1291 Saracens capture Acre, ending the Crusades.
1281 Mongol invaders' fleet driven from Japan by the Kamikaze, or "Divine Wind."
c.1294 Persians convert to Islam.

Marco Polo and fellow travelers in the Far East

1271 Aged only 16, Marco Polo begins his journeys around the Far East, traveling from Venice, Italy, to China.
1273 Rudolf Hapsburg becomes ruler of Germany and founds the powerful Hapsburg dynasty.

c. 1250 Restoration of Mayan Empire and building of a new capital at Mayapan in Mexico. Incas expand their capital at Chan-chan in northern Peru.

c. 1250 Stone platforms later used to erect religious statues built in Polynesia.

	1300–1339	1340–1379
AFRICA	**1300** Origins of Benin kingdom in Nigeria. **1324** Mansa Musa makes pilgrimage to Mecca.	**1348** Population of Egypt devastated by the Black Death plague. **1352** Moroccan scholar Ibn Battuta makes his great journey across the Sahara to Mali.
ASIA	**c. 1300** Osman I establishes Ottoman dynasty in Turkey. **1321** Tughluq dynasty founded in Delhi, India.	**1340** Indian Hindu empire of Vijayanagar becomes center of resistance to Islam. **1350** Majapahit Empire founded in Java. **1368** Mongols driven from China by Tai Tsu, founder of the Ming dynasty.
EUROPE	**1309** The Pope moves from Rome, Italy, to Avignon, France, creating a rift in the Western Church.	**1346** The 100 Years War between England and France begins with the Battle of Crécy. **1347** The Black Death reaches Europe. **1358** Peasant revolt near Paris, France.
AMERICAS	**c.1300** Major expansion of Incas through Andes. **1325** Aztecs found capital at Tenochtitlán.	**1350** Acamapitchli becomes Aztec ruler and begins expansion of the empire.
OCEANIA		**1350** Maoris create rock art in New Zealand.

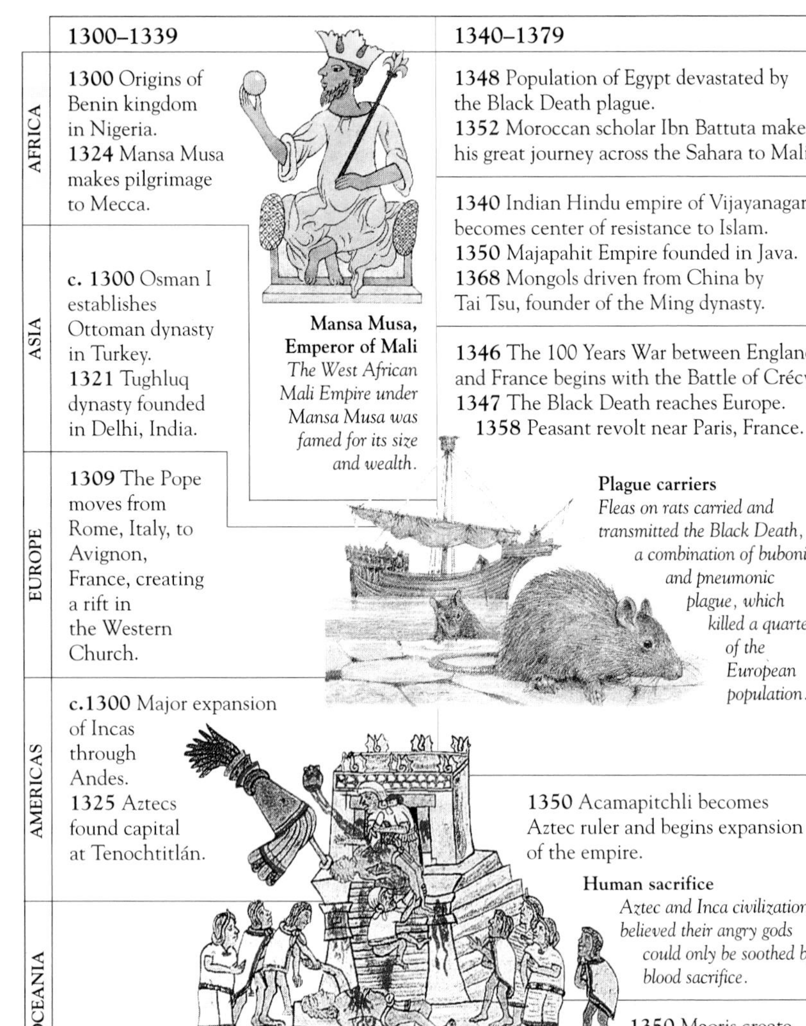

Mansa Musa, Emperor of Mali
The West African Mali Empire under Mansa Musa was famed for its size and wealth.

Plague carriers
Fleas on rats carried and transmitted the Black Death, a combination of bubonic and pneumonic plague, which killed a quarter of the European population.

Human sacrifice
Aztec and Inca civilizations believed their angry gods could only be soothed by blood sacrifice.

1380–1419

c.1400 Kingdom of Zimbabwe thrives on gold trade.

1398 Mongol leader Tamerlane sacks Indian city of Delhi.
1404–33 Chinese navigator Chang Ho explores India and East Africa.
1405 Death of Tamerlane leads to fall of Mongol Empire.
1411 Ahmad Shah founds Ahmadabad, an important commercial city in India.

The murder of Wat Tyler
Peasant revolts in the years following the Plague were ruthlessly put down.

1381 Wat Tyler and John Ball lead Peasants' Revolt in England against high taxes and low pay. The uprising is crushed and the leaders killed.
1389 Ottoman Turks crush Christian Serbs at Kossovo, Serbia.
1415 French defeated by the English at the Battle of Agincourt in France.

c. 1400 Viracocha becomes first Inca empire builder, establishing permanent rule over conquered neighboring lands.

1420–1459

1432 Portuguese explorers reach the Azores Islands.

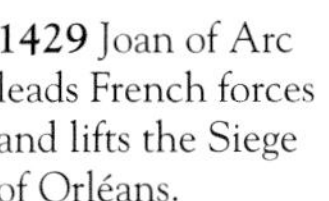

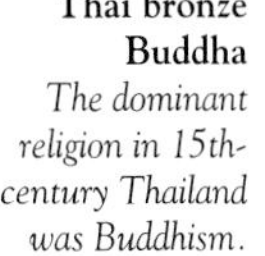

Thai bronze Buddha
The dominant religion in 15th-century Thailand was Buddhism.

1448 Major reforms begin in Thailand under King Traillok.

1429 Joan of Arc leads French forces and lifts the Siege of Orléans.
1450 Italian cities of Florence, Milan, and Naples form an alliance.
1450s German craftsman Johannes Gutenberg produces the first printed books in Europe.
1453 Constantinople falls to Ottoman sultan Muhammad II, ending the centuries-old Byzantine Empire.

Muhammad II
Ottoman leader Muhammad II dragged 70 ships overland to avoid a huge iron chain protecting the waterway into Byzantium when he invaded the city.

1438 Inca overlord Pachacuti greatly enlarges the Inca Empire.

	1460–1479	1480–1499
AFRICA	**1464** Sonni Ali becomes ruler of Songhai people in West Africa.	**1482** First Portuguese settlements established on Gold Coast of West Africa. **1488** Sea route from Europe to Asia opened by Portuguese navigator Bartolomeu Diaz, sailing around the Cape of Good Hope, South Africa.
ASIA	**1467** Beginning of the Onin War in Japan, which continues for more than 10 years. It leads to the end of the feudal system and the rise of large territories.	**1497–98** Portuguese explorer Vasco da Gama sails to India via Africa.
EUROPE	**1463–79** Ottoman Turks and Venetians from Italy fight for control of the Mediterranean. The Turks are the eventual victors. **1479** Kingdoms of Aragon and Castille in Spain united by the marriage of King Ferdinand and Queen Isabella.	**1492** Christian conquest of Granada ends Islamic regional control in Spain and results in expulsion of Jews. **1494** Treaty of Tordesillas leads Spain and Portugal to agree to divide the unexplored world between their two nations.
AMERICAS	**1470s** Collapse of Chimu culture in Northern Peru. **1473** Aztec capital Tenochtitlán absorbs neighboring city of Tlatelolco.	**1492** Italian explorer Christopher Columbus reaches the Caribbean islands of the Americas. **1497** John Cabot of Italy discovers Newfoundland, present-day Canada.
OCEANIA	**1450–1500** Widespread cultivation of wet taro, a starchy root vegetable, in the Hawaiian islands.	

Battling warriors in the Onin civil war

Portuguese caravel
The caravel ships used by Portuguese explorers were longer, narrower, and easier to manuever than earlier craft.

The Renaissance
The rediscovery or "renaissance" of Greek and Roman ideas on art, literature, and science spreads through Europe from Italy during the 14-1500s.

1500–1519

1500s Southern African Bantus trade with Europeans. Hausa states develop in West Africa.
1517 Ottomans conquer Eygpt.

1502 Safavid dynasty begins in Persia.

c. 1503 Italian artist Leonardo da Vinci begins painting the Mona Lisa.
1512 Michelangelo paints ceiling of the Sistine Chapel, Italy.
1517 European Reformation begins.

The Reformation
Protestant (protesting) churches were formed after Martin Luther called for reform of the corrupt Catholic Church in a list he nailed to his church door in 1517.

1501–02 Amerigo Vespucci of Italy explores the coast of Brazil. First African slaves taken to the West Indies.
1519 Portuguese explorer Ferdinand Magellan sails across the Pacific Ocean.
1520 Spaniard Hernando Cortés brings down the Aztec Empire.

Moctezuma's headdress
This is a replica of a headdress said to have belonged to the last Aztec ruler Moctezuma, who was murdered by Cortés of Spain in 1520.

1520–1539

1520–21 Portuguese traders reach China.
1526 Babur I becomes first Moghul Emperor of India.

Babur I of India
A descendant of Genghis Khan, Babur I was a brilliant military leader who also took an interest in art and poetry.

1529 Ottoman Turks besiege Vienna.
1533 Ivan the Terrible comes to the throne in Russia.

1532 Francisco Pizarro of Spain overthrows Incas in South America by kidnapping and murdering their Emperor, Atahualpa. The leaderless Inca Empire then crumbles.
1534 French explorer Jacques Cartier sails along the St. Lawrence River in Canada.

Inca knife

1526 Portuguese begin landings in Polynesia.

	1540–1564	1565–1589
AFRICA	**c. 1540s** Portuguese begin organization of the transatlantic slave trade.	**1566** Sulayman I, ruler of the Ottoman Empire, dies as his empire reaches its peak.
ASIA	**1542** Traders from Portugal reach Japan. **1546** King Tabinshweti unites Burma. **1556** Akbar the Great becomes Moghul emperor of India.	**1577** Akbar the Great completes unification of northern India, providing a structured system of government. **Akbar the Great in religious discussion** *The Islamic Moghul emperor Akbar was renowned for his tolerance of other religions.*
EUROPE	**1541** French Protestant reformer John Calvin sets up Puritan state in Geneva, Switzerland. **1545** Meeting of Catholic leaders at Council of Trent in northern Italy begins Catholic Counter-Reformation. **1564** Birth of English playwright William Shakespeare.	**1571** European alliance defeats Ottoman Turkish fleet at Battle of Lepanto, Greece. **1572** St. Bartholomew's Day Massacre of Protestants (Huguenots) in France. **1588** English navy defeats the Armada, Spain's huge invasion fleet.  **St. Bartholomew's Day Massacre**
AMERICAS	**1540s** Spanish arrive in California on the west coast of North America.	**1567** Portuguese establish Rio de Janeiro in Brazil. **1579** Francis Drake claims the west coast of North America for England.
OCEANIA	**1550** Maoris sail from North Island, New Zealand, to settle on South Island. **Maori migration**	**1567** Spanish explorer Mendaña becomes first European to reach Solomon Islands.

1590–1614

1591 Moroccans and European mercenaries destroy Songhai Empire.
1600s Trading posts set up on African coast by all major European powers.

1590 Shah Abbas of Persia makes peace with Ottoman Turkey.
1592 Japan invades Korea under commander Hideyoshi.
1603 Ieyasu of Tokugawa clan becomes ruler of Japan. English East India Company established.
1602 Dutch East India Company founded.

1598 Edict of Nantes ends civil war in France, giving Catholics and Huguenots equal rights.
1604 Russians settle in Siberia.
1605 Failure of Gunpowder Plot in London, England, and arrest of ringleader Guy Fawkes.
1610 French King Henry IV assassinated.
1613 Michael Romanov becomes first Russian Romanov Tsar (king).

1607 John Smith establishes a colony in Virginia at Jamestown.
1608 Foundation of Quebec in Canada.
1609 Henry Hudson sails up the Hudson River on the east coast of North America.

1595 Mendaña lands on Marquesas Islands in the central South Pacific.
1606 Spanish explorer Luis Vaez de Torres sails between Australia and New Guinea.

1615–1639

1620s Queen Nzinga of Ndongo defeats the Portuguese in Angola.

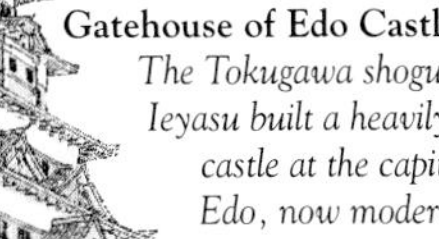

Gatehouse of Edo Castle, Japan
The Tokugawa shogun (ruler) Ieyasu built a heavily fortified castle at the capital city of Edo, now modern Tokyo.

1620s Formation of Japanese national policy restricting contact with the outside world.

1618 Beginning of Thirty Years' War in Europe between Catholic and Protestant powers.

1620 *Mayflower* pilgrims set sail from England for North America.
1625 French begin to settle West Indies.
1626 Dutch found New Amsterdam on site of present-day New York.
1630 Dutch East India Company seizes part of Brazil for its sugar and silver.

Building Manhattan
The first brick house on the site of present-day Manhattan, New York, was built on The Strand in New Amsterdam, now Whitehall Street.

	1640–1669	1670–1699
AFRICA	**1652** Dutch found colony at Cape Town in southern Africa. **1663** Death of Queen Nzinga of Ndongo in Angola.	**1670s** French colonists settle in Senegal. **1690s** Ashanti kingdom established on Gold Coast of West Africa.
ASIA	**1644** Manchus invade China, replacing Ming dynasty. **1657** City of Edo on site of present-day Tokyo, Japan, is destroyed by fire.	**1683** K'ang Hsi of China conquers Formosa, now modernTaiwan. **1690** Job Caharnock of the English East India Company founds city of Calcutta.
EUROPE	**1642** Civil War in England. **1643** Louis XIV of France begins reign. **1648** End of the Thirty Years' War in Europe. **1649** Oliver Cromwell executes Charles I of England and sets up Commonwealth.	**1672** Third Anglo-Dutch trade war begins. **1677** Ottoman Empire at war with Russia. **1682** Peter the Great of Russia starts reign. **1685** Louis XIV of France abolishes Edict of Nantes' protection of the rights of Huguenot protestants. Many flee to England as a result. **1688** Protestant William of Orange defeats Catholic James II at the Battle of the Boyne and becomes king of England.
AMERICAS	**1642** French explorer De Maisonneuve founds Ville-Marie (Montreal) in Canada. **1664** English forces seize New Amsterdam from Dutch and rename it New York.	**1670** Colony founded in South Carolina. English Hudson's Bay Company established. **1675** War between colonists and Native Americans devastates New England. **1680** French explorer Robert Cavalier de la Salle claims Mississippi valley for France. **1692** Salem witch trials begin in New England.
OCEANIA	**1642** Dutch explorer Abel Tasman becomes first European to reach Van Dieman's Land, Tasmania.	**1680** The dodo becomes extinct.

Manchu lord with Chinese subjects, pigtailed to show inferiority

Louis XIV of France in classical costume

Dodo

1700–1729

1702 French win "Asiento," or monopoly on shipping of African slaves to Spanish colonies.
1712 Rise of Futa Jalon kingdom in West Africa.

1707 Death of Moghul leader Aurangzeb leads to breakup of the empire and new opportunities for European traders.
1727 Border fixed between China and Russia.

1700 Death of Charles II of Spain, leaving a French heir, leads to War of Spanish Succession.
1703 Russian Czar Peter the Great founds St. Petersburg.
1707 Act of Union joins England and Scotland.
1709 Abraham Darby's use of coke instead of charcoal to extract metal from iron ore (smelting) starts English Industrial Revolution.

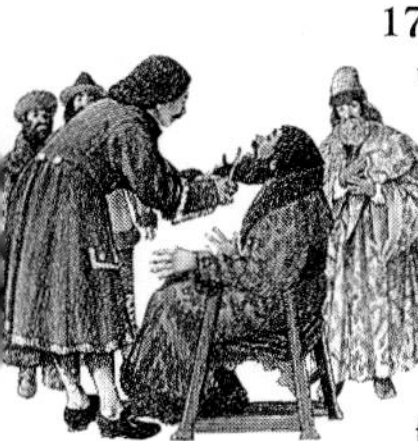

Peter the Great forced nobles to shave

1709 Mass emigration of Germans to America begins.
1710 South Sea Company increases British trade with South America.
1720–22 Spanish occupation of Texas. Collapse of English South Sea and French Mississippi Companies.

1722 Dutch navigator Roggeveen reaches Samoa and Easter Island.

1730–1759

1739 Nadir Shah of Persia defeats the Moghuls and captures city of Delhi, India.
1740s Anglo/French rivalry in India.
1750 China conquers Tibet.
1757 Bengali army defeated by the British at the Battle of Plassey.

1746 Victory of English at Battle of Culloden, Scotland, ends Scottish revolt.
1748 Marie Theresa becomes Empress of Austria.
1755 Earthquake at Lisbon in Portugal.
1756–1763 Seven Years War between Britain and France.

Captured slaves assembled for sale
Slaves transported from Africa to the Americas were often worked to death on plantations owned by European settlers.

1733 England passes the Molasses Act, forbidding trade between American and West Indian colonies. Colony of Georgia founded.
1739 Slave uprising in South Carolina.
1759 English forces defeat French on Plains of Abraham in Quebec, Canada.

	1760–1779	1780–1799
AFRICA	**1764** Osei Kwadwo becomes Ashanti ruler in western Africa. **1768** Independent Eygpt under Ali Bey.	**1794** Beginning of Qaja dynasty's rule in Persia.
ASIA	**1761** Marathas defeated by Afghans at Battle of Panipat. **1763** Treaty of Paris makes Britain dominant power in India.	**1789** French Revolution begins in Paris. **1795** Formation of France's Directoire government. **1796** Edward Jenner introduces smallpox vaccine in England. French general Napoleon Bonaparte begins Italian campaigns.
EUROPE	**1762** Catherine the Great begins reign over Russia. **1751–1786** Ideas of Enlightenment thinkers published in *L'Encyclopedie*.	
AMERICAS	**1773** Rebel colonists throw English tea into the harbor at the Boston Tea Party. **1775–83** American colonists fight against British rule in Revolutionary War. **1776** Signing of US Declaration of Independence.	**1780** Tupac Amara leads Incas of Peru in revolt against Spain. **1787–9** US Constitution and Bill of Rights written and ratified. **1791** Revolution in Haiti led by former slave Toussaint L' Ouverture. **1793** City of York founded on site of present-day Toronto in Canada.
OCEANIA	**1770** Captain James Cook reaches Australia.	**1788** Foundation of British colony of New South Wales in Australia.

Ashanti gold weight

ENCYCLOPEDIE,
OU
DICTIONNAIRE RAISONNÉ
DES SCIENCES,
DES ARTS ET DES MÉTIERS,
TOME PREMIER

Inspirational reading
L'Encyclopedie expressed the ideals of justice, equality, and rational thought proposed by followers of the Enlightenment movement.

Storming the Bastille
The Bastille prison in Paris was a symbol of aristocratic tyranny. Its overthrow by the people in 1789 launched the French Revolution.

Captain Cook trades with Islanders
English navigator James Cook explored the South Pacific and was renowned for taking great care of his crews.

1800–1819	1820–1839
1804 British win control of Cape of Good Hope. **1816** Shaka becomes leader of the Zulu warriors. 	**1822** Liberian republic for freed slaves founded in west Africa. **1830** French invade Algeria. British and Dutch South Africans (Boers) clash in South Africa. **1836** Start of Great Trek of the Boer farmers to establish independent republics in Transvaal and the Orange Free State.
1815 Java restored to Dutch by the British. **1819** Singapore founded by Stamford Raffles. **Zulu warrior**	**1824** Britain and Burma at war. **1839–42** China seizes opium imports from India, starting First Opium War.
1805 English admiral Horatio Nelson dies victorious against the French at the Battle of Trafalgar. **1812** French rule under Emperor Napoleon Bonaparte in almost all of Europe. **1815** Napoleon finally defeated at Battle of Waterloo. **Napoleon Bonaparte**	**1821–9** Greek War of Independence from Ottoman Turkey. **1825** First passenger railroad opens in England. **1830** French King Charles X overthrown in July Revolution. **1832** First Reform Act extends voting rights in Britain. **1837** Queen Victoria begins reign in England.  **The Rocket** *English engineer George Stephenson built this early steam-powered locomotive in 1829.*
1811 Paraguay and Venezuela gain independence from Spain. **1812–1815** British Canada resists invasion from the US.	**1821** Mexico wins independence from Spain. Mexicans rule Texas until 1836. **1822** Brazil gains independence from Portuguese. **1832** Samuel Morse invents electric telegraph in US. ... ‒ ‒ ‒ ... S. O. S. **Morse code**
1806 First white women arrive in New Zealand. **1817** First European emigrants settle Australian grasslands.	**1825** Charles Darwin begins a five-year voyage to the Pacific for scientific research.

	1840–1844	1845–1849
AFRICA	**1840** Iman Sayid Said, ruler of Oman, makes the island of Zanzibar off the east African coast his capital. **1843** British take over Boer colony in northeastern province of Natal.	**1847** Bantus defeated by British in southern Africa.
ASIA	**1842** Treaty of Nanking gives Hong Kong to Britain and opens trading links with China.	**1845–9** Anglo/Sikh war ends in defeat for Sikhs and the beginning of British rule over their homeland, the Punjab. **1848** Nasir ud-Din begins reign as Shah (ruler) of Persia.
EUROPE	**1840** The introduction of the Penny postage stamp leads to a low-cost, universally priced British postal service.	**1845–46** Failure of potato crop in Ireland leads to severe famine. **1848** Year of Revolution in Europe. **1849** Collapse of revolutionary movements.
AMERICAS	**1840** First general anesthetic used in America by C.W. Long. Upper and Lower Canada form self-governing union.	**1845** Texas and Florida become US states. **1846** US and Mexico at war over Texas. **1848** California Gold Rush leads to rapid population growth in western United States. First US women's rights convention in New York State.
OCEANIA	**1840** Treaty of Waitangi signed in New Zealand.	

Penny Black stamp

Native Americans defend their land
Increased numbers of European settlers threatened Native American territories.

British and Maoris at Waitangi
The Treaty of Waitangi gave Britain possession of New Zealand in return for recognizing ancient Maori land rights.

1850–1854

1854 Independent Orange Free State set up in South Africa.

1850–64 Taiping revolt in China.
1852–53 Second war between England and Burma.
1853–54 US Navy forces Japan to open up to Western trade.

1851 Great Exhibition celebrating the industrial age held at the Crystal Palace in London.
1853–56 Crimean War between Russia, Britain, and France.

Crystal Palace

1850 California becomes a US state.
1851 First pedal-powered sewing machine made by I.S. Singer.
1853 Completion of railroad from New York to Chicago.

1850 Australian Colonies Act enables New South Wales, Tasmania, and South Australia to have virtual self-government.
1851 Australian Gold Rush begins.

Gold miners

1855–1859

1855 Discovery of Victoria Falls by English explorer Livingstone leads to European exploration of African interior.

1856–57 Persia's seizure of Herat, Afghanistan, leads to war with Britain.

Uprising in India
The refusal of Hindu and Muslim soldiers to comply with an order on religious grounds led to a major protest against British rule in 1857.

1857 Britain governs India directly after "Indian Mutiny."
1858 Treaty of Tientsin forces China to trade with the West.

1856 Henry Bessemer invents industrial steelmaking process in England.
1859–61 Giuseppe Garibaldi leads the "red shirts" in the War of Italian Unification, capturing Sicily and southern Italy to form a new Italian state.

Garibaldi

1858 Reformer Benito Juarez becomes president of Mexico.
1856 Formation of anti-slavery Republican party in US.

1856 Major Australian colonies achieve self-government.

1860–1869

AFRICA

1860s Britain, France, Belgium, Germany, and Portugal begin to explore and colonize inner Africa.
1869 Opening of the Suez Canal in Egypt links the Mediterranean Sea with the Indian Ocean.

ASIA

1861 Empress Tze Hsi begins her 47-year rule of China.
1862 French occupation of Indo-China in Southeast Asia.

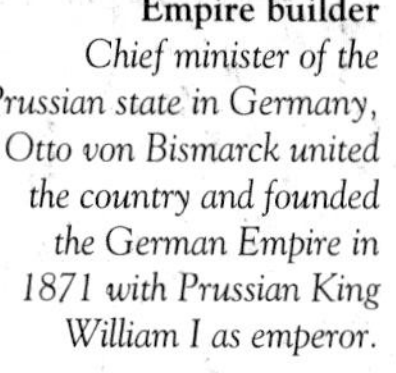

Empire builder
Chief minister of the Prussian state in Germany, Otto von Bismarck united the country and founded the German Empire in 1871 with Prussian King William I as emperor.

EUROPE

1864–66 Prussian forces defeat Denmark and Austria.
1866 Swedish chemist Alfred Nobel invents dynamite.

AMERICAS

1861 US Civil War begins.
1865 Union victory in Civil War. President Abraham Lincoln assassinated.
1867 British North America Act creates Dominion of Canada.

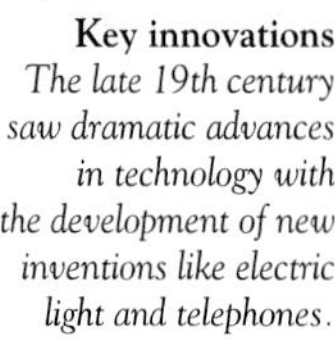

North v. South
The split of 11 Southern states from the Union in 1861 led to civil war in the US.

OCEANIA

1860–70 War between Maoris and white settlers in New Zealand.
1868 Last convict-settlers arrive in Australia.

1870–1879

AFRICA

1879 British defeat Zulu uprising led by King Cetshwayo at Ulundi, South Africa.
1881 Boers rebel against British rule in South Africa, leading to First Boer War.

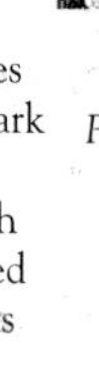

Zulu shield
The South African Zulu people fought the British and Boer settlers to protect their land.

ASIA

1870s Japan begins industrialization.
1872 Feudal control of Japan ends. Compulsory education is introduced.

EUROPE

1870s Most Western European countries start industrialization.
1871 Otto von Bismarck invades and defeats France. Britain legalizes trade unions.
1876 French build refrigerated cargo ships.

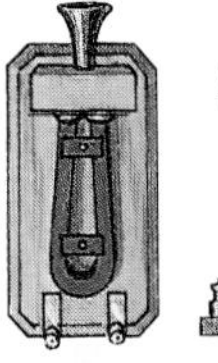

Key innovations
The late 19th century saw dramatic advances in technology with the development of new inventions like electric light and telephones.

AMERICAS

1876 Sioux and Cheyenne tribes defeat Custer at the Battle of Little Bighorn.
1876–1911 Porfirio Diaz begins rule as President of Mexico.
1879–84 Chile defeats Peru and Bolivia in the War of the Pacific.
1883 Thomas Edison invents the lightbulb.

1880–1889	1890–1899
1882 British rule of Egypt begins. **1886** Gold discovered in South Africa.	**1896** Ethiopians defeat Italian army. **1899** Second Boer War begins in South Africa.
1880s Britain and France move into Burma and Vietnam. **1885** Indian National Congress Party formed.  **Chinese revolt against Western power**	**1899-1901** Chinese government supports peasant revolt by the Society of Harmonious Fists to rid China of all foreigners. This so-called "Boxer Rebellion" is crushed by Western forces.
1884 Berlin Conference decides colonial divisions in Africa. First deep underground railroad built in London. **1885** Karl Benz builds first car driven by internal combustion engine in Germany. **1888** Scottish surgeon John Dunlop patents pneumatic (air-filled) tire. Kaiser (Emperor) William II starts German reign. **Benz Motorwagen**	**1896** Modern Olympic Games introduced in Greece. **1897** Greece and Turkey at war.
1882 Thomas Edison designs the first hydroelectric power station. **1884** First skyscraper built in Chicago. **1889** King Pedro II deposed by army revolt and Brazil declared a republic.	**1890** Last massacre of Native Americans in US at Battle of Wounded Knee in Dakota. First moving picture (film) shows appear in New York. **1895** Cuban revolt against Spanish rule. **1896** Gold struck in Klondike, Canada. **1898** US wins Spanish-American War and takes over the Philippines. Cuban independence from Spain. **Sioux warrior** *About 300 members of the Sioux tribe were slaughtered at the Battle of Wounded Knee.*
1880 Tahiti becomes a French colony. **1884** Volcano erupts on Krakatoa, Indonesia. **1885-86** Opening up of gold fields in New Guinea.	**1893** New Zealand Prime Minister Richard Seddon introduces advanced social reforms, including granting women the vote.

	1900–1904	1905–1909
AFRICA	**1902** Ovimbundu people of Angola revolt against Portuguese rule. **1904** Federation of French West Africa created.	**1905** Independent Union of former Boer republics founded in South Africa.
ASIA	**1904-5** Russo-Japanese war in Manchuria, ending in defeat for Russia and the total destruction of its fleet. 	**1907** Discovery of oil in Persia, now modern Iran. **1909** Conflict between China and Tibet.
EUROPE	**1900** Expansion of German navy begins arms race with Britain. **1903** Votes for Women Movement formed in Britain by suffragette Emmeline Pankhurst. First Tour de France bicycle race. **1904** French and British empires agree to Entente Cordiale (friendly understanding).	**1905** Czar of Russia forced to grant democratic rights in October Manifesto. Physicist Albert Einstein formulates his Special Theory of Relativity. **1908** The AEG turbine factory in Berlin, Germany is built. It is the world's first steel and glass building.
AMERICAS	**1900** Coca-Cola first produced in US. **1901** Theodore Roosevelt becomes youngest-ever US president after assassination of President McKinley. **1902** Plastic invented in US. **1903** Orville and Wilbur Wright build the first airplane and make a successful powered flight. 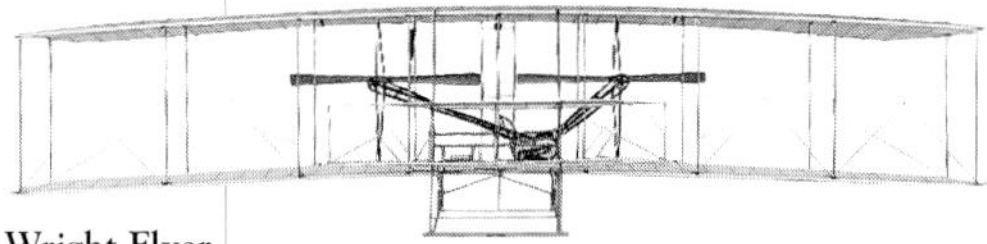	**1906** US forces occupy Cuba. Major earthquake damage in San Francisco. **1907** First comic strips appear in US. **1908** Henry Ford manufactures first Model T motor car.
OCEANIA	**1901** Australia becomes a Commonwealth. New Zealand takes over the Cook Islands.	**1907** New Zealand becomes a dominion. Minimum basic wage law set in Australia.

Russians fight the Japanese at the Battle of Liaio-Yang

Wright Flyer

1910–1914	1915–1919
1911 Lamogi people of Uganda rebel against British rule. **1912** African National Congress formed to fight for black people's rights.	**1917** Ras (Prince) Tafari takes power in Ethiopia.
1910 Japan takes over Korea. **1911** Chinese revolution overthrows Manchu dynasty and founds a republic.	**1915** Mohandas Gandhi becomes leader of the Indian National Congress Party. **1919** British troops fire on peaceful Indian protest in Amritsar Massacre, killing 379 people.
 **The sinking of the *Titanic*** **1910** Halley's Comet appears. **1911** Norwegian explorer Roald Amundsen reaches South Pole. **1912** The *Titanic*, the world's largest ocean liner, strikes an iceberg on her maiden voyage, sinking with the loss of 1,513 lives. **1912–13** Greece, Serbia, Bulgaria, and Montenegro unite to defeat Ottoman Turkey in the Balkan War. **1914** European alliances break down with the assassination of Archduke Ferdinand, heir to the Austro-Hungarian Empire. World War I begins. **German soldiers, World War I**	**1915** Bulgaria aligns with Central Powers (Germany, Austro-Hungary) and Italy joins Allies (Britain, France, Russia, Serbia) in World War I. **1916** Irish revolt against British rule in Easter Rising. **1917** Communists take over from Czar in Russian Revolution, leading to civil war. Greece joins the Allies. **1918** World War I ends with Allied victory. **Comrades in arms** *Russian workers overthrew Czar Nicholas II in February 1917. Vladimir Lenin and his Communist Bolshevik Party soon seized control of Russia.*
1911 Mexican dictator Diaz overthrown in revolution. **1912–33** US troops occupy Nicaragua. **1914** Opening of Panama Canal.	**1915–16** Unrest in Haiti and Dominican Republic put down by US troops. **1917** US enters World War I.
1914 Australia and New Zealand join the Allies in World War I.	**1919** Australia acquires former German colonies in the Pacific.

	1920–1924	1925–1929
AFRICA	**1922** Egypt under King Faud wins conditional independence from Britain. **1923** Ethiopia joins League of Nations.	**1926** End of Berber and Arab revolt against Europeans in North Africa.
ASIA	**1923** Major earthquake in Tokyo, Japan. End of Ottoman Empire as Mustafa Kemal becomes president of new Republic of Turkey.	**1927** Communists, led by Mao Tse-tung, attempt to overthrow Chinese government. **1929** Arabs attack Jews in Jerusalem, Palestine, in a conflict over the Wailing Wall.
EUROPE	**1920** Communist Red Army under Leon Trotsky wins Russian Civil War. **1922** Benito Mussolini becomes prime minister of Italian government. **1923** Partial Irish independence from Britain with creation of Irish Free State. **1924** Russian leader Vladimir Lenin dies. Josef Stalin later succeeds him.	**1925** Mussolini, Fascist leader of Italy, rules the country as a dictator. **1926** Police and army defeat general strike in Britain.
AMERICAS	**1920** Prohibition (banning) of the manufacture and sale of alcohol begins in USA. **1924** US military planes make first airborne trip around the world.	**1927** *The Jazz Singer*, starring Al Jolson, is released in the US. It is the first "talkie," or film including a synchronized speech and music soundtrack. **1929** Prices of shares on American stock exchange fall rapidly in Wall Street Crash.
OCEANIA	**1923** Ross area of Antarctica becomes New Zealand dependency.	**1927** Canberra becomes capital of Australia.

Dictator of Italy
Fascist leader Benito Mussolini led Italy into World War II on Germany's side in 1940. He was captured and executed in 1945.

The Great Depression
In October 1929, panicking share dealers on Wall Street, sold 13 million shares in one day. This contributed to the worldwide economic crisis called the Great Depression, in which millions of people lost their jobs, businesses, savings, and homes.

1930–1934

1930 Ras Tafari crowned as Haile Selassie I in Ethiopia.
1934 Lagos Youth Movement formed, demanding self-government of Nigeria.

1930s Indian leader Gandhi leads nonviolent opposition to British rule in India.
1934–35 Long March of Communists across China to find sanctuary in the Shaanxi province. Troops supporting the Nationalist leader Chiang Kai-shek pursue them daily.

Chinese Communist troops on the Long March

1933 Adolf Hitler, Führer (leader) of the Nazi Party, becomes German Chancellor.

Führer of the Nazis
Hitler's dreams of German world domination contributed to the outbreak of World War II. The war resulted in the mass murder, or holocaust, of 6 million Jews in Nazi concentration camps.

1931 British Parliament grants Canada full independence.
1933 Franklin D. Roosevelt becomes US President, introducing the New Deal to end the Depression. Prohibition ends.

1931 First solo trans-Tasmanian flight. Airmail service between Australia and Britain introduced.

1935–1939

1935 Italian forces invade Ethiopia.

1936 Signing of alliance between Japan and Germany.
1937 Japan occupies much of Chinese coast, leading to war between the nations.

The rise of Japan
Military rule of Japan in the late 1930s led to displays of the nation's strength in warfare and empire building.

1936 Olympic Games in Berlin, Germany.
1936–39 Spanish Civil War ends in victory for General Franco and defeat for the Republic.
1937 Frank Whittle invents the jet engine in Britain.
1938 Germany takes over Austria and part of Czechoslovakia.
1939 Britain and France declare war on Germany after Hitler invades Poland.

1935 US National Labor Relations Act comes into force.

1937 Formation of Royal New Zealand Air Force.
1939 Australia and New Zealand join Allied forces against Germany.

	1940–1941	1942–1943
AFRICA	**1940** British Navy sinks French fleet at Oran to prevent its capture by Germany. **1941** Allied troops overrun Italy's African colonies. German forces led by Erwin Rommel arrive in Libya to help Italy.	**1942** Allied troops land in Morocco. Rommel's troops are defeated by the Allies, led by General Montgomery, at El Alamein.
ASIA	**1941** French colonies in Southeast Asia taken over by Japanese. **1941–42** Japan captures the Philippines, Malaya, Hong Kong, Singapore, Burma, and Indonesia.	**1942** US Navy defeats Japan in Coral Sea of New Guinea and at Midway Island. **1943–44** Series of victories by US in Pacific islands pushes back Japanese forces.
EUROPE	**1940** Germany occupies Denmark, Norway, France, Belgium, and the Netherlands. Winston Churchill becomes Prime Minister of Britain. British air force prevents German invasion in the Battle of Britain. **1941** Hungary, Bulgaria, Greece, and parts of Yugoslavia and Russia under Germans.	**1943** Allied troops take over Sicily, then invade Italian mainland. **1943** German forces driven out of Russia.
AMERICAS	**1940** Xerox photocopying machine invented. Development of penicillin and other early antibiotics. **1941** US joins Allies in World War II after Japanese attack on US Navy at Pearl Harbor in Hawaii.	**1942** Enrico Fermi builds first US nuclear reactor. Mexico and Brazil join Allies. Nylon used for hosiery and parachutes first produced in US.
OCEANIA	**1940s** Australia prepares for the eventuality of a Japanese invasion.	**1942** Japanese bomb Darwin, Australia, and invade New Guinea and part of Papua.

Winston Churchill
The many rousing speeches given on the radio by Britain's wartime leader Winston Churchill helped inspire the Allies to victory.

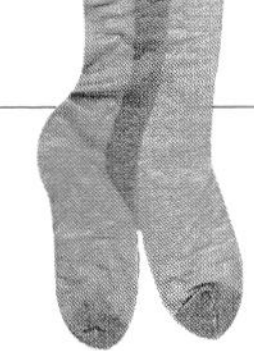

Nylon stockings

Attack on Pearl Harbor
The surprise assault by Japanese forces on the US Navy fleet at Pearl Harbor, Hawaii, in 1941 sank or damaged 18 ships and destroyed 200 aircraft.

1944–1945

1944 Japan attacks India but is defeated at Kohima.
1945 US drops first atomic bombs on Japanese cities of Hiroshima and Nagasaki. Emperor Hirohito authorizes Japanese surrender.

Emperor Hirohito of Japan
Japanese pilots thought of Emperor Hirohito as a god and considered it an honor to die for him on "kamikaze" missions, which involved crash-diving explosive-packed planes into Allied ships.

1944 Allies invade France and drive back Germans.
1945 German forces surrender.

1945 Roosevelt, US President, dies. US tests first atomic bomb in New Mexico.

Dawn of the Nuclear Age
The first atomic bomb was dropped on Hiroshima, Japan, in 1945, killing about 80,000 people. A second bomb was dropped on the city of Nagasaki three days later, leading to Japan's surrender and the end of World War II.

1944 Mass breakout of Japanese prisoners of war in Australia.
1945 Australia recovers New Guinea and Papua territory from Japan.

1946–1947

Gandhi and followers

1947 India and Pakistan gain independence from Great Britain amid riots that kill 500,000 people. Indian leader Gandhi begins a protest fast against the continuing violence.

1947 Marshall Plan offers US aid to help European countries rebuild their economies after World War II.

United Nations flag
The United Nations (UN) was established in 1945 to foster friendly relations between nations and to try to solve international disputes without war.

1947 US government promises to aid any country resisting communism.

1947 South Pacific Commission formed to discuss economic and health issues of South Pacific islands.

	1948–1950	1951–1953
AFRICA	**1950** Group Areas Act enforcing racial segregation (apartheid) passed in South Africa.	**1951** Libyan independence from Italy sanctioned by US. **1953** Military coup in Egypt ends anarchy and establishes a republic.
ASIA	**1948** Gandhi assassinated in India. State of Israel created in Palestine. **1949** Founding of Mao Tse-tung's new Communist Republic in China.	**1950** Communist North Korea invades US-backed South Korea, starting Korean War. **1953** Korean War ends. Edmund Hillary and Sherpa Tenzing Norgay are first people to reach summit of Mount Everest.
EUROPE	**1948** Berlin Airlift of supplies defeats USSR's blockade of West Berlin. **1949** Germany divided into two states, West Germany and communist East Germany. Western Europe and US form defensive NATO alliance against attack by USSR.	**1952** Greece and Turkey join NATO.
AMERICAS	**1948** Harry Truman wins Presidential election in US. **1950** Senator Joseph McCarthy begins anti-communist "witch-hunts" in US.	**1950s** Black Americans intensify their campaign for civil rights. **1953** Link between smoking and lung cancer first established in US.
OCEANIA		**1951** Australia, New Zealand, and US sign ANZUS Pact defense alliance.

Jewish nation
In 1948, the United Nations recognized the state of Israel in the ancient Jewish homeland of Palestine. The resulting conflict over territory between Israelis and Arab Palestinians has continued ever since.

Hillary and Tensing

Post-war Europe
After World War II, Europe was divided into the USSR-controlled East and the US-backed West. The uneasy peace between each side, known as the Cold War, led to an arms race between the US and USSR in which both superpowers began to stockpile nuclear weapons.

1954–1956	1957–1959
1954 National Liberation Front formed in Algeria to fight French rule. **1955** African National Congress (ANC) pressure group in South Africa adopts antiracist Freedom Charter. **1956** Egyptian leader Nasser takes over the Suez Canal.	**1957** Ghana becomes first country in sub-Saharan Africa to gain independence.
1954 French defeated by communist forces at Dien Bien Phu, North Vietnam. Vietnam divided into communist North and US-backed South. **1956** Israel captures Sinai peninsula from Arab forces in eight days.	**1958** King Faisal II of Iraq is removed by a military revolt and a new republic founded. **1959** Tibetan uprising against Chinese occupation crushed. The Dalai Lama, Tibet's spiritual leader, is forced to flee the country.
Symbol of Soviet Communism	**The Dalai Lama**
1955 Warsaw Pact defense treaty signed by communist nations, allowing Soviet (USSR) troops to be stationed in any communist Eastern European country. West Germany joins NATO and East Germany becomes part of Warsaw Pact. **1957** USSR launches Sputnik I, the world's first artificial satellite.	**1958** Charles de Gaulle begins strong presidential rule in France.
	1958 US's first atomic-powered submarine, *USS Nautilus*, makes undersea crossing of North Pole. **1959** Revolution in Cuba brings communist Fidel Castro to power, creating close Cuban ties with the Soviets. **Sputnik I satellite**
1955 Military coup in Argentina overthrows President Juan Perón.	**1959** Antarctic Treaty preserves the area for research.
1956 Olympics held in Melbourne, Australia.	

	1960–1963	1964–1967
AFRICA	**1960** Independence gained by 17 African colonies. A peaceful demonstration in Sharpeville against white rule in South Africa ends in the death of 69 protestors and banning of the ANC.	**1964** ANC leader Nelson Mandela jailed in South Africa. **1965** White-ruled Rhodesia declares independence from Britain. **1967** Dr. Christiaan Barnard completes first heart transplant in South Africa.
ASIA	**1963** Diem, leader of South Vietnam, is assassinated in a military coup.	
EUROPE	**1961** Berlin Wall built. Russian cosmonaut Yuri Gagarin is first man in space. **1962** British pop group The Beatles release *Love Me Do,* their first hit record.	**1965** US troops start arriving in South Vietnam to help in the fight against communist North Vietnam. **1966** Chinese Cultural Revolution begins. **1964** Fighting between Greeks and Turks in Cyprus. **1967** Military coup in Greece.
AMERICAS	**1960** Election of John F. Kennedy, the youngest US president. **1962** Cuban Missile Crisis. **1963** President Kennedy assassinated.	**1965** Malcolm X, campaigner for black civil rights, assassinated. Riots break out in Chicago and Los Angeles.
OCEANIA	**1960** Aborigines granted the same social security benefits as the rest of Australian society.	**1967** Aboriginal people gain Australian citizenship.

Cultural revolution in China
Mao Tse-tung's "cultural revolution" closed schools and colleges, forcing teachers and students to work on the land. Any opposition was brutally put down by the Red Guards – enthusiastic young Communists inspired by the thoughts of Chairman Mao.

Fidel Castro
In 1962, Cuban dictator Fidel Castro allowed the USSR to build missile bases on Cuban soil. The US Navy blockaded Cuba and the Russians withdrew.

Martin Luther King Jr.
During the 1960s, civil rights leaders such as Martin Luther King and Malcolm X campaigned for the rights of black Americans.

1968–1971	1972–1975
1970 Biafra region defeated by Federal Nigerian government in civil war.	**1975** Portuguese colonies in Africa win independence.

1968 US soldiers kill hundreds of civilians in Vietnamese village of My Lai.
1971 East Pakistan gains independence from Pakistan, becoming Bangladesh.

Allied troops in Vietnam

1968 Riots in Paris as students call for educational and social reform and workers demand a new minimum wage. Anti-communist uprising in Prague, Czechoslavkia.
1969 Britain sends troops to Northern Ireland.

1968 Assassination of Martin Luther King in Memphis.
1969 US astronauts Neil Armstrong and Edwin "Buzz" Aldrin walk on the moon.

Men on the Moon
The live television broadcast of Neil Armstrong taking humankind's first steps on the lunar surface was seen by about 600 million people.

1972 Ceylon becomes Republic of Sri Lanka.
1973 US troops withdraw from Vietnam. Arab states attack Israel in October War and cut oil production, leading to a world economic crisis.

Arabian oil
Many countries dependent on Arabian oil faced economic disaster when the Arab states cut their oil production in 1973.

1972 "Bloody Sunday" in Londonderry, Northern Ireland, as British troops fire on civil rights marchers.

1973 Elected Chilean president Allende killed in military coup led by General Pinochet.
1974 US President Richard Nixon resigns in disgrace after Watergate scandal.

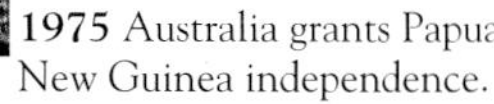

1975 Australia grants Papua New Guinea independence.

	1976–1980	1981–1985
AFRICA	**1976** Riots in black townships across South Africa. **1979** Ugandan leader Idi Amin ousted by Tanzanian-backed rebels. **1980** Independent Zimbabwe formed under leadership of Robert Mugabe.	**1983** War and drought lead to famine in Ethiopia. **Ethiopian Famine**
ASIA	**1976** North and South Vietnam reunited as a communist country after 22 years of separation. **1979** Camp David peace treaty between Egypt and Israel. Islamic revolution in Iran.	**1982** Israeli troops invade southern Lebanon. Palestinians massacred in Beirut refugee camp. **1984** Siege at Amritsar, India, ends with Sikh extremists being forced out of Golden Temple. Indian Prime Minister Indira Gandhi assassinated by her Sikh bodyguards. **Iranian Revolution** *Ayatollah Khomeini, a fundamentalist (strict) Muslim hostile to the West, led the Islamic revolution that overthrew the Shah (King) of Iran in 1979. The exiled Shah's entry into the USA led to Iranian students taking 53 Americans hostage in the US embassy in Tehran.*
EUROPE	**1976** Adoption of Helsinki Convention on human rights. **1978** Margaret Thatcher becomes Britain's first woman Prime Minister. **1980** President Tito of Yugoslavia dies. Lech Walesa leads Solidarity trade union in Poland.	**1981** Death of 11 Irish republican prisoners on hunger strike. **1984** French and US scientists independently identify the AIDS virus.
AMERICAS	**1977** Jimmy Carter elected US President. **1979** Sandinista guerillas defeat government forces and take power in Nicaragua. **Personal computing** *The first personal desktop computer (PC) was developed by the American company IBM in 1981.*	**1980s** First personal computers developed in US. **1980** Victory for Ronald Reagan in US Presidential elections. **1982** Britain defeats Argentine forces occupying British-held Falkland islands in Falklands War. Creation of Canadian constitution independent from UK.
OCEANIA	**1978** The Solomon islands of Tuvalu and Dominica become independent nations.	**1984** New Zealand declares itself a nuclear-free zone.

1986–1990	1991–2004
1990 Dismantling of apartheid begins in South Africa as Nelson Mandela is freed after 27 years in prison. Namibia gains independence from South Africa. **1990** Civil war begins in Liberia.	**1991** Collapse of government rule in Somalia. **1992** US leads UN troops into Somalia. **1993** Eritrea gains independence from Ethiopia. **2003** Families of Apartheid victims compensated.
1988 Ceasefire in Iran-Iraq war ends eight years of conflict. **1989** Chinese security forces kill pro-democracy protestors in Beijing's Tiananmen Square. **1990** Iraq invades Kuwait.  **Protester at Tiananmen Square**	**1994** Palestinian self-rule over the Gaza Strip under 1993 peace treaty between Israel and the Palestinian Liberation Organization (PLO).  **Yasser Arafat, leader of the PLO** **1991** Gulf War ends with Iraq being driven from Kuwait by UN forces. **2001** US-led forces invade Afghanistan. **2003** Second Gulf War in Iraq.
1986 New Soviet leader Mikhail Gorbachev introduces the policies of *glasnost* (openess) and *perestroika* (remodeling), eventually resulting in the breakup of the Soviet Union. **1989** Communist governments overthrown in Romania, Hungary, East Germany, and Czechoslovakia.	**1991** Dissolution of Soviet Union into Commonwealth of Independent States. 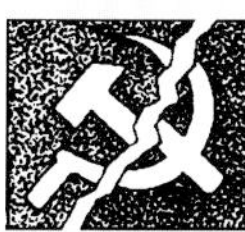 **Fall of USSR** **1992–95** Civil war between countries in former Yugoslavia. **1999** Single European currency, the Euro, is launched.
1986 "Irangate" revelations as US President Reagan questioned on secret arms deals with Iran. **1989** George Bush becomes US President.	**2000** George W. Bush elected US President. **2001** Terrorists fly jets into New York's World Trade Center.
1986 Treaty of Rarotonga sets up South Pacific Nuclear-Free Zone.	**1999** Australia votes to remain a constitutional monarchy.

2416
2417
2418

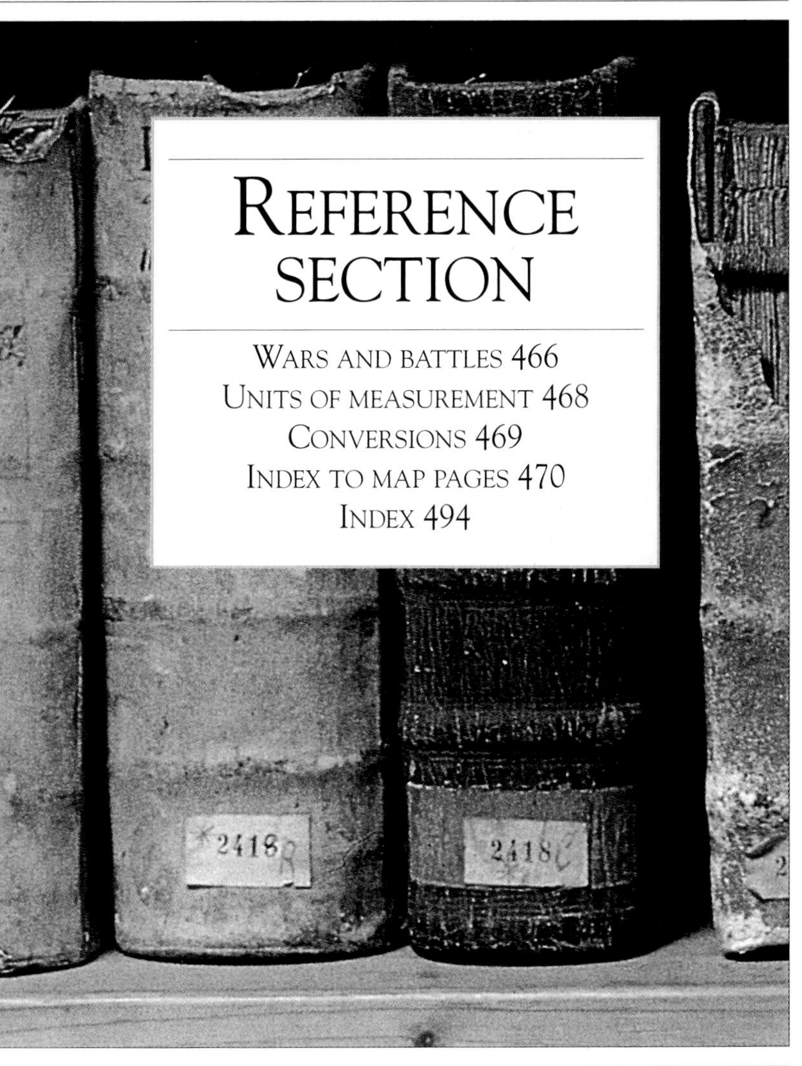
2418
2418

REFERENCE SECTION

Major wars

3100 B.C. First recorded war. Pharaoh Narmer unites Upper and Lower Egypt.
c.1200 B.C. Trojan War War between Greeks and Trojans, as in Homer's *Iliad*.
264–146 B.C. Punic Wars Three wars between Rome and Hannibal's Carthage.
c. A.D. 1096–1291 Crusades Religious wars in which European Christians try to recapture the Holy Land from Muslims.
1337–1453 Hundred Years War English and French battle for control of France.
1455–1485 Wars of the Roses English war between Houses of York and Lancaster for control of English throne.
1618–1648 Thirty Years War Initially between German Catholics and Protestants, but later involves all Europe.
1756–1763 Seven Years War Prussia and England fight against Austria and France for control of Germany.
1775–1783 American Revolution American colonists fight for independence from British rule. After they win, they form the US.
1800–1815 Napoleonic Wars Fought between Napoleon's France and Britain, Austria, Prussia, and Russia.
1821–1829 Greek War of Independence Greeks fight Turkish rule.
1839–1842 Opium War Trade war between Britain and China.
1846–1848 Mexican-American War Mexico and US battle over Texas.
1853–1856 Crimean War Turkey, allied with Britain, France, and Sardinia, fights Russia in the Black Sea.
1861–1865 American Civil War Conflict between Unionists from the North and Confederates from the South.
1870–1871 Franco-Prussian War Prussian war against France ends with establishment of German Empire.
1894–1895 Chinese-Japanese War Japanese defeat Chinese.
1899–1902 Boer War Britain fights Boers for control of South Africa.
1914–1918 World War I Britain, France, Russia, US, and others in global war against Germany, Austria-Hungary, and Turkey.
1939–1945 World War II Global war between Axis powers of Germany, Italy, and Japan and Allied powers of Britain, US, and USSR.
1950–1953 Korean War Communist North Korea fights against South Korea and UN forces led by the US.
1965–1975 Vietnam War Communist North Vietnam fights against South Vietnam and US allies.
1967 Six Day War Egypt against Israel.
1980–88 Iran-Iraq War
1991 Gulf War Saddam Hussein's Iraq defeated by United Nations forces.
1991–1995 Bosnian War Civil war in former Yugoslavia.
1999 Kosovan War NATO forces drive Serbians out of Kosovo province.
2002 War in Afghanistan US-led coalition deposes Taliban leadership.
2003 Iraq war US-led coalition deposes Saddam Hussein's regime.

Famous battles

490 B.C. Marathon (Greece) Athenians defeat Persians and save Greece.
331 B.C. Gaugamela (Persia) Alexander the Great's greatest victory, defeating the Persian King Darius II.
31 B.C. Actium (Greece) Octavian defeats Mark Antony and Cleopatra of Egypt and becomes Emperor Augustus, ending the Roman civil wars.
A.D. 378 Adrianople (Turkey) Goths (Germanic tribes) defeat Romans.
636 Yarmuk (Israel) Arabs under Khalid ibn–al Walid defeat Byzantines in desert sandstorm.
732 Tours (France) Charles Martel leads Franks to victory over Moors to halt their advance in Europe.
1066 Hastings (Britain) Normans under William the Conqueror invade England and beat the Saxons.
1429 Orléans (France) French heroine Joan of Arc lifts English siege of Orléans.
1453 Constantinople (Turkey) Turks besiege and capture Constintinople (Istanbul), ending Byzantine Empire.
1526 Panipat (India) Babur conquers Delhi and establishes Mughal empire
1571 Lepanto (Greece) End of Turkish seapower in the Mediterranean.
1588 Spanish Armada (Britain) English ships and storms defeat great Spanish invasion fleet of 130 ships.
1704 Blenheim (Germany) British-Austrian army led by Duke of Marlborough beats French, limiting French power in Europe.
1709 Poltava (Ukraine) Peter the Great of Russia defeats Swedes under Charles XII to control the Baltic Sea.
1759 Quebec (Canada) Britain gains control of Canada.
1777 Saratoga (USA) Decisive battle in American Revolution. British, led by Gen. Burgoyne, surrender to Americans.
1781 Yorktown (USA) George Washington leads Americans to final victory over British, ending American Revolution.
1805 Trafalgar (South of Spain) Nelson's British fleet destroys French and Spanish fleet.
1815 Waterloo End of Napoleonic wars. Allies under Wellington crush Napoleon.
1863 Gettysburg (USA) Decisive battle of American Civil War. Unionists defeat Confederates.
1914 Marne (France) Allies halt German advance on Paris.
1916 Somme (France) The deadliest battle of World War I. 1,265,000 men are killed.
1940 Battle of Britain Aircraft of British Royal Air Force (RAF) drive off German bombing raids.
1942 Midway (Pacific) Japanese aircraft fail to capture Midway Island from the USA.
1944 D–day (Normandy, France) Allies invade German-occupied France.
1991 Operation Desert Storm (Iraq) Airborne attack on Iraq by United Nations forces turns Gulf War.

Units of measurement

The metric system, based on the number ten, is the most common system of measurement and is used by scientists worldwide. Certain countries, such as the USA, use the older imperial system.

Temperature conversions

To convert Fahrenheit (°F) into centigrade (°C), use the formula:
°C = (°F – 32) ÷ 1.8

To convert centigrade (°C) into Fahrenheit (°F), use the formula:
°F = (°C x 1.8) + 32

Volume

1 cubic in (in^3)	
1 cubic ft (ft^3)	144 in^3
1 cubic yd (yd^3)	9 ft^3
1 fluid oz (fl oz)	4,840 yd^3
1 pint (pt)	20 fl oz
1 gallon (gal)	
1 cubic mm (mm^3)	
1 cubic cm (cm^3)	100 mm^3
1 cubic meter (m^3)	1,000,000 cm^3
1 liter (l)	1,000 cm^3

Length

1 inch (in)	
1 foot (ft)	12 in
1 yard (yd)	3 ft
1 mile	1,760 yd
1 millimeter (mm)	
1 centimeter (cm)	10 mm
1 meter (m)	100 cm
1 kilometer (km)	1,000 m

Area

1 square inch (in^2)	
1 sq foot (ft^2)	144 in^2
1 sq yard (yd^2)	9 ft^2
1 acre	4,840 yd^2
1 sq mile	640 acres
1 sq millimeter (mm^2)	
1 sq centimeter (cm^2)	100 mm^2
1 sq meter (m^2)	10,000 cm^2
1 hectare	10,000 m^2
1 sq kilometer (km^2)	1,000,000 m^2

Mass and weight

1 ounce (oz)	
1 pound (lb)	16 oz
1 stone	14 lb
1 hundredweight (cwt)	8 stones
1 ton	20 cwt
1 gram (g)	
1 kilogram (kg)	1,000 g
1 tonne (t)	1,000 kg

Conversions

You can convert between the metric and imperial systems of measurement by using the following conversion tables.

Length

To convert	Into	X by
in	cm	2.54
ft	m	0.3048
yd	m	0.9144
miles	km	1.6093
cm	in	0.3937
m	f	3.2808
m	yd	1.0936
km	miles	0.6214

Area

To convert	Into	X by
sq in	sq cm	6.4516
sq ft	sq m	0.0929
sq yd	sq m	0.8361
acres	hectares	0.4047
sq miles	sq km	2.59
sq cm	sq in	0.155
sq m	sq ft	10.7639
sq m	sq yd	1.1960
hectares	acres	2.4711
sq km	sq miles	0.3861

Mass and Weight

To convert	Into	X by
oz	g	28.3495
lb	kg	0.4536
stones	kg	6.3503
cwt	kg	50.802
tons	tonnes	1.0161
g	oz	0.0352
kg	lb	2.2046
kg	stones	0.1575
kg	cwt	0.0197
tonnes	tons	0.9842

Volume

To convert	Into	X by
in^3	cm^3 (milliliters)	16.3871
ft^3	liters	28.3169
yd^3	m^3	0.7646
fl oz	cm^3	28.4131
pints	liters	0.5683
gallons	liters	4.5461
cm^3	in^3	0.0610
cm^3	fl oz	0.0352
liters	ft^3	0.0353
m^3	yd^3	1.3080
litres	pints	1.7598
litres	gallons	0.2200

Prefixes

kilo	= 1000		centi	=	1/100
hecto	= 100		milli	=	1/1,000
deci	= 1/10		micro	=	1/1,000,000

Index to map pages

Grid references in the Index help find places on the map. If you look up Nairobi in the Index, you will see 302 F4. The first number, 302, is the page number on which the map of Nairobi appears. Next, find the letters and numbers which border the page and trace a line across from the letter and down from the number. This will direct you to the exact grid square in which the city of Nairobi is located.

A

B

C

T

Index

C

Acknowledgments

PAGEO*ne* and Dorling Kindersley would like to thank:
Christiane Gunzi for editorial assistance; Sarah Watson for general assistance; Thomas Keenes for design assistance; Hilary Bird for the index; Gordon Models, Peter Griffiths, and John Holmes for model making; Ashmolean Museum; Beaulieu Motor Museum; The British Library; Capotine Museum; Ermine Street Guard Museum; Louisiana State Museum; Musée du Louvre; Museum of London; Museum of Mankind; Museum of the Moving Image; Museum of Natural History; National Railway Museum; Pitt Rivers Museum; Royal Academy of Arts; The Science Museum, London; Uffizi, Florence; University Museum of Archaeology and Anthropology, Cambridge.

Photographs by:
Geoff Brightling, Jane Burton, P. Chadwell, Peter Chadwick, Andy Crawford, Geoff Dann, Philip Dowell, Mike Dunning, Neil Fletcher, Philip Gatward, Steve Gorton, Frank Greenaway, Colin Keates, Gary Kevin, Dave King, Nick Nicholls, Andrew McRobb, Ray Moller, Stephen Oliver, Roger Phillips, Tim Ridley, Karl Shone, James Stevenson, Clive Streeter, Kim Taylor, Andreas Von Einsiedel, Matthew Ward, Jerry Young, Christian Zuber.

Illustrations by:
Evi Antoniou, Rick Blakely, Peter Bull, Mike Courtney, John Crawford Fraser, Bill Donohoe, Simone End, Eugene Fleury, Giuliano Fornari, Ann George-Marsh, Jeremy Gower, Elizabeth Gray, Andrew Green, Ray Grinaway, Nick Hewetson, Dave Hopkins, Aziz Khan, Jason Lewis, Stuart Mackay, Judith Maguire, Janos Marffy, Kevin Marks, Angus Mcbride, Sean Milne, Sergio, Colin Salmon, Michael Saunders, Rodney Shackell, Rob Shone, Clive Spong, Roger Stewart, John Temperton, Pete Visscher, Richard Ward, John Woodcock, Dan Wright.

Picture credits:
a = above, b = below, l = left,
t = top, c = center
The publisher would like to thank the following for their kind permission to reproduce the photographs:

Aardman Animations 403bl; Action Plus/Glyn Kirk 412ac; AKG, London, 349acl; AKG, Berlin, 442bcr; Ancient Art and Architecture 437tc; Directed and produced by Animation City/A.C. Live 402cl; Austin Brown and The Aviation Picture Library 197br; Aviation Images, 196c; Biology Media 142cl; Bettmann Archive 443br; Bridgeman Art Library/Glraudon 389acl; Museum of Mankind 370bc; Museum of Natural History, London, 99br; The British Museum 371tr, 371ac, 376ar, 376bl, 376br, 377acl, 377acr, 377br, 378al, 378acl, 378br, 379ac, 427ar, 428br, 430tc, 439cl; Neill Bruce Motoring Photolibrary 185crb; Stefan Luscher 185br; The Peter Roberts Collection 185clb, 185bl; Camera Press/Ian Stone 460ac; Carolco 1991, courtesy of

Kobal collection 402tr; J. Allan Cash 430cr; Christie's Colour Library 313br; Bruce Coleman Ltd/Jeff Foott Productions 224cl; Christian Zuber 307tr; Colorsport © Duono; David Madlen 404bl; Comstock 432ar; Corbis/Roger Ressmeyer 32tr; Ferdaus Shamim/Corbis Sygma 399bc; James Davis 375bl; et archive 427acl, 434tr, 436al, 437cr, 439br, 452ac; Mary Evans Picture Library 69ac, 370tr, 375bc, 375br, 380tr, 397bcl; The British Library 372cl, 446acl, 446acr, 449br, 454bc; Exeter Maritime Museum 190acr, 190bcl; Gilbert and George, courtesy of Anthony d'Offay Gallery, London, 389br; Ronald Grant Archive 396bl, 403cr; Sonia Halliday 371br; Robert Harding Picture Library 181tr, 423bcl, 436bl, 439tr, 444bc; Michael Holford 377ar, 429acl, 432br, 434bc; Hulton-Getty Picture Collection 380cr; Robert Hunt Library 454acl; Hutchison Library, 373br, 374bl; J.G. Fuller 235bl; Image Bank/Kaz Mori 66-67; Image Select 395tcl, 399tcl, 444tcl; Ann Ronan 394cr; Simon James 377bl; David King 380cl; Kobal Collection 403bc; Magnum/ Cagnoni 460cl; Mander & Mitcheson 397cr; Museum of the Moving Image/ © Academy of Motion Picture Arts and Sciences R 3br, 403br; NASA 5al, 33c, 35tr, 36acr, 36bcr, 37cl, 37tr, 461bc; NASA/CXC/SAO 32cr; W.M. Keck Obs 32cl; Palomar Obs 32bc; National Maritime Museum, 190bcr, 190b, 193br, 440acr; Peter Newark Pictures 435c, 451cr; Oxford Scientific Films/Root; Okapia 111cl; Ann and Bury Peerless, 372bc, 374acr; Photostage/Donald Cooper 397br; Popperfoto 456ac, 457bc, 459acr; Press Association 380bcl; Redferns 395br; Rex features 381tl; 461tc, 462ar; Cheryl Hatch, Sipa Press, 463acr; Coll. Privé, Sipa 457tl; Setbon, Sipa Press 462c; Royal Geographical Society/Paul Harris 288ac; The Royal Ballet School 396bcl, 396acr; Scala 371bcl, 377tl; Biblioteca Nazionale Centrale, Florence 438bc; Science Photo Library/George Bernard 144-5; Biology Media 142cl; Chris Bjornberg 12-13; Jeremy Burgess 84tr; Cern 149tl; CNRI 79bcl; Tony Hallas 16tr; Adam Jones 38-39; James King-Holmes 171br; Thomas Ligon 198-99; Lawrence Migdale 171cr; Prof. P. Motta, Dept. of Anatomy, University Lasapienza, Rome 114-115; Professors P.M. Motta, K.R Porter & P.M Andrews 123tr; Novostl 36cl, 329bl; Omikron 128tr; David Parker 171tr; John Sanford 32ar; David Sharfe 133cr; Simon Terrey 146tr; Sporting Pictures (UK) Ltd 156tr, 187tc, 189tc, 404bcr, 413tl, 413tr; Tony Stone Images/Tony Craddock 257tr; Sepp Dietrich 273br, Ian Murphy 396br; Hugh Sitton 306cl; Warner Brothers/courtesy Kobal Collection 403cl; Werner Forman Archives 370acl, 396tl, 420-421, 428cl; Jerry Young 103br, Michael Zabé 441bc; Zefa Pictures 379bl, 464-465; Ian Bradshaw 368-369; Stockmarket 322c; Krebs 176-177; Joe Cornish 281.

Every effort has been made to trace the copyright holders and we apologize in advance for any unintentional omissions. We would be pleased to insert the appropriate acknowledgment in any subsequent edition of this publication.